Where to watch birds in

Asia

THE *WHERE TO WATCH BIRDS* SERIES

Where to watch birds in Africa
Nigel Wheatley

Where to watch birds in Asia
Nigel Wheatley

Where to watch birds in South America
Nigel Wheatley

Where to watch birds in

Asia

Nigel Wheatley

Princeton University Press

Princeton, New Jersey

Published by Princeton University Press,
41 William Street, Princeton, New Jersey 08540

In the United Kingdom, published by
Christopher Helm (Publishers) Ltd, a subsidiary of
A & C Black Ltd, 35 Bedford Row, London WC1R 4JH

Library of Congress Cataloging-in-Publication Data

Wheatley, Nigel, 1960–
Where to watch birds in Asia / Nigel Wheatley.
p. cm.
Includes bibliographical references and index.
ISBN 0-691-01214-8 (cloth)
1. Bird watching—Asia—Guidebooks. 2. Asia—Guidebooks.
I. Title.
QL691.A1W48 1996
598'.072345—dc20 96-27112

This book has been composed in 9 pt Cheltenham Light

Printed and bound by Biddles Limited, Guildford,
Surrey, in Great Britain

1 3 5 7 9 10 8 6 4 2

CONTENTS

ACKNOWLEDGEMENTS

It would have been impossible to write this book without the help of many birders who have not just travelled to Asia to see the wonderful birds, but who have been unselfish enough to record their experiences for the benefit of others. These people have made their information generally available and, to me, are some of the heroes of the birding world.

I would like to express my heartfelt thanks to the following birders and organisations who have either kindly allowed me to use the information contained within their reports, papers, books and letters and/or covered some draft country accounts in honest red ink: Ian Andrews, John Ash, BirdLife International, Birdquest, Bill Blake, Neil Bostock, John Bowler, Chris Bradshaw, Mark Brazil, Alan Brown, Jon Curson, Cygnus, David Diskin, Nigel Driver, John Edge, Hanne and Jens Eriksen, Foggy (Simon Fogg), Annika Forsten, Michael Gallagher, Brian Gee, Chris Gibbins, Gary Grant, John and Penny Hale, Henk Hendriks, Erik Hirschfeld, Remco Hofland, Juha Honkala, Jon Hornbuckle, Carol and Tim Inskipp, Anders Jihmanner, David Johnson, Krys Kazmierczak, Guy Kirwan, Ken Kraayeveld, Alan Lewis, Graham Lobley, Steve Madge, Guy Manners, Edward Massiah, Saeed Mohamed, Glenn Morris, Pete Morris, Rob Morris, Tony Morris, Eddie Myers, Bob Nation, Christine and John Oldfield, Urban Olsson, John Palfrey, Charles Pilcher, Nick Pope, Gerry Richards, Colin Richardson, Lim Kim Seng, Noel Shillcock, Hadoram Shirihai, Solve Sondbo, Spotter (John Mason), Barry Stidolph, Sunbird, Paul Thompson, Philip Verbelen, Jan Vermeulen, Alan Vittery, Paul Willoughby and Jan Zwaaneveld.

Naturally, many thanks also go to the many birders who accompanied these people in the field, helped to find the birds and no doubt contributed their own information.

I have spoken with numerous other people on the telephone or in the field about minor, but important, matters, who I have unwittingly omitted from the above list. I sincerely hope these people will accept my profuse apologies if I have failed to acknowledge their help in this edition, and hope they will let me know before the next edition.

It has to be said at this juncture that there are some birders, including a few with a wealth of experience in Asia, who have *never* written any trip reports. Or, if they have done so, they have not made their information generally available. Fortunately, such people are few and far between, and sharing information comes naturally to the vast majority of birders.

Once I had come up with the idea for the book I had to convince a publisher it would be popular. Fortunately, Robert Kirk, the editor at Helm, saw the potential and deserves thanks for taking on the original idea and developing it. When I started writing the book it seemed as though every bird had at least three different names. This major headache was cured by James Clements, to whom I am very grateful for giving me permission to use his *Check List* as the baseline for this book.

Finally, special thanks must go to Mark Hardwick, who lent me a pile of books for the price of a pint, and Chief (Nick Cobb), Nick Gardner and Alun Hatfield, who all lent me an ear when the critics caused consternation.

INTRODUCTION

My first experience of birding in Asia was from the Awam Express, the far from express train which traverses the 1000 km from Karachi in south Pakistan to Rawalpindi in the north. I had never been beyond Britain and northern Europe before, so the Green Bee-eaters and Indian Rollers which adorned the trackside wires were nothing short of incredible to my inexperienced eyes. It was October 1985 and I was on my way to look for snow leopards in the Karakoram Range at the western end of the Himalayas on an adventure organised by my old friend Rob Roberts. The chances of seeing a snow leopard were slim, but I could hardly wait to get there because I thought there had to be some great birds up in those mountains.

The trouble was, there was hardly any information readily available on the birds of north Pakistan. It was not until two months after our first failed attempt to see a snow leopard, while I was sipping firewater at KS Nepali's house in Kathmandu, that I discovered the little beauty of a bird we had seen in the Nar Valley near Skardu, Pakistan was a White-browed Tit-Warbler, and that the bird which fed us for three days in that valley, but was never seen alive, was a Himalayan Monal. One of the Forestry Department guides shot the tasty bird while we were in another part of the valley and it was in the pot when we got back! I had to wait until I got home to confirm that the bird I saw on our second miserable attempt to see a snow leopard was a Wood Snipe, and it was years later when I heard the earth-shattering news that we had passed the Palas Valley, where the rare and beautiful Western Tragopan occurs, no fewer than three times.

I missed many other great birds when I was in the Karakoram and that is partly how this book, and the others in this mini-series, evolved. I wanted to produce a book which would have helped me to research our trip more thoroughly in 1985 and which, hopefully, will help today's birders to plan their own successful trips for years to come. This book is also an attempt to inspire birders to travel to the world's wild places in search of the birds they dream of, catalysed by my own personal memories of birding in Asia during the last decade. I will never forget the multitude of birds at Bharatpur (India), my first gaggle of White-crested Laughingthrushes at Phulchowki (Nepal), a brilliant Blue-headed Pitta lighting up the gloomy forest at Danum Valley (Borneo), the shiny beard of a Purple-bearded Bee-eater on Sulawesi, beautiful Blue Nuthatches on Java, a Spoonbill Sandpiper among 2,000 summer-plumaged shorebirds in Hong Kong and, best of all, January 10th 1986 when, after seeing White-browed Tit-Warblers, Wallcreepers and White-winged (Guldenstadt's) Redstarts while walking up to a remote *nulla* (high valley) beyond the village of Chu Tran, near K2, to look for snow leopards, Rob and I came across five Ibisbills. Thanks to the presence of some hot springs they were feeding in the only stretch of unfrozen river for miles, shuffling in and out of the steam as they swept their bills from side to side through the shallow water. Having missed these unique birds in Nepal and having had no idea that they occurred on the river at Ramnagar, where we stopped on our way to Corbett National Park in India, we were ecstatic.

The first question birder's usually ask themselves before planning a trip is not 'where could I see a snow leopard', but 'where could I see certain species'. First-time visitors to Asia may be thinking about such birds as Ibisbill and White-browed Tit-Warbler, along with many other goodies, perhaps including Steller's Sea-Eagle*, Great Philippine Eagle*, many superb pheasants, Masked Finfoot*, Pheasant-tailed and Bronze-winged Jacanas, Spoonbill Sandpiper*, numerous kingfishers, Red-, Blue- and Purple-bearded Bee-eaters, many hornbills, some wonderful woodpeckers, 25 of the world's 30 pittas, ten of the world's 14 broadbills, Malaysian Rail-babbler, Wallace's Standardwing*, Bornean Bristlehead*, Asian Fairy-bluebird, thrushes galore, Siberian and White-tailed Rubythroats, some superb redstarts, seven forktails, four cochoas, Krueper's, Blue, Giant* and Beautiful* Nuthatches, Hypocolius, lots of laughingthrushes, Silver-eared Mesia, Red-billed Leiothrix, Cutia, Fire-tailed Myzornis, Sultan Tit, some cracking sunbirds and numerous buntings.

Those birders thinking about returning to the continent for the second, third, fourth or fortieth time may be wondering about the whereabouts of more obscure species and little known endemics such as Scaly-sided Merganser*, the seven species of peacock-pheasant, Swinhoe's Rail*, Solitary and Wood* Snipes, Sunda Ground-Cuckoo*, many owls, a number of bulbuls and babblers and a few flowerpeckers.

Once birders have decided what they would like to see, further questions may spring to mind. Which country supports the best selection? When is the best time to visit that country? Where are the best sites within that country? How easy is it to get from site to site? How long will I need to spend at each one? What other species are there at these sites? Which birds should I concentrate on? Are there any endemics? How many species am I likely to see? The list goes on.

Such questions need careful consideration if the proposed birding trip is going to be an enjoyable success. Without months of painstaking preparation a trip may not be anywhere near as exciting as it could be. Hence this book's major aim is to answer those questions birders may ask themselves before venturing to Asia for the first or fortieth time. It is not meant to direct you to every site and bird in the minutest detail, but to be a first point of reference — *a guiding light*. There can be no substitute for an up-to-date report and I urge readers to seek these reports out (see p. 426) once they have decided on their destination, and to write their own reports on their return.

Birders are notoriously hard to please, so writing this book has been all-consuming. I began by compiling a list of sites, and the species recorded at them, from every imaginable source. Birders' reports were the major goldmine and without the generous permission of the writers (see Acknowledgements) this book would not exist. While compiling the site lists I soon realised that every birder seemed to have a different name for every bird. It was not as bad as that, but it was becoming a major headache. Hence I decided I needed a list of species as the baseline for names used and the taxonomic order of the species lists for each site. I chose *Birds of the World: A Check List*, by James Clements (Fourth Edition 1991, together with Supplements 1 and 2; 1992 and 1993, respectively), simply because the names and taxonomic order used seemed the most logical and James was kind enough to allow me to use it.

The names of birds in this *Check List* are spelt in 'American'. For example, 'coloured' is spelt 'colored' and 'grey' is spelt 'gray'. Although the

'English' names of New World birds should be spelt in the American way, I have written all bird names in English in this edition, simply because I think its easier on the English eye and because my busy fingers refused *not* to press the 'u' in 'coloured' or *to* press the 'a' in 'grey' instead of the 'e', while whizzing (no, stumbling) across the keyboard. Some of the names used by James are different to those used in many Asian bird books, hence a comparison table has been included (p. 430).

Using these databases, most, if not all, of the best birding sites, spectacular and endemic species, as well as those birds hard to see beyond the continent's boundaries, have been included, albeit in varying amounts of detail. Absolute coverage and precision would have resulted in the staggered publication of several thick volumes.

The result is over 250 major sites, listed in the Contents, over 100 maps, endemic and near-endemic species-lists (at the end of each country account) where appropriate and a species index. Hence birders interested in a particular species can look it up in the species index, see the page number(s) and turn straight to the site(s) it occurs at. Birders with an interest in a site or sites they have heard about can refer to the Contents, see the page number(s) and turn directly to the required site(s) or refer to the Index of Sites (listed under country name) on page 433.

After much consideration the book has taken the following shape. Countries are treated alphabetically, with those in the Middle East in a separate section. Details for each country are dealt with as follows:

The **Country Introduction** includes:

A brief **summary** of the features discussed below.
The **size** of the country in relation to England and Texas.
How easy or difficult **getting around** the country is.
What the **accommodation and food** are like.
Details relating to **health and safety**, where, although general advice is given, it is best to check the latest immunisation requirements (immunisation against Yellow Fever may be compulsory, not 'just' recommended) and personal safety levels before planning your trip.
Climate and timing, where the best times to visit are given (summarised in the Calender, p. 424).
A brief outline of the **habitats** within the country.
Any pertinent **conservation** issues.
The total number of **bird species** recorded in the country (where known), followed by a short list of non-endemic specialities and spectacular species which is intended to give a brief taste of what to expect (rarely seen species are not usually included in this brief list).
The total number of **endemic species** and near-endemic species (where appropriate), followed by a short list of the most spectacular birds in this category.
Expectations, where an idea of how many species to expect is given.

Some of these sections may be missing for the less well-known countries and the details given are intended to be as brief as possible. There seems little point here in repeating the vast amount of information now available in travel guides and it makes much more sense to save room for more information on the birds and birding in this book.

FIGURE 1: LIST OF BIRD FAMILIES WHICH REGULARLY OCCUR IN ASIA

The six families listed below in **BOLD CAPITAL** type are endemic to Asia. The two families listed in ***bold italics*** are only present in south-west Arabia.

Cassowaries
Grebes
Albatrosses
Shearwaters and petrels
Storm-Petrels
Tropicbirds
Frigatebirds
Gannets and boobies
Cormorants
Anhingas
Pelicans
Waterfowl
Flamingoes
Herons
Hamerkop
Ibises and spoonbills
Storks
Osprey
Vultures, hawks and eagles
Falcons
Megapodes
Guineafowl
Pheasants
Buttonquails
Rails
Sungrebes (Masked Finfoot*)
Cranes
Bustards
Jacanas
Painted-Snipes (Greater Painted-Snipe)
Snipes and sandpipers
Crab Plover
Thick-knees
Oystercatchers
IBISBILLS
Stilts and avocets
Coursers and pratincoles
Plovers and lapwings
Gulls and terns
Skuas and jaegers
Skimmers (Indian Skimmer*)
Auks
Divers
Sandgrouse
Pigeons and doves
Parrots
Cockatoos
Lories
Cuckoos
Coucals
Barn-Owls
Owls
Frogmouths
Owlet-Nightjars
Eared-Nightjars
Nightjars
Treeswifts
Swifts
Trogons
Kingfishers
Bee-eaters
Rollers
Hoopoes
Hornbills
ASIAN BARBETS
Honeyguides
Woodpeckers
Pittas
Broadbills
Gerygones
Honeyeaters
Australian robins
Whistlers
Quail-thrushes (Malaysian Rail-babbler)
Fantails, paradise-flycatchers and monarchs
Drongos
Corvids
Birds-of-paradise
Woodswallows
IORAS
Orioles
Cuckoo-Shrikes
LEAFBIRDS
Shrikes
Bushshrikes
Waxwings
Dippers

Thrushes
Starlings
Old World flycatchers (niltavas, robins, redstarts, forktails, etc.)
Nuthatches
Treecreepers
Wrens (Winter Wren)
Long-tailed Tits
Swallows
Kinglets (crests)
Bulbuls
White-eyes
HYPOCOLIUS
Cisticolas
Warblers
Babblers
Parrotbills
RHABDORNISES
Tits
Penduline-tits
Larks
Old World sparrows
Waxbills
Wagtails and pipits
Accentors
Weavers
Flowerpeckers
Sunbirds
Finches
Buntings

Total = 116

On each country map the **sites** are numbered, roughly, along a more or less logical route through the country, or in 'bunches', and discussed in that order under each country account. Naturally, different birders will prefer their own routes, but I felt this was a better method than dealing with the sites alphabetically because those birders intending to visit just one region of a country will find all the sites in that region dealt with in the same section of the book.

Sites are dealt with as follows:

The **site name** usually refers to the actual site. However, if it is nameless, or it involves a number of birding spots which are in close proximity, the best city, town, village, lodge or road name, however remote, from which to explore the site, is used.

The **site introduction** gives its general location within the relevant country before describing its size, main physical characteristics, habitat make-up and avifauna, including the number of species recorded (if known) and particular reference to endemic and speciality species best looked for at that site. It is *important* to remember here that specialities of the given site are mentioned in the introduction and do not include all the birds listed under the section headed **Specialities** in the list for that site (see full explanation opposite).

The site's altitude (where known) is also given, in feet and metres. Both measurements are given as some birders prefer metres and some prefer feet, whereas only kilometre readings are given for distances because most birders now have a grasp of kilometres. For those that don't, remember that one mile equals 1.6093, or roughly, 1.6 km.

Restrictions on access, if there are any, are also given in the site introduction. Such a negative start is designed to eliminate the extreme disappointment of discovering the site is inaccessible to all but the most well-prepared and adventurous *after* reading about the wealth of avian riches present at the site. It is *imperative* to check the situation in some countries with the relevant authorities before even considering a visit. Birds are beautiful, but so is life.

The **species lists** for the site follow the introduction and include:

Endemics: species only found in the country the site is in (not species endemic to the site). Some birds listed here may only occur at one or two sites within the country, so it is important to make a special effort to see them. Such species are mentioned in the site introduction. Others are more widespread, but *still* endemic to the relevant country.

Specialities: species which have: restricted ranges which cross country boundaries; wider distributions throughout Asia but are generally scarce, rare or threatened; or rarely been mentioned in the literature consulted in preparing this book.

It is important to remember here that the species listed under **Specialities** are *not* specialities of the site (such species are mentioned in the site introduction). Some species which are listed under **Specialities** may be very rare at the given site. Nevertheless, they *still* fit the criteria given above and merit the 'status' of speciality as far as this book is concerned.

Others: species that are widely distributed, but uncommon, spectacular or especially sought after for a variety of reasons.

Some species are **Specialities** in one country, but not in others, hence they may appear under **Specialities** for one country and **Others** for another, and some species may appear under **Specialities** for one country and **Others** for another because they are more likely to be seen at the site where they are listed under **Specialities**, and are difficult to see at sites where they are listed under **Others**.

At the end of the bird lists there is also a list of **Other wildlife**, which includes species of mammals, reptiles, amphibians, fish, insects, etc., which are listed in alphabetical order.

The lists, particularly the **Others** section, are not comprehensive and many more species may have been recorded at the given site. Such species are common and likely to be seen at many sites in that region of the country, or throughout a large part of Asia. These abundant, widespread, but no less spectacular species which are not normally listed include White-rumped Vulture, Crested Serpent-Eagle, Black Eagle, Changeable and Mountain Hawk-Eagles, Kalij Pheasant, Barred Buttonquail, White-breasted Waterhen, River and Red-wattled Lapwings, Oriental Turtle-Dove, Emerald Dove, Green and Mountain Imperial-Pigeons, Asian Koel, Greater and Lesser Coucals, Collared Scops-Owl, Brown Hawk-Owl, Large-tailed Nightjar, Collared and Pied Kingfishers, Dollarbird, Oriental Pied-Hornbill, Grey-capped Woodpecker, Black-naped Monarch, Asian Paradise-Flycatcher, most drongos, Common Iora, Black-naped Oriole, White-browed Shortwing, Common and Hill Mynas, Rufous-gorgeted, White-gorgeted, Snowy-browed, Little Pied, Blue-and-white and Verditer Flycatchers, Orange-flanked Bush-Robin (Red-flanked Bluetail), Oriental Magpie-Robin, White-rumped Shama, Blue-fronted, White-capped and Plumbeous Redstarts, Pied and Grey Bushchats, Ashy, Mountain and Black Bulbuls, Mountain Tailorbird, Dusky, Radde's, Arctic, Greenish, Golden-spectacled and Chestnut-crowned Warblers, Pygmy Wren-Babbler, White-browed Wagtail, Thick-billed, Plain and Fire-breasted Flowerpeckers, and Little and Yellow-breasted Buntings. By restricting the numbers of species listed under **Others** I have hoped to avoid repetition.

No one, not even the most experienced observer, is likely to see all the species listed under each site in a single visit or over a period of a few days, or, in some cases, during a prolonged stay of weeks or more. This is because a number of Asian species, especially the forest species, apart from being hyper-skulkers, are very thin on the ground.

Although you may not wish to take this book into the field once you have decided on your destination and itinerary, it, or a photocopy of the relevant section, may prove useful if you are prepared to scrawl all over it. For, by crossing out those species you have seen on a previous trip, or at a previously visited site, or already at the site you are at, you will be able to see what species you need to concentrate on. It is all too easy, in the haze of excitement generated by birding in a new country or at a new site, to see a lot of good birds and be satisfied with your visit, only to discover later that you have missed a bird at that site which does not occur at any other, or that you have just left a site offering you the last chance to see a certain species (on your chosen route) and are unable to change your itinerary.

Within these lists those species which have been marked with an **asterisk** (*) have been listed as threatened, conservation-dependent, data-deficient or near-threatened by BirdLife International/IUCN in *Birds to Watch 2: The World List of Threatened Birds*, Collar N *et al*, 1994. It is important to report any records of these species, and those described as rare in the text, to BirdLife International, Wellbrook Court, Girton Road, Cambridge CB3 0NA, UK. The BirdLife book deals in detail with Asia's rarest and often most spectacular species, hence all birders planning a trip to the region should seriously consider scrutinising it as part of their pre-trip planning research.

After the bird lists, directions to the site from the nearest large city, town or village, or previous site, are given under access. Then the best trails, birding 'spots' and birds are dealt with. Most distances are given to the nearest kilometre because speedometers and tyres vary so much, and directions are usually described as points of the compass rather than left or right so as not to cause confusion if travelling from a different direction to that dealt with. These directions are aimed at birders with cars. However, it is important to note that in most countries, buses and taxis go virtually anywhere there is habitation and will drop the passenger off at birding sites on request. I have decided not to repeat the vast amount of information regarding means of public transport given in reports or compete with the mindboggling detail presented in the various guidebooks. These can be used by those birders requiring them, thus allowing more room in this book to talk birds.

Where access is limited or permission required this is stated and a contact address given, sometimes in the **Additional Information** section at the end of each country account. If the detail under the access section seems scant, this is usually because one or more severely endangered species are present at that site.

Under **Accommodation** I have included the names of hotels, etc. recommended by birders for their safety, economy, comfort, position and, especially, opportunities for birding in their grounds. I have not listed all types of accommodation available at every site, as it would be foolish to waste so much space on repeating all the information which exists in the general guide books.

Hotels etc. are marked as follows: (A) = over £10/$15 (usually a long way over.); (B) = £5 to £10/$7.5 to $15; and (C) = under £5/$7.5 (all prices per person per night). In a few cases these price codes have also been used to indicate other costs, such as boat hire and guide fees.

Under each main site other nearby spots worth visiting are also mentioned. These usually offer another chance of seeing those species already listed under the main sites, but, in some cases, include sites, especially new ones, where information is scant and a deal of pioneer spirit is required. Asia veterans may wish to find out more about such sites (and send me the details for inclusion in the next edition.).

At the end of each country account there is an **Additional Information** section which includes lists of **Books and Papers**, for further research and field use, and **Addresses** to contact for more information or advanced booking of permits, accommodation etc.

Each country account ends, where relevant, with a list of **Endemic Species** and the best sites at which to look for them. There may be no specific site for some species. This is the time to leave this book in the car, put your exploring boots on and set out to find these little known birds. If successful, please send the details to me for inclusion in the next edition (see **Request**, p. 423).

Finally, lists of **Near-endemic Species** are also given where appropriate. The birds listed here have restricted ranges which cross two or three country boundaries. Birders with a particular interest in the endemics and near-endemics may wish to plan their trip around these sections, especially if many of the near-endemics are difficult to get to, or see, in the neighbouring countries, and a return trip is unlikely.

It is important to remember that this book is not an up-to-the-minute trip report. Some sites will have changed when you get there, some may not even be there and some new ones may have been discovered. Still, a little uncertainty is what makes birding so fascinating. It would be one hell of a poor pastime if every bird was lined up on an 'x' on the map, and while some birds are lined up like that in this book, I hope there are not too many. I have aimed to leave enough room, in the major part of the book, for you to 'find' your own birds and, perhaps even more importantly, to provide just the right amount of guidance to help birders to plan a successful and enjoyable birding trip to Asia.

INTRODUCTION TO BIRDING IN ASIA

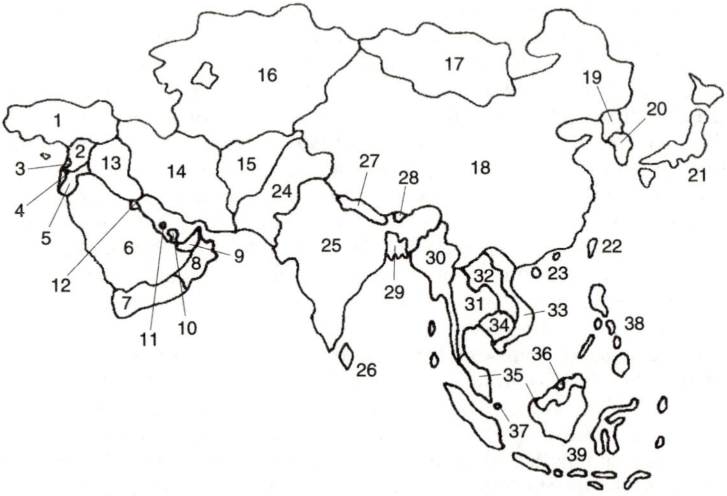

1 Turkey
2 Syria
3 Lebanon
4 Israel
5 Jordan
6 Saudi Arabia
7 Yemen
8 Oman
9 United Arab Emirates
10 Qatar
11 Bahrain
12 Kuwait
13 Iraq
14 Iran
15 Afghanistan
16 Turkestan
17 Mongolia
18 China
19 North Korea
20 South Korea
21 Japan
22 Taiwan
23 Hong Kong
24 Pakistan
25 India
26 Sri Lanka
27 Nepal
28 Bhutan
29 Bangladesh
30 Burma (Myanmar)
31 Thailand
32 Laos
33 Vietnam
34 Cambodia
35 Malaysia
36 Brunei Darussalam
37 Singapore
38 Philippines
39 Indonesia

Over a quarter of the world's birds occur in Asia. The total number of species recorded is nearly 2,700, which is around 400 less than in South America, but some 400 more than in Africa. The majority of species are concentrated along the Himalayas through north India, Nepal, Bhutan and Burma, and through southeast Asia to Malaysia.

Habitat Diversity

This massive continent, which stretches from Turkey and the Middle East in the west through the Himalayas to Japan, the Philippines and Halmahera in the east, supports a great variety of major habitats.

The western and southern slopes of Turkey and, to a lesser extent, the west-facing slopes of Syria, Lebanon and north Israel, support the char-

FIGURE 2: SPECIES LISTS OF THE WORLD'S MAJOR ZOOGEOGRAPHICAL ZONES

Approximate figures based on *Birds of the World: A Check List* (Fourth Edition), Clements J, 1991, and Supplements 1 and 2, 1992 and 1993, which list some 9,700 species.

Region	List	% of world total	% of Asian total
SOUTH AMERICA	3,083	32	115
ASIA	2,689	28	—
AFRICA	2,313	24	86
PALEARCTIC	950	10	35
AUSTRALASIA	900	9	34
NEARCTIC	800	8	30

acteristic scrub of the Mediterranean region, known as maquis. This gives way at higher and usually more inland locations to broadleaf and coniferous forests which stretch across the whole of mainland Asia in various forms. Although much of the Arabian Peninsula is desert, the major part of Asia is dominated by mountains. A multitude of magnificent peaks stretch across the centre of the continent, from Mount Ararat on the border between Turkey and Iran, which rises to 5165 m (16,946 ft), through the west Himalayas where K2 reaches 8611 m (28,251 ft) to the east Himalayas which reach 8848 m (29,029 ft) at Mount Everest. The mountains are less impressive southeast of the Himalayas, but they reach 4101 m (13,455 ft) at Mount Kinabalu in north Borneo.

The mountain meadows of the Himalayas and Tibetan Plateau, home to many fine pheasants, give way to oak–rhododendron forests, temperate forests and subtropical forests on their lower slopes. These habitats support distinct avifaunas and together they harbour a rich diversity of species which reaches a peak in the east Himalayas — one the richest areas for birds in Asia. To the north of the Tibetan Plateau the pine forests give way to vast areas of grassy steppe in north China and Mongolia. To the south and east of the Himalayas lie the huge floodplains of the Indus, Ganges, Brahmaputra, Irrawaddy, Mekong and Yangtze Rivers, all of which begin as mere trickles in the mountains, but end in massive deltas. Otherwise the coasts of Asia are strewn with mangrove-lined mud flats and beaches which support numerous shorebirds, many of which breed in Siberia.

The two major rivers away from the Himalayas, the Tigris and Euphrates, drain the mountains of eastern Turkey and form linear oases through Syria and Iraq before linking up to form one delta at the Arabian Gulf. Their floodplains give way to desert, steppe and forested mountains to the east, and the vast desert known as the 'Empty Quarter' to the south. This desert is bordered to the west by the Red Sea escarpment, which rises to 3666 m (12,028 ft) in Yemen and supports some surprisingly luxuriant monsoon forests and juniper stands with a unique avifauna.

ASIA: MAIN PHYSICAL FEATURES AND HABITATS

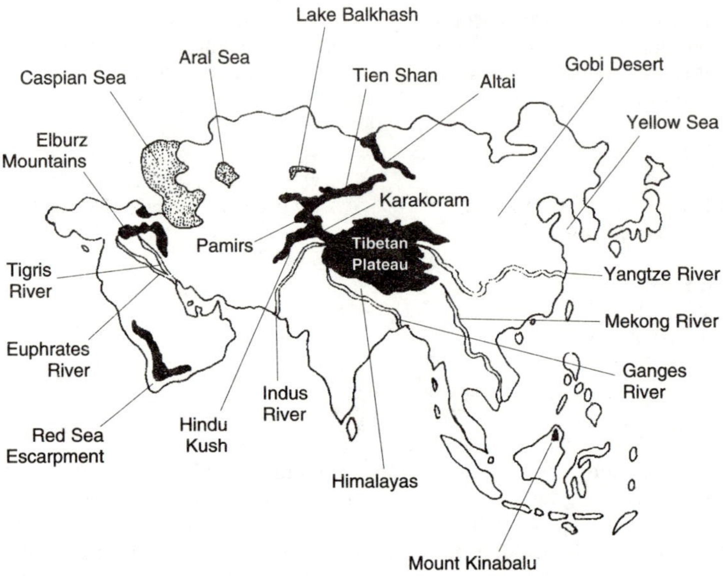

In southeast Asia and Malaysia the lowlands are far from being deserts. Although much of these lowlands have been turned over to paddies and plantations of palms and rubber, some fine stretches of lowland rainforest remain and they support the richest avifauna in Asia. These forests are only second in terms of diversity to those of Amazonia and they are full of broadbills, bulbuls and babblers, particularly in Malaysia. The numerous islands of the Philippines and Indonesia to the east support their own endemic avifaunas, which are usually restricted to remnant lowland and montane forest patches.

Country Lists

Asia's top three country lists all exceed 1,200. All three are higher than any African country, but lower than the top four South American countries.

Indonesia supports more birds than any other country in Asia. Around 1,500 species have been recorded there, 270 more than in India, which is nearly twice the size, and 250 more than China, which is five times larger. Indonesia's exceptionally rich diversity, a result of the country's high degree of endemism, still seems a little limited, however, when compared with Ecuador, which, despite being nearly seven times smaller, manages to support around 500 more species. Ecuador, however, only supports 12 endemics compared with Indonesia's 338. Africa's highest country lists are also surpassed by India and China, although India only supports around 150 more birds than Kenya, despite being nearly six times larger.

Three countries from Asia, Africa and South America which lie just north of the equator and support substantial areas of forest are worth comparing. Thailand's list of about 920 is slightly higher than similar sized Cameroon's 874 and compares favourably with Venezuela's 1,360, as this South American country is nearly twice as big.

Birders hoping to see the widest possible diversity of species on a short trip to Asia should read the accounts for north India, Nepal, Thailand and Malaysia first.

FIGURE 3: TOP FIVE COUNTRY SPECIES LISTS (approximate figures) (see Figure 4)

	Country	Species
1	INDONESIA	1,500
2	CHINA	1,244
3	INDIA	1,230
4	BURMA	970
5	THAILAND	920

FIGURE 4: COUNTRIES WITH OVER 900 SPECIES (see Figure 3)

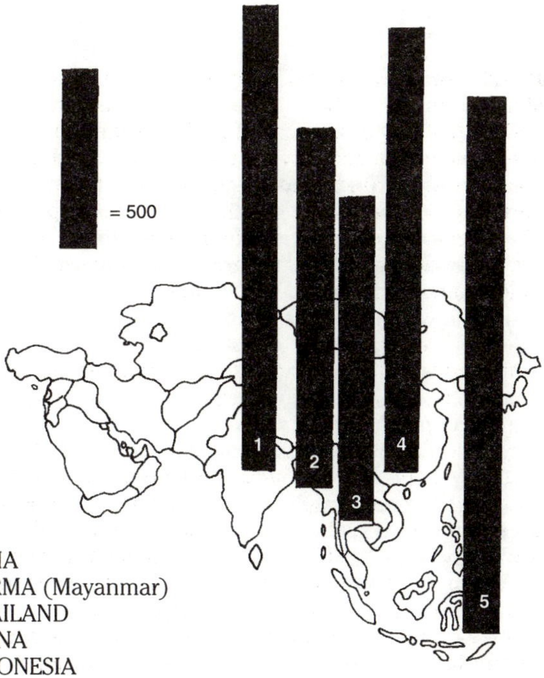

1 INDIA
2 BURMA (Mayanmar)
3 THAILAND
4 CHINA
5 INDONESIA

Site Lists

The top five sites in Asia support between 350 and at least 480 species, but these impressive totals fall short of the top nine sites in South America and even Asia's best is below Africa's top three. Asia's top site for species diversity is Chitwan National Park in Nepal, where over 480 species have been recorded in the fine habitat mosaic of rivers, forests and grassland. The similar Ruwenzori National Park in Uganda has a total somewhere around 550. The best forested sites in South American have lists which exceed 500, but Taman Negara, a forested site in Malaysia, can only muster around 350. Other readily accessible Asian sites with high species diversity include Bharatpur in India, Kaeng Krachan National Park in Thailand and Gunung Mulu National Park in Malaysian Borneo.

FIGURE 5: THE TOP FIVE SITE LISTS IN ASIA (approximate figures)

Site	List
CHITWAN NP (NEPAL)	480+
NAKAI-NAM THUEN (LAOS)	400+
XISHUANGBANNA (CHINA)	400+
BHARATPUR (INDIA)	400
TAMAN NEGARA (MALAYSIA)	350+

The above does not include the migration hot spots of Eilat, Israel (420+), Beidaihe, China (400+) and Aqaba, Jordan (350+), where many of the species recorded are vagrants.

Trip and Day Lists

In Asia the best places to visit to see the most species on trips lasting three or four weeks are northeast India, where a total of 440 is possible, north India, Malaysia and Thailand, where it is possible to see between 350 and 420 species, and Nepal and Vietnam, where up to 350 species are likely. At the lower end of the scale serious birders can expect to see around 200 species on short trips to Israel, Japan, Sri Lanka (in winter), Turkey, the United Arab Emirates (in spring) and Yemen.

Unfortunately, Asia is unable to compete with Africa and South America when it comes to long trip lists, and the highest Asian trip totals fall a long way short of the 730 species possible on Sunbird's three-week thrashes to Kenya, the 25-day tour to Kenya led by Brian Finch in November 1991 which amassed an amazing 797 species, Birdquest's 707 species in three weeks in Ecuador or the unofficial 'world bird tour record', which belongs to the Danish Ornithological Society, who recorded a mindblowing 844 species on a 27-day trip to Ecuador in 1992.

Although high trip totals are usually only possible on organised tours led by leaders equipped with masses of experience of the sites, birds and birding, and tape-recorders to lull out the many skulkers, thorough preparation by independent birders can result in similar totals for small 'teams' of fanatics.

Top Asian day lists are also put in the shade by Africa and South America. Although it is possible to record over 180 species in a day at Bharatpur (India) and over 150 at Chitwan National Park (Nepal), Kosi (Nepal) and Hong Kong (in spring) the African and South American day list records are 342 in Kenya on a November day in 1986 and 331 in Manu National Park, Peru, also in November in 1986.

Family Diversity

Asia does boast the greatest family diversity of the big three continents. A total of 116 families of birds are present here (see Figure 1, p. 15), eight more than Africa and 24 more than South America. However, only six families are endemic to Asia, three less than the nine which only occur in South America (25 including Central America) and four less than the ten which are endemic to Africa (15 including Malagasy). The six families unique to Asia are Ibisbill, Asian Barbets (26 species), Ioras (four species), Leafbirds (ten species), Hypocolius and Rhabdornises (three species). Hypocolius is more or less restricted to the Middle East, where it is most likely to be seen in Bahrain or the United Arab Emirates, and Rhabdornises are restricted to the Philippines, but the other four families are more widespread and it is possible to come across all four on trips to either south China, Nepal, India or Bhutan.

Asia is particularly rich in pheasants, cranes, treeswifts, kingfishers, hornbills, woodpeckers, pittas, broadbills, monarch flycatchers, orioles, cuckoo-shrikes, flycatchers, nuthatches, bulbuls, brightly coloured babblers, parrotbills and flowerpeckers, while unique genuses include the malkohas, shortwings, forktails, cochoas, laughingthrushes and the bizarre Malaysian Rail-babbler.

Endemic Species

Regions of the world with concentrations of restricted range birds have been identified as Endemic Bird Areas (EBAs) in BirdLife International's *Putting Biodiversity on the Map*, 1992. Out of the world total of 221 EBAs, Asia has 57 (see Figure 6), two more than South America and 20 more than Africa.

The distribution of Asian EBAs is reflected in country endemics lists. Indonesia has the most EBAs (15) and the most endemics (338), followed by the Philippines with nine EBAs and 185 endemics, China with 11 EBAs and 59 endemics, and mainland India with six EBAs and 39 endemics. The islands of Indonesia support far more endemics than any African or South American country, and even the Philippines has more endemics than Brazil, South America's richest country for endemics with 179 unique species, and Madagascar, whose total of 102 is the highest in Africa. On the other hand, China (59) and Colombia (59), and mainland India (39) and Venezuela (41) have equal or very similar totals.

FIGURE 6: ASIAN ENDEMIC BIRD AREAS (57)

CAUCASUS, CYPRUS, IRAQ MARSHES, ARABIAN MOUNTAINS (Saudi Arabia and Yemen), WESTERN HIMALAYAS, INDUS VALLEY (Pakistan), WESTERN GHATS (India), SRI LANKA, ASSAM PLAINS (India), TIRAP FRONTIER (India and Burma), ANDAMAN ISLANDS,

NICOBAR ISLANDS, EASTERN HIMALAYAS, TIBETAN VALLEYS, SOUTH TIBET, WEST CHINA, QINGHAI MOUNTAINS, CENTRAL SICHUAN, WEST SICHUAN, SOUTH CHINA, YUNNAN MOUNTAINS, SHANXI MOUNTAINS, FUJIAN MOUNTAINS, HAINAN, TAIWAN, NANSEI ISLANDS (Japan), OGASAWARA ISLANDS (Japan), BURMESE PLAINS, ANNAMESE LOWLANDS (Laos and Vietnam), DA LAT PLATEAU (Vietnam), COCHINCHINA (Vietnam), LUZON MOUNTAINS, LUZON LOWLANDS, MINDORO, NEGROS and PANAY, CEBU, PALAWAN, SAMAR-LEYTE-BOHOL-MINDANAO LOWLANDS, MINDANAO MOUNTAINS, SULU ARCHIPELAGO (all Philippines), BORNEAN MOUNTAINS, SUMATRA and PENINSULAR MALAYSIA, ENGGANO ISLANDS (Sumatra), JAVAN and BALINESE MOUNTAINS, JAVAN LOWLANDS, FLORES, SUMBA, TIMOR, TANIMBAR, TALAUD and SANGIHE, SULAWESI MOUNTAINS, SULAWESI LOWLANDS, BANGGAI and SULA, BURU, SERAM, NORTH MOLUCCAS and CHRISTMAS ISLAND.

It is impossible to see all or even a high percentage of the endemic birds of Indonesia and the Philippines on short, or even long, trips because so many are so rare, but a month's hard birding in the Philippines may produce as many as 130 of the 185 endemics (70%). Similar percentages are possible in China and on mainland India but only on extensive trips, whereas higher percentages may be achieved with Sulawesi's 67, Borneo's 37, Java's 20, Taiwan's 14, Japan's 12 and Vietnam's 10, even on short trips, and ten days or so on Sri Lanka is usually enough to clinch the magical 100% — all 23 endemics.

FIGURE 7: COUNTRY ENDEMIC LISTS (see Figure 8)

1	INDONESIA	338
2	PHILIPPINES	185
3	CHINA	59
4	INDIA (Mainland)	39*
5	(BORNEO, MALAYSIA and INDONESIA)	37
6	SRI LANKA	23
7	ANDAMAN and NICOBAR ISLANDS	17
8	TAIWAN	14
9	JAPAN	12
10	VIETNAM	10
11	BURMA	4

Countries with two endemics: Nepal and Thailand. Countries with single endemics: Afghanistan, Iran and Turkestan.

*Not including the 17 species endemic to the Andaman and Nicobar Islands.

FIGURE 8: COUNTRIES WITH OVER 20 ENDEMICS (see Figure 7)

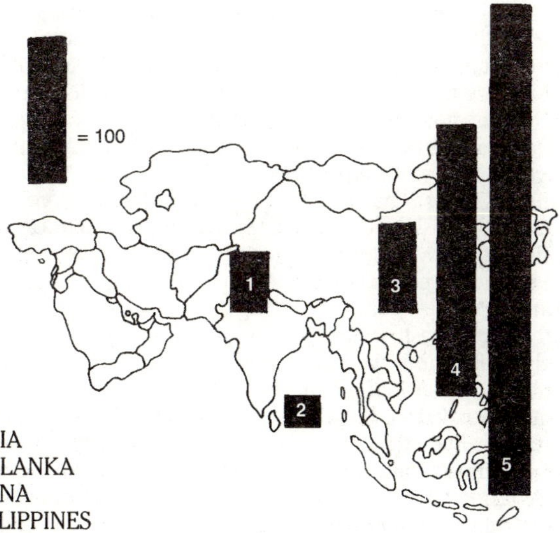

1 INDIA
2 SRI LANKA
3 CHINA
4 PHILIPPINES
5 INDONESIA

Exploration

Only a few birders have seen over 1,500 species in Asia, but the leading lister for the continent, Ben King, has seen over 1,970, including all but 40 of China's 1,200 or so species. This is a remarkable achievement, considering the logistical and political problems that still prevent easy access to many areas, but Ben has been birding his favourite continent for many years and knows Asia better than many birders know their local patches.

Those birders in search of Asia's little known and rarely seen species will be busy planning possible trips to areas which may become accessible in the near future, such as northern Burma, having carried out extensive and painstaking research into old records, habitat preferences and the present day distribution of those habitats. A number of species which were thought to be extinct have been relocated in recent years, especially in Indonesia, where many islands were not visited by birders for decades, and even new species have been discovered during the 1990s. The fact that a woodcock remained undetected on the Philippines, a popular birding destination for many years, until 1993, suggests that there may be a few more new species out there, perhaps even a pitta.

CONSERVATION

More than half of the earth's human population lives in Asia. Almost a quarter (1.2 billion) are crammed into China and nearly 100 million somehow manage to exist on the small islands of Java and Bali. The densely populated parts of China are an ecological disaster area and what little remains of the original natural forest cover on Java and Bali is virtually restricted to the steepest, infertile mountain slopes. In the equally overpopulated Philippines less than 2% of the original forest cover remains. Birders have to find the trees there before they even think about birding. The continent's high human population is the reason why five of the top ten countries in the world with the most bird species in danger of extinction are Asian.

Burgeoning human populations need somewhere to live, land to grow food on and fresh water, basic requirements that result in deforestation, desertification, wetland reclamation and drainage, pollution and potentially catastrophic climate changes.

As our numbers increase, so it seems do the numbers of us who live low-quality lives. Even those of us who think the quality of our lives has improved with time should stop and think. Is living in a concrete box surrounded by tarmac better than a hut in the woods? Is our quality of life better if we live in a centrally heated house with all the modern conveniences alongside birdless, chemically sterilised farmland, or if we live in more primitive accommodation surrounded by forests, meadows and birdsong? Most people would, given the choice, probably plump for a combination of both, but most don't have a choice, because there are so many of us.

Ironically, it seems we need to think about ourselves first and then perhaps we will be able to help the birds. It is no good trying to persuade governments to protect areas, even those where the current land use by local people benefits birds, when they advocate increasing human populations as a necessary prerequisite of economic growth and stability. Unless the quality of life is to sink to even greater depths, whatever areas such governments do protect will ultimately come under pressure from an increased human population. Logically, we will continue to increase in numbers until all that is left of the natural world is small oases among vast deserts of concrete and sterile green spaces.

The only way we can ensure that there will be enough room for us and the birds in the future is to stabilise human population growth. Better still, we should aim to decrease it. However, as stemming population growth seems impossible and, indeed, undesirable to some governments, it may be worth considering some smaller initiatives to help preserve what we have left. For example, integrating local needs with sustainable use of the natural habitat, through such schemes as ecotourism, could be implemented. Some governments have catered for ecotourists interested in Asia's wild places for many years, but providing specifically for birders is still in its infancy. Bird tourism has the potential to boost the economy of many local communtities and this is a strong argument for conserving natural resources at a given site. When visiting any of the sites described in this book, please make sure every person in the area, especially local business people, knows why you are there and why more will follow you if the birds and their habitats are protected.

I hope this book, in its own small way, will help to convince governments, via encouraging bird tourism to their countries, that protecting birds and their habitats is more important than encouraging population growth.

GENERAL TIPS

Any birding guide necessitates the inclusion of some miscellaneous tips on how to see the most birds, how to see them well, how to get the most out of a birding trip and, most importantly of all, how to enjoy the experience. The following tips are by no means comprehensive and they are little more than a mishmash of points resulting from personal experience and birding tales shared between friends. However, they may help maximise the enjoyment of a birding trip to Asia.

The best birding trips usually result from extensive pre-trip research. Find out where you are most likely to find the species you wish to see before embarking on any trip and work out an itinerary very carefully. It usually takes much longer to see many birds in the forests of Asia than most people imagine, so allow plenty of time in the itinerary for forested sites.

Once at your chosen destination, walk quietly and slowly, especially in forests, and use vegetation for patient stalking. These basic field skills are well known to most birders, but they are all too easily forgotten in the frenzy of new and exciting birds. Early morning is usually the best time for birding anywhere in the world and Asia is no exception. The middle of the day is a good time to move from one site to another or, if this is not appropriate, to take a siesta before a late afternoon bash, the evening owl and nightjar search, and the appropriate celebration of another great day in the field. Some fanatical birders will argue that it is still possible to see plenty of birds around midday, especially where there is some shade or water, and the hours of darkness after the owls and nightjars have been seen are the best time to move from site to site. Travelling at night can be dangerous in some Asian countries, especially where the roads are bad, but overnight drives do help to keep accommodation costs down and may produce a few birds and mammals. However, while a couple of night drives may save some money, being constantly tired could impair your enjoyment of the whole trip. Its not much fun returning home only to discover that you can't remember anything because you were too tired.

Asian forest birding is often very frustrating, especially compared with South America, and many hours may pass without seeing a single bird (you may hear plenty), but when a wave (feeding flock) appears, or an avian jewel in the form a pitta pops out on to the trail, all the hours of planning and patient scanning will suddenly seem worthwhile. Bird waves are a feature of Asian forests and may contain anything up to 20 different species. They often seem to appear from nowhere and move all too quickly, but try sticking with them as long as possible, even after it seems like they have all passed, because the stragglers often turn out to be the real goodies. If all is quiet in the canopy it is worth remembering that many of the rarest and most spectacular of Asian forest birds are ground dwellers such as pheasants and pittas, and that walking silently and slowly with your eyes riveted to the ground on and either side of the trail may turn out to be the best birding method. Tracking down every call, especially whistles (pittas), is essential, but more often than not requires the patience of a saint. It is easy to get the tape recorder out in such a situation, but this devious birding method is *not* appropriate for use with threatened species (not knowing the call means it could be a threatened species), if any species at all. It distracts birds from feeding and causes them undue excitement. If you cannot see a calling bird it is frustrating, but, surely, there is more joy and satisfaction to be gained from seeing the bird after a long and hard stalk, than standing by a tape recorder waiting for the unfortunate creature to come and peck at it.

Pigeons, parrots, hornbills, barbets, leafbirds, thrushes, bulbuls, flowerpeckers and sunbirds are good examples of birds which are attracted to flowering and fruiting trees. While such trees may seem devoid of life as the birds feed quietly, they can slowly come alive, and standing next to one for a few hours may be more productive than frantic wandering. The same goes for bamboo, which is the haunt of specialists such as parrotbills and parrotfinches.

Rain and mist is prevalent in many lowland and montane forest sites, but this rarely seems to affect bird activity, hence it is worth carrying on birding in such conditions. Air- and water-tight binoculars are essential in these damp, humid and often downright wet forests.

Altitude sickness is a potentially serious problem in the Himalayas and on the Tibetan Plateau, hence it is worth remembering the following; most people can travel up to 3000 m (9843 ft) in a short time and manage 4500 m (14,764 ft) after a night at 3000 m (9843 ft), but going straight to 4500 m (14,764 ft) can be dangerous and one in three people who attempt it usually end up with a severe headache or, even worse, feel dizzy and begin to vomit. If that person then turns blue or coughs up pink mucus they should descend immediately to below 3000 m (9843 ft), where a quick recovery is normal. High-altitude health problems can be alleviated by eating lightly, taking it easy, using maximum sunblock and keeping warm when the sun goes down.

It is worth taking an altimeter and a compass if you are unsure of the terrain you are visiting, or if the only information you have on a certain species is the altitude at which it has been recorded. Vehicles may be a problem at high altitudes. If you have difficulty starting your engine in the early mornings, try pouring petrol directly into the carburetter.

Two of the joys of birding in Asia, especially compared with Africa, are that hiring a car is rarely essential for getting to, or birding at, most of the best sites and that it is possible to bird on foot almost everywhere. However, it pays to be aware of the fact that tigers still roam the grasslands and forests of India, lowland Nepal, southeast Asia and Sumatra. If you come across one while birding, there is little you will be able to do, except make a wish.

GLOSSARY

2WD: Two-wheel-drive vehicle.
4WD: Four-wheel-drive vehicle.
FR: Forest Reserve.
Gallery forest/woodland: Waterside (riparian) forest and woodland, usually where forested areas merge into more open areas such as savanna, alongside watercourses.
Garrigue: Overgrazed maquis, usually dominated by thorny bushes, which is common around the Mediterranean.
Maquis: A natural scrub community of low and high bushes usually dominated by heath, rosemary and sage, which grows on the rocky slopes around the Mediterranean.
NP: National Park.
NR: Nature Reserve.
Secondary: This term usually refers to forested areas which have been cleared, but since regenerated, albeit usually in fragments alongside the newly established land use.
WS: Wildlife Sanctuary.

MAPS

Birders, understandably, are more interested in finding birds than noting down distances and directions when in the field, so although every effort has been made to make the maps in this book as precise as possible, they may not be entirely accurate, at least in terms of exact scale and compass points. The main purpose of the maps is to facilitate birding at the sites, so more often than not 'direction-pointers' such as rivers and buildings, and on-site detail such as trails, have been exaggerated and are not drawn to scale. Each country account begins with a map of the country with the main sites numbered, and there are also some maps of regions within countries to show how 'bunches' of sites are distributed. These are intended to aid birders in their production of trip routes and itineraries during the planning stage.

It is important to remember that Asia is a fast-changing continent, hence trails may have become tracks, tracks may have become roads, buildings may have been knocked down, buildings may have been put up, marshes, lakes and rivers may have dried up, rivers may have changed course, signs may have fallen down, habitats may have been totally destroyed and some sites may no longer exist by the time you come to use these maps. If you arrive at a site which no longer exists or which looks totally different to what you have perceived as a result of reading this book. don't blame the birders who have been before you and don't blame me, blame the ever-increasing human population on the planet. And, remember, this book is a guiding light, not a substitute for up-to-the-minute information.

The **map symbols** used are as follows:

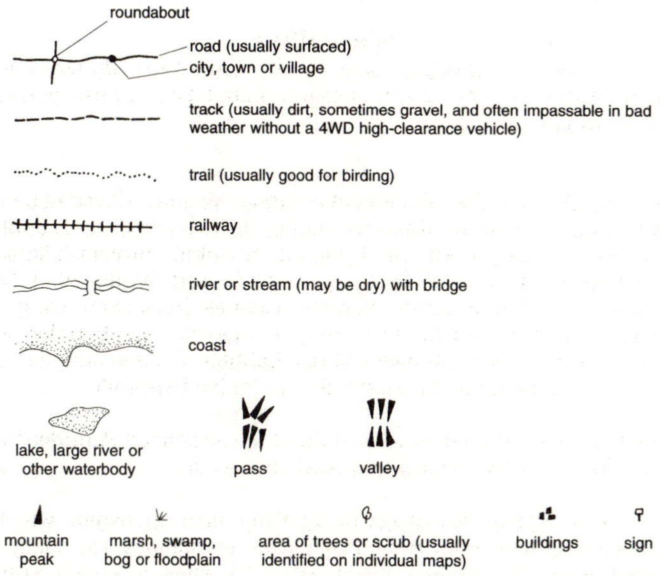

BANGLADESH

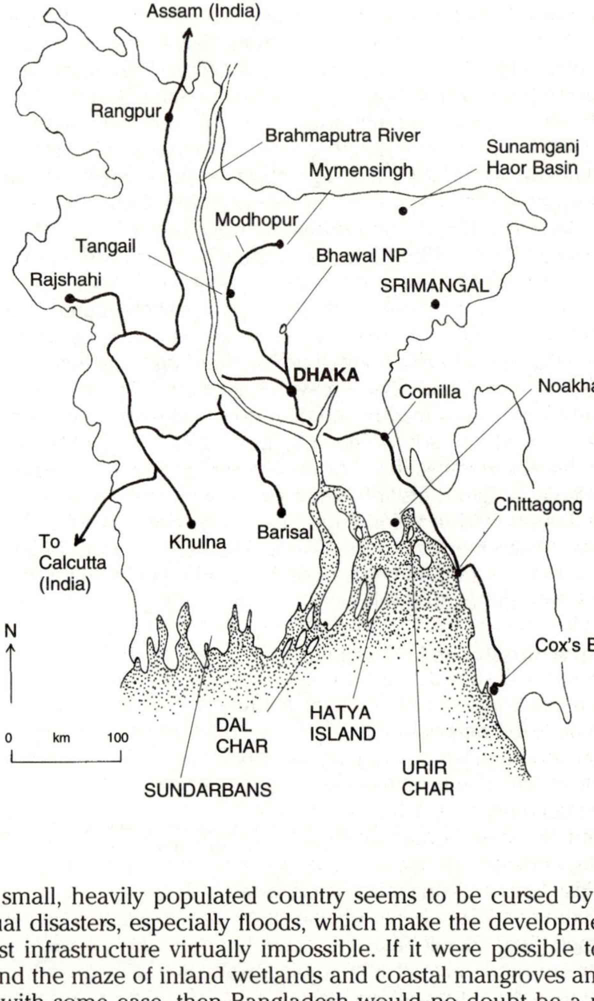

This small, heavily populated country seems to be cursed by almost annual disasters, especially floods, which make the development of a tourist infrastructure virtually impossible. If it were possible to travel around the maze of inland wetlands and coastal mangroves and mudflats with some ease, then Bangladesh would no doubt be a popular destination, for this country is the major wintering ground of Spoonbill Sandpiper*.

At 143,998 sq km, this small country is slightly larger than England and one fifth the size of Texas. The best way to bird Bangladesh is to join the local conservationists on their January survey trips and help them to count the masses of wintering waterbirds. To arrange places on these reasonably priced excursions which last around ten days write to Anisuzzaman Khan, NACOM (Nature Conservation Movement), 128–129 (2nd Floor), Mohammadia Super Market, Sobhanbagh (near Dhanmondi), Dhaka (tel: 819237), a few months in advance. Otherwise it will be necessary to hire vehicles (only available with drivers) and boats, both of which are expensive, to get the best out of Bangladesh on a short trip. It is possible to reach some sites on the crowded public transport network which includes a few internal flights, trains (the best way to reach sites in the eastern half of the country), buses, rickshaws and 'babytaxis' (motorised three-wheelers), but the wintering grounds of Spoonbill Sandpiper* are only accessible by boat. Independent birders will find a knowledge of Bangla, the national language, useful when organising boats etc. There is a wide range of accommodation in Dhaka, the capital, and a number of cheap, basic hotels, resthouses and missions elsewhere in the country. Away from Dhaka where a wide range of food is available, menus are dominated by meat and fish curries which are served with rice or dal (lentils). Immunisation against hepatitis, polio, typhoid and yellow fever is recommended, as are precautions against Malaria. The prime time for Spoonbill Sandpiper* and a sprinkling of rare wintering passerines is between December and February, and this also happens to be the driest and least humid time of year, although it can be rather cool at night. The hot, humid rainy season usually lasts from June to September.

The mighty, braided Brahmaputra River flows north to south through the middle of Bangladesh, spilling out to sea through a maze of mangroves, mudflats and sandy islands known as chars, all of which support numerous wintering waterbirds, especially shorebirds. The eastern half of the delta is dominated by chars and the western half by the world's largest remaining area of mangroves — the Sundarbans. Inland, there are large flooded basins in the northeast of the country, known as haors. These dry up to some extent during the winter but permanent wetlands known as beels remain and also support spectacular concentrations of wintering waterbirds. There are also a few fragments of evergreen and semi-deciduous forest in the east, but much of this badly degraded country has been turned over to rice cultivation. Conservation is almost non-existent and with such a massive human population struggling to survive in such a small area, most of the remaining forests and wetlands look likely to be felled and drained before the end of the millennium. Unless the population can be controlled and, ultimately, reduced, the birds of Bangladesh will continue to suffer, especially the 63 threatened and near-threatened species which occur here.

Around 687 species have been recorded and non-endemic specialities and spectacular species include Baer's Pochard*, Lesser Adjutant*, Pallas' Fish-Eagle*, White-cheeked Partridge*, Spoonbill Sandpiper*, Indian Skimmer*, Spot-bellied Eagle-Owl*, Brown-winged Kingfisher*, Blue-naped Pitta*, Black-breasted Thrush* and Yellow-vented Warbler*. There are no endemics. It is possible to see over 250 species in two weeks during a winter visit and over 300 species on a more extensive winter trip. During the summer it would be hard to find 200 species, even on a long trip.

In **Dhaka** the zoo and adjacent botanical gardens are worth visiting if there is time to kill. The zoo is very popular but it opens early at 0700 and this is the best time to be there. Check the lake (turn right at the monkey cage) for ducks and the botanical gardens for Striated Babbler. Spring (April) and Autumn (September) migrants include Forest Wagtail, and rare winter visitors include Smoky Warbler. The extensive but degraded Sal forest at **Modhupur**, three hours by road north of Dhaka, is an excellent place for nightbirds including Spot-bellied* and

Dusky Eagle-Owls, Brown and Tawny* Fish-Owls, Brown Wood-Owl and Hodgson's Frogmouth, as well as Indian Pitta (May), Orange-headed Thrush and Yellow-vented Warbler* (Dec–Feb). To reach this forest turn west just southwest of Rasalpur Bazar (on the Mymensingh–Tangail road) on to the entrance road which leads to a lake (after 4 km) and the Juneer Resthouse (after 8 km). Concentrate on the forest alongside the first five km or so of the entrance road, part of which is accessible via tracks and trails leading north and south from the lake.

The best birding area in Bangladesh, in terms of variety, is that around **Srimangal** in the northeast. Over 375 species have been recorded within a 10-km radius of this town which is just five hours by train from Dhaka. **Hail Haor**, just to the west of town, supports wintering Pied Harrier, Grey-headed Lapwing* and Bengal Weaver. To bird the west shore turn north off the Dhaka road on to Bunobir Road 7 km west of Srimangal and after 5.5 km along here turn east to reach the lakeshore after one km. Boats can be hired here. The small (9 sq km) **Lawachara/West Bhanugach Reserve Forest**, a plantation dating back to the 1920s, has attracted nearly 240 species including virtually all of the forest species regularly recorded in Bangladesh. Notable species include White-cheeked Partridge*, Red-headed Trogon, Blue-bearded Bee-eater, Blue-naped Pitta*, Silver-breasted Broadbill (scarce), Black-breasted Thrush* (Dec–Feb), White-tailed Robin and Yellow-vented Warbler* (Dec–Feb). This reserve is accessible from the Srimangal-Kamalganj road which bisects it 5–12 km east of Srimangal.

Accommodation: Niaz Hotel (basic); Mission (C), bookable in advance via HEED, Plot 19, Main Road, Section 11, Mirpur, Dhaka; British High Commission (A — tel: 08626 207); Forest Resthouse, bookable in advance via Divisional Forest Officer, Sylhet (tel: 0821 716358).

The large and complex **Sunamganj Haor Basin** in north Bangladesh supports masses of wintering waterbirds including Falcated Duck and Baer's Pochard*, and is a major world stronghold of the Pallas' Fish-Eagle*. Concentrate on Tangua Haor and Pasua Beel where around 200,000 duck roosted in January 1993. From Sylhet, accessible by air, rail and road from Dhaka, it is 2 hours by road to Sunamganj where the boat called *Al Amin*, which is used for waterfowl census work, can be hired via the Country Boat Association on the river front.

Bangladesh is the main wintering ground of the rare Spoonbill Sandpiper*. Counts in the eastern delta on the south coast off **Noakhali** around Urir Char, Hatya Island and Dal Char have ranged from as many as 257 (January 1989) to as few as two (January 1993), although the most recent count (January 1996) revealed about 100. This is a difficult area to bird independently and it is best to join the local conservationists on the January surveys organised by NACOM in order to enjoy this superb area to the full. Counting all the birds amongst the mass of ever-changing chars and mudflats usually takes around ten days, based on Forest Department trawlers. Other species which occur here include Bar-headed Goose (Dec–Feb), Great Knot, Indian Skimmer*, Black-capped Kingfisher and rarities such as Nordmann's Greenshank* and Asian Dowitcher*.

The most accessible site for wintering shorebirds in Bangladesh is **Patenga** near Chittagong in the southeast, but only small numbers of Spoonbill Sandpiper* occur here on an irregular basis. Once at Patenga, accessible by overnight train from Dhaka, head for the Steel Mill Colony, 500 m south of the naval base, and turn west to Catgor. If using a babytaxi make sure the driver understands that you do not want to go to the tourist beach farther south. Walk north from the end of the road at Catgor and check the mudflats for shorebirds which include Great Knot and Broad-billed Sandpiper, and occasional Nordmann's Greenshanks* and Spoonbill Sandpipers*.

Accommodation: plenty of hotels in Chittagong.

Species recorded in the **Sundarbans** in southwest Bangladesh include Lesser Adjutant*, Masked Finfoot* (Katka Khal in Kochikhali Tiger Reserve), Great Thick-knee (Egg Island) and Brown-winged Kingfisher*. The best area is the extreme southeast of the mangrove belt and this is accessible by boats which can be hired at Mongla but to bird here it is necessary to obtain a permit from the Forest Department and to book accommodation in their resthouses in advance. This may prove to be a bureaucratic nightmare, so it is probably wise to contact The Guide, 47 New Eskaton Road, Dhaka (tel: 400511; fax: 833544), a tour company which runs regular cruises (with comfortable cabins) through the best area. There are more tigers in the Sundarbans than anywhere else in Asia, so it would be foolish to try and bird this area alone.

ADDITIONAL INFORMATION

Books and Papers

Birding in Bangladesh. Thompson P and Johnson L, 1996. Privately published (available via OBC).
Birds in Bangladesh. Harvey W, 1990. Dhaka University Press.
Birds of Bangladesh. Husain Z, 1979. Government of Bangladesh.

Near-endemics

White-bellied Heron*, Swamp Francolin*, Manipur Bush-Quail*, White-cheeked Partridge*, Firethroat, Rufous-vented* and Swamp Prinias, Smoky Warbler, Bristled Grassbird*, Yellow-throated Laughingthrush*, Marsh Babbler*, Spotted Wren-Babbler*, Nepal Fulvetta, White-naped Yuhina, Black-breasted Parrotbill*, Fire-tailed Sunbird, Scarlet Finch.

BHUTAN

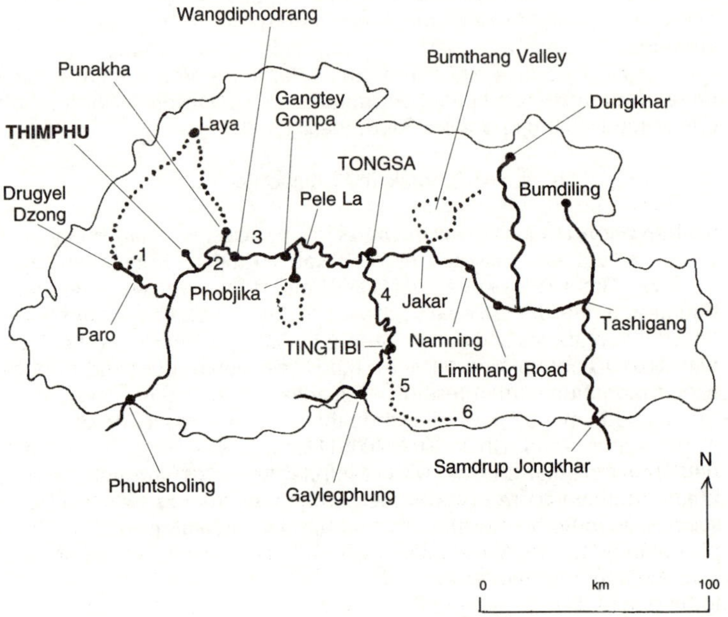

1 Paro Valley
2 Dochu La
3 Wangdiphodrang–Tongsa Road
4 Tongsa–Tingtibi Road
5 Shemgang Trek
6 Manas Wildlife Sanctuary

INTRODUCTION

Summary

Most of the pristine forest which is left in the eastern Himalayas is in sparsely populated Bhutan, hence this tiny country supports a wonderfully rich avifauna which includes many of the most beautiful babblers. Although numerous birders have been fortunate enough to go birding in Bhutan, most have been on expensive, organised tours because, unfortunately, this is a difficult country for the independent traveller to visit.

Size

At 47,000 sq km, Bhutan is one-third the size of England and 15 times smaller than Texas.

Getting Around

A birding trip to Bhutan involves a mini-expedition, based on a drive across the middle of the country or a long trek, hence the vast majority of birders visit Bhutan on organised tours. A strict limit is imposed on the number of visitors allowed into the country each year and every visitor must pay for the privilege.

Accommodation and Food

There are few places to stay in Bhutan and most places, like the food, are basic.

Health and Safety

Immunisation against hepatitis, polio, typhoid and yellow fever is recommended, as are precautions against malaria.

Climate and Timing

The best time to visit Bhutan is between November and March when winter visitors such as Black-necked Crane* are present.

Habitats

Bhutan is a little gem of a wild place where over 60% of the land is still forested, and what is even more amazing about this beautiful country is that most of these forests, as well as the high Himalayan meadows and wide river valleys, are in pristine condition.

Conservation

Bhutan is one of those rare countries where it seems the birds have a bright future, and that includes the 36 threatened and near-threatened species. So long as the human population remains stable, the local people continue to care about their environment and the government manages the country's modernisation with the utmost care, Bhutan is likely to be one of those very rare places where it will be possible to go birding in pristine forests full of birds in the future.

Bird Families

Babblers are particularly well represented in Bhutan, with over 10 laughingthrushes and five scimitar-babblers.

Bird Species

Over 590 species have been recorded in Bhutan. Non-endemic specialities and spectacular species include White-bellied Heron*, Satyr Tragopan*, Black-necked Crane*, Ibisbill, Long-billed Plover, Ward's Trogon*, Ruddy and Crested Kingfishers, Rufous-necked Hornbill*, Yellow-rumped Honeyguide*, Collared Treepie, Sapphire Flycatcher, Blue-fronted Robin*, Green Cochoa*, Yellow-vented Warbler*, Rufous-chinned, Grey-sided and Scaly Laughingthrushes, Red-faced Liocichla, Slender-billed Scimitar-Babbler*, Silver-eared Mesia, Cutia, Red-tailed Minla, Yellow-throated* and Rufous-throated* Fulvettas, White-naped Yuhina, Fire-tailed Myzornis, Great, Black-browed* and Rufous-headed* Parrotbills, Sultan and Fire-capped Tits, Maroon-backed Accentor, Gould's and Fire-tailed Sunbirds, Crimson-browed Finch.

Endemics

There is no endemic species, but Bhutan is a good place to see a number of eastern Himalayan specialities.

Expectations

It is possible to see 300 species on a thorough three or four week trip.

From Bagdogra (accessible by air from Delhi), near Darjeeling in northeast India, it is four hours by road to the Bhutan border at **Phuntsholing**. This busy town lies near the Torsa River where Ibisbill winter (Nov–Mar) and the degraded sal forest on the slopes above the town support Blue-bearded Bee-eater, Pygmy Blue-Flycatcher, White-naped Yuhina, Grey-headed Parrotbill, Sultan Tit and Gould's Sunbird. From Phuntsholing it is one day by road to the Paro Valley, via steep, forested hills where Rufous-bellied Eagle, Red-headed Trogon, Coral-billed Scimitar-Babbler and Fire-capped Tit occur.

PARO VALLEY

This wide valley is situated at 2150 m (7054 ft) below the snow-capped peak of Chomolhari in northwest Bhutan. Paddies line the Paro River at the bottom of the valley where Ibisbill is a winter visitor, while birds such as Black-faced Laughingthrush occur on the surrounding slopes which support mixed temperate forests and subalpine pastures interspersed with patches of juniper and rhododendron scrub.

Specialities

Ibisbill (Nov–Apr).

Others

Crested Kingfisher, Eurasian Nutcracker, Grey-backed Shrike, White-collared Blackbird, White-browed Bush-Robin, Hodgson's Redstart, Little Forktail, Wallcreeper, Rusty-flanked Treecreeper, Black-browed Tit, Nepal Martin, Chestnut-headed Tesia, Aberrant and Grey-sided Bush-Warblers, Buff-barred Warbler, Blyth's Leaf-Warbler, Grey-hooded Warbler, Black-faced Laughingthrush, Red-billed Leiothrix, Green Shrike-Babbler, White-browed Fulvetta, Stripe-throated Yuhina, Green-backed Tit, Rufous-breasted and Maroon-backed Accentors, Gould's and Fire-tailed Sunbirds, Beautiful Rosefinch.

The Paro Valley is accessible by road (one day) from Phuntsholing on the border with India, or by air from Delhi and Calcutta. Bird the Paro River, the riverside paddies, the trail to the famous Tuktsang (Tiger's Nest) Monastery at 3680 m (12,074 ft), which passes through excellent forest, and the ruins of Drugyel Dzong at the northern end of the valley.

Accommodation: Paro — Olathang Hotel.

From Drugyel Dzong at the northern end of the Paro Valley it is possible to hike into the highest mountain region of northwest Bhutan on the long, hard, high-altitude **Tashitang Trek**, which ends in Tashitang, near Punakha, and usually takes around three weeks to complete. Birds recorded on this trek include Tibetan Snowcock, Himalayan Monal, Ibisbill and Snow Pigeon, but they may be eclipsed by the sighting of a snow leopard, for this is probably the best place on earth to see this beautiful cat. Other mammals present include bharal, black and brown bears, Himalayan tahr, red panda and the rare takin, a large 'goat'. The best time to try this trek is April, although even then some passes may be blocked by snow. It is also possible to trek from Drugyel Dzong to

Chimding, and birds recorded on this route include Blood Pheasant and Spotted Laughingthrush.

Satyr Tragopan* and the very rare Blue-fronted Robin* (close to Tashigong Monastery), have been recorded on the one-day walk between Thimphu and the Dochu La pass.

DOCHU LA

The mossy, oak–rhododendron forests either side of this 3050 m (10,007 ft) pass support some superb birds, including Slender-billed Scimitar-Babbler*, Rufous-breasted Bush-Robin*, Red-tailed Minla, Fire-tailed Myzornis and Fire-capped Tit.

Specialities

Slender-billed Scimitar-Babbler*, Fire-tailed Myzornis, Fire-capped Tit.

Others

Lammergeier, Himalayan Griffon, Speckled Wood-Pigeon, Gold-billed Magpie, Rufous-bellied Niltava, Slaty-blue Flycatcher, Hodgson's Redstart, Rufous-breasted Bush-Robin*, White-tailed Nuthatch, Black-browed Tit, Yellowish-bellied Bush-Warbler, White-throated, Striated and Black-faced Laughingthrushes, Rufous-capped Babbler, Blue-winged, Chestnut-tailed and Red-tailed Minlas, Rufous-winged Fulvetta, Rufous Sibia, Whiskered and Rufous-vented Yuhinas, Black-throated Parrotbill, Grey-crested, Green-backed, Yellow-cheeked and Yellow-browed Tits, Rufous-breasted Accentor, Red-headed Bullfinch.

Dochu La is accessible from the capital, Thimphu, and a few hours by road east of Olathang. Bird around the pass, especially on the eastern side, and check areas of bamboo for Slender-billed Scimitar-Babbler*.

Accommodation: Thimphu — Druk Hotel. Dochu La — lodge.

From Dochu La the road north descends to Punakha, the former capital of Bhutan. The **Mo Cho (Chuu) Valley**, which runs north from Punakha to subtropical forest near Tashitang, supports Pallas' Fish-Eagle*, Ibisbill, Crested Kingfisher, Blue-bearded Bee-eater, Slaty-backed and Spotted Forktails, Yellow-vented Warbler*, Cutia, Black-eared Shrike-Babbler, Rusty-fronted Barwing and Red-tailed Minla. From Tashitang it is possible to explore the Sankosh River by boat, one of the few known sites for White-bellied Heron*.

South of Punakha the **Wangdiphodrang–Tongsa Road** passes a number of good sites. The stretch of road before Gangtey Gompa passes through oak–rhododendron forests which support Yellow-rumped Honeyguide* (usually near cliffs where there are bees' nests) and Rufous-breasted Bush-Robin* (stream sides), as well as Brown-throated Treecreeper, Red-billed Leiothrix, Black-eared Shrike-Babbler, Red-tailed Minla, Russet Sparrow, Green-tailed Sunbird and Yellow-breasted Greenfinch. The village of Gangtey Gompa, which lies at 2740 m (8990 ft) is situated in the wide **Popshika Valley**, where the bogs and fields support wintering Black-necked Cranes* (Nov–Mar), viewable from a hide at their roost site. East of Gangtey Gompa the road ascends to the 3300 m (10,827 ft) **Pele La pass**, where the stunning Fire-tailed Myzornis has been recorded on the east side, along with Hill Partridge, Yellow-rumped Honeyguide*, Rufous-bellied Woodpecker, Chestnut Thrush, Stripe-throated Yuhina, Brown Parrotbill, Maroon-backed Accentor, Crimson-browed Finch and Red-headed Bullfinch, as well as golden langur.

The **Tongsa–Tingtibi Road**, south of Tongsa, passes through superb birding country. The broadleaf and subtropical forests from just north of Shemgang (in the Wangdechhu Valley) south to Mangdechu support Blue-bearded Bee-eater, Long-tailed Broadbill, White-crested Laughingthrush, Yellow-throated Fulvetta*, Sultan Tit, Gould's Sunbird and Yellow-rumped Honeyguide*, which has been recorded at the Ishgongchhu Bridge near Buju and 4 km below Shemgang (check branches near pendulous honeycombs of giant honeybees which hang from the cliffs). The subtropical forests near Tingtibi, especially between there and Tshanglajong, support Grey-bellied Cuckoo, Rufous-necked* and Wreathed Hornbills, Collared Treepie, White-throated Bulbul, Grey-crowned Prinia*, White-spectacled and Black-faced Warblers, Rufous-chinned Laughingthrush, Red-faced Liocichla, Spotted Wren-Babbler*, Cutia, Striated, White-naped and Black-chinned Yuhinas and Black-browed Parrotbill*. 'Honey Rocks', south of Tingtibi, *en route* to Gaylegphung, is another good site for Yellow-rumped Honeyguide* and the rare Blyth's Kingfisher* has been recorded in this area. It is also possible to see golden langur along the Tongsa–Tingtibi road.

Accommodation: camping only.

SHEMGANG TREK

It is possible to see over 250 species during the week it takes to walk from Shemgang south to Manas. This strenuous trail traverses the many steep side-valleys of the Mangdechu Valley, passing through lowland, subtropical and temperate oak–rhododendron forests where the specialities include Rufous-necked Hornbill*, Green Cochoa* and Rufous-headed Parrotbill*.

Specialities

Rufous-necked Hornbill*, Green Cochoa*, Cutia, Yellow-throated* and Rufous-throated* Fulvettas, Black-browed* and Rufous-headed* Parrotbills, Fire-capped Tit.

Others

Red-headed Trogon, Wreathed Hornbill, Pale-headed Woodpecker, Long-tailed Broadbill, White-throated Bulbul, White-spectacled, Rufous-faced and Black-faced Warblers, Red-faced Liocichla, Coral-billed Scimitar-Babbler, Silver-eared Mesia, Black-headed Shrike-Babbler*, White-hooded Babbler, Rusty-fronted Barwing, White-naped Yuhina, Streaked Spiderhunter.

Other Wildlife

Assamese macaque, capped, common and golden langurs, leopard.

Accommodation: camping only.

MANAS WILDLIFE SANCTUARY

The sal forests and grasslands surrounding the wide, shallow Manas River within this huge sanctuary which straddles the Bhutan–India border support such scarce and localised species as Long-billed Plover* and Ruddy Kingfisher, but Manas is more famous for its mammals, which include Indian rhinoceros and tiger.

Specialities

Long-billed Plover* (Nov–Mar), Ruddy Kingfisher, Pale-chinned Blue-Flycatcher.

Others

Pallas' Fish-Eagle*, Small Pratincole, Black-bellied* and River Terns, Orange-breasted Pigeon, Pompadour Green-Pigeon, Black-backed Kingfisher, Long-tailed Broadbill, Crow-billed Drongo, Rosy Minivet, Black-backed Forktail, Sultan Tit.

Other Wildlife

Asian elephant, gaur, golden langur, hispid hare, hog deer, Indian rhinoceros, leopard, pygmy hog, sambar, swamp deer, tiger, water buffalo.

Manas is accessible from Gaylegphung or via the trek from Shemgang to the north.

It is possible to take a week-long trek through the **Bumthang Valley**, east of Tongsa. The trail starts at Jakar, where Black-necked Crane* and Ibisbill have been recorded in winter near the lodge, and winds its way through some excellent forests where Satyr Tragopan* occurs.

East of Jakar the road crosses the 3800 m (12,467 ft) Thrumsing La pass where Snow Pigeon, Blue-fronted Redstart and White-winged Grosbeak occur. Many east Himalayan specialities occur in the forest alongside the **Limithang Road** (which descends, via numerous hairpin bends, from this pass to 650 m (2,133 ft) in just 80 km) including Ward's Trogon*, Rufous-necked Hornbill*, Collared Treepie, Blue-fronted Robin*, Yellow-vented Warbler*, Golden-breasted and Yellow-throated* Fulvettas, White-naped Yuhina and Rufous-headed Parrotbill*. In southeast Bhutan the foothill forest near the border town of **Samdrup Jongkhar** supports Rufous-throated Partridge, Pin-tailed Pigeon, Pale-headed Woodpecker and Silver-breasted Broadbill.

ADDITIONAL INFORMATION

Books and Papers

The Birds of Bhutan. Ali S *et al.*, in prep. *Rec. Zool. Surv. India Occ. Pap. No. 136:* 1–263.

Near-endemics

White-bellied Heron*, Chestnut-breasted Partridge*, Satyr* and Blyth's* Tragopans, Black-necked Crane*, Ward's Trogon*, Pied Thrush*, Rufous-breasted Bush-Robin*, Grey-crowned Prinia*, Smoky Warbler, Striated, Rufous-necked, Rufous-vented and Grey-sided Laughingthrushes, Rufous-throated*, Bar-winged and Spotted* Wren-Babblers, Rusty-fronted and Hoary-throated Barwings, Ludlow's and Nepal Fulvettas, White-naped and Rufous-vented Yuhinas, Fire-tailed Myzornis, Great, Brown and Fulvous Parrotbills, Tibetan Lark, Robin and Maroon-backed Accentors, Fire-tailed Sunbird, Tibetan Serin, Blanford's, Beautiful and Dark-rumped Rosefinches, Crimson-browed and Scarlet Finches, Red-headed and Grey-headed Bullfinches, Gold-naped Finch.

BRUNEI DARUSSALAM

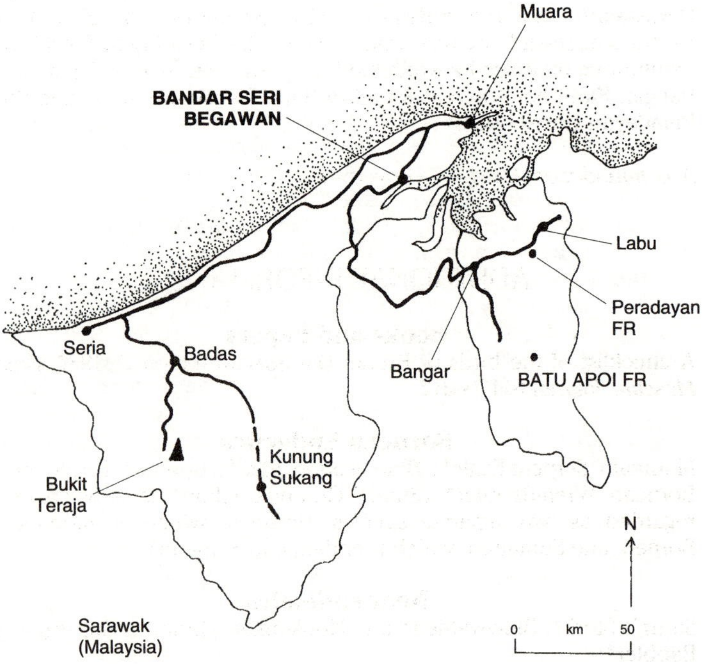

Brunei Darussalam is a small, friendly country on the west coast of Borneo. Very few birders have been to Brunei, but recent sightings of such rare birds as Sunda Ground-Cuckoo* and Blue-wattled Bulbul* may see more make it there in the future.

At just 5765 sq km, Brunei is a very small country. The bus network is unreliable and a hired vehicle is recommended for a thorough birding trip. However, it is possible to reach some sites by river. Transport, accommodation and food are all more expensive than most southeast Asian countries and birders who like a cold beer after a long, hard day in the field will be disappointed to learn that the sale of alcohol was banned in 1991. Immunisation against hepatitis, polio, typhoid and yellow fever is recommended. The wettest time of the year is from September to January and best avoided. Much of Brunei is still forested and some areas have been designated as reserves, which will help to conserve the 44 threatened and near-threatened species. Spectacular species include Mountain Serpent-Eagle*, Bulwer's Pheasant*, Blue-headed Pitta* and Bornean Bristlehead*, all of which are endemic to Borneo, and Sunda Ground-Cuckoo* and Blue-wattled Bulbul*.

The very rare Blue-wattled Bulbul*, a debatable species which may be a morph of Puff-backed Bulbul, was recorded in **Batu Apoi FR** in 1992. This reserve covers most of southern Temburong, the eastern part of Brunei, which is surrounded by Sarawak. The bulbul, which was known previously only from specimens taken in northeast Kalimantan in 1900 and northwest Sumatra in 1937, was seen along the river near the Kuala Belalong Field Studies Centre. It is possible to stay at the centre, where Sunda Ground-Cuckoo* has also been recorded, by booking in advance through the Biology Department of the Universiti Brunei Darussalam, Bandar Seri Begawan 3186, Brunei (tel: 02 427001). The centre is accessible by boat from Bangar. The **Peradayan FR** in north Temburong may also be worth exploring. The entrance is 15 km east of Bangar. From here there is a trail to Bukit Patoi (one hour) and Bukit Peradayan (three hours).

Accommodation: Bangar — government rest house.

ADDITIONAL INFORMATION

Books and Papers

A checklist of the birds of Brunei Darussalam. Mann C, 1987. *Brunei Museum Journal* 6: 170–212.

Bornean Endemics

Mountain Serpent-Eagle*, Blue-headed Pitta*, Bornean Bristlehead*, Bornean Wren-Babbler* (Sunda Ground-Cuckoo* is now generally regarded as two separate species: Bornean, which is endemic to Borneo, and Sumatran, which is endemic to Sumatra).

Near-endemics

Storm's Stork*, Blue-wattled* and Hook-billed* Bulbuls, Grey-breasted Babbler*.

BURMA (MYANMAR)

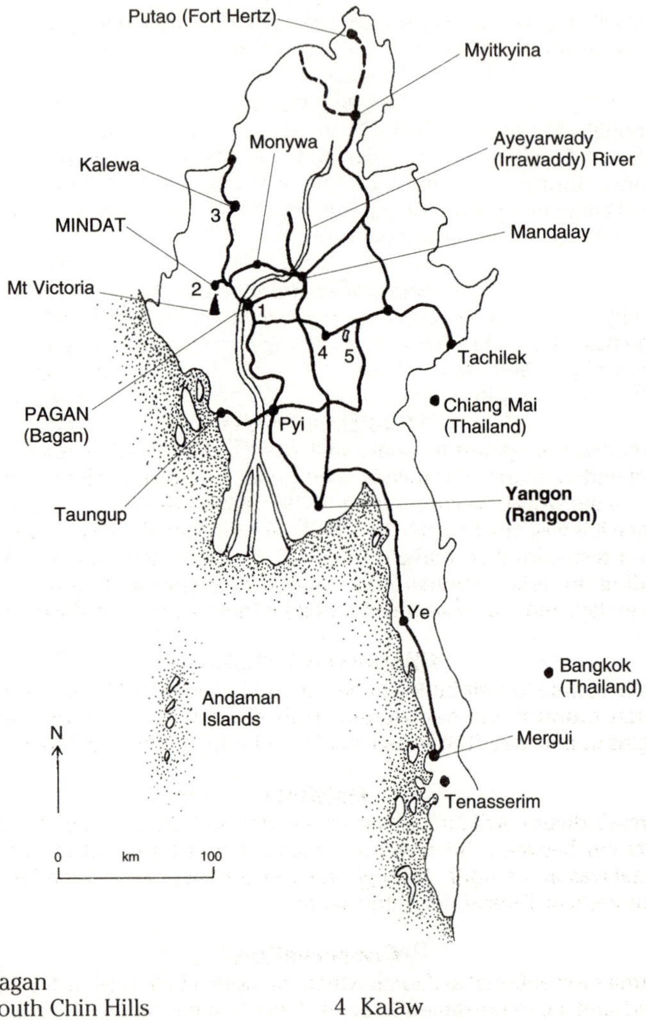

1 Pagan
2 South Chin Hills
3 North Chin Hills
4 Kalaw
5 Inle Lake

INTRODUCTION

Summary

Burma has the most diverse avifauna in southeast Asia and now that long-term travel restrictions seem to be on the way out, many birders may want to make their way in. The tourist infrastructure is still in its infancy, especially away from the major towns, and a 4WD vehicle will be needed to cover the country thoroughly, but the rewards for roughing it on an expensive trip could include four endemics and plenty of birds which are hard to see in neighbouring countries.

Size

At 676,552 sq km, Burma is five times larger than England and virtually the same size as Texas.

Getting Around

Although 30-day tourist visas have been available since 1994, travel within the country is still restricted and many areas remain out of bounds. Birders on a tight schedule will need a 4WD vehicle, as most roads are in need of repair, but those with more time will find extensive internal bus and air networks.

Accommodation and Food

Foreigners are usually required to stay in designated hotels, which tend to be basic, but expensive, and mild curries washed down with Mandalay beer will probably dominate the daily diet of most visiting birders.

Health and Safety

Immunisation against hepatitis, polio, typhoid and yellow fever is recommended, as are precautions against malaria. As one might expect in one of the world's poorest countries, the standards of hygiene are low, hence it is wise not to drink the water unless it is sterilised or boiled. The travel restrictions do make some sense. It is definitely not wise to go birding in rebel strongholds, especially north and northeast of Mandalay, and it also worth avoiding pro-democracy demonstrations.

Climate and Timing

The best time to visit Burma is between December and February. From March onwards the temperature rises steadily until the wet season begins in mid-May. The rains usually continue until mid-October.

Habitats

Burma's diverse avifauna reflects the variety of habitats which lie in the 2000 km between the montane meadows and forests of the eastern Himalayas in the north, through the arid central plains, to the lowland rainforests of Tenasserim in the south.

Conservation

Burma's exceptional avifauna, which includes a high total of 118 threatened and near-threatened species, faces a bleak future because the major habitats of importance, the forests, are under serious threat from all sides. For example, proposed dams look set to destroy the already degraded forests of eastern Burma, including parts of the Kahilu Wildlife Sanctuary and Pakchan Permanent FR, and in the north most evidence points to the fact that the forests are being logged by rebel groups who sell the timber to China.

Bird Species

Over 970 species have been recorded in Burma, the highest total for a southeast Asian country. Non-endemic specialities and spectacular species include Baer's Pochard*, White-rumped Falcon*, Blyth's Tragopan*, Hume's Pheasant*, Great Thick-knee, Pale-capped Pigeon*,

Rufous-necked Hornbill*, Blue-naped Pitta*, White-bellied Minivet*, Black-breasted* and Grey-sided* Thrushes, Collared Myna*, White-tailed Stonechat, Jerdon's Bushchat*, Giant Nuthatch*, Moustached, Striped and Brown-capped* Laughingthrushes, Red-faced Liocichla, Chinese Babax, Silver-eared Mesia, Cutia, Red-tailed Minla, Black-bibbed and Sultan Tits, Gould's and Fire-tailed Sunbirds, Scarlet Finch.

Endemics

Four species are endemic to Burma: Hooded Treepie*, White-browed Nuthatch*, White-throated Babbler and Rusty-capped Fulvetta.

Pale-capped Pigeon* and Daurian Starling (Nov–Mar) have been recorded in Hlawgaw (Hlawa) Park, 45 minutes by road from **Yangon (Rangoon)** *en route* to Pyi.

The endemic White-throated Babbler occurs in the thorn scrub and palm groves that surround the numerous pagodas near the capital, **Pagan (Bagan)**. This city is situated on the Ayeyarwady (Irrawaddy) River in Burma's rather arid central plains. The river supports Bar-headed Goose (Nov–Mar), Great Thick-knee, Small Pratincole, River Lapwing, Black-bellied* and River Terns, and Indian Skimmer*, while Rain Quail, Indian Nightjar, Blue-tailed Bee-eater, Burmese Shrike, Vinous-breasted Starling, Sand Lark and winter visitors such as Siberian Rubythroat, and Thick-billed and Yellow-streaked Warblers, occur in nearby open country. The endemic Hooded Treepie* occurs in the open scrubby areas at the base of **Mount Popa** near Pagan, and in remnant dry deciduous forest alongside the road west from Pagan to Mindat, along with Black Baza, White-eyed Buzzard, White-rumped Falcon*, Grey-headed and Red-breasted Parakeets, Greater Yellownape, Black-collared Starling, White-vented Myna and Plain-backed Sparrow.

SOUTH CHIN HILLS

These hills are in fact steep mountains which are situated in west Burma near northeast India, and form a southern extension of the Himalayas. They rise to 2600 m (8530 ft) and support pine, broadleaf evergreen and oak–rhododendron forests, where such terrific birds as Blyth's Tragopan*, Blue-naped Pitta*, the endemic White-browed Nuthatch*, Brown-capped Laughingthrush* and Red-tailed Minla occur.

Burmese Endemics

White-browed Nuthatch*.

Specialities

Blyth's Tragopan*, Rufous-necked Hornbill*, Blue-naped Pitta*, Broad-billed Warbler*, Brown-capped Laughingthrush*, Slender-billed Scimitar-Babbler*, Long-tailed Wren-Babbler, Chinese Babax, Cutia, Grey Sibia*, Black-bibbed Tit.

Others

Hill and Rufous-throated Partridges, Mountain Bamboo-Partridge,

Speckled and Ashy Wood-Pigeons, Wedge-tailed Pigeon, Red-headed Trogon, Great and Golden-throated Barbets, Stripe-breasted, Crimson-breasted, Darjeeling and Bay Woodpeckers, Gold-billed and Green Magpies, Long-tailed Minivet, Chestnut-bellied Rock-Thrush, Long-tailed, Long-billed*, Chestnut and Grey-sided* (Nov–Mar) Thrushes, Slaty-backed and Slaty-blue Flycatchers, Large, Rufous-bellied and Vivid Niltavas, Pygmy Blue-Flycatcher, White-bellied Redstart, Brown-throated Treecreeper, Black-throated and Black-browed Tits, Crested Finchbill, Striated and Flavescent Bulbuls, Chestnut-headed Tesia, Aberrant and Brown Bush-Warblers, Buff-barred and Ashy-throated Warblers, Blue-winged Laughingthrush, Spot-throated Babbler, Streak-breasted and Coral-billed Scimitar-Babblers, Black-headed*, Green and Black-eared Shrike-Babblers, Rusty-fronted and Streak-throated Barwings, Chestnut-tailed and Red-tailed Minlas, Rufous-winged, White-browed and Nepal Fulvettas, Rufous-backed Sibia, Whiskered and Stripe-throated Yuhinas, Grey-headed, Spot-breasted and Black-throated Parrotbills, Yellow-browed Tit, Russet Sparrow, Fire-tailed Sunbird, Scarlet Finch, Brown Bullfinch, Spot-winged Grosbeak.

Bird the high, forested mountain slopes to the northwest of Mindat. White-browed Nuthatch*, which has only been recorded here and on Mount Victoria a few kilometres to the south, occurs in the high-level oak forests which also support Blyth's Tragopan*, Brown-capped Laughingthrush* (in bamboo), Black-headed Shrike-Babbler*, Streak-throated Barwing and Black-browed Tit.

Accommodation: Mindat.

The endemic White-browed Nuthatch*, as well as Blyth's Tragopan* and Slender-billed Scimitar-Babbler* also occur on **Mount Victoria**, to the south of Mindat. Black-backed Forktail occurs at **Bonzon**, a small riverside town to the north of Mindat, and the surrounding dry deciduous forest supports Chestnut-headed Bee-eater, Yellow-crowned, White-bellied and Great Slaty Woodpeckers, Blue Magpie and Rosy Minivet.

NORTH CHIN HILLS

The broadleaf and evergreen forests on these hills support a number of birds which have not been recorded further south around Mindat, including Black-breasted Thrush* and Moustached and Striped Laughingthrushes.

Specialities

Black-breasted Thrush*, Moustached and Striped Laughingthrushes, Spotted Wren-Babbler*, Streak-throated and Dusky Fulvettas.

Others

Jungle Nightjar, Blue-bearded Bee-eater, Blue-throated Barbet, Lesser Yellownape, Black-winged Cuckoo-shrike, Short-billed Minivet, Blue-throated Flycatcher, Little, Slaty-backed and Spotted Forktails, White-tailed Nuthatch, Grey-bellied Tesia, Brownish-flanked and Russet Bush-

Warblers, Black-faced Warbler, Red-faced Liocichla, Spot-breasted Scimitar-Babbler, Scaly-breasted Wren-Babbler, Silver-eared Mesia, White-browed Shrike-Babbler, Striated Yuhina, Yellow-cheeked Tit, Gould's and Green-tailed Sunbirds, Yellow-breasted Greenfinch.

(Other species recorded here include Black-tailed Crake, Wood Snipe*, Hodgson's Frogmouth, Yellow-throated Laughingthrush* and Collared Myna*.)

Based in Ramhtlow, north of Haka, bird roadside mid-level broadleaf forest (Black-breasted Thrush*, Spotted Wren-Babbler*) and higher level evergreen forest.

Accommodation: Ramhtlow.

The lowland evergreen and dry deciduous forests around **Aung Chan Tha**, east of Kalewa, support Asian Emerald and Drongo Cuckoos, Brown Hornbill*, Indochinese Cuckoo-Shrike, Golden-crested Myna, White-throated and Olive Bulbuls, White-crested Laughingthrush, Brown-cheeked Fulvetta, Sultan Tit, Yellow-vented Flowerpecker and Ruby-cheeked Sunbird, as well as hoolock gibbon. The scarce White-bellied Minivet* occurs in open country between **Monywa** and **Mandalay**.

KALAW

The remnant evergreen broadleaf and pine forests near the hill resort of Kalaw on the Shan Plateau in central Burma support a similar avifauna to that of northwest Thailand, just to the east, and it includes Hume's Pheasant* and Giant Nuthatch*.

Specialities

Hume's Pheasant*, Collared Myna*, Giant Nuthatch*, White-headed Bulbul.

Others

Crimson-breasted Woodpecker, Burmese Shrike, White-browed Laughingthrush, Red-faced Liocichla, Spectacled Barwing, Black-headed Sibia, Gould's Sunbird.

Bird around Kalaw which is situated on the Thazi-Taunggyi road.

Accommodation: Kalaw — Kalaw Hotel (B).

INLE LAKE

This shallow lake and its surrounding marshes and paddies support a fine range of marshbirds, including the rare and local Jerdon's Bushchat*.

Specialities

White-tailed Stonechat, Jerdon's Bushchat*.

Others

Cotton Pygmy-goose, Falcated Duck (Nov–Mar), Baer's Pochard* (Nov–Mar), Pied Harrier (Nov–Mar), Greater Spotted Eagle* (Nov–Mar), Ruddy-breasted Crake, Sarus Crane*, Pheasant-tailed and Bronze-winged Jacanas, Spotted Bush-Warbler, Striated Grassbird, Rosy Pipit.

Bird on the lake itself, via boats which can be hired (B) in Yaunghwe at the northern end, to check the floating mats of emergent vegetation for the chats, and around Mong Pai at the southern end of the lake (Sarus Crane*).

Accommodation: Yaunghwe.

Rumours about the possible presence of Pink-headed Duck* in north Burma continue to circulate, but they mainly revolve around reports of sightings by hunters. The last confirmed record of this species, which is otherwise thought to be extinct, is of one in India in 1935.

ADDITIONAL INFORMATION

Books and Papers

The Birds of Burma. Smythies B, 1986. Nimrod.

ENDEMICS (4)

Hooded Treepie*	Central: Mount Popa and Pagan–Mindat Road
White-browed Nuthatch*	Central/West: South Chin Hills and Mount Victoria
White-throated Babbler	Central: Pagan
Rusty-capped Fulvetta	South: pine forests

Near-endemics

White-cheeked Partridge*, Blyth's* and Temminck's* Tragopans, Sclater's Monal*, Hume's* and Lady Amherst's* Pheasants, White-fronted Scops-Owl*, Mottled Wood-Owl, Ward's Trogon*, Plain-pouched Hornbill*, Streak-breasted and Bamboo Woodpeckers, Gurney's Pitta*, White-bellied Minivet*, Collared* and Crested Mynas, Pale-chinned Blue-Flycatcher, Rufous-breasted Bush-Robin*, Chestnut-vented, Giant* and Beautiful* Nuthatches, Olive and White-headed Bulbuls, Striated, Rufous-necked, Chestnut-backed*, Yellow-throated*, Rufous-vented, Moustached, Grey-sided, Striped* and Brown-capped* Laughing-thrushes, Bar-winged, Spotted* and Wedge-billed* Wren-Babblers, Jerdon's* and Slender-billed* Babblers, Chinese Babax, Rusty-fronted and Streak-throated Barwings, Nepal Fulvetta, Grey* and Beautiful Sibias, White-naped, Burmese*, White-collared and Rufous-vented Yuhinas, Fire-tailed Myzornis, Great, Brown, Black-breasted*, Brown-winged*, Fulvous and Short-tailed* Parrotbills, Black-bibbed Tit, Maroon-backed Accentor, Purple-rumped and Fire-tailed Sunbirds, Black-headed Greenfinch, Vinaceous Rosefinch, Grey-headed Bullfinch.

CAMBODIA

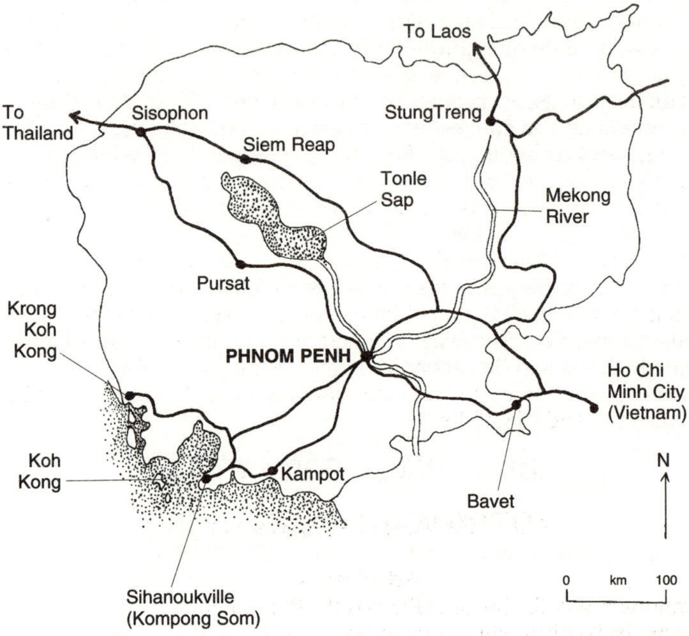

After 20 years of violent war, including four years of genocide under the Khmer Rouge, Cambodia has calmed down a little since 1993. It is still too dangerous to do any serious birding here but, perhaps in the future, if any forests are left, it may be possible for birders to look for such great rarities as Giant Ibis*.

At 181,035 sq km, Cambodia is 1.4 times the size of England and four times smaller than Texas. Travelling beyond the few government controlled areas is a risky business and it is wise to stick to the beaten track anyway because the countryside is littered with unexploded land mines and other military paraphernalia. There are buses and trains, but both are slow, crowded and dangerous. Accommodation is reasonably priced and the food, which consists mainly of variations on noodle soup, is cheap. Immunisation against hepatitis, polio, typhoid and yellow fever is recommended, as are precautions against malaria. The best time to visit would be the dry season, which normally lasts from November to March. Cambodia is a maze of mountains and rivers, with the mighty Mekong meandering from north to south in the east. There are mountains in the northeast along the borders with Laos and Vietnam, in the north (Dangkrek Range) and the southwest (Cardamom Range). In 1974 it was estimated that 74% of the country was covered in forests, but they are disappearing fast and in 1995 only

30–35% of Cambodia remained forested. It seems likely that little will be left by the end of the century, and yet the felling of these great forests where so many wonderful birds reside is already causing droughts and floods, and in 1994 many rice-growing areas failed to produce a harvest, leading to starvation throughout the country. Most of the logging is taking place in the west near the border with Thailand, in areas still under the control of the Khmer Rouge. Even the coastal 'mangrove forests' can't escape destruction and many areas have been cleared to make way for shrimp and fish ponds. The end seems nigh for many of Cambodia's birds, including the 35 threatened and near-threatened species which occur there. Non-endemic specialities and spectacular species include Spot-billed Pelican*, Milky* and Painted* Storks, Lesser* and Greater* Adjutants, Chestnut-headed Partridge* and Blue-rumped* and Bar-bellied* Pittas. There is no endemic species.

The coastal areas in **Koh Kong** province, **Tonle Sap** and the flooded forest along the Mekong River from **Stung Treng** to the border with Laos have all been idenitified as potential Ramsar sites by the Asian Wetlands Bureau. Spot-billed Pelican* (Chunuk Tru), Milky* and Painted* Storks and Greater Adjutant* all occur around Tonle Sap and local people have reported sightings of White-winged Duck* and White-shouldered* and Giant* Ibises.

ADDITIONAL INFORMATION

Addresses

Cambodian Wildlife Society, PO Box 82, Phnom Penh.
Ministry of Tourism, Phnom Penh (tel: 2 2107).

Books and Papers

A bird's eye view of Cambodia. Archibald G, 1992. *ICF Bugle* 18: 1–3.
Survey of Waterbirds in Cambodia (March–April 1994). Mundkur T, 1994. Report submitted to the IUCN by the AWB (Asian Wetlands Bureau).

Near-endemics

White-shouldered* and Giant* Ibises, Chestnut-headed Partridge*, Siamese Fireback*, Bengal Florican*, Coral-billed Ground-Cuckoo*, Blue-rumped* and Bar-bellied* Pittas, Silver Oriole*.

CHINA

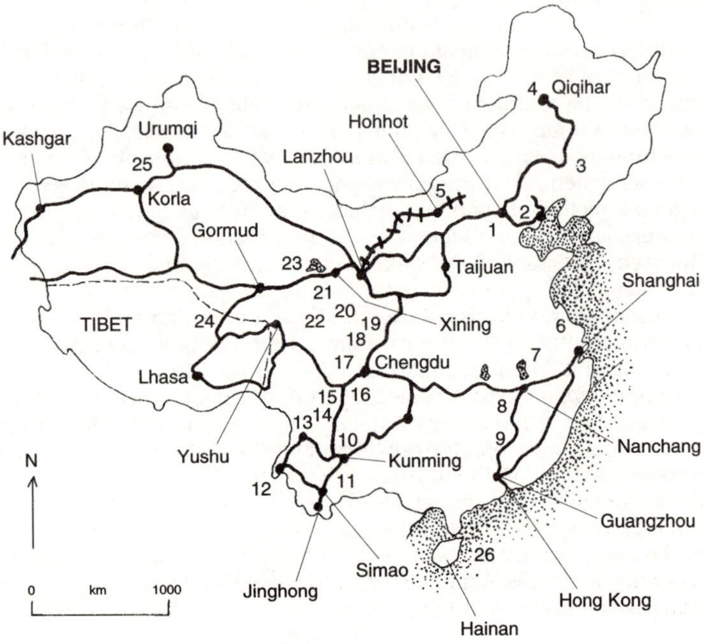

1 Beijing
2 Beidaihe
3 Xianghai NR
4 Zhalong NR
5 Zhaohe
6 Yancheng Marshes
7 Poyang Hu
8 Guan Shan NR
9 Ba Bao Shan
10 Kunming
11 Xishuangbanna Reserve
12 Ruili
13 Lijiang
14 Cao Hai Reserve
15 Tuoda NR
16 Omei Shan
17 Wolong Reserve
18 Wolong–Jiuzhaigou Road
19 Jiuzhaigou
20 Ganzi Prefecture
21 Xining–Nangqen Road
22 Nangqen
23 Qinghai Hu (Koko Nor)
24 Qingzang Road
25 Xinjiang Province
26 Hainan

INTRODUCTION

Summary

Although many habitats in this huge, over-populated country have been severely degraded and birds are few and far between in many areas, the avifauna is diverse and ranges from the rare pheasants, snowfinches and rosefinches of the remote mountainous areas of the southwest, to the vast array of eastern Palearctic specialities in the northeast. Most major birding sites are accessible by public transport, but an extensive birding trip could take some time.

Size

China is a massive country. At 9,596,961 sq km, including Tibet, it is nearly twice the size of Europe and a little larger than the United States of America.

Getting Around

Birders planning an extensive trip to China will need plenty of patience and time. While Beidaihe, the hot spot for eastern Palearctic specialities, is readily accessible from Beijing and easy to work, many of the other sites, especially in Sichuan and on the Tibetan Plateau, are a long way from the major cities (which are all connected by good air and rail networks), hence it is necessary to cover long distances by road to see a good selection of the 60 endemics and many near-endemics. The bus network is extensive, but slow, especially in the remoter areas where the buses have to cover long distances on bad roads. The transport system as a whole is crowded, especially during the summer, and getting a ticket at short notice is not always straightforward, so it is best to book in advance if possible. The roads are terrible in Sichuan and birders planning a short trip there are advised to hire a 4WD with a driver/guide/interpreter in Chengdu, in advance through a travel agent.

Accommodation and Food

Accommodation and food are relatively cheap and basic away from the major cities, even though foreigners must pay much more than the Chinese for any type of accommodation and are usually forced to stay in the most expensive places available. In the remotest areas accommodation and food are both poor, but it is usually possible to get a beer. Tsingtao, pronounced 'Ching Dow' is one of the best brews.

Health and Safety

Immunisation against hepatitis, polio, rabies, typhoid and yellow fever is recommended, as are precautions against malaria in the south. Beware of altitude sickness in Sichuan and Tibet, where many of the best birding areas are above 3048 m (10,000 ft).

Climate and Timing

The best times to visit Beidaihe in the northeast are the first half of May or late September to early October, whereas Sichuan and the grasslands of Inner Mongolia are best in May and June. It is bitterly cold and often windy in the north from December to March, but usually hot from May to August. The south is hot, wet and humid from April to September, but drier and cooler between November and March.

Habitats

China's great diversity of habitats ranges from numerous coastal estuaries, west through densely populated agricultural plains where barely a bird survives, except around the huge lakes, to the Tibetan Plateau which rises above 4500 m (14,764 ft). Steep, remote eastern slopes of this plateau are still forested, but the plateau itself is a barren landscape with some grasslands and lakes. Sparsely populated steppe and desert lies to the north and northwest of the plateau, and remnant pine and subtropical forests to the southeast.

Conservation

China has numerous nature reserves, but much of the country, especially the east, is an ecological disaster area thanks to the presence of 1.2 billion people. Although there are over 400 reserves, most of these are in name only, and even in flagship reserves such as Wolong, which was set up to protect giant pandas, the habitat is being destroyed and degraded. Unless the Chinese can be persuaded, by humane methods, to settle for smaller families, there will be no future for the birds of China, especially the 180 threatened and near-threatened species. Eighty-six of these are threatened, the third highest total, with the Philippines, for any country in the world.

Bird Species

A total of 1,244 species has been recorded in China, over 600 of which occur in Sichuan. Notable birds of the north and east include Scaly-sided Merganser*, Chinese Egret*, Oriental Stork*, Swinhoe's Rail*, Hooded*, Red-crowned*, White-naped* and Siberian* Cranes, Oriental Plover, Saunders'* and Relict* Gulls, Pallas' Sandgrouse, Japanese Waxwing*, Siberian Accentor and many buntings. Spectacular species of the south and southeast include Sclater's Monal*, Silver Oriole*, Purple Cochoa*, Giant Nuthatch*, Red-tailed Laughingthrush*, Chinese Babax, Cutia and Sultan Tit. Non-endemic Sichuan specialities include Temminck's Tragopan*, Black-necked Crane*, Solitary Snipe, Ibisbill, Tibetan Ground-Jay, Siberian and White-tailed Rubythroats, Firethroat*, Grandala, White-browed Tit-Warbler, Red-winged Laughingthrush*, Giant Babax*, Red-tailed Minla, many snowfinches and numerous rosefinches. Western goodies include White-winged Woodpecker, Mongolian Ground-Jay, Rufous-backed Redstart, Azure Tit and Saxaul Sparrow.

Endemics

China supports more endemics than any other mainland Asian country. The 59 endemics, of which 25 are only found in Sichuan and the surrounding provinces, include 14 'pheasants', Sichuan Jay*, Rufous-headed Robin*, a nuthatch, Crested Tit-Warbler*, seven laughingthrushes, four parrotbills and four rosefinches.

Expectations

It is possible to see 230–240 species during a two-week spring trip to Beidaihe, but it will be necessary to travel some distance from there to see just one or two endemics. A similar number of species, including over 20 endemics, is possible on a two- or three-week trip to Sichuan.

BEIJING

It is possible to see some good birds in and around China's capital, including three endemics and any of the 17 species of bunting which have been recorded in the area.

Most of the species listed below are only present during the summer (Apr–Sep).

Chinese Endemics

Pere David's Laughingthrush, White-browed Chinese Warbler, Chinese Leaf-Warbler (Apr–May).

Specialities

Blunt-winged Warbler, Siberian Accentor (Nov–May).

Others

Mandarin Duck*, Falcated Duck, Baer's Pochard*, Chinese Pond-Heron, Yellow and Cinnamon Bitterns, Amur Falcon, Common Pheasant, White-throated Needletail (Apr–May), Rufous-bellied Woodpecker (Apr–May), Blue and Azure-winged Magpies, Daurian Jackdaw, Dusky Thrush, Yellow-rumped (Apr–May) and Narcissus (*elisae* race) (Apr–May) Flycatchers, Daurian Redstart, Black-browed Reed-Warbler, Thick-billed (late May) and Yellow-streaked Warblers, Pale-legged Leaf-Warbler, Eastern Crowned-Warbler, Vinous-throated Parrotbill, Willow (Songar) Tit, Forest Wagtail, Buff-bellied Pipit, Grey-capped Greenfinch, Long-tailed and Pallas' Rosefinches, Pine (Nov–May), Rock, Meadow (Nov–May), Ochre-rumped* (Nov–May), Tristram's, Yellow-browed, Yellow-throated, Black-faced and Pallas' (Nov–May) Buntings.

(Other species recorded in and around Beijing include Baikal Teal*, Japanese Waxwing*, Chinese Thrush*, Snowy-browed Nuthatch*, Streaked Reed-Warbler* (early June) and Rufous-backed Bunting*.)

Birders with a day to spare in Beijing may find a morning at the **Summer Palace** and an afternoon on the **Fragrant Hills** the best way to spend it. The grounds of the Summer Palace (Yihe Yuan), especially Longevity Hill and around Kunming Lake, 12 km northwest of the city centre, attract many of the species listed above. Kunming Lake, in front of the palace, is the best place for ducks and breeding Blunt-winged Warbler. The Fragrant Hills, 40 minutes northwest of the city, support White-browed Chinese Warbler (on scrubby hilltops), Pere David's Laughingthrush (on wooded slopes) and Meadow Bunting, and attract migrants such as raptors, White-throated Needletail, Narcissus Flycatcher and Chinese Leaf-Warbler. Take the chair-lift to the top and explore. Nearby, the paddies, fishponds, woodland and scrub at the northern end of the **Old Summer Palace** (Yuan Ming Yuan) have attracted migrants such as Rufous-bellied Woodpecker, Thick-billed Warbler and Ochre-rumped Bunting*. Further afield, the best birding site is **Badaling**, although this is a very degraded area crowded with tourists visiting the Great Wall. Bird the wooded valleys near the railway station, 85 km northwest of Beijing, and the area between there and the Great Wall, where Daurian Jackdaw, Daurian Redstart, Vinous-throated Parrotbill, Siberian Accentor, Long-tailed and Pallas' Rosefinches, and Rock Bunting occur. The Great Wall is less crowded at **Mutianyu** and Snowy-browed Nuthatch* has been recorded here.

BEIDAIHE

This big seaside resort, 280 km east of Beijing, lies on the Gulf of Bohai at the northern end of the Yellow Sea. It has become a major birding destination in recent years because it is arguably the best site in the world for eastern Palearctic specialities, including many species which are rarities in Europe and America, and in spring 1994 there were up to

BEIDAIHE

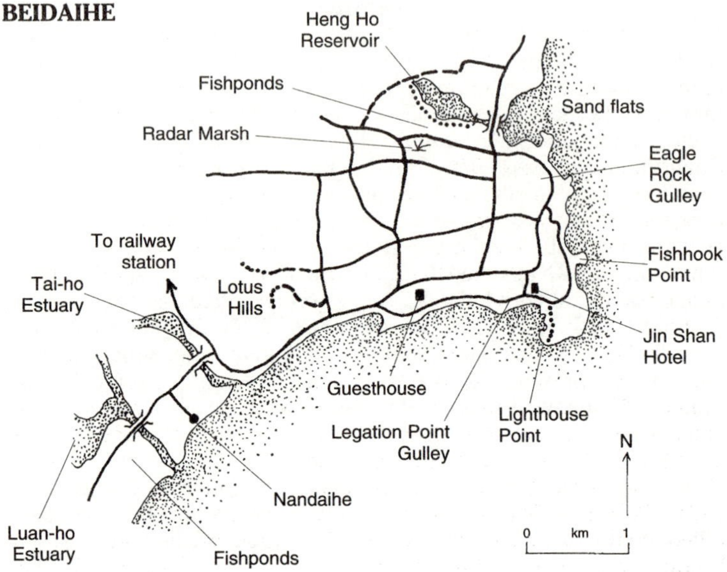

150 birders present at any one time. The variety of habitats in the region of this resort, from wooded gullies to paddies and estuaries, has attracted over 400 species, including six cranes, nearly 60 shorebirds, a fine selection of thrushes including Pale and Brown-headed, plenty of warblers including Streaked Reed-Warbler* and Marsh Grassbird*, and at least ten buntings including Ochre-rumped* and Pallas', but only around ten species are actually resident.

Spring passage begins in March when migrant cranes mix with winter visitors such as Siberian Accentor. More migrants appear in April and the variety of passerines peaks during the first half of May, which is also a good time for Pied Harrier, Asian Dowitcher* and Relict Gull*. Autumn migrants begin to turn up in late August. In early September Pied Harriers pass through in large numbers, but most passerine migrants are around in late September and early October. Six species of crane pass the visible migration watchpoints from mid-October to early November and in 1994 over 250 Red-crowned*, nearly 200 Siberian*, over 100 White-naped* and nearly 40 Hooded* were seen during early November.

Many of the birds listed below are spring and/or autumn migrants.

Chinese Endemics

Chinese Leaf-Warbler (Apr–May).

Specialities

Chinese Egret*, Oriental Stork*, Hooded*, Red-crowned*, White-naped* and Siberian* Cranes, Swinhoe's Snipe, Japanese Waxwing*, Pale and Brown-headed Thrushes, Streaked Reed-Warbler* (late May–early June), Blunt-winged Warbler, Marsh Grassbird*, Chinese Penduline-Tit, Siberian Accentor.

Others

Japanese Cormorant (Sep–Oct), Swan Goose*, Mandarin* and Falcated Ducks, Baer's Pochard*, Chinese Pond-Heron, Yellow and Schrenck's* Bitterns, Eastern Marsh-Harrier, Pied Harrier, Grey-faced and Upland (autumn) Buzzards, White-tailed*, Greater Spotted* and Imperial* Eagles, Amur and Saker (autumn) Falcons, Daurian Partridge, Japanese Quail, Baillon's Crake, Watercock, Great Bustard* (autumn), Greater Painted-Snipe, Pintail Snipe, Grey-tailed Tattler, Rufous-necked and Long-toed Stints, Sharp-tailed Sandpiper, Oriental Pratincole, Grey-headed Lapwing*, Black-tailed Gull, Oriental Scops-Owl, Jungle Nightjar, White-throated Needletail, Black-capped Kingfisher, Dollarbird, Grey-capped and Rufous-bellied Woodpeckers, Asian Paradise-Flycatcher (autumn), Blue Magpie, Daurian Jackdaw, Tiger, Brown and Chinese Grey Shrikes, White-throated Rock-Thrush, Siberian, Scaly, Grey-backed and Dusky Thrushes, Daurian and White-cheeked Starlings, Yellow-rumped, Narcissus (*elisae* race) and Mugimaki Flycatchers, Rufous-tailed Robin, Siberian Rubythroat, Siberian Blue Robin, Orange-flanked Bush-Robin, Daurian Redstart, Light-vented Bulbul, Chestnut-flanked White-eye, Asian Stubtail, Manchurian Bush-Warbler, Lanceolated and Pallas' Warblers, Black-browed Reed-Warbler, Paddyfield and Thick-billed Warblers, Pale-legged Leaf-Warbler, Eastern Crowned-Warbler, Vinous-throated Parrotbill, Asian Short-toed Lark, Forest Wagtail, Blyth's, Pechora and Buff-bellied Pipits, Grey-capped Greenfinch, Long-tailed and Pallas' (autumn) Rosefinches, Yellow-billed and Japanese Grosbeaks, Meadow, Ochre-rumped*, Tristram's, Chestnut-eared, Yellow-browed, Yellow-throated, Yellow-breasted, Chestnut, Black-faced and Pallas' Buntings.

(Other species recorded here include Baikal Teal*, Swinhoe's Rail* and Little Curlew.)

Beidaihe (pronounced Bay-die-her) is accessible by train from Beijing (5–6 hours). Although there are some good birding areas within a few minutes walk of town, birding by bicycle is the best way to see Beidaihe. Bicycles can be hired at the Jin Shan Hotel. The best sites are the Jin Shan Hotel garden, Lighthouse Point, Legation Point Gulley, Fish Hook Point, Eagle Rock Gulley, Pagoda Hill (visible migration), any poplar plantations around the town, the sand flats, the Heng Ho Reservoir area (Swinhoe's Rail*, Pechora Pipit), the small estuaries south of town and the Lotus Hills (Lianfengshan Park). The quiet gullies

Yellow-rumped Flycatcher is one of the star spring migrants at Beidaihe

on the northern side of the Lotus Hills are good for thrushes and flycatchers, but the hills are more famous for visible migration. In autumn it is possible to see six species of crane and other exceptional birds such as White-throated Needletail passing low over the tops, especially from the southeasternmost peak.

Accommodation: Jin Shan Hotel (A/B) (fax: 0335 442478), Diplomatic Personnel Guesthouse (C) and possibly at the Bird Banding Centre (tel: 0335 441756).

Siberian Cranes can be seen migrating over the Lotus Hills, Beidaihe, in autumn*

The **Luanhe** estuary, 45 km south of Beidaihe (at least 2 hours via a busy road), is also a good place for migrants, especially the south side, as well as Saunders' Gull*, which breeds nearby. Beidaihe is a hot birding spot, but many birders believe **Happy Island**, 3–4 hours by road to the south, is even better. Spectacular falls of passerines (including over 100 Siberian Rubythroats) have been recorded here, as well as Daurian Starling, Asian Stubtail, Chinese Penduline-Tit and Yellow-billed and Japanese Grosbeaks, while vagrants have included Japanese Night-Heron* and Fairy Pitta*. The island, which is only 2.5 km long and 1 km wide, can be reached by boat (organise in advance at the travel service in Laoting or hire at Lao Yu Jian) and on the short crossing it is possible to see Far Eastern Curlew*, Asian Dowitcher*, Great Knot and Saunders'* and Relict* Gulls on the mud flats which surround the island. The large shorebird and gull roost at the western end of the island has held Spoonbill Sandpiper*, up to 1,000 Asian Dowitchers* and, in autumn 1994, 865 Relict Gulls* (there are usually fewer than ten). It is possible to stay on the island, albeit in very basic hut accommodation, or in Laoting. The woods around Daqinghe, on the mainland opposite the island, are also worth exploring.

The endemic White-browed Chinese Warbler occurs near the Great Wall at **Shanhaiguan**, on the hill west of town, 30 km north of Beidaihe. Three endemics (Chinese Thrush*, Chinese Leaf-Warbler and Yellow-bellied Tit) as well as Koklass Pheasant, Bull-headed Shrike, Grey-sided Thrush*, Narcissus Flycatcher, Snowy-browed Nuthatch*, Asian Stubtail, Yellow-streaked Warbler, Blyth's Leaf-Warbler and Yellow-throated Bunting occur in the remnant forest around **Old Peak** (Lao Ling), near Qinhuangdao, 3–4 hours by road north of Beidaihe. Migrant raptors have included Upland Buzzard and Saker Falcon. Qinhuangdao is connected to Beijing by rail.

Accommodation: Qinhuangdao — hostel (basic).

XIANGHAI NATURE RESERVE

The reedy wetlands, grasslands and scattered elm woods in this large reserve in northeast China support three cranes, Asian Dowitcher* and the highly localised Rufous-backed Bunting*.

Most of the birds listed below are only present during summer (May–Sep).

Specialities

Oriental Stork*, Red-crowned*, White-naped* and Demoiselle* Cranes, Chinese Penduline-Tit, Rufous-backed Bunting*.

Others

Swan Goose*, Falcated Duck, Baer's Pochard*, Schrenck's Bittern*, Daurian Partridge, Japanese Quail, Great Bustard*, Asian Dowitcher*, Oriental Pratincole, Grey-headed Lapwing*, Pallas' Sandgrouse, Daurian Jackdaw, Chinese Grey Shrike, White-cheeked Starling, Pallas' and Gray's Warblers, Mongolian Lark.

The reserve is about 1 hour by road from Kaitong, which is connected to Qinhuangdao (near Beidaihe), Beijing and Qiqihar, near Zhalong NR (see next site) by rail. Rufous-backed Bunting*, which was first discovered to be breeding here in 1990, is fairly widespread.

Accommodation: guesthouse.

ZHALONG NATURE RESERVE

The wetlands within this reserve in northeast China support the rare and local Marsh Grassbird*, as well as Red-crowned* and White-naped* Cranes (some of which are feral).

Most of the birds listed below are only present in summer (May–Sep).

Specialities

Red-crowned* and White-naped* Cranes, Marsh Grassbird*, Chinese Penduline-Tit.

Others

Swan Goose*, Baer's Pochard*, Schrenck's Bittern*, Pied Harrier, Amur Falcon, Daurian Partridge, Japanese Quail, Great Bustard*, Oriental Pratincole, White-cheeked Starling, Gray's, Paddyfield and Thick-billed Warblers, Ochre-rumped*, Yellow-throated and Chestnut Buntings.

Zhalong NR is about 25 km from Qiqihar, which is accessible by air and rail (24 hours) from Beijing, and rail (6 hours) from Kaitong. There are two lakes worth checking either side of the entrance road, just before the HQ, and at KM 24 a 1 km track leads to an area of fields worth prolonged birding.

Accommodation: NR HQ or Qiqihar.

Scaly-sided Merganser* and Band-bellied Crake*, as well as Mandarin Duck*, Ural Owl, Grey-backed and Pale Thrushes, Rufous-tailed Robin, Gray's Warbler, Japanese Grosbeak and Tristram's Bunting occur around **Dailing** in the Lesser Hinggan Mountains, which are situated in extreme northeast China.

The **Panquangou NR** near Taijuan in Shaanxi province, west of Beijing, supports Brown Eared-Pheasant*, Grey-sided* and Chinese* Thrushes, Snowy-browed Nuthatch* and Long-tailed Rosefinch. The pheasant also occurs at Donglingshan NR, approximately 100 km west of Beijing, at Xiaowutaishan NR in Hebei province and Luyiashan NR in Shaanxi province.

Relict Gull* has been recorded near **Zhaohe** (Wolantouge), a popular tourist attraction 81 km north of Hohhot in Nei Mongol (Inner Mongolia) province. The grasslands here also support breeding Demoiselle Crane, Oriental Plover and Pallas' Sandgrouse. Bird the riverside at Zhaohe, the roadside grasslands between there and KM 91 and the lake 2 km from the road at KM 91 (Relict Gull*). The rare Relict Gull* has also been recorded near Wuliangsuhai and Baotou in Inner Mongolia, and more grasslands are accessible from **Hailar**, which is connected to Beijing by air. One of the best birding areas near here is to the southwest around the riverside village of Medamuji, where Swan Goose*, Red-crowned*, White-naped* and Demoiselle Cranes, Great Bustard*, Asian Dowitcher*, Oriental Plover and Reed Parrotbill* have been recorded.

On China's east coast near Shanghai, the **Yancheng Marshes**, where there is a small reserve, support up to 35,000 Swan Geese*, a few Black-faced Spoonbill*, up to 600 Red-crowned Cranes* and Ochre-rumped* and Pallas' Buntings during the winter, while Saunders' Gull* breeds here and the grassy marshes also support the rarely seen Swinhoe's Rail*.

ZHAOHE

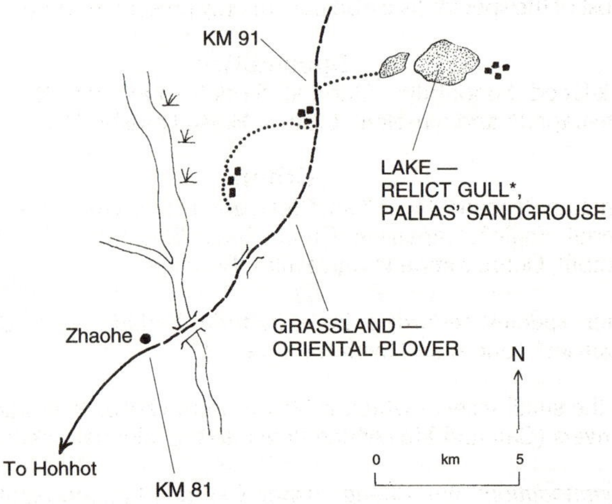

The superb Oriental Plover breeds in the grasslands of northern China

POYANG HU

The massive complex of seasonal freshwater lakes centred on Poyang Hu in east-central China is an immensely important wintering ground for waterbirds, with as many as 500,000 birds present in some years. It is especially important for cranes, including virtually all of the world's Siberian Cranes* (up to 2800 but only 100 in 1995–96), up to 2,000 White-naped Cranes*, over 800 Red-crowned Cranes* and up to 800 Hooded Cranes*, as well as up to 50,000 Swan Geese and 200 Oriental Storks*. Despite these amazing statistics, less than 10% of the area is protected and the delicate ecosystem could easily be damaged by proposals to dam the rivers upstream. In normal circumstances as many as 4600 sq km may be flooded during the summer, but by the middle of winter, when the water levels may be as much as 10 m lower, the area of water usually shrinks to around 460 sq km, leaving a wilderness of shallow lagoons, marshes, mud flats and wet grasslands absolutely alive with birds. There are few passerines, but they include wintering Marsh Grassbird*.

Most of the species listed below are only present in winter (Nov–Mar).

Specialities

Black-faced Spoonbill*, Oriental Stork*, Hooded*, Red-crowned*, White-naped* and Siberian* Cranes, Marsh Grassbird*.

Others

Dalmatian Pelican*, Swan* and Bean and Lesser White-fronted* Geese, Imperial Eagle*, Japanese Quail, Great Bustard*, Vinous-throated Parrotbill, Ochre-rumped* and Pallas' Buntings.

(Other species recorded here include Baikal Teal*, Scaly-sided Merganser* (once) and Swinhoe's Rail*.)

Bird the small reserve which is 50 km northwest of Nanchang and the two rivers (Gan and Xiu) which flow into the lake near here.

Accommodation: Wu Cheng Visitor Centre (A+), bookable through Jiangxi Forest, Beijing West Road, Nanchang.

GUAN SHAN NATURE RESERVE

The degraded forest within this reserve supports Silver and Elliot's* Pheasants, as well as Chinese Bamboo-Partridge.

Chinese Endemics

Elliot's Pheasant*.

Specialities

Chinese Bamboo-Partridge, Silver Pheasant, Chestnut Bulbul.

Others

Great Barbet, Bay Woodpecker, Orange-bellied Leafbird, White-crowned Forktail, Brownish-flanked Bush-Warbler, Rufous-faced Warbler, Greater Necklaced Laughingthrush, Hwamei, Rufous-capped Babbler, Red-billed Leiothrix, Grey-cheeked Fulvetta, Striated Yuhina, Grey-headed Parrotbill, Tristram's and Yellow-browed Buntings.

The reserve is accessible by road from Nanchang.

Accommodation: resthouse (basic).

BA BAO SHAN

This remnant montane forest in Guangdong province, southeast China, supports the endemic Cabot's Tragopan*, as well as the rarely seen Silver Oriole* and the fabulous Red-tailed Laughingthrush*.

Chinese Endemics

Cabot's Tragopan*, Yellow-bellied Tit.

Specialities

Chinese Bamboo-Partridge, Silver Oriole* (Apr–Sep), Brown-chested Jungle-Flycatcher* (Apr–Sep), Chestnut Bulbul, Grey*, Rusty and Red-tailed* Laughingthrushes.

Others

Speckled Piculet, Bay Woodpecker, Blue Magpie, Chestnut-bellied Rock-Thrush, Daurian Redstart, Little, Slaty-backed and Spotted Forktails, Black-throated Tit, Collared Finchbill, Brownish-flanked, Brown and Russet Bush-Warblers, Blyth's and White-tailed Leaf-Warblers, Sulphur-breasted Warbler, Greater Necklaced Laughing-thrush, Rufous-capped Babbler, Spot-breasted Scimitar-Babbler, Red-billed Leiothrix, White-browed Shrike-Babbler, Golden-breasted and Grey-cheeked Fulvettas, Striated Yuhina, Golden Parrotbill.

(Other species recorded here include White-necklaced Partridge* and Varied Tit, but these records may relate to escapes.)

The reserve is near the village of Ru Yang, near Shaoguan, which is accessible by train from Hong Kong. Bird all altitudes, especially the summit of Shi Keng Kong at 1900 m (6234 ft), where it is often misty.

Accommodation: Ru Yang — guesthouse (basic).

KUNMING

Nearly 330 species have been recorded around this large city in south China, mostly in the remnant evergreen broadleaf and pine forests on the nearby Western Hills. The mixture of eastern Himalayan and south-east Asian species present here ranges from Lady Amherst's Pheasant* to Maroon-backed Accentor.

Chinese Endemics

White-backed and Chinese* Thrushes, Yellow-bellied Tit.

Specialities

Chinese Bamboo-Partridge, Lady Amherst's Pheasant*, Pale Thrush (Nov–Mar), Buff-throated Warbler, Spectacled* and Dusky Fulvettas, White-collared Yuhina, Ashy-throated Parrotbill, Vinaceous Rosefinch.

Others

Speckled Piculet, Ashy Woodswallow, Rosy, Long-tailed and Short-billed Minivets, Chestnut-bellied Rock-Thrush, Long-tailed, Scaly, Chestnut and Dusky Thrushes, Blue-throated Flycatcher, Daurian Redstart, Black-throated Tit, Brown-breasted Bulbul, Striated Prinia, Tickell's Leaf-Warbler, Buff-barred Warbler, Hwamei, Spot-breasted Scimitar-Babbler, Blue-winged Minla, Black-headed Sibia, Green-backed Tit, Russet Sparrow, Rufous-breasted and Maroon-backed Accentors, Gould's Sunbird, Black-headed Greenfinch, Dark-breasted Rosefinch.

(Other species recorded here include Black-breasted Thrush* and Slaty Bunting*.)

Kunming is situated at 1895 m (6217 ft). Birding can be good in the vicinity of the Golden Peacock Hotel at the northeast corner of Dian Chi lake, where there is plenty of bamboo (Ashy-throated Parrotbill), but it is best to concentrate on the Western Hills 15 km from the city, west of Dian Chi lake. While there is little forest left on the western slopes of these hills, the presence of three temples, linked by a good road, has helped to preserve much of the forest on the eastern slopes. The best way to bird these hills is probably to get one of the regular buses from Gaoyao at the base of the hills up to Sanqingge and then descend the 5 km road on foot, concentrating on the rubbish tip at Sanqingge Temple (thrushes), the areas around the Taihua and Huating Temples and the gardens by Gaoyao bus station (Buff-throated Warbler). The road to, and the vicinity of, Anning, 40 km southwest of Kunming, the Golden Temple (Jin Dian), 7 km to the north of Kunming, and the Bamboo Temple (Qiong Zhu), 12 km northwest of Kunming, are also worth birding.

Accommodation: Kunming — Golden Peacock Hotel. Western Hills — Green Lake Hotel.

South of Kunming the road to Mengla passes through Pu'er. The forest on the ridge above the village of **Yongde**, west of Pu'er, supports White-bellied Redstart, Crested Finchbill, Red-faced Liocichla, Chinese Babax, Rusty-fronted Barwing, Dusky Fulvetta, Whiskered and White-collared Yuhinas, Spot-breasted Parrotbill, Yellow-browed Tit and Vinaceous Rosefinch. Simao, south of Pu'er, is the entry point to the huge **Xishuangbanna** nature protection zone (2000 sq km) in southwest Yunnan, where over 400 species have been recorded, including Mountain Bamboo-Partridge, Grey Peacock-Pheasant, Silver-breasted Broadbill, Ashy-throated Warbler, Red-faced Liocichla and Sultan Tit. Good birding areas include the remnant forest patches 20 km to the north of Simao, alongside the road to Kunming, and the forests 10 km and 65 km to the south of Simao. Further south there is some remnant forest around Mandian, near Jinghong, where Blue-bearded Bee-eater, Black-faced Warbler and Buff-breasted and Rufous-capped Babblers have been recorded. Turn right some 5 km northwest of Jinghong on to the 20–25 km track to the village of Mandian, where it is possible to stay. Rufous-breasted Bush-Robin* has been recorded in the Menghun Botanical Gardens, which lie on an island in the river alongside the Jinghong–Mengla road. A permit (obtainable in Jinghong) may still be needed to visit the Mengla area, where the main road south through Yunnan ends near the Laos border. Red-headed Trogon and Gould's Sunbird occur in the Wangtianshu NR, 19 km east of Mengla, where there are trails and a canopy boardwalk was under construction in 1992. About 15 km west of Mengla there is another nature reserve (on the south side of the river) where Pin-tailed Parrotfinch has been recorded, and the old road up Nangong Shan, a nearby hill, is also worth birding.

RUILI

This town in extreme southwest Yunnan on the border with Burma lies next to the broad, shallow Shelwi River and near some excellent deciduous forest which supports a number of localised species including Rusty-naped Pitta, Black-breasted Thrush* and Collared Myna*.

Specialities

Rusty-naped Pitta, Black-breasted Thrush*, Collared Myna*, Grey Sibia*, Black-browed Parrotbill*.

Others

Speckled Wood-Pigeon, Red-headed Trogon, White-browed Piculet, Stripe-breasted Woodpecker, Green Magpie, White-vented and Crested Mynas, Large Niltava, White-bellied Redstart, Chestnut-vented Nuthatch, Flavescent and White-throated Bulbuls, Grey-bellied Tesia, Pale-footed Bush-Warbler, Blyth's and White-tailed Leaf-Warblers, White-crested, Greater Necklaced, Rufous-necked, Black-throated and White-browed Laughingthrushes, Red-faced Liocichla, Red-billed Scimitar-Babbler, White-hooded Babbler, Rusty-fronted Barwing, Grey-cheeked Fulvetta, Rufous-backed and Long-tailed Sibias, Striated Yuhina, Grey-headed Parrotbill, Yellow-cheeked Tit, Gould's and Fire-tailed Sunbirds, Streaked Spiderhunter, Tibetan Serin.

Bird the forested hills northwest of town.

West of Kunming the road to Lijiang passes through **Chuxiong**, where the nearby Zizhu Forest Park supports Giant Nuthatch* and Red-tailed Minla.

LIJIANG

The remnant pine forests near Lijiang in northwest Yunnan support the endemic Yunnan Nuthatch* and Rufous-tailed Babbler, as well as a number of localised goodies such as Szecheny's Partridge*, Giant Nuthatch* and Black-bibbed Tit.

Chinese Endemics

Yunnan Nuthatch*, Giant Laughingthrush, Rufous-tailed Babbler*.

Specialities

Szecheny's Partridge*, Koklass Pheasant, White-throated Redstart, Giant Nuthatch*, Buff-throated Warbler, Chinese Babax, Spectacled* and Dusky Fulvettas, White-collared Yuhina, Black-bibbed Tit.

Others

Blood Pheasant, Chestnut Thrush, Hodgson's Redstart, Chestnut-vented Nuthatch, Bar-tailed Treecreeper, Black-browed Tit, Brown-breasted Bulbul, Chestnut-tailed Minla, Black-headed Sibia, White-browed Fulvetta, Russet Sparrow, Rufous-breasted and Maroon-backed Accentors, Black-headed Greenfinch, Beautiful and White-browed Rosefinches, Grey-headed Bullfinch.

Lijiang is 6 hours by bus from Dali. Bird the park and the hills beyond, to the north of town (Yunnan* and Giant* Nuthatches), the low hills alongside the Dali road, 3 km west of town (Chestnut-tailed Minla) and especially Jack Dragon Snow Mountain. This mountain, visible from town to the northwest, is 1.5 hours from the town and it takes 4 hours hard hiking to get up to the remaining forest above the temple, which is a popular tourist site.

The **Gaoligong Shan NR** in northwest Yunnan supports Sclater's Monal*, as well as Hill Partridge, Mountain Bamboo-Partridge, Blood Pheasant, Temminck's Tragopan*, Lady Amherst's Pheasant*, Purple Cochoa*, Blue-winged and Scaly Laughingthrushes, Slender-billed Scimitar-Babbler*, Long-tailed Wren-Babbler, Cutia, Streak-throated Barwing, Beautiful Sibia and Brown-winged Parrotbill*.

CAO HAI RESERVE

Cao Hai, which means 'Sea of Grass', consists of a large lake (10 by 5 km) surrounded by extensive marshes. This important wetland, which lies at 2200 m (7218 ft), supports one of the largest concentrations of wintering Black-necked Cranes* in the world (nearly 400 in 1992).

Access to the reserve area may still be restricted and potential visitors will need to check with the Guizhou Provincial Environmental Protection Bureau, No. 83, Zun Yi Road, Guiyang, People's Republic of China.

Specialities

Black-necked Crane* (Nov–Mar), White-collared Yuhina, Black-backed Wagtail (Nov–Mar).

Others

Bar-headed Goose (Nov–Mar), Falcated Duck, Baer's Pochard*, White-tailed Eagle*, Upland Buzzard, Imperial Eagle*, Daurian Jackdaw, Brown-breasted Bulbul, White-browed Laughingthrush, Russet Sparrow, Buff-bellied Pipit (Nov–Mar), Grey-capped and Black-headed Greenfinches.

Weining, a town on the shores of Cao Hai, is accessible by road from Liu Pan Shui, which is connected to Kunming by rail. The visitor centre, at the edge of Weining, overlooks the lake from the northeast and provides good views from the balcony. The conifer-clad headland of Yang Guan Shan in the northwest corner also enables good views over the lake. Otherwise, it is best to explore the south shore, between the villages of Bo Li Wan and Wang Jia Yuan Zi, and the area around Xi Jia Hai Zi lake and Lo Lo Shan, near Dongshan, on the southwest side of the lake. On calm days, it is possible to bird by punt.

Accommodation: Weining.

Tuoda NR, some 60 km northwest of Weining, is the best site in China for Reeves' Pheasant*. This site also supports Lady Amherst's Pheasant*, Black-browed Tit, Spectacled Fulvetta* and Spot-breasted Parrotbill, while rarities include Silver Oriole*, Purple Cochoa* and Yunnan Nuthatch*.

The city of **Chengdu** in central China, 2.5 hours by air from Beijing, is the gateway to Sichuan Province, where many of China's endemics occur. During a spare morning or afternoon here it is worth birding the popular **Du Fu's Cottage Park** (Du Fu Caotang Park) on the western outskirts of the city, because Brown-rumped Minivet*, Chestnut Thrush, Red-billed* (Nov–May) and White-cheeked (Nov–May) Starlings, Buff-throated Warbler (Apr–Sep), Large-billed Leaf-Warbler (Apr–Sep), Rufous-faced Warbler (Apr–Sep), White-browed Laughingthrush, Vinous-throated Parrotbill, Grey-capped Greenfinch, Yellow-billed Grosbeak and Slaty Bunting* (Nov–May) all occur here.

Accommodation: Jin Jiang Hotel (quite good birding in grounds), Tibet Hotel (tel: 3333988).

OMEI SHAN

This sacred Buddhist mountain, which rises to 3099 m (10,167 ft), south of Chengdu, is very popular with pilgrims and birders. The evergreen and temperate forests on its steep slopes support the richest montane avifauna in the country. Over 280 species have been recorded, including two birds which are virtually endemic to the mountain and its immediate vicinity: Grey-faced Liocichla* and Grey-hooded Parrotbill*, as well as Temminck's Tragopan*, Lady Amherst's Pheasant*, Brown-rumped Minivet*, Purple Cochoa*, four forktails, an incredible 12 species of *Phylloscopus* warblers, the beautiful Red-tailed Minla and seven other parrotbills.

Many of the species listed below are only present from April to September and the peak time to visit is late April–early May. However, some species are more conspicuous during the winter when snow may lie on the summit. Rain and mist are prevalent throughout the year.

Chinese Endemics

Brown-rumped Minivet*, Chinese Leaf-Warbler, Elliot's Laughingthrush, Grey-faced Liocichla*, Three-toed and Grey-hooded* Parrotbills, Pere David's and Yellow-bellied Tits, Slaty Bunting*.

Specialities

Chinese Bamboo-Partridge, Temminck's Tragopan*, Lady Amherst's Pheasant*, Fujian Niltava*, Purple Cochoa*, Chestnut-crowned Bush-Warbler, Buff-throated Warbler, Moustached and Red-winged* Laughingthrushes, Bar-winged Wren-Babbler, Chinese Babax, Streaked Barwing*, Streak-throated Fulvetta, White-collared Yuhina, Ashy-throated and Fulvous Parrotbills, Fork-tailed Sunbird, Vinaceous Rosefinch.

Others

Black Baza, Speckled Wood-Pigeon, Wedge-tailed Pigeon, Lesser and Drongo Cuckoos, Collared Owlet, Himalayan Swiftlet, Speckled Piculet, Crimson-breasted, Darjeeling and Bay Woodpeckers, Tiger Shrike, Scaly and Dusky Thrushes, Brown-breasted*, Ferruginous, Slaty-backed, Slaty-blue and Blue-throated Flycatchers, Vivid Niltava, Golden Bush-Robin, Little, Slaty-backed, White-crowned and Spotted Forktails, Black-throated Tit, Collared Finchbill, Brown-breasted Bulbul, Striated Prinia, Chestnut-headed Tesia, Aberrant, Grey-sided and Russet Bush-Warblers, Buff-barred, Ashy-throated and Pale-rumped Warblers, Large-billed Leaf-Warbler, Eastern Crowned-Warbler, Blyth's and White-tailed Leaf-Warblers, Sulphur-breasted and Rufous-faced Warblers, White-throated, Spotted, White-browed and Black-faced Laughingthrushes, Streak-breasted Scimitar-Babbler, Red-billed Leiothrix, Green Shrike-Babbler, Red-tailed Minla, Golden-breasted, Dusky and Grey-cheeked Fulvettas, Black-headed Sibia, Stripe-throated and Black-chinned Yuhinas, Great, Brown, Spot-breasted and Golden Parrotbills, Rufous-vented, Grey-crested, Green-backed and Yellow-browed Tits, Russet Sparrow, Forest Wagtail, Robin, Rufous-breasted and Maroon-backed Accentors, Gould's Sunbird, Dark-breasted, Dark-rumped and White-browed Rosefinches, Crimson-browed Finch, Grey-headed Bullfinch, Collared Grosbeak, Yellow-throated, Meadow and Tristram's Buntings.

Other Wildlife

Ferret-badger, leopard cat, tufted deer.

(Other species recorded here include Chestnut Thrush, White-bellied Redstart and Gold-fronted Fulvetta*, while the 'Omei Leaf-Warbler'

OMEI SHAN

seems destined to become a separate species.)

Omei Shan is accessible from Omei, which is connected by road (3–4 hours) and rail (2 hours) to Chengdu. The main trail, which is often crowded with pilgrims, is steep and paved. It begins at Bao Guo Temple, which lies at 550 m (1805 ft), 10 km from the railway station, and is a good place to start birding (Brown-rumped Minivet*, Ashy-throated Parrotbill). Further up, Brown-breasted Flycatcher* occurs around Fuhu. The 5 km side-trail which runs along an old irrigation ditch to a gorge at Wannian is good for Lady Amherst's Pheasant*, Moustached Laughingthrush, Grey-faced Liocichla* and Streaked Barwing* (Nov–Mar). The Wannian–Hongchun stretch via Qingyin runs through good forest where all four forktails occur, with Red-winged Laughingthrush* and Golden Parrotbill in the bamboo near Hongchun. Temminck's Tragopan* has been recorded along the narrow side-trail behind Hongchun and along the side-trail below Xianfeng, where Purple Cochoa* and Bar-winged Wren-Babbler also occur. Pere David's Tit occurs between Xixiang and Jieyin Hall. There are large expanses of bamboo around the Golden Monastery and these support specialists such as bush-warblers and parrotbills including Grey-hooded*, Brown and Fulvous. The Golden Monastery lies at 2450 m (8038 ft), 1 km below the summit, and is also a good area for Streaked Barwing (Apr–Oct), Grey-crested Tit, Maroon-backed Accentor and Vinaceous Rosefinch (most reliable around the rubbish tip). The road to the Cable Car Station is also worth birding.

Accommodation: Bao Guo — Hotel Hongzhushan. Trail — temples (C), monasteries (C).

The remote **Dafengding Reserve** in south Sichuan, west of Mabian, supports such great rarities as Blue-fronted Robin*, Gold-fronted

Fulvetta* and Grey-hooded Parrotbill*, as well as Purple Cochoa*. The cochoa has also been recorded at **Huang Nian Shan**, 25 km east of Mabian, along with Sichuan Partridge* and Silver Oriole*.

Slaty-backed Forktail is one of four species of forktail which occur on Omei Shan

WOLONG RESERVE

This large (1700 sq km), scenic reserve in the mountains of Sichuan is the base for the WWF Giant Panda Project. The panda and birds such as Black-throated Blue Robin* are rarely seen in the forests, bamboo thickets and meadows, but it is still possible to see a good selection of Chinese endemics and a number of other rarely reported species such as Firethroat*.

Chinese Endemics

Verreaux's Partridge*, Chinese Monal*, White Eared-Pheasant*, Golden Pheasant*, White-backed Thrush, Sooty Tit*, Chinese Leaf-Warbler, Barred*, Giant and Elliot's Laughingthrushes, Chinese Fulvetta, Spectacled Parrotbill*, Pere David's and Yellow-bellied Tits, Pink-rumped Rosefinch, Slaty Bunting*.

Specialities

Snow and Tibetan Partridges, Temminck's Tragopan*, Koklass Pheasant, Fujian Niltava*, Firethroat*, Grandala, Buff-throated Warbler, Red-winged Laughingthrush*, Chinese Babax, Streak-throated Fulvetta, White-collared Yuhina, Fire-capped Tit, Red-fronted Rosefinch.

Others

Lammergeier, Himalayan Griffon, Upland Buzzard, Tibetan Snowcock, Blood Pheasant, Snow Pigeon, White-throated Needletail, Crimson-breasted and Bay Woodpeckers, Eurasian Nutcracker, Long-tailed Minivet, Grey-backed Shrike, Plain-backed, Long-tailed and Chestnut Thrushes, Ferruginous, Slaty-backed, Slaty-blue and Blue-throated Flycatchers, White-tailed Rubythroat, Golden Bush-Robin, White-bellied Redstart, Little and White-crowned Forktails, Wallcreeper, Black-browed Tit, Collared Finchbill, Chestnut-headed Tesia, Yellowish-bellied, Grey-sided and Spotted Bush-Warblers, Tickell's Leaf-Warbler, Buff-barred and Pale-rumped Warblers, Large-billed, Blyth's and White-tailed Leaf-Warblers, Streak-breasted Scimitar-Babbler, Golden-breasted

Fulvetta, Great and Brown Parrotbills, Rufous-vented and Grey-crested Tits, Hume's Lark, Forest Wagtail, Rufous-breasted and Maroon-backed Accentors, Gould's Sunbird, Tibetan Serin, Plain and Black-headed Mountain-Finches, Dark-breasted, Beautiful, Dark-rumped and White-browed Rosefinches.

Other Wildlife

Black bear, giant panda, golden monkey, red panda, snow leopard.

(Other species recorded here include Solitary and Wood* Snipes, Black-throated Blue Robin* and Giant Laughingthrush.)

Wolong village is about 100 km west of Chengdu (6 hours by rough road). After crossing a small suspension bridge about 10 km out of Wolong village, bird the track up to the observation station (a 2 hour walk), which is situated in bamboo thickets where both Black-throated Blue-Robin* and Firethroat* are possible. Otherwise, bird by road and on the few trails, especially at the meadows and scree slopes beyond the 4300 m (14,108 ft) Balang Shan pass (Snow Partridge, Wood Snipe*, Grandala, Red-fronted Rosefinch), the HQ area in the Valley of the Heroes (Firethroat* in bamboo thickets) and the 3658 m (12,000 ft) Ting Fang Pass (pheasants, Grandala, Chinese Fulvetta, Red-fronted Rosefinch).

Accommodation: Wolong — Wolong Hotel.

The **Wolong–Jiuzhaigou Road** traverses the 4000 m (13,123 ft) Zhegu Shan pass and the eastern edge of the Tibetan Plateau where Chinese Grey Shrike and Wallcreeper may be seen before reaching Hongyuan, where there is a 'hotel'. The small marsh known as Wa Qie, 42 km north-east of Hongyuan, supports Pallas' Fish-Eagle* and Black-necked Crane*. Between Hongyuan and Ruoergai look out for Tibetan Ground-Jay, White-browed Tit and Black-winged Snowfinch. High altitude scrub between Ruoergai and Jiuzhaigou supports White-browed Tit-Warbler and Streaked and Przevalski's Rosefinches. Species recorded between Sunpang and Jiuzhaigou include Sichuan Jay, as well as Blood Pheasant, Snow Pigeon, Pere David's Owl*, Crested Tit-Warbler*, Chinese Fulvetta, White-browed and Grey-crested Tits and White-winged Grosbeak. From Sunpang it is possible to visit the Huanlong Pass where Tibetan Partridge, Blood Pheasant and White-browed Tit-Warbler occur. If returning to Chengdu via Wenchuan it is worth stopping at **Qingcheng Shan**, where Brown-rumped Minivet* has been recorded.

JIUZHAIGOU RESERVE

Jiuzhaigou (or Xiaozhaizigou) in north Sichuan is a wonderfully wild land of lakes, streams and waterfalls set among forested snow-capped peaks, and the scene is completed by some great birds, including Blue Eared-Pheasant*, Severtzov's Grouse*, Sichuan Jay*, Rufous-headed Robin*, Sukatschev's Laughingthrush*, Rusty-throated Parrotbill* and Three-banded Rosefinch.

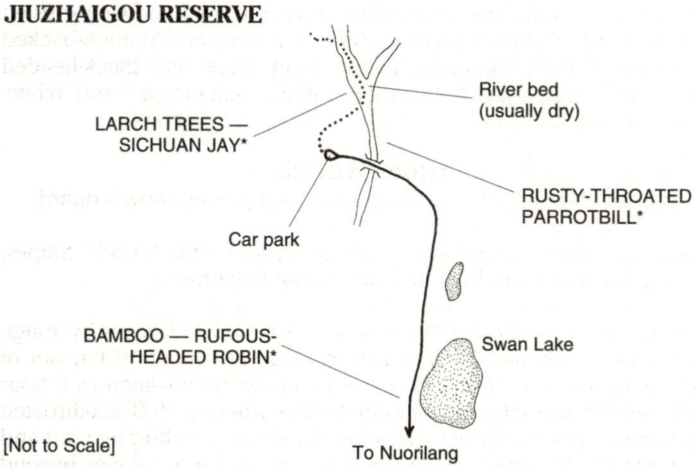

Chinese Endemics

Verreaux's Partridge*, Blue Eared-Pheasant*, Golden Pheasant*, Severtzov's Grouse*, Pere David's Owl*, Sichuan Jay*, White-backed and Chinese* Thrushes, Rufous-headed Robin*, Sooty Tit*, Crested Tit-Warbler*, Chinese Leaf-Warbler, Pere David's, Sukatschev's*, Barred*, Giant and Elliot's Laughingthrushes, Chinese Fulvetta, Three-toed, Spectacled* and Rusty-throated* Parrotbills, Pere David's Tit, Pink-rumped and Three-banded Rosefinches.

Specialities

White-throated Redstart, Grandala, Snowy-browed Nuthatch*, Chinese Babax, Spectacled Fulvetta*, Vinaceous Rosefinch.

Others

Upland Buzzard, Tibetan Snowcock, Blood Pheasant, Snow Pigeon, Lesser Cuckoo, Jungle Nightjar, Crimson-breasted, Three-toed and Black Woodpeckers, Eurasian Nutcracker, Long-tailed Minivet, Grey-backed Shrike, White-throated Rock-Thrush, Long-tailed and Chestnut Thrushes, Slaty-backed Flycatcher, Hodgson's, Daurian and White-bellied Redstarts, Wallcreeper, Bar-tailed Treecreeper, Yellowish-bellied and Spotted Bush-Warblers, Tickell's Leaf-Warbler, Yellow-streaked Warbler, Large-billed and Blyth's Leaf-Warblers, Spot-breasted Scimitar-Babbler, Great Parrotbill, Rufous-vented and Grey-crested Tits, Russet Sparrow, Rufous-breasted and Maroon-backed Accentors, Tibetan Serin, Long-tailed, Beautiful and White-browed Rosefinches, Grey-headed Bullfinch, Collared and White-winged Grosbeaks.

Other Wildlife

Chinese marten, giant panda.

Jiuzhaigou is about 430 km north of Chengdu via Sunpang. Snowy-browed Nuthatch* occurs alongside the 15 km road from the reserve entrance to Nuorilang. From Nuorilang continue straight on and after crossing the river 3 km above the village of Zechawa, walk left alongside the river (Rufous-headed Robin*), cross a tributary of this river, then cross the main river and bird the steep yak trail south (Chinese Fulvetta) which leads to meadows and scrub around a yak shed where White-throated Redstart and Crested Tit-Warbler* occur. Back at the main road continue to the car park at Long Lake and walk right, up through coniferous forest to an area of dwarf rhododendrons and meadows where Tibetan Snowcock, Verreaux's Partridge* and Grandala occur. Back at Nuorilang take the 15 km road to Swan Lake. Rufous-headed Robin* occurs in the bamboo opposite this lake. From the car park above Swan Lake (Sukatschev's Laughingthrush* in scrub around car park) walk the trail along the normally dry river bed into forest where Sichuan Jay* and Rusty-throated Parrotbill* occur.

Accommodation: Hotel Sichuan Jiuzhai Villa.

Ganzi Prefecture in extreme northwest Sichuan is an excellent birding area, especially the road between Kangding, Luhuo, Ganzi and Shiqu where Tibetan Ground-Jay occurs, and the 70 km road between Shigu and Luoxu which traverses the Obala Valley, north of Luoxu (Diankog). This road crosses the 4730 m (15,518 ft) Chawzhela Pass and traverses secondary spruce forest and juniper stands. Species occurring in this area include Tibetan Snowcock, Tibetan Partridge, Blood Pheasant (Obala Valley), Ibisbill (Ganzi-Shigu), Snow Pigeon, Tibetan Ground-Jay, White-backed Thrush (Obala Valley), White-throated and White-winged Redstarts, White-browed and Crested* (Obala Valley) Tit-Warblers, Giant (Obala Valley) and Elliot's Laughingthrushes, Spot-breasted Scimitar-Babbler (Obala Valley), Chinese Fulvetta (Obala Valley), White-browed Tit, Tibetan Lark, Black-winged, White-rumped and Rufous-necked Snowfinches, Robin Accentor, Long-tailed (Obala Valley), Pink-rumped, White-browed and Red-fronted (Chawzhela Pass) Rosefinches, White-winged Grosbeak and Przevalski's Rosefinch.

Przevalski's* and Daurian Partridges, Mongolian Finch, Pale Rosefinch and Meadow Bunting occur on the barren hills above the railway station in **Xining**, a large town which is situated at 2500 m (8202 ft) at the northeastern edge of the Tibetan Plateau in Qinghai province. The remnant mixed forest on the north side of **Laoye Shan**, a mountain near Xining, supports White-browed and Crested* Tit-Warblers. The forest is a 10 minute walk from the centre of Datong, a town 35 km northwest of Xining. To the south of Xining the **Xining–Nangqen Road** ascends the Tibetan Plateau (Daurian Partridge, Tibetan Ground-Jay) *en route* to Gonghe. The road southwest from Gonghe to Madoi passes through cultivated valleys, then grasslands where Pere David's Snowfinch occurs. The road then ascends to the 4482 m (14,705 ft) Er La Pass, beyond which the species to look out for include White-rumped and Rufous-necked Snowfinches. Madoi lies at 4313 m (14,250 ft) close to the marshes at the head of the Huang Ho (Yellow River). These marshes and the lakes Erling and Zhaling support breeding Pallas' Fish-Eagle* and Black-necked Crane* (May–Sep), as well as Bar-headed Goose (May–Sep) and Great Black-headed Gull. After crossing a 5000 m (16,404 ft) pass south of Madoi, the star birds to look out for are Tibetan Babax* and the smart Tibetan Bunting*, with Kanda Shan, 25 km north of Nangqen, being a good area for both.

NANGQEN

This remote town in central China lies on the banks of the Mekong River in an arid valley. Its surrounds and the fir forests and juniper stands in nearby side-valleys support a extraordinary assortment of rare and beautiful birds, including White-throated Redstart, White-browed and Crested* Tit-Warblers, Tibetan Babax* and Tibetan Bunting*.

Chinese Endemics

White Eared-Pheasant*, White-backed Thrush, Crested Tit-Warbler*, Giant and Elliot's Laughingthrushes, Tibetan Babax*, White-browed Tit, Przevalski's Rosefinch, Tibetan Bunting*.

Specialities

Szecheny's Partridge*, Solitary Snipe, Ibisbill, White-throated Redstart, Grandala, White-throated Bushchat*, White-browed Tit-Warbler.

Others

Lammergeier, Himalayan Griffon, Tibetan Snowcock, Tibetan Partridge, Blood Pheasant, Grey-backed Shrike, Hodgson's and White-winged Redstarts, Wallcreeper, Tickell's Leaf-Warbler, Grey-crested Tit, Robin and Brown Accentors, Plain Mountain-Finch, Beautiful, White-browed and Streaked Rosefinches, White-winged Grosbeak.

Other Wildlife

Bharal.

Head up to the high pass across the river and walk down through the alpine meadows (Tibetan Partridge), juniper stands (Tibetan Babax*) and bushy gullies (redstarts). The nearest forest is 55 km away on a terrible road (allow 4 hours), but it is possible to see Solitary Snipe *en route*, and, once in the forest, pheasants, Giant Laughingthrush and Crested Tit-Warbler*. Tibetan Bunting* occurs to the south of Nangqen, along with Przevalski's Rosefinch.

Tibetan Snowcock, Tibetan Partridge, White-browed Tit-Warbler and Przevalski's Rosefinch have been recorded in roadside valleys west of Xining *en route* to Heimahe and Qinghai Hu.

QINGHAI HU (KOKO NOR)

The marshes, meadows and scrubby mountain slopes surrounding China's largest lake (100 km long and 60 km wide), which is situated at 3200 m (10,500 ft), supports Black-necked Crane* and six of the world's seven snowfinches, including Black-winged and White-rumped.

Many of the birds listed below are only present during the summer (May–Sep).

Chinese Endemics

White-backed Thrush, White-browed Tit, White-rumped Snowfinch, Przevalski's Rosefinch.

Specialities

Tibetan Partridge, Black-necked* and Demoiselle (May/Sep–Oct) Cranes, Solitary Snipe, Tibetan Ground-Jay, White-browed Tit-Warbler, Black-winged, Pere David's, Rufous-necked and Blanford's Snowfinches.

Others

Bar-headed Goose, Pallas' Fish-Eagle*, Lammergeier, Himalayan Griffon, Upland Buzzard, Imperial Eagle*, Tibetan Snowcock, Great Black-headed Gull, Pallas' Sandgrouse, Daurian Jackdaw, Chinese Grey Shrike, Siberian and White-tailed Rubythroats, White-winged Redstart, Wallcreeper, Tickell's Leaf-Warbler, Tibetan, Mongolian and Hume's Larks, White-winged Snowfinch, Robin and Rufous-breasted Accentors, Plain Mountain-Finch, Beautiful and Streaked Rosefinches.

Other Wildlife

Black-lipped pika, wolf.

The extensive wet meadows along the southwest shore near the town of Heinahe, 200 km west of Xining, are particularly good, as are the scrubby hillsides and the high plateau behind the town (Solitary Snipe, White-winged Redstart, Przevalski's Rosefinch). Most of the geese and gulls nest on Bird Island (Neotoh) in the northwest corner of the lake, about 70 km from Heimahe and 16 km from the nearest accommodation at Bird Island Village near Shinahe.

Accommodation: Heimahe, Bird Island Village.

Tibet is politically part of China, although many of its people would prefer this remote, lofty land to be treated as a separate country. The most popular overland tourist route to Lhasa, its capital, is the **Qingzang Road**, which heads south from Gormud, a town which lies at the southern edge of the huge (820 km by 350 km) Zaidam Depression. Around Gormud it is worth birding the reservoirs a few kilometres north of the town (between the Golmud–Dunhuang road and the railway), where Solitary Snipe and Little Curlew have been recorded on passage in late August and early September, and the sand dunes on the southeast outskirts of the town where Mongolian Ground-Jay occurs. The road south to Lhasa traverses the Kunlun Range via a 4000 m (13,123 ft) pass before crossing the plains of Chang Tang where Chiru (an antelope) occurs. South of Tuotuohe, where there is accommodation, the road climbs even further, to the Tanggula Pass at a dizzy 5180 m (16,995 ft). In 1993 the little known Tibetan Rosefinch* was recorded here, the first sighting for over 50 years, and it has also been seen since. The huge Nam Tso (Tengri Nor) lake near Damxung, where it is possible to stay, is surrounded by grasslands which support the little known Tibetan Sandgrouse and localised Blanford's Snowfinch. To the east of Nam Tso lake is **Retinga Gompa**, an ancient monastery surrounded by juniper stands where two species only found in southeast Tibet occur; Tibetan Eared-Pheasant* and Prince Henry's Laughingthrush, as well as the near-endemic Giant Babax*.

Accommodation: Lhunzhub.

Tibetan Sandgrouse is one of the hardest Tibetan Plateau endemics to find

Most travellers visit **Lhasa**, which is situated at an altitude of 3683 m (12,083 ft), to see the Potala Palace, perched on top of Marpori (Red Mountain), and the Jokhang Temple. Even the most fanatical birders will probably be impressed by these man-made wonders, but in the valley below the Yongbulagong Castle more excitement is possible in the form of Prince Henry's Laughingthrush.

Accommodation: Tibet Hotel.

Permits may still be required to visit much of **Xinjiang Province** in extreme west China and they may be obtained from the Wildlife and Conservation Office, Xinjiang Uygur Autonomous Region, Forestry Bureau, 12 Heilongjiang Road, Urumqi (tel: 51061). Send itinerary and at least two letters of introduction. White-winged Woodpecker* and Saxaul Sparrow occur in the poplars at the northern edge of **Puhui**, and Pallas' Sandgrouse and Xinjiang Ground-Jay* in the most barren areas of desert halfway between Puhui and Korla, to the north. Great Black-headed Gull, Azure Tit and Desert Finch occur on and around **Boshteng Hu** lake 12 km from Bofur, which is northeast of Korla near Yanqi. It is possible to stay in Bofur and to hire bicycles to visit the lake. The pine forests alongside the roads around **Nalatie** (near the junction of the Bayanbolak and Yining–Korla roads), to the north of Bayanbolak, support White-backed Woodpecker, Azure Tit and Black-throated Accentor. The semi-desert between Kuytun, to the north of Nalatie, and Altai, supports Mongolian Ground-Jay. The localised Asian Rosy-Finch, as well as Pallas' Fish-Eagle*, White-backed and Three-toed Woodpeckers and Pine Bunting occur in the forested hills surrounding **Hanas Hu** lake, some 25 km north of Chardingjy Lingcha (obtain permission to visit this area in Burqin). Near **Urumqi** the surrounds of Tien Che Hu (Heavenly Lake) are worth a look. Although the west end is popular with tourists, the foothills to the south and east, north of Bogda Feng mountain, support Himalayan Snowcock, Rufous-backed and Blue-capped Redstarts and Black-throated Accentor. Birds seen from the train east of Urumqi include Mongolian Ground-Jay.

HAINAN

The two birds endemic to this island off the south China coast, a partridge and a leaf-warbler, occur in the Bawangling, Jianfengling and

Wuzhishan NRs. Jianfengling also supports Grey Peacock-Pheasant, Blue-rumped Pitta*, White-winged Magpie* and Ratchet-tailed Treepie, while other species recorded on Hainan include Black-faced Spoonbill (Nov–Mar), Collared Crow, Yellow-billed Nuthatch* (Bawangling NR), Chestnut Bulbul and Fork-tailed Sunbird.

ADDITIONAL INFORMATION

Books and Papers

The Birds of China. Meyer de Schauensee R, 1984. Oxford University Press.
A Field Guide to the Birds of Japan. Wild Bird Society of Japan, 1982. Kodansha.
A Field Guide to the Rare Birds of Britain and Europe. Alstrom P *et al.*, 1991. Harper Collins.
Birdwatching in the summer palaces of Beijing. Palfrey J, 1990. *OBC Bulletin* 12: 21–26.
Hainan Island bird notes. King B and Liao W, 1989. *Hong Kong Bird Report* 1988: 88–101.

CHINESE ENDEMICS (59)

White-eared Night-Heron*	Southeast: recorded at five sites between 1990 and 1994 in south Guangxi Province, including Mount Langu Shan
Crested Ibis*	Northeast: Qinling Mountains, south Shaanxi (only 25 birds left in the wild in 1994)
Verreaux's Partridge*	Central: Wolong and Jiuzhaigou
Przevalski's Partridge	North-central: Xining
Sichuan Partridge*	Central: south-central Sichuan
White-necklaced Partridge*	Southeast
Hainan Partridge*	Hainan Island: Bawangling, Jianfengling and Wuzhishan NRs
Cabot's Tragopan*	Southeast: Ba Bao Shan
Chinese Monal*	Central: Wolong
Tibetan Eared-Pheasant*	Central: Retinga Gompa (this species may also occur in extreme northeast India)
White Eared-Pheasant*	Central: Wolong and Nangqen
Brown Eared-Pheasant*	Northeast: Pangquangou NNR, and Donglingshan, Luyiashan and Wulushan NRs, in Shaanxi Province, and Xiaowutaishan NR in Hebei Province
Blue Eared-Pheasant*	Central: Jiuzhaigou
Elliot's Pheasant*	South and East: Guan Shan NR
Reeve's Pheasant*	Central: Tuoda NR
Golden Pheasant*	Central: Wolong and Jiuzhaigou
Severtzov's Grouse*	Central: Jiuzhaigou
Pere David's Owl*	Central: Wolong–Jiuzhaigou Road and Jiuzhaigou

Vaurie's Nightjar*	West: west Xinjiang; only known from a single specimen taken near Guma in 1929
Sichuan Jay*	Central: Wolong–Jiuzhaigou Road and Jiuzhaigou
Xinjiang Ground-Jay*	West: Puhui
White-backed Thrush	Central: widespread (has also occurred outside China)
Chinese Thrush*	Central and East: widespread
Rufous-headed Robin*	Central: very rare, Jiuzhaigou (a single bird has also been trapped as a migrant or vagrant in Malaysia)
Black-throated Blue Robin*	Central: very rare, Wolong, southeast Gansu, South Shaanxi and north-central Sichuan (has also been recorded in Thailand)
Ala Shan Redstart*	Southwest
Yunnan Nuthatch*	Central: Lijiang and Panguangou NR
Sooty Tit*	Central: Wolong, Jiuzhaigou and Dafengding
White-browed Chinese Warbler	North and west: Beijing and Shanhaiguan
Crested Tit-Warbler*	Central: widespread
Hainan Leaf-Warbler*	Hainan Island: Bawangling and Jianfengling NRs
Chinese Leaf-Warbler	Central: widespread
Pere David's Laughingthrush	North and central: Beijing, Jiuzhaigou
Sukatschev's Laughingthrush*	Central: Jiuzhaigou
Barred Laughingthrush*	Central: Wolong and Jiuzhaigou
Biet's Laughingthrush*	Southwest: Sichuan and north Yunnan
Giant Laughingthrush	Central: widespread
Elliot's Laughingthrush	Central: widespread
Prince Henry's Laughingthrush	Central: Retinga Gompa and Lhasa
Grey-faced Liocichla*	Central: Omei Shan
Rufous-tailed Babbler*	Central: Lijiang
Tibetan Babax*	Central: Nangqen
Gold-fronted Fulvetta*	Central: Huang Nian Shan (near Dafengding) and Laba He, south Sichuan
Chinese Fulvetta	Central: Wolong, Wolong–Jiuzhaigou Road, Jiuzhaigou and Ganzi
Three-toed Parrotbill	Central: Omei Shan and Jiuzhaigou
Spectacled Parrotbill*	Central: Wolong and Jiuzhaigou
Grey-hooded Parrotbill*	Central: Omei Shan and Dafengding
Rusty-throated Parrotbill*	Central: Jiuzhaigou
White-browed Tit	Central: widespread
Pere David's Tit	Central: Omei Shan, Wolong and Jiuzhaigou
Yellow-bellied Tit	North, east and central: widespread
White-rumped Snowfinch	Central: Ganzi, Xining–Nangqen Road and Qinghai Hu (has also occurred in India and Nepal)
Pink-rumped Rosefinch	Central: Wolong, Jiuzhaigou and

	Ganzi
Three-banded Rosefinch	Central: Jiuzhaigou
Tibetan Rosefinch*	Central: Qingzang Road
Przevalski's Rosefinch	Central: widespread
Slaty Bunting*	Central: widespread
Tibetan Bunting*	Central: Xining–Nangqen Road and Nangqen

Sillem's Mountain-Finch (*Leucosticte sillemi*) has been described from two specimens collected in 1929 on the barren plateau between the upper Kara Kash and upper Yarkand Rivers in south Xinjiang province.

Near-endemics

North and East
Scaly-sided Merganser*, Chinese Bamboo-Partridge, Swinhoe's Rail*, Hooded*, Red-crowned*, White-naped* and Siberian* Cranes, Black-tailed, Saunders'* and Relict* Gulls, Blakiston's Fish-Owl*, Collared Crow, Silver Oriole*, Bull-headed and Chinese Grey Shrikes, Japanese Waxwing*, Streaked Reed-Warbler*, Marsh Grassbird*, Reed Parrotbill*, Varied Tit, Chinese Penduline-Tit, Mongolian Lark, Black-backed and Japanese Wagtails, Mongolian Accentor, Japanese Grosbeak, Rufous-backed*, Ochre-rumped*, Tristram's, Yellow-throated and Yellow* Buntings.

North
Pallas' Sandgrouse, Mongolian Ground-Jay.

West
Turkestan and Yellow-breasted Tits, Saxaul Sparrow, Streaked Rosefinch.

South-Central
Szecheny's*, Tibetan, White-cheeked* and Chestnut-breasted* Partridges, Satyr*, Blyth's* and Temminck's* Tragopans, Sclater's Monal*, Hume's* and Lady Amherst's* Pheasants, Black-necked Crane*, Tibetan Sandgrouse, Brown-rumped Minivet*, Indian Grey Thrush, Rusty-bellied Shortwing*, Red-billed Starling*, Collared* and Crested Mynas, Fujian Niltava*, Pale-chinned Blue-Flycatcher, Firethroat*, Rufous-breasted Bush-Robin*, Chestnut-vented, White-cheeked and Giant* Nuthatches, Collared Finchbill, Light-vented and Chestnut Bulbuls, Striated, Grey*, Rufous-necked, Yellow-throated*, Moustached and Grey-sided Laughingthrushes, Hwamei, Red-winged Laughingthrush*, Bar-winged, Spotted* and Wedge-billed* Wren-Babblers, Chinese and Giant* Babaxes, Rusty-fronted, Hoary-throated, Streak-throated and Streaked* Barwings, Spectacled*, Ludlow's and Nepal Fulvettas, Grey* and Beautiful Sibias, White-naped, White-collared and Rufous-vented Yuhinas, Fire-tailed Myzornis, Great, Brown, Brown-winged*, Ashy-throated, Fulvous, Golden and Short-tailed* Parrotbills, Black-bibbed Tit, Tibetan Lark, Black-winged, Pere David's, Rufous-necked and Blanford's Snowfinches, Robin, Rufous-breasted and Maroon-backed Accentors, Fire-tailed Sunbird, Tibetan Serin, Black-headed Greenfinch, Blanford's, Beautiful, Pink-browed, Vinaceous and Dark-rumped Rosefinches, Crimson-browed and Scarlet Finches, Red-headed and Grey-headed Bullfinches, Gold-naped Finch.

Southwest
Brown-fronted, White-winged* and Himalayan Woodpeckers, Tibetan Ground-Jay, Long-billed Bush-Warbler*.

Southeast
Blue-rumped Pitta*, White-winged Magpie*, Ratchet-tailed Treepie, Yellow-billed Nuthatch* (Hainan Island), Masked and Rusty Laughingthrushes, Fork-tailed Sunbird, Yellow-browed Bunting.

More or Less Throughout
Snowy-browed Nuthatch*, Grey-capped Greenfinch.

HONG KONG

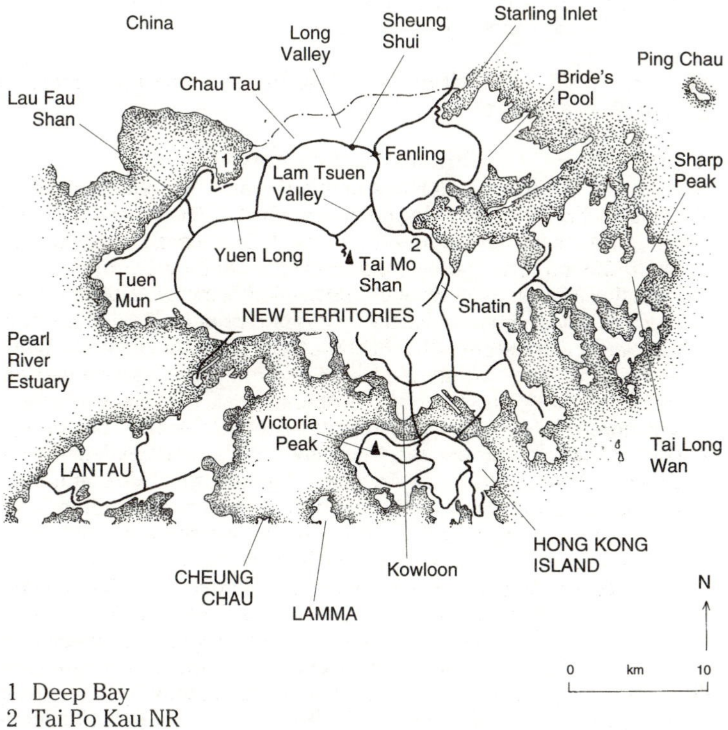

1 Deep Bay
2 Tai Po Kau NR

INTRODUCTION

Summary

The siberian shorebird express passes through Hong Kong and on a good day in April or May, Deep Bay is capable of producing the most spectacular shorebird show on earth. The sheer variety and concentration of species, most of which are in summer plumage, is staggering, and among 40 species or so there might just be a Spoonbill Sandpiper*. Passerine migration is less pronounced, but, along with lingering winter visitors, includes a fine selection of eastern Palearctic specialities.

Size

At just 1074 sq km, Hong Kong is merely a 'dot in China'.

Getting Around

Hiring a car is a luxury in such a small place as Hong Kong where there is a superb public transport system. This includes the KCR (overground train), MTR (underground train), buses, taxis and ferries, all of which are modern, cheap and very efficient. It is best to stay on the mainland where the best birding sites are.

Accommodation and Food

Accommodation is Hong Kong's downfall as far as budget birders are concerned. Apart from the basic hostel at Mai Po NR, virtually all types of accommodation are excessively expensive. However, cheap Chinese food can be found almost anywhere and can be washed down with the excellent Tsingtao beer (pronounced Ching Dow).

Health and Safety

Immunisation against hepatitis, polio and typhoid is recommended.

Climate and Timing

Shorebird fanatics must visit Hong Kong in April, which just happens to be the best time for passerine migrants too. It can be hot, wet and humid at this time, but the weather is rarely bad enough to spoil the birding. June to September is usually far too hot and humid for enjoyable birding, and even many local birders rarely venture out at this time of the year, unless a typhoon promises a movement of seabirds. From October to January the weather is cooler and generally dry and sunny.

Habitats

Parts of urban Hong Kong resemble scenes from science fiction movies, especially at night, but the sprawling metropolis is relieved here and there by small patches of secondary forest, barren hills, fishponds and, best of all, the mangrove-fringed mud flats of Deep Bay.

Conservation

Virtually the whole of Hong Kong has been deforested and its value to wildlife now lies primarily in its coastal habitats, especially those around Deep Bay. This bay is of immense importance as a wintering ground for world rarities such as Black-faced Spoonbill* and as a refuelling station for rare shorebirds. At high tide many birds seek refuge in the bay's hinterland, mainly at Mai Po NR, but this isn't enough, and if Deep Bay is to maintain its importance to birds, local conservationists must start working with, instead of against, those developers willing to listen, in order to provide the right combination of sensitive development and the provision of suitable habitats around the bay. Otherwise, the fate of most of the 21 threatened and near-threatened species which occur in Hong Kong will be left in the hands of the government, which, after 1997, will ultimately be controlled by Beijing.

Bird Species

Over 380 species have been recorded in Hong Kong, the vast majority of which are passage migrants and winter visitors. Non-endemic specialities and spectacular species include Dalmation Pelican*, Falcated Duck, Chinese Egret*, Black-faced Spoonbill*, Swinhoe's Snipe, Far Eastern Curlew*, Nordmann's Greenshank*, Asian Dowitcher*, Great Knot, Spoonbill Sandpiper*, Saunders' Gull*, Aleutian Tern, Japanese Paradise-Flycatcher*, Blue Magpie, Collared Crow, Grey-backed and Japanese Thrushes, Red-billed*, White-shouldered and White-cheeked Starlings, Siberian Rubythroat, Chestnut Bulbul, Black-throated and White-browed Laughingthrushes, Chinese Babax, Chinese Penduline-Tit, Fork-tailed Sunbird and Yellow-billed Grosbeak.

Endemics

There is no endemic species and the only Chinese endemic which has been recorded, Yellow-bellied Tit, is an irruptive winter visitor.

Expectations

It is possible to see 200 species during a two-week spring trip, including 40 species or so of shorebird. Birders from all over the world take part in the annual Birdrace, held in April, when around 170 species are usually recorded in 24 hours.

The unique Spoonbill Sandpiper is the star of the spring shorebird show in Hong Kong, but is by no means guaranteed to appear*

DEEP BAY

Deep Bay is, in fact, a big, shallow backwater of the massive Pearl River estuary, surrounded by mangrove, shrimp ponds (gei wais) and fishponds. It supports masses of wintering waterbirds (over 60,000 in winter 1994–95), including important populations of world rarities such as Black-faced Spoonbill* (99 in November 1995) and Saunders' Gull* (122 in January 1995), and in spring it acts as crucial refuelling stop for

DEEP BAY

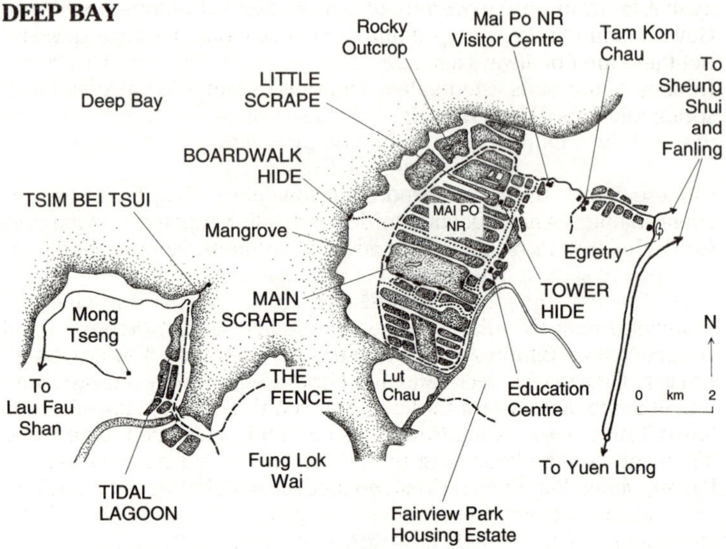

Siberian shorebirds such as Nordmann's Greenshank*, Asian Dowitcher* and Spoonbill Sandpiper*. In spring it is possible to see over 100 species in a day around Deep Bay, including over 35 species of shorebird, and, when conditions are right, the highlight of the day may be the stunning scene of thousands of summer-plumaged shorebirds crammed together on a mud flat or scrape.

Anyone with even a passing interest in shorebirds who has not experienced Deep Bay should start planning their trip now. And such a trip does take a lot of planning, unfortunately. The procedures outlined below are subject to change, especially in 1997, so it is probably best to write to WWF Hong Kong, No. 1 Tramway Path, Hong Kong (tel:2526 1011, fax: 2845 2734), or GPO Box 12721, for the latest details on how to see the birds of Deep Bay. At present, to obtain a permit to visit Mai Po NR it is necessary to send details, at least two weeks in advance, of the purpose and intended dates of your visit, as well as your passport number and expiry date, to The Director of Agriculture and Fisheries, Canton Road Government Offices, 393 Canton Road, Kowloon. Officially, only members of WWF Hong Kong are allowed to use the hides on the reserve, and access can be arranged on site or by writing to WWF Hong Kong. Another permit is required to visit the Boardwalk Hide which overlooks the mud flats at the edge of the mangroves and is essential for close-up views of shorebirds and Saunders' Gull. It is not possible to obtain a permit to visit this hide outside Hong Kong, but once there it can be obtained by taking photocopies of your Mai Po NR permit and passport, as well as a letter from the reserve, to The Permit Office, Fanling Police Station, 5 minutes walk from Fanling KCR station, where processing normally takes around an hour.

It is important to check the tide times before venturing to the bay because shorebirds are distant specks at low tide and are usually only seen at close range from the Boardwalk Hide or on the scrapes at Mai Po NR when the tide exceeds 1.7 m at Tsim Bei Tsui. Tide timetables are available from the Government Publications Centre, Queensway Government Offices, near Admiralty MTR Station, Hong Kong Island, but these are not always accurate.

Many of the birds listed below are winter visitors (Nov–Apr) and/or spring migrants (Apr–May).

Specialities

Chinese Egret*, Black-faced Spoonbill*, Swinhoe's Snipe, Nordmann's Greenshank*, Asian Dowitcher*, Spoonbill Sandpiper*, Saunders' Gull*, Collared Crow, Red-billed Starling*, Chinese Penduline-Tit.

Others

Dalmatian Pelican*, Falcated and Spot-billed Ducks, Chinese Pond-Heron, Yellow Bittern (Apr–Oct), Eurasian Spoonbill, Eastern Marsh-Harrier, Greater Spotted* and Imperial* Eagles, Slaty-breasted Rail, Pintail Snipe, Far Eastern Curlew*, Marsh and Terek Sandpipers, Grey-tailed Tattler, Great Knot, Rufous-necked and Long-toed Stints, Sharp-tailed and Broad-billed Sandpipers, Oriental Pratincole, Pacific Golden-Plover, Mongolian Plover, Greater Sandplover, Grey-headed Lapwing*, Oriental Turtle-Dove, Black-capped Kingfisher, Brown Shrike, White-shouldered, White-cheeked and Black-collared Starlings, Siberian Rubythroat, Light-vented Bulbul, Yellow-bellied and Plain Prinias, Chinese Bush-Warbler, Black-browed Reed-Warbler, Yellow-breasted and Black-faced Buntings.

(Rare winter visitors include Baikal Teal*, Baer's Pochard*, Oriental Stork*, Black-tailed, Slaty-backed, Great Black-headed and Relict* Gulls; scarce spring migrants include Little Curlew, Oriental Plover and Yellow Bunting*; and scarce spring and autumn migrants include Schrenck's* and Cinnamon Bitterns, Pied Harrier, Blue-tailed Bee-eater and Lanceolated and Pallas' Warblers.)

The best place to see most of the species listed above is **Mai Po NR** (400 ha), in the northwest New Territories, mainland Hong Kong. Public transport does not serve the reserve, but buses run from Sheung Shui KCR station to Mai Po village, from where it is a 30 minute walk west, through fishponds. Most taxi drivers outside Sheung Shui KCR station also know where Mai Po NR is and visitors travelling from Hong Kong Island who use the KCR and a taxi will need 1.5 hours to get to the reserve. The Main Scrape failed to attract roosting shorebirds on a regular basis in springs 1994 and 1995, but most of the rare shorebirds, including Spoonbill Sandpiper*, were seen from the Boardwalk Hide just before and just after high tide. Unfortunately, this hide is usually packed to the rafters with birders, so it is wise to arrive well before high tide to guarantee a seat and, more importantly, a decent view, and to be prepared to stay until the tide recedes. A second, larger hide was moored alongside this hide in spring 1996 and was due to be moved to a permanent position to the south in June 1996. The Little Scrape, at the north end of the reserve in front of the Tower Hide, has attracted large numbers of roosting shorebirds in recent springs and is a good place for Black-faced Spoonbill*, which also seem to spend a lot of time in the gei wais at the northern end of the reserve, east of the Rocky Outcrop.

Alternatively, many of the birds listed above can be seen between

Tsim Bei Tsui and the end of **'The Fence'** (erected to keep out illegal immigrants from China), along the 3.5 km track at the southern edge of Deep Bay. Tsim Bei Tsui, pronounced 'Chim Bay Choi', is accessible by bus via Yuen Long and Lau Fau Shan. Yellow-billed Grosbeaks frequent the roadside trees between Lau Fau Shan and Tsim Bei Tsui in winter. The tidal lagoons at the beginning of the track are a reliable site for wintering Grey-headed Lapwing* and they attract small numbers of roosting shorebirds, including Nordmann's Greenshank*.

Spring dates of Spoonbill Sandpiper* since 1990

1990	March 31 to June 3	(mostly April 10 to April 18)
1991	April 4 to May 12	(mostly May 2 to May 5)
1992	April 3 to May 16	(mostly April 3 to April 11)
1993	April 8 to April 30	(mostly April 8 to April 14)
1994	March 10 to May 5	(mostly March 28 to April 11)
1995	April 21 only	

Accommodation: Mai Po NR (tel: 2471 6306) — Field Studies Centre (A). To book in advance, write to WWF Hong Kong well before dates of travel. Sha Tin — Regal Riverside Hotel (A+), Royal Park (A+). Tai Po — Tai Po Hotel (A+), 1–2F, 6 Wun Tau Kok Lane, Tai Po Market (tel: 2658 6121. fax: 2650 2170) — convenient for Tai Po Kau NR.

The paddies at **Lok Ma Chau** near Mai Po NR are one of the best sites in Hong Kong for wintering and/or passage Pintail and Swinhoe's Snipes. Bird the small area of wet fields to the east of the junction of the road to the Lok Ma Chau Lookout Point and Castle Peak Road, accessible from the village of Pun Uk Tsuen at the northern end of the fields. A little further east along Castle Peak Road turn left to reach **Chau Tau**, where the barren hillsides on the east side of the road before the pig farm support Great Spotted* (Nov–Mar), Imperial* (Nov–Mar) and Bonelli's Eagles, Chinese Francolin, Lesser Coucal and Savanna Nightjar (Apr–Sep). The bus from Sheung Shui KCR station to Mai Po village passes these roads and stops nearby. Greater Painted-Snipe occurs at **Long Valley**, which is also accessible from Castle Peak Road. Bird the wet fields (beware of dogs) north of Tsung Pak Long village, near Sheung Shui.

TAI PO KAU NATURE RESERVE

When the tide is out in Deep Bay, one of the best sites to bird in Hong Kong is the secondary forest in this reserve near Tai Po. Birding here can be depressingly slow compared with the bay, but patient and persistent birders may find such star spring migrants as Japanese Paradise-Flycatcher*. Forget trying a couple of hours after dawn on Sundays though.

Specialities

Japanese Paradise-Flycatcher* (Apr–May/Sep–Oct), Chestnut Bulbul, Fork-tailed Sunbird.

TAI PO KAU NR

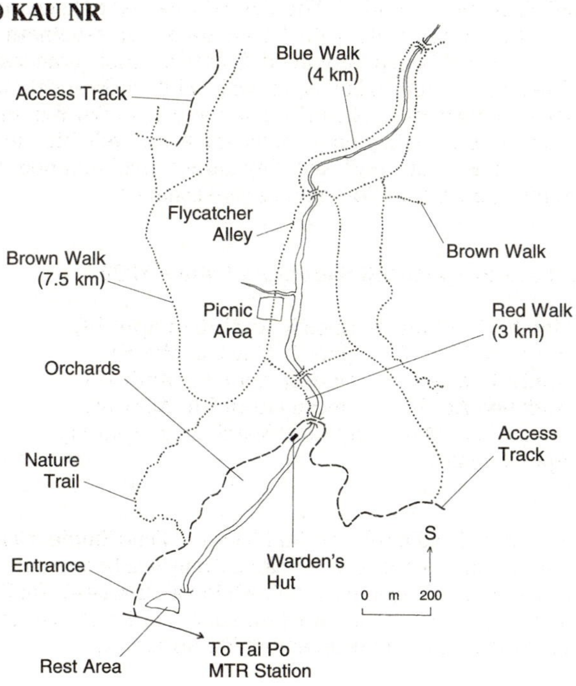

Others

Crested Serpent-Eagle, Crested Goshawk, Oriental Turtle-Dove (Nov–Apr), Chestnut-winged Cuckoo (Apr–Sep), Asian Barred Owlet, Dollarbird (Apr–May/Sep–Oct), Great Barbet, Asian Paradise-Flycatcher (Apr–May/Sep–Oct), Grey-chinned and Scarlet Minivets, Grey-backed (Nov–Apr), Japanese (Nov–Apr) and Eye-browed (Nov–Apr) Thrushes, Dark-sided (Sep–Oct), Ferruginous (Apr), Yellow-rumped (Sep–Oct) and Narcissus (Apr–May) Flycatchers, Hainan Blue-Flycatcher (Apr–Sep), Grey-headed Canary-Flycatcher (Nov–Apr), Rufous-tailed Robin (Nov–Apr), Black-throated Tit, Light-vented Bulbul, Japanese White-eye, Asian Stubtail (Nov–Apr), Pale-legged Leaf-Warbler (Sep–Oct), Eastern Crowned-Warbler (Sep–Oct), Greater Necklaced Laughingthrush, Hwamei, Red-billed Leiothrix, White-bellied Yuhina, Yellow-cheeked Tit, Forest Wagtail (Sep–Oct), White-rumped Munia, Fire-breasted and Scarlet-backed Flowerpeckers, Tristram's Bunting (Nov–Apr).

(Other species recorded here include Orange-headed, Scaly (Nov–Apr) and Pale (Nov–Apr) Thrushes and Japanese Robin (Feb); those species whose status is obscure, but are probably best treated as 'escapes', include Velvet-fronted Nuthatch and Silver-eared Mesia.)

The reserve entrance is at the milestone 42 lay-by, accessible by bus and taxi southeast of Tai Po. There are a number of trails worth exploring, though the stretch from the entrance to the picnic area and the tall forest (known locally as 'Flycatcher Alley') beyond is often the best.

Rufous-rumped Grassbird, Chinese Babax, Vinous-throated Parrotbill and Upland Pipit (along with the much commoner *sinensis* race of Richard's Pipit) occur near the top of **Tai Mo Shan**, Hong Kong's highest peak at 957 m (3140 ft) in the central New Territories. Walk up from the barrier, accessible via Route Twisk between Tsuen Wan and Shek Kong. Sites worth birding in the northeast New Territories include the **Starling Inlet** area, especially Luk Keng, where the freshwater marsh is good for bitterns, and **Bride's Pool**, which is the best site for the scarce Crested Kingfisher in Hong Kong. The island of **Ping Chau** in Mirs Bay off the northeast New Territories is good for passerine migrants in spring. The twice-daily ferry leaves from Ma Liu Shui near University KCR station. Once on the 2 km long island the best area is the woodland around the Police Post, reached by walking northwest from the pier.

Before the new airport is completed in 1998, first-time visitors to Hong Kong will soon discover, when the plane flies alongside the skyscrapers to land at Kai Tak airport, that Kowloon is one of the most densely populated urban areas in the world. **Kowloon Park** is a tiny green oasis in this concrete desert and has attracted a number of interesting migrants, including Slaty-legged Crake, Grey-backed Thrush and Rufous-tailed Robin. The park is adjacent to Tsim Sha Tsui MTR station (take Exit A from the station). **Kai Tak Airport** is one of the best sites in Hong Kong for Little Curlew and Oriental Plover, which occasionally visit the short grass areas alongside the runways in spring, some of which can be viewed from near the taxi rank outside the arrival hall.

The best place to go birding on **Hong Kong Island** is Victoria Peak, which rises steeply from the harbour to 552 m (1811 ft). Blue Magpie, Blue Whistling-Thrush, wintering thrushes, flycatchers, Asian Stubtail (Nov–Apr), Black-throated and White-browed Laughingthrushes, Hwamei and Fork-tailed Sunbird occur here. The peak is accessible via the Peak Tram (prepare to travel at a new angle!), the No. 15 bus from near the Star Ferry terminal and No. 1 bus from Edinburgh Place. From the 'tourist' area at the peak walk up Mount Austin Road to the Victoria Peak Garden and The Governor's Walk, a small park, or walk the Lugard Road–Harlech Road loop lower down. In the typhoon season (Jul–Sep) seabirds such as Streaked Shearwater, and Aleutian and Bridled Terns have been recorded from **Cape D'Aguilar** at the southeast corner of Hong Kong Island. The best passage has been recorded in 'No. 8 Signal' conditions, when gusts may exceed 180 km per hour and people are advised to stay indoors, but it is possible to reach the cape with a hire-car in such conditions, although such a journey is dangerous, especially in heavy rain. Buses, which only get to within 2–3 km anyway, stop running and taxi drivers are very reluctant to make the trip. The Cape is definitely not the best place to be in rare 'No. 9 or 10 Signal' conditions, but, then again, nowhere is.

Pacific Reef-Egret, White-bellied Sea-Eagle and Black-naped Tern all occur on and around the smaller outer islands, and in mid August to mid September Aleutian Tern is possible (85–190 in autumn 1992–95), especially from the **Cheung Chau** ferry. There are regular ferries to Lamma, Cheung Chau and Lantau from Hong Kong Island and the HKBWS organises occasional boat trips to look for seabirds.

ADDITIONAL INFORMATION

Addresses

The Hong Kong Bird Watching Society (HKBWS), GPO Box 12460, Hong Kong, publishes an excellent annual *Bird Report*, available in the United Kingdom from Wendy Young, 12 Denman's Close, Lindfield, West Sussex RH16 2JX. Please submit records to the HKBWS.

Hong Kong Birdline

2667 4537.

Books and Papers

Birds of Hong Kong and South China, Sixth Edition. Viney C *et al.*, 1994. Government Information Services.

A Field Guide to the Rare Birds of Britain and Europe. Alstrom P *et al.*, 1991. HarperCollins.

Birding Hong Kong. Diskin D, 1995. Available from David Diskin, PO Box 952, Shatin Central Post Office, New Territories, Hong Kong.

Chinese Endemics

Yellow-bellied Tit (irruptive winter visitor).

Near-endemics

Saunders' Gull*, Collared Crow, Red-billed Starling*, Crested Myna, Light-vented and Chestnut Bulbuls, Masked Laughingthrush, Hwamei, Chinese Penduline-Tit, Fork-tailed Sunbird, Tristram's and Yellow* Buntings.

INDIA

INTRODUCTION

Summary

Birders who like seeing a bag full of brilliant birds, who are prepared to see real poverty and squalor, who are unaffected by almost unbelievable hustle and bustle, and who enjoy overcoming bureaucratic barriers, will enjoy India. This is a huge country which stretches from the Himalayas in the north, where there are many specialities, via the famous bird-filled wetlands of Bharatpur, to the remnant forests of the far south, where most of the 39 endemics are present and a further 17 species are shared only with Sri Lanka. India is a budget birders dream and many have lasted months here without breaking the bank, thanks to the incredibly cheap public transport network and, as birders with a better cash flow will be pleased to learn, the presence of a wide variety of accommodation almost everywhere.

1	Delhi	9	Darjeeling	18	Goa
2	Ramnagar	10	Sandakphu Trek	19	Sri Lankamalles-wara
3	Corbett NP	11	Pemayangtse	20	Rajiv Gandhi NP
4	Naini Tal	12	Lava	21	Mudumalai NP
5	Kashmir and Ladakh	13	Manas NP	22	Ootacamund
6	Bharatpur	14	Kaziranga NP	23	Indira Gandhi NP
7	Ranthambore NP	15	Dibru-Saikhowa	24	Periyar NP
8	Desert NP	16	Namdapha NP		
		17	Jatinga		

Size

At 3,287,590 sq km, India is 25 times larger than England and five times the size of Texas.

Getting Around

Public transport is so cheap and efficient that hiring a vehicle would be an extreme extravagance. However, the Indians do not travel lightly and every bus and train appears to be overflowing with them and their belongings. Fortunately, it is possible to book sleeping compartments for the longer journeys, in advance, and as this luxurious form of transport is still ridiculously cheap, it makes great sense to take advantage of it if you wish to arrive at the next birding site in a fit birding state. In the towns there are also cheap taxis and auto-rickshaws which will take foreigners almost anywhere within range, but negotiate and agree the price before setting off.

Political instability may result in access being restricted in some areas (e.g. Kashmir, Ladakh, Assam and Sikkim) and, at times, good birding sites such as Kaziranga and Manas have been closed to visitors. In such cases Restricted Area Permits may be required and these may be obtained at the relevant Foreigners Regional Registration Office, or by applying to home consulates months in advance, in the major cities such as Delhi, Calcutta and Darjeeling (for Sikkim).

Accommodation and Food

There is a wide range of accommodation and food virtually everywhere. People who like Indian food will enjoy eating, although, for some strange reason, the curries cooked here rarely match those made in foreign countries. In the south the curries are usually very spicy hot. People who don't like curries will have to get by on western-style food such as omelettes. The national drink is tea, which is usually thick, milky and sweet — a bit like drinking toffee — and known as chai. Beer is available in all but a few states where it is prohibited.

Health and Safety

Immunisation against hepatitis, meningitis, polio, typhoid and yellow fever is recommended, as are precautions against malaria. Very few visitors to India manage to survive a whole trip without some sort of stomach upset. To avoid being ill, or, more realistically, to lessen the effects, stick to sterilised or boiled water and stay away from meat, salads and ice cream.

In the summer of 1995 the guerrilla war, which has been going on since 1990 in the Muslim-dominated state of Kashmir, intensified when western hostages were taken into the mountains. Naturally, it is wise to check with the relevant Foreign Office before even considering a birding trip to this part of northwest India.

Climate and Timing

The best time to visit northwest, northeast and south India is between November and March, whereas April is the peak time to go to Sikkim and West Bengal, and April to September to the far northwest (Kashmir and Ladakh). In general, the temperature rises steadily from November (cool) to May (very hot) before the monsoon season, which usually lasts from June to September.

Habitats

India is a huge country with a wide range of major habitats. The mountain meadows and montane forests of the Himalayas in the north give way to sal forests and grasslands in the foothills, and to the south lies desert, thorn scrub, agricultural plains and wetlands. In southern India there are two north–south mountain ranges running parallel to the west (Western Ghats) and east (Eastern Ghats) coasts. The Western Ghats rise to 2695 m (8842 ft) and, among the numerous tea plantations, still retain some areas of evergreen and dry deciduous forests which support a distinctive avifauna.

Conservation

One of the most striking features of India is the close co-existence of people and some of the wildlife. Even small ponds in major towns, where the local people wash everything from themselves to their clothes and cars, can be crammed full of waterbirds. However, while the common species may be able to cope, many birds are unable to adapt when their habitats are degraded or destroyed, so when the government come up with such projects as that in the Mahadayi Valley in the Western Ghats, where a proposed hydroelectric project threatens to drown 1600 ha of forest, one wonders how much longer there will be room in India for all the people and all the wildlife. The government has established numerous national parks and reserves throughout the country, but many are little more than lines on a map, and if the human population is not stabilised it will be difficult to protect the country's amazing birdlife in the future. The avifauna includes 171 threatened and near-threatened species, of which 71, the fifth highest total for any country in the world, are threatened with extinction.

Bird Species

About 1,230 species have been recorded in India, the highest total for a mainland Asian country. Non-endemic specialities and spectacular species in the north include Black-necked Stork, Sarus Crane*, Great Thick-knee, Ibisbill, Indian Courser, Crested Kingfisher, Black-headed Jay, White-tailed Iora, Siberian and White-tailed Rubythroats, White-browed Bushchat*, Fire-capped Tit and Black-throated Accentor. Notable birds of the extreme northwest include Tibetan Sandgrouse, Orange Bullfinch and Black-and-yellow Grosbeak. Notable birds of the northeast are White-winged Duck*, White-bellied Heron*, Swamp Francolin*, Satyr* and Blyth's* Tragopans, Sclater's Monal*, Masked Finfoot*, Bengal Florican*, Ward's Trogon*, Yellow-rumped Honeyguide*, Long-tailed Broadbill, Black-breasted Thrush*, Blue-fronted Robin*, Jerdon's Bushchat*, Beautiful Nuthatch*, Red-faced Liocichla, Rufous-throated Wren-Babbler*, Silver-eared Mesia, Cutia, Red-tailed Minla, Fire-tailed Myzornis, Rufous-headed Parrotbill*, Sultan Tit, Maroon-backed Accentor, Gould's and Fire-tailed Sunbirds and Scarlet and Gold-naped Finches. Southern specialities include Heart-spotted Woodpecker and Indian Pitta.

Endemics

A total of 39 species are endemic to mainland India, of which 24 are only found in the south. Northern endemics include Rock Bush-Quail, Indian Bustard* and Green Avadavat* and southern endemics include Jerdon's Courser*, White-bellied Treepie*, Black-and-rufous Flycatcher* and three laughingthrushes. Seventeen species are shared with Sri Lanka and these include Blue-faced Malkoha, Ceylon Frogmouth* and Malabar Trogon. The Andaman and Nicobar Islands support a further 17 endemics, of which five are confined to the Nicobar Islands and eight, including a serpent-eagle, a woodpecker and a treepie, are confined to the Andaman Islands.

Expectations

It is possible see 350–400 species in two or three weeks on a trip to northern India which includes Bharatpur, Corbett and Naini Tal, around 440 species on a three-week trip to the northeast which includes sites in Sikkim and Assam, and 340–350 during a similar period in the south.

NORTHWEST INDIA

There are a few sites worth birding in **Delhi** if time allows. It is possible to see 50 species during a short visit to **Okhla Island**, in the Yamuna River, on the outskirts of the city, including widespread species such as Indian Pond-Heron, Red-naped Ibis*, Indian Peafowl, Black-bellied* and River Terns, Green Bee-eater and Indian Roller, but the birds to concentrate on here are White-tailed Stonechat, Yellow-bellied Prinia, Striated Grassbird and Striated Babbler, all of which are hard to find elsewhere in the country. The **Buddha Jayanti Gardens** support Grey

DELHI AREA

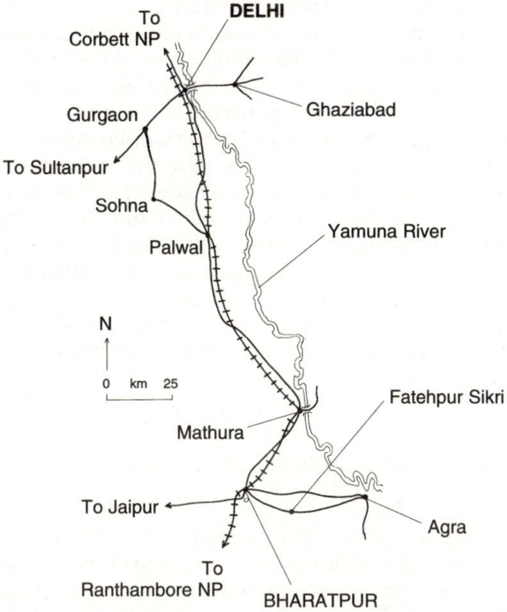

Francolin, Sirkeer Malkoha, Rufous-fronted Prinia and Brooks' Leaf-Warbler. **Delhi Zoo** and the nearby old Fort is a good site for Wire-tailed Swallow and Large Grey Babbler. A little further afield, the semi-desert areas in and around the **Tuglakhabad Ruins**, several kilometres to the southeast of the city, support Jungle Bush-Quail, Sirkeer Malkoha, White-tailed Iora, Rufous-fronted and Jungle Prinias, Sulphur-bellied Warbler (Nov–Mar) and Brooks' Leaf-Warbler. The shallow **Sultanpur Jheel**, 1.5 hours by road (50 km) southwest of Delhi, is a mini-Bharatpur and supports many birds including Greater Flamingo, Red-naped Ibis*, Painted* and Black-necked Storks, Sarus Crane*, Pheasant-tailed and Bronze-winged Jacanas and White-tailed Lapwing,

Ramnagar is one of the best sites in Asia for the bizarre Ibisbill

with occasional Demoiselle Cranes joining the Common Cranes which use the jheel as a roost site. There are several observation towers around the jheel which lies behind a hotel complex, and the dry area south of the jheel is worth checking for Indian Courser.

The road north from Delhi to Corbett National Park and Naini Tal crosses the River Ganges where Great Black-headed Gull, Black-bellied Tern*, Streak-throated Swallow and Sand Lark occur, as well as Ganges dolphin. Further north, at **Ramnagar**, where accommodation in Corbett NP must be booked at the park HQ, the road crosses the rocky Kosi River where Ibisbill occurs between November and March. Birders who have never seen this bizarre bird would be wise to spend some time here before moving on to the greater variety of birds in Corbett and at Naini Tal, for this is one of the most accessible sites in the world for Ibisbill, a bird which could well end up as 'bird of the trip'. They are usually present in small numbers north of the bridge and have been accompanied by other delights such as Great Thick-knee, Crested Kingfisher and Wallcreeper

Accommodation: Govind Restaurant, tourist bungalow.

CORBETT NATIONAL PARK

The extensive sal forests and grasslands of this large park in the Himalayan foothills 300 km northeast of Delhi support a superb range of birds, including Great Thick-knee and Tawny Fish-Owl*. However, the birding experience here is tainted by tigers. Their presence means it is not possible to bird on foot away from the small Dhikala compound, leaving many visiting birders to wonder what they might have seen in the forests and grasslands that stretch far beyond the fence.

Specialities

Great Thick-knee, Sirkeer Malkoha, Tawny Fish-Owl*, Long-billed Thrush*, Black-chinned Babbler, Black-throated Accentor (Nov–Mar).

Others

Black-necked Stork, Pallas'* and Lesser* Fish-Eagles, White-eyed Buzzard, Rufous-bellied Eagle, Collared Falconet, Grey and Black Francolins, Red Junglefowl, Indian Peafowl, River Lapwing, Slaty-headed and Plum-headed Parakeets, Brown Fish-Owl, Jungle Owlet, Crested Treeswift, Himalayan Swiftlet, White-rumped Needletail, Stork-billed and Crested Kingfishers, Blue-bearded and Chestnut-headed Bee-eaters, Great Hornbill, Brown-headed, Lineated and Blue-throated Barbets, Fulvous-breasted and Rufous Woodpeckers, Lesser Yellownape, Streak-throated Woodpecker, Himalayan and Black-rumped Flamebacks, Rufous and Grey Treepies, Large Cuckoo-Shrike, Small Minivet, Golden-fronted and Orange-bellied Leafbirds, Grey-backed Shrike, Large Woodshrike, Grey-winged Blackbird, Chestnut-tailed Starling, Jungle Myna, Slaty-blue Flycatcher, Rufous-bellied Niltava, White-tailed Rubythroat (Nov–Mar), Spotted Forktail, Chestnut-bellied and Velvet-fronted Nuthatches, Wallcreeper (Nov–Mar), Black-crested Bulbul, Golden-headed Cisticola, Grey-breasted Prinia, Chestnut-headed Tesia, Aberrant and Grey-sided Bush-Warblers, Tickell's Leaf-Warbler, Scaly-breasted Wren-Babbler, Chestnut-capped and Yellow-eyed Babblers, Rosy Pipit, Crested and Chestnut-eared (Nov–Mar) Buntings.

Other Wildlife

Asian elephant, chital, common langur, gharial, hog-deer, Indian smooth otter, mugger crocodile, rhesus macaque, sambar, tiger, yellow-throated marten.

Permits and accommodation must be arranged in Ramnagar, 19 km south of the park entrance. The park hub is at Dhikala. From here it is possible to scan the huge lake, formed by damming the River Ramganga, where Great Thick-knee and Gharial may be seen, to check the stretch of river nearby where Lesser Fish-Eagle* and Crested Kingfisher occur, and to visit an observation tower set in the forest where flocks of feeding birds often pass through, especially early in the day. Otherwise all birding must be done from jeeps or elephants, neither of which are ideal for forest birding. At times groups have been allowed to bird on foot outside the compound in the presence of armed guards. Outside the park it is worth birding at Dhangarhi and near the Quality Inn Kumaria (A), which overlooks the Kosi River and is surrounded by forest where it is possible to bird on foot.

CORBETT NP

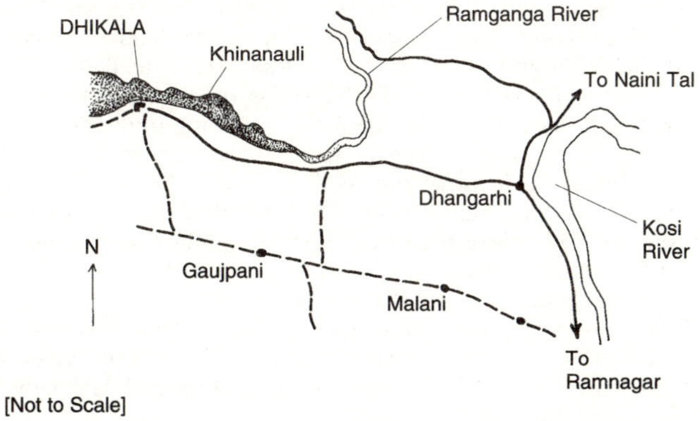

Great Thick-knee can be seen alongside Gharial on the lake at Corbett National Park

NAINI TAL

This cool Himalayan hill resort is situated at 2000 m (6562 ft). Although the town is a shabby relic of the Raj, it is an excellent base from which to explore nearby coniferous forests and open country which support some west Himalayan specialities such as Black-headed Jay, as well as Long-billed Thrush* and Fire-capped Tit.

Many of the species listed below are only present during the winter (Nov–Mar).

Specialities

Koklass Pheasant, Black-headed Jay, Long-billed Thrush*, Black-chinned Babbler, Fire-capped Tit, Black-throated Accentor, Spectacled Finch, Pink-browed Rosefinch.

Others

Lammergeier, Himalayan Griffon, Cinereous Vulture*, Hill Partridge, Brown Fish-Owl, Brown Wood-Owl, Great and Blue-throated Barbets, Speckled Piculet, Brown-fronted and Himalayan Woodpeckers, Greater Yellownape, Scaly-bellied Woodpecker, Yellow-bellied Fantail, Blue Magpie, Grey Treepie, Maroon Oriole, Long-tailed Minivet, Chestnut-bellied Rock-Thrush, Plain-backed, Long-tailed and Scaly Thrushes, White-collared and Grey-winged Blackbirds, Chestnut and Dark-throated Thrushes, Ultramarine Flycatcher, Small and Rufous-bellied Niltavas, Siberian and White-tailed Rubythroats, Golden Bush-Robin, Blue-capped Redstart, Little, Slaty-backed and Spotted Forktails, Chestnut-bellied, White-tailed and Velvet-fronted Nuthatches, Wallcreeper, Bar-tailed Treecreeper, Black-throated Tit, Nepal Martin, Himalayan Bulbul, Chestnut-headed Tesia, Brownish-flanked, Aberrant and Grey-sided Bush-Warblers, Buff-barred, Ashy-throated, Pale-rumped and Grey-hooded Warblers, White-throated, White-crested, Striated, Rufous-chinned and Streaked Laughingthrushes, Red-billed Leiothrix, White-browed and Green Shrike-Babblers, Blue-winged Minla, Rufous Sibia, Whiskered Yuhina, Black-crested, Black-lored and Yellow-browed Tits, Russet Sparrow, Himalayan and Rufous-breasted Accentors, Green-tailed, Black-throated and Fire-tailed Sunbirds, Fire-fronted Serin, Yellow-breasted Greenfinch, Plain Mountain-Finch, Dark-breasted Rosefinch, Brown Bullfinch, Collared and Spot-winged Grosbeaks, Chestnut-breasted Bunting.

(Other species recorded here include Red-headed Bullfinch.)

Around Naini Tal bird the fields between the Tourist Resthouse and the beginning of the Tiffin Top trail (Himalayan Accentor), the trail to Tiffin Top (Black-headed Jay), the area around the church near the Swiss Hotel (Russet Sparrow), the forest and ridge above the Swiss Hotel, and Snow View (Long-tailed Thrush and rarities such as Red-headed Bullfinch). There are two sites near Naini Tal, both accessible by bus and taxi, which also deserve prolonged attention. At **Mangoli** walk up from behind the stalls where the bus stops for 150 m, follow the path through some fields (Black-throated Accentor, Fire-tailed Sunbird) past the school to a stream, then follow the stream down the valley to a larger stream and bird the well-vegetated banks (Small Niltava, Chestnut-headed Tesia, Blue-winged Minla). At **Sat Tal** bird the roadside fields (White-tailed Rubythroat, Black-throated Accentor, Chestnut-breasted Bunting) 2.5 km before the turn-off to Sat Tal (coming from Bhowali) and the forest around the lakes at Sat Tal (Scaly Thrush, White-crested and Rufous-chinned Laughingthrushes, Red-billed Leiothrix).

Accommodation: numerous places to choose from in Naini Tal.

In 1995 it again became dangerous to visit Kashmir, hence birders in search of west Himalayan specialties may wish to consider birding in the **Great Himalayan NP** (620 sq km) in Himachal Pradesh. This park supports Western Tragopan*, Himalayan Monal, Cheer Pheasant*, Snow Pigeon, Gold-billed Magpie, Long-billed Thrush*, Rusty-tailed Flycatcher, Grandala, White-cheeked Nuthatch, White-throated Tit*, Spectacled Finch, Red-headed Bullfinch and Black-and-yellow Grosbeak. Unfortunately, the park is not geared towards ecotourism at

NAINI TAL

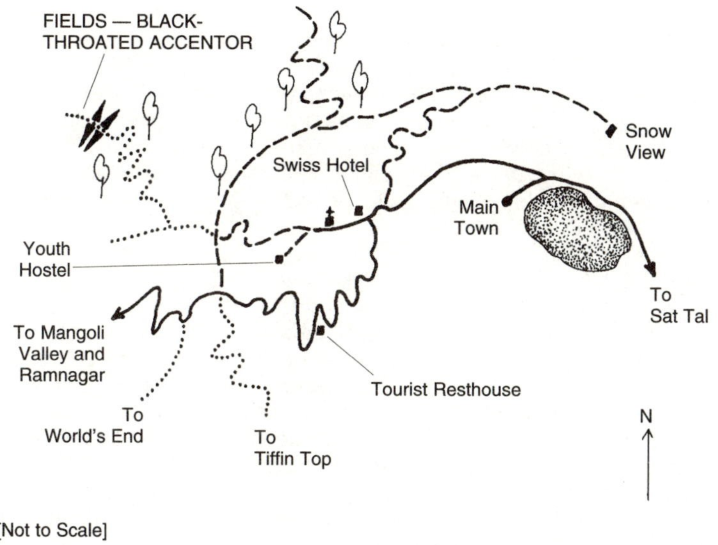

the moment, but there are several trails and some huts in which to stay. To arrange a visit contact the Park Director, Great Himalayan NP, Department of Forest Farming and Conservation, Shamshi, Kullu District, Himachal Pradesh. A number of the species listed above can be seen with more ease in the forest at 'The Glen' (ask locals for directions) within 1 hour's walk from **Shimla**, and on treks out of Manali, and alpine species occur at **Rohtang Pass** between Manali and Lahul.

KASHMIR AND LADAKH

The montane meadows and forests of Kashmir and Ladakh in extreme northwest India support a number of western Himalayan specialities such as Orange Bullfinch* and Black-and-yellow Grosbeak, as well as a few species such as Tibetan Sandgrouse which are hard to see elsewhere.

Unfortunately, due to the activities of religious extremists Kashmir was not a safe area to visit in 1996. Check with the relevant Foreign Office for details on the latest situation.

Many of the species listed below are only present during the summer (Apr–Sep).

Specialities

Koklass Pheasant, Solitary Snipe, Ibisbill, Tibetan Sandgrouse, Kashmir Flycatcher*, White-cheeked Nuthatch, Tytler's Leaf-Warbler*, Black-breasted and Fire-capped Tits, Black-winged and Blandford's Snowfinches, Black-headed Mountain-Finch, Spectacled Finch, Orange Bullfinch*, Black-and-yellow Grosbeak.

Others

Pallas' Fish-Eagle*, Lammergeier, Himalayan Griffon, Himalayan Snowcock, Chukar, Speckled Wood-Pigeon, Brown-fronted, Himalayan and Scaly-bellied Woodpeckers, Gold-billed Magpie, Blue-capped Rock-Thrush, Plain-backed, Indian Grey and Chestnut Thrushes, Rusty-tailed and Ultramarine Flycatchers, Indian Blue Robin, White-winged and White-bellied Redstarts, Wallcreeper, Bar-tailed Treecreeper, Tickell's Leaf-Warbler, Sulphur-bellied Warbler, Western Crowned-Warbler, Black-crested Tit, Hume's Lark, Russet Sparrow, Rosy Pipit, Robin and Rufous-breasted Accentors, Fire-fronted Serin, Yellow-breasted Greenfinch, Mongolian Finch, Great Rosefinch, Grey-hooded and Chestnut-breasted Buntings.

The Mogul Emperor Gardens and lake edge in **Srinagar**, the gateway to Kashmir, are worth birding, before moving on to the Dachigam Sanctuary to the east where Gold-billed Magpie, Kashmir Flycatcher* and Orange Bullfinch occur, Hokarsar Lake, which supports Pallas' Fish-Eagle*, and the area around the resort of Gulmarg at 2600 m (8530 ft) where Himalayan Snowcock, White-cheeked Nuthatch, Spectacled Finch and Black-and-yellow Grosbeak occur. **Leh**, accessible by air from Delhi, is situated in the upper Indus Valley at 3505 m (11,500 ft) on the edge of the Tibetan Plateau, in a land of small terraced fields and poplar and willow groves set among a cold, stony semi-desert and surrounded by magnificent mountain scenery. Although birds are few and far between, there are a handful of specialities, including Tibetan Sandgrouse and Blandford's Snowfinch, which have been recorded at the Tanglang La pass, on the road south to Manali. At 5359 m (17,582 ft) this is the second highest road pass in the world, and is a mighty fine area in which to go birding. Leh is also accessible by road (via a 4267 m (14,000 ft) pass and through a good birding area) from Srinagar. Explore the general area, especially the shingle banks of the Indus where Ibisbill breeds. From Leh it is possible to trek to **Zanskar**, via three passes over 5000 m (16,404 ft) into a wild, rugged, treeless land where snow leopard and wolf are present. The trek ends at Padum, three days by track from Srinagar.

BHARATPUR (KEOLADEO NATIONAL PARK)

Bharatpur is a birder's paradise. There are so many birds here during the winter months (Nov–Mar) that the wetlands appear to support more birds than seems possible in such a small area. Over 400 species have been recorded in the 29 sq km oasis of shallow lakes, known as jheels, surrounded by woodland, savanna and scrub, which lies at the edge of

BHARATPUR

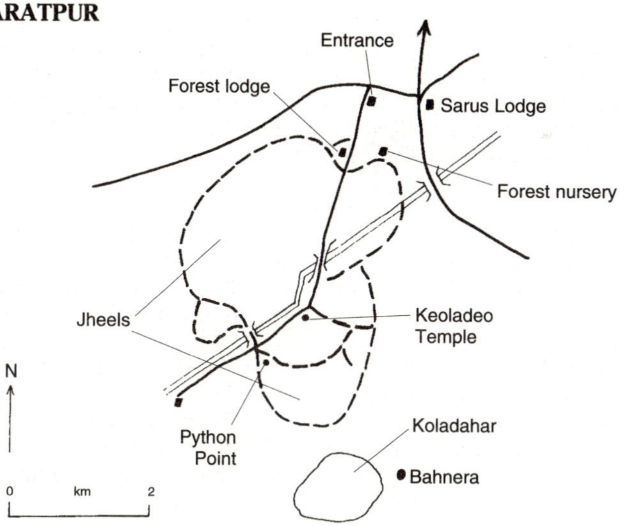

the heavily populated and heavily cultivated Gangetic Plain, and, in winter, it is possible to see around 180 species in a day, including masses of waterbirds, a fine selection of passerines and over 25 species of raptor. The beautiful black-and-white blackbuck is one of the site's mammalian bonuses. Many egrets, herons, storks and ibises nest on the acacias in autumn, after the monsoon rains have flooded the reserve, and, in winter, they roost in the same trees, but, unfortunately, one of the site's star avian attractions, Siberian Crane*, no longer winters here on a regular basis.

Specialities

Sirkeer Malkoha, Dusky Eagle-Owl, White-tailed Iora, Spotted Creeper, Brooks' Leaf-Warbler (Nov–Mar), Large Grey Babbler.

Others

Little and Indian Cormorants, Oriental Darter*, Great White (Nov–Mar) and Dalmatian* (Nov–Mar) Pelicans, Bar-headed Goose (Nov–Mar), Comb Duck, Cotton Pygmy-Goose, Indian Pond-Heron, Black-headed Ibis*, Painted Stork*, Asian Openbill*, Black-necked Stork, Pallas' Fish-Eagle*, Long-billed* and Red-headed* Vultures, White-eyed Buzzard, Lesser Spotted (Nov–Mar), Greater Spotted* (Nov–Mar) and Imperial* (Nov–Mar) Eagles, Laggar Falcon, Grey Francolin, Rain Quail, Indian Peafowl, Brown Crake, Sarus Crane*, Pheasant-tailed and Bronze-winged Jacanas, Greater Painted-snipe, Yellow-wattled, Red-wattled and White-tailed (Nov–Mar) Lapwings, Black-bellied* and River Terns, Chestnut-bellied Sandgrouse, Red Collared-Dove, Yellow-footed Pigeon, Pied Cuckoo, Indian Scops-Owl, Brown Fish-Owl, Spotted Owlet, Brown Hawk-Owl, Jungle, Large-tailed and Indian Nightjars, Green Bee-eater, Indian Roller, Indian Grey Hornbill, Coppersmith Barbet, Brown-capped and Yellow-crowned Woodpeckers, Black-rumped Flameback, Asian Paradise-Flycatcher, Rufous Treepie, Small

Pheasant-tailed Jacana is one of the many wonderful waterbirds which throng the wetlands of Bharatpur

Minivet, Bay-backed Shrike, Common Woodshrike, Orange-headed and Indian Grey Thrushes, Brahminy and Asian Pied Starlings, Bank Myna, Tickell's Blue-Flycatcher, Siberian Rubythroat (Nov–Mar), Indian Robin, Wire-tailed and Streak-throated Swallows, Ashy Prinia, Blyth's (Nov–Mar) and Clamorous Reed-Warblers, Sykes' Warbler (Nov–Mar), Small Whitethroat, Orphean Warbler (Nov–Mar), Yellow-eyed, Common and Jungle Babblers, Ashy-crowned Sparrow-Lark, Rufous-tailed and Bimaculated Larks, Chestnut-shouldered Petronia, Red Avadavat, White-throated Munia, Long-billed Pipit, Bengal and Baya Weavers, Purple Sunbird, Chestnut-breasted (Nov–Mar), Black-headed (Nov–Mar) and Red-headed (Nov–Mar) Buntings.

Other Wildlife

Blackbuck, fishing cat, Indian python, Indian smooth otter, jungle cat, nilgai, porcupine, rhesus macaque, small Indian mongoose.

(Other species recorded here include Falcated Duck, Yellow, Cinnamon and Black Bitterns, Red-naped Ibis*, Lesser Adjutant*, Indian Courser, Grey-headed* and Sociable* Lapwings, Mottled Wood-Owl and Hume's Lark. In the early 1960s over 125 Siberian Cranes* wintered at Bharatpur, but numbers have decreased rapidly since then to 13 in 1986–87, six in 1991–92, three to five in 1992–93 and none in 1993–94 and 1994–5. Some have since been introduced and four wild birds appeared in February 1996.)

The town of Bharatpur (Indian Chat, Streak-throated Swallow) is accessible by road and rail, 177 km south of Delhi and 50 km west of Agra. The reserve is a couple of kilometres outside the town and best explored by bicycles. These can be hired in town or at some of the lodges near the reserve. Guides are also available and some of them know exactly where to find most of the specialities, especially night-birds. Bird throughout the reserve and its surroundings and concentrate on the forest nursery for passerines including White-tailed Iora.

Accommodation: Shanti Kutir, inside the reserve — forest lodge (A), forest resthouse. Outside reserve — Sarus lodge (B/C), Tourist lodge (C), Falcon Guesthouse (B/C).

Although Bharatpur is famous for its masses of waterbirds, it also supports a number of localised terrestrial species including White-tailed Iora

Indian Cormorant, the endemic Rock Bush-Quail, Great Thick-knee, River Tern, Indian Skimmer*, White-tailed Iora, Blyth's Reed-Warbler (Nov–Mar), Tickell's Leaf-Warbler (Nov–Mar) and Sulphur-bellied Warbler (Nov–Mar) occur at the **Bund Bharata Reservoir**, 45 km by road from Bharatpur. Vehicles can be hired at Bharatpur to bird this excellent site.

Between Bharatpur and Agra, a distance of about 50 km, Indian Chat and Dusky Crag-Martin may be seen at the deserted sandstone city of Fatehpur Sikri. While touring the Taj Mahal in **Agra**, fanatical birders may wish to check out the Yamuna River behind the building, where Black-necked Stork, Small Pratincole, River Lapwing, Great Black-headed Gull and Black-bellied* and River Terns occur. Indian Grey Hornbill and Brown-headed Barbet occur in the grounds and the main town park.

Accommodation: Gulsham Lodge (C).

Small numbers of Indian Bustard* may still be present at **Karera**, which is half a day's drive from Bharatpur. This wildlife sanctuary, on the Shivpuri–Jhansi road in Madhya Pradesh, is accessible from Gwalior, which is 110 km from Agra. The best area for the bustards used to be 20 km north of Karera town, where it is advisable to seek assistance from the sanctuary superintendent.

RANTHAMBORE NATIONAL PARK

The dry, deciduous forests and grasslands in this large park (400 sq km) used to be one of the best places in India to see tiger. Although they are now scarce here, birders will find plenty of birds, inside and outside the park, to occupy them, including Painted Spurfowl, Indian Courser, Painted Sandgrouse and White-naped Woodpecker, all of which are hard to see elsewhere.

RANTHAMBORE NP

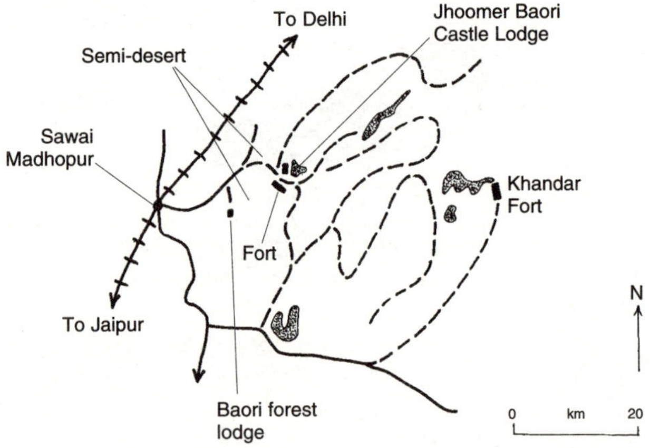

Indian Endemics

Painted Spurfowl.

Specialities

Jungle Bush-Quail, Demoiselle Crane (Nov–Mar), Great Thick-knee, Indian Courser, Painted Sandgrouse, Sirkeer Malkoha, White-naped Woodpecker, White-tailed Iora, Brooks' Leaf-Warbler (Nov–Mar), Large Grey Babbler.

Others

Cotton Pygmy-Goose, Red-naped Ibis*, Painted Stork*, Painted Francolin, Indian Peafowl, Brown Crake, Pheasant-tailed and Bronze-winged Jacanas, Yellow-wattled Lapwing, Chestnut-bellied Sandgrouse,

Yellow-footed Pigeon, Plum-headed Parakeet, Indian Scops-Owl, Brown Fish-Owl, Spotted Owlet, Stork-billed Kingfisher, Brown-capped Woodpecker, Black-rumped Flameback, Rufous Treepie, Large Cuckoo-Shrike, Small Minivet, Bay-backed Shrike, Tickell's Blue-Flycatcher, Indian Chat, Variable Wheatear (Nov–Mar), Rufous-fronted and Jungle Prinias, Sulphur-bellied Warbler (Nov–Mar), Tawny-bellied Babbler, Rufous-winged Bushlark, Ashy-crowned Sparrow-Lark, Rufous-tailed and Bimaculated (Nov–Mar) Larks, Spanish Sparrow, Chestnut-breasted Bunting (Nov–Mar).

Other Wildlife

Chinkara, chital, common langur, jungle cat, leopard, mugger crocodile, nilgai, rhesus macaque, ruddy mongoose, sambar, sloth bear, tiger.

(Other species recorded here include Dalmatian Pelican*, White-browed Bushchat* and Grey-hooded Bunting (Nov–Mar)).

Ranthambore is accessible by road from Sawai Madhopur, which is connected to Delhi by rail. Access within the reserve is restricted to expensive vehicles only, but it is possible to stay in Sawai Madhopur, hire bicycles and explore the reserve fringes where many of the best birds occur. The best sites outside the reserve are the entrance road (Painted Spurfowl, White-naped Woodpecker, Tawny-bellied Babbler) and the fort complex near the reserve HQ (Jungle Bush-Quail, Painted Sandgrouse, Jungle Prinia, Chestnut-breasted Bunting).

Accommodation: Jhoomer Baori Castle Lodge (A+). Sawai Madhopur — Hotel Vishal (B/C).

Jungle Bush-Quail, Red and Painted Spurfowls, Painted Sandgrouse, Indian Pitta (May–Jun) and Spotted Creeper occur in **Sariska Tiger Reserve** (800 sq km), Rajasthan. This reserve lies in the semi-arid Aravali Hills and contains two lakes, dry deciduous forest, gallery forest, woodland and thorn scrub.

The semi-desert around the Mandore Gardens, **Jodhpur**, supports Chestnut-bellied and Painted Sandgrouse, while Indian Bustard*, Lesser Florican* (Jun–Sep) and Demoiselle Crane (on passage) occur in the **Sonkhaliya Closed Area** (17 sq km), on the Nazirabad-Kekri road between Ranthambore and Jaipur, 40 km from Ajmer. A special permit, obtainable from the Divisional Forest Officer in Ajmer, is needed to visit this area, along with a 4WD.

DESERT NATIONAL PARK

Although there are 37 villages and many other homesteads within this park and the fragile arid grasslands are under severe pressure from overgrazing, the park is still sufficiently large enough at 3162 sq km to support such rarities as Indian* and Houbara Bustards, White-bellied Minivet* and White-browed Bushchat*. However, one wonders how long these, and many other, arid country specialists will survive if the human population continues to increase.

It is necessary to arrange permission to visit this NP in advance via the District Magistrate's Office, the Superintendent of Police and, finally, the park HQ, all of which lie at opposite ends of Jaisalmer.

Many of the species listed below are only present during the winter (Nov–Mar).

Indian Endemics

Indian Bustard*.

Specialities

Houbara Bustard, Indian Courser (Jun–Sep), White-bellied Minivet*, White-browed Bushchat*, Plain Leaf-Warbler.

Others

Imperial Eagle*, Laggar Falcon, Rain Quail (Jun–Sep), Cream-coloured Courser, Chestnut-bellied, Spotted and Black-bellied Sandgrouse, Variable and Red-tailed Wheatears, Graceful Prinia, Small Whitethroat, Desert Warbler, Black-crowned and Ashy-crowned Sparrow-Larks, Rufous-tailed, Desert and Bimaculated Larks, Chestnut-shouldered Petronia, Long-billed Pipit, Trumpeter Finch, House Bunting.

Bicycles and 4WD vehicles can be hired in Jaisalmer. Bird Fossil Park, 16 km to the southeast (Red-tailed Wheatear), the 50 km road west to Sam and the 13 km road south from there to the **Sudaseri Enclosure**, a protected area of grassland, where Indian Bustard* is usually present.

Accommodation: Jaisalmer — Fort View Hotel (C).

Up to 150 (December 1993) Hypocolius have been recorded in winter (Nov to early Apr) near the village of Fulay and between there and Chhari, in **Kutch**, Gujarat, west of Ahmadabad.

The **Rann of Kutch**, a vast, shallow inland lake is inaccessible during the monsoon season (Jun–Sep), but by February–March much of it has dried out and the remaining shallow lagoons still support wintering wetland species such as Demoiselle Crane. Other species recorded in the area include Rock Bush-Quail, Sarus Crane*, Houbara Bustard, Indian Courser, White-browed Bushchat* (around Banni) and Paddyfield Warbler, as well as Asiatic Wild Ass. Rann of Kutch is accessible by road (3 hours) from Ahmadabad.

Accommodation: Camp Zainabad.

The **Gir Lion Sanctuary**, at the southern tip of Gujarat, supports 300 lions, the only 'Asiatic lions' left in the wild.

NORTHEAST INDIA

Yellow-vented Warbler* has been recorded in riverside vegetation at **Sukna FR** near Siliguri (accessible by road from Bagdogra) and this reserve also supports Collared Falconet, Pin-tailed Pigeon, Blue-bearded Bee-eater, Long-tailed Broadbill and Gould's Sunbird, as well as

Asian elephant and hoolock gibbon. The Siliguri–Kalimpong road runs beside the River Teesta where Black-backed Forktail occurs.

Accommodation: Siliguri — Sinclairs Hotel (A), Siliguri Lodge (C).

Red-tailed Minla is one of a number of beautiful babblers which occur in northeast India

DARJEELING

This famous hill resort sits on a ridge at 1981 m (6500 ft) within sight of Kangchenjunga, the world's third highest mountain. Although there are plenty of good birds around Darjeeling, including Satyr Tragopan*, Rusty-throated Wren-Babbler* and Red-tailed Minla, most of the species here, and many more, can be seen on the Sandakphu Trek (p. 106) and at other sites in northeast India.

Specialities

Satyr Tragopan*, Sapphire Flycatcher, Rufous-throated Wren-Babbler*, Hoary-throated Barwing, Yellow-throated Fulvetta*.

Others

Great Barbet, Rufous-bellied and Darjeeling Woodpeckers, Gold-billed Magpie, Scaly and Long-billed* Thrushes, White-collared and Grey-winged Blackbirds, Ferruginous Flycatcher, Large Niltava, Golden and White-browed Bush-Robins, Spotted Forktail, Brown-throated Treecreeper, Chestnut-headed Tesia, Brownish-flanked, Aberrant and Yellowish-bellied Bush-Warblers, Broad-billed Warbler*, Scaly Laughingthrush, Coral-billed and Slender-billed* Scimitar-Babblers, Scaly-breasted Wren-Babbler, Rufous-capped Babbler, Red-billed Leiothrix, Silver-eared Mesia, Black-headed Shrike-Babbler*, Red-tailed Minla, Golden-breasted and White-browed Fulvettas, Rufous Sibia, Stripe-throated Yuhina, Black-throated Parrotbill, Maroon-backed Accentor, Gould's Sunbird, Streaked Spiderhunter, Dark-breasted and Dark-rumped Rosefinches, Brown and Red-headed Bullfinches, Gold-naped Finch.

Other Wildlife

Assamese macaque, yellow-throated marten.

(Other species recorded here include Blue-fronted Robin*, Rusty-fronted Barwing and Grey-headed Parrotbill.)

Much of the forest around Darjeeling has been destroyed, but remnant patches still survive around the nearby tourist hot spot of Tiger Hill. From the top of this hill, at 2573 m (8442 ft), it is usually possible to see Mount Everest at dawn. Satyr Tragopan* has been recorded along the track which leads off to the right about 1 km from the top, a few kilometres above Jorebungalow (which is 10 km from Darjeeling). Red-tailed Minla has been recorded on the slope behind the cages at Darjeeling Zoo, which is 10 minutes walk west from the town centre.

Accommodation: Windamere Hotel (A), Bellevue Hotel (B), Youth Hostel (C).

SANDAKPHU TREK

The mossy oak–rhododendron forests, coniferous forests and bamboo stands on the Singalila Ridge adjacent to the border with Nepal support some beautiful high-altitude specialities including White-throated Redstart and Fire-tailed Myzornis.

Specialities

Satyr Tragopan*, White-throated Redstart, Hoary-throated Barwing, Fire-tailed Myzornis, Great Parrotbill, Pink-browed Rosefinch.

Others

Himalayan Griffon, Hill Partridge, Blood Pheasant, Crimson-breasted and Darjeeling Woodpeckers, Eurasian Nutcracker, Long-tailed Minivet, Plain-backed, Scaly and Long-billed* Thrushes, White-collared Blackbird, Slaty-blue Flycatcher, Golden and White-browed Bush-Robins, Hodgson's Redstart, Rusty-flanked Treecreeper, Black-browed Tit, Yellowish-bellied and Grey-sided Bush-Warblers, Broad-billed Warbler*, Spotted, Scaly and Black-faced Laughingthrushes, Slender-billed Scimitar-Babbler*, Rufous-capped Babbler, Black-headed* and Green Shrike-Babblers, Red-tailed Minla, Golden-breasted Fulvetta, Brown, Fulvous and Black-throated Parrotbills, Rufous-vented, Grey-crested and Yellow-browed Tits, Hume's Lark, Rufous-breasted and Maroon-backed Accentors, Fire-tailed Sunbird, Tibetan Serin, Plain Mountain-Finch, White-browed Rosefinch, Collared and White-winged Grosbeaks, Gold-naped Finch.

Other Wildlife

Red panda.

(Other species recorded here include Blue-fronted Robin*.)

It is best to start the trek at Manebhanjang, accessible by bus from Darjeeling. Although most of the forest has been cleared between here and Tonglu (a distance of 11 km), there are some good birds to be seen before the 15 km Tonglu–Garibas–Kalipokhari stretch which passes through some good oak–rhododendron forest where Satyr Tragopan* occurs. After passing the Singalila National Park building above Tonglu, take the old right-hand track to descend through excellent forest to Garibas. After Garibas again take the right-hand track to reach Kalipokhari. At Kalipokhari, bird the cattle track down to the old jeep track, reached by crossing the sandy, grassy area opposite the football pitch (which is to the left of the new track to Sandakphu). This cattle track hangs left before descending into forest with lots of bamboo (Satyr Tragopan*, Fire-tailed Myzornis, Brown Parrotbill, red panda). At Sandakphu, bird the cattle tracks along the ridges to the east of the settlement and to the east of the track to Phalut, up to 2 km north of Sandakphu (Blood Pheasant, Great Parrotbill). Instead of walking back the same way, it is possible to return via Rimbik on a trail which leads east approximately 2 km north of Kalipokhari. Buses run from Rimbik to Darjeeling.

Accommodation: trekker's lodges (basic) at Megma, Tonglu, Garibas, Kalipokhari, Sandakphu and Rimbik.

PEMAYANGTSE

This Buddhist settlement is situated on a ridge in northwest Sikkim at an altitude over 2200 m (7218 ft) and is surrounded by patches of mossy oak–rhododendron forest which support such localised species as Yellow-rumped Honeyguide* and Collared Treepie.

Specialities

Yellow-rumped Honeyguide*, Collared Treepie, Yellow-vented Warbler*, Grey-sided and Blue-winged Laughingthrushes, Cutia, Hoary-throated Barwing, Fire-tailed Myzornis.

Others

Himalayan Swiftlet, Bay Woodpecker, Green Magpie, Maroon Oriole, Orange-bellied Leafbird, Blue-capped and Chestnut-bellied Rock-Thrushes, Plain-backed, Long-tailed, Scaly and Indian Grey Thrushes, Grey-winged Blackbird, Ferruginous and Sapphire Flycatchers, Large and Small Niltavas, Pygmy Blue-Flycatcher, Black-throated Tit, Nepal Martin, Chestnut-headed and Slaty-bellied Tesias, Brownish-flanked Bush-Warbler, Striated Laughingthrush, Streak-breasted Scimitar-Babbler, Scaly-breasted Wren-Babbler, Red-billed Leiothrix, Rusty-fronted Barwing, Blue-winged, Chestnut-tailed and Red-tailed Minlas, Rufous Sibia, Stripe-throated Yuhina, Green-backed and Yellow-cheeked Tits, Gould's Sunbird, Yellow-breasted Greenfinch.

Pemayangtse is accessible by road from Darjeeling (10 hours) and Kalimpong. This road follows the River Rangit in places, where Ibisbill, Small Pratincole and Crested Kingfisher occur. Bird the forested hills around Pemayangtse, or take the trek from Yoksam, near Pemayangtse, to Lake Samiti at 4267 m (14,000 ft).

Accommodation: Mount Pandim Hotel (B).

LAVA

The mid-altitude forest below the village of Lava, which lies at 2184 m (7165 ft) near Kalimpong supports the very rare Blue-fronted Robin*, as well as a number of other eastern Himalayan specialities.

Specialities

Blue-fronted Robin*, Grey-sided and Blue-winged Laughingthrushes, Rufous-throated Wren-Babbler*, Cutia, Hoary-throated Barwing, Yellow-throated* and Nepal Fulvettas, Scarlet Finch.

Others

Ashy Wood-Pigeon, Lesser Cuckoo, Himalayan Swiftlet, Bay Woodpecker, Short-billed Minivet, Grey-backed Shrike, Chestnut-bellied Rock-Thrush, Long-billed Thrush*, Ferruginous and Sapphire Flycatchers, Pygmy Blue-Flycatcher, Indian Blue Robin, White-tailed Nuthatch, Black-throated Tit, Hill Prinia, Grey-bellied Tesia, Brownish-flanked Bush-Warbler, Buff-barred and Ashy-throated Warblers, Large-billed and Blyth's Leaf-Warblers, Grey-cheeked and Black-faced Warblers, White-throated, Striated, Scaly and Black-faced Laughing-thrushes, Red-faced Liocichla, Streak-breasted Scimitar-Babbler, Silver-eared Mesia, Red-billed Leiothrix, Black-headed* and Black-eared Shrike-Babblers, Rusty-fronted Barwing, Blue-winged, Chestnut-tailed and Red-tailed Minlas, Rufous-winged Fulvetta, Rufous Sibia, White-naped, Whiskered, Stripe-throated and Rufous-vented Yuhinas, Black-throated Parrotbill, Yellow-cheeked Tit, Rufous-breasted and Maroon-backed Accentors, Gould's, Green-tailed and Fire-tailed Sunbirds, Tibetan Serin, Brown Bullfinch, Gold-naped Finch.

Kalimpong is accessible by road east from Darjeeling (4 hours by bus). From Kalimpong it is 2 hours by road east to Lava (Labha) via Algarah. Bird the tracks which descend in a northerly direction from behind the village and, especially, from just east of the monastery. The very rare Blue-fronted Robin* (12 records between 1900 and 1992 throughout its known range) has been recorded in gardens at Lava and in ravines (e.g. 3 km below Lava) alongside the road back towards Algarah.

Accommodation: Lava — forest resthouse (permission needed from Forest Department in Kalimpong). Kalimpong — Himalayan Hotel (A).

The huge **Manas National Park** (3280 sq km) on the border with Bhutan (p. 43) is 4 hours by road northwest of Gauhati, which is accessible by air from Delhi. Although over 300 species have been recorded here, including Swamp Francolin* and Bengal Florican*, it is perhaps better known for its mammalian fauna, which includes Asian elephant, capped and golden langurs, hoolock gibbon, Indian rhinoceros and tiger. Ward's Trogon*, Beautiful Nuthatch* and Bar-winged Wren-Babbler have been recorded in the **Eagle's Nest Wildlife Sanctuary** north of Tezpur, near the Bhutan border in west Arunachal Pradesh.

KAZIRANGA NATIONAL PARK

The marshes, grasslands and lowland forest in this park (470 sq km), which is situated on the floodplain of the Brahmaputra River in Assam, support a fine selection of rarities, including White-bellied Heron*, Swamp Francolin*, Bengal Florican*, Black-breasted Thrush*, Black-breasted Parrotbill* and the endemic Yellow Weaver*, as well as good numbers of Indian rhinoceros. Around 200 species may be seen in three days.

Indian Endemics

Yellow Weaver*.

Specialities

Spot-billed Pelican*, White-bellied Heron*, Swamp Francolin*, Bengal Florican*, Swinhoe's Snipe (Nov–Apr), Tawny Fish-Owl*, Black-breasted Thrush*, Pale-chinned Blue-Flycatcher, Rufous-vented Prinia, Yellow-vented Warbler*, Bristled Grassbird*, Jerdon's*, Striated and Slender-billed* Babblers, Black-breasted Parrotbill*.

Others

Oriental Darter*, Falcated Duck (Nov–Apr), Baer's Pochard* (Nov–Apr), Black-necked Stork, Lesser* and Greater* Adjutants, Pallas'* and Grey-headed* Fish-Eagles, Long-billed Vulture*, Eastern Marsh-Harrier, Pied Harrier (Nov–Apr), Watercock, Pheasant-tailed and Bronze-winged Jacanas, Pintail Snipe (Nov–Apr), Grey-headed Lapwing* (Nov–Apr), Black-bellied* and River Terns, Grey-headed and Red-breasted Parakeets, Green-billed Malkoha, Brown Fish-Owl, Jungle Owlet, Red-headed Trogon, Blue-eared and Stork-billed Kingfishers, Blue-bearded and Blue-tailed Bee-eaters, Indian Roller, Great and Wreathed Hornbills, Lineated, Blue-throated and Blue-eared Barbets, White-browed Piculet, Fulvous-breasted and Rufous Woodpeckers, Lesser Yellownape, Streak-throated Woodpecker, Common and Black-rumped Flamebacks, Long-tailed Broadbill, Ashy Woodswallow, Large and Black-winged Cuckoo-Shrikes, Short-billed Minivet, Asian Fairy-bluebird, Blue-winged and Golden-fronted Leafbirds, Large Woodshrike, Orange-headed Thrush, Spot-winged and Chestnut-tailed Starlings, White-vented Myna, Slaty-backed Flycatcher, Siberian (Nov–Apr) and White-tailed (Nov–Apr) Rubythroats, Black-backed Forktail, Black-crested and White-throated Bulbuls, Paddyfield (Nov–Apr), Blunt-winged (Nov–Apr), Smoky (Nov–Apr) and White-spectacled Warblers, Striated and Rufous-rumped Grassbirds, Greater Necklaced Laughingthrush, White-hooded Babbler, Sultan Tit, Sand Lark, Black-headed Munia, Forest Wagtail (Nov–Apr), Rosy Pipit, Bengal and Streaked Weavers, Scarlet-backed Flowerpecker, Ruby-cheeked and Crimson Sunbirds, Little Spiderhunter.

Other Wildlife

Asian elephant, black giant squirrel, capped langur, Ganges dolphin, hog-deer, Hoolock gibbon (in the adjacent Panbari Reserve Forest), Indian rhinoceros, rhesus macaque, swamp deer, tiger, water buffalo, yellow-throated marten.

Kaziranga is 220 km (6 hours) by road from Gauhati, which is accessible by air from Delhi. Elephant rides are available and advisable in the 3 m high grasslands, and it is possible to bird by jeep. In Panbari RF birding can be done on foot in the company of a forest guard.

Accommodation: Wild Grass Hotel (A), Aranya Lodge (B).

DIBRU-SAIKHOWA

This wildlife sanctuary (640 sq km), together with the nearby Bherjan and Podumoni Forest Reserves, in east Assam supports marshes, grasslands and lowland forests where the avifauna is similar to Kaziranga National Park (p. 108). There are some notable exceptions, however, among the 250 or so species which have been recorded, and these include White-winged Duck*.

It is necessary to obtain permission to stay here from the office of the Chief Conservator of Forests in Gauhati.

Indian Endemics

Yellow Weaver*.

Specialities

Spot-billed Pelican*, White-winged Duck*, Swamp Francolin*, Bengal Florican*, Swinhoe's Snipe (Nov–Apr), Spot-winged Starling*, Pale-chinned Blue-Flycatcher, Bristled Grassbird*, Marsh* and Striated Babblers.

Others

Oriental Darter*, Black-necked Stork, Lesser* and Greater* Adjutants, Pallas'* and Grey-headed* Fish-Eagles, Pied Harrier (Nov–Apr), Watercock, Pheasant-tailed and Bronze-winged Jacanas, Pintail Snipe (Nov–Apr), Grey-headed Lapwing* (Nov–Apr), Black-bellied* and River Terns, Red-breasted Parakeet, Green-billed Malkoha, Brown Fish-Owl, Jungle Owlet, Red-headed Trogon, Stork-billed Kingfisher, Blue-tailed Bee-eater, Great and Wreathed Hornbills, Blue-eared Barbet, Rufous and Streak-throated Woodpeckers, Common and Black-rumped Flamebacks, Ashy Woodswallow, Asian Fairy-bluebird, Golden-fronted Leafbird, Large Woodshrike, Chestnut-tailed Starling, White-vented Myna, Smoky Warbler (Nov–Apr), Striated and Rufous-rumped Grassbirds, Greater Necklaced and Rufous-necked Laughingthrushes, Abbott's and White-hooded Babblers, Sultan Tit, Sand Lark, Black-headed Munia, Rosy Pipit, Bengal and Streaked Weavers, Scarlet-backed Flowerpecker, Ruby-cheeked and Crimson Sunbirds, Little Spiderhunter.

(Rarities include White-bellied Heron*, Manipur Bush-Quail*, Jerdon's Bushchat*, Swamp Prinia, Jerdon's Babbler* and Black-breasted* and Rufous-headed* Parrotbills.)

Accommodation: resthouse (basic dormitory) at Guijan, near Tinsukia.

Nearly 300 species have been recorded in the **Mehao Wildlife Sanctuary** in Arunachal Pradesh, including White-winged Duck*, Temminck's Tragopan*, Himalayan Monal, the rare Rusty-bellied Shortwing*, Firethroat* and Green Cochoa*.

NAMDAPHA NATIONAL PARK

This huge park (1985 sq km) in the mountains of Arunachal Pradesh adjacent to the Burmese border covers the greatest altitudinal range of any park in the world, from 200 m (656 ft) to over 4500 m (14,764 ft) at the summit of Mount Daphabum. Hence there is a great range of habitats, from lowland forest through temperate montane forest to mountain meadows and rhododendron scrub, where the wide range of birds includes the endemic Snowy-throated Babbler*, as well as Blyth's Tragopan*, Sclater's Monal*, Ward's Trogon*, Rusty-bellied Shortwing* and Beautiful Nuthatch*, all of which are very difficult to see elsewhere.

Permission to visit Arunachal Pradesh is usually only given to groups of four or more for a maximum of ten days and permits are very expensive.

Indian Endemics

Snowy-throated Babbler* (Nov–Apr).

Specialities

White-bellied Heron*, White-cheeked Partridge*, Blyth's Tragopan*, Sclater's Monal*, Ibisbill, Ward's Trogon*, Rufous-necked Hornbill*, Silver-breasted Broadbill, Collared Treepie, Rusty-bellied Shortwing*, Beautiful Nuthatch*, Yellow-vented Warbler*, Chestnut-backed*, Yellow-throated*, Grey-sided and Blue-winged Laughingthrushes, Long-billed*, Bar-winged and Spotted* Wren-Babblers, Cutia, Hoary-throated and Streak-throated Barwings, Yellow-throated* and Rufous-throated* Fulvettas, Grey* and Beautiful Sibias, White-naped and Rufous-vented Yuhinas, Fire-tailed Myzornis, Black-throated, Black-browed* and Rufous-headed* Parrotbills, Scarlet Finch.

Others

Collared and Pied* Falconets, Blood Pheasant, Grey Peacock-Pheasant, Small Pratincole, Crested Kingfisher, Blue-bearded Bee-eater, Brown Hornbill*, Long-tailed Broadbill, Blue and Green Magpies, Plain-backed, Long-tailed and Long-billed* Thrushes, White-collared and Grey-winged Blackbirds, Ultramarine, Slaty-blue and Blue-throated Flycatchers, Large Niltava, Pale and Pygmy Blue-Flycatchers, Golden, White-browed and Rufous-breasted* Bush-Robins, Hodgson's Redstart, Chestnut-bellied and White-tailed Nuthatches, Brown-throated and Rusty-flanked Treecreepers, Black-throated and Black-browed Tits, Hill Prinia, Chestnut-headed and Grey-bellied Tesias, Yellowish-bellied and Grey-sided Bush-Warblers, Grey-cheeked, Broad-billed* and Black-faced Warblers, Striated, Rufous-necked, Rufous-vented, Spotted, Scaly and Black-faced Laughingthrushes, Slender-billed Scimitar-Babbler*, Scaly-breasted Wren-Babbler, Black-headed* and Green Shrike-Babblers, Spectacled Barwing, Chestnut-tailed and Red-tailed Minlas, Golden-breasted, Rufous-winged and White-browed Fulvettas, Rufous Sibia, Stripe-throated Yuhina, Brown and Fulvous Parrotbills, Rufous-vented, Grey-crested, Green-backed, Yellow-cheeked and Yellow-browed Tits, Maroon-backed Accentor, Gould's, Green-tailed and Fire-tailed Sunbirds, Yellow-breasted Greenfinch, Crimson-browed Finch, Brown and Grey-headed Bullfinches, Collared Grosbeak, Gold-naped Finch.

Other Wildlife

Clouded leopard, leopard, snow leopard, tiger.

Namdapha is accessible by road from Dibrugarh, which is connected by air to Calcutta. Bird around the Deban resthouse, which lies close to the River Noa Dihing, and in the upper reaches of the park via trekking and camping (allow a week to get to the treeline and back). Snowy-throated Babbler* has been recorded along the Deban–Hornbill Trek.

Accommodation: Deban — resthouse (basic dormitory).

JATINGA

The hills near Jatinga in southeast Assam support a few birds which are hard to see elsewhere in India, including Pale-headed Woodpecker and Beautiful Nuthatch*.

Specialities

Pale-headed Woodpecker, Beautiful Nuthatch*, Yellow-vented Warbler*, Striped* and Blue-winged Laughingthrushes, Wedge-billed Wren-Babbler* (rare), Nepal Fulvetta.

Others

Hill Partridge, Mountain Bamboo-Partridge, Pin-tailed Pigeon, Grey-headed Parakeet, Golden-throated Barbet, White-browed Piculet, Bay Woodpecker, Maroon Oriole, Black-winged Cuckoo-Shrike, Small Niltava, Black-backed, Slaty-backed and Spotted Forktails, Flavescent and White-throated Bulbuls, Rufescent Prinia, Brownish-flanked Bush-Warbler, Buff-barred, White-spectacled and Rufous-faced Warblers, Red-faced Liocichla, Streak-breasted, Red-billed and Coral-billed Scimitar-Babblers, Streaked Wren-Babbler, Rufous-fronted and Grey-throated Babblers, Silver-eared Mesia, Black-eared Shrike-Babbler, Spectacled Barwing, Blue-winged Minla, White-browed and Dusky Fulvettas, Whiskered and Black-chinned Yuhinas, Black-throated Sunbird, Streaked Spiderhunter.

Bird Hau Phu Ped Peak (with guide arranged via village head) near the village of Jatinga, which is near Haflong and accessible by road from Gauhati.

Accommodation: Haflong — Hotel Elite (C). Jatinga — Birdwatching Centre (very basic, C)

CENTRAL INDIA

Kanha NP in Madhya Pradesh is currently one of the most reliable sites in India to see tiger. The 940 sq km of sal forest and grassland also supports a good cross-section of India's birds and many other mammals including blackbuck, chousingha, dhole, gaur, leopard, nilgai, sloth bear and swamp deer. April, when there are fewer waterholes for the tiger's prey to gather around and the grass is shorter, is the best time to visit Kanha, which is 6 hours by road from Jabalpur (accessible by train from Delhi) and 2 hours by road from Gondia (accessible by train from Calcutta).

SOUTH INDIA

Most of India's endemic birds only occur in the south, along with 17 species which are otherwise only found on Sri Lanka. The majority of these birds are restricted to the Western Ghats, a mountain range which runs parallel to the southwest coast and rises to 2695 m (8842 ft).

GOA

This tiny province on India's west coast is a popular package tour destination for European sunseekers and, fortunately, an excellent birding area. The paddies, marshes, mangroves, mud flats, rocky scrub, remnant lowland forest and nearby foothill forests of the Western Ghats combine to support 14 of the 24 southern Indian endemics and nine of the 17 species which only occur in southern India and Sri Lanka. There is also a good selection of more widespread species, including plenty of waterbirds and the delightful Heart-spotted Woodpecker. The best time to visit Goa is between November and March when it is possible to see over 200 species in two weeks.

Indian Endemics

Red Spurfowl, Grey Junglefowl*, Nilgiri Wood-Pigeon* (rare), Malabar Parakeet, Malabar Grey Hornbill*, White-cheeked Barbet, Spot-breasted Fantail, Malabar Whistling-Thrush, Nilgiri Flycatcher*, White-bellied Blue-Flycatcher*, Grey-headed Bulbul*, Rufous Babbler, Malabar Lark, Crimson-backed Sunbird.

Specialities

Indian Swiftlet, Malabar Trogon (scarce), Malabar Pied-Hornbill*, Crimson-fronted Barbet, Rusty-tailed Flycatcher (Nov–Mar), White-browed and Yellow-browed Bulbuls, Indian Scimitar-Babbler, Dark-fronted Babbler, Long-billed Sunbird.

Others

Little and Indian Cormorants, Oriental Darter*, Comb Duck, Cotton Pygmy-Goose, Western Reef-Egret, Indian Pond-Heron, Cinnamon Bittern, Lesser Adjutant*, Brahminy Kite, White-bellied Sea-Eagle, Pallid Harrier (Nov–Mar), Indian Peafowl, Watercock, Pheasant-tailed and Bronze-winged Jacanas, Greater Painted-Snipe, Pintail Snipe (Nov–Mar), Great Knot (Nov–Mar), Small Pratincole, Yellow-wattled and Red-wattled Lapwings, Great Black-headed Gull (Nov–Mar), River Tern, Vernal Hanging-Parrot, Plum-headed Parakeet, Brown Fish-Owl, Spotted Owlet, Black-backed, Stork-billed and Black-capped Kingfishers, Blue-bearded, Green, Blue-tailed and Chestnut-headed Bee-eaters, Indian Roller, Rufous Woodpecker, Black-rumped Flameback, Heart-spotted Woodpecker, Rufous Treepie, Ashy Woodswallow, Black-headed Cuckoo-Shrike, Small Minivet, Asian Fairy-bluebird, Golden-fronted Leafbird, Common Woodshrike, Orange-headed Thrush, Chestnut-tailed Starling, Jungle Myna, Brown-breasted Flycatcher* (Nov–Mar), Tickell's Blue-Flycatcher, White-rumped Shama, Indian Robin, Wire-tailed and Streak-throated Swallows, Black-crested Bulbul, Grey-breasted and Ashy Prinias, Paddyfield Warbler (Nov–Mar), Blyth's (Nov–Mar) and Clamorous Reed-Warblers, Western Crowned-Warbler

GOA

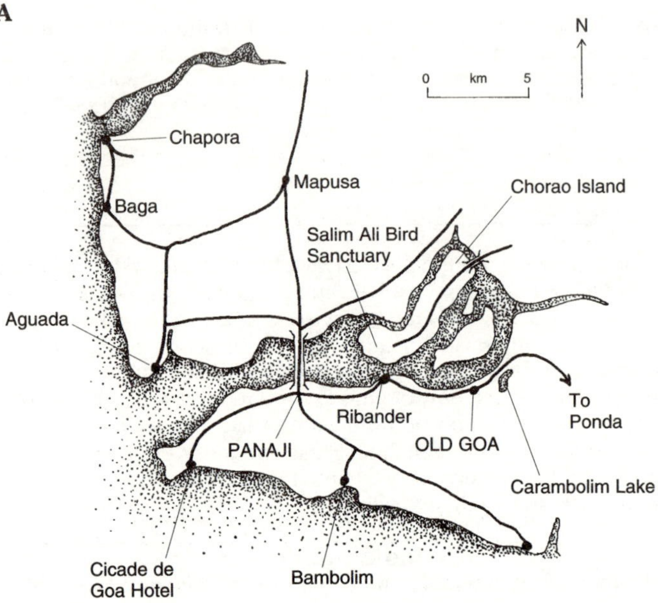

(Nov–Mar), Puff-throated and Tawny-bellied Babblers, Brown-cheeked Fulvetta, Black-lored Tit, Forest Wagtail (Nov–Mar), Baya Weaver, Pale-billed Flowerpecker, Purple-rumped Sunbird.

The best bases at the coast are Bambolim, where the hotel is surrounded by remnant lowland forest (Red Spurfowl), and Baga, where there is a good variety of habitats close to the resort (Brown Fish-Owl, Paddyfield Warbler, Malabar Lark, Long-billed Sunbird). Sites worth visiting near these include Chapora, 4 km north of Baga (Great Black-headed Gull), the Salim Ali Bird Sanctuary on Chorao Island in the mouth of the Mandovi River, accessible by ferry from Ribander (Lesser Adjutant*, Great Knot, Small Pratincole, River Tern), the small marsh to the east of the Cicade de Goa Hotel (Red Spurfowl, Malabar Lark) and Carambolim Lake, 2 km east of old Goa (Cinnamon Bittern, Black-backed Kingfisher, Chestnut-headed Bee-eater). The best birds near Goa are arguably those in the foothills of the Western Ghats, an hour or so by road inland. The **Bondla WS** (80 sq km), 10 km east of Ponda, and the **Molem WS** (best along the track to Dudhsagar Falls), 28 km east of Ponda, support most of the endemics listed above.

Accommodation: Goa — plenty to choose from. Bondla WS and Molem WS — chalets (basic), bookable in advance through the Goa Tourism Development Corporation Ltd., Trionora Apartments, Panaji, Goa 403001 (tel: 0832 226515, fax: 223926), or in Ponda at the Hotel President.

Some good birds occur near **Pune**, north of Goa near Bombay. Rock Bush-Quail, Rock Eagle-Owl and White-bellied Minivet* occur in the

Parvati Temple area to the southeast of town; the bush-quail also occurs in the Katraj Valley to the northeast of town, and Demoiselle Crane* occurs at Vir Dam, between Shirwal and Lonand to the south.

The **Sri Lankamalleswara** wildlife sanctuary near Cuddapah in the low, rocky Eastern Ghats, is one of the few known localities for Jerdon's Courser*, which, until its rediscovery here in 1986, was thought to be extinct because it had not been recorded for 86 years. This rare nocturnal bird is one of the most difficult species to see in the world, and when the bureaucratic barriers, which may take days to break down, have been overcome, be prepared to spend more than one night looking for it with the local guides. Contact the Chief Wildlife Warden in Hyderabad or Forest Office in Tirupati a month in advance to see if it is possible to visit this highly sensitive site.

The small, but important, **Ranganthitoo** bird sanctuary on the River Cauvery near Mysore west of Bangalore supports breeding cormorants, egrets, herons and storks, as well as Great Thick-knee.

RAJIV GANDHI NATIONAL PARK (NAGARHOLE)

This park (540 sq km) lies in the eastern foothills of the Western Ghats and is dominated by dry deciduous forests which support five endemics and White-naped Woodpecker.

Indian Endemics

Red Spurfowl, Grey Junglefowl*, Malabar Parakeet, White-cheeked Barbet, Malabar Lark.

Specialities

Jerdon's Nightjar, Malabar Trogon, Malabar Pied-Hornbill*, White-naped Woodpecker, Indian Pitta (Nov–Mar).

Others

Red-naped Ibis*, Lesser Adjutant*, Grey-headed Fish-Eagle*, Indian Peafowl, Bronze-winged Jacana, Black-bellied Tern*, Vernal Hanging-Parrot, Plum-headed Parakeet, Brown Fish-Owl, Stork-billed Kingfisher, Blue-tailed Bee-eater, Chestnut-tailed Starling, Pale-billed Flowerpecker.

Other Wildlife

Asian elephant, chital, dhole, gaur, Hanuman langur, leopard, sambar, sloth bear, tiger.

This park is 85 km southeast of Mysore. Indian Pitta has been recorded in the Kabini River Lodge gardens, along with Brown Fish-Owl. Bird the gardens, the nearby fields where Malabar Lark occurs, the dam near the lodge (coracles available) and the forest and open areas (dawn and dusk jeep rides available) within the park, which lies just across the Kabini River from the lodge.

Accommodation: Kabini River Lodge (A+).

MUDUMALAI NATIONAL PARK

The dry deciduous forest, evergreen gallery forest and bamboo stands within this park support five endemics, including the localised Grey-headed Bulbul*, as well as White-bellied Minivet* and 12 species of woodpecker.

Indian Endemics

Painted Bush-Quail, Red Spurfowl, White-cheeked Barbet, Grey-headed Bulbul*, Malabar Lark.

Specialities

Blue-faced Malkoha, Jerdon's Nightjar, Indian Swiftlet, White-naped Woodpecker, Indian Pitta (Nov–Mar), White-bellied Minivet*, Tawny-bellied Babbler.

Others

Rufous-bellied Eagle, Yellow-footed Pigeon, Plum-headed Parakeet, Crested Treeswift, Blue-bearded Bee-eater, Yellow-crowned Woodpecker, Lesser Yellownape, Common and Black-rumped Flamebacks, Streak-throated Woodpecker, Golden-fronted Leafbird, Tickell's Blue-Flycatcher, Chestnut-bellied Nuthatch, Thick-billed Warbler (Nov–Mar), Pale-billed Flowerpecker.

Other Wildlife

Asian elephant, dhole, gaur, leopard, mouse deer, sloth bear, tiger.

The park HQ is situated at the junction of the roads to Masinagudi, Mysore and Gudalur near Ooty (Ootacamund). Grey-headed Bulbul* occurs in the bamboo stands along the river which runs alongside the Mysore–Gudalur Road. Beware of elephants.

Accommodation: book in advance at the Forestry Office, Coonoor Road, Ooty.

White-bellied Minivet* and Malabar Lark, as well as Bonnet macaques and Nilgiri langurs may be seen alongside the road between Mudumalai NP and Ootacamund.

OOTACAMUND

'Ooty' is a large rundown hill resort which lies at 2268 m (7441 ft) in the 'Nilgiri Hills', part of the Western Ghats. Most of the original evergreen forest has been destroyed in the vicinity of Ooty, to make way for tea, eucalypt and pine plantations, but a few remnants survive in the steepest ravines and these oases of local birdlife support the lovely Black-and-rufous Flycatcher and four Nilgiri specialities, notably Rufous-breasted Laughingthrush*.

Indian Endemics

Painted Bush-Quail, Grey Junglefowl*, Nilgiri Wood-Pigeon*, White-cheeked Barbet, Spot-breasted Fantail, White-bellied Treepie*, Malabar

Whistling-Thrush, White-bellied Shortwing*, Black-and-rufous* and Nilgiri* Flycatchers, Rufous-breasted Laughingthrush*, Malabar Lark, Crimson-backed Sunbird.

Specialities

Blue-faced Malkoha, Indian Swiftlet, White-naped Woodpecker, Indian Pitta (Nov–Mar), White-bellied Minivet*, Kashmir Flycatcher* (Nov–Mar), Yellow-browed Bulbul, Indian Scimitar-Babbler, Long-billed Sunbird.

Others

Blue-capped Rock-Thrush, Orange-headed Thrush, Tickell's Blue-Flycatcher, Indian Blue Robin (Nov–Mar), Velvet-fronted Nuthatch, Ashy Prinia, Blyth's Reed-Warbler (Nov–Mar), Tickell's Leaf-Warbler (Nov–Mar), Western Crowned-Warbler (Nov–Mar), Puff-throated Babbler, Brown-cheeked Fulvetta, Black-lored Tit, Forest Wagtail (Nov–Mar).

Other Wildlife

Bonnet macaque.

Bird the roadside forest on the Ooty side of **Naduvattam** village, between KMS 31 and 34, on the road north from Ooty to Gudalur (Malabar Whistling-Thrush, Black-and-rufous Flycatcher*, Rufous-breasted Laughingthrush*), the **Cairn Hill Reserved Forest**, which is a small wooded ravine 3 km west of Ooty along Avalanche Road, and the Masinagudi Road, which descends steeply through remnant dry, deciduous forest and tall grassland north of Ooty, between the villages of Kalhatty, 11 km from Ooty, and Mavanalle, near Masinagudi, 22 km from Ooty (Painted Bush-Quail, on road early in the day, and, possibly, White-bellied Minivet*).

Nilgiri Wood-Pigeon* and Spot-breasted Fantail occur alongside the roads to Dolphin's Nose and Lamb's Rock, up to 10 km away from **Coonoor**, a hill resort 45 minutes by road from Ooty.

The striking White-bellied Treepie is a widespread southern Indian endemic*

INDIRA GANDHI NATIONAL PARK

The selectively logged evergreen and dry deciduous forests, which survive among the tea plantations within this park, support a good selection of endemics including Wynaad Laughingthrush*, as well as many near-endemics such as Ceylon Frogmouth*.

INDIRA GANDHI NP

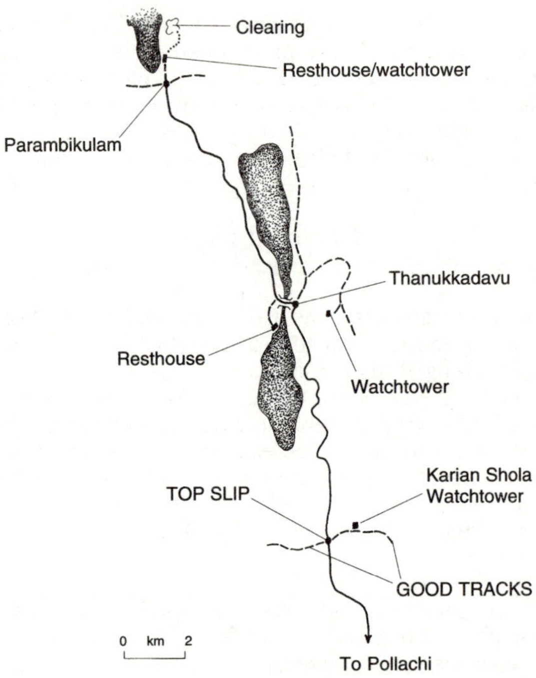

Indian Endemics

Red Spurfowl, Grey Junglefowl*, Malabar Parakeet, Malabar Grey Hornbill*, White-cheeked Barbet, White-bellied Treepie*, Malabar Whistling-Thrush, White-bellied Blue-Flycatcher*, Wynaad Laughingthrush*, Rufous Babbler, Nilgiri Pipit, Crimson-backed Sunbird.

Specialities

Blue-faced Malkoha, Spot-bellied Eagle-Owl*, Ceylon Frogmouth*, Jerdon's Nightjar, Malabar Trogon, Crimson-fronted Barbet, Indian Pitta (Nov–Mar), Rusty-tailed Flycatcher (Nov–Mar), White-browed and Yellow-browed Bulbuls, Indian Scimitar-Babbler, Dark-fronted Babbler, Black-throated Munia.

Others

Black Baza, Grey-headed Fish-Eagle*, Indian Peafowl, Pompadour Green-Pigeon, Vernal Hanging-Parrot, Plum-headed Parakeet, White-rumped and Brown-backed Needletails, Blue-bearded and Chestnut-headed Bee-eaters, Great Hornbill, Heart-spotted Woodpecker, Black-headed Cuckoo-Shrike, Large Woodshrike, Orange-headed Thrush, Brown-breasted Flycatcher* (Nov–Mar), Black-crested Bulbul, Large-billed Leaf-Warbler (Nov–Mar), Western Crowned-Warbler (Nov–Mar).

Other Wildlife

Asian elephant, chital, gaur, leopard, lion-tailed macaque, Nilgiri langur, sambar, tiger.

This park, also known as Anamalai, is accessible from Pollachi. Head from there to Top Slip, a former logging camp, and bird Karian Shola opposite Bison Lodge, and Anagunti (Anai Kundi) Shola (lion-tailed macaque), which is only accessible with a guide. The Thanukkadavu and Parambikulam (Grey-headed Fish-Eagle*) areas are also worth visiting if time allows.

Accommodation: Top Slip — book resthouse (basic) in advance at Pollachi — Forest Department.

Nilgiri Pipit occurs in the scrubby grassland alongside the road to **Rajamalai NP** from Munnar, along with Nilgiri Tahr, and other species recorded here include Painted Bush-Quail, Nilgiri Wood-Pigeon*, Malabar Whistling-Thrush, Nilgiri Flycatcher*, White-bellied Shortwing* and Grey-breasted Laughingthrush*.

The localised endemic, Yellow-throated Bulbul*, as well as Blue-faced Malkoha, occur in roadside scrub 57 km east of Munnar, 13 km west of Bodinayakanur.

PERIYAR NATIONAL PARK

This park, at the southern end of the Western Ghats, is one of India's largest (777 sq km) and most popular reserves, mainly because it is one of the easiest places to see elephants in India. The evergreen forests, dry deciduous forests and grasslands, which have survived being turned over to teak plantations, encircle a huge central lake, formed by the damming of the River Periyar. Over 260 species have been recorded, including 14 of the 24 southern Indian endemics and eight of the 17 species which only occur in southern India and Sri Lanka.

Indian Endemics

Red Spurfowl, Grey Junglefowl*, Nilgiri Wood-Pigeon*, Malabar Parakeet, Malabar Grey Hornbill*, White-cheeked Barbet, White-bellied Treepie*, Malabar Whistling-Thrush, Black-and-rufous Flycatcher* (scarce), White-bellied Blue-Flycatcher*, Grey-headed Bulbul*, Wynaad Laughingthrush*, Rufous Babbler, Crimson-backed Sunbird.

Specialities

Ceylon Frogmouth*, Malabar Trogon, Crimson-fronted Barbet, Indian Pitta (Nov–Mar), Rusty-tailed Flycatcher (Nov–Mar), White-browed and Yellow-browed Bulbuls, Indian Scimitar-Babbler, Dark-fronted Babbler, Long-billed Sunbird.

Others

Black Baza, Grey-headed Fish-Eagle*, Rufous-bellied Eagle, Pintail Snipe (Nov–Mar), Pompadour Green-Pigeon, Vernal Hanging-Parrot, Chestnut-winged and Drongo Cuckoos, Jungle Owlet, Great Eared-Nightjar, White-rumped Needletail, Chestnut-headed Bee-eater, Indian Roller, Great Hornbill, Rufous Woodpecker, Lesser Yellownape, Greater, Black-rumped and Common Flamebacks, Heart-spotted Woodpecker, Black-headed Cuckoo-Shrike, Asian Fairy-bluebird, Orange-headed Thrush, Brown-breasted* (Nov–Mar) and Blue-throated Flycatchers, Tickell's Blue-Flycatcher, Indian Blue Robin (Nov–Mar), Black-crested Bulbul, Blyth's Reed-Warbler (Nov–Mar), Thick-billed Warbler (Nov–Mar), Large-billed Leaf-Warbler (Nov–Mar), Western Crowned-Warbler (Nov–Mar), Puff-throated Babbler, Brown-cheeked Fulvetta, Black-lored Tit, Forest Wagtail (Nov–Mar), Little Spiderhunter.

Other Wildlife

Asian elephant, black bear, Bonnet macaque, dhole, gaur, leopard, Nilgiri langur, sambar.

The park entrance is 2 km outside the small town of Kumilly, accessible by road (5 hours) from Munnar. Bird the track to the Mangla Devi Temple (Wynaad Laughingthrush*), the scrub behind the Ambadi Hotel at the entrance (Red Spurfowl) and throughout the park. Boat trips are possible on the lake to look for elephants and gaur.

Accommodation: Kumilly — Nice Lodge (C). NP Entrance — Ambika Lodge. Boat landing — Periyar Lodge (B), Aranya Nivas (A).

Great Hornbill is one of Periyar's most spectacular birds

One of the richest areas for birds in Kerala, southwest India, is the **Wynaad WS** (344 sq km). Whereas the forest of the Western Ghats is evergreen, this sanctuary supports moist deciduous forest (at Muthanga and Kupadi) where the birds include Nilgiri Wood-Pigeon*, Malabar Parakeet, Ceylon Frogmouth*, Malabar Trogon, Black-and-rufous Flycatcher*, White-bellied Blue-Flycatcher*, Yellow-browed Bulbul, Wynaad*, Rufous-breasted* and Grey-breasted* Laughingthrushes, Dark-fronted and Rufous Babblers and Nilgiri Pipit.

Accommodation: basic lodges at Sultan's Battery.

Point Calimere on India's southeast coast near Vederanyam, south of Madras, is an internationally important site for migrant and wintering shorebirds, and in November large numbers of Indian Pittas pass through. The wintering shorebirds have included small numbers of Spoonbill Sandpiper*, although they are hard to find among 40,000 Little Stints. Bicycles are available for hire in Kodikkarai to explore the salt lagoons to the west of the resthouse and Lighthouse Lagoon, the most likely place for Spoonbill Sandpiper*, in Koddikkarai NP, 8 km to the east. Other species present in the area include Great Black-headed Gull (Nov–Mar), Grey-bellied Cuckoo and Blue-faced Malkoha.

Accommodation: Kodikkarai — basic lodge. Vederanyam — basic lodge.

ANDAMAN ISLANDS

While these islands are politically part of India, they lie a long way to the east, far closer to the Burmese coast than the Indian coast, and are ornithologically part of southeast Asia. They support eight endemics plus four near-endemics, which are shared with the Nicobar Islands to the south. Despite being under Indian administration, only South Andaman Island is normally accessible to foreigners without special permits, although other islands in the archipelago are slowly opening up to tourists. If arriving by air permits to stay up to 30 days are issued on arrival. Flights leave three times a week from Madras and Calcutta and must be booked weeks in advance. If arriving by sea it is necessary to obtain a permit before departure from the Immigration Offices at Calcutta or Madras airports. Boats leave on an irregular basis, take three to four days and may be booked in advance at the Shipping Corporation of India, Jawahar Building, Rajaji Salai, Madras (tel: 52 4964) or on the 1st Floor, 13 Strand Road, Calcutta.

SOUTH ANDAMAN

Most of the eight Andaman Island endemics and four near-endemics shared with the Nicobar Islands are easy to see in the remnant lowland forest on South Andaman Island, which rises to 800 m (2625 ft). There are plenty of other birds here and it is possible to see over 100 species on a two-week visit.

The best time to visit is between February and April, the driest period. It can be very wet here between May and October.

Andaman Endemics

Andaman Serpent-Eagle*, Andaman Coucal*, Andaman Woodpecker*, Andaman Drongo*, Andaman Treepie*.

Andaman and Nicobar Endemics

Andaman Wood-Pigeon*, Andaman Cuckoo-Dove*, White-headed Starling*.

SOUTH ANDAMAN

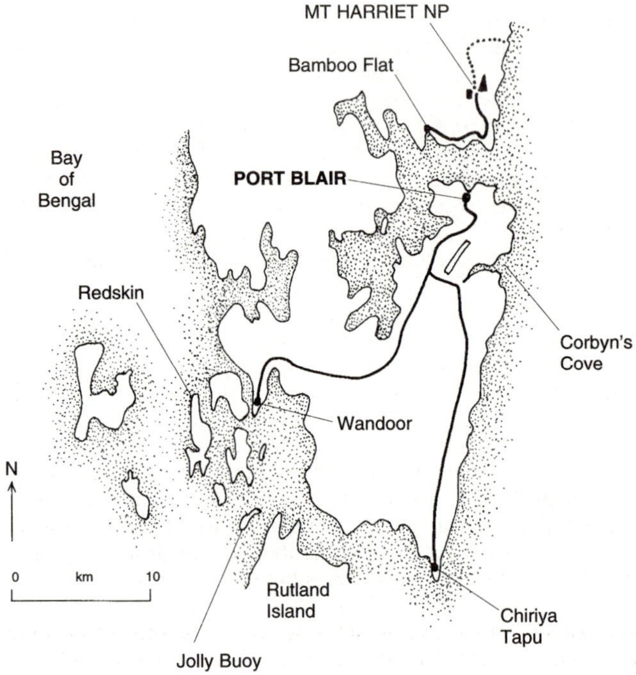

Others

Sunda Teal, Pacific Reef-Egret, Cinnamon Bittern, White-bellied Sea-Eagle, Slaty-breasted Rail, Baillon's Crake (Nov–Mar), Watercock, Pintail Snipe (Nov–Mar), Long-toed Stint (Nov–Mar), Black-naped Tern, Pompadour Green-Pigeon, Vernal Hanging-Parrot, Red-breasted and Long-tailed Parakeets, Asian Emerald (Nov–Mar) and Violet Cuckoos, Glossy and Edible-nest Swiftlets, Brown-backed Needletail, Stork-billed, Black-capped and Collared Kingfishers, Blue-tailed and Chestnut-headed Bee-eaters, Fulvous-breasted Woodpecker, Mangrove Whistler, White-breasted Woodswallow, Bar-bellied Cuckoo-shrike, Small and Scarlet Minivets, Asian Fairy-bluebird, Orange-headed Thrush, Asian Glossy Starling, Black-headed Bulbul, Pale-footed Bush-Warbler, Pallas' Warbler (Nov–Mar), Black-browed Reed-Warbler (Nov–Mar), Thick-billed Warbler (Nov–Mar), Forest Wagtail (Nov–Mar).

(The three remaining endemics are Andaman Crake*, which is rarely reported, Narcondam Hornbill*, which only occurs on the virtually inaccessible island of Narcondam, and Andaman Scops-Owl*, which is also rarely reported. The one remaining near-endemic is Andaman Hawk-Owl*, which, again, is rarely reported.)

From Port Blair it is possible to reach the birding sites on local buses and ferries, in taxis or via hired scooters and motorcycles. The best birding site by far is Mount Harriet NP, which is accessible via the ferry from Phoenix

Bay to Bamboo Flat or Hope Town. Bird the trail north from Hope Town, the track from here to the forest resthouse and, if time permits, the 6 km track down to the beach beyond. The forest-dwelling Andaman Crake* is rarely reported, but Mount Harriet is probably as good a place as any for this elusive species. The marsh and tidal creek at the south end of Corbyn's Cove, just to the southeast of Port Blair, support Cinnamon Bittern and Pallas' Warbler and Sunda Teal has also been recorded here. There is a narrow strip of forest at Chiriya Tapu, some 30 km south of Port Blair, at the southern tip of the island, where the serpent-eagle, woodpecker, drongo and treepie occur, along with Mangrove Whistler, Orange-headed Thrush and Pale-footed Bush-Warbler. Bird the forest alongside the last few kilometres of road before the tea stalls and alongside the track to the beach beyond. The Mahatma Gandhi Marine NP is also worth visiting, although the snorkelling, especially off Jolly Buoy Island, is likely to be much more exciting than the birding. The park is accessible by boat from Wandoor, 30 km southwest of Port Blair. Ask to be dropped off on Red Skin Island where a 2 km trail is planned through the forest. Sunda Teal has been recorded in the southwest of this island, as well as north of Wandoor and on Havelock Island, north of Port Blair.

The Narcondam Hornbill* only exists on the tiny, uninhabited island of Narcondam. To visit this island it is necessary to apply for a permit at least six months in advance and, even then, one will only be issued with good reason. If the aim of your visit is to 'twitch the hornbill' your application for a permit will almost certainly result in refusal.

Accommodation: there is a wide range of accommodation, from the cheap Youth Hostel to the expensive Andaman Beach Resort.

The **Nicobar Islands** have been closed to foreigners since 1992. They support five endemics (a serpent-eagle, a sparrowhawk, a scrubfowl, a parakeet and a bulbul) and four near-endemics, which are shared with the Andaman Islands (a wood-pigeon, a cuckoo-dove, a hawk-owl and a starling).

NICOBAR ISLANDS

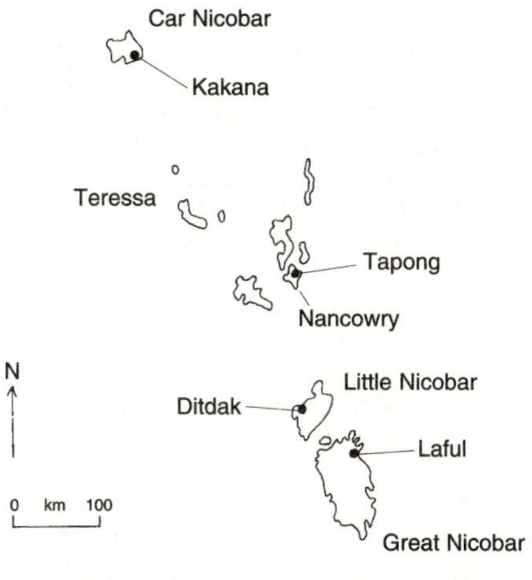

The **Maldive Islands** are a very popular tourist destination and one of the best scuba-diving sites in the world. A total of 147 bird species has been recorded, including Wedge-tailed, Flesh-footed and Audubon's Shearwaters, White-tailed Tropicbird, Great and Lesser Frigatebirds, Crab Plover, Oriental Pratincole (Nov–Mar), Pacific Golden Plover (Nov–Mar), Mongolian Plover (Nov–Mar), Greater Sandplover (Nov–Mar), Black-naped and Saunders' Terns, Brown and Lesser Noddies and Common White-Tern. However, birds are few and far between here because bird collecting is rife and flightless flocks of shorebirds and terns are a common sight in the settlements throughout the islands. If only the local people thought these birds looked better in the wild.

There are colonies of Sooty Tern and Brown Noddy on Pitti Island, one of the **Lakshadweep Islands**, which also includes the Laccadives, 220–440 km offshore from Kerala, southwest India. Many seabirds also breed on the **Chagos Islands**, to the south.

ADDITIONAL INFORMATION

Addresses

The Bombay Natural History Society, Hornbill House, Shahid Bhagat Road, Bombay 400 023, publishes a newsletter and journal.

Delhi Bird Club, c/o Ravi Singh, EG 1/6 Garden Estate, Vil., Sikandarpur, Khosi Gurgaon, Haryana (tel: 3326895/8353553)

The local conservation organisation on the Andaman Islands, the Indian National Trust for Art and Cultural Heritage (INTACH) can be contacted at Tarangs, Middle Point, Port Blair 744101 (tel: 03192 20929), a few doors along from the Hotel Shompen.

Books and Papers

A Birdwatchers Guide to India. Kaymiercyak K and Singh R. In press. Prion.

A Pictorial Guide to the Birds of the Indian Subcontinent. Ali S and Ripley D, 1983. Bombay Natural History Society.

Birds of the Andaman and Nicobar Islands. Tikader B, 1984. Zoological Society of India.

South India, Sri Lanka and The Andaman Islands (Trip Report). Gee B, 1995. Privately published (available via OBC)

The birds of Great and Car Nicobars. Abdulali H, 1978. *Journal of the Bombay Natural History Society* 75: 744–772.

Birds of the Maldive Islands, Indian Ocean. Ash J and Shafeeg A, 1994. *Forktail* 10: 3–32.

The birds of the Chagos group, Indian Ocean. Bourne W, 1971. *Atoll Research Bulletin* 149: 175–207.

INDIAN ENDEMICS (39)

Rock Bush-Quail	North-central: Bund Baratah Reservoir, near Bharatpur, Rann of Kutch and Pune
Painted Bush-Quail	South: Mudumalai, Ootacamund

	and Rajamalai
Red Spurfowl	North-central and south: widespread
Painted Spurfowl	North-central: Ranthambore and Sariska
Himalayan Quail*	North: known only from a few specimens collected near Mussooree and Naini Tal, during the nineteenth century
Grey Junglefowl*	South: widespread
Indian Bustard*	North/west: Sonkhaliya and Desert NP
Jerdon's Courser*	East-central: Sri Lankamalleswara
Nilgiri Wood-Pigeon*	South: widespread
Intermediate Parakeet*	North: known only from seven specimens and small numbers of live birds in bird markets, reputedly collected on the plains of Uttar Pradesh
Malabar Parakeet	South: widespread
Forest Owlet*	Central: known only from ten or so specimens taken before 1914 and a possible sight record in 1968 near Nagpur, Madhya Pradesh
Dark-rumped Swift*	East: Khasi Hills, Meghalaya
Malabar Grey Hornbill*	South: Goa, Indira Gandhi NP and Periyar
White-cheeked Barbet	South: widespread
Spot-breasted Fantail	South: Goa and Ootacamund
White-bellied Treepie*	South: Ootacamund, Indira Gandhi NP and Periyar
Malabar Whistling-Thrush	South: widespread
White-bellied Shortwing*	South: Ootacamund and Rajamalai
Black-and-rufous Flycatcher*	South: Ootacamund and Periyar
Nilgiri Flycatcher*	South: Goa, Ootacamund and Rajamalai
White-bellied Blue-Flycatcher*	South: Goa, Indira Gandhi NP and Periyar
Grey-headed Bulbul*	South: Goa, Mudumalai and Periyar
Yellow-throated Bulbul*	South: Bodinayakanur
Broad-tailed Grassbird*	Southwest
Wynaad Laughingthrush*	South: Indira Gandhi NP, Periyar and Wynaad
Rufous-breasted Laughingthrush*	South: Ootacamund and Wynaad
Grey-breasted Laughingthrush*	South: Rajamalai and Wynaad
Mishmi Wren-Babbler*	Northeast: one 1947 specimen from the Mishmi Hills, Arunachal Pradesh
Tawny-breasted Wren-Babbler*	Northeast: Khasi Hills and Shillong Peak, Meghalaya, Cachar Hills, Assam and Manipur
Snowy-throated Babbler*	Northeast: Namdapha NP
Rufous Babbler	South: Goa, Indira Gandhi NP and Periyar

White-winged Tit*	North-central and south: Jaisamand
Malabar Lark	South: Goa, Nagarhole, Mudumalai and Ootacamund
Tawny Lark	Central plateau: Rollapadu and Shamirpet
Green Avadavat*	Central: Kumbhalgarh
Nilgiri Pipit	South: Indira Gandhi NP, Rajamalai and Wynaad
Yellow Weaver*	Northeast: Kaziranga and Dibru-Saikhowa
Crimson-backed Sunbird	South: widespread

The single 1905 specimen of Large-billed Reed-Warbler*, taken in Himachal Pradesh, is now considered to be a Blyth's Reed-Warbler.

Near-endemics

Species Shared with Sri Lanka (17)
Painted Francolin, Jungle Bush-Quail, Blue-faced Malkoha, Ceylon Frogmouth*, Jerdon's Nightjar, Indian Swiftlet, Malabar Trogon, Malabar Pied-Hornbill*, Crimson-fronted Barbet, Hill Swallow, White-browed and Yellow-browed* Bulbuls, Indian Scimitar-Babbler, Dark-fronted and Yellow-billed Babblers, Black-throated Munia, Long-billed Sunbird

North (Both Sides of the Himalayas)
Rufous-vented Prinia*, Tibetan Lark, Black-winged Snowfinch, Robin and Rufous-breasted Accentors, Spectacled Finch, Beautiful, Pink-browed and Streaked Rosefinches, Red-headed Bullfinch, Gold-naped Finch.

Northwest
Western Tragopan*, Cheer Pheasant*, Siberian Crane*, Lesser Florican*, Tibetan Sandgrouse, Pale-backed Pigeon*, Sykes' Nightjar, Brown-fronted and Himalayan Woodpeckers, Black-headed Jay, White-tailed Iora, Rusty-tailed (winters in south) and Kashmir (winters in south) Flycatchers, White-browed Bushchat*, Indian Chat, Kashmir and White-cheeked Nuthatches, White-cheeked and White-throated* Tits, Rufous-fronted Prinia, Long-billed Bush-Warbler*, Tytler's Leaf-Warbler*, Western Crowned-Warbler (winters in south), Variegated Laughingthrush, Black-chinned and Large Grey Babblers, Black-crested Tit, Sind Sparrow, Orange Bullfinch*, Black-and-yellow Grosbeak.

Northeast
White-bellied Heron*, Szecheny's Partridge*, Swamp Francolin*, Tibetan Partridge, Manipur Bush-Quail*, White-cheeked* and Chestnut-breasted* Partridges, Satyr*, Blyth's* and Temminck's* Tragopans, Sclater's Monal*, Hume's Pheasant*, Black-necked Crane*, Bengal Florican*, Derbyan Parakeet*, Ward's Trogon*, Tibetan Ground-Jay, Pied Thrush* (winters on Sri Lanka), Rusty-bellied Shortwing*, Collared Myna*, Pale-chinned Blue-Flycatcher, Firethroat*, Rufous-breasted Bush-Robin*, Chestnut-vented and Beautiful* Nuthatches, Olive Bulbul, Swamp and Grey-crowned* Prinias, Smoky Warbler, Striated,

Rufous-necked, Chestnut-backed*, Yellow-throated*, Rufous-vented, Moustached, Grey-sided, Striped* and Brown-capped* Laughing-thrushes, Marsh Babbler*, Rufous-throated*, Bar-winged, Spotted* and Wedge-billed* Wren-Babblers, Jerdon's* and Slender-billed* Babblers, Chinese and Giant* Babaxes, Rusty-fronted, Hoary-throated and Streak-throated Barwings, Ludlow's and Nepal Fulvettas, Grey* and Beautiful Sibias, White-naped and Rufous-vented Yuhinas, Fire-tailed Myzornis, Great, Brown, Black-breasted* and Fulvous Parrotbills, Rufous-necked and Blanford's Snowfinches, Maroon-backed Accentor, Fire-tailed Sunbird, Tibetan Serin, Blanford's and Dark-rumped Rosefinches, Crimson-browed and Scarlet Finches, Grey-headed Bullfinch.

More or Less Throughout
Indian Courser, Painted Sandgrouse, Mottled Wood-Owl, White-naped Woodpecker, White-bellied Drongo, White-bellied Minivet*, Indian Grey Thrush, Streak-throated Swallow, Jungle Prinia, Bristled Grassbird*, Tawny-bellied Babbler, Black-lored Tit, Rufous-tailed Lark, Purple-rumped Sunbird.

ANDAMAN ISLANDS ENDEMICS (8)

Andaman Serpent-Eagle*, Andaman Crake*, Andaman Coucal* (also recorded in Burma), Andaman Scops-Owl*, Narcondam Hornbill* (Narcondam Island), Andaman Woodpecker*, Andaman Drongo* (also recorded in Burma), Andaman Treepie*.

NICOBAR ISLANDS ENDEMICS (5)

Nicobar Serpent-Eagle*, Nicobar Sparrowhawk*, Nicobar Scrubfowl*, Nicobar Parakeet*, Nicobar Bulbul*.

ANDAMAN and NICOBAR ISLANDS ENDEMICS (4)

Andaman Wood-Pigeon*, Andaman Cuckoo-Dove*, Andaman Hawk-Owl*, White-headed Starling*.

INDONESIA

Indonesia lies within Asia and Australasia. East of Wallace's Line, which falls between Bali and Lombok, the islands of the Lesser Sundas, Moluccas and Sulawesi form the transition zone, known as Wallacea, between the Asian and Australasian avifaunas. Wallacea is covered in this book, because the avifauna is partly Asian and because many birders visit Asian and Wallacean Indonesia during a single trip. The western half of the island of New Guinea, known as Irian Jaya, is politically part of Indonesia, but because its avifauna is essentially Australasian and most birders visit this part of the world on a separate trip, it is not covered in this book but will be included in the next volume in this series.

INTRODUCTION

Summary

Indonesia is such a huge and complex archipelago it would be impossible to see a good cross-section of its avifauna during a single short trip, unless half of it was spent airborne. However, there are so many endemics (338), the people are so friendly and getting around is so easy, that Indonesia is the kind of place that merits trip after trip, or, better still, a year off work. Although some parts of the country have been catering for tourists for many years, most of the accommodation at the best birding sites is basic, but clean and cheap.

Size

At 1,904,569 sq km, Indonesia is nearly 15 times larger than England and three times the size of Texas. The numerous islands are sprinkled across the equator over a distance of 5000 km.

---

1 Barito Ulu (Kalimantan)
2 Berestagi (Sumatra)
3 Kerinci-Seblat NP (Sumatra)
4 Mauro Sako (Sumatra)
5 Way Kambas NP (Sumatra)
6 Christmas Island
7 Gunung Gede-Pangrango NP (Java)
8 Carita (Java)
9 Baluran NP (Java)
10 Bali Barat NP (Bali)
11 Bedugul (Bali)
12 Denpasar (Bali)
13 Lombok
14 Sumbawa
15 Komodo Island
16 Ruteng (Flores)
17 Kisol (Flores)
18 Waingapu (Sumba)
19 Lewapaku (Sumba)
20 Bipolo (Timor)
21 Camplong (Timor)
22 Wetar
23 Yamdena (Tanimbar Islands)
24 Kai Islands
25 Ambon
26 Manusela NP (Seram)
27 Buru
28 Taliabu (Sula Islands)
29 Kali Batu Putih (Halmahera)
30 Tangkoko NR (Sulawesi)
31 Dumoga-Bone NP (Sulawesi)
32 Lore Lindu NP (Sulawesi)

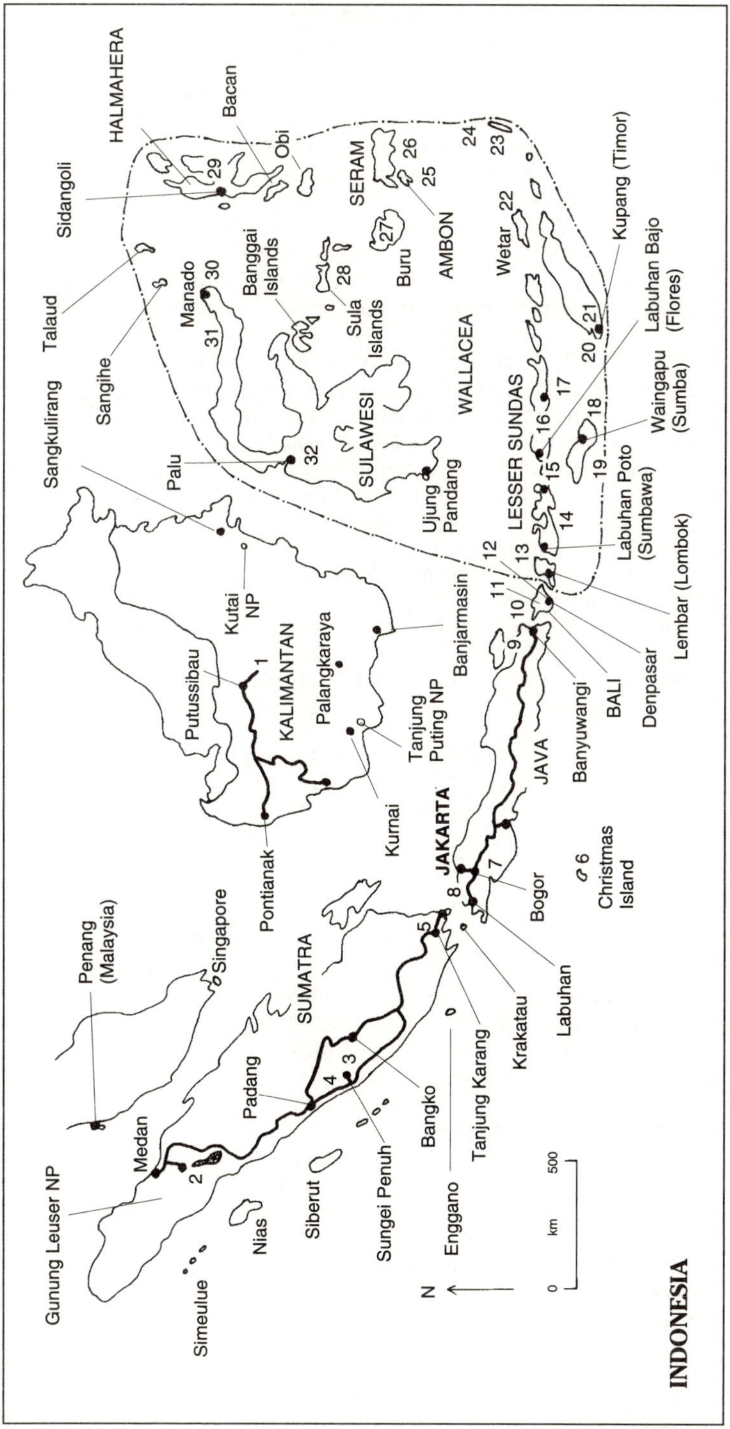
INDONESIA
N
0 km 500
Gunung Leuser NP
Simeulue
Nias
Siberut
Enggano
Sungei Penuh
Bangko
Tanjung Karang
Krakatau
Labuhan
Bogor
JAKARTA
Christmas Island
Medan
Padang
SUMATRA
Penang (Malaysia)
Singapore
Pontianak
Kurnai
Tanjung Puting NP
Putussibau
KALIMANTAN
Palangkaraya
Banjarmasin
Kutai NP
Sangkulirang
JAVA
Banyuwangi
BALI
Denpasar
Lembar (Lombok)
Labuhan Poto (Sumbawa)
Waingapu (Sumba)
Labuhan Bajo (Flores)
Kupang (Timor)
LESSER SUNDAS
WALLACEA
Wetar
Ujung Pandang
SULAWESI
Palu
Manado
Sangihe
Talaud
Sidangoli
Banggai Islands
Sula Islands
Buru
AMBON
SERAM
Obi
Bacan
HALMAHERA
1
2
3
4
5
6
7
8
9
10
11
12
13
14
15
16
17
18
19
20
21
22
23
24
25
26
27
28
29
30
31
32

Getting Around

Travelling around Indonesia is delightfully easy, thanks to the extensive internal flight network (the Garuda-Merpati Airlines airpass makes travelling to more than two islands relatively cheap), the far-reaching bus system (even in remote areas there are usually mini-buses or converted trucks (bemos) which carry passengers) and the regular ferries which operate between the major islands. Car hire need not be considered, although it is necessary to hire a 4WD with driver at a couple of sites. A good grasp of Bahasa Indonesian would greatly assist getting around some of the remoter islands, where it is usually necessary to speak to village chiefs about the possibilities of accommodation and birding. A letter of introduction, perhaps from BirdLife, would also help in such areas.

Accommodation and Food

Most sites on the main birding circuit have some form of cheap, clean, basic accommodation, often 'right next to the birds'. Off the beaten track it is necessary to arrange accommodation, be it in a tent or a village house, with the local village chiefs. The staple diet is nasi goreng (fried rice), although satay dishes and Chinese-style food are also widely available.

Health and Safety

Immunisation against hepatitis, polio, typhoid and yellow fever is recommended, as are precautions against malaria. *Falciparum* malaria, which can be fatal, is particularly prevalent in east Indonesia and it is important to take all possible precautions here, including wearing long-sleeved shirts and long trousers and sleeping under a mosquito net.

Climate and Timing

The climate is complex, but bascially the wet season lasts from October to April except for the Moluccas, where it is wet from April to August. Hence the best time to visit much of Indonesia is June–October, the peak time being August–September.

Habitats

Indonesia's islands support a great variety of habitats, including coral reefs, beaches, mud flats, mangroves, paddies, lowland forests and montane forests. Most of the islands are mountainous and the highest peak is Gunung Kerinci, which rises to 3805 m (12,484 ft) in Sumatra, where the mountains are confined to the west coast.

Conservation

Only Amazonia has more forest cover than Indonesia, but 54 million hectares have been lost since 1970 and in the early 1990s the forests were disappearing at about 1.2 million hectares per annum, hence there are more threatened species (104) in Indonesia than in any other country in the world. A further 183 species are near-threatened. Unless the human population can be stabilised (the most densely populated island of Java lost 90% of its forest long ago), these, and many other birds, face extinction.

Bird Species

Over 1500 species have been recorded in Indonesia, the highest country total outside of South America. Over 675 species have been recorded in Wallacea alone, including 243 endemics, and over 600 species have been recorded on Sumatra. Non-endemic specialities and spectacular species present on Sumatra include White-winged Duck*, Storm's Stork*, Fire-tufted Barbet, Dusky Broadbill, Malaysian Rail-Babbler and Silver-eared Mesia. Notable non-endemics on Sumatra and Java include Blue Nuthatch and Pin-tailed Parrotfinch, while widespread goodies which occur on Java include Green Peafowl*, Chestnut-fronted Shrike-Babbler and Mountain Serin. Non-endemic spectacular species which occur at the eastern end of the archipelago, on islands such as Seram and the Moluccas, include Gurney's Eagle*, Common Paradise-Kingfisher, Rainbow Bee-eater and Red-bellied Pitta, while Great-billed Heron*, Beach Thick-knee and Island Thrush occur, more or less, throughout Indonesia.

Endemics

The islands of Indonesia support an amazing total of 338 endemic species, the majority of which are confined to the Moluccas (97), Sulawesi (67) and the Lesser Sundas (63). A further 61 species are confined to Sumatra, Java and Bali, where Sumatra has 18 of its own and Java has 20. Other islands and archipelagos with ten or more endemics include Halmahera and its satellites (22), Tanimbar and its satellites (13), Timor (11) and Buru (10). The endemics are discussed in more detail under island headings, but they include such spectacular species as Blue-tailed Trogon, 13 kingfishers, Purple-bearded Bee-eater, two rollers, four pittas, eight fantails, eight monarchs, Wallace's Standardwing*, ten thrushes, Bali Myna*, Sumatran* and Javan* Cochoas, 21 white-eyes and four sunbirds.

KALIMANTAN

Virtually all of Borneo's endemics (p. 219) are fairly easy to see in north Borneo (Malaysia), hence few birders have ventured to the remoter south where there are few roads and very little accommodation. However, those who enjoy overcoming such obstacles will find plenty of river transport and some internal flights.

The lowland swamp forest in **Tanjung Puting NP**, accessible by boat from Palangkaraya in south-central Kalimantan, supports Storm's Stork*, Lesser Adjutant*, Bulwer's Pheasant*, Bornean Peacock-Pheasant*, Cinnamon-headed Pigeon* and Mangrove Whistler, and is a good place to see orang-utan and proboscis monkey. In east Kalimantan, Hose's and Whitehead's Broadbills (near the summit) occur on **Mount Lunjut**, Whitehead's Spiderhunter has been recorded in the upper reaches of the **Bahan River Valley** and the lowland forest around the Mentoko research centre in **Kutai NP** supports Wallace's Hawk-Eagle*, Short-toed Coucal*, Blue-headed Pitta*, Rufous-chested Flycatcher and Grey-bellied and Grey-cheeked Bulbuls.

BARITO ULU

The forests of the upper Barito River Valley in central Kalimantan support a good selection of Bornean endemics, including Bulwer's Pheasant* and Pygmy White-eye, as well as Blue-banded Kingfisher and Hook-billed Bulbul*. This is a remote site and birding it will involve a mini-expedition.

Bornean Endemics

Red-breasted Partridge, Bulwer's Pheasant*, Mountain and Bornean Barbets, Blue-headed* and Blue-banded Pittas, Bornean Whistler, Bornean Bristlehead*, Pygmy White-eye, Bornean Stubtail, Bornean Wren-Babbler*.

Specialities

White-shouldered Ibis*, Black Partridge*, Crestless* and Crested* Firebacks, Great Argus, Oriental Bay-Owl, Blue-banded Kingfisher, Malaysian Rail-babbler, Chestnut-tailed Jungle-Flycatcher, Rufous-chested Flycatcher, Chestnut-naped Forktail, Hook-billed Bulbul*, Grey-breasted Babbler*, Pin-tailed Parrotfinch, Dusky Munia.

Others

Oriental Darter*, Jerdon's Baza*, Bat Hawk, Rufous-bellied Eagle, Blyth's Hawk-Eagle, Brown Wood-Owl, Malaysian Nightjar, Orange-breasted Trogon, Blue-eared Kingfisher, Rhinoceros Hornbill, Black Magpie*, Rufous-winged and Maroon-breasted Philentomas, Malaysian* and Pygmy Blue-Flycatchers, Straw-headed Bulbul*, Rufous-tailed and Ashy Tailorbirds, White-chested* and Moustached Babblers, Brown Fulvetta, White-bellied Munia.

Other Wildlife

Binturong, Malay civet, proboscis monkey, slow loris, western tarsier.

(Bornean Peacock-Pheasant* probably occurs here as well.)

This site is only accessible by boat via Muaratewe and Muarajulai and there is no accommodation.

SUMATRA

Over 600 species have been recorded on this 1000 km long island, which still supports large areas of forest. Eighteen species are endemic and most of them only occur in the Barisan Range (Marching Mountains) which runs along the west side of the island.

The main entry point in the north is Medan, which is accessible by air or ferry from Penang in Malaysia. Look out for Milky Stork* and Lesser Adjutant* at Belawan, where the ferry docks. **Gunung Leuser NP** (9000 sq km) in north Sumatra has been neglected by birders for a long time, despite the fact that old records from here include such great rarities as Sumatran Pheasant*, Sunda Ground-Cuckoo* (Gunung Singgalang and Padang Highlands), White-fronted Scops-Owl* and

Sumatran Cochoa*. The park is accessible via Kutacane and Gurah, where there is basic bungalow accommodation. Plenty of birders have been to **Berestagi**, however, because species recorded in the remnant forests near this small hill town, 1.5 hours by bus from Medan, include Bronze-tailed Peacock-Pheasant*, Rajah Scops-Owl, Barred Eagle-Owl, Short-tailed Frogmouth*, Salvadori's Nightjar*, Blue-tailed Trogon, Schneider's Pitta*, Shiny Whistling-Thrush, Rufous-browed and Indigo Flycatchers, Rufous-vented Niltava, Pygmy Blue-Flycatcher, Orange-spotted Bulbul, Black-capped White-eye, Yellow-breasted Warbler, Long-billed* and Rusty-breasted Wren-Babblers, Spot-necked Babbler and Pin-tailed Parrotfinch. The best birding area is alongside the road to the transmitter, but birds such as Schneider's Pitta* are rarely seen here these days and, as with a number of the species listed above, is reported more regularly from Kerinci-Seblat NP (see below).

Accommodation: Losmen Sibayak.

KERINCI-SEBLAT NATIONAL PARK

Gunung Kerinci, which rises to 3805 m (12,484 ft) and is Sumatra's highest peak, is situated roughly halfway along the Barisan Range, the island's endemic base. Hence the remnant montane forest on its slopes support most of the Sumatran endemics, including Salvadori's Pheasant*, Bronze-tailed Peacock-Pheasant*, Schneider's Pitta*, Blue-masked Leafbird* and the fabulous Sumatran Cochoa*, as well as many species which are restricted to Sumatra, Java and Peninsular Malaysia, including Dusky Woodcock, Blue-tailed Trogon, Fire-tufted Barbet, Sunda Forktail, Blue Nuthatch and Marbled Wren-Babbler*.

Although it can be wet here throughout the year, the driest period tends to be from June to September.

Sumatran Endemics

Red-billed Partridge, Salvadori's Pheasant*, Bronze-tailed Peacock-Pheasant*, Schneider's Pitta*, Blue-masked Leafbird*, Shiny Whistling-Thrush, Sumatran Cochoa*, Cream-striped and Spot-necked Bulbuls, Rusty-breasted Wren-Babbler.

Specialities

Dusky Woodcock, Green-spectacled Pigeon*, Pink-headed Fruit-Dove, Whiskered Treeswift, Waterfall Swift* (Jun–Sep), Blue-tailed Trogon, Fire-tufted Barbet, Sunda Cuckoo-Shrike, Sunda Minivet, Sunda ('Chestnut-winged') Whistling-Thrush, Indigo Flycatcher, Rufous-vented Niltava, White-tailed Flycatcher, Sunda Robin, Sunda Forktail, Blue Nuthatch, Orange-spotted and Sunda Bulbuls, Black-capped White-eye, Bar-winged Prinia, Sunda Bush-Warbler, Sunda Warbler, Sunda and Black Laughingthrushes, Long-billed* and Marbled* Wren-Babblers, Spot-necked Babbler, Scarlet Sunbird.

Others

Jerdon's Baza*, Rufous-bellied Eagle, Wedge-tailed Pigeon, Blue-crowned Hanging-Parrot, Violet and Drongo Cuckoos, Black-bellied and Green-billed Malkohas, Mountain and Rajah Scops-Owls, Barred

KERINCI-SEBLAT NP

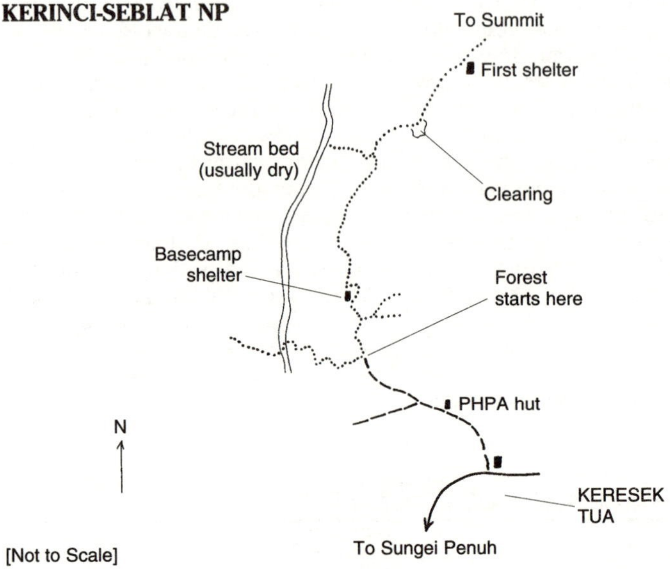

Eagle-Owl, Red-bearded Bee-eater, Bushy-crested and Wreathed Hornbills, Gold-whiskered, Red-throated, Black-browed and Brown Barbets, Lesser and Greater Yellownapes, Maroon and Buff-necked Woodpeckers, Black-and-yellow and Long-tailed Broadbills, Spotted Fantail, Green Magpie, Black-and-crimson Oriole, Greater Green and Golden-fronted Leafbirds, Grey-bellied, Red-eyed, Spectacled, Grey-cheeked, Yellow-bellied, Hairy-backed and Streaked Bulbuls, Mountain White-eye, Hill Prinia, Rufous-tailed Tailorbird, Mountain Leaf-Warbler, Short-tailed Babbler, Eyebrowed Wren-Babbler, Grey-headed and White-necked Babblers, Silver-eared Mesia, White-browed Shrike-Babbler, Brown Fulvetta, White-headed Munia, Yellow-breasted and Crimson-breasted Flowerpeckers, Plain and Crimson Sunbirds, Grey-breasted Spiderhunter.

Other Wildlife

Banded langur (orange morph), siamang, yellow-throated marten.

(This is also the site where the 'Sumatran Yeti', a 4 ft tall bipedal primate, known locally as Orang-pendek, has been reported.)

Sungei Penuh, where permits to visit this park must be obtained from the PHPA office, is about 250 km (12–14 hours by bus) southeast of Padang, which is accessible by air or road from Medan, and road from Berestagi (6 hours via Prapat) to the north, and by road from Bangko (5–8 hours by bus) to the east. The best base for birding is Keresek Tua, 1.5 hours by bus from Sungei Penuh, from where it is an hour's hike, or a short motorbike ride, through tea plantations to the trail at the start of the forest on Gunung Kerinci. Motorbike rides can be arranged at Homestay Keluarga Subandi, where there is also a birder's logbook. It may be more worthwhile, however, to stay in the basecamp shelter, just inside the forest, so that birding in the best habitat can begin at dawn, when birds such as Bronze-tailed Peacock-Pheasant* are most likely to be seen. The rare and hyper-elusive Schneider's Pitta* is one of the hardest birds to see in the world, although when flushed from the trail birds have settled at head-height and provided excellent views. Most recent sightings have been in June and July, a little way above and below the basecamp shelter, and in the ravine and along the small trail just below the first shelter, a 2–3 hour climb from the basecamp shelter. Species seemingly restricted to higher altitudes (above and below the first shelter) include Dusky Woodcock. Prepare to work hard for the birds here on a steep trail that is usually muddier than most. Away from the mountain, Waterfall Swift*, Blue-masked Leafbird* and Sunda Forktail occur at the Letter-W waterfall, east of Keresek Tua.

Accommodation: Keresek Tua — Homestay Keluarga Subandi. Sungei Penuh — Mata Hari Losmen.

The blue and black Sumatran Cochoa is one of Sumatra's most beautiful endemics*

The endemic Blue-masked Leafbird* occurs in the roadside forest above **Mauro Sako**, a small village 3 hours by bus from Sungei Penuh towards Padang. The forest here is at a lower elevation than that above Keresek Tua in Kerinci-Seblat NP, hence the avifauna is a little different and includes Blyth's Hawk-Eagle, Great Argus, Blue-tailed and Diard's Trogons, Banded Kingfisher, Helmeted Hornbill*, Sumatran Drongo*, Sunda Forktail, Cream-striped and Spot-necked* Bulbuls, Black Laughingthrush, Marbled Wren-Babbler* and Spot-necked Babbler. Mammals such as agile gibbon and tiger are also present, so beware!

Accommodation: Mauro Sako — basic room next to restaurant.

WAY KAMBAS NATIONAL PARK

The selectively logged lowland forest, grassland and riverine pools in this large park (1235 sq km) in southeast Sumatra support a similar avifauna to that of Taman Negara in Malaysia (p. 198). As is the case at Taman Negara, the birds of Way Kambas include many malkohas, hornbills, woodpeckers, broadbills, bulbuls and babblers, as well as spe-

WAY KAMBAS NP

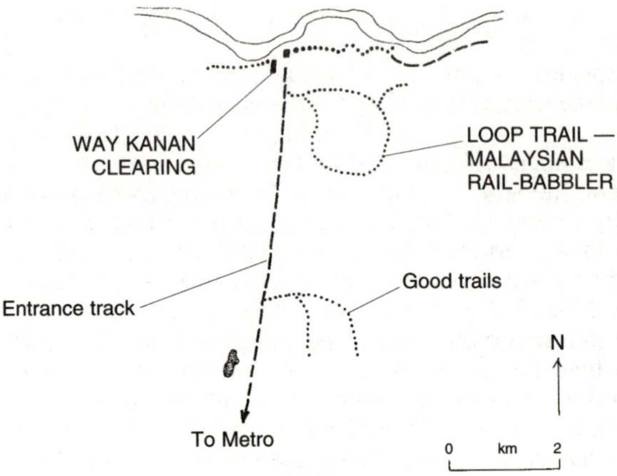

cialities such as Malaysian Rail-babbler, but the exceptions here include White-winged Duck* and Long-billed Blue-Flycatcher*.

Specialities

White-winged Duck*, Storm's Stork*, Ferruginous Partridge, Crested Fireback*, Reddish Scops-Owl, Gould's and Sunda Frogmouths, Wrinkled Hornbill*, Sunda Woodpecker, Dusky Broadbill, Malaysian Rail-babbler, Long-billed Blue-Flycatcher*, Grey-breasted Babbler*, Javan Munia.

Others

Oriental Darter*, Lesser Adjutant*, Lesser Fish-Eagle*, Black-thighed Falconet, Crested Partridge, Cinnamon-headed Pigeon*, Little Green-Pigeon, Blue-rumped Parrot*, Blue-crowned Hanging-Parrot, Violet Cuckoo, Black-bellied, Chestnut-bellied, Raffles', Red-billed and Chestnut-breasted Malkohas, Brown Wood-Owl, Malaysian Nightjar, Grey-rumped and Whiskered Treeswifts, Silver-rumped Needletail, Blue-eared and Banded Kingfishers, Red-bearded and Blue-throated Bee-eaters, Black, Rhinoceros, Helmeted* and Bushy-crested Hornbills, Gold-whiskered, Red-crowned* and Brown Barbets, White-bellied, Crimson-winged, Checker-throated, Maroon, Orange-backed, Buff-rumped, Buff-necked and Grey-and-buff Woodpeckers, Banded Pitta, Black-and-red, Banded, Black-and-yellow and Green Broadbills, Black Magpie*, Green Iora, Dark-throated Oriole, Lesser Cuckoo-Shrike, Fiery Minivet, Rufous-winged Philentoma, Grey-chested Jungle-Flycatcher, Malaysian Blue-Flycatcher*, Rufous-tailed Shama, Olive-winged, Cream-vented, Red-eyed, Spectacled, Yellow-bellied, Hairy-backed and Buff-vented Bulbuls, Rufous-tailed and Ashy Tailorbirds, White-chested*, Ferruginous*, Short-tailed, Black-capped, Moustached, Sooty-capped and Scaly-crowned Babblers, Chestnut-backed Scimitar-Babbler, Black-throated, Chestnut-rumped and Chestnut-winged Babblers, Fluffy-backed Tit-Babbler, White-bellied Munia, Plain, Ruby-cheeked, Purple-throated and Crimson Sunbirds, Little Spiderhunter.

Other Wildlife

Asian elephant, banded leaf-monkey, dark-handed gibbon, pig-tailed macaque, red giant flying squirrel, siamang, silvered leaf-monkey, slow loris.

(Other species recorded here include Malayan Night-Heron, Milky Stork*, Large Green-Pigeon* and Buffy Fish-Owl.)

The park is accessible by road and track from Tanjung Karang, near Bakauheni, the southern gateway to Sumatra, which is connected to Jakarta by air and sea (via Bakauhuni), and to Sungei Penuh in central Sumatra (see previous site) by road (22 hours via Bangko). Head to Metro, then towards Way Jepara, and turn off at the village of Raja Basalam, 15 km before Way Jepara, on to the 12 km entrance track. It is possible to hire a motorbike in the village to travel the 12 km to Way Kanan where the accommodation is, but the entrance track is well worth birding (beware of elephants). From Way Kanan bird the small trails (beware of leeches) and the river (by boat). White-winged Duck* is most reliably seen 30 minutes upstream from Way Kanan in the swampy areas at Rawagajah, where there is a small observation hut, and at Rawapasir, which is 1 hour upstream. Rawagajah is also a good area for Wrinkled Hornbill* and White-chested Babbler*, while the elusive Storm's Stork* has been recorded at Rawapasir, as well as in pools alongside the entrance track, and, most frequently, flying overhead.

Accommodation: Way Kanan — chalets (B/basic/take food).

CHRISTMAS ISLAND

Red-tailed and White-tailed (apricot race) Tropicbirds, Christmas Island Frigatebird*, Abbott's* (road along north side of island) and Red-footed Boobies, Brown Goshawk, Christmas Island Imperial-Pigeon* (central plateau), Moluccan Hawk-Owl and Christmas Island White-eye* all occur on Christmas Island and the best time to see them is August. The island, which is Australian territory, is 360 km south of Java, accessible by air from Jakarta, Java, Kuala Lumpur, Malaya and Perth, Australia. For more information write to Administration for the Territory of Christmas Island, Government Offices, Christmas Island, Indian Ocean, WA 6798, Australia.

The **Cocos (Keeling) Islands**, 900 km southwest of Christmas Island, support White-tailed Tropicbird, Masked Booby and Common White-Tern. They are also Australian territory and accessible by air from Perth. For more information write to Administration for the Territory of the Cocos (Keeling) Islands, Government Offices, Cocos (Keeling) Islands, Indian Ocean, WA 6799, Australia.

JAVA

Despite the fact that Java accounts for a mere 7% of the land area of Indonesia, 60% of the archipelago's population lives on this grossly overpopulated island. Hence very little of the natural lowland habitats remain and virtually all of the endemics, which are mostly montane species, are confined to remnant forests on the steepest slopes, especially those in Gunung Gede-Pangrango NP. Over 430 species have been recorded.

The western end of the island is accessible by sea from Padang (31 hours to Tanjung Priok, Jakarta) or Bakauheni (1.5 hours to Merak) in Sumatra, and from Tanjung Pinang (36 hours to Tanjung Priok, Jakarta), an island 2.5 hours by ferry from Singapore. The eastern end of the island can be reached from Gilimanuk (30 minutes to Ketapang, 8 km from Banyuwangi) in Bali. **Jakarta**, the huge, sprawling capital city of Java, at the western end of the island, lies close to some fine, but fast disappearing, wetlands where Christmas Island Frigatebird*, Milky Stork*, Javan Plover*, Sunda Coucal*, Small Blue Kingfisher, Black-winged Starling* and Bar-winged Prinia occur, as well as Javan Pond-Heron, Yellow, Cinnamon and Black Bitterns, Ruddy-breasted and White-browed Crakes, Island Collared-Dove, Chestnut Munia and Streaked and Asian Golden* Weavers. The best birding areas near the city are the wet fields near Cilincing, east of Tanjung Priok (head for the Madura Wood Company), the pools alongside airport road (difficult to access) and the large heron and cormorant colony at Pulau Dua, near Banten (3 hours by bus west of Jakarta), where Milky Stork* and Javan White-eye* are most likely.

Black-naped Fruit-Dove and Java Sparrow*, as well as Grey-cheeked Pigeon, Sooty-headed Bulbul, Bar-winged Prinia, Javan Munia and Scarlet-headed Flowerpecker occur in **Bogor Botanical Gardens**, 60 km south of Jakarta and 45 km northeast of Gunung Gede-Pangrango NP (see below). The gardens are in the centre of the town and best avoided at weekends. If travelling by bus in Java, while in Bogor it is wise to buy a ticket to Wonorejo, the gateway to Baluran NP in east Java, in advance.

Accommodation: Firman Pensione.

GUNUNG GEDE-PANGRANGO NATIONAL PARK

The forested slopes of Gede and Pangrango volcanoes, which rise to 3019 m (9905 ft), in west Java, support 15 of the 20 Javan endemics, many of the species confined to Sumatra, Java and Bali, including Dusky Woodcock, Blue-tailed Trogon and Sunda Forktail, and a superb assortment of more widespread but localised specialities such as Island Thrush, Blue Nuthatch, Chestnut-fronted Shrike-Babbler, Tawny-breasted and Pin-tailed Parrotfinches and Mountain Serin. Taking into account the presence of so many good birds and the fact that most are easy to see, this is easily the best birding site on Java and one of the finest in Indonesia.

Javan Endemics

Javan Hawk-Eagle*, Chestnut-bellied Partridge, Javan Scops-Owl*, Volcano Swiftlet*, Brown-throated Barbet*, Rufous-tailed and White-bellied* Fantails, Javan Cochoa*, Pygmy Tit, Javan Tesia, Rufous-front-

GUNUNG GEDE-PANGRANGO NP

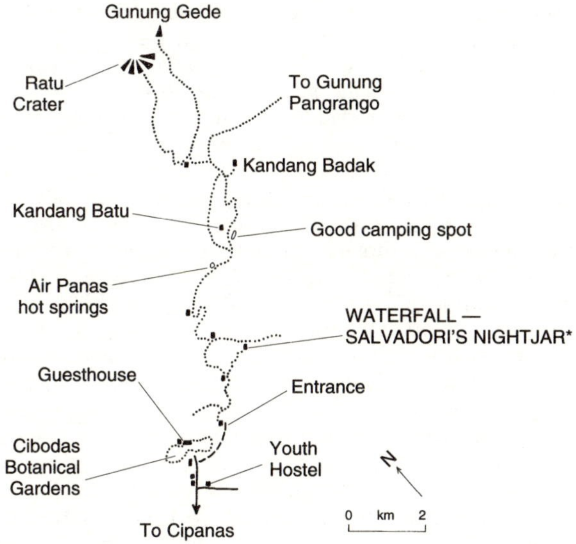

ed Laughingthrush*, White-bibbed Babbler, Javan Fulvetta, Spotted Crocias*, White-flanked Sunbird.

Specialities

Dusky Woodcock, Green-spectacled Pigeon*, Yellow-throated Hanging-Parrot*, Rajah Scops-Owl, Salvadori's Nightjar*, Waterfall Swift*, Blue-tailed Trogon, Flame-fronted Barbet, Sunda Cuckoo-Shrike, Sunda Minivet, Sunda Whistling-Thrush, Sunda, Horsfield's and Island Thrushes, Indigo Flycatcher, Sunda Robin, Sunda Forktail, Blue Nuthatch, Orange-spotted and Sunda Bulbuls, Javan Grey-throated White-eye, Bar-winged Prinia, Sunda Warbler, Crescent-chested Babbler, Chestnut-fronted Shrike-Babbler, Tawny-breasted and Pin-tailed Parrotfinches, Javan Munia, Blood-breasted and Scarlet-headed Flowerpeckers, Mountain Serin.

Others

Spotted Kestrel, Wedge-tailed Pigeon, Cave Swiftlet, Crimson-winged and Orange-backed Woodpeckers, Banded Broadbill, Lesser Cuckoo-Shrike, Siberian Thrush (Nov–Mar), Lesser Shortwing, White-crowned Forktail, Sunda Bush-Warbler, Mountain Leaf-Warbler, Yellow-bellied Warbler, Horsfield's Babbler, Chestnut-backed Scimitar-Babbler, Eyebrowed and Pygmy Wren-Babblers, White-browed Shrike-Babbler, Little Spiderhunter.

Other Wildlife

Crab-eating macaque, Javan gibbon, Javan stink badger, red giant flying squirrel, Sunda leaf-monkey.

(Other species recorded here include Pink-headed Fruit-Dove, Dark-backed Imperial-Pigeon, Javan Kingfisher and Short-tailed Magpie*.)

The park is accessible by road from Jakarta (2.5 hours by bus) via Bogor and Cipanas. Permits to enter the forest must be obtained on a daily basis from the office in the Cibodas Botanical Gardens, 4 km uphill from Cipanas. The botanical gardens, which are situated at 1400 m (4593 ft), are worth a good look, but it is best to concentrate on the trails through the forest above. It is usually necessary to visit the waterfall (Cibeureum) at dawn to see Waterfall Swift*, and at dusk for Salvadori's Nightjar*, although the nightjar has been seen in the trees above the waterfall during daylight. Dusky Woodcock occurs around the open areas much higher up, above and below Kandang Badak at 2400 m (7874 ft). There is a ruined house and a hut here, both of which are used by climbers and birders for shelter, although a tent would-be more suitable for would be woodcock watchers. Above Kandang Badak the elfin moss forest supports Chestnut-bellied Partridge and Horsfield's Thrush, and above there (several hours walk from the botanical gardens) it is possible to reach the Ratu Crater of the Gede volcano, where the endemic Volcano Swiftlet* and Javan Grey-throated White-eye occur.

Accommodation: guesthouse (A/B) in the botanical gardens.

Four endemics (Javan Frogmouth*, Black-banded Barbet, White-breasted Babbler* and Grey-cheeked Tit-Babbler) occur at **Carita** on Java's west coast. Other species recorded here include Javan Owlet, Banded and Javan Kingfishers, a distinctive and spectacular race of Banded Pitta, Racket-tailed Treepie, Chestnut-capped Thrush, Fulvous-chested Jungle-Flycatcher and Large Wren-Babbler*. Carita is an expensive beach resort 7 km north of Labuhan, which is accessible by road from Jakarta (4 hours) and Bogor, via Panderglang. From Carita, accessible by bemo, head inland and bird alongside the track through degraded dry lowland forest, which continues as a path through better forest to a waterfall, a couple of hours away. It is possible to visit Krakatau from Labuhan, where in 1883 the biggest volcanic eruption of recent times occured. **Ujung Kulon NP** in Java's southwest corner is an expensive place to get to, but it does support a fine selection of lowland specialities, including Green Junglefowl, Green Peafowl* and White-breasted Babbler*, as well as Great-billed Heron*, Beach Thick-knee, Ruddy Kingfisher and Banded Pitta. The park's major mammalian attraction, the rare Javan rhinoceros, is very difficult to see. The park is accessible by boat from Labuhan, where it is necessary to obtain a permit and book accommodation in advance at the PHPA office on the road 2 km towards Carita.

Green Junglefowl and Black-banded Barbet have been recorded in the small, forested NP on the headland just south of **Pangandaran**, a popular tourist resort on the south coast. This town is accessible by road from Bogor, via Banjar. **Segara Anakan**, a huge tidal lagoon to the east of Pangandaran, is one of the few sites where Sunda Coucal* has been recorded in the recent past. The lagoon is only accessible by boat (ask at Kalipucang, 17 km northeast of Pangandaran) and the coucal has been seen around Cibelus Island at the eastern edge. Other species recorded in the Kalipucang area include Sunda Teal, Milky Stork*, Lesser Adjutant*, Small Blue and Javan Kingfishers, Racket-tailed Treepie and Streaked Weaver. (Sunda Coucal* has also been recorded around Indramaya, on the north coast of Java near Ciberon, along with Javan White-eye*.)

BALURAN NATIONAL PARK

This area of open, lowland deciduous forest, grassland and acacia savanna at the eastern end of Java is probably the most accessible site in the world for Green Peafowl*. Apart from this species and the endemic Grey-cheeked Tit-Babbler, the avifauna is otherwise virtually identical to that of Bali Barat NP (p. 142), just across the water in Bali, although one vital ingredient, Bali Myna*, is missing.

Javan Endemics

Grey-cheeked Tit-Babbler.

Specialities

Green Junglefowl, Green Peafowl*, Oriental Bay-Owl, Small Blue and Javan Kingfishers, Racket-tailed Treepie, Javan Cuckoo-Shrike, White-shouldered Triller, Black-winged Starling*, Crescent-chested Babbler, Java Sparrow* (Aug–Oct), Scarlet-headed Flowerpecker.

Others

Black-thighed Falconet, Island Collared-Dove, Zebra Dove, Orange-breasted and Grey-cheeked Pigeons, Red-breasted Parakeet, Barred Eagle-Owl, Buffy Fish-Owl, Brown Wood-Owl, Savanna Nightjar, Grey-rumped Treeswift, Banded Kingfisher, Wreathed Hornbill, Coppersmith Barbet, Fulvous-breasted Woodpecker, Common Flameback, Banded Pitta, Small Minivet, Asian Fairy-bluebird, Asian Glossy and Asian Pied Starlings, Hill and Mangrove Blue-Flycatchers, Brown Prinia, Horsfield's Babbler, Australasian Bushlark.

Other Wildlife

Banteng, silver leaf-monkey, Timor deer.

Baluran is easier to get to from Bali (via the Gilimanuk–Banyuwangi Ferry) than west Java, which is a very long bus or train ride away. The park entrance is at Wonorejo (Wolorejo), which is accessible by road from Banyuwangi. From Wonorejo it is 12 km to Bekol where the hostel is situated. The best time to see Green Peafowl* is between August and October when they are displaying, and when the park is dry enough to force them in to visiting the waterholes more regularly. They can also be seen going to roost from the watchtower. Grey-cheeked Tit-Babbler occurs in the forest patch by the beach.

Accommodation: Bekol — hostel (basic/take food). Beach (2 km from Bekol) — hostel (basic/take food).

BALI

To some people this island is a tropical paradise, to others it is an over-crowded, ecologically degraded, westernised holiday resort. Land birds are scarce, mainly because the island is largely deforested, and although they include the gravely endangered Bali Myna* it is virtually impossible to see this beautiful bird because the only place where they occur is currently closed to casual visitors.

BALI BARAT NATIONAL PARK

The open, lowland deciduous forest within this park (777 sq km), which lies next to the coast in northwest Bali, is the only site in the world where Bali Myna* occurs. Around 40 birds maintain a toehold on existence here, but because they are still the target of hunters and collectors, the areas within the park where they occur are currently out of bounds to all casual visitors, including birders. However, the park and its surrounds are still worth visiting for the off chance of seeing the snow-white myna, and because Great-billed Heron*, Beach Thick-knee, Javan Plover* and Yellow-bellied White-eye also possible. Otherwise, the avifauna is very similar to that of Baluran NP, just across the water in Java (p. 141).

BALI BARAT NP

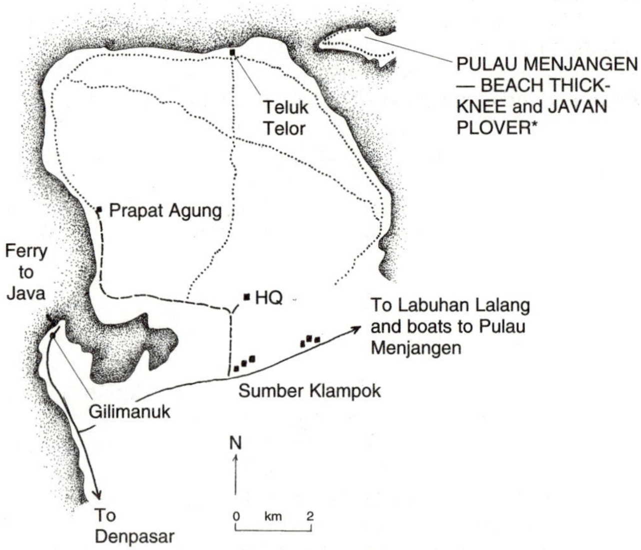

Bali Endemics

Bali Myna*.

Specialities

Great-billed Heron*, Green Junglefowl, Beach Thick-knee, Javan Plover*, Yellow-throated Hanging-Parrot*, Small Blue and Javan Kingfishers, Sunda Woodpecker, Javan Cuckoo-Shrike, White-shouldered Triller, Black-winged Starling*, Yellow-bellied White-eye, Javan Munia, Java Sparrow*.

Others

Lesser Frigatebird, Wandering Whistling-Duck, Lesser Adjutant*, Brahminy Kite, Grey-headed Fish-Eagle*, Rufous-bellied Eagle, Black-thighed Falconet, Great Crested-Tern, Black-naped Tern, Island Collared-

Dove, Zebra Dove, Orange-breasted Pigeon, Buffy Fish-Owl, Savanna Nightjar, Grey-rumped Treeswift, Blue-tailed and Chestnut-headed Bee-eaters, Coppersmith Barbet, Fulvous-breasted Woodpecker, Banded Pitta, Golden-bellied Gerygone, Mangrove Whistler, Pied Fantail, White-breasted Woodswallow, Small Minivet, Fulvous-chested Jungle-Flycatcher, Horsfield's Babbler, Australasian Bushlark.

Other Wildlife

Silver leaf-monkey.

Bali Barat is accessible by road from Denpasar, the capital of Bali, or by ferry from Java. For the latest information on whether or not it is possible to look for Bali Myna*, inquire at the PHPA office in Labuhan Lalang, 16 km east of Gilimanuk, where the ferry from Java docks. Otherwise bird around Gilimanuk where the mud flats and mangroves are worth checking for shorebirds, and on the island of **Pulau Menjangen** where Beach Thick-knee, Javan Plover* and Yellow-bellied White-eye occur. This island is not always accessible (ask in Labuhan Lalang).

Accommodation: Gilimanuk, Labuhan Lalang.

The beautiful Bali Myna is one of the rarest birds in the world*

BEDUGUL

The remnant montane forests around the crater lakes near Bedugul in Bali's central highlands support Indonesian Honeyeater, the only member of its family west of Wallace's Line, and some localised species such as Dark-backed Imperial-Pigeon.

Specialities

Black-backed Fruit-Dove, Dark-backed Imperial-Pigeon, Yellow-throated Hanging-Parrot*, Flame-fronted Barbet, Indonesian Honeyeater, Sunda Whistling-Thrush, Orange-spotted Bulbul, Javan Grey-throated White-eye, Sunda Warbler, Crescent-chested Babbler, Javan Munia, Blood-breasted Flowerpecker.

Others

White-browed Crake, Grey-cheeked Pigeon, Golden Whistler, Orange-headed Thrush, Lesser Shortwing, Asian Glossy Starling, Fulvous-chested Jungle-Flycatcher, Sunda Bush-Warbler, Mountain Leaf-Warbler, Chestnut-backed Scimitar-Babbler.

(Other species recorded here include Sunda Thrush.)

Bird the botanical gardens (take the first track on left once through main gate) and the forest around Bali Handara Country Club.

Accommodation: Bali Handara Country Club and numerous Losmen to choose from.

DENPASAR

Bali's capital lies close to the island's main tourist beaches, as well as mud flats, mangroves and some fishponds, where a surprisingly good variety of birds occur. Scarce species such as Great-billed Heron* and Javan Plover* have been recorded, as well as a good selection of wintering shorebirds such as Far Eastern Curlew* and Asian Dowitcher*.

Specialities

Christmas Island Frigatebird*, Great-billed Heron*, Javan Plover*, Small Blue Kingfisher, Bar-winged Prinia, Javan Munia.

Others

Lesser Frigatebird, Little Pied Cormorant, Sunda Teal, White-faced Heron, Pacific Reef-Egret, Javan Pond-Heron, Ruddy-breasted and White-browed Crakes, Far Eastern Curlew* (Nov–Mar), Grey-tailed Tattler (Nov–Mar), Asian Dowitcher* (Nov–Mar), Rufous-necked (Nov–Mar) and Long-toed (Nov–Mar) Stints, Oriental Pratincole (Nov–Mar), Island Collared-Dove, Little Cuckoo-Dove, Zebra Dove, Savanna Nightjar, Grey-rumped Treeswift, Cave Swiftlet, Sacred Kingfisher, Blue-tailed Bee-eater, Golden-bellied Gerygone, Grey-cheeked Bulbul, White-headed Munia, Red Avadavat, Streaked Weaver.

The gardens of the hotels in **Sanur** and **Nusa Dua** are worth a look, but most of the best birds to be seen in this area can be found at the mud flats and mangroves near Benoa Port (at the end of a 2 km long causeway at the north side of Benoa Bay), on the mud flats opposite Pulau Serangan (Turtle Island), accessible on foot along the beach from Sanur or by track from near the Surya Beach Hotel in Tanjung (Javan Plover), and around the fishponds at Suwung, 5 km or so south of Sanur, alongside the road to the airport.

Accommodation: many hotels, etc.

The localised Javan Kingfisher occurs at the paddies around **Ubud**, in the foothills of the central highlands, 25 km north of Denpasar. White-tailed Tropicbird may breed on the cliffs at **Ulu Watu** on the tip of the Bukit Peninsula, south of Denpasar.

LESSER SUNDAS (NUSA TENGGARA)

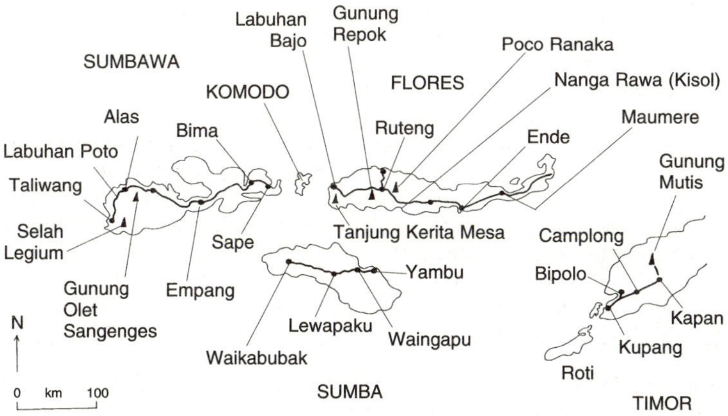

The islands east of Bali, including Lombok, Sumbawa, Komodo, Flores, Lembata (Lomblen), Alor, Timor and Sumba are known as the Lesser Sundas or Nusa Tenggara. Most are accessible by air and ferry, but even though some of the islands have been on the tourist circuit for some time now, many of the endemic birds are restricted to the forests, most of which lie off the beaten track at some distance from towns. Hence to see these birds a spirit of adventure is needed and it may be necessary in some places to camp or to stay with the local people. At such sites always seek permission from the chief of the nearest village to go birding, and ask if it is possible to stay in their village. The people are almost invariably very friendly and helpful.

LOMBOK

Lombok is accessible by ferry (4 hours) from Padanbai, east Bali. This island has no endemics, but Black-backed Fruit-Dove, White-rumped Kingfisher, Elegant Pitta, Sunda Honeyeater, Wallacean Drongo, Chestnut-backed and Sunda Thrushes, and Red-chested Flowerpecker have been recorded on the slopes of **Gunung Rinjani** volcano. This is Lombok's highest mountain at 3726 m (12,224 ft) and it is accessible by trail from Batu Koq and Senaru in the north of the island. From Senaru it is a 6 hour trek to basecamp and a further 2 hours to the rim.

SUMBAWA

The mountainous island of Sumbawa has no endemic species, but it supports a few species which otherwise only occur on Flores and Sumba. Labuhan Poto, at the western end of the island, is accessible by ferry (2 hours) from Lombok. Milky Stork*, Beach Thick-knee, Javan Plover*, Small Blue Kingfisher and Flame-breasted Sunbird occur around the rivermouth at **Labuhan Lalar** to the west of Taliwang, south of Labuhan Poto. Two good forested areas at the western end of the island are the lowland forest at **Selah Legium** (Selalu Legini) and the lowland and montane forests at **Gunung Olet Sangenges**. Species recorded at both sites include Wallace's Scops-Owl*, White-rumped Kingfisher, Elegant Pitta, Bare-throated Whistler, Brown-capped Fantail, Sumba Cuckoo-Shrike*, Flores Minivet, Chestnut-backed Thrush, Yellow-spectacled, Dark-crowned* and Flores White-eyes, Russet-capped Tesia, Golden-rumped and Black-fronted Flowerpeckers and Flame-breasted Sunbird. Otherwise, Nicobar Pigeon*, Flores Green-Pigeon*, Yellow-crested Cockatoo*, Sunda Honeyeater and Flores Jungle-Flycatcher* have only been recorded at Selah Legium and Dark-backed Imperial-Pigeon and White-browed White-eye only at Gunung Olet. At Selah Legium bird inland from the coastal village of Babar, especially around the Batu Hijau mining camp and the meteorological station. At Gunung Olet bird the Aipok Ridge, about 5 km from the village of Marente, which is 3 km from the town of Alas. Green Junglefowl, Flores Green-Pigeon*, Yellow-crested Cockatoo*, Small Blue and White-rumped Kingfishers, Elegant Pitta, Brown-capped Fantail, Flores Minivet, Russet-capped Tesia, Dark-crowned* and Flores White-eyes, and Golden-rumped Flowerpecker have been recorded near the village of **Empang** in the centre of the island, in forest, which may still exist, 2 hour's walk to the southeast.

Red-tailed Tropicbird has been seen from the Sumbawa–Flores ferry, which travels between Sape (Sumbawa) and Labuhan Bajo (Flores) and takes 8 hours. Some ferries stop at **Komodo Island**, a national park which is more easily accessible by boat from Labuhan Bajo (4 hours) on Flores, or Bima on Sumbawa. This island of parched hills and dry gullies is famous for its monstrous monitor lizards known as Komodo dragons. Although seeing these magnificent beasts is easy, it usually involves watching them come to bait, in the form of a tethered goat, and some people have not enjoyed the experience, which resembles 'feeding time at the zoo'. Komodo is a good place to see Yellow-crested Cockatoo*, and the ferry crossing provides the chance of seeing seabirds such as Bulwer's Petrel, Streaked Shearwater, Lesser Frigatebird, Black-naped Tern and, sometimes, Red-tailed Tropicbird, as well as Great-billed Heron* and dolphins including spinner dolphin. It is worth birding around the HQ at Loh Liang, which is a 30 minute walk north of Kampung Komodo village, where the ferry from Flores docks. Other birds present on the island include Orange-footed Scrubfowl, Yellow-spectacled White-eye, Golden-rumped and Black-fronted Flowerpeckers and Flame-breasted Sunbird.

FLORES

This rugged volcanic island supports some of the best forest in the Lesser Sundas, and four endemics: Wallace's Hanging-Parrot*, Flores Scops-Owl*, Flores Monarch* and Flores Crow*.

Secondary forest, mangroves and mud flats near **Labuhan Bajo**, at the western end of the island, support Green Junglefowl, Beach Thick-knee and Wallacean Cuckoo-Shrike. Three endemics (Wallace's Hanging-

Parrot*, Flores Monarch* and Flores Crow*) occur at **Tanjung Kerita Mese** near Paku in southwest Flores, where some 15,000 ha of lowland forest still remain. Bird the Mata Wae Ndeo area, adjacent to the small village of Paku (13 km from the village of Werang) and around the small village of Kampung Langka on the plain below Mata Wae Ndeo.

RUTENG

The montane forest on the active volcano of Poco Ranaka, the second highest peak on Flores at 2140 m (7021 ft), does not support any endemics, but the restricted range species present here include Sunda Thrush, four species of white-eye and Tawny-breasted Parrotfinch.

Specialities

Black-backed Fruit-Dove, Dark-backed Imperial-Pigeon, Wallace's Scops-Owl*, White-rumped Kingfisher, Sunda Woodpecker, Elegant Pitta, Sunda Honeyeater, Bare-throated Whistler, Brown-capped Fantail, Wallacean Drongo, Sumba Cuckoo-Shrike*, Flores Minivet, Chestnut-backed and Sunda Thrushes, Short-tailed Starling, Flores Jungle-Flycatcher*, Yellow-spectacled, White-browed, Dark-crowned* and Flores White-eyes, Russet-capped Tesia, Timor Leaf-Warbler, Tawny-breasted Parrotfinch, Five-coloured Munia, Golden-rumped, Black-fronted and Blood-breasted Flowerpeckers.

Others

Red-cheeked Parrot, Mountain White-eye, Yellow-breasted Warbler, Pygmy Wren-Babbler.

The town of Ruteng, in west Flores, is accessible by road (5 hours) from Labuhan Bajo, or by air from Kupang, Timor. Bird alongside the road south of the Golo Lusang Pass, which is about 7 km south of Ruteng, and the 9 km road from Kampung Robo to the transmitter station on Poco Ranaka, to the east of town. There may still be some forest near **Mano**, which can be reached in less than an hour from Ruteng by heading east towards Bajawa and taking the left fork after Mano to Benteng Jawa. The montane forest on **Gunung Repok**, southwest of Ruteng, also supports similar species to those listed above, and is accessible from Kampung Repok.

Accommodation: Ruteng — Wisma Dahlia, Hotel Sindha.

KISOL

This village near the south coast of Flores lies at the base of Gunung Pacendeki, an isolated forested mountain which rises from coastal scrub and gallery forest which support Flores Green-Pigeon* and Flores Crow*.

Flores Endemics

Flores Crow*.

Specialities

Green Junglefowl, Flores Green-Pigeon*, Yellow-crested Cockatoo*, Wallace's Scops-Owl*, White-rumped Kingfisher, Elegant Pitta, Brown-capped Fantail, Wallacean Drongo, Wallacean and Sumba* Cuckoo-Shrikes, Flores Minivet, Chestnut-backed Thrush, Yellow-spectacled, Dark-crowned* and Flores White-eyes, Russet-capped Tesia, Black-faced Munia, Golden-rumped and Black-fronted Flowerpeckers, Flame-breasted Sunbird.

Others

Little Pied Cormorant, Pacific Baza, Spotted Kestrel, Orange-footed Scrubfowl, Metallic Pigeon, Island Collared-Dove, Barred Dove, Black-naped Fruit-Dove, Rainbow Lorikeet, Moluccan Scops-Owl, Helmeted Friarbird, Golden Whistler, Plain-throated Sunbird.

Gunung Pacendeki is accessible via the road south from Kisol, which is on the Ruteng–Bajawa road. Before reaching a banana plantation, 3 km south of Kisol, a bad road leads east then south for 12 km to the coastal village of Nanga Rawa. It is possible to hire an expensive 4WD at the Catholic Seminary to visit the wooded ravines west of here where Flores Crow* occurs. Also bird the valley west of the banana plantation where White-rumped Kingfisher, Elegant Pitta and Chestnut-backed Thrush have been recorded.

Accommodation: none, but the Catholic Seminary may be persuaded to take guests, especially those with letters of introduction.

The main tourist attraction on Flores is the three crater lakes of **Keli Mutu** volcano in the centre of the island. The forest near the summit, 13 km from the village of Moni, supports White-rumped Kingfisher, Flores Jungle-Flycatcher* and Tawny-breasted Parrotfinch. From Ende, near Moni and 6 hours by bus east of Kisol, it is possible to fly to Kupang on Timor. Otherwise occasional ferries leave Ende and Larantuka (at the eastern end of Flores) for Kupang.

Chestnut-backed Thrush is a typically striking Zoothera *thrush which occurs at a number of sites on Sumbawa, Flores and Sumba*

SUMBA

By 1992 only 10% of Sumba's forest had survived the axe and the island is now primarily covered in rough pasture, hence the eight endemics which are forest species include some of the rarest birds in the world.

Even the remaining endemic, Sumba Buttonquail*, appears to be rare. The best time to visit Sumba is in September, at the end of the dry season.

WAINGAPU

Sumba's main town lies close to patches of gallery forest, dry grassland, scrub, mangroves and mud flats where three endemics occur, including Sumba Buttonquail*.

Sumba Endemics

Sumba Buttonquail*, Sumba Green-Pigeon*, Apricot-breasted Sunbird.

Specialities

Malaysian Plover*, White-shouldered Triller, Yellow-spectacled White-eye.

Others

Brown and Blue-breasted Quails, Red-backed Buttonquail, Barred Dove, Sacred Kingfisher, Australasian Bushlark, Five-coloured and Pale-headed Munias, Plain-throated Sunbird.

Sumba Buttonquail* has been recorded in the dry grassland either side of the road near Yumba, 5 km east of Watumbaka, east Waingapu. Malaysian Plover* has been recorded at the mouth of the Melolo River near Melolo, east of Waingapu.

Accommodation: camping.

LEWAPAKU

Remnant forest near Lewapaku supports all of Sumba's forest-dwelling endemics, as well as Elegant Pitta and Chestnut-backed Thrush.

Sumba Endemics

Sumba Green-Pigeon*, Red-naped Fruit-Dove*, Sumba Boobook*, Sumba Hornbill*, Sumba Myzomela, Sumba Brown* and Sumba* Flycatchers, Apricot-breasted Sunbird.

Specialities

Green Junglefowl, Yellow-crested Cockatoo*, Elegant Pitta, Wallacean Drongo, Wallacean and Sumba* Cuckoo-shrikes, Chestnut-backed Thrush, Flores Jungle-Flycatcher*, Yellow-spectacled White-eye, Blood-breasted Flowerpecker.

Others

White-faced Heron, Brown Goshawk, Spotted Kestrel, Orange-footed Scrubfowl, Brown Quail, Red-backed Buttonquail, Little Cuckoo-Dove, Red-cheeked, Great-billed and Eclectus Parrots, Rainbow Lorikeet, Channel-billed Cuckoo, Blue-tailed and Rainbow Bee-eaters, Helmeted Friarbird, Golden Whistler, Rufous Fantail, Short-tailed Starling, Red Avadavat.

(Other species recorded here include an unidentified scops-owl.)

Lewapaku is 51 km west of Waingapu. Bird the forest to the south of the road 7 km east of Lewapaku and along the side-road at km 48.

Accommodation: camping.

Sumba Green-Pigeon*, Red-naped Fruit-Dove*, Sumba Boobook*, Sumba Hornbill*, Sumba Flycatcher* and Apricot-breasted Sunbird have also been recorded in the southeast corner of the island, along with Spectacled Monarch and Ashy-bellied White-eye, at **Pengadu-hahar** north of Baing, and in the **Tabundung–Laiwangi** area near Pringkareha.

TIMOR

Timor is the largest and most easterly of the Lesser Sundas. It lies 500 km northwest of Darwin and one of the major habitats, arid savanna, resembles much of northwest Australia. However, there are also lowland and montane forests, and more endemics are present here than on any other island in the Lesser Sundas. It is very difficult and perhaps unwise to get into troubled east Timor, but, fortunately, all 11 endemics can be seen in the safe southwest corner.

Sunda Teal, Ashy-bellied White-eye, Black-faced and Five-coloured Munias and Flame-breasted Sunbird occur in and around **Kupang**, the main town in the southwest. Most of the remnant forest patches in west Timor lie within three hours by bemo from Kupang. The nearest area is around **Buan**, where Black-breasted Myzomela*, Orange-banded Thrush*, Timor Blue-Flycatcher, Timor Stubtail*, Buff-banded Bushbird* and Red-chested Flowerpecker occur.

BIPOLO

The evergreen coastal forest near this small town north of Kupang, together with surrounding scrub and farmland, supports six Timor endemics, including Timor Green-Pigeon* and Timor Sparrow*.

Timor and Satellite Endemics

Timor Green-Pigeon*, Black-breasted Myzomela*, Streak-breasted Honeyeater*, Timor Friarbird*, Timor Bushchat*, Timor Sparrow*.

Timor and Wetar Endemics

Slaty Cuckoo-Dove*, Olive-shouldered Parrot*, Iris Lorikeet*, Plain Gerygone, Fawn-breasted Whistler*, Timor Oriole, Orange-banded Thrush*, Timor Blue-Flycatcher.

Specialities

Black-backed Fruit-Dove, Pink-headed Imperial-Pigeon, Olive-headed Lorikeet, Cinnamon-backed Kingfisher*, Elegant Pitta, Wallacean

Drongo, Wallacean Cuckoo-Shrike, Ashy-bellied White-eye, Tricoloured Parrotfinch, Flame-breasted Sunbird.

Others

Pacific Baza, Brown Quail, Dusky Cuckoo-Dove, Barred Dove, Red-cheeked Parrot, Rainbow Lorikeet, Morepork, Rainbow Bee-eater, Helmeted Friarbird, Northern and Rufous Fantails, Black-faced Woodswallow, Green Figbird, Short-tailed Starling, Tree Martin, Zebra Finch, Black-faced Munia.

From Kupang head east towards Camplong, then turn north towards Parati at the village of Oelmasi. Bird around Bipolo, especially the forest alongside the river just to the north.

Accommodation: Taupkole — possibly in village (take food and ask permission from village head) or camping (take food).

CAMPLONG

The small town of Camplong lies at the base of Timor's central plateau where nine Timor endemics occur in the remnant semi-deciduous forest, including Black-banded Flycatcher* and Timor White-eye*.

Timor and Satellite Endemics

Yellow-eared Honeyeater, Black-breasted Myzomela*, Streaky-breasted Honeyeater*, Timor Friarbird*, Black-banded Flycatcher*, Timor Bushchat*, Timor White-eye*, Timor Stubtail*, Buff-banded Bushbird*.

Timor and Wetar Endemics

Slaty Cuckoo-Dove*, Olive-shouldered Parrot*, Iris Lorikeet*, Plain Gerygone, Fawn-breasted Whistler*, Timor Oriole, Orange-banded Thrush*, Timor Blue-Flycatcher.

Specialities

Dusky Cuckoo-Dove, Pink-headed Imperial-Pigeon, Cinnamon-backed Kingfisher*, Elegant Pitta, Spectacled Monarch, Wallacean Drongo, Wallacean Cuckoo-Shrike, Ashy-bellied White-eye, Timor Leaf-Warbler, Tricoloured Parrotfinch, Red-chested Flowerpecker.

Others

Brown Goshawk, Metallic Pigeon, Rose-crowned Fruit-Dove, Gould's Bronze-Cuckoo, Australian Koel, Rainbow Bee-eater, Golden Whistler, Northern and Rufous Fantails, Green Figbird, Common Cicadabird, Short-tailed Starling.

Bird alongside the road east out of Camplong towards Soe, which runs through excellent forest for 4–5 km, and side-trails.

Accommodation: Catholic Wisma de Hat Honis.

Timor Imperial-Pigeon* is the island's only montane endemic and it occurs on **Gunung Mutis**, which rises to 2400 m (7874 ft) and which is accessible via a rough road and track north of Kapan. Bird around the end of the road and near the summit where the pigeon, Chestnut-backed, Sunda and Island Thrushes, Sunda and Russet Bush-Warblers and Blood-breasted Flowerpecker occur. Yellow-eared Honeyeater, Black-breasted Myzomela* and Black-banded Flycatcher* have been recorded in the remnant roadside forest 7 km south of **Kapan** on the Soe–Nitibe road.

WETAR

Three species are endemic to this mountainous island, which rises to 1414 m (4639 ft). Two (Black-chested Honeyeater* and Wetar Figbird*) as well as Dusky and Slaty* Cuckoo-Doves, Olive-shouldered Parrot*, Plain Gerygone, Fawn-breasted Whistler*, Timor Oriole and Tricoloured Parrotfinch occur in the logged forest near the coast north of **Perai**. The third endemic, Crimson-hooded Myzomela*, is fairly common in secondary forest and gardens.

TANIMBAR ISLANDS

The Tanimbar Islands, which support 13 endemics, lie in the Banda Sea between Timor and New Guinea. The main town, Saumlaki, on the island of Yamdena, is accessible by air from Ambon (opposite), where it is necessary to obtain a permit from the PHPA office before heading for Tanimbar.

YAMDENA

All of the Tanimbar endemics, plus three of the four species confined to the Tanimbar and Kai Islands, occur on this 45 km wide island.

Tanimbar Endemics

Tanimbar Cockatoo*, Blue-streaked Lory*, Banda Myzomela, Golden-bellied Flyrobin*, Cinnamon-tailed* and Long-tailed* Fantails, Loetoe* and Black-bibbed* Monarchs, White-browed Triller, Slaty-backed* and Fawn-breasted* Thrushes, Tanimbar Starling*, Tanimbar Bush-Warbler*.

Specialities

Great-billed Heron*, Wallace's Fruit-Dove, Elegant and Pink-headed Imperial-Pigeons, Pied Bronze-Cuckoo, Moluccan Hawk-Owl, Cinnamon-backed Kingfisher*, Elegant Pitta, Rufous-sided Gerygone, White-tufted Honeyeater, Black-faced Friarbird, Drab and Wallacean Whistlers, Island Monarch, Buru Oriole, Tricoloured Parrotfinch.

Others

Great and Lesser Frigatebirds, Australian Pelican, Orange-footed Scrubfowl, Dusky Cuckoo-Dove, Wallace's and Rose-crowned Fruit-Doves, Broad-billed Flycatcher.

(Other species recorded here include Lesser Masked-Owl*, which was seen in the south in January 1996.)

The only road on Yamdena runs north from Saumlaki to the forested areas, which can be reached via vehicles with drivers for hire in Saumlaki. About 20 km north of Saumlaki, bird the track to the west, 500 m or so north of the garden compound, and the forest to the east, just south of the tidal channel 15 km north of the compound (Slaty-backed Thrush*). The small islands off Saumlaki Bay support Island Monarch (boats available for hire), while Great-billed Heron* occurs around the bay itself.

Accommodation: Saumlaki — Harapan Indah (B, including food) and Pantai Indah (B, including food).

KAI ISLANDS

The Kai Islands are accessible by air from the Tanimbar Islands and Ambon (below), where it is necessary to obtain a permit from the PHPA office before venturing to Kai. The island of **Tual** supports two of the four endemics (Kai Coucal* and Little Kai White-eye), as well as Great and Lesser Frigatebirds, Red-backed Buttonquail, White-breasted Fruit-Dove, Black-faced Friarbird, Kai Cuckoo-Shrike* (which has also been recorded on the Tanimbar Islands) and Mistletoebird. The town of Tual lies on the island of the same name and is a short distance, via a road bridge, from the airport on the island of Kai Kecil. Most of the birds listed above occur in the remnant forest patch known locally as Taman Angrekk, on the right just before Dullah village (accessible by bus from the harbour). The other two Kai endemics (White-tailed Monarch* and Great Kai White-eye*) are confined to the narrow, rugged island of **Kai Besar**, which is accessible by ferry (2 hours) from Tual. The endemics, as well as Kai Coucal*, occur in the degraded forest around Voko village, accessible by road from Elat where the ferry docks (vehicles are available for hire). Introduce yourself to the village chief here before exploring.

Accommodation: Tual — Hotel Mira (C).

SERAM

Around 200 species, including eight endemics, have been recorded on this wild, mountainous island, which still boasts extensive areas of forest. It is accessible via ferry from **Ambon**, where it is necessary to obtain a permit from the PHPA office before moving on to Seram. There is also a BirdLife International field office here which is worth a visit. Ambon is a major hub for air traffic in Indonesia and it is also accessible by ferry from Jakarta. This sails every 10–12 days, takes 3–4 days and usually stops off at Bau-Bau on Buton Island, off south Sulawesi, where Maleo*, Platen's Rail* and Rusty-backed Thrush* occur. Much of Ambon is deforested, but it is still possible to see the endemic white-eye, as well as Salmon-crested Cockatoo*, Red Lory, Red-flanked Lorikeet, Lazuli Kingfisher and Ashy Flowerpecker around the airport and Haya, while Oriental Plover has been recorded on the airport runways.

MANUSELA NATIONAL PARK

This huge park (1860 sq km), which covers over 10% of Seram, is situated in the centre of the island around Gunung Binaia, which rises to 2490 m (8169 ft). Over 140 species have been recorded in the lowland and mossy, montane forests, including all eight Seram endemics and the four species which are restricted to Seram and Ambon.

It is usually very wet here between October and March.

Seram Endemics

Blue-eared Lory*, Seram Honeyeater, Seram Friarbird, Streaky-breasted Fantail, Seram Oriole, Long-crested Myna, Rufescent and Grey-hooded White-eyes.

Seram and Ambon Endemics

Salmon-crested Cockatoo*, Purple-naped Lory*, Lazuli Kingfisher, Seram Myzomela.

Seram and Buru Endemics

Long-tailed Mountain-Pigeon*, Wakolo Myzomela, Pale-grey Cuckoo-Shrike, Moluccan Thrush*.

Specialities

Southern Cassowary* (possibly feral), Rufous-necked Sparrowhawk, White-eyed and Elegant Imperial-Pigeons, Great-billed Parrot, Moluccan King-Parrot*, Red Lory, Moluccan Scops-Owl, Moluccan Hawk-Owl, Moluccan Swiftlet, Drab Whistler, Moluccan Flycatcher, Moluccan Cuckoo-Shrike, Island Thrush, Cinnamon-chested Flycatcher, Golden Bulbul, Black-crowned White-eye, Chestnut-backed Bush-Warbler, Blue-faced Parrotfinch, Ashy Flowerpecker.

Others

Radjah Shelduck, Pacific Baza, Grey and Meyer's Goshawks, Gurney's Eagle*, Spotted Kestrel, Orange-footed Scrubfowl, Blue-breasted Quail, Rufous-tailed Bush-hen, Metallic Pigeon, Slender-billed and Great Cuckoo-Doves, Nicobar Pigeon*, Superb, White-breasted and Claret-breasted Fruit-Doves, Red-breasted Pygmy-Parrot, Eclectus Parrot, Red-flanked Lorikeet, Moustached Treeswift, Variable Kingfisher, Common Paradise-Kingfisher, Rainbow Bee-eater, Blyth's Hornbill, Red-bellied Pitta, Golden Whistler, Willie-Wagtail, Spectacled Monarch, Common Cicadabird, Moluccan Starling, Island Flycatcher, Mountain White-eye, Gray's Warbler (Nov–Mar), Island Leaf-Warbler, Black-faced Munia, Black Sunbird.

(Lesser Masked-Owl* may also be present on the island.)

The park is accessible from Wahai on the north coast and Moso (via Amahai and Tehoru) on the south coast, both of which are accessible from Tulehu on Ambon by ferry (look out for seabirds such as Streaked Shearwater and Matsudaira's Storm-Petrel). A road was under construction between Tehoru and the park in the early 1990s and, if complete, may afford better access to the area than Wahai. If approaching the park from the south, assuming the road is incomplete, arrange porters and food at Moso before walking to Sinahari village. Bird around Sinahari and above Liang-Liang on the outskirts of the park before continuing to Murkele Ridge (see below).

If arriving in the north, check the secondary coastal forest behind the quay at Air Besar, near Wahai, for Common Paradise-Kingfisher. One of the best areas on Seram for the localised Lazuli Kingfisher is between Wahai and the park entrance to the east. There are few trails around Solea, inside the park, but in the dry season it is possible to walk along the Wae Toluorang River through lowland forest which supports Southern Cassowary*, Streaky-breasted Fantail and Pale-grey Cuckoo-Shrike, while upstream is best for Seram Myzomela, Drab Whistler, Seram Oriole and Long-crested Myna. From Solea it is possible to take truck rides on logging tracks to the villages of Kaloa and Wasa, the access points to the area known as The Enclave where Purple-naped Lory*, Wakolo Myzomela, Cinnamon-chested Flycatcher and Rufescent White-eye occur. The best bases from which to explore the forest in this area are the villages of Manusela (which may accessible by road from the southern port of Tehoru by the time you get there) and Kineke. From Kineke there is a steep trail which ascends the northern slopes of the Merkele Ridge up to mossy montane forest. It will take four days to get to the best habitat and back, but the rewards could be Long-tailed Mountain-Pigeon*, Blue-eared Lory*, Seram Honeyeater and Grey-hooded White-eye. The lower Kobipoto Ridge where the rare Moluccan Thrush* was recorded in 1987 can be reached via an even steeper trail from Solimena.

Accommodation: Wahai — two losmen. Tehoru — Losmen Susi.

Spotted Whistling-Duck, Rufous Night-Heron, White-browed Crake and Comb-crested Jacana occur on and around the small pool at **Air Merah**, 10 km west along the coast road from Wahai, in north Seram. The small islands off Wahai (accessible by boat) support Beach Thick-knee and Olive Honeyeater (both on Pulau Lusaolate), Claret-breasted Fruit-Dove (Pulau Sawai) and Island Monarch (on Pulau Sawai and Pulau Radjah), while Great-billed Herons* frequent the mangroves surrounding these islands.

BURU

This remote island is accessible from Ambon (p. 153), where it is necessary to obtain a permit from the PHPA office before departing for Buru. Seven of Buru's ten endemics (Buru Racquet-tail*, Blue-fronted Lorikeet*, Buru Honeyeater*, Cinnamon-backed Fantail*, Black-tipped Monarch*, Buru Cuckoo-Shrike* and Buru White-eye) have been recorded in the **Lake Rana** (Lake Wakolo) area near Waenibe on the north coast, particularly around the village of Wafawel, and at Bara on the northwest tip of the island. Other species recorded in this area include Orange-footed and Moluccan* Scrubfowls, Long-tailed Mountain-Pigeon*, Red-breasted Pygmy-Parrot, Eclectus Parrot, Moluccan King-Parrot*, Red Lory, Red-bellied Pitta, Black-faced Friarbird, Pale-grey Cuckoo-Shrike, Golden Bulbul, Flame-breasted Flowerpecker and Black Sunbird. The remaining three endemics (Black-lored Parrot*, Buru Jungle-Flycatcher* and Rufous-throated White-eye*) are restricted to high-altitude forests where they were recorded in late 1995 on Kelapat Mada, a remote mountain range. The best time to visit is November to December, at the driest time of year.

SULA ISLANDS

The islands of Taliabu, Mangole and Sanana support four endemics and a further four species which are only shared with the Banggai Islands to the west.

TALIABU

The selectively logged lowland and montane forests, and mangroves and mud flats of Taliabu, the largest of the Sula Islands, support all of the archipelago's endemics and the four species shared with the Banggai Islands.

Sula Endemics

Taliabu Owl*, Sula Pitta*, Sula Cuckoo-Shrike, Bare-eyed Myna*.

Sula and Banggai Endemics

Sula Scrubfowl*, Slaty Cuckoo-Shrike, Helmeted Myna*, Henna-tailed Jungle-Flycatcher*.

Specialities

Great-billed Heron*, Vinous-breasted Sparrowhawk, Sulawesi Serpent-Eagle, Sulawesi Hawk-Eagle*, Beach Thick-knee, Malaysian Plover*, White-faced Cuckoo-Dove, Maroon-chinned Fruit-Dove, White-bellied and White Imperial-Pigeons, Golden-mantled Racquet-tail, Azure-rumped Parrot, Moluccan King-Parrot*, Moluccan Hanging-Parrot, Yellow-and-green Lorikeet, Black-billed Koel, Black-billed and Ruddy Kingfishers, Elegant Pitta, Sulawesi Myzomela, Drab Whistler, Rusty-flanked Fantail, Island Monarch, White-backed Woodswallow, White-rumped Triller, Rusty-backed Thrush*, Moluccan Starling, Golden Bulbul, Black-crowned White-eye.

Others

Cinnamon Bittern, Spotted Harrier (Apr–Sep), Spotted Kestrel, Blue-breasted Quail, Barred and Buff-banded Rails, White-browed Crake, Dusky Moorhen, Little Curlew (Nov–Mar), Australian Pratincole (Apr–Sep), Oriental Plover (Nov–Mar), Nicobar Pigeon*, Black-naped Fruit-Dove, Rusty-breasted and Channel-billed (Apr–Sep) Cuckoos, Variable Kingfisher, Rainbow Bee-eater (Apr–Sep), Island Flycatcher, Mountain White-eye, Gray's Warbler (Nov–Mar), Island Leaf-Warbler, Black-faced Munia, Pechora Pipit (Nov–Mar).

(A possible new species of owl has been heard on this island, as well as on Mangole and Sanana.)

Taliabu is accessible by boat from Falabisahaya on Mangole. A network of logging tracks and trails enables access to the coastal plain and adjacent hills at the northern and western ends of the island, and to montane forest in the centre. It is also possible to hire boats from the logging company to reach the north coast. Most of the endemics occur in the lowland forest, including Sula Pitta*, which prefers areas near bamboo.

Accommodation: guesthouse, logging camps, camping.

BANGGAI ISLANDS

Peleng, the largest of the Banggai Islands, which lie off east Sulawesi, supports Spotted and Wandering Whistling-Ducks, Sunda Teal, Barred Rail, White Imperial-Pigeon, Moluccan Hanging-Parrot, Black-billed Kingfisher and White-rumped Triller. The rare Bare-faced Rail* and Rusty-backed Thrush*, both of which are otherwise endemic to Sulawesi, have also been recorded here.

HALMAHERA

To visit Halmahera, the largest of the Moluccan or 'Spice' Islands, it is necessary to fly to the island of **Ternate** (from Manado on Sulawesi, or Ambon) where ferries to Sidangoli, on Halmahera, depart daily. Ternate's gently smoking volcano, which last erupted in 1987, rises to 1700 m (5577 ft) and dominates the island, which, although largely deforested, supports White Cockatoo*, Variable Kingfisher, Rufous-bellied Triller and Black Sunbird. A single road circumnavigates the island, enabling access to a lake where Spotted Whistling-Duck occurs. Once on the ferry to Halmahera, look out for Wedge-tailed Shearwater, Great and Lesser Frigatebirds, Brown Booby, White-bellied Sea-Eagle and Black-naped Tern.

KALI BATU PUTIH

In the forest at Kali Batu Putih it is possible to see 20 of the 22 species which are endemic to Halmahera and its satellite islands, including three fruit-doves, two kingfishers, a roller and such extraordinary birds as the huge Ivory-breasted Pitta, the strange Paradise-crow and the bizarre Wallace's Standardwing*.

The best time to visit Halmahera is during the dry season (Sep–Mar).

Halmahera Endemics

Moluccan Goshawk, Scarlet-breasted, Blue-capped* and Grey-headed Fruit-Doves, Chattering Lory*, Goliath Coucal, Moluccan Owlet-Nightjar, Blue-and-white and Sombre* Kingfishers, Purple Roller, Ivory-breasted Pitta, White-streaked and Dusky* Friarbirds, Long-billed Crow, Paradise-crow, Wallace's Standardwing*, Halmahera Oriole, Halmahera Cuckoo-shrike, Rufous-bellied Triller, Cream-throated White-eye.

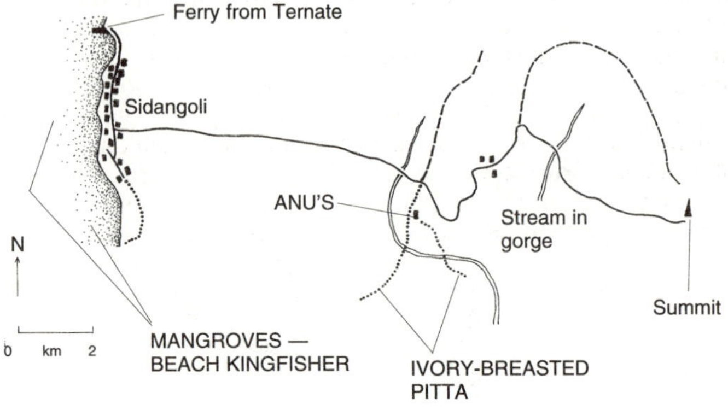

Moluccan Endemics

Rufous-necked Sparrowhawk, White-eyed and Cinnamon-bellied Imperial-Pigeons, White Cockatoo*, Moluccan Cuckoo-shrike, Flame-breasted Flowerpecker.

Specialities

Dusky Scrubfowl, Moluccan King-Parrot*, Moluccan Hanging-Parrot, Violet-necked Lory, Moluccan Scops-Owl, Moluccan Hawk-Owl, Moluccan Swiftlet, Drab Whistler, White-naped Monarch, Moluccan Flycatcher, Moluccan Starling, Golden Bulbul, Black-faced Munia.

Others

Rufous Night-Heron, Pacific Baza, Grey Goshawk, Gurney's Eagle*, Spotted Kestrel, Oriental Hobby, Rufous-tailed Bush-hen, Far Eastern Curlew* (Nov–Mar), Grey-tailed Tattler (Nov–Mar), Slender-billed and Great Cuckoo-Doves, Nicobar Pigeon*, Superb Fruit-Dove, Pied Imperial-Pigeon, Red-cheeked, Great-billed and Eclectus Parrots, Red-flanked Lorikeet, Moustached Treeswift, Azure, Variable and Beach Kingfishers, Common Paradise-Kingfisher, Rainbow Bee-eater (Mar–Sep), Blyth's Hornbill, Dusky Myzomela, Golden Whistler, Willie-Wagtail, Spectacled Monarch, Shining Flycatcher, White-bellied Cuckoo-Shrike, Common Cicadabird, Metallic Starling, Gray's Warbler (Nov–Mar), Island Leaf-Warbler, Black Sunbird.

(The two remaining endemics are Invisible Rail*, a rarely seen bird which was recorded in the sago swamps near Ake Tajawe in the proposed Lolobata Protected Area on the island's northeast peninsula in 1995, and Moluccan Cuckoo* which is known only from five specimens taken in 1931, on Halmahera and Bacan.)

On arriving in the small town of Sidangoli it is possible to take a bus (irregular) or bemo to Kali Batu Putih, 9 km inland. The basic lodge here is run by Anu (Demianus Bagali), who also knows where to see most of the top birds and is an excellent guide. If he is not around, bird around the lodge, along the tracks and trails, and alongside the 3 km track to the summit. It is best to arrange a trip to the area northeast of Sidangoli, where open-country species such as Purple Roller occur, with Anu, who will help to organise transport in Sidangoli. Beach Kingfisher is restricted to the mangroves around Sidangoli and may be seen in those opposite the harbour (accessible by boat), or to the south of town.

Accommodation: Ternate — Wisma Alhilal, Wisma Sejahtera. Kali Batu Pituh — lodge (B/basic/including food).

The extraordinary Wallace's Standardwing is one of Halmahera's two birds-of-paradise*

OBI

This mountainous island rises to 1611 m (5285 ft) and supports one endemic, Carunculated Fruit-Dove*, which was recorded during the last survey in 1992. Moluccan Woodcock*, which is endemic to Obi and Bacan, was not found during this survey, but a local guide has reported flushing birds in recent years which may well be this species.

SULAWESI

Birding on Sulawesi is an amazing experience because nearly 100 of the 330 or so birds which have been recorded are endemic (67) or near-endemic (26) and first-time visitors will be forgiven for thinking that they are in that avian paradise they have always dreamt of, where almost every different species they see is a new one. Furthermore, it is possible to see a high percentage of these unique and often extraordinary birds by visiting just three sites: Tangkoko NR and Dumoga-Bone NP at the northeastern corner of the island, and Lore Lindu NP in the centre.

The modern city of **Manado** at the island's northeastern tip is the gateway to the north. Few birders have been to **Bunaken Island**, a major destination for scuba-divers 30 minutes by boat from Manado, but one of those who did go there in October 1995 saw two Bristle-thighed Curlews*.

TANGKOKO NATURE RESERVE

This area of coastal and montane forest on the northeast coast of Sulawesi is one of the best sites on earth for kingfishers. An incredible nine species occur here, including Lilac, Black-billed, Ruddy and Green-backed, as well as a fine selection of other endemics and near-endemics.

TANGKOKO NR

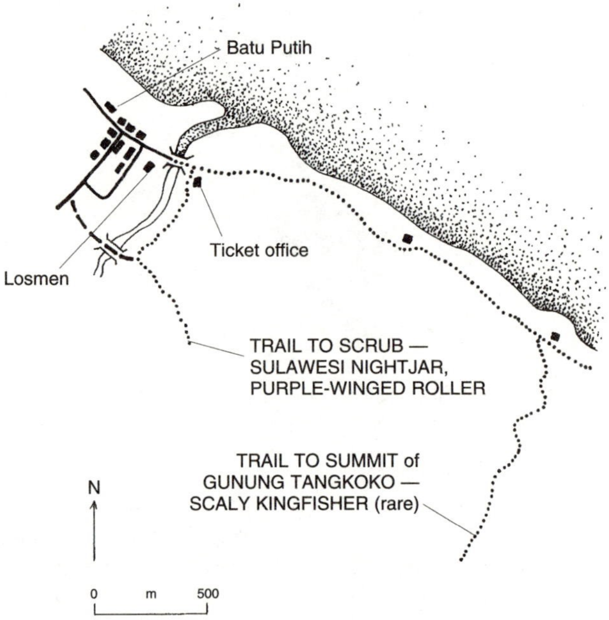

Sulawesi Endemics

Sulawesi and Spot-tailed Goshawks, Maleo*, Isabelline Waterhen, Yellowish-breasted Racquet-tail*, Pygmy Hanging-Parrot, Ornate Lorikeet, Yellow-billed Malkoha, Sulawesi Owl, Sulawesi Scops-Owl, Green-backed and Scaly (rare) Kingfishers, Purple-winged Roller, Sulawesi and Knobbed Hornbills, Sulawesi and Ashy Woodpeckers, Cerulean, Pied*, White-rumped and Sulawesi Cuckoo-Shrikes, White-necked and Finch-billed Mynas, Sulawesi Babbler, Yellow-sided, Crimson-crowned and Grey-sided Flowerpeckers.

Specialities

Vinous-breasted Sparrowhawk, Sulawesi Hawk-Eagle*, Tabon Scrubfowl*, White-faced Cuckoo-Dove, White Imperial-Pigeon, Golden-mantled Racquet-tail, Azure-rumped Parrot, Black-billed Koel, Sulawesi Nightjar, Moluccan Swiftlet, Sulawesi, Lilac, Black-billed and Ruddy Kingfishers, White-backed Woodswallow, White-rumped Triller, Rusty-backed Thrush*, Black-crowned White-eye, Black-faced Munia.

Others

Great and Lesser Frigatebirds, Blue-breasted Quail, Red Junglefowl, Barred and Buff-banded Rails, Stephan's Dove, Pink-necked Pigeon, Superb and Black-naped Fruit-Doves, Great Eared-Nightjar, Grey-rumped Treeswift, Common, Collared and Sacred Kingfishers, Rainbow Bee-eater (May–Sep), Hooded and Red-bellied Pittas, Pechora Pipit (Nov–Mar), Plain-throated and Black Sunbirds.

Other Wildlife

Bear phalanger, black macaque, cuscus, spectral tarsier.

Batu Putih, a small fishing village adjacent to the reserve, is 3 hours from Manado via bus to Girian and jeep from then on. Bird the creek (Ruddy Kingfisher), the trail through the coastal forest, the trail which ascends Gunung Tangkoko and the scrub southwest of the hut at the entrance (Sulawesi Nightjar). At first, it is best to bird with the guides who live in Batu Putih, especially on the Gunung Tangkoko trail where it is easy to get lost. These guides are especially adept at locating the kingfishers and Spectral Tarsiers, one of the world's smallest and most amazing mammals. It is also possible to travel by boat to Remesun to look for Maleo* and the mangroves at Batuangus, 40 minutes away, where Black-billed Kingfisher occurs. Beware of sandflies on and near the black, volcanic beaches.

Accommodation: losmen, owned by Tulende Wodi (B, including food).

DUMOGA-BONE NATIONAL PARK

The lowland and montane forests in this large park (3000 sq km) in northeast Sulawesi support over 30 endemics and plenty of near-endemics, including Maleo*, Lilac Kingfisher and Purple-bearded Bee-eater.

DUMOGA-BONE NP: DOLODUA

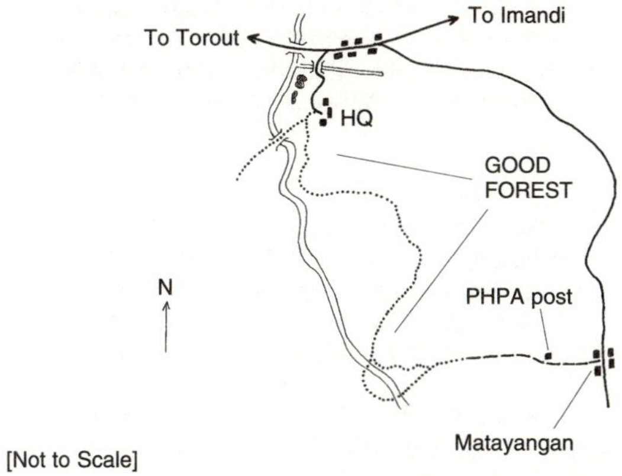

DUMOGA-BONE NP: TOROUT

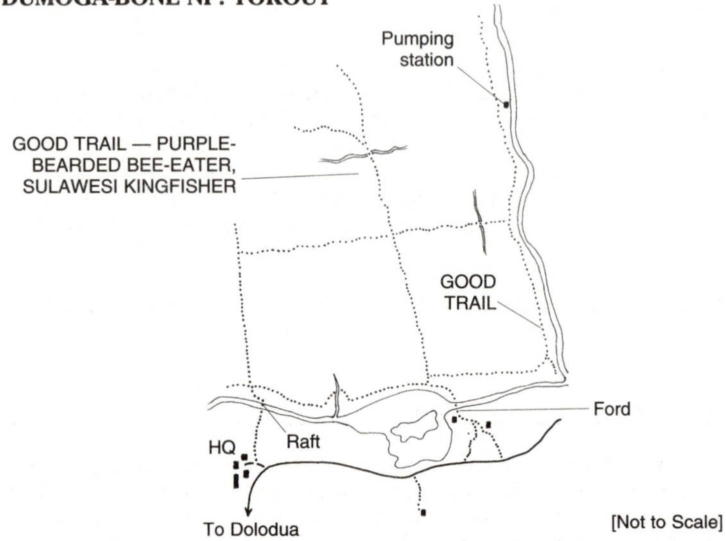

Sulawesi Endemics

Spot-tailed Goshawk, Small Sparrowhawk*, Maleo*, Isabelline Waterhen, Sulawesi Ground-Dove, Grey-headed Imperial-Pigeon, Yellowish-breasted Racquet-tail*, Sulawesi and Pygmy Hanging-Parrots, Ornate Lorikeet, Yellow-billed Malkoha, Bay Coucal, Sulawesi Owl, Sulawesi Scops-Owl, Speckled Hawk-Owl, Green-backed Kingfisher, Purple-bearded Bee-eater, Purple-winged Roller, Sulawesi and Knobbed Hornbills, Sulawesi and Ashy Woodpeckers, Pied* and Sulawesi Cuckoo-Shrikes, Sulawesi, White-necked and Finch-billed Mynas, Rufous-throated Flycatcher*, Sulawesi Babbler, Yellow-sided and Grey-sided Flowerpeckers.

Specialities

Sulawesi Serpent-Eagle, Vinous-breasted Sparrowhawk, Sulawesi Hawk-Eagle*, Tabon Scrubfowl*, White-faced Cuckoo-Dove, Maroon-chinned Fruit-Dove, White-bellied and White Imperial-Pigeons, Golden-mantled Racquet-tail, Azure-rumped Parrot, Black-billed Koel, Moluccan Swiftlet, Sulawesi, Lilac, Black-billed and Ruddy Kingfishers, Sulawesi Myzomela, White-backed Woodswallow, Rusty-backed Thrush*, Black-crowned White-eye, Black-faced Munia.

Others

Oriental Darter*, Wandering Whistling-Duck, Sunda Teal, Cinnamon Bittern (Nov–Mar), Lesser Fish-Eagle*, Spotted Harrier, Spotted Kestrel, Red Junglefowl, Barred and Buff-banded Rails, Slender-billed Cuckoo-Dove, Stephan's Dove, Grey-cheeked Pigeon, Black-naped Fruit-Dove, Great Eared-Nightjar, Grey-rumped Treeswift, Red-bellied Pitta.

Other Wildlife

Bear cuscus, Celebes ape, reticulated python, spectral tarsier, Sulawesi pig.

(Other species recorded here include Bare-faced Rail*, Minahassa Owl* and Matinan Flycatcher*.)

This park is accessible by road from Manado via Kotamobagu. It takes 4–5 hours by bus to reach the HQ at **Dolodua**. Bird the trails alongside the river and to the waterfall. The nearby **Torout** area is probably better, however, and this site is a more convenient base for visiting Tambun, where Maleo* occurs. At Torout bird the the lowland forest north of the river (Maroon-chinned Fruit-Dove, Purple-bearded Bee-eater, Red-bellied Pitta) and around the lodge at night (Sulawesi Owl, Sulawesi Scops-Owl).

Accommodation: Dolodua — lodge (basic). Torout — lodge (basic).

LORE LINDU NATIONAL PARK

The lowland and montane forests in this large park (2500 sq km) in central Sulawesi are badly degraded, but they still support virtually all of the island's 20 or so montane endemics, including Sulawesi Woodcock*, Purple-bearded Bee-eater, Geomalia*, Great Shortwing, Fiery-browed Myna and Crimson-crowned Flowerpecker.

Before entering the park it is necessary to obtain a permit from the Sub Balai Kawasan Pelestarian Alam office on Jalan Mohammed Yamin road in Palu. It is also important to arrange the use of a 4WD with driver, with a chap called Rolex who works at these offices, unless you are prepared to walk the 22 km from the accommodation at Kamarora to the montane forests at Anaso.

LORE LINDU NP

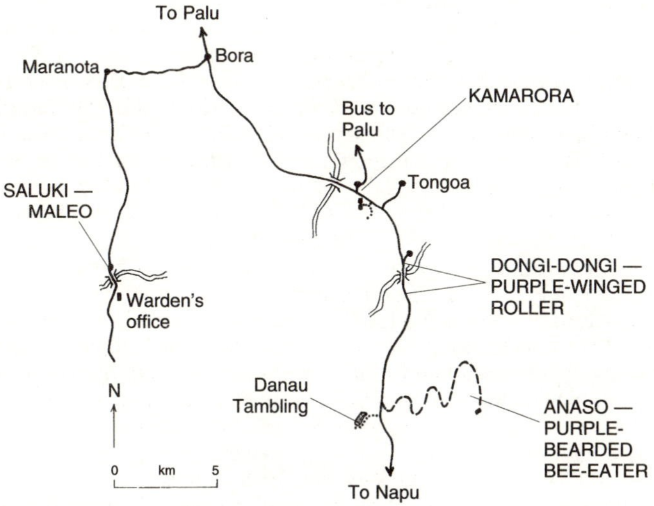

The Maleo is Sulawesi's endemic megapode*

Sulawesi Endemics

Spot-tailed Goshawk, Isabelline Waterhen, Sulawesi Woodcock*, Sulawesi Ground-Dove, Red-eared Fruit-Dove, Grey-headed Imperial-Pigeon, Sombre Pigeon*, Sulawesi and Pygmy Hanging-Parrots, Ornate Lorikeet, Sulawesi Hawk-Cuckoo, Yellow-billed Malkoha, Bay Coucal, Sulawesi Scops-Owl, Ochre-bellied and Speckled Hawk-Owls, Purple-bearded Bee-eater (Jul–Sep), Purple-winged Roller, Sulawesi and Knobbed Hornbills, Sulawesi and Ashy Woodpeckers, Dark-eared and Greater Streaked Honeyeaters, Olive-flanked, Maroon-backed and Sulphur-bellied Whistlers, Sulawesi Drongo, Piping Crow, Cerulean, White-rumped, Pygmy and Sulawesi Cuckoo-Shrikes, Geomalia*, Sulawesi Thrush, Great Shortwing, Sulawesi, White-necked, Fiery-browed and Finch-billed Mynas, Rufous-throated* and Blue-fronted Flycatchers, Sulawesi Blue-Flycatcher, Streak-headed White-eye, Sulawesi Leaf-Warbler, Malia, Sulawesi Babbler, Yellow-sided, Crimson-crowned and Grey-sided Flowerpeckers.

Specialities

Barred Honey-buzzard, Sulawesi Serpent-Eagle, Sulawesi Hawk-Eagle*, White-faced Cuckoo-Dove, Maroon-chinned Fruit-Dove, White-bellied Imperial-Pigeon, Golden-mantled Racquet-tail, Azure-rumped Parrot, Yellow-and-green Lorikeet, Black-billed Koel, Moluccan Swiftlet, Purple Needletail, Red-bellied Pitta, Sulawesi Myzomela, Rusty-flanked Fantail, White-backed Woodswallow, White-rumped Triller, Short-tailed Starling, Island Flycatcher, Black-crowned White-eye, Chestnut-backed Bush-Warbler, Blue-faced Parrotfinch, Black-faced and Pale-headed Munias, Mountain Serin.

Others

Sunda Teal, Jerdon's Baza*, Lesser Fish-Eagle*, Spotted Kestrel, Oriental Hobby, Slender-billed Cuckoo-Dove, Grey-cheeked Pigeon, Superb and Black-naped Fruit-Doves, Grey-rumped Treeswift, Blue-tailed Bee-eater, Hooded Pitta, Asian Glossy Starling, Citrine Canary-Flycatcher, Golden-headed Cisticola, Mountain and Yellow-bellied White-eyes, Plain-throated, Black and Crimson Sunbirds.

(Other species recorded here include Sulawesi Goshawk, Platen's* and Bare-faced* Rails, Green-backed and Scaly Kingfishers, Rusty-backed Thrush* and a probable Diabolical Nightjar*, which was seen here in July 1993.)

The park HQ at Kamarora is 40 km south of Palu, which is accessible by air from Ujung Pandang, Jakarta and Lahad Datu in Sabah, Borneo (via Kalimantan). Spotted Harrier has been recorded at Palu airport. It is possible to travel by bus to Kamarora but, if time is short, a 4WD is recommended, as this will be needed to reach the montane forest at Anaso, 22 km away on a old logging track which resembles a vertical dry river bed in places. Allow 3 hours each way, and expect to be stuck at Kamarora in heavy rain. The small patch of forest at Kamarora supports a number of lowland endemics, including Rufous-throated Flycatcher*, but the area to concentrate on here is around Anaso at over 2000 m (6562 ft). Bird alongside the track for a few kilometres below the deserted logging camp, where there is now a forest nursery. Also bird alongside the road either side of Dongi-Dongi (Sulawesi Babbler) and around Danau Tambling lake, both of which are roughly halfway between Kamarora and Anaso.

Accommodation: Kamarora (basic cabins — the warden cooks for guests on request).

At **Saluki**, accessible by bus from Kamarora via Maranota, it is possible to hire guides to visit a Maleo* breeding ground along the Saluki River, to the east of the village. The birds are usually absent from the nesting sites in July and August.

In southwest Sulawesi, Black-ringed White-eye* has been recorded at **Bantimurung NR**, northeast of Ujung Pandang, and near the popular tourist destination of **Tanatoraja**, 7–8 hours (320 km) north of Ujung Pandang, above Rante Pao near Batutumonga, in the company of Yellow-bellied White-eye.

The superb White-backed Woodswallow occurs at Lore Lindu

ADDITIONAL INFORMATION

Addresses

The Indonesian Ornithological Society (IOS), PO Box 4087, Jakarta 12040, Java, publishes the regular *Kukila* journal.

PHPA: Permits (Surat Jalans) may be obtained from the Directorate Jenderal PHPA (Perlindungan Hutan dan Pelestarian Alam), Jl. Ir. H. Juanda, Bogor, Java.

Books and Papers

A Field Guide to the Birds of Borneo, Sumatra, Java and Bali. Mackinnon J, 1993. Oxford University Press.
The Avifauna of Barito Ulu, Central Borneo. Dutson G and Wilkinson R, 1991. BirdLife Study Report No. 48.
The Birds of Borneo, Third Edition. Smythies B, 1981. Sabah and Malayan Nature Societies.
Pocket Guide to the Birds of Borneo. Francis C, 1984. WWF Malaysia.
A Field Guide to the Mammals of Borneo. Payne J and Francis C, 1985. WWF Malaysia.
The Birds of Sumatra. van Marle J and Voous K, 1988. BOU Checklist 10.
The Birds of Wallacea. Bruce and White, 1986. BOU. (Although there are no plates, this book does contain descriptions of many endemics and is essential for islands such as Sulawesi and Halmahera.)
Wallacea (Trip Report). Gibbs D, 1990. Privately published.
Birding in the Sula Islands. Davidson P and Stones T, 1993. *OBC Bulletin* 18: 59–63.
Manusela National Park, Seram. Bowler J and Taylor J, 1993. *OBC Bulletin* 18: 21–25.
Birds of the Cocos (Keeling) Islands, Indian Ocean. Stokes T, Sheils W and Dunn K, 1984. *Emu* 84: 23–28.
Birds of New Guinea. Beehler B, 1986. Princeton.

INDONESIAN ENDEMICS (338)

KALIMANTAN

Black-browed Babbler	Known only from a nineteenth century specimen

(For a full list of Bornean endemics, see p. 219).

SUMATRA, JAVA and BALI (61)

SUMATRA (18)

Red-billed Partridge	Barisan Range: Kerinci-Seblat
Sumatran Pheasant*	Northwest: Gunung Leuser (possibly a subspecies of the following species)
Salvadori's Pheasant*	Barisan Range: Kerinci-Seblat (and Gunung Kaba)
Bronze-tailed Peacock-Pheasant*	Barisan Range: Berestagi and Kerinci-Seblat
Semulu Scops-Owl	Offshore islands: Simeulue Island, off northwest coast
Mentawai Scops-Owl	Offshore islands: Siberut and Sipura Islands, off west coast
Short-tailed Frogmouth*	Barisan Range: Berestagi
Schneider's Pitta*	Barisan Range: Berestagi, Kerinci-Seblat and Dolok Sibual Bual NR
Sumatran Drongo*	Barisan Range: Kerinci-Seblat (at

	Mauro Sako)
Blue-masked Leafbird*	Barisan Range: Kerinci-Seblat
Shiny Whistling-Thrush	Barisan Range: Berestagi and Kerinci-Seblat
Rueck's Blue-Flycatcher*	North: known only from two specimens taken in 1917 and 1918
Sumatran Cochoa*	Barisan Range: Kerinci-Seblat
Cream-striped Bulbul	Barisan Range: Kerinci-Seblat
Spot-necked Bulbul*	Barisan Range: Berestagi and Kerinci-Seblat
Enggano White-eye	Offshore islands: Enggano Island
Vanderbilt's Babbler*	North: known only from a 1939 specimen taken at Keungke in the Alas Valley
Rusty-breasted Wren-Babbler	Barisan Range: Berestagi and Kerinci-Seblat

Sunda Ground-Cuckoo* is now generally regarded as two separate species; Sumatran, which is endemic to Sumatra, and Bornean, which is endemic to Borneo. Sumatran Ground-Cuckoo* has not been seen since 1916. It is only known from the Barisan Range where it has been recorded at five sites including Mauro Sako.

Sumatra and Peninsular Malaysia (4)
Fire-tufted Barbet, Mangrove Pitta*, Rufous-vented Niltava, Marbled Wren-Babbler*.

Sumatra and Borneo (10)
Silvery Wood-Pigeon*, Bonaparte's Nightjar*, Black-crowned Pitta, Sunda Treepie, Long-billed Blue-Flycatcher*, Blue-wattled* and Hook-billed* Bulbuls, Black-capped White-eye, Sunda Laughingthrush.

Sumatra and Java (7)
Green-spectacled Pigeon*, Salvadori's Nightjar*, Blue-tailed Trogon, Sunda Minivet, Sunda Robin, Sunda Forktail, Sunda Bulbul.

Sumatra, Java and Peninsular Malaysia (1)
Waterfall Swift*.

Sumatra, Java and Borneo (3)
Rajah Scops-Owl, Sunda Cuckoo-Shrike, Indigo Flycatcher.

CHRISTMAS ISLAND (3)
Abbott's Booby*, Christmas Island Imperial-Pigeon*, Christmas Island White-eye*.

JAVA (20)

Javan Hawk-Eagle*	Throughout: local, but widespread
Chestnut-bellied Partridge	West: Gunung Gede-Pangrango
Sunda Coucal*	Coastal lowlands: near Jakarta, Pangandaran and Indramaya (may also occur on Sumatra)
Javan Scops-Owl*	West: Gunung Gede-Pangrango
Javan Frogmouth*	West: Carita

Volcano Swiftlet*	West: Gunung Gede-Pangrango
Brown-throated Barbet*	West: Gunung Gede-Pangrango
Black-banded Barbet	West: Carita, Ujung Kulon and Pangandaran
Rufous-tailed Fantail	West: Gunung Gede-Pangrango
White-bellied Fantail*	West: Gunung Gede-Pangrango
Javan Cochoa*	West: Gunung Gede-Pangrango
Pygmy Tit	West: Gunung Gede-Pangrango
Javan Tesia	West: Gunung Gede-Pangrango
Rufous-fronted Laughingthrush*	West: Gunung Gede-Pangrango
White-breasted Babbler*	West: Carita and Ujong Kulon
White-bibbed Babbler	West: Gunung Gede-Pangrango (may also occur in south Sumatra)
Grey-cheeked Tit-Babbler	Throughout: Carita and Baluran (also on Kangean Islands)
Javan Fulvetta	West: Gunung Gede-Pangrango
Spotted Crocias*	West: Gunung Gede-Pangrango
White-flanked Sunbird	West: Gunung Gede-Pangrango

Sunda Lapwing is believed to be extinct. This bird was regularly reported in the northwest of Java until 1930 and from river deltas on the south coast until at least 1940. However, recent surveys have drawn a depressing blank.

Java and Borneo (2)
Javan White-eye*, Temminck's Babbler.

BALI (1)

Bali Myna*	Northwest: Bali Barat NP, where 36–40 birds were recorded in 1994

Java and Bali (10)
Javan Plover*, Yellow-throated Hanging-Parrot*, Javan Owlet, Javan Kingfisher, Flame-fronted Barbet, Javan Cuckoo-shrike, Javan Grey-throated White-eye, Crescent-chested Babbler, Java Sparrow*, Chestnut Munia.

Java, Bali and Sumatra (5)
Pink-headed Fruit-Dove, Horsfield's Thrush, Orange-spotted Bulbul, Bar-winged Prinia, Sunda Warbler.

Java, Bali, Sumatra and Lombok (1)
Javan Munia.

Java, Bali and Lombok (2)
Black-winged Starling*, Olive-backed Tailorbird.

Java, Bali, Lombok, Flores and Sumbawa (1)
Dark-backed Imperial-Pigeon.

Java, Bali and Lesser Sundas (1)
Green Junglefowl.

Java, Bali and south Sulawesi (1)

Pale-bellied Myna.

Bali and Lesser Sundas (1)
Black-backed Fruit-Dove.

LESSER SUNDAS (63)

THROUGHOUT (8)
Dusky Cuckoo-Dove, Indonesian Honeyeater, Wallacean Drongo, Wallacean Cuckoo-Shrike, Chestnut-backed Thrush, Five-coloured Munia, Red-chested Flowerpecker, Flame-breasted Sunbird.

Lesser Sundas and Moluccas (6)
Barred Dove, Pink-headed and Elegant Imperial-Pigeons, Cinnamon-backed Kingfisher*, Elegant Pitta, Tricoloured Parrotfinch.

Lesser Sundas and Sulawesi (2)
Yellow-crested Cockatoo*, Pale-headed Munia.

SUMBA (9)
Sumba Buttonquail*, Sumba Green-Pigeon*, Red-naped Fruit-Dove*, Sumba Boobook*, Sumba Hornbill*, Sumba Myzomela, Sumba Brown* and Sumba* Flycatchers, Apricot-breasted Sunbird.

Sumba, Flores and Sumbawa (3)
Sumba Cuckoo-Shrike*, Flores Jungle-Flycatcher*, Yellow-spectacled White-eye.

FLORES (4)
Wallace's Hanging-Parrot*, Flores Scops-Owl* (only known from three specimens collected in 1896, which may have originated in Sumba, not Flores, and may only be a red phase of Moluccan Scops-Owl), Flores Monarch*, Flores Crow*.

Tanahjampea Island, Flores Sea (1)
White-tipped Monarch*.

Flores and Lombok (1)
Flores Green-Pigeon*.

Flores and Sumbawa (10)
Wallace's Scops-Owl, Bare-throated Whistler, Brown-capped Fantail, Flores Minivet, White-browed, Dark-crowned* and Flores White-eyes, Russet-capped Tesia, Golden-rumped and Black-fronted Flowerpeckers.

Flores, Sumbawa and Lombok (2)
White-rumped Kingfisher, Sunda Honeyeater.

Flores and Timor (1)
Timor Leaf-Warbler.

TIMOR (11)
Timor Green-Pigeon*, Yellow-eared Honeyeater, Black-breasted Myzomela*, Streak-breasted Honeyeater*, Timor Friarbird*, Black-

banded Flycatcher*, Timor Bushchat*, Timor White-eye*, Timor Stubtail*, Buff-banded Bushbird*, Timor Sparrow*.

Timor and Wetar (10)
Wetar Ground-Dove*, Slaty Cuckoo-Dove*, Timor Imperial-Pigeon*, Olive-shouldered Parrot*, Iris Lorikeet*, Plain Gerygone, Fawn-breasted Whistler*, Timor Oriole, Orange-banded Thrush*, Timor Blue-Flycatcher.

WETAR (3)
Black-chested Honeyeater*, Crimson-hooded Myzomela*, Wetar Figbird*.

Wetar and Tanimbar Islands (1)
White-tufted Honeyeater.

MOLUCCAS (97)

THROUGHOUT (6)
Rufous-necked Sparrowhawk, White-eyed Imperial-Pigeon, Red Lory, Drab Whistler, Moluccan Flycatcher, Flame-breasted Flowerpecker.

South Moluccas (1)
Ashy Flowerpecker.

Moluccas and islands off east Sulawesi (2)
Moluccan Hanging-Parrot, Golden Bulbul.

Moluccas and islands off west New Guinea (4)
Moluccan Scrubfowl*, Violet-necked Lory, Olive Honeyeater, Island Whistler.

Boano Island (off west Seram) (1)
Black-chinned Monarch*.

TANIMBAR ISLANDS (including Babar, Banda and Damar) (13)
Tanimbar Cockatoo*, Blue-streaked Lory*, Banda Myzomela, Golden-bellied Flyrobin*, Cinnamon-tailed* and Long-tailed* Fantails, Black-bibbed* and Loetoe* Monarchs, White-browed Triller, Slaty-backed* and Fawn-breasted* Thrushes, Tanimbar Starling*, Tanimbar Bush-Warbler*.

Tanimbar and Kai Islands (4)
Pied Bronze-Cuckoo, Rufous-sided Gerygone, Wallacean Whistler, Kai Cuckoo-Shrike*.

KAI ISLANDS (4)
Kai Coucal*, White-tailed Monarch*, Great Kai* and Little Kai* White-eyes.

Tanimbar and Buru Islands (2)
Lesser Masked-Owl* (recorded in January 1996), Buru Oriole.

Tanimbar, Kai and Buru Islands (1)
Black-faced Friarbird.

Tanimbar, Kai, Buru and Seram Islands (1)
Cinnamon-chested Flycatcher.

Central and North Moluccas (3)
Cinnamon-bellied Imperial-Pigeon, White Cockatoo*, Moluccan Cuckoo-Shrike.

SERAM (8)
Blue-eared Lory*, Seram Honeyeater, Seram Friarbird, Streaky-breasted Fantail, Seram Oriole, Long-crested Myna, Rufescent and Grey-hooded White-eyes.

Seram and Ambon (4)
Salmon-crested Cockatoo*, Purple-naped Lory*, Lazuli Kingfisher, Seram Myzomela.

AMBON (1)
Ambon White-eye*.

Seram and Buru (4)
Long-tailed Mountain-Pigeon*, Wakolo Myzomela, Pale-grey Cuckoo-Shrike, Moluccan Thrush*.

Seram, Buru and Sulawesi (1)
Chestnut-backed Bush-Warbler.

BURU (10)
Buru Racquet-tail*, Black-lored Parrot*, Blue-fronted Lorikeet*, Buru Honeyeater*, Cinnamon-backed Fantail*, Black-tipped Monarch*, Buru Cuckoo-Shrike*, Buru Jungle-Flycatcher*, Buru and Rufous-throated* White-eyes.

Buru and Halmahera (1)
White-naped Monarch.

HALMAHERA (and satellite islands) (22)
Moluccan Goshawk, Invisible Rail*, Scarlet-breasted, Blue-capped* and Grey-headed Fruit-Doves, Chattering Lory*, Moluccan Cuckoo, Goliath Coucal, Moluccan Owlet-Nightjar, Blue-and-white and Sombre* Kingfishers, Purple Roller, Ivory-breasted Pitta, White-streaked and Dusky* Friarbirds, Long-billed Crow, Paradise-crow, Wallace's Standardwing*, Halmahera Oriole, Halmahera Cuckoo-shrike, Rufous-bellied Triller, Cream-throated White-eye.

OBI (1)
Carunculated Fruit-Dove*.

Obi and Bacan (1)
Moluccan Woodcock*.

Bacan and Sulawesi (1)
Sulawesi Myzomela.

SULA ISLANDS (4)
Taliabu Owl*, Sula Pitta*, Sula Cuckoo-Shrike, Bare-eyed Myna*.

Sula and Banggai Islands (4)
Sula Scrubfowl*, Slaty Cuckoo-Shrike, Helmeted Myna*, Henna-tailed Jungle-Flycatcher*.

Sula and Sulawesi (14)
Sulawesi Serpent-Eagle, Vinous-breasted Sparrowhawk, Sulawesi Hawk-Eagle*, White-faced Cuckoo-Dove, Maroon-chinned Fruit-Dove, White-bellied and White Imperial-Pigeons, Golden-mantled Racquet-tail, Yellow-and-green Lorikeet, Black-billed Koel, Sulawesi Nightjar, Black-billed Kingfisher, Rusty-flanked Fantail, White-rumped Triller.

Sula, Banggai and Sulawesi (1)
White-backed Woodswallow.

Moluccas and Sulawesi (1)
Moluccan Swiftlet.

SULAWESI (and satellite islands) (67)

Sulawesi Goshawk	North: Tangkoko
Spot-tailed Goshawk	North and central: widespread
Small Sparrowhawk*	North: Dumoga-Bone
Maleo*	North and central: widespread
Platen's Rail*	Central: Lore Lindu
Bare-faced Rail*	North and central: Dumoga-Bone and Lore Lindu (has also been recorded on Peleng in the Banggai Islands)
Isabelline Waterhen	North and central: widespread
Sulawesi Woodcock*	Central: Lore Lindu
Sulawesi Ground-Dove	North and central: Dumoga-Bone and Lore Lindu
Red-eared Fruit-Dove	Central: Lore Lindu
Grey-headed Imperial-Pigeon	North and central: Dumoga-Bone and Lore Lindu
Sombre Pigeon*	Central: Lore Lindu
Yellowish-breasted Racquet-tail*	North: Tangkoko and Dumoga-Bone
Sulawesi Hanging-Parrot	North and central: Dumoga-Bone and Lore Lindu
Pygmy Hanging-Parrot	North: Tangkoko and Dumoga-Bone
Ornate Lorikeet	North and central: widespread
Sulawesi Hawk-Cuckoo	Central: Lore Lindu
Yellow-billed Malkoha	North and central: widespread
Bay Coucal	North and central: Dumoga-Bone and Lore Lindu
Minahassa Owl*	North: Dumoga-Bone
Sulawesi Owl	North: Tangkoko and Dumoga-

	Bone
Sulawesi Scops-Owl	North and central: widespread
Ochre-bellied Hawk-Owl	Central: Lore Lindu
Speckled Hawk-Owl	Throughout: Dumoga-Bone, Lore Lindu and Tanatoraja
Diabolical Nightjar*	Central: probably seen at Lore Lindu in July 1993. Otherwise known only from a 1931 specimen
Green-backed Kingfisher	North and central: Tangkoko and Dumoga-Bone
Scaly Kingfisher	North and central: Tangkoko (rare)
Purple-bearded Bee-eater	North and central: Dumoga-Bone and Lore Lindu
Purple-winged Roller	North and central: widespread
Sulawesi Hornbill	North and central: widespread
Knobbed Hornbill	North and central: widespread
Sulawesi Woodpecker	North and central: widespread
Ashy Woodpecker	North and central: widespread
Dark-eared Honeyeater	Central: Lore Lindu
Greater-streaked Honeyeater	Central: Lore Lindu
Olive-flanked Whistler	Central: Lore Lindu
Maroon-backed Whistler	Central: Lore Lindu
Sulphur-bellied Whistler	Central: Lore Lindu
Sulawesi Drongo	Central: Lore Lindu
Piping Crow	Central: Lore Lindu
Cerulean Cuckoo-Shrike	North and central: Tangkoko and Lore Lindu
Pied Cuckoo-Shrike*	North: Tangkoko and Dumoga-Bone
White-rumped Cuckoo-Shrike	North and central: Tangkoko and Lore Lindu
Pygmy Cuckoo-Shrike	Central: Lore Lindu
Sulawesi Cuckoo-Shrike	North and central: widespread
Geomalia*	Central: Lore Lindu
Sulawesi Thrush	Central: Lore Lindu
Rusty-backed Thrush*	North: Tangkoko and Dumoga-Bone (also occurs on Peleng in the Banggai Islands)
Great Shortwing	Central: Lore Lindu
Sulawesi Myna	North and central: Dumoga-Bone and Lore Lindu
White-necked Myna	North and central: widespread
Fiery-browed Myna	Central: Lore Lindu
Finch-billed Myna	North and central: widespread
Rufous-throated Flycatcher*	North and central: Dumoga-Bone and Lore Lindu
Lompobattang Flycatcher*	Southwest: Gunung Lompobattang (seen 1995)
Matinan Flycatcher*	North: one 1981 record from Gunung Kabila in Dumoga-Bone, one 1985 record from Gunung Muajat, and several specimens
Blue-fronted Flycatcher	Central: Lore Lindu

Sulawesi Blue-Flycatcher	Central: Lore Lindu (also occurs on islands in the Flores Sea)
Sulawesi White-eye	Southeast
Black-ringed White-eye*	Southwest: Bantimurung NR and Tanatoraja
Streak-headed White-eye	Central: Lore Lindu
Sulawesi Leaf-Warbler	Central: Lore Lindu
Malia	Central: Lore Lindu
Sulawesi Babbler	North and central: widespread
Yellow-sided Flowerpecker	North and central: widespread
Crimson-crowned Flowerpecker	North and central: Tangkoko and Lore Lindu
Grey-sided Flowerpecker	North and central: widespread

Sulawesi and Philippines (4)
Barred Honey-buzzard, Azure-rumped Parrot, Philippine Nightjar, Purple Needletail.

Sulawesi and Sangihe Islands (2)
Sulawesi and Lilac Kingfishers.

SANGIHE ISLANDS (2)
Sangihe Hanging-Parrot, Cerulean Paradise-Flycatcher*.

Sangihe and Siau Islands (1)
Elegant Sunbird*.

Sangihe and Talaud Islands (1)
Red-and-blue Lory (Karakelong Island).

TALAUD ISLAND (1)
Talaud Kingfisher.

Near-endemics

White-shouldered Ibis*, Storm's Stork*, Barred Honey-buzzard, Tabon* and Dusky Scrubfowls, Grey-breasted Partridge, Dusky Woodcock, Silvery Wood-Pigeon*, Ruddy Cuckoo-Dove, Grey Imperial-Pigeon*, Blue-naped* and Azure-rumped Parrots, Violet-necked Lory, Sunda Ground-Cuckoo*, Moluccan and Rajah Scops-Owls, Sunda Frogmouth, Philippine Nightjar, Waterfall Swift*, Grey Swiftlet, Purple Needletail, Plain-pouched Hornbill*, Fire-tufted Barbet, Black-crowned Pitta, Olive Honeyeater, Island Whistler, Rufous Paradise-Flycatcher*, Sunda Treepie, Sunda Thrush, Moluccan and Short-tailed Starlings, Chestnut-tailed Jungle-Flycatcher, Island Flycatcher, Rufous-vented Niltava, Citrine Canary-Flycatcher, Blue Nuthatch, Blue-wattled* and Hook-billed* Bulbuls, Black-capped, Yellow-bellied and Ashy-bellied White-eyes, Black Laughingthrush, Temminck's and Grey-breasted* Babblers, Large* and Marbled* Wren-Babblers, Dusky Munia, Brown-backed Flowerpecker*, Mountain Serin.

JAPAN

1 Karuizawa	Ferry	10 Hakata Bay
2 Mount Fuji	6 Hokkaido	11 Arasaki (Izumi)
3 Katano Kamo-ike	7 Miyake-jima	12 Mi-ike
4 Hegura-jima	8 Torishima	13 Amami-oshima
5 Honshu–Hokkaido	9 Hahashima	14 Okinawa

INTRODUCTION

Summary

Birders planning their first visit to this lengthy archipelago are faced with a major dilemma: whether to go in the very cold winter to see Steller's Sea-Eagles* and cranes, or in the summer, which is the best time to search for Fairy Pitta*, rare warblers and the seven endemics confined to the Nansei Shoto archipelago in the subtropical south. Budget birders must also decide whether the excitement matches the expense, for public transport, hire-cars and accommodation are all costly, and it is necessary to visit five different islands to see all 12 endemics and the many specialities.

Size

At 377,708 sq km, Japan is three times bigger than England and approximately half the size of Texas.

Getting Around

Although travelling alone in Japan can be a daunting experience because so few people speak English and there are no English signs, it is by no means impossible. Indeed, once settled in, the very efficient, but expensive, air, sea, road and rail (passes available outside the country) networks make virtually every site easily accessible, except on the islands of Hokkaido and Okinawa, where a vehicle is more or less a necessity.

Accommodation and Food

Apart from Youth Hostels and campsites, most of which are only open in July and August, accommodation is very expensive, even in the relatively basic, but clean, minshukus (futon and breakfast) and the 'capsule hotels', which are popular with drunks who don't mind spending the night in what resembles a coffin. Food is also expensive apart from noodles and Western fast-food. The Japanese like alcohol and beer is even dispensed by vending machines. Sake (rice wine) is very popular, but takes some swallowing for those not used to spirits.

Health and Safety

Immunisation against hepatitis, polio and typhoid is recommended.

Minor earthquakes are part of everyday life in Japan (watch out for swinging ceiling lights) and it is best to stay indoors when these occur. In the event of a major earthquake the most sensible action to take is to cower under a strong table, or, better still, head for a major structural part of a building (e.g. a pillar).

Climate and Timing

The best time to visit Japan to see Steller's Sea-Eagle* and cranes is February, despite the fact that at this time the island of Hokkaido, where the eagles occur, is covered in snow and surrounded by sea-ice. To see most of the endemics, Fairy Pitta* and rare breeding warblers it is best to visit after the first week of June. The rainy season begins in June in the south and gradually moves north, arriving in Honshu by July.

Habitats

This Japanese archipelago stretches 3500 km from the subarctic to the subtropical zones, hence there is a great range of habitats, from coniferous forests in the north, through deciduous and broadleaf evergreen forests, to subtropical forests in the south. There are also grasslands, many lakes and estuaries, and, in the south, paddies and mangroves. A chain of steep mountains and volcanoes, rising to 3776 m (12,389 ft) at Mount Fuji on Honshu, forms the backbone of the islands.

Conservation

Despite Red-crowned Cranes* being symbols of happiness and longevity in Japanese culture, they were almost hunted to extinction by the 1930s. There were just 20 left then, but there are over 500 now, thanks to hunting bans and supplementary feeding during the winter months. Japan's other cranes are also fed in the winter, but they still annoy the farmers of Arasaki, even though these people are compensated financially. Overall though, Japan's birds, which include a high total of 53 threatened and near-threatened species, are fairly well protected.

Bird Species

Over 580 species have been recorded in Japan. Non-endemic specialities and spectacular species which are present on and around the main islands all year round include Short-tailed*, Black-footed and Laysan Albatrosses, Mandarin Duck*, Hazel Grouse, Red-crowned Crane*, Long-billed Plover*, Japanese Murrelet*, Japanese Wood-Pigeon*, White-bellied Pigeon*, Blakiston's Fish-Owl*, Crested Kingfisher, Brown-headed Thrush, White-cheeked Starling, Varied Tit, Black-backed and Japanese Wagtails, Long-tailed Rosefinch, Pine and Japanese Grosbeaks and Ochre-rumped* and Grey Buntings. Summer specialities include Band-rumped, Swinhoe's and Tristram's* Storm-Petrels, Latham's Snipe*, Ruddy Kingfisher, Fairy Pitta*, Japanese Paradise-Flycatcher*, Japanese Thrush, Chestnut-cheeked Starling*, Siberian Rubythroat, Middendorff's and Gray's Warblers, Marsh Grassbird* and Yellow Bunting. In winter, notable species include Baikal Teal*, Harlequin Duck, Black-faced Spoonbill*, Steller's Sea-Eagle*, Hooded* and White-naped* Cranes, Sanders' Gull*, Pale and Dusky Thrushes, Japanese Waxwing*, Asian Rosy-Finch and Yellow-billed Grosbeak. Resident specialities of the Nansei Shoto archipelago include Whistling Green-Pigeon*.

Endemics

Japan's 12 endemics include a pheasant, a rail, a woodcock, two woodpeckers, a jay, a minivet and an accentor.

Expectations

It is possible to see over 200 species on a three-week winter or summer trip which includes Hokkaido, Honshu, Kyushu and the Nansei Shoto archipelago.

In **Tokyo**, which is on the island of Honshu, Azure-winged Magpie occurs at the Imperial Palace and Meiji Jingu, a shrine set in 73 ha of grounds which also support Mandarin Duck* (Nov–Mar), Chinese Bamboo-Partridge (introduced), Pygmy Woodpecker, Bull-headed Shrike, Pale (Nov–Mar), Brown-headed (Nov–Mar), and Dusky (Nov–Mar) Thrushes, White-cheeked Starling, Brown-eared Bulbul and Varied Tit.

The marshes at **Omigawa**, 3 hours by train east of Tokyo, support two very localised breeding species (Jun–Aug): Marsh Grassbird* and Ochre-rumped Bunting*. From Omigawa Station, cross the Tonegawa (Tone River) via the Ohashi bridge and explore the riverside up or down stream. Rock Sandpiper has been recorded in winter at **Choshi**, at the mouth of the Tonegawa south of Omigawa. Scan the rocks near the port, 2 km northeast of the railway station, from the shrine near the Kawaguchi-sennin-zuka bus stop on an obvious bend in the road.

KARUIZAWA

The forested hills and river around Karuizawa, which is situated at the foot of the gently smoking Asamayama Volcano, which rises to 2542 m (8340 ft) in central Honshu, support two resident endemics, as well as Long-billed Plover* and Brown-headed Thrush.

Japanese Endemics

Copper Pheasant*, Japanese Woodpecker.

Specialities

Mandarin Duck* (Nov–Mar), Long-billed Plover*, Lesser Cuckoo (May–Sep), Pygmy Woodpecker, Japanese Waxwing* (Dec–Mar), Brown-headed Thrush (May–Sep), Japanese Robin (May–Sep), Brown-eared Bulbul, Varied Tit, Japanese Skylark, Japanese Wagtail, Asian Rosy-Finch (Dec–Mar), Japanese Grosbeak.

Others

Hodgson's Hawk-Cuckoo (May–Aug), Jungle Nightjar (May–Sep), White-backed Woodpecker, Azure-winged Magpie, Bull-headed Shrike, Siberian (May–Sep), Scaly, Japanese (May–Sep) and Dusky (Oct–Apr) Thrushes, Narcissus (May–Sep) and Blue-and-white (May–Sep) Flycatchers, Siberian Blue Robin (May–Sep), Daurian Redstart (Nov–Mar), Asian Stubtail (Apr–Sep), Long-tailed Rosefinch (Oct–Mar), Meadow and Chestnut-eared (May–Sep) Buntings.

(Other species recorded here include Solitary Snipe (Nov–Mar), Ural Owl, Ruddy Kingfisher (May–Sep), Japanese Paradise-Flycatcher* (May–Sep), Japanese Accentor and Yellow Bunting* (May–Sep).)

Karuizawa, a popular summer resort area 145 km northwest of Tokyo, is 2 hours by express (tokkyu) train from Ueno station in Tokyo. From Naka-Karuizawa railway station there are plenty of possible walks, but the best is probably north along the Yukawa River via Hoshino Onsen to the **Yacho no Mori Reserve**.

Accommodation: Karuizawa — Hoshino Onsen Hotel (owned by birders and complete with hot spring baths).

Yellow* (May–Sep) and Grey (Apr–Oct) Buntings, as well as Hodgson's Hawk-Cuckoo (May–Aug), Ural Owl, Tiger Shrike (May–Aug), Japanese (May–Sep) and Brown-headed (May–Sep) Thrushes and Japanese Waxwing* (Dec–Mar) occur at **Togakushi** in the Central Alps, accessible via Nagano railway station, an hour or so beyond Karuizawa. From Nagano head for Chusha, walk up the main street and turn left after 2 km on to the track signposted 'Kamauko Pond'. Bird around the pond, 2 km away.

The best site for the endemic Japanese Accentor is **Mount Fuji**. From Kawaguchi-ko railway station (2.5 hours by train or bus from Shinjuku station in Tokyo) take a bus to the tree-line at the Kawaguchi-ko 5th Station. Head up from here as early in the day as possible and check the dwarf conifers for the accentor, while other species to look out for include White-bellied Pigeon* (May–Sep), Japanese Woodpecker, Siberian Thrush (May–Sep), Japanese Robin (May–Sep), Pale-legged Leaf-Warbler (May–Sep), Eastern Crowned-Warbler (May–Sep), Alpine Accentor and Yellow Bunting* (May–Sep).

The only regular wintering site of Baikal Teal* in Japan is **Katano Kamo-ike**, a small lake near Kaga in western Honshu. The lake, run as a sanctuary by the Wild Bird Society of Japan, is 20 minutes by road from Komatsu Airport and 1–2 hours by train from Kanazawa. Other species recorded here, in the woods between the lake and the Sea of Japan, and on the coast itself, include Japanese Cormorant, Mandarin Duck* (Nov–Mar), Azure-winged Magpie, Japanese Waxwing* (Dec–Mar), White-cheeked Starling (Nov–Mar) and Yellow-billed Grosbeak (Nov–Mar).

The tiny island of **Hegura-jima** (2 sq km), 50 km north of Wajima in the Sea of Japan, is Japan's 'Fair Isle', a magnet for migrants which have included Japanese Night-Heron*, Fairy Pitta*, Rufous-tailed Robin, Middendorff's Warbler and many buntings including Yellow* and Grey. The island is accessible by boat from Wajima, which is connected to Kanazawa by train and bus. Bird the lighthouse area, the northern and southern capes and the line of pines which runs north–south across the island. The best time to visit is May and October.

Accommodation: Minshuku Tsukasa (A), which resembles a typical bird observatory at peak times.

HONSHU–HOKKAIDO FERRY

Seabird fanatics can spend a whole day and an early morning in paradise on this ferry which runs daily between Tokyo and Kushiro. The rich waters of the north Pacific support an exciting selection of seabirds and on a good day it is possible to see three species of albatross, which may be joined by some rare storm-petrels in summer or numerous auks in winter.

Specialities

Black-footed and Laysan Albatrosses, Streaked Shearwater (Feb–Oct), Band-rumped (May–Oct), Swinhoe's* (May–Sep) and Tristram's* (Mar–Sep) Storm-Petrels, Black-tailed and Slaty-backed Gulls.

Others

Flesh-footed and Short-tailed Shearwaters, Leach's Storm-Petrel (Apr–Sep), Japanese Cormorant, South Polar Skua (Apr–Jun), Thick-billed Murre (Nov–Apr), Spectacled Guillemot, Ancient Murrelet (Nov–Apr), Crested (Oct–Mar), Least (Feb–Jun) and Rhinoceros Auklets, Pacific Loon (Nov–Apr).

Other Wildlife

Bottle-nosed dolphin, Dall's porpoise, northern fur seal, Steller's sealion.

(Other possible seabirds include Short-tailed Albatross*, Fork-tailed Storm-Petrel, Marbled (Nov–Mar) and Japanese* Murrelets and Tufted Puffin.)

The ferry leaves Tokyo late at night and reaches Kushiro after a second night. Prepare for low temperatures, especially in winter.

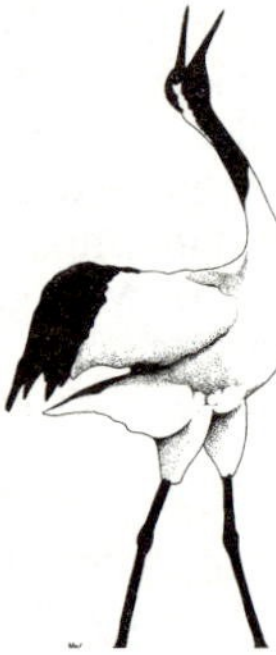

A 'dancing' and bugling Red-crowned Crane is one of nature's most beautiful sights*

HOKKAIDO

In February Japan's northernmost island offers birders the chance of a glorious double delight, in the form of the world's largest concentration of the truly magnificent Steller's Sea-Eagles*, and the sight of 100 or so beautiful bugling and 'dancing' Red-crowned Cranes*, which when set against the backdrop of snow represents nature's art at its finest.

In summer, this mountainous, forested island also supports Latham's Snipe*, Chestnut-cheeked Starling*, Middendorff's and Gray's Warblers, Sakhalin Leaf-Warbler and Grey Bunting, while resident species include the rare Blakiston's Fish-Owl*.

Japanese Endemics

Japanese Accentor.

Specialities

Mandarin Duck* (Apr–Oct), Steller's Sea-Eagle* (Nov–Mar), Red-crowned Crane*, Latham's Snipe* (Apr–Aug), Black-tailed and Slaty-backed Gulls, Spectacled Guillemot, White-bellied Pigeon* (Jun–Sep), Blakiston's Fish-Owl*, Pygmy Woodpecker, Chestnut-cheeked Starling* (Apr–Aug), Middendorff's Warbler (Jun–Sep), Sakhalin Leaf-Warbler (May–Sep), Japanese Skylark, Asian Rosy-Finch (Dec–Feb), Grey Bunting (Apr–Oct).

Others

Japanese and Pelagic Cormorants, Whooper Swan (Nov–Mar), Falcated (Apr–Oct) and Harlequin Ducks, White-tailed Eagle*, Japanese

Sparrowhawk (May–Sep), Hazel Grouse, Rock Sandpiper (Mar–Apr), Pigeon Guillemot (Dec–Mar), Oriental Scops-Owl (May–Sep), Jungle Nightjar (May–Sep), White-throated Needletail (Apr–Sep), Crested Kingfisher, White-backed and Black Woodpeckers, Eurasian Nutcracker, Brown Shrike (May–Jul), Scaly Thrush (May–Sep), Narcissus Flycatcher (May–Sep), Siberian Rubythroat (May–Sep), Lanceolated (Jun–Sep) and Gray's (Jun–Sep) Warblers, Black-browed Reed-Warbler (May–Sep), Pale-legged Leaf-Warbler (May–Sep), Eastern Crowned-Warbler (May–Sep), Long-tailed (May–Sep) and Pallas' (Nov–Mar) Rosefinches, Pine Grosbeak, Chestnut-eared (May–Sep) and Yellow-breasted (May–Sep) Buntings.

Other Wildlife

Brown bear, harbour seal (Nov–Mar), Steller's sealion (Nov–Mar).

(Other species recorded here include Red-faced Cormorant, Steller's Eider (Jan–Mar), Gyrfalcon (Dec–Mar), Tufted Puffin (May–Sep) and Ural Owl.)

KUSHIRO

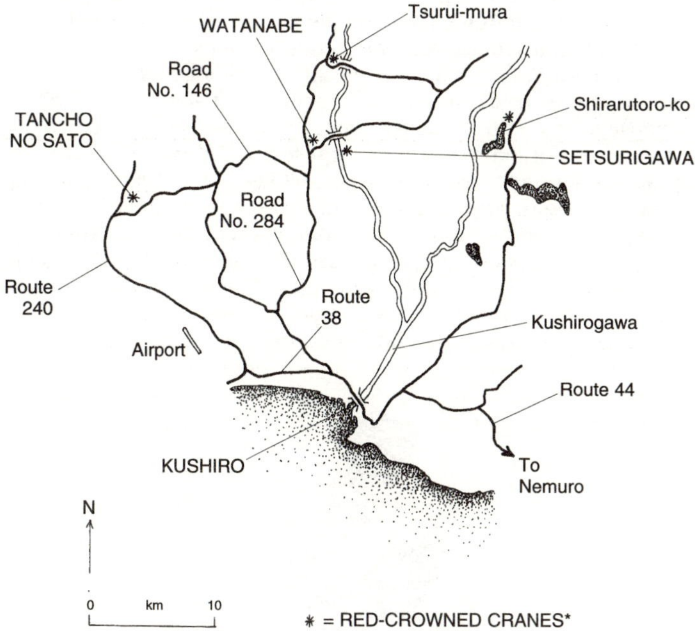

Hokkaido is accessible by air and sea from Tokyo. The best starting point is **Kushiro**. In winter, flocks of Red-crowned Cranes* feed near the observatory at Tancho no Sato, 35 km northwest of Kushiro, and at Watanabe, 30 km or so to the east. They roost in the Setsurigawa, a shallow river a few kilometres east of Watanabe, where they can be seen from the bridge before 0900 or after 1630. East of Kushiro the first place worth stopping at is **Nosappu Misaki**, a headland where Steller's Eider has been recorded in winter. The next major headland is **Ochiishi**, where Latham's Snipe* and Middendorff's Warbler are present in summer. In addition, the scarce Red-faced Cormorant (walk left from the lighthouse) and wintering Gyrfalcon have been recorded here. Further east (1.5 hours out of Kushiro by road) is the rocky promontary of **Kiritappu**, where Rock Sandpiper (in spring) and Tufted Puffin (best in July when feeding young) have been recorded. At the western end of this headland **Furen-ko** is the best place to see large numbers of Steller's Sea-Eagles* in winter and three *locustella* warblers (alongside the south shore of the huge coastal lagoon) in summer. There is also a feeding station for Blakiston's Fish-owl* at Furo-so.

At the base of the mountainous, forested **Shiretoko Peninsula**, which protrudes into the Sea of Okhotsk north of Furen-ko, lies the bustling port of Rausu (4 hours by direct road from Kushiro), a good place for gulls in the afternoon. The peninsula is also a good place for Steller's Sea-Eagles*, especially in February when peak numbers are usually present. They roost in the steep wooded valleys, mainly at Sashiruigawa, 10 km north of Rausu, and Mosekarubetsugawa, further north along the coast road, arriving from 1500 and departing at dawn to feed out on the sea-ice, where it is possible to see them at close range from boats which run from Rausu. During the summer Grey Bunting occurs at **Shiretoko-toge**, a pass in the middle of the peninsula. Walk up the trail to Rausudake from the campsite opposite Kumanoyu.

The wooded Wakoto-hanto peninsula on **Kusharo-ko**, a steaming crater lake in Akan NP, supports summering White-bellied Pigeon* and Jungle Nightjar, and the lake is a winter Whooper Swan roost. The forest to the west of the road about 1 km south of **Kawayu** village, near Kusharo-ko, supports Hazel Grouse and White-bellied Pigeon*, although this area was being logged in the early 1990s. In central Hokkaido, the fish farm and river mouth near the northwest corner of **Shikaribetsu-ko** may still be a good spot for Blakiston's Fish-Owl* (this site is only accessible in summer). The lake lies at the southern end of **Daisetsuzan NP** near Obihiro, where Mandarin Duck*, Crested Kingfisher, Gray's Warbler, Japanese Accentor and Pine Grosbeak occur.

The massive Steller's Sea-Eagle appears on Hokkaido in spectacular numbers during the winter*

Accommodation: Kawayu — Kanko Hotel. Rausu — Daiichi Hotel. Furen-ko — Furen Minshuku (run by a birder). Furo-so — Takada-san's Minshuku.

MIYAKE-JIMA

The grassy headlands and evergreen forests on this island, one of the seven Izu Islands southeast of Tokyo, support the endemic Izu Thrush*, the breeding endemic Ijima's Leaf-Warbler* and the localised Pleske's Warbler. In addition, the ferry between the island and Tokyo offers the best chance of seeing Japanese Murrelet* in Japan.

Japanese Endemics

Izu Thrush*.

Specialities

Tristram's Storm-Petrel* (Mar–Sep), Japanese Murrelet*, White-bellied Pigeon*, Japanese Robin (May–Sep), Pleske's Warbler (Jun–Sep), Ijima's Leaf-Warbler* (May–Sep), Varied Tit.

Others

Streaked Shearwater (Mar–Oct), Grey-faced Buzzard (Apr–Sep), Lesser Cuckoo (May–Sep).

(Other species recorded here in summer include Japanese Night-Heron*.)

Miyake-jima is accessible by air and sea (6–7 hours). Buses run regularly round the circular island (8 km by 8 km). Head for the Toga Jinja shrine in the southwest and walk from there to the cape beyond, where Izu Thrush* and Ijima's Leaf-Warbler*, as well as White-bellied Pigeon* and Pleske's Warbler occur. Also bird the forested surrounds of Tairo-ike, a small lake at the south end of the island where Japanese Robin and Ijima's Leaf-Warbler* occur, and Japanese Night-Heron* has been recorded.

Accommodation: Ako — Youth Hostel.

It is possible to travel by boat (three days) from Yokohama, near Tokyo, to the island of **Torishima**, also one of the Izu Islands. Such a trip, best taken in early April, provides the chance of seeing a 500-strong breeding colony of Short-tailed Albatrosses* (Oct–Jun), as well as Black-footed and Laysan Albatrosses, Bonin and Bulwer's (Apr–Oct) Petrels, Streaked Shearwater (Mar–Oct), Tristram's Storm-Petrel* (Mar–Sep) and Japanese Murrelet*. Landing on the island is not permitted. There is a smaller Short-tailed Albatross* colony on Minami-kojima, one of the Senkaku Islands.

Bonin Honeyeater* is widespread on **Hahashima** island in the Ogasawara Shoto Islands, 1000 km south of Tokyo. A good place to look for this endemic is around the village of Motochi. The island can be reached by ferry (30 hours via Chichi-jima) from Tokyo and a summer visit by sea will involve a round-trip of six days. Possible seabirds, from the ferry, include Short-tailed Albatross* (Oct–Jun), Bonin and Bulwer's (Apr–Oct) Petrels, Red-tailed Tropicbird (May–Aug) and Brown Noddy (Apr–Sep).

Hakata Bay, alongside Fukuoka city in northwest Kyushu Island, supports up to 70,000 waterbirds during the winter, including small numbers of Black-faced Spoonbills* and Saunders' Gulls*. At this time of year it is possible to see 100 species in a day, also including Pacific Loon, Pale and Dusky Thrushes, Chinese Penduline-Tit and Grey Bunting, while rarities include Baikal Teal*. The bay also attracts many migrants and nearly 50 species of shorebird have been recorded, including Little Curlew (Apr–May/Sep), Nordmann's Greenshank* (Aug–Sep), Asian Dowitcher* (Apr–May/Aug–Sep), Great Knot (Apr–May/Aug–Oct), Spoonbill Sandpiper* (Sep–Oct) and Long-billed Plover* (Muromi River, east of Fukuoka), although only Great Knot appears regularly. The best birding sites around the bay are **Wajiro** (shorebirds in spring) and **Imazu** (walk from railway station to Zuibaijigawa estuary for spoonbills and gulls).

In spring (May) or autumn (Sep) many migrants occur on the twin islands of **Tsushima**, accessible by air or sea from Fukuoka. The best sites here are the Sapo River valley at the north end of the north island and the Kisaka Yacho no Mori forest at Mine in the west.

The huge coastal bay known as **Ariake-kai** in west Kyushu attracts similar birds to those listed for Hakata Bay, including migrant shorebirds and wintering Saunders' Gulls*. Good birding sites around this bay include Daijugarami, 10 km south of Saga, at the northern end, and Isahaya (Saunders' Gull*) in the southwest corner. Copper Pheasant*, Pygmy Woodpecker, Japanese Waxwing* (Nov–Mar) and Long-tailed Rosefinch (Oct–Mar) occur on the wooded slopes above Miyayi, around **Mount Aso**, the world's biggest caldera, on the east side of Ariake-kai.

ARASAKI (IZUMI)

The paddies at Arasaki on Kyushu host the most spectacular gathering of wintering cranes in the world. Over 10,000 birds, including nearly 8,000 Hooded* and over 2,000 White-naped* may be present between December and February, as well as a fine selection of other birds including Long-billed Plover* and Crested Kingfisher.

Many of the species listed below are only present during the winter (Nov–Mar).

Specialities

Hooded* and White-naped* Cranes, Long-billed Plover*, Black-tailed Gull, White-bellied Pigeon*, Chinese Penduline-Tit, Japanese Skylark, Black-backed and Japanese Wagtails, Buff-bellied Pipit, Yellow-billed and Japanese Grosbeaks, Ochre-rumped* and Grey Buntings.

ARASAKI

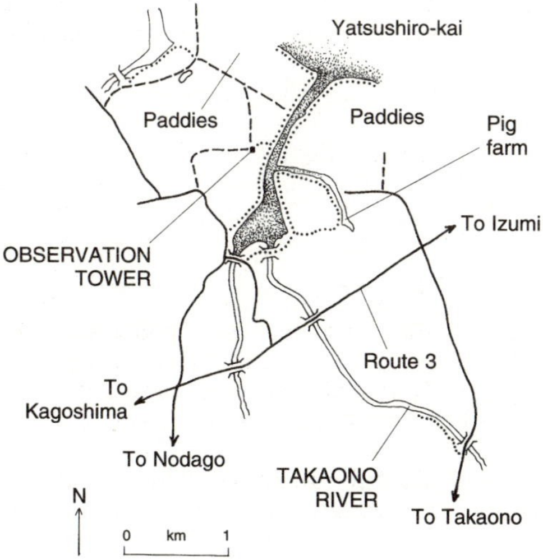

Others

Japanese Cormorant, Greater Painted-Snipe, Crested Kingfisher, Daurian Jackdaw, Bull-headed Shrike, Scaly, Pale and Dusky Thrushes, White-cheeked Starling, Japanese Bush-Warbler, Russet Sparrow, Grey-capped Greenfinch, Meadow, Chestnut-eared, Yellow-throated and Black-faced Buntings.

(Other species recorded here include Swan Goose*, Oriental Stork*, Common, Sandhill, Siberian* and Demoiselle Cranes, Little Curlew (Apr–May), Oriental Plover (Feb–Apr), Ural Owl (nearby) and Pallas' Bunting.)

Arasaki is 2 hours by road (83 km) northwest of Kagoshima Airport in south Kyushu (Copper Pheasant* is possible *en route*). Trains run from Kagoshima to the nearest town, Izumi. The cranes range over a wide area, but can usually be seen in large numbers from the observation tower near the minshuku. Other sites worth concentrating on are the coast, farmland, woodland and the Takaono River, south of Route 3, where Long-billed Plover*, Crested Kingfisher and Japanese Wagtail occur, and Tachibanayama (Standing Flower Mountain) where Ural Owl and Grey Bunting occur.

Accommodation: Arasaki — Minshuku Tsurumitei (in the midst of the cranes and run by the warden). Izumi — Hotel Tsuru.

Ruddy Kingfisher and Fairy Pitta* are summer visitors to the evergreen broadleaf forest around **Mi-ike**, a small lake 1 hour by road northeast of Kagoshima Airport. Other species recorded here include Scaly-sided Merganser* (rare in Nov–Mar), Copper Pheasant*, White-bellied Pigeon*, White-backed and Japanese Woodpeckers, Japanese Paradise-Flycatcher* (May–Sep), Ashy Minivet (May–Sep), Narcissus (May–Sep) and Blue-and-white (May–Sep) Flycatchers, Varied Tit and

Japanese Grosbeak. From Kagoshima head for Takaharu (2.5 hours by train) and on to Mi-ike. Once there bird the nature trails around the campsite at the west end of the lake and look for the pitta in shady areas near streams. Wintering minivets are believed to be Ryukyu Minivets, otherwise endemic to the Nansei Shoto archipelago.

Accommodation: cabins, camping (take food).

AMAMI-OSHIMA

This subtropical island, in the Nansei Shoto archipelago, 400 km south-west of Kyushu, supports five endemics, two of which only occur on this island: Lidth's Jay* and Amami Thrush*. The best time to look for all the endemics is between March and May.

Japanese Endemics

Amami Woodcock*, Lidth's Jay*, Ryukyu Minivet, Amami Thrush*, Ryukyu Robin*.

Specialities

Japanese Wood-Pigeon*, Whistling Green-Pigeon*, Ryukyu Scops-Owl.

Others

Pacific Reef-Egret, Grey-faced Buzzard (Sep–Apr), Barred Buttonquail (May–Sep), Eurasian Woodcock (Nov–Mar), Roseate (May–Sep) and Black-naped (May–Sep) Terns, White-backed Woodpecker.

Other Wildlife

Amami black rabbit.

Amami-Oshima is accessible by air and sea. To see the endemics head north out of the island's capital, Naze, along the west side of the harbour, then take the left fork where the main road bends right, towards Yamato. A few hundred metres along this track, turn left on to the **Supa-rindo** track and bird along here for 5–10 km. Dawn is the best time for the jay, minivet, thrush and robin, and after dark is the best time for the woodcock and scops-owl. The woodcock occurs along the trackside, but be prepared for the presence of wintering Eurasian Woodcocks as well.

Accommodation: Naze — Sunplaza Hotel.

OKINAWA

This subtropical island in the Nansei Shoto archipealgo supports five endemics, two of which only occur here: Okinawa Rail* and Okinawa Woodpecker*. The best time to look for all the endemics is between March and May.

Japanese Endemics

Okinawa Rail*, Amami Woodcock*, Okinawa Woodpecker*, Ryukyu Minivet, Ryukyu Robin*.

Specialities

Mandarin Duck*, Saunders' Gull* (Nov–Mar), Japanese Wood-Pigeon*, Whistling Green-Pigeon*, Ryukyu Scops-Owl, Ruddy Kingfisher (May–Sep), Japanese Paradise-Flycatcher* (May–Sep).

Others

Cinnamon Bittern, Japanese Sparrowhawk (May–Sep), Grey-faced Buzzard (Sep–Apr), Barred Buttonquail (May–Sep), Pintail Snipe (Sep–Apr), Grey-tailed Tattler (Aug–Apr), Rufous-necked (Aug–Apr) and Long-toed (Aug–Apr) Stints, Roseate (May–Sep) and Black-naped (May–Sep) Terns, Brown Hawk-Owl, Light-vented Bulbul.

(Other species recorded here include Black-faced Spoonbill* (Nov–Mar), Oriental Stork* (Nov–Mar), Nordmann's Greenshank* (Sep–Oct) and Spoonbill Sandpiper* (Sep–Oct).)

Okinawa is accessible by air and sea. The rare and endangered rail and woodpecker are confined to the remnant forest at the north end of the island in an area known as **Yambaru**. To reach this forest turn east off Route 58 at Yona, 104 km north of Naha Airport (at the south end of the island), on to Road No. 2. The track to the right 6 km along here is known as Okuni-rindo, the track to the left 7.6 km along here is known as Teakubi-rindo and the track to the left 9 km along is known as Pipeline Road. Explore all three tracks at night for the rail, which roosts in trackside trees, and woodcock, and at dawn for the woodpecker. The area at the southern end of Fungawa Dam, 11 km along Road No. 2, is also worth exploring, as is the area around Benoki Dam, north of Yona on Route 58. The wet fields at **Kijyoka**, alongside Route 58 between Naha and Yona, and the paddies and rushy fields just north of **Kin**, on the southern side of the island, support migrant and wintering shorebirds. The **Man-ko Estuary**, 4 km northeast of Naha airport, and the estuary off the south end of the airport support a few Saunders' Gulls* and shorebirds in winter.

Accommodation: Hentona.

The subtropical **Yaeyama Islands** at the south end of the Japanese archipelago support Malayan Night-Heron (in the mangrove-lined estuaries of northern Iriomote Island and southeast Ishigaki Island), a subspecies of Crested Serpent-Eagle, considered to be a separate species, Ryukyu Serpent-Eagle, by some taxonomists (most easily seen on Iriomote) and Slaty-legged Crake. In summer (Apr–Jun) seabirds such as Wedge-tailed and Flesh-footed Shearwaters, Swinhoe's Storm-Petrel*, Sooty Tern and Brown Noddy may be seen from the Okinawa-Yaeyama Islands ferry and ferries between the main Yaeyama Islands of Iriomote, Ishigaki and Yonaguni.

ADDITIONAL INFORMATION

Addresses

Local birdwatchers may be willing to help visitors and they can be contacted via the Wild Bird Society of Japan, 5th Floor, Aoyama Flower Building, Tokyo.

Books and Papers

A Birdwatcher's Guide to Japan. Brazil M, 1987. Kodansha.
A Field Guide to the Birds of Japan. Wild Bird Society of Japan, 1982. Kodansha.
The Birds of Japan. Brazil M, 1991. Helm.
A Budget Traveller's Guide to Japan. McQueen I, 1992. Kodansha.

ENDEMICS (12)

Main Islands

Copper Pheasant*	Honshu (Karuizawa) and Kyushu (Mt Aso and Mi-ike)
Japanese Woodpecker	Honshu (Karuizawa and Mt Fuji) and Kyushu (Mi-ike)
Izu Thrush*	Izu Islands: Miyake-jima
Japanese Accentor	Honshu (Mt Fuji) and Hokkaido (Daisetsuzan NP)

Nansei Shoto Archipelago

Okinawa Rail*	Okinawa only
Amami Woodcock*	Amami and Okinawa
Okinawa Woodpecker*	Okinawa only
Lidth's Jay*	Amami only
Ryukyu Minivet	Amami, Okinawa and Yaeyama Islands
Amami Thrush*	Amami only
Ryukyu Robin*	Throughout

Bonin Islands

Bonin Honeyeater*	Hahajima

('Ryukyu Serpent-Eagle', which occurs on the Yaeyama Islands of Iriomote and Ishigaki, is considered to be a separate species from Crested Serpent-Eagle by some authorities.)

Near-endemics

Short-tailed Albatross*, Bannerman's Shearwater, Tristram's* and Matsudaira's* Storm-Petrels (both endemic breeding species), Japanese Cormorant, Steller's Sea-Eagle*, Swinhoe's Rail*, Hooded*, Red-crowned* and White-naped* Cranes, Latham's Snipe*, Black-tailed, Slaty-backed and Saunders'* Gulls, Spectacled Guillemot, Japanese Murrelet*, Japanese Wood-Pigeon*, Whistling Green-Pigeon*, Ryukyu Scops-Owl, Blakiston's Fish-Owl*, Bull-headed Shrike, Japanese Waxwing*, Japanese Robin, Light-vented Bulbul, Sakhalin and Ijima's* (endemic breeding species) Leaf-Warblers, Marsh Grassbird*, Varied Tit, Chinese Penduline-Tit, Black-backed and Japanese Wagtails, Grey-capped Greenfinch, Japanese Grosbeak, Ochre-rumped*, Yellow-throated, Yellow* (endemic breeding species) and Grey Buntings.

LAOS

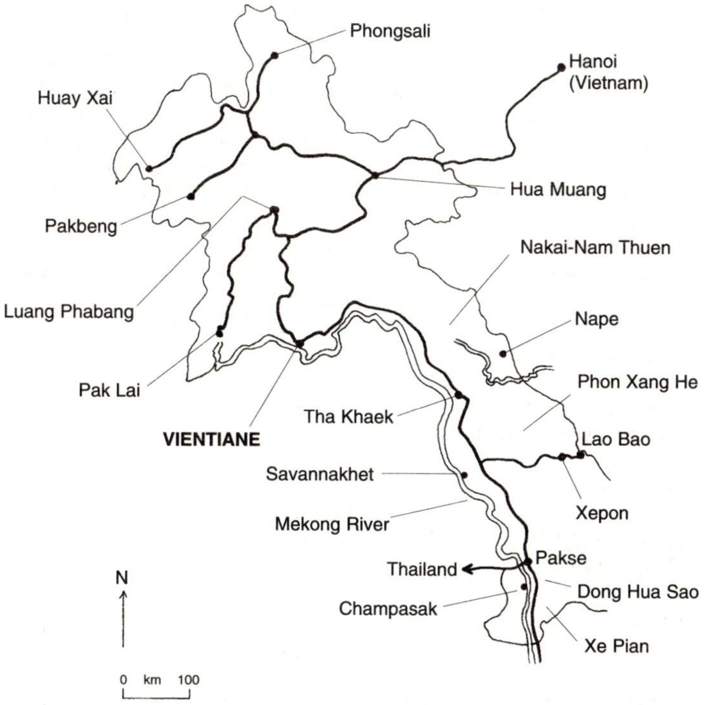

Travelling independently in Laos is virtually impossible because visitor visas are normally only issued to people taking part in cultural tours authorised by the Lao Tourism Authority (LTA). If only the government, which allows logging in its so-called reserves, could be convinced that its natural resources, which include vast forests full of birds such as Beautiful Nuthatch*, are a major asset and that these wild places have a tremendous potential for generating revenue from ecotourists.

At 231,800 sq km, Laos is nearly twice the size of England and three times smaller than Texas. With the exception of a good road between Vientiane, the capital, and Luang Phabang, most of the few other roads are little more than rough tracks. There are some internal flights, but these are very difficult to get on, hence rivers remain the major highways in Laos. There are few places to stay and virtually all of the expensive fairly modern hotels and basic government resthouses are situated in the provincial capitals. The Thai-like food, which also includes excellent French bread, is cheap. Immunisation against hepatitis, polio, typhoid and yellow fever is recommended, as are precautions against malaria. Liver flukes, a type of worm which causes the liver to swell, may be 'taken on board' if undercooked fish is eaten. The best time to visit would be the dry season, which usually lasts from November to

April. Laos is primarily a land of mountains and plateaus, and because the majority of the people live along the Mekong and other river valleys there are still extensive areas of forest. Seventeen so-called reserves were designated in the early 1990s, but logging and hydroelectric power schemes are all allowed within these reserves, so there is little hope for the birds of Laos, especially the 68 threatened and near-threatened species which occur there.

Nearly 640 species have been recorded in Laos. Non-endemic specialities and spectacular species include White-winged Duck*, White-shouldered* and Giant* Ibises, Greater Adjutant*, Rufous-winged Buzzard*, White-rumped Falcon*, Siamese Fireback*, Crested Argus*, Green Peafowl*, Masked Finfoot*, Sarus Crane*, Long-billed Plover*, Pale-capped*, Yellow-vented* and White-bellied* Pigeons, Coral-billed Ground-Cuckoo*, Blyth's* and Crested Kingfishers, Rufous-necked Hornbill*, Red-vented Barbet, Red-collared Woodpecker*, Blue-naped*, Blue-rumped* and Bar-bellied* Pittas, Japanese Paradise-Flycatcher*, White-winged* and Short-tailed* Magpies, Fujian Niltava*, Blue-fronted Robin*, Purple* and Green* Cochoas, Jerdon's Bushchat*, Beautiful Nuthatch*, Grey*, Spot-breasted* and Red-tailed* Laughingthrushes, Short-tailed Scimitar-Babbler*, Sooty Babbler*, Grey-faced Tit-Babbler*, Yellow-throated*, Spectacled* and Rufous-throated* Fulvettas and Short-tailed*, Black-browed* and Rufous-headed* Parrotbills. There is no endemic species.

Small Pratincole has been recorded on the Mekong River, 5 minutes walk from the centre of **Vientiane**. The small Houay Nhang Nature Reserve 14 km north of the city is degraded but may be worth a visit if it is not possible to reach the sites discussed below.

Four large sites in central and south Laos were surveyed extensively in the early 1990s, revealing the continuing presence of many rare and threatened species. The **Nakai-Nam Thuen** national biodiversity conservation area (3500 sq km) on the Nakai Plateau in central Laos is dominated by pristine dry evergreen forest, although there are also mixed and gallery forests, all of which are being degraded and destroyed by logging and which are now subject to a proposed dam, despite being in a 'reserve'. Over 400 species have been recorded here including Crested Argus* and Beautiful Nuthatch*, as well as White-winged Duck*, Lesser* and Grey-headed* Fish-Eagles, Pied Falconet*, Siamese Fireback*, Yellow-vented* and White-bellied* Pigeons, Coral-billed Ground-Cuckoo*, Blyth's* and Crested Kingfishers, Rufous-necked Hornbill*, Red-collared Woodpecker*, White-winged Magpie*, Ratchet-tailed Treepie, Purple Cochoa*, Yellow-vented Warbler*, Short-tailed Scimitar-Babbler* and Spectacled Fulvetta*, while Imperial Pheasant* may also be present.

The semi-evergreen and mixed deciduous forests in the **Phou Xang He** national biodiversity conservation area (1140 sq km), about 85 km east of Savannakhet in south-central Laos, support Rufous-winged Buzzard*, Bar-backed Partridge, Siamese Fireback*, Grey Peacock-Pheasant, Red-vented Barbet, Red-collared*, Black-headed and Pale-headed Woodpeckers, Bar-bellied Pitta, Dusky Broadbill, Brown-rumped Minivet*, Grey-faced Tit-Babbler* and Rufous-throated Fulvetta*. Similar species occur in the semi-evergreen and hill forests in the **Dong Hua Sao** national biodiversity conservation area (900 sq km) on the Bolovens Plateau northeast of Champasak, as well as Malayan Night-Heron, Silver Pheasant, Green Peafowl*, Green Cochoa* and Red-tailed Laughingthrush*. Over 300 species have been recorded in and around the **Xe Pian** national biodiversity conservation area (1500 sq km) southeast of Champasak in the extreme south. The semi-evergreen forest, wetlands and adjacent river valleys support White-winged Duck*, White-shouldered* (on the Xe Khong plains to the east) and Giant* (on the Xe Pian and Houay Kaliang Rivers) Ibises, Rufous-winged Buzzard*, White-rumped Falcon*, Siamese Fireback*, Grey Peacock-Pheasant, Green Peafowl*, Masked Finfoot*, Grey-headed Lapwing (Nov–Jan), Yellow-footed Pigeon, Red-collared*, Black-headed and Pale-headed Woodpeckers, Blue-rumped* and Bar-bellied* Pittas, Short-tailed Magpie*, Brown-rumped Minivet* and Grey-faced Tit-Babbler*.

ADDITIONAL INFORMATION

Books and Papers

Ornithological records from Laos, 1992–1993. Thewlis R *et al.*, 1996. *Forktail* 11: 47–100.
Wildlife and Habitat Surveys of the Xe Piane National Biodiversity Conservation Area, and the Phou Xang He and Dong Hua Sao Proposed Protected Areas. Duckworth J, Timmins R *et al.*, 1993. National Office for Nature Conservation and Watershed Management, Laos.
Wildlife in Lao P.D.R.: a Status Report. Salter R, 1993. IUCN.

Near-endemics

White-shouldered* and Giant* Ibises, Siamese Fireback*, Crested Argus*, Yellow-vented Pigeon*, Coral-billed Ground-Cuckoo*, Indochinese Swiftlet, Red-vented Barbet, Red-collared* and Bamboo Woodpeckers*, Blue-rumped* and Bar-bellied* Pittas, White-winged Magpie*, Ratchet-tailed Treepie, Crested Myna, Fujian Niltava*, Beautiful Nuthatch*, Grey*, White-cheeked and Rufous-vented Laughingthrushes, Hwamei, Short-tailed Scimitar-Babbler*, Sooty Babbler*, Grey-faced Tit-Babbler*, Spectacled* and Mountain Fulvettas, Golden and Short-tailed* Parrotbills, Black-headed Greenfinch.

MALAYSIA

INTRODUCTION

Summary

Only Amazonian forests have a greater diversity of birds than those in Malaysia and this country is full of birds, especially trogons, hornbills, pittas, broadbills and babblers, many of which are easy to see thanks to the excellent tourist infrastructure. There are only two true endemics, but the Malaysian states of Sabah and Sarawak support virtually all of the 37 species which are endemic to the island of Borneo.

Size

At 329,749 sq km, Malaysia is 2.5 times larger than England and about half the size of Texas.

Getting Around

Malaysia is a relatively modern country and getting around is generally cheap and easy thanks to the short distances, reasonably priced long-distance taxis, and the extensive bus and air networks, all of which make hiring a car an unnecessary expense.

Accommodation and Food

There is a wide range of accommodation and food throughout most of Malaysia, although it is necessary to book accommodation in advance at some of the best birding sites.

Health and Safety

Immunisation against hepatitis, polio, typhoid and yellow fever is recommended, as are precautions against malaria.

Climate and Timing

The best time to visit Malaysia is from March to September, when rain is still possible, especially in the afternoons, but the weather tends to be drier than during the October to February period. The peak period is March and April when many species are breeding and thus easier to locate by their songs and calls. For example, pittas, which are hard to find at the best of times, are usually quiet by the end of April, making it even more difficult to locate them.

Habitats

Malaysia's rich birdlife is primarily sustained by luxuriant lowland dipterocarp forests, montane forests and a long coastline where there are many mangrove-lined mud flats. Most of the lowland forest survives on the island of Borneo, although there are also montane forests here, including that on Mount Kinabalu in Sabah, which is the highest peak between the Himalayas and New Guinea at 4101 m (13,455 ft). The central highlands of Peninsular Malaysia, which rise to 2179 m (7150 ft) at Gunung Tahan, also support remnant montane forests.

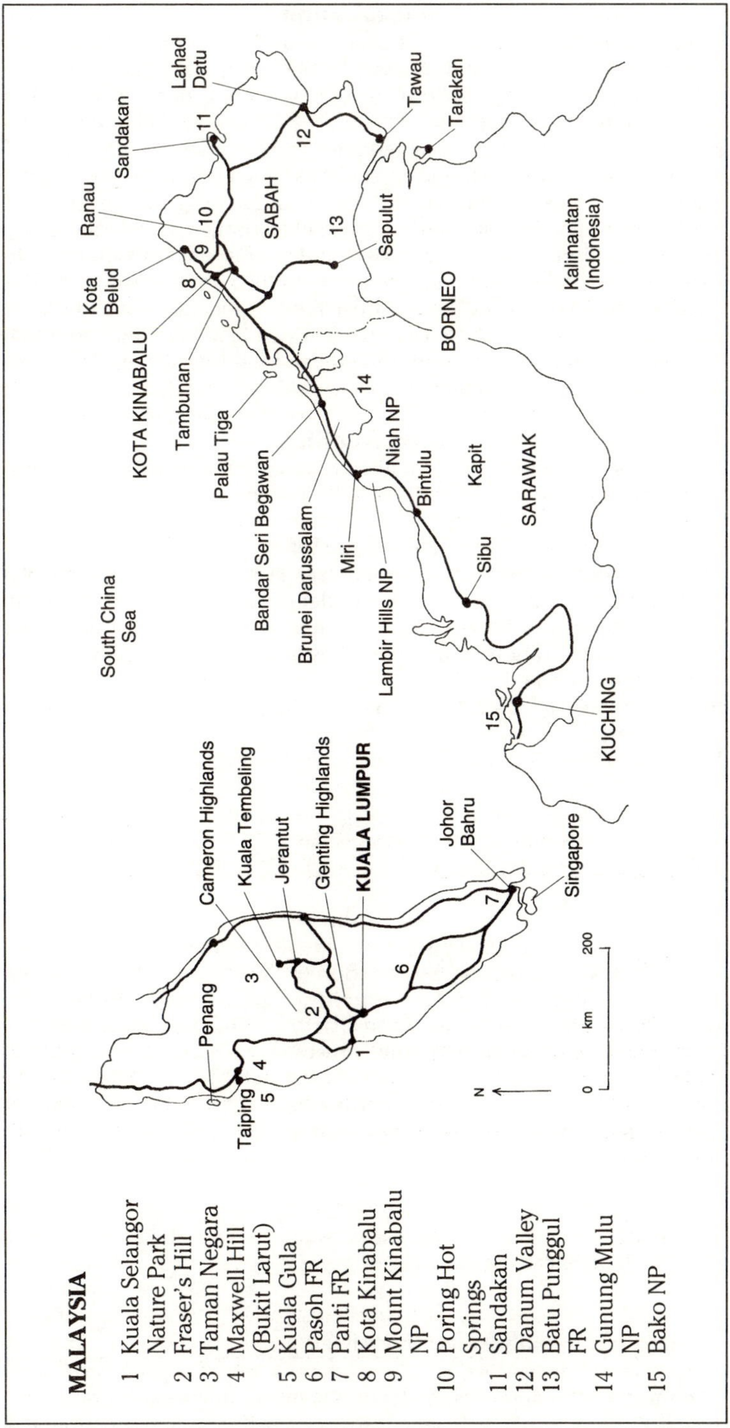

MALAYSIA
1 Kuala Selangor Nature Park
2 Fraser's Hill
3 Taman Negara
4 Maxwell Hill (Bukit Larut)
5 Kuala Gula
6 Pasoh FR
7 Panti FR
8 Kota Kinabalu
9 Mount Kinabalu NP
10 Poring Hot Springs
11 Sandakan
12 Danum Valley
13 Batu Punggul FR
14 Gunung Mulu NP
15 Bako NP
N
0
km
200
Taiping
Penang
Cameron Highlands
Kuala Tembeling
Jerantut
Genting Highlands
KUALA LUMPUR
Johor Bahru
Singapore
South China Sea
KUCHING
Lambir Hills NP
Brunei Darussalam
Bandar Seri Begawan
Miri
Palau Tiga
Tambunan
KOTA KINABALU
Kota Belud
Ranau
Sandakan
Lahad Datu
Tawau
Tarakan
SABAH
Sapulut
BORNEO
Kalimantan (Indonesia)
Niah NP
Bintulu
Kapit
SARAWAK
Sibu

Conservation

Most of Peninsular Malaysia's forest has already been replaced with rubber and oil-palm plantations, and in 1992 the remaining forests were being logged at a rate of 700,000 ha per annum, despite the World Bank's guideline of just(?) 270,000 ha. By 1995 virtually all of the peninsula's forest, outside of the few reserves, had been logged. Over 50% of Borneo is still forested, but such statistics only encourage the logging companies, whose proposals, together with those of the government who are planning to build dams in some of Sarawak's so-called reserves, not only spell disaster for the birds, but threaten to drive tribal people to extinction. The government's promises to the people who will be displaced include providing them with all the 'modern conveniences', but these people would prefer to keep what is their land, and the forests that grow there. Their future and that of Malaysia's birds, especially the 87 threatened and near-threatened species which occur there, looks grim.

Bird Families

Malaysia is rich in pheasants, malkohas, frogmouths, trogons, hornbills, barbets, pittas, broadbills, bulbuls, babblers and spiderhunters.

Bird Species

Over 720 species have been recorded in Malaysia, including around 580 in the Bornean state of Sabah. Non-endemic specialities and spectacular species include Chinese Egret*, Great-billed Heron*, Milky* and Storm's* Storks, Tabon Scrubfowl*, Crestless* and Crested* Firebacks, Great Argus, Masked Finfoot*, Nordmann's Greenshank*, Malaysian Plover*, Nicobar Pigeon*, six trogons, Blue-banded, Brown-winged*, Ruddy and Rufous-collared Kingfishers, Red-bearded Bee-eater, 11 hornbills, Fire-tufted Barbet, Malaysian Honeyguide*, Rusty-naped, Giant*, Garnet, Black-crowned and Mangrove* Pittas, seven broadbills, Malaysian Rail-babbler, Short-tailed Magpie, Chestnut-capped and Island Thrushes, Chestnut-naped Forktail, Blue Nuthatch, Marbled Wren-Babbler*, Silver-eared Mesia, Cutia, Sultan Tit and Scarlet Sunbird.

Endemics

Borneo boasts 37 endemics and these include a falconet, a trogon, two pittas, two broadbills, the bizarre Bornean Bristlehead*, the unique Fruit-hunter, three wren-babblers and two spiderhunters. In addition, two species are endemic to Peninsular Malaysia: Mountain Peacock-Pheasant* and Malayan Whistling-Thrush*.

Expectations

It is possible to see around 350 species on a three-week trip to Peninsular Malaysia and Sabah.

PENINSULAR MALAYSIA

KUALA SELANGOR NATURE PARK

The mud flats, mangroves, pools and scrub in this small reserve (350 ha) at the mouth of the Selangor River near Kuala Lumpur support a

KUALA SELANGOR NP

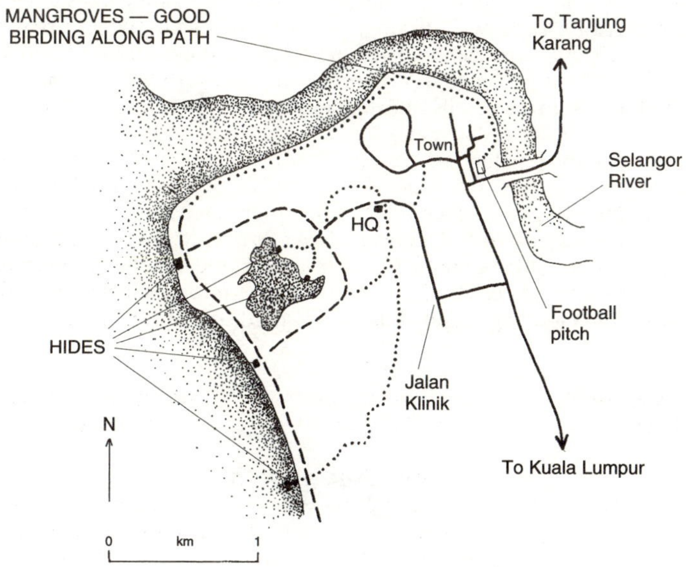

fine selection of birds, including mangrove specialities such as Mangrove Pitta*.

Specialities

Nordmann's Greenshank* (Nov–Mar), Sunda and Laced Woodpeckers, Mangrove Pitta*, Mangrove Blue-Flycatcher.

Others

Yellow and Cinnamon Bitterns, Lesser Adjutant*, Brahminy Kite, White-bellied Sea-Eagle, Red Junglefowl, Slaty-breasted Rail, Watercock, Greater Painted-Snipe, Asian Dowitcher* (Nov–Mar), Zebra Dove, Pink-necked Pigeon, Chestnut-bellied Malkoha, Collared Scops-Owl, Buffy Fish-Owl, Stork-billed, Black-capped (Nov–Mar) and Collared Kingfishers, Blue-tailed Bee-eater, Coppersmith Barbet, Common and Greater Flamebacks, Golden-bellied Gerygone, Mangrove Whistler, Pied Triller, Asian Glossy Starling, Jungle Myna, Ashy Tailorbird, Black-headed Munia, Forest Wagtail (Nov–Mar), Scarlet-backed Flowerpecker, Plain-throated Sunbird.

Other Wildlife

Crab-eating macaque, leopard cat, Malay pangolin, silver leaf-monkey, small-clawed and smooth-coated otters.

(A Milky Stork* re-introduction project was scheduled to take place here in 1995, and Masked Finfoot* has also been recorded.)

The park is just to the southwest of the town of Kuala Selangor, 35 km northwest of Kuala Lumpur. Bird the six, signposted trails within the park and the riverside trail to the north, which is particularly good for the mangrove specialities. On the reserve there are five hides, two of which overlook a 55 ha brackish lagoon, and one of which is situated at the end of a boardwalk through the mangroves and overlooks the tidal mud flats. It is possible to see the amazing synchronised flashing of fireflies near the village of Karang Kuantan, east of Kuala Selangor. Ask in the village for details of excursions.

Accommodation: chalets.

Blyth's Hawk-Eagle, Red-naped Trogon, Rhinoceros and Helmeted* Hornbills, Great Slaty Woodpecker, Green Broadbill, Fiery Minivet and Sultan Tit, as well as migrants (Feb–Mar) such as Tiger Shrike, have been recorded along the Old Gombak Road which ascends the Ulu Gomback Valley in the **Genting Highlands**, 50 km northeast of Kuala Lumpur.

The delightful Forest Wagtail, which waves its tail from side to side, is a winter visitor to Kuala Selangor and much of south Asia

FRASER'S HILL

This cool hill resort, which is situated at 1524 m (5000 ft) in the central highlands, is one of the best birding sites in Malaysia. The remnant montane forest which surrounds the resort supports some superb birds, including both Peninsular Malaysia endemics, Fire-tufted Barbet, Rusty-naped Pitta, Blue Nuthatch, Marbled Wren-Babbler*, Cutia and Black-eared Shrike-Babbler. The best time to visit the hill is in March and April, when most species are breeding, and winter visitors such as Siberian Thrush are still around.

Peninsular Malaysia Endemics

Mountain Peacock-Pheasant* (rare), Malayan Whistling-Thrush*.

Specialities

Grey-breasted Partridge, Yellow-vented Pigeon*, Jambu Fruit-Dove, Fire-tufted Barbet, Rusty-naped Pitta, Blue Nuthatch, Black Laughingthrush, Marbled Wren-Babbler*, Cutia, Pin-tailed Parrotfinch.

FRASER'S HILL

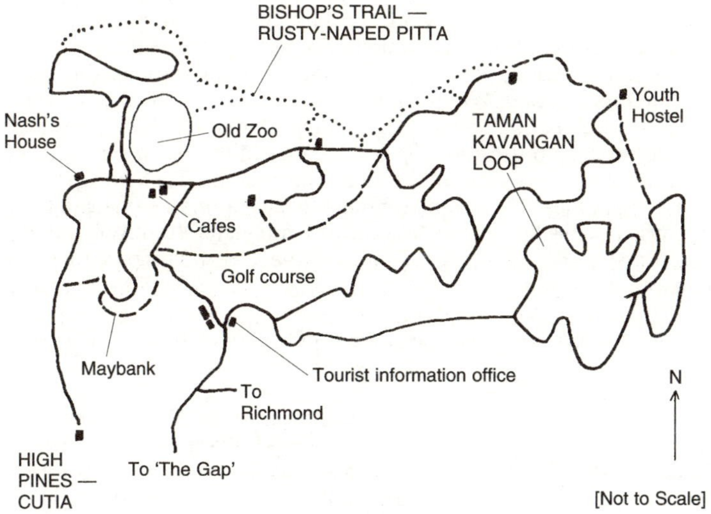

Others

Rufous-bellied Eagle, Blyth's Hawk-Eagle, Black-thighed Falconet, Little Green-Pigeon, Wedge-tailed Pigeon, Mountain Scops-Owl, Collared Owlet, Jungle Nightjar, Brown-backed Needletail, Orange-breasted and Red-headed Trogons, Banded Kingfisher, Red-bearded and Blue-throated Bee-eaters, Helmeted Hornbill*, Red-throated, Black-browed and Yellow-crowned Barbets, Speckled Piculet, Lesser and Greater Yellownapes, Maroon and Bay Woodpeckers, Banded, Black-and-yellow and Long-tailed Broadbills, Green Magpie, Black-and-crimson Oriole, Asian Fairy-bluebird, Orange-bellied Leafbird, Tiger Shrike (Nov–Mar), Orange-headed and Siberian (Nov–Mar) Thrushes, Lesser Shortwing, Ferruginous, Mugimaki (Nov–Mar) and Rufous-browed Flycatchers, Large Niltava, Hill and Pygmy Blue-Flycatchers, Black-crested, Scaly-breasted and Ochraceous Bulbuls, Eastern Crowned-Warbler (Nov–Mar), Mountain Leaf-Warbler, Yellow-bellied Warbler, Chestnut-capped Laughingthrush, Buff-breasted Babbler, Large Scimitar-Babbler, Streaked Wren-Babbler, Silver-eared Mesia, White-browed and Black-eared Shrike-Babblers, Grey-throated and White-hooded Babblers, Blue-winged Minla, Mountain Fulvetta, Long-tailed Sibia, Sultan Tit, Yellow-breasted Flowerpecker, Black-throated Sunbird, Streaked Spiderhunter, Brown Bullfinch.

Other Wildlife

Banded leaf-monkey, pig-tailed macaque, siamang.

(Other species recorded here include Long-billed and Ferruginous Partridges, while in spring (Apr–May) and autumn (Oct–Nov) migrants have included Red-legged Crake, Black-backed and Ruddy Kingfishers, Hooded and Blue-winged Pittas and Brown-chested Jungle-Flycatcher*.)

Fraser's Hill is 103 km north of Kuala Lumpur. There is a one-way 8 km road between 'The Gap', at the bottom of the hill, and the resort, at the top, where vehicles are allowed up and down during alternate hours. If you miss the 'up' hour it is worth birding the forest around 'The Gap' (Helmeted Hornbill*) while waiting. In fact, the road between 'The Gap' and the resort is worthy of a full day's birding because this is the best area for Marbled Wren-Babbler* (1 km above 'The Gap'), White-hooded Babbler and Pin-tailed Parrotfinch. One way to bird this road is to walk down and get a bus back up. Around the resort bird the network of roads, tracks and trails, including Bishop's Trail (Rusty-naped Pitta), High Pines (Cutia, Brown Bullfinch), the Taman Kavangan Loop (Malaysian Whistling-Thrush*) and, unfortunately, the rubbish dump area (Red-bearded Bee-eater). Beware of leeches and prepare for chilly dawn starts.

Accommodation: Nash's House (C), a variety of other hotels and a Youth Hostel.

Two montane species which have not been recorded at Fraser's Hill, Rufous-vented Niltava and Yellow-breasted Warbler, occur in the **Cameron Highlands**, another hill resort to the north. The resort is 60 km east of Tapah, which is on the Kuala Lumpur–Ipoh road.

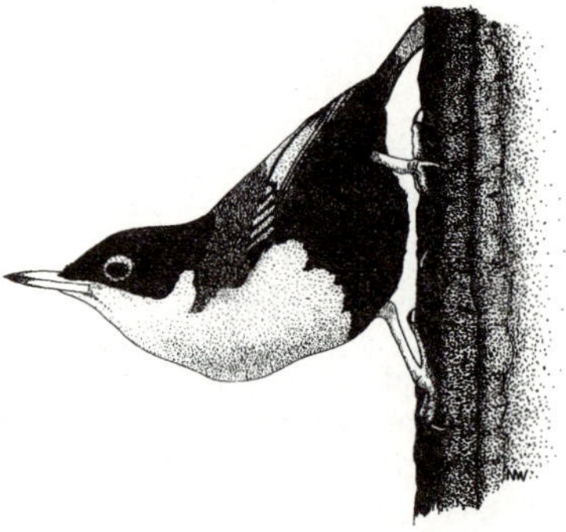

The fabulous Blue Nuthatch is one of the many exceptional birds which occur at Fraser's Hill

TAMAN NEGARA

The largest tract of more or less pristine lowland forest left on mainland southeast Asia lies within this huge National Park (4343 sq km), hence it is one of the finest birding sites in the region. Over 350 species have been recorded, including plenty of malkohas, trogons, hornbills, pittas, broadbills, bulbuls and babblers to keep most birders more than happy. Some birders will no doubt want to concentrate on the specialities, however, and these include Malayan Peacock-Pheasant*, Blue-banded Kingfisher, Garnet Pitta and last, but by no means least, the bizarre Malaysian Rail-babbler.

Taman Negara is a very popular tourist attraction and it is best to book accommodation well in advance, through Taman Negara Resort, Kuala Lumpur Office, 2nd Floor, Istana Hotel, Jalan Raja Chulan, 50250 Kuala Lumpur (tel: 03 2455585, fax: 03 2610615). The park is closed between mid November and mid January because much of the area is usually flooded.

TAMAN NEGARA

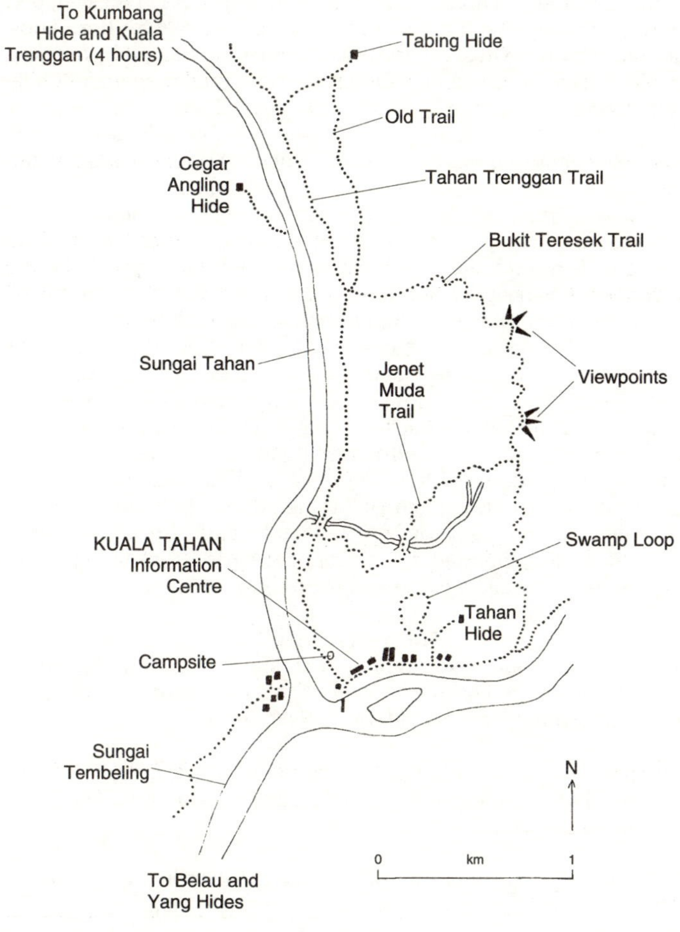

Specialities

Crestless* and Crested* Firebacks, Malayan Peacock-Pheasant*, Great Argus, Red-legged Crake, Masked Finfoot*, Jambu Fruit-Dove, Short-toed Coucal*, Reddish Scops-Owl, Barred Eagle-Owl, Gould's Frogmouth, Cinnamon-rumped Trogon, Blue-banded and Rufous-collared Kingfishers, Wrinkled Hornbill*, Garnet Pitta, Dusky Broadbill, Malaysian Rail-babbler, Chestnut-naped Forktail, Black-and-white and Finsch's Bulbuls, Striped and Large* Wren-Babblers.

Others

Bat Hawk, Lesser Fish-Eagle*, Wallace's Hawk-Eagle*, Black-thighed Falconet, Crested Partridge, Red Junglefowl, Little and Large* Green-Pigeons, Blue-rumped Parrot*, Blue-crowned Hanging-Parrot, Moustached Hawk-Cuckoo, Violet and Drongo Cuckoos, Black-bellied, Chestnut-bellied, Raffles', Red-billed and Chestnut-breasted Malkohas, Oriental (Nov–Mar) and Collared Scops-Owls, Buffy Fish-Owl, Malaysian Nightjar, Whiskered Treeswift, Silver-rumped, Silver-backed and Brown-backed Needletails, Red-naped, Diard's, Scarlet-rumped and Orange-breasted Trogons, Banded, Stork-billed and Black-capped (Nov–Mar) Kingfishers, Red-bearded and Blue-throated Bee-eaters, Black*, Rhinoceros, Great, Helmeted*, White-crowned and Wreathed Hornbills, Yellow-crowned and Brown Barbets, Rufous Piculet, White-bellied, Banded, Orange-backed and Great Slaty Woodpeckers, Banded, Hooded (Nov–Mar) and Blue-winged Pittas, Black-and-red, Banded, Black-and-yellow and Green Broadbills, Spotted Fantail, Crow-billed Drongo (Nov–Mar), Crested Jay, Black Magpie*, Green Iora, Dark-throated Oriole, Bar-bellied Cuckoo-Shrike, Fiery Minivet, Asian Fairy-bluebird, Greater Green and Lesser Green Leafbirds, Rufous-winged and Maroon-breasted Philentomas, Chestnut-capped Thrush, Grey-chested Jungle-Flycatcher, Rufous-chested Flycatcher, Malaysian* and Tickell's Blue-Flycatchers, Siberian Blue Robin (Nov–Mar), White-rumped and Rufous-tailed Shamas, White-crowned Forktail, Straw-headed, Grey-bellied, Stripe-throated, Olive-winged, Grey-cheeked and Yellow-bellied Bulbuls, Rufous-tailed Tailorbird, White-chested*, Ferruginous*, Short-tailed, Black-capped, Moustached, Sooty-capped, Scaly-crowned and Rufous-crowned Babblers, Chestnut-backed Scimitar-Babbler, Rufous-fronted, Grey-headed, White-necked and Black-throated Babblers, Fluffy-backed Tit-Babbler, Brown Fulvetta, Sultan Tit, White-bellied Munia, Crimson-breasted and Scarlet-breasted Flower-peckers, Plain, Red-throated and Scarlet Sunbirds, Thick-billed, Long-billed, Spectacled, Yellow-eared and Grey-breasted Spiderhunters.

Other Wildlife

Common gibbon, gaur, lesser mouse-deer, Malayan tapir, red giant flying squirrel, slow loris. (Asian elephant, clouded leopard, leopard, leopard cat and tiger are also present, but rarely seen.)

(Other species recorded here include Storm's Stork*, Long-billed and Ferruginous Partridges, Crested Argus*, Large Frogmouth*, Malaysian Honeyguide* and Giant Pitta*.)

Taman Negara is 300 km northeast of Kuala Lumpur. It is accessible by boat only and the HQ at Kuala Tahan is 60 km (2–3 hours) upstream on the River Tembeling from Kuala Tembeling, which is 16 km north of Jerantut. Boats leave and return at 0900 and 1400. It is possible to bird on foot on the many trails (those around the HQ at Kuala Tahan are excellent), by boat (a number of outlying trails can only be reached by boat) and from the six large hides which overlook grassy clearings and salt-licks. These hides are best at night and sleep 6–8 people (take food and sleeping bag). The Kumbang Hide, a 7 hour walk away (it is much quicker by boat) is usually the best and it is situated in a good birding area (Crestless Fireback*, Helmeted Hornbill*). Other previously productive spots include the Swamp Loop (frogmouths), the Kumbang–

Kuala Trenggan Trail (Chestnut-capped Thrush), the Jenet Muda Trail (Malayan Peacock-Pheasant*, Great Argus, Short-toed Coucal*, Dusky Broadbill), the Sungai Keniam Trail (Malaysian Rail-babbler), the Tabing (1.5 hours on foot from Kuala Tahan) and Yang (3 hours) hides and Lubok Lehson. It is also possible to climb the 2179 m (7150 ft) Gunung Tahan, where Crested Argus* has been recorded, but this will involve a 110 km round trip which takes nine days. Beware of leeches throughout the park.

Accommodation: Kuala Tahan Resort — chalets (A), hostel (C), camping (C), all of which should be booked in advance. Kuala Tahan Village (on opposite side of the river) — Tembeling Camp (C). Nusa Camp (15 minutes upriver) — cottages (A), huts (B), hostel (C), bookable in advance through Nusa Camp Desk, Tourist Centre, Jalan Ampang, Kuala Lumpur (tel: 03 242 3929, extension 112). Kuala Trenggan (35 minutes upriver) — Trenggan Lodge (A), camping (C).

Whiskered Treeswift is one of the many wonderful birds which occur at Taman Negara

Over 200 species have been recorded in the montane forests around the old hill resort of **Maxwell Hill** (Bukit Larut), which lies at 1035 m (3396 ft), 9 km east of Taiping in north Peninsular Malaysia. The avifauna, which is almost identical to that of Fraser's Hill (p. 196), includes Blyth's Hawk-Eagle, Grey-breasted Partridge, Rusty-naped Pitta, Dusky and Silver-breasted Broadbills, Slaty-backed Forktail, Everett's White-eye, Marbled Wren-Babbler*, Cutia and Tawny-breasted Parrotfinch. Bukit Larut is only accessible, to those who have booked accommodation in advance, by jeeps which leave from the bottom of the road every 30 minutes or so from 0800 to 1800 hours. These jeeps can be booked in advance by phoning 05 827243. Few people visit this small place in the week, hence birding can be a delight alongside the road up from Taiping, the road beyond to the telecommunications tower on Gunung Hijau at 1448 m (4750 ft), and on the few tracks. Beware of leeches.

Accommodation: Gunung Hijau Resthouse, bookable in advance through the Officer-in-Charge, Bukit Larut Hill Resort, Taiping, Perak 34020 (tel: 05 827241) or by writing direct to the Resthouse at Rumah Rehat Gunung Hijau, Bukit Larut, Taiping, Perak 34020 (tel: 05 827240).

KUALA GULA

The mangroves and mud flats near the fishing village of Kuala Gula in the northwest corner of Peninsular Malaysia are one of the best sites for Milky Stork* in Asia, as well as some mangrove specialists.

Specialities

Milky Stork*, Sunda and Laced Woodpeckers, Mangrove Blue-Flycatcher.

Others

Chinese Pond-Heron, Yellow and Cinnamon Bitterns, Lesser Adjutant*, Pink-necked Pigeon, Golden-bellied Gerygone, Mangrove Whistler, Olive-winged Bulbul, Ashy Tailorbird, Lanceolated Warbler (Nov–Mar), Plain-throated and Copper-throated Sunbirds.

Other Wildlife

Crab-eating macaque, dusky leaf-monkey, smooth-coated otter.

(Other species recorded here include Chinese Egret*, Red-legged Crake, Masked Finfoot*, Asian Dowitcher*, Great Knot, Cinnamon-headed Pigeon*, Oriental Bay-Owl, Ruddy Kingfisher and Mangrove Pitta*.)

Kuala Gula is 40 km northwest of Taiping. Birding is good throughout the surrounding area (from Kuala Kurau to the north to Kuala Sepetang (Port Weld) to the south), especially in the Matang Mangrove FR, the northern part of which is a Bird Sanctuary. The best way to bird this area, however, is by boat, bookable in advance through the park office which is situated behind the school (signposted 'Projek Konservasi Burung-Burung Laut') just north of Kuala Gula village (tel: 04 557207). The ranger here may be willing to act as a guide. Milky Stork* and Lesser Adjutant* occur around the lake on Pular Kelumpang, 2 km south of the park office.

Accommodation: Kuala Gula (basic, but better accommodation is planned), bookable in advance through the Wildlife and National Parks Department (address at end of section).

Malayan Peacock-Pheasant*, Malaysian Honeyguide*, Crimson-winged and Olive-backed Woodpeckers, Garnet Pitta, Malaysian Rail-babbler, Japanese Paradise-Flycatcher* (Nov–Mar), Rufous-tailed Shama and Grey-breasted Babbler* have been recorded at **Pasoh Forest Reserve**, a small area of peat-swamp forest about 150 km southeast of Kuala Lumpur. To reach this reserve turn off the main road south in response to the 'Felda Pasoh Dua' sign, 0.5 km before Simpang Pertang. From here it is 6 km to the reserve where there are a few trails, but birding is very hard work here and leeches abound.

Accommodation: hostel (C/take food).

PANTI FOREST RESERVE

Over 250 species have been recorded in the lowland, swamp and montane forests in this reserve (275 sq km) at the southern end of Peninsular Malaysia. Few foreign birders have made it here because it is a long way from the well beaten birding circuit near Kuala Lumpur, but the site is readily accessible from Singapore and the rewards for those who do make the effort to spend some time here could include such scarce species as Chestnut-necklaced Partridge*, Garnet Pitta and Malaysian Rail-babbler.

Specialities

Chestnut-necklaced Partridge*, Crestless Fireback*, Great Argus, Short-toed Coucal*, Oriental Bay-Owl, Reddish Scops-Owl, Gould's Frogmouth, Cinnamon-rumped Trogon, Wrinkled Hornbill*, Laced Woodpecker, Garnet Pitta, Dusky Broadbill, Malaysian Rail-babbler, Chestnut-naped Forktail, Black-and-white Bulbul, Brown-backed Flowerpecker*.

Others

Schrenck's* (Nov–Mar) and Black (Nov–Mar) Bitterns, Lesser Fish-Eagle*, Wallace's Hawk-Eagle*, Black-thighed Falconet, Crested Partridge, Cinnamon-headed Pigeon*, Little Green-Pigeon, Blue-rumped Parrot*, Blue-crowned Hanging-Parrot, Chestnut-breasted Malkoha, Malaysian and Savanna Nightjars, Red-naped, Diard's and Scarlet-rumped Trogons, Banded Kingfisher, Red-bearded Bee-eater, Black*, Rhinoceros, Helmeted*, Bushy-crested and Wreathed Hornbills, Red-crowned and Yellow-crowned Barbets, Rufous Piculet, White-bellied, Buff-rumped and Great Slaty Woodpeckers, Black-and-red, Banded, Black-and-yellow and Green Broadbills, Mangrove Whistler, Black Magpie*, Green Iora, Dark-throated Oriole, Lesser Cuckoo-Shrike, Fiery Minivet, Siberian Thrush (Nov–Mar), Siberian Blue-Robin (Nov–Mar), White-crowned Forktail, Straw-headed*, Puff-backed, Hairy-backed and Buff-vented Bulbuls, Ferruginous*, Black-capped, Grey-headed, Chestnut-rumped and Chestnut-winged Babblers, Brown Fulvetta, Yellow-breasted Flowerpecker, Scarlet Sunbird.

Other Wildlife

Asian elephant, cream-coloured giant squirrel, flying lemur, leopard, Malayan tapir, slow loris, sun bear, Sunda pangolin, tiger.

The reserve is 20 km north of the town of Kota Tinggi, which is 41 km north of Johor Bahru at the southern tip of Peninsular Malaysia, just across the water from the island of Singapore. To reach the **Gunung Panti Trail**, take the road northwest out of Kota Tinggi towards Lombong Waterfall and look out for a police station on the right after 6 km. Turn east into the road beside the station and continue 4 km to Batu Empat village. Ask permission to leave vehicles here and, if granted, take the trail left of the road through farmland, old rubber plantations and scrub for 2 km (Laced Woodpecker, Mangrove Whistler, Straw-headed Bulbul*), then the trail which leads through logged foothill forest on the slopes of flat-topped Gunung Panti (Black-thighed Falconet, Green Broadbill). It is easy to get lost here, but guides are available for hire in the village. To reach the **Ridge Trail** head north-east out of Kota Tinggi towards Kuantan and Mersing. The trail heads west from the 270 KM post, approximately 40 km north of Kota Tinggi.

PANTI FR

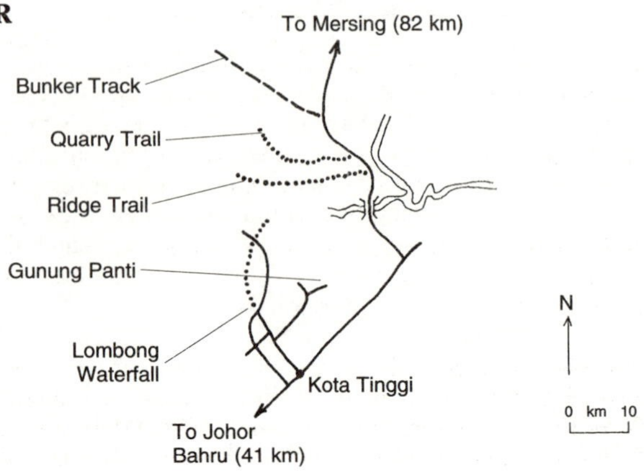

The first kilometre of this trail is particularly good for Crestless Fireback*, as well as bird waves which may contain up to 20 species. After another 1.5 km the trail enters swamp forest where Wrinkled Hornbill* and Puff-backed Bulbul occur, and leeches abound. Wallace's Hawk-Eagle*, Garnet Pitta, Malaysian Rail-babbler and Black-and-white Bulbul have been recorded along the **Quarry Trail**, which leads west 1 km north of the Ridge Trail. The **Bunker Track** heads west from near the 266 KM post where there are two World War II bunkers on either side of the road. This track is very busy on weekdays with trucks heading to and from quarries within the reserve, hence weekends are the best time to look for the track's specialities which include Black Bittern, Helmeted Hornbill*, and a selection of nightbirds. Beware of Asian elephants and tigers throughout the area.

Accommodation: Kota Tinggi.

SABAH (Malaysian Borneo)

KOTA KINABALU

The town of Kota Kinabalu on Sabah's west coast is the major gateway to north Borneo. It is surrounded by coastal lagoons, marshes, farmland and grasslands which support such scarce species as Chinese Egret* and Malaysian Plover*, while Christmas Island Frigatebird* and Tabon Scrubfowl* occur on the nearby offshore islands.

Specialities

Chinese Egret* (Nov–Apr), Tabon Scrubfowl*, Swinhoe's Snipe (Nov–Mar), Malaysian Plover*, Blue-naped Parrot*, Mangrove Blue-Flycatcher, Striated Grassbird, Dusky Munia.

Others

Lesser and Christmas Island* Frigatebirds, Pacific Reef-Egret, Yellow, Cinnamon and Black Bitterns, Eastern Marsh-Harrier (Nov–Mar), Pied Harrier (Nov–Mar), White-browed Crake, Greater Painted-Snipe, Pintail Snipe (Nov–Mar), Grey-tailed Tattler (Sep–Apr), Great Knot (Sep–Apr), Rufous-necked (Sep–Apr) and Long-toed (Sep–Apr) Stints, Oriental Pratincole (Sep–Apr), Pink-necked Pigeon, Blue-throated Bee-eater, Mangrove Whistler, White-breasted Wood-swallow, Pied Triller, Asian Glossy-Starling, Fulvous-chested Jungle-Flycatcher, Olive-winged and Red-eyed Bulbuls, Pallas' Warbler (Nov–Mar), Black-headed Munia, Plain-throated and Crimson Sunbirds.

Kota Kinabalu is accessible by air from Kuala Lumpur and Singapore. Areas worth birding in and near the town include the **Museum Botanic Gardens** (Blue-naped Parrot*), **Summit Hill**, at the eastern edge of town (Blue-throated Bee-eater), the lagoons alongside **Likas Bay**, 3 km to the northeast, which support wintering Chinese Egret* and shorebirds including Grey-tailed Tattler, the paddies at **Kota Belud**, 70–80 km to the northeast (2 hours by bus), near Tempassuk, which support bitterns, harriers, shorebirds, Blue-throated Bee-eater and Striated Grassbird, and the **Papar** paddies (crakes), which are to the south of Kota Kinabalu near a river estuary and beach which supports Great Knot and Malaysian Plover*. It is possible to take boat trips from Kota Kinabalu to **Palau Manukan**, one of five offshore islands in Tunku Abdul Rahman NP, where Tabon Scrubfowl* and Malaysian Plover* occur, as well as Lesser and Christmas Island* Frigatebirds, Blue-naped Parrot*, Mangrove Whistler, Mangrove Blue-Flycatcher and Olive-winged and Red-eyed Bulbuls. Boats leave on a regular basis from the jetties behind the Hyatt Hotel, or the marina at Tanjong Aru, and take just 20 minutes. The scrubfowl occurs alongside the 1.5 km paved path which runs through the dry woodland left of the reception area. Another island here, **Pulau Sapi**, supports the scrubfowl and Fulvous-chested Jungle-Flycatcher. Snorkelling and scuba-diving off these islands is recommended.

Accommodation: Kota Kinabalu — traveller's resthouse (C), Farida's B & B, near Likas Bay, (C). Kota Belud — Hotel Kota Belud (A), Century Hotel (A), Palace Hotel (A), government resthouse (A). Palau Manukan — chalets (A).

Lesser and Christmas Island* Frigatebirds, Chinese Egret* (Nov–Apr), Tabon Scrubfowl*, Nicobar Pigeon*, Ruddy Kingfisher, Mangrove Whistler, Mangrove Blue-Flycatcher and Pechora Pipit (Nov–Mar) occur on **Pulau Tiga**, another island off west Sabah. To bird this island obtain a permit and book accommodation at the Sabah Parks Office in Kota Kinabalu, then head for Kuala Penyu, 3.5 hours by road, where the ferry usually leaves for Pulau Tiga at 1100 on weekdays. Otherwise, it is possible to charter a local fishing boat. There are a number of trails to explore on the island, but Tabon Scrubfowl* is a rather tame bird here and often seen in the campsite.

Accommodation: chalets, camping (C/take food).

MOUNT KINABALU NATIONAL PARK

The forest on this 4101 m (13,455 ft) mountain, the highest between the Himalayas and New Guinea, supports most of Borneo's montane endemics, including the amazing 'Whitehead's' trogon, broadbill and spiderhunter hat-trick, the unique Fruit-hunter and Friendly Bush-Warbler, all of which are supported by stunners such as Short-tailed Magpie and Scarlet Sunbird. Hence any Bornean birding itinerary should allow for at least a few days here.

MOUNT KINABALU NP

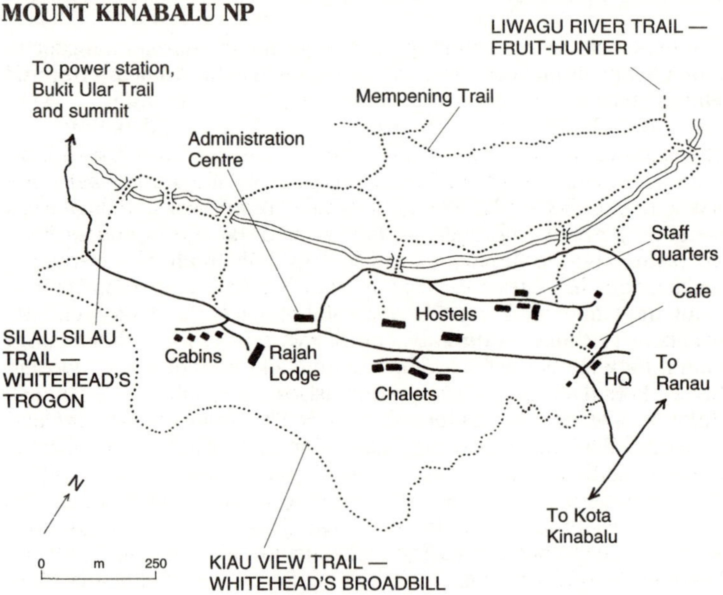

Bornean Endemics

Mountain Serpent-Eagle*, Red-breasted and Crimson-headed Partridges, Whitehead's Trogon, Mountain and Golden-naped Barbets, Whitehead's Broadbill, Bornean Whistler, Everett's Thrush*, Fruit-hunter, Eyebrowed Jungle-Flycatcher, Mountain Black-eye, Bornean Stubtail, Friendly Bush-Warbler, Mountain Wren-Babbler, Chestnut-crested Yuhina, Black-sided Flowerpecker, Whitehead's Spiderhunter.

Specialities

Cave Swiftlet, Cinnamon-rumped Trogon, Sunda Treepie, Sunda Cuckoo-Shrike, Sunda Whistling-Thrush, Island Thrush, Indigo Flycatcher, Black-capped and Everett's (Nov–Mar) White-eyes, Sunda Bush-Warbler, Yellow-breasted Warbler, Sunda and Black Laughing-thrushes, Temminck's Babbler, Dusky Munia, Scarlet Sunbird.

Others

Blyth's Hawk-Eagle, Mountain Scops-Owl, Collared Owlet, Jungle Nightjar (Nov–Mar), Wreathed Hornbill, Crimson-winged, Checker-throated, Maroon and Orange-backed Woodpeckers, Short-tailed Magpie*, Black-and-crimson Oriole, Bar-bellied Cuckoo-Shrike, Blue-winged Leafbird, White-tailed Flycatcher, Pygmy Blue-Flycatcher, White-crowned Forktail, Velvet-fronted Nuthatch, Flavescent and Ochraceous Bulbuls, Mountain Leaf-Warbler, Grey-throated Babbler, White-browed Shrike-Babbler, Grey-breasted Spiderhunter.

Other Wildlife

Moonrat, mountain tree-shrew, red leaf-monkey, spotted giant flying squirrel, yellow-throated marten, nine species of pitcher-plant, over 1,500 species of orchid, and butterflies including Rajah Brooke's Birdwing.

(Other species recorded here include Brown Wood-Owl, Bornean Frogmouth*, Bornean Barbet, Pygmy White-eye and Tawny-breasted Parrotfinch.)

The HQ, situated at 1623 m (5325 ft), is 2 hours by road (88 km) from Kota Kinabalu. The mountain is very popular with tourists, but fortunately very few stray from the summit trail. The areas around the hostels are good for birds, especially at dawn when a number of species feed on the insects attracted to the lights overnight, including Sunda Treepie and laughingthrushes. In the early morning it is also worth checking the dead trees behind Rajah Lodge for Whitehead's Spiderhunter. The excellent network of trails includes the Kiau View (Red-breasted Partridge, Whitehead's Broadbill, Whitehead's Spiderhunter), Liwagu River (Fruit-hunter, Mountain Wren-Babbler, Temminck's Babbler), Bukit Ular (Everett's Thrush*) and Silau-Silau (Crimson-headed Partridge, Whitehead's Trogon, Sunda Whistling-Thrush). The 4.5 km road up to the power station (accessible by foot and bus) at 1950 m (6398 ft) is also worth birding. From the power station it is possible to walk to Carson's Camp, at 2650 m (8694 ft), and back in a day, with enough time to find Island Thrush, Flavescent Bulbul and the endemic Friendly Bush-Warbler, all of which usually only occur above 2150 m/7054 ft, in the process. It is necessary to obtain a permit and arrange a guide at the HQ to walk to the bare granite summit of Mount Kinabalu.

The unique Fruit-hunter is one of many Bornean endemics which occur on Mount Kinabalu

Most people start from the power station at 0700, from where it is a punishing 6–7 hours up to the Laban Rata Resthouse at around 3353 m (11,000 ft), just above the treeline. From here most people leave at 0300 the following morning to reach Low's Peak at dawn. It is then possible to return to the HQ area by 1300 in time for an afternoon's birding.

Accommodation: chalets (A), hostel (C), Laban Rata Resthouse (B). All accommodation should be booked in advance through Sabah Parks, PO Box 10626, 88806 Kota Kinabalu (tel: 088 211881. fax: 088 211585).

PORING HOT SPRINGS

The upper dipterocarp forest which surrounds Poring Hot Springs at 457 m (1500 ft) supports a small, but superb, selection of Bornean endemics, including the brilliant Blue-banded Pitta, although, as is the case with most pittas, this is one hell of a bird to find. Other localised avian jewels which occur here and deserve special attention include Blue-banded and Rufous-collared Kingfishers.

PORING HOT SPRINGS

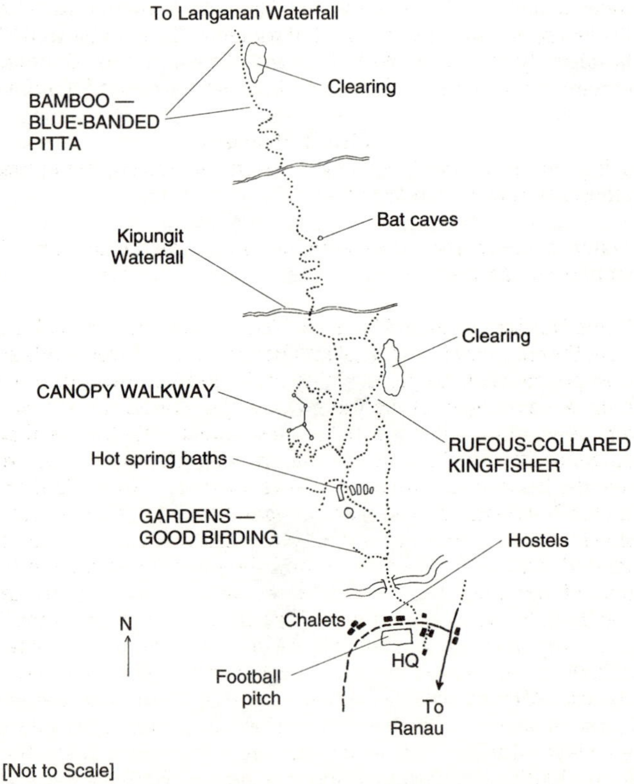

Bornean Endemics

White-fronted Falconet*, Bornean Barbet, Blue-banded Pitta, Bornean Blue-Flycatcher, White-crowned Shama, Chestnut-crested Yuhina, Yellow-rumped Flowerpecker, Bornean and Whitehead's Spiderhunters.

Specialities

Ruddy Cuckoo-Dove, Jambu Fruit-Dove, Cinnamon-rumped Trogon, Blue-banded and Rufous-collared Kingfishers, Sunda Treepie, Chestnut-tailed Jungle-Flycatcher, Chestnut-naped Forktail, Everett's White-eye, Temminck's Babbler, Dusky Munia, Scarlet Sunbird.

Others

Blue-crowned Hanging-Parrot, Black-bellied, Raffles', Red-billed and Chestnut-breasted Malkohas, Grey-rumped Treeswift, Silver-rumped Needletail, Red-naped, Scarlet-rumped and Orange-breasted Trogons, Banded Kingfisher, Red-bearded Bee-eater, Bushy-crested, White-crowned and Wreathed Hornbills, Gold-whiskered, Red-throated and Brown Barbets, Rufous Piculet, Banded, Crimson-winged, Checker-throated, Olive-backed, Maroon, Buff-rumped, Buff-necked and Grey-and-buff Woodpeckers, Banded Pitta, Black-and-red, Banded, Black-and-yellow and Green Broadbills, Spotted Fantail, Crested Jay, Dark-throated Oriole, Maroon-breasted Philentoma, Orange-headed Thrush, White-tailed Flycatcher, Siberian Blue Robin (Nov–Mar), White-crowned Forktail, Straw-headed*, Scaly-breasted, Red-eyed, Spectacled, Grey-cheeked, Yellow-bellied and Hairy-backed Bulbuls, Horsfield's, Black-capped and Moustached Babblers, Chestnut-backed Scimitar-Babbler, Eyebrowed Wren-Babbler, Grey-headed Babbler, Plain Sunbird, Long-billed, Yellow-eared and Grey-breasted Spiderhunters.

Other Wildlife

Flying lemur, slender tree-shrew, western tree-shrew, flying lizards and rafflesia (the world's largest flower).

(Other species recorded here include Red-legged Crake and Chestnut-capped Thrush.)

Poring Hot Springs are 43 km from Mount Kinabalu NP, via Ranau. This is another popular tourist spot and best avoided at weekends, although most people seem to prefer sitting in the red hot water to scouring the trails. A dawn walk along the forest edge around the springs can be very rewarding. After dawn the best trail to explore is that to the Langanan Waterfall. Rufous-collared Kingfisher has been recorded near the beginning of this trail, before the first clearing. Further up look out for Red-bearded Bee-eater, Bornean Barbet, Banded Pitta, Bornean Blue-Flycatcher, Yellow-rumped Flowerpecker and, especially, Blue-banded Pitta, which occurs around the clearing below the first large area of bamboo. It is a 2–3 hour climb to the superb Langanan Waterfall, by which time the rock pools at the bottom of the fall may seem very inviting, especially to those fortunate few who are able to wallow in memories of Blue-banded Pitta. This trail also passes Kipungit Waterfall where Chestnut-capped Thrush has been recorded. The steel canopy walkway, just behind the spring baths, allows excellent views of some birds which are rarely seen at eye-level, but at over 30 m (100 ft) above the ground it is best avoided by those who fear heights. The area around the hostel is also worth birding, especially the road to the generator.

Accommodation: chalets (A), hostel (C), camping (C). It is best to take food, which can be cooked in the hostel, and to book in advance through the Sabah Parks office in Kota Kinabalu (see previous site for address).

The tiny White-fronted Falconet is endemic to Borneo*

Sandakan, the gateway to Pulau Selingaan, Uncle Tan's Jungle Camp, Gomantong Caves and Sepilok FR, is accessible by air from Kuala Lumpur and by air and road from Kota Kinabalu. The best base for budget birders here is Uncle Tan's Guesthouse (C), which is 29 km from Sandakan and 4 km from the turn-off to the 3 km Sepilok FR entrance road. To book Uncle Tan's in advance write to PPM 245 Elopura, 9000 Sandakan (tel: 089 531639). Another good place to stay is the Wildlife Lodge (A–C) opposite the Sepilok FR. To book in advance write to Wildlife Lodge, Sepilok Jungle Resort Phase 1, Mile 14, Labuk Road, Sepilok Orangutan Sanctuary, PO Box 1034, 90008 Sandakan, Sabah, Malaysia (tel: 089 533031, fax: 089 533029). Brown-backed Flowerpecker* has been recorded in the vicinity and nearly 220 species have been recorded at the **Sepilok FR** (44 sq km), including Rufous-collared Kingfisher, Giant* and Blue-headed* Pittas and Bornean Bristlehead*. Access is restricted because this reserve surrounds an orang-utan rehabilitation project, but if it is possible to bird beyond the buildings, try the Waterfall Trail where Giant Pitta* has been recorded. Uncle Tan arranges trips (A) to Pulau Selingaan, Gomantong Caves and his own Jungle Camp on the Kinabatangan River. **Pulau Selingaan** is one of three small islands in the Turtle Island NP, where Tabon Scrubfowl*, Nicobar Pigeon* and Pied Imperial-Pigeon occur, as well as green and hawksbill turtles (Aug–Sep). Boats also visit the Kinabatangan River near Sandakan Bay, where the mangrove-lined creeks and mud flats support Lesser Frigatebird, Chinese Egret* (Nov–Mar), Storm's Stork*, Lesser Adjutant*, Great Knot (Sep–Apr) and Ruddy Kingfisher, as well as proboscis monkey and mangrove catsnake. Alternatively, Great-billed Heron*, Storm's Stork*, Jerdon's Baza* and Wrinkled Hornbill*, as well as proboscis monkey, have been recorded in the Kinabatangan tributaries which are accessible by boat from Sukau. **Uncle Tan's Jungle Camp** (basic, food included) is 1 hour downstream from the bridge over the Kinabatangan River, which is 1 hour by road from

Sandakan towards Lahad Datu. The camp is set among a number of oxbow lakes (with viewing platforms) and secondary forest, and is a good site for Storm's Stork*, as well as Bornean Bristlehead* and Brown-backed Flowerpecker*, plus proboscis monkey. Other species recorded here include Malayan Night-Heron, Wallace's Hawk-Eagle*, Crested Fireback*, Large Green-Pigeon*, Rufous-backed and Rufous-collared Kingfishers, Wrinkled Hornbill*, Blue-headed*, Hooded and Black-crowned Pittas, Bornean Blue-Flycatcher, White-chested* and Black-throated Babblers and Yellow-rumped Flowerpecker. The massive **Gomantong Caves**, 32 km south of Sandakan, support millions of bats and swiftlets (Mossy-nest, Black-nest and mostly Edible-nest), while the surrounding secondary forest avifuana includes Bat Hawk, Whiskered Treeswift, Red-bearded Bee-eater, Dusky Broadbill, Dusky Munia and Brown-backed Flowerpecker*. If travelling independently of Uncle Tan it is necessary to obtain a permit from the Wildlife Department (Pejabat) at Mile 7 on the outskirts of Sandakan before visiting the caves. Prepare for the smell and take a torch to get the best views of the swiftlets and hang around for dusk if you want to see Bat Hawks attacking the bats as they emerge in their millions from the caves to feed.

DANUM VALLEY

Although the biggest trees are usually seen on the huge logging trucks, making their way out of the valley as visitors make their way in, 438 sq km of lowland dipterocarp forest has been preserved in the Danum Valley, northeast Borneo, and this is one of the best places for birds on earth. Around 275 species have been recorded here, over 130 are possible in a week and 70 in a day; astonishing totals for a small area of Asian lowland forest. The impressive list is headlined by the dazzling Blue-headed* and Blue-banded Pittas, but there are a further five pittas here, including Giant* and Black-crowned, as well as a bag full of broadbills, bulbuls and babblers, and this is one of the best sites in Asia to see orang-utan. A week, a month, even a year, is not long enough, but few birders leave here without fond memories.

Permits, transport and accommodation should all be booked well in advance.

Bornean Endemics

White-fronted Falconet*, Bulwer's Pheasant*, Blue-headed* and Blue-banded Pittas, Bornean Bristlehead*, Bornean Blue-Flycatcher, White-crowned Shama, Bornean* and Black-throated Wren-Babblers, Yellow-rumped Flowerpecker.

Specialities

Chestnut-necklaced Partridge*, Crested Fireback*, Great Argus, Short-toed Coucal*, Reddish Scops-Owl, Large Frogmouth*, Blue-banded and Rufous-collared Kingfishers, Wrinkled Hornbill*, Malaysian Honeyguide*, Giant* and Black-crowned Pittas, Dusky Broadbill, Chestnut-tailed Jungle-Flycatcher, Long-billed Blue-Flycatcher*, Chestnut-naped Forktail, Finsch's Bulbul, Temminck's Babbler, Striped Wren-Babbler, Dusky Munia.

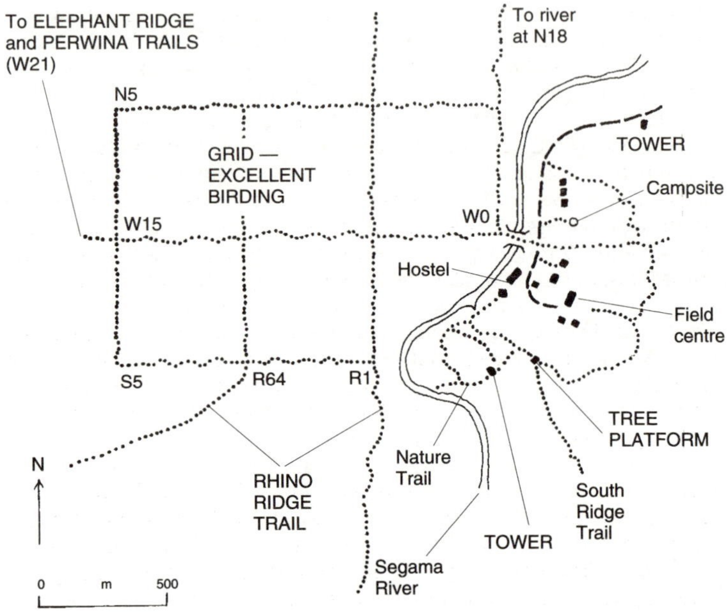

Others

Schrenck's Bittern* (Nov–Mar), Jerdon's Baza*, Bat Hawk, Wallace's Hawk-Eagle*, Crested Partridge, Little and Large* Green-Pigeons, Blue-rumped Parrot*, Blue-crowned Hanging-Parrot, Violet and Drongo Cuckoos, Black-bellied, Raffles', Red-billed and Chestnut-breasted Malkohas, Buffy Fish-Owl, Brown Wood-Owl, Whiskered Treeswift, Black-nest Swiftlet, Silver-rumped and Brown-backed Needletails, Red-naped, Diard's and Scarlet-rumped Trogons, Black-backed and Banded Kingfishers, Red-bearded and Blue-throated Bee-eaters, Black*, Rhinoceros, Helmeted*, Bushy-crested, White-crowned and Wreathed Hornbills, Gold-whiskered, Red-throated, Yellow-crowned and Brown Barbets, White-bellied, Banded, Crimson-winged, Checker-throated, Olive-backed, Orange-backed, Buff-rumped, Buff-necked, Grey-and-buff and Great Slaty Woodpeckers, Banded, Hooded (Nov–Mar) and Blue-winged (Nov–Mar) Pittas, Black-and-red, Banded, Black-and-yellow and Green Broadbills, Spotted Fantail, Crested Jay, Black Magpie*, Green Iora, Dark-throated Oriole, Lesser Cuckoo-Shrike, Fiery Minivet, Asian Fairy-bluebird, Greater Green and Lesser Green Leafbirds, Rufous-winged and Maroon-breasted Philentomas, Chestnut-capped Thrush, Grey-chested Jungle-Flycatcher, Rufous-chested and White-tailed Flycatchers, Pale and Malaysian* Blue-Flycatchers, Rufous-tailed Shama, White-crowned Forktail, Straw-headed*, Scaly-breasted, Grey-bellied, Puff-backed, Olive-winged, Cream-vented, Red-eyed, Spectacled, Grey-cheeked, Yellow-bellied, Hairy-backed and Buff-vented Bulbuls, Rufous-tailed Tailorbird, White-chested*, Ferruginous*, Horsfield's, Short-tailed, Black-capped, Moustached, Sooty-capped, Scaly-crowned and Rufous-crowned Babblers, Chestnut-backed Scimitar-Babbler, Grey-headed, White-necked, Chestnut-rumped and

Chestnut-winged Babblers, Fluffy-backed Tit-Babbler, Brown Fulvetta, Yellow-breasted Flowerpecker, Plain, Red-throated, Ruby-cheeked and Purple-throated Sunbirds, Little, Thick-billed, Long-billed, Spectacled and Grey-breasted Spiderhunters.

Other Wildlife

Banteng, bearded pig, Bornean gibbon, clouded leopard (rare), flat-headed cat, flying lemur, grey leaf-monkey, Hose's langur, leopard cat, marbled cat, maroon leaf-monkey, orang-utan, otter civet, pig-tailed macaque, red giant flying squirrel, red leaf-monkey, slow loris, western tarsier, yellow-throated marten, many butterflies and moths including atlas moths, and spectacular beetles including rhinoceros beetles.

(Other species recorded here include Great-billed Heron*, Malayan Night-Heron, Red-legged Crake, Moustached Hawk-Cuckoo, Sunda Ground-Cuckoo*, Oriental Bay-Owl, Barred Eagle-Owl, Cinnamon-rumped Trogon, Malaysian Rail-babbler, Narcissus Flycatcher and Scarlet-breasted and Brown-backed Flowerpeckers.)

It used to be possible to stay at the Danum Valley Field Centre, 85 km by rough road west of Lahad Datu. However, in 1994 the much more expensive Borneo Rainforest Lodge, 97 km west of Lahad Datu and 36 km from the field centre, opened and birders have since been deterred from staying at the Field Centre (students, researchers and 'serious naturalists' are welcomed). The birds are the same at both sites except for Crested Fireback*, which is not usually seen near the lodge. However, it is possible to visit the Field Centre area even if based at the lodge. Around the lodge, bird the short Danum Trail just behind the lodge (Great Argus, Malaysian Rail-babbler), the Segama Trail (on the opposite side of the river from the suspension bridge which is a good spot for Whiskered Treeswift) and the canopy walkway (Wallace's Hawk-Eagle*, Bornean Bristlehead*). It is also worth scanning the forest from the verandah of the lodge, for any fruiting trees are likely to be full of birds. The lodge also organises night-drives during which it is possible to see some nocturnal species, mainly mammals. The area around the Field Centre, alongside the River Segama, supports Buffy Fish-Owl, a pair of which usually appear on the badminton court at dusk to take the easy pickings of the myriad of moths, beetles and other insects which fly into the net. Bat Hawks are often seen flying over the centre around dusk. Schrenck's Bittern* usually winters on the lily-pond.

Most of the species which occur at Danum have been recorded on the superb 2 km square grid, across the Segama River, and this area deserves nothing but thorough and prolonged birding. Towards dusk the swing bridge across the river is a good place to sit and wait for the red giant flying squirrel to glide across the wide river, sometimes just as the 'six o'clock cicada' starts up its incredible racket. If based at the Field Centre also bird the 6.4 km Rhino Ridge Trail (Blue-banded Pitta, Temminck's Babbler), the Elephant Ridge Trail (two Great Argus dancing grounds) and the Perwina Trail (Blue-banded Pitta around PO5 and Blue-banded Kingfisher on the stream at the end), which leaves the Elephant Ridge Trail at E13. To the south of the Field Centre the short Nature and Sungai Palum Trails are worth walking at dawn, in search of Chestnut-necklaced* and Crested Partridges, Crested Fireback*, Finsch's Bulbul and Yellow-rumped Flowerpecker. There is also an unnerving 35 m tree platform here, overlooking fig trees which are full of birds when in fruit. Another shorter tree platform, a few kilometres north of the Field Centre, alongside the road in, also provides good views of fig trees, which are particularly good for hornbills and broadbills, while spectacular species such as Black-and-yellow Broadbill have been seen down to just a few feet in front of the screen. A walk along the entrance track at night may produce Reddish Scops-Owl and Large Frogmouth* (which also occurs along the Nature Trail), as well as a few nocturnal mammals. There are also jeep rides (A).

Accommodation: Borneo Rainforest Lodge (A+), bookable in advance by phoning (011 817624) or faxing (011 817619) the lodge direct, or by writing to Innoprise Jungle Lodge, Sadong Jaya Boulevard, PO Box 11622, 88817 Kota Kinabalu, Sabah (tel: 6 088 243245, fax: 6 088 254227). The office is located on the 3rd Floor, Lot 10, Block D, Sadong Jaya Complex. The Lahad Datu office is on the ground floor, Block 3, Fajar Centre and can be contacted by writing to PO Box 61174, 91120 Lahad Datu, Sabah (tel: 6 089 885051, fax: 6 089 883091). Field centre (A), hostel (B/take food) or campsite (C/take food), which used to be bookable in advance through the Sabah Foundation Office in Kota Kinabalu, or in Lahad Datu, at the Yayasan Sabah Regional Office, 2nd Floor, Hap Seng Building (tel: 6 089 81092).

From Lahad Datu it is possible to enter Indonesia (providing a visa has already been obtained) by flying to Balikpapan in Kalimantan via Tawau and Tarakan. From Balikpapan it is possible to fly to Sulawesi or Java.

All pittas are special, but Blue-headed Pitta is among the best and is usually easy to see at Danum Valley*

BATU PUNGGUL FOREST RESERVE

This small area of lowland forest (20 sq km), bisected by the Sapulut River and dominated by an impressive limestone pinnacle, is, along with Gunung Mulu, one of the few known sites for the endemic Hose's Broadbill.

This reserve is managed by the Korporasi Pembangunan Desa (KPD — Rural Development Corporation) and access and accommodation should be booked in advance via KPD, Beg Berkunci 86, 88998 Kota Kinabalu (tel: 088 428910, extension 247).

Bornean Endemics

Blue-headed Pitta*, Hose's Broadbill, Bornean Blue-Flycatcher, White-crowned Shama, Yellow-rumped Flowerpecker.

Specialities

Great Argus, Malaysian Honeyguide*, Black-crowned Pitta, Chestnut-naped Forktail, Finsch's Bulbul, Striped Wren-Babbler, Dusky Munia.

Others

Moustached Hawk-Cuckoo, Violet Cuckoo, Raffles' Malkoha, Red-naped, Diard's and Scarlet-rumped Trogons, Red-bearded Bee-eater, Rhinoceros, Helmeted*, Bushy-crested and Wreathed Hornbills, Red-throated and Brown Barbets, Olive-backed Woodpecker, Black-and-red, Black-and-yellow and Green Broadbills, Spotted Fantail, Crested Jay, Chestnut-capped Thrush, Rufous-tailed Shama, Straw-headed Bulbul*.

Other Wildlife

Bornean gibbon, crab-eating macaque, Hose's langur, pig-tailed macaque, yellow-throated marten and rafflesia (the world's largest flower).

This reserve is 3–5 hours by boat (A) up-river from the small settlement of Sapulut, accessible from Kota Kinabalu via bus to Keningau (2.5 hours) and jeep (3.5 hours) from there. Hose's Broadbill has been recorded along the short trail to the suspension bridge and along the trail behind the pinnacle which leads up to the ridge. There is also a 2 km loop Nature Trail and a network of old logging and hunting trails, all worth birding.

Accommodation: Sapulut — KPD resthouse. Reserve — resthouse, huts, mock longhouse, camping.

The second highest mountain in Sabah, **Mount Trus Madi**, accessible from Tambunan (no accommodation), supports most of Borneo's montane endemics including Bornean Barbet, as well as Bonaparte's Nightjar* and Tawny-breasted Parrotfinch. The **Malau Basin** in west-central Sabah supports Pygmy White-eye, as well as Bornean Bristlehead*.

SARAWAK (Malaysian Borneo)

GUNUNG MULU NATIONAL PARK

This large park (544 sq km) lies in a land of limestone on the northern slopes of Gunung Mulu, which rises to 2376 m (7795 ft). Spectacular pinnacles rise high above the forest, which supports more Bornean endemics than any other site on the island (25 out of 37), including Black Oriole*, which is rarely seen elsewhere, and Hose's Broadbill, which occurs at few other sites. The other major avian attractions on the park list that exceeds 300 are Mountain Serpent-Eagle*, Bulwer's Pheasant*, Garnet Pitta, Everett's Thrush*, Fruit-hunter and Hook-billed Bulbul*. Allow at least a week to see some of these.

The cave system at Gunung Mulu is reputed to be the most extensive on earth, and these caves, which include the 600 m long and 100 m high Sarawak Chamber, are a very popular tourist attraction, hence access and accommodation must be booked in advance. Unfortunately, independent travellers usually have to join an expensive organised tour to get in.

Bornean Endemics

Mountain Serpent-Eagle*, Red-breasted and Crimson-headed Partridges, Bulwer's Pheasant*, Whitehead's Trogon, Mountain, Golden-naped and Bornean Barbets, Blue-headed Pitta*, Hose's and Whitehead's Broadbills, Bornean Whistler, Black Oriole*, Everett's Thrush*, Fruit-hunter, Bornean Blue-Flycatcher, Mountain Black-eye, Bornean Stubtail, Bornean*, Black-throated and Mountain Wren-Babblers, Chestnut-crested Yuhina, Yellow-rumped and Black-sided Flowerpeckers, Whitehead's Spiderhunter.

Specialities

Storm's Stork*, Black Partridge*, Crestless* and Crested* Firebacks, Great Argus, Jambu Fruit-Dove, Reddish Scops-Owl, Large Frogmouth*, Cinnamon-rumped Trogon, Rufous-collared Kingfisher, Malaysian Honeyguide*, Garnet Pitta, Sunda Treepie, Sunda Cuckoo-Shrike, Sunda Whistling-Thrush, Chestnut-tailed Jungle-Flycatcher, Indigo Flycatcher, Long-billed Blue-Flycatcher*, Chestnut-naped Forktail, Black-and-white and Hook-billed* Bulbuls, Black-capped White-eye, Sunda Bush-Warbler, Sunda and Black Laughingthrushes, Temminck's and Grey-breasted* Babblers, Tawny-breasted Parrotfinch, Dusky Munia, Scarlet Sunbird.

Others

Lesser Adjutant*, Bat Hawk, Jerdon's Baza*, Blyth's and Wallace's* Hawk-Eagles, Black-thighed Falconet, Crested Partridge, Little and Large* Green-Pigeons, Blue-crowned Hanging-Parrot, Violet and Drongo Cuckoos, Black-bellied and Raffles' Malkohas, Buffy Fish-Owl, Brown Wood-Owl, Malaysian Nightjar, Whiskered Treeswift, Mossy-nest and Black-nest Swiftlets, Silver-rumped Needletail, Red-naped, Diard's and Orange-breasted Trogons, Red-bearded Bee-eater, Helmeted Hornbill*, Yellow-crowned and Brown Barbets, Olive-backed and Maroon Woodpeckers, Long-tailed and Green Broadbills, Crow-billed Drongo (Nov–Mar), Crested Jay, Black Magpie*, Green Iora, Greater Green and Lesser Green Leafbirds, Rufous-winged and Maroon-breasted Philentomas, Grey-chested Jungle-Flycatcher, Pale and Pygmy Blue-Flycatchers, Rufous-tailed Shama, Straw-headed*, Flavescent and Ochraceous Bulbuls, Mountain Leaf-Warbler, Yellow-breasted Warbler, White-chested*, Rufous-fronted and White-necked Babblers, White-bellied Munia, Plain Sunbird, Long-billed and Yellow-eared Spiderhunters.

Other Wildlife

Slow loris, Sunda tarsier and butterflies including Rajah Brooke's birdwing.

(Other species recorded here include Malayan Night-Heron, Sunda Ground-Cuckoo*, Short-toed Coucal*, Oriental Bay-Owl, Dusky Broadbill, Malaysian Rail-babbler and Fulvous-chested Jungle-Flycatcher.)

The park is accessible from Miri, which is connected by air to Kota Kinabalu in Sabah. It takes a day or more to get from Miri to Marudi by boat, but the 15 minute flight costs roughly the same. From Marudi it is a short jeep ride to the HQ and a short boat trip to Long Pala. The area around the HQ is excellent for birds, especially along the banks of the Melinau River. Birding is also good along the 3–4 km trail through some swamp forest to Long Pala and Deer Cave, but guides are compulsory. At Deer Cave (prepare for the smell) there is an observatory from which millions of bats can be seen streaming out of the cave at dusk, often attended by a Bat Hawk. The forest opposite the picnic site at Clearwater Cave, one of the world's largest caves (51 km long), supports Hose's Broadbill, while Black Oriole* occurs around Lamut Hut, a 10 hour ascent from the Nipa River Camp. Most of the montane specialities listed above as well as Bulwer's Pheasant* can only be seen on treks to the limestone pinnacles (3–4 days round trip) and the summit of Gunung Mulu (4 days round trip), with compulsory guides. The best birding areas are beyond Camp 5 on the Pinnacles Trail, and above Camp 3 on the Gunung Mulu Trail.

Accommodation: HQ — resthouse (A), chalets (B), hostel (C), Melinan canteen (C/on opposite side of river). Long Pala (15 minutes by boat from the HQ) — guesthouses, hostels. Accommodation, permits and guides should be booked in advance through the National Parks and Wildlife Office, 1st Floor, Wisma Sumber Alam, 93050 Kuching, Sarawak. (tel: 082 442180/201), or via the Section Forest Office, 98000 Miri, Sarawak (tel: 085 36637).

BAKO NATIONAL PARK

This small rugged headland (27 sq km), just 37 km northeast of Kuching, supports a variety of habitats where a fine selection of shore and lowland forest species occur side by side. Only 150 species have been recorded, but these include the scarce Red-crowned Barbet* and passage migrants such as Chinese Egret* and Nordmann's Greenshank*.

Permits and accommodation should be booked in advance at the booking office, Tourist Information Centre, Main Bazaar, Kuching 93000 (tel: 082 248088/410944).

Specialities

Chinese Egret* (Sep–Nov), Nordmann's Greenshank* (Sep–Nov), Red-crowned Barbet*, Sunda Woodpecker, Long-billed* and Mangrove Blue-Flycatchers, Dusky Munia.

Others

Lesser Frigatebird (Sep–Nov), Pacific Reef-Egret, Brahminy Kite, Grey-tailed Tattler (Sep–Nov), Asian Dowitcher* (Sep–Nov), Black-naped Tern, Pink-necked Pigeon, Drongo Cuckoo, Chestnut-bellied Malkoha, Buffy Fish-Owl, Malaysian Nightjar, Edible-nest Swiftlet, Silver-rumped Needletail, Scarlet-rumped Trogon, Rufous-backed, Stork-billed and Black-capped Kingfishers, Blue-throated Bee-eater, Common Flame-back, Mangrove Whistler, White-breasted Woodswallow, Green Iora, Pied Triller, Fiery Minivet, Asian Fairy-bluebird, Greater Green Leafbird, Tiger Shrike, Asian Glossy-Starling, Straw-headed Bulbul*, Ashy Tailorbird, White-chested Babbler*, Copper-throated Sunbird, Little Spiderhunter.

Other Wildlife

Bearded pig, crab-eating macaque, proboscis monkey, silver leaf-monkey.

(Other species recorded here include Bulwer's Petrel, Great-billed Heron*, Lesser Adjutant*, Beach Thick-knee, Malaysian Plover*, Sooty Tern, Oriental Bay-Owl, Sunda Frogmouth and Malaysian Honey-guide*.)

The HQ is at Telok Assam, accessible by boat (30 minutes) from Kampung Bako, which is 45 minutes by road from Kuching. Mangrove specialities can be found just north of Telok Assam where there is an elevated boardwalk, or at Telok Delima, an hour's walk south of Telok Assam, which is also the best area for proboscis monkey. There are 30 km of well-marked trails, but the best one is probably the 5 km Lintang Loop as it traverses most of the habitats. Snorkelling is excellent in the Telok Limau/Pulau Lakei area, northeast of Telok Assam.

Accommodation: Telok Assam — resthouse (A), hostels (C), camping (C).

Sunda Ground-Cuckoo* has been recorded at the **Samunsam WS** at the extreme western tip of Sarawak. Approach the Wildlife and National Parks Department to seek permission to visit this remote reserve.

ADDITIONAL INFORMATION

Addresses

The Malayan Nature Society, PO Box 10750, 50724 Kuala Lumpur, Malaysia, publishes a quarterly journal and annual bird report.
Wildlife and National Parks Department, KM 10, Jalan Cheras 56100 Kuala Lumpur (tel: 03 9052872).

Books and Papers

A Guide to the Birds of Thailand. Lekagul B and Round P, 1991. C of P: Thailand.
The Birds of Borneo, Third Edition. Smythies B, 1981. Sabah and Malayan Nature Societies.
Pocket Guide to the Birds of Borneo. Francis C, 1984. WWF Malaysia.

A Guide to the Birds of Borneo, Sumatra, Java and Bali. Mackinnon J and Phillipps K, 1993. Oxford University Press.
A Birdwatcher's Guide to Malaysia. Bransbury J, 1993. Waymark.
A Field Guide to the Mammals of Borneo. Payne J and Francis C, 1985. WWF Malaysia.

MALAYSIAN ENDEMICS

Mainland Peninsula (2)

Mountain Peacock-Pheasant*	Fraser's Hill (rare)
Malayan Whistling-Thrush*	Fraser's Hill

Borneo (37)

Mountain Serpent-Eagle*	Northwest: Mt Kinabalu and Gunung Mulu (also Mt Trus Madi, Gunung Murad and Bukit Tudal (Brunei)
White-fronted Falconet*	North: Poring and Danum Valley
Red-breasted Partridge	Northwest: Mt Kinabalu and Gunung Mulu
Crimson-headed Partridge	Northwest: Mt Kinabalu and Gunung Mulu
Bulwer's Pheasant*	North: Danum Valley and Gunung Mulu
Bornean Peacock-Pheasant*	Throughout: rare, with only a few recent records, mostly from Kalimantan
Dulit Frogmouth*	Central: known only from seven specimens taken at Mt Dulit (Sarawak), Usun Apau Plateau, Kelabit Uplands and Mt Liang Kubung
Bornean Frogmouth*	Throughout: known only from a few specimens, but probably heard at Mt Kinabalu
Whitehead's Trogon	Northwest: Mt Kinabalu and Gunung Mulu
Mountain Barbet	Northwest: Mt Kinabalu and Gunung Mulu
Golden-naped Barbet	Northwest: Mt Kinabalu and Gunung Mulu
Bornean Barbet	Northwest: Poring and Gunung Mulu
Blue-headed Pitta*	Throughout: widespread
Blue-banded Pitta	North: Poring and Danum Valley
Hose's Broadbill	Northwest: Batu Punggul and Gunung Mulu
Whitehead's Broadbill	Northwest: Mt Kinabalu and Gunung Mulu
Bornean Whistler	Northwest: Mt Kinabalu and Gunung Mulu
Bornean Bristlehead*	North: Uncle Tan's Jungle Camp, Sepilok and Danum Valley

Black Oriole*	Northwest: Gunung Mulu and Mt Dulit (Sarawak)
Everett's Thrush*	Northwest: Mt Kinabalu and Gunung Mulu
Fruit-hunter	Northwest: Mt Kinabalu and Gunung Mulu
Eyebrowed Jungle-Flycatcher	Northwest: Mt Kinabalu
Bornean Blue-Flycatcher	North: widespread
White-crowned Shama	North: widespread
Pygmy White-eye	Northwest: Mt Kinabalu (rare)
Mountain Black-eye	Northwest: Mt Kinabalu and Gunung Mulu
Bornean Stubtail	Northwest: Mt Kinabalu and Gunung Mulu
Friendly Bush-Warbler	Northwest: Mt Kinabalu (also Mt Trus Madi and Mt Tam Boyukan)
Black-browed Babbler	South: known only from one mid nineteenth century specimen taken in south Kalimantan
Bornean Wren-Babbler*	North: Danum Valley and Gunung Mulu
Black-throated Wren-Babbler	North: Danum Valley and Gunung Mulu
Mountain Wren-Babbler	Northwest: Mt Kinabalu and Gunung Mulu
Chestnut-crested Yuhina	Northwest: Mt Kinabalu, Poring and Gunung Mulu
Yellow-rumped Flowerpecker	North: widespread
Black-sided Flowerpecker	Northwest: Mt Kinabalu and Gunung Mulu
Bornean Spiderhunter	Northwest: Poring
Whitehead's Spiderhunter	Northwest: Mt Kinabalu, Poring and Gunung Mulu

(Sunda Ground-Cuckoo* is now generally regarded as two separate species; Bornean, which is endemic to Borneo, and Sumatran, which is endemic to Sumatra.)

Near-endemics

Storm's Stork*, Tabon Scrubfowl*, Grey-breasted Partridge, Malayan Peacock-Pheasant*, Crested Argus*, Silvery Wood-Pigeon*, Ruddy Cuckoo-Dove, Yellow-vented Pigeon*, Grey Imperial-Pigeon*, Blue-naped Parrot*, White-fronted*, Mantanani and Rajah Scops-Owls, Sunda Frogmouth, Waterfall Swift*, Germain's and Grey Swiftlets, Fire-tufted Barbet, Streak-breasted and Bamboo Woodpeckers, Black-crowned Pitta, Sunda Treepie, Chestnut-tailed Jungle-Flycatcher, Rufous-vented Niltava, Citrine Canary-Flycatcher, Blue Nuthatch, Hook-billed Bulbul*, Black-capped White-eye, Black Laughingthrush, Temminck's and Grey-breasted* Babblers, Large* and Marbled* Wren-Babblers, Mountain Fulvetta, Dusky Munia, Brown-backed Flowerpecker*.

MONGOLIA

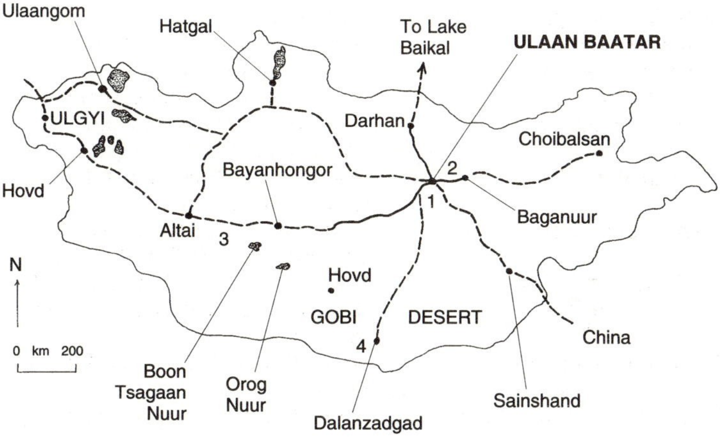

1 Ulaan Baatar
2 Terelj
3 Khujirt to Boon Tsagaan Nuur
4 Bayanzag

INTRODUCTION

Mongolia has a low diversity of birds, at least as far as Asia is concerned, but what this country lacks in quantity it more than makes up for in quality. Unfortunately, there are a number of bureaucratic barriers to cross to get in and visas are usually only issued to people on organised tours, which are expensive.

At 1,565,000 sq km, Mongolia is 12 times larger than England and over twice the size of Texas. There are some internal flights which are subject to fuel shortages, few public buses and the roads are terrible or non-existent in many steppe and desert areas, hence a 4WD is absolutely essential for an extensive birding trip. In fact, such a trip would necessitate a mini-camping expedition, for accommodation is sparse to say the least, apart from a few cheap hotels and the odd tourist camps which are composed of basic tents, known locally as *gers* (yurts). Food shortages are frequent away from the capital, but mutton, noodles and soups dominate the local cuisine otherwise. The locals like salty tea and the local brew is a low-alcohol drink made from horse milk. Immunisation against hepatitis, polio and typhoid is recommended.

The best time to visit Mongolia is June when the breeding birds are in peak plumage and migrants *en route* to Siberia are still passing through. The climate is extreme, with very hot, dry summers and very cold, mainly dry winters, and it is usually windy. The southern edge of the Siberian forests (taiga) stretches into north Mongolia, giving way to vast steppe grasslands in the centre and the sands of the Gobi Desert in the south and east. Much of the country lies between 1000 m (3281 ft) and 2000 m (6562 ft), but in the west the 1000 km long Altai mountain range rises to 4374 m (14,350 ft) at Tavanbogd. As well as other smaller mountain ranges in the middle of the country and the northeast there are numerous lakes and marshes. Mongolia is one of the most sparsely populated countries in the world and huge parts of the country can safely be described as wilderness. If these wonderful wild places survive, so may the birds, which include 17 threatened and near-threatened species and the following specialities and spectacular species: Altai Snowcock, Black-billed Capercaillie, Demoiselle Crane, Swinhoe's Snipe, Oriental Plover, Great Black-headed and Relict* Gulls, Pallas' Sandgrouse, Ural Owl, Siberian Jay, Mongolian Ground-Jay, Siberian Rubythroat, White-throated Bushchat*, Azure Tit, Saxaul Sparrow, Pere David's Snowfinch and Mongolian Accentor. There is no endemic species. It is possible to see around 225 species on an extensive three-week trip.

ULAAN BAATAR

Mongolia's sprawling capital city is situated in north-central Mongolia at the southern edge of the taiga and a few good birds can be seen in its vicinity.

Specialities

Daurian Partridge, Azure Tit, White-crowned Penduline-Tit.

Others

Azure-winged Magpie, Brown Shrike (May–Sep), Isabelline Wheatear (May–Sep), Long-tailed Rosefinch, Meadow, Yellow-breasted (May–Sep) and Black-faced (May–Sep) Buntings.

The best birding areas near the city include the steppe and scrub of the Tuul Gol River Valley, Lord's Hill Valley and the coniferous forests of Bogd Uul NR, just south of the city.

TERELJ

The broadleaf and coniferous forests around Terelj, which is situated at 1600 m (5249 ft) in the Hentiy Mountains northeast of Ulaan Baatar support a fine selection of Siberian and eastern Palearctic birds, including Black-billed Capercaillie, Ural Owl and Siberian Jay.

Most of the species listed below are only present in summer (May–Sep).

Others

Black Stork, Oriental Honey-buzzard, Black-billed Capercaillie, Hazel Grouse, Swinhoe's Snipe, Ural Owl, Three-toed and Black Woodpeckers, Siberian Jay, Eurasian Nutcracker, Brown Shrike, Eyebrowed and Dark (Red)-throated Thrushes, White-cheeked Starling, Dark-sided Flycatcher, Siberian Rubythroat, Siberian Blue Robin, Daurian Redstart, Isabelline Wheatear, Chinese Bush-Warbler, Lanceolated, Pallas' and Thick-billed Warblers, Long-tailed Rosefinch, Pine, Meadow, Chestnut-eared, Chestnut and Black-faced Buntings.

Terelj is 80 km northeast of Ulaan Baatar by road.

Accommodation: tourist camp.

KHUJIRT TO BOON TSAGAAN NUUR

The lake-dotted steppe and desert between Khujirt and Boon Tsagaan Nuur, a large lake situated at 1420 m (4659 ft), support a superb selection of little known birds, not least Relict Gull* and Mongolian Accentor.

Most of the species listed below are only present during the summer (May–Sep).

Specialities

Demoiselle Crane, Oriental Plover, Relict Gull*, Pallas' Sandgrouse, Mongolian Ground-Jay, Mongolian Lark, Pere David's Snowfinch, Mongolian Accentor.

Others

Swan* and Bar-headed Geese, Falcated Duck, Black Stork, Pallas' Fish-Eagle*, Cinereous Vulture*, Upland Buzzard, Steppe Eagle, Amur and Saker Falcons, Swinhoe's Snipe, Asian Dowitcher*, Long-toed Stint, Greater Sandplover, Great Black-headed Gull, Daurian Jackdaw, Pied and Isabelline Wheatears, Lanceolated, Pallas', Paddyfield and Desert Warblers, Asian Short-toed Lark, Rock Petronia, Brown Accentor, Mongolian Finch, Pallas' Bunting.

Other Wildlife

Souslik.

Khujirt is accessible by air and road from Ulaan Bataar. Bird around here and along the 480 km track south to Boon Tsagaan Nuur.

It is 235 km east from Boon Tsagaan Nuur to Orog Nuur and the nearby Yellow Pools, a journey which may produce similar species to those listed above. **Bayanzag**, near South Gobi Tourist camp at Dalanzadgad, is a site famous among fossil-hunters for dinosaur remains and well-known to birders as the haunt of the Saxaul Sparrow, which inhabits the drought-resistant *Saxual* bushes in the area.

The rare Relict Gull promises to be a major highlight for anyone who goes birding in Mongolia during the summer*

Species recorded in the **Gobi Altai** mountain range in south Mongolia include Altai Snowcock and Mongolian Accentor, as well as Lammergeier, Saker Falcon, Wallcreeper and Beautiful and Great Rosefinches. The Gobi Altai is accessible from Hovd, which is connected by air to Ulaan Baatar. The Valley of Yol and its surroundings is the best area, although it is possible to trek into the mountains from the tourist camp at Hovd.

The town of **Ulgyi** (Olgiy) in west Mongolia is the best base from which to explore the Kobdo Delta, Har Us Nuur (Black Water Lake), the Zabkhan River, the Turgen Ul Mountains and the lowlands around the Urgen Nur lake, which support some very localised and little-known birds, including Relict Gull* (Har Us Nuur, 30 km east of Hovd) and White-throated Bushchat*, as well as Mongolian Ground-Jay. It is possible to enter west Mongolia from Tashanta in the Russian Altai and White-throated Bushchat* occurs alongside the road between the two passes through the border range.

Near-endemics

Altai Snowcock, Red-crowned* and White-naped* Cranes, Relict Gull*, Pallas' Sandgrouse, Mongolian Ground-Jay, Mongolian Lark, Saxaul Sparrow, Pere David's Snowfinch, Mongolian Accentor, Grey-capped Greenfinch.

NEPAL

INTRODUCTION

Summary

This small, friendly Himalayan country with a long established tourist infrastructure supports a very diverse avifauna and, especially on the various treks, offers the chance to see numerous great birds, including pheasants, Ibisbill and many beautiful babblers, in some wonderfully wild landscapes.

Size

At 140,747 sq km, Nepal is a little larger than England and five times smaller than Texas.

Getting Around

The good, if somewhat expensive, flight network and the excellent bus system allows access to virtually all of the best birding sites, so hiring a vehicle is an unnecessary extravagance.

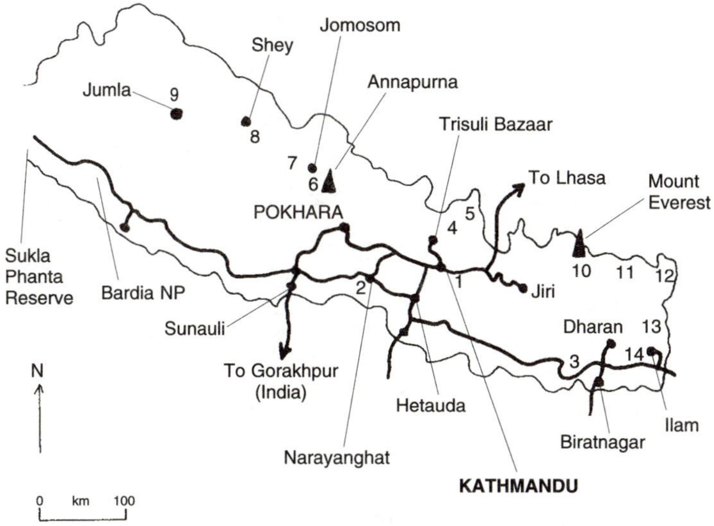

1	Phulchowki	8	Shey-Phoksundo NP
2	Chitwan NP	9	Rara Lake Trek
3	Kosi	10	Everest Trek
4	Langtang Valley Trek	11	Barun Valley Trek
5	Gosainkund Trek	12	Kangchenjunga Trek
6	Jomosom Trek	13	Hanga Tham Trek
7	Mustang Trek	14	Sunischare Trek

Trekking
The paths and trails through the Himalayas have been there for centuries and for many years now they have been used to great effect by birders in search of the many Himalayan specialities. Large stretches are paved and there are numerous rest stops, complete with tea houses, restaurants and accommodation, hence trekking in the Nepalese Himalayas is, on the whole, relatively easy. It is, however, necessary to obtain permits before embarking on the trails and these can be obtained at the Central Immigration Offices in Kathmandu and Pokhara.

Accommodation and Food

Although there is a wide range of accommodation and food available in the major towns, such as Kathmandu and Pokhara, and at some of the National Parks, such as Chitwan, accommodation is much more basic on the treks. On the major treks Western-style food, including chips and apple pie, is available at the major rest stops.

Health and Safety

Immunisation against hepatitis, meningitis, polio, typhoid and yellow fever is recommended, as are precautions against malaria and rabies. Hygiene leaves more than something to be desired in Nepal and few budget travellers manage to avoid at least some kind of stomach upset. However, such health problems rarely last more than day or so and, remember, the birding will more than justify the suffering. To avoid being ill or, at least, to lessen the effects, stay away from meat and salads, and only drink boiled or sterilised water.

Climate and Timing

The best time to visit the Kathmandu Valley, Pokhara, Kosi and Chitwan is between November and March, when winter visitors from the north and high Himalayas are present in the relatively dry lowlands. The best time to trek is between late March and late May when the middle and high altitude Himalayan specialities are breeding and the lowlands are already becoming almost unbearably hot. The lowland monsoon season lasts from June to September.

Habitats

Only 150 km separate the highest point on earth, 8848 (29,029 ft) at Mount Everest, and the lowlands of southern Nepal, which are less than 100 m (328 ft) above sea level. Thanks to this vast altitudinal range, Nepal supports a wide range of habitats, despite the fact that it is a small, mainly mountainous, land-locked country. These habitats range from high mountain meadows and oak–rhododendron forests, down to temperate and subtropical forests, to the fertile lowlands, known as the terai, where, among the farmland, there are still large stretches of sal forest and grasslands, as well as wide rivers and wetlands.

Conservation

At least one travel guide to Nepal states that 'development is hampered by the lack of roads'. Long may this remain the case, because there has already been plenty of 'development' here, especially in the form of forest clearance, which has left many mountain slopes bare, particularly around Kathmandu, and allowed much of the lowlands to be turned over to agriculture. As deforestation continues and even reserves, such as Kosi Tappu where overgrazing and chemical fishing are major problems, are not sacrosanct, a lot remains to be done if the exceptionally rich avifauna of Nepal, including 62 threatened and near-threatened species, is to survive.

Bird Species

Over 840 species have been recorded in Nepal, an amazing total for such a small, land-locked country. Non-endemic specialities and spectacular species include Swamp Francolin*, Snow Partridge, Tibetan Snowcock, Blood Pheasant, Satyr Tragopan*, Koklass and Cheer* Pheasants, Bengal Florican*, Solitary and Wood* Snipes, Ibisbill, Long-billed Plover*, Great Black-headed Gull, Crested Kingfisher, Yellow-rumped Honeyguide*, Indian Pitta, Long-tailed Broadbill, Pied Thrush*, Siberian and White-tailed Rubythroats, Rufous-backed and White-throated Redstarts, Grandala, four forktails, White-throated Bushchat*, White-browed Tit-Warbler, Grey-sided Laughingthrush, Rufous-throated Wren-Babbler*, Cutia, Red-tailed Minla, Fire-tailed Myzornis, Sultan Tit, Maroon-backed Accentor, Gould's and Fire-tailed Sunbirds, Blanford's and Red-fronted Rosefinches and Scarlet and Gold-naped Finches.

Endemics

There are two endemics: Immaculate Wren-Babbler* and Spiny Babbler.

Expectations

It is possible to see over 330 species on a two- to three-week trip if Phulchowki, Chitwan and Kosi Tappu are included in the itinerary, and around 200 species on a two- to three-week trek.

PHULCHOWKI

Most of the wide Kathmandu Valley, which lies at 1500 m (4921 ft), has been deforested, but the steep slopes of Phulchowki, a mountain at the southern rim of the valley, have avoided the axe so far. The mossy oak–rhododendron forests near the 2767 m (9078 ft) summit, and the subtropical forests lower down this mountain are full of birds and the star-studded show includes White-crested and Grey-sided Laughingthrushes, Cutia, Black-eared Shrike-Babbler and Gold-naped Finch.

Specialities

Grey-sided Laughingthrush, Cutia.

KATHMANDU VALLEY

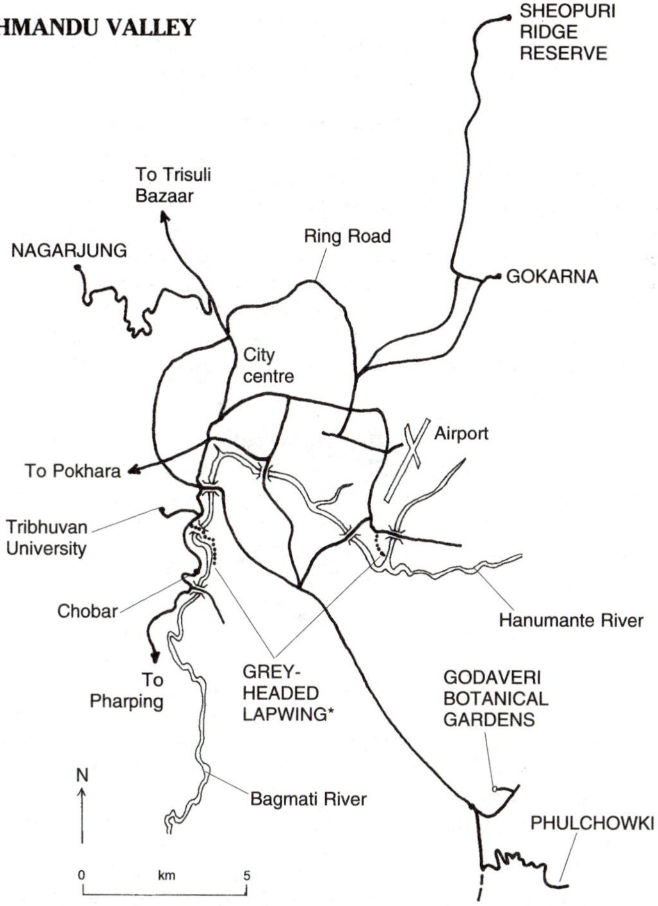

Others

Hill and Rufous-throated Partridges, Golden-throated Barbet, Rufous-bellied Woodpecker, Yellow-bellied Fantail, Blue Magpie, Grey Treepie, Maroon Oriole, Long-tailed Minivet, Scaly Thrush, White-collared Blackbird, Dark-throated Thrush (Nov–Mar), Slaty-backed Flycatcher, Rufous-bellied Niltava, Golden Bush-Robin, Slaty-backed and Spotted Forktails, Black-throated Tit, Chestnut-headed and Grey-bellied Tesias, Yellowish-bellied Bush-Warbler, Buff-barred and Ashy-throated Warblers, Blyth's Leaf-Warbler, White-throated, White-crested and Rufous-chinned Laughingthrushes, Scaly-breasted Wren-Babbler, Grey-throated Babbler, Red-billed Leiothrix, White-browed and Black-eared Shrike-Babblers, Chestnut-tailed Minla, Rufous Sibia, Whiskered and Stripe-throated Yuhinas, Black-throated Parrotbill, Black-lored Tit, Yellow-bellied Flowerpecker, Green-tailed, Black-throated and Fire-tailed Sunbirds, Tibetan Serin (Nov–Mar), Gold-naped Finch.

Other Wildlife

Yellow-throated Marten.

(Other species recorded here include Blue-naped Pitta*, Long-billed Thrush*, Blue-winged Laughingthrush, Maroon-backed Accentor, Crimson-browed and Scarlet Finches and Spot-winged Grosbeak.)

The best way to bird Phulchowki, which is about 20 km south of Kathmandu, is to travel by road to the summit and descend on foot. The Godaveri Botanical Gardens (forktails, Tibetan Serin) at the base of the mountain are also worthy of thorough investigation.

Other sites worth birding near Kathmandu include **Sheopuri Ridge Reserve**, 12 km to the north, where the endemic Spiny Babbler occurs

The beautiful Cutia could be 'bird of the day' on Phulchowki

(around Pati Banjiyang), as well as Wedge-tailed Pigeon, Indian Grey Thrush and Scarlet Finch, the mainly secondary forest on the slopes of **Nagarjung**, 5 km northwest of town, where the species are similar to Phulchowki, the royal forest at **Gokarna**, 8.5 km northeast of town, where Ashy Wood-Pigeon and Blue-throated Flycatcher (May–Sep) occur, the **Swayhambu Temple**, the **Monohari–Hanumauti River Confluence**, on the southeastern outskirts of town, where winter visitors include Grey-headed Lapwing* and Yellow-breasted Bunting and last, but by no means least, the **River Bagmati** at Chobar, a few kilometres south of town, where winter visitors include Pintail Snipe, Long-billed Plover*, Grey-headed Lapwing* and Wallcreeper. Cross the footbridge from the west to the east side of the river and explore the paddies and river to the south. Ibisbill was recorded here in the distant past, but the best wintering site near Kathmandu for this strange shorebird now is near **Bairini**, about 50 km west of Kathmandu on the Pokhara road. From Bairini continue west for a few kilometres towards the village of Belchu, then check the rapids of the Trisuli River just before the village. Chestnut-bellied Rock-Thrush and Wallcreeper also occur here.

CHITWAN NATIONAL PARK

Nepal's largest remaining expanse of lowland sal forest and grassland lies within this park (970 sq km) and they support one of the most diverse ranges of birds and mammals in Asia. Over 480 species of bird have been recorded, including grassland specialities such as Bengal Florican*, Jerdon's Babbler* and Bristled Grassbird*, as well as many spectacular species such as breeding Indian Pitta and both Siberian and White-tailed Rubythroats in winter. It is possible to see up to 150 species in a day here, and the otherwise rare Indian rhinoceros is relatively common and easy to see.

Specialities

Bengal Florican*, Grey-bellied Cuckoo, Sirkeer Malkoha, Indian Pitta (May–Sep), Pale-chinned Blue-Flycatcher, White-tailed Stonechat, Grey-crowned Prinia*, Bristled Grassbird*, Black-chinned, Jerdon's*, Striated and Slender-billed* Babblers, Nepal Fulvetta.

Others

Oriental Darter*, Red-naped Ibis*, Lesser Adjutant*, Black Baza, Grey-headed Fish-Eagle*, White-eyed Buzzard, Collared Falconet, Red Junglefowl, Indian Peafowl, Brown Crake, Greater Painted-snipe, Small Pratincole, River Lapwing, Great Black-headed Gull (Nov–Mar), Orange-breasted Pigeon, Pompadour Green-Pigeon, Plum-headed and Red-breasted Parakeets, Green-billed Malkoha, Oriental Scops-Owl, Brown Fish-Owl, Brown Wood-Owl, Jungle Owlet, Brown Hawk-Owl, Savanna Nightjar, Crested Treeswift, White-rumped and Silver-backed Needletails, Red-headed Trogon, Blue-eared and Stork-billed Kingfishers, Blue-bearded, Green and Chestnut-headed Bee-eaters, Indian Roller, Great Hornbill, Lineated and Blue-throated Barbets, White-browed Piculet, Lesser Yellownape, Streak-throated Woodpecker, Himalayan and Greater Flamebacks, Long-tailed Broadbill, Green Magpie, Rufous Treepie, Ashy Woodswallow, Large and Black-winged Cuckoo-Shrikes, Small and Scarlet Minivets, Golden-fronted Leafbird, Large and Common Woodshrikes, Orange-headed Thrush (May–Sep), Spot-winged and Chestnut-tailed Starlings, Slaty-blue Flycatcher, Siberian (Nov–Mar) and White-tailed (Nov–Mar) Rubythroats, White-rumped Shama, Black-backed Forktail, Chestnut-bellied Nuthatch, Black-crested Bulbul, Grey-breasted and Ashy Prinias, Pale-footed, Chestnut-crowned and Spotted Bush-Warblers, Paddyfield Warbler (Nov–Mar), Blyth's Reed-Warbler (Nov–Mar), Smoky Warbler (Nov–

CHITWAN NP

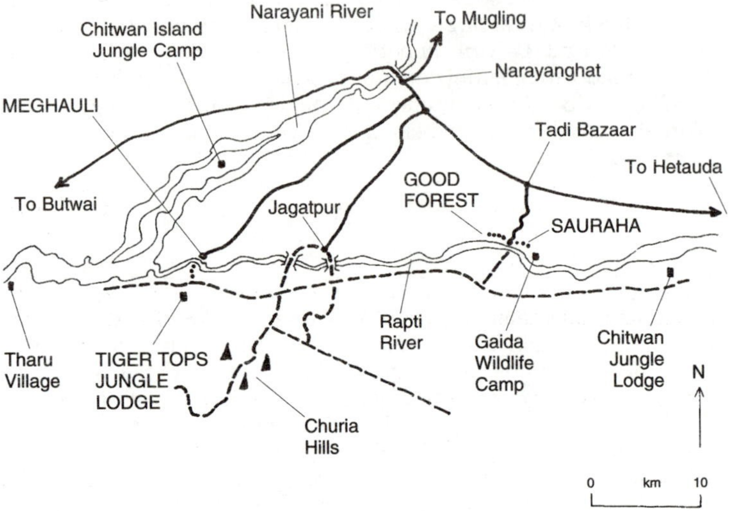

Mar), Striated and Rufous-rumped Grassbirds, Rufous-necked Laughingthrush, Puff-throated Babbler, White-browed Scimitar-Babbler, Chestnut-capped, Yellow-eyed and Jungle Babblers, Sultan Tit, Rufous-winged Bushlark, Red Avadavat, White-rumped Munia, Bengal and Baya Weavers, Crested Bunting.

Other Wildlife

Gaur, gharial, grey langur, hog-deer, Indian rhinoceros, jungle cat, leopard, mugger crocodile, rhesus macaque, sambar, sloth bear, tiger, yellow-throated marten.

Chitwan is accessible by air (via Meghauli) and road (4–6 hours via Narayanghat) from Kathmandu. It is possible to bird on foot in most areas, as well as by jeep, boat and elephant-back. Staying in the park is expensive, but budget birders can head for Meghauli or Sauraha villages, both of which are just outside the NP, where there is plenty of cheap, but clean and convenient accommodation to choose from. It is possible to enter the park on a daily basis from these two villages by crossing the Rapti River. From **Meghauli**, cross the river, to bird the grassland and ditches, especially around Bhimle Checkpoint (Bengal Florican* and both rubythroats), and the sal forest around **Tiger Tops Jungle Lodge** (Red-headed Trogon, Great Hornbill, Indian Pitta, Grey-crowned Prinia*, Rufous-necked Laughingthrush). From **Sauraha**, accessible via Tadi Bazaar, bird the sal forest to the west (Blue-bearded Bee-eater) and cross the river to reach the grassland and sal forest within the park (Bengal Florican*, Indian Pitta). Sauraha is an excellent area for Indian rhinoceros and, while it is exciting, and a little unnerving, to know that it is possible to come across such a huge creature at any moment, it is downright dangerous to startle a mother and a young calf. Also watch out for the equally dangerous, but much rarer, sloth bears and tigers throughout the park. The drier and more open forest at the eastern end of the reserve, around **Chitwan Jungle Lodge**, supports specialities such as Collared Falconet, while Green Magpie, Long-tailed Broadbill and Sultan Tit are confined to the **Churia Hills** in the southwest. A number of the rare birds here are grassland specialities and because the grass grows over head-height the best time to look for these species is from February to April, after large areas of grass have been cut in January.

Accommodation: Inside — Tiger Tops Jungle Lodge (A+), PO Box 242, Durbar Marg, Kathmandu. Chitwan Jungle Lodge (A+), PO Box 1281, Durbar Marg, Kathmandu. Machan Wildlife Resort (A+), PO Box 3140, Durbar Marg, Kathmandu. Outside — Meghauli: Chital Lodge (C). Sauraha: Gaida Wildlife Camp (A+), PO Box 2056, Durbar Marg, Kathmandu. Gaida Tented Camp (A+). Wendy's (C). Park View Lodge (C).

The rare and local Bengal Florican is a Chitwan speciality*

The shingle banks of the Rapti River at **Hetauda**, east of Narayanghat, support wintering Ibisbill, Long-billed Plover* and Wallcreeper. Bird along the river south of the road where the Ibisbills have been seen up to 5 km away, but not during times of heavy disturbance.

Accommodation: Neelam Lodge.

Swamp Francolin*, Bengal Florican* and White-tailed Stonechat occur in the **Sukla Phanta** reserve (155 sq km) in the far west terai close to Dudwa NP in India, but access to this site is usually restricted. Bengal* and Lesser* (Apr–Sep) Floricans and Ibisbill (Nov–Mar) occur in **Bardia NP**, also in the western terai. Bardia is 2 hours by road from Nepalgunj, which is connected by air to Kathmandu. The best place to stay is Karnali Tented Camp, which is bookable through Tiger Tops, PO Box 242, Durbar Marg, Kathmandu.

KOSI

The wetlands, grasslands and farmland near the 1 km long barrage across the Kosi River and at the nearby Kosi Tappu reserve in southeast Nepal support numerous wintering waterbirds, as well as Swamp

KOSI

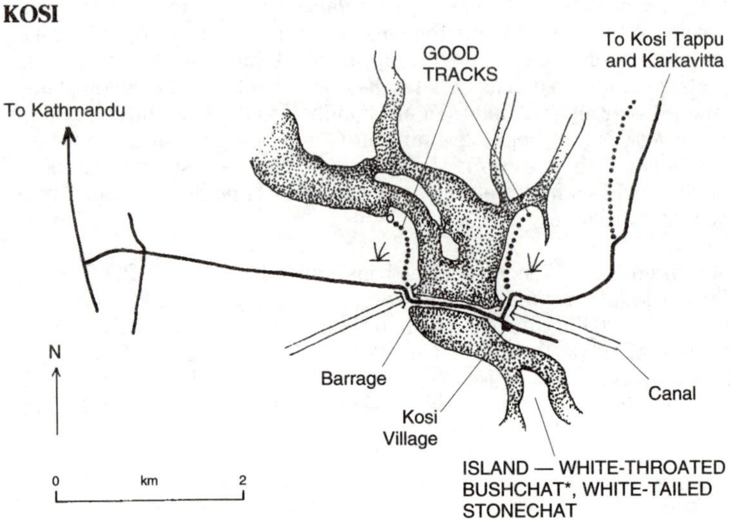

Francolin* and White-throated Bushchat*, and during the winter it is possible to see over 150 species in a day.

Specialities

Spot-billed Pelican* (Apr–Sep), Swamp Francolin*, Grey-bellied Cuckoo, White-throated Bushchat* (Nov–Apr), White-tailed Stonechat, Striated Babbler, Hume's Lark (Nov–Mar).

Others

Little Cormorant, Oriental Darter*, Comb and Falcated (Nov–Mar) Ducks, Indian Pond-Heron, Yellow and Cinnamon Bitterns, Black-headed* and Red-naped* Ibises, Asian Openbill*, Black-necked Stork, Lesser* and Greater* (Apr–Sep) Adjutants, White-tailed Eagle* (Nov–Mar), Long-billed Vulture*, Pied Harrier (Oct–Apr), White-eyed Buzzard, Imperial Eagle* (Nov–Mar), Red-necked Falcon*, Black Francolin, Ruddy-breasted Crake, Watercock (Jun–Sep), Pheasant-tailed and Bronze-winged Jacanas, Greater Painted-Snipe, Small Pratincole, River Lapwing, Great Black-headed (Nov–Mar) and Brown-headed (Nov–Mar) Gulls, Black-bellied* and River Terns, Spotted Owlet, Stork-billed Kingfisher, Green and Blue-tailed Bee-eaters, Indian Roller, Coppersmith Barbet, Rufous Treepie, Brown Shrike (Nov–Mar), Brahminy Starling, Asian Pied Starling, Bank Myna, Siberian Rubythroat (Nov–Apr), Yellow-bellied and Plain Prinias, Spotted Bush-Warbler (Nov–Mar), Pallas' Warbler (Nov–Mar), Blyth's Reed-Warbler (Nov–Mar), Paddyfield (Nov–Mar), Thick-billed (Nov–Mar) and Smoky (Nov–Mar) Warblers, Striated Grassbird, Ashy-crowned Sparrow-Lark, Sand Lark, Rosy Pipit, Red Avadavat, Bengal Weaver, Chestnut-eared (Nov–Mar), Yellow-breasted (Nov–Mar) and Black-faced (Nov–Mar) Buntings.

Other Wildlife

Fishing cat, Ganges dolphin, gharial, leopard, nilgai, water buffalo (mostly feral).

(Other species recorded here include Baer's Pochard* (Nov–Mar), Pallas' Fish-Eagle*, Great Thick-knee, Indian Courser and Indian Skimmer*.)

At the **Kosi Barrage**, near Karkavitta, bird west and east of the barrage, the islands to the north, and the island to the south (White-throated Bushchat*, White-tailed Stonechat, Hume's Lark). Swamp Francolin* occurs at **Kosi Tappu** (175 sq km), 15 km north of the barrage. This reserve is accessible by bus or by foot along the embankment from the barrage, or by bus (2 hours) from Biratnagar, which is connected by air and road to Kathmandu. Bird the tracks which run through the reserve (bicycles available for hire).

Accommodation: Kosi Barrage — tea shops. Kosi Tappu — Kosi Camp (A), PO Box 536, Kamaladi, Kathmandu (tel: 977 1 226130, fax: 977 1 224237), or Naturetrek, Chautara, Bighton, Alresford, Hampshire SO24 9RB, UK (tel: 01962 733051, fax: 01962 733368).

Dharan Forest, accessible from Kosi or, better still, Itahari, supports Collared Falconet, Pompadour Green-Pigeon, Silver-backed Needletail, Blue-bearded Bee-eater, Black-headed Cuckoo-Shrike, Spot-winged Starling*, Pale-chinned Blue-Flycatcher and Pale-billed Flowerpecker.

Accommodation: Itahari — Hotel Jay Nepal.

LANGTANG VALLEY TREK

This trek passes through subtropical, temperate and oak–rhododendron forests which support the endemic Immaculate Wren-Babbler*, which was only discovered here in 1991, as well as a quartet of 'pheasants', Ibisbill, Yellow-rumped Honeyguide* and Pied Thrush*. Together with a section of the Gosainkund Trek, all the habitats can be covered in two weeks, but three would be better.

Most of the birds listed below are only present in the summer, and the best time to go is the second half of May.

Nepalese Endemics

Immaculate Wren-Babbler*.

Specialities

Snow Partridge, Ibisbill, Yellow-rumped Honeyguide*, Pied Thrush*, Rusty-tailed Flycatcher, Yellow-vented Warbler*, Variegated Laughingthrush, Rufous-vented Yuhina, Hume's Lark, Pink-browed and Spot-winged Rosefinches, Scarlet Finch.

Others

Lammergeier, Himalayan Griffon, Tibetan Snowcock, Blood Pheasant, Himalayan Monal, Snow Pigeon, Speckled Wood-Pigeon, Wedge-tailed Pigeon, Lesser Cuckoo, Collared Owlet, Jungle Nightjar, Himalayan Swiftlet, White-throated Needletail, Great and Golden-throated Barbets, Rufous-bellied, Crimson-breasted, Darjeeling, Scaly-bellied and Bay Woodpeckers, Gold-billed Magpie, Maroon Oriole, Short-billed Minivet,

LANGTANG VALLEY AND GOSAINKUND TREKS

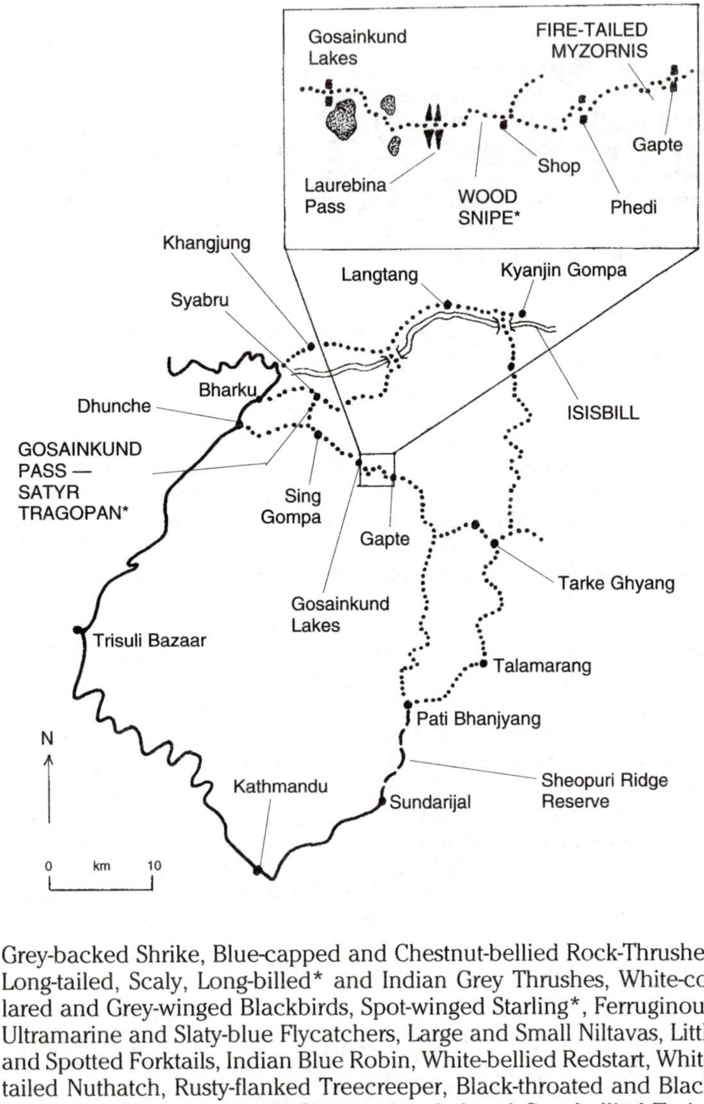

Grey-backed Shrike, Blue-capped and Chestnut-bellied Rock-Thrushes, Long-tailed, Scaly, Long-billed* and Indian Grey Thrushes, White-collared and Grey-winged Blackbirds, Spot-winged Starling*, Ferruginous, Ultramarine and Slaty-blue Flycatchers, Large and Small Niltavas, Little and Spotted Forktails, Indian Blue Robin, White-bellied Redstart, White-tailed Nuthatch, Rusty-flanked Treecreeper, Black-throated and Black-browed Tits, Striated Prinia, Chestnut-headed and Grey-bellied Tesias, Aberrant and Grey-sided Bush-Warblers, Tickell's Leaf-Warbler, Buff-barred and Ashy-throated Warblers, Large-billed and Blyth's Leaf-Warblers, Black-faced Warbler, White-throated, Striated, Streaked and Black-faced Laughingthrushes, Red-billed Leiothrix, Chestnut-tailed Minla, Rufous-winged Fulvetta, Rufous Sibia, Whiskered and Stripe-throated Yuhinas, Rufous-vented, Grey-crested and Black-lored Tits, Rosy and Upland Pipits, Rufous-breasted Accentor, Gould's, Green-tailed and Fire-tailed Sunbirds, Yellow-breasted Greenfinch, Beautiful and White-browed Rosefinches, Crimson-browed Finch, Brown Bullfinch, Collared and White-winged Grosbeaks.

Other Wildlife

Common goral, Himalayan tahr, mainland serow, musk deer.

It is possible to save two days walking through relatively poor habitat (Spot-winged Starling*) by starting at **Dhunche**, which is accessible by track from Trisuli Bazaar, near Kathmandu. Just out of Dhunche the trail crosses a number of wet, vegetated ravines where the superb Pied Thrush* occurs, along with Blue-capped and Chestnut-bellied Rock-Thrushes, Little and Spotted Forktails and Grey-bellied Tesia. From here the trail descends to the Trisuli River then climbs to Bharku at 1845 m (6053 ft), passing through some forest. Leave the new road at Bharku and follow the path over a ridge towards **Syabru**, where there are a number of lodges on a steep, terraced hillside. From Syabru the trail descends through the terraced paddies, then climbs again before descending into the **Langtang Gorge** where the trail enters excellent moist deciduous forest, alongside the Langtang River. Birds to look out for along this stretch include the endemic Immaculate Wren-Babbler* (in thick riverside undergrowth), Yellow-rumped Honeyguide* (on branches near the pendulous bees' nests which hang from the cliffs), Pied Thrush*, Chestnut-headed Tesia and Scarlet Finch, while Himalayan Monal, as well as Common Goral, Himalayan Tahr and Mainland Serow may be seen on the steep grassy slopes above.

The trail then crosses the Langtang River before ascending to Chongdong at 2380 m (7808 ft) and **Ghore Tabela** at 2880 m (9449 ft) via coniferous forest where Long-tailed and Long-billed* Thrushes occur. Above Ghore Tabela the trail reaches the large village of **Langtang**, which lies at 3305 m (10,843 ft) in a U-shaped glacial valley surrounded by spectacular snow-capped peaks. There are few birds beyond Langtang, but most of them are spectacular. Between there and Kyanjin Gompa look out for Snow Pigeon, White-bellied Redstart (in the first ravine east of Langtang), Black-browed Tit, Fire-tailed Sunbird, and Pink-browed and Spot-winged Rosefinches. At **Kyanjin Gompa**, which is situated at 3750 m (12,303 ft) the river is broad and stony: ideal Ibisbill habitat. The birch wood alongside the river supports Blood Pheasant, as well as Musk Deer. Snow Partridge and Tibetan Snowcock also occur around Kyanjin, especially towards Yala Hill, which is a little more than a hill at 4985 m (16,355 ft).

Accommodation: basic lodges, camping.

The stunning Pied Thrush is a summer visitor to the Langtang Valley. In winter this species moves south and Sri Lanka is a good place to see it.*

At Syabru on the Langtang Valley Trek it is possible to take a short cut to the **Gosainkund Trek** (see below). The brilliant Satyr Tragopan* occurs in the mixed forest of the Gosainkund Pass along this short cut (best to look at dawn), along with a number of other species which are not usually seen on the Langtang Valley Trek. These include Spotted Laughingthrush, Green Shrike-Babbler, White-browed Fulvetta, Black-throated Parrotbill and Red-headed Bullfinch. Turn left at the end of the short-cut to join the Gosainkund Trek to Sing Gompa.

GOSAINKUND TREK

This trek traverses higher ground than the Langtang Valley Trek, passing through oak–rhododendron forests before reaching the high-altitude meadows and barren stony wastes around the 4600 m (15,092 ft) Laurebina Pass. This pass may seem like a long way to go for what amounts to a few birds, but these birds are a bit special. They include Wood Snipe*, Gould's Shortwing*, Grandala, Red-tailed Minla, Fire-tailed Myzornis and Red-fronted Rosefinch.

Nepalese Endemics

Spiny Babbler.

Specialities

Snow Partridge, Wood Snipe*, Gould's Shortwing*, Grandala, Hoary-throated Barwing, Fire-tailed Myzornis, Red-fronted Rosefinch, Red-headed Bullfinch.

Others

Blood Pheasant, Himalayan Monal, Lesser Cuckoo, Plain-backed, Long-tailed, Scaly, Long-billed* and Indian Grey Thrushes, White-collared Blackbird, Ultramarine Flycatcher, Golden, White-browed and Rufous-breasted* Bush-Robins, White-bellied Redstart, Rusty-flanked Tree-creeper, Black-browed Tit, Aberrant and Grey-sided Bush-Warblers, Smoky Warbler, White-throated Laughingthrush, White-browed Scimitar-Babbler, Red-tailed Minla, Yellow-browed Tit, Fire-tailed Sunbird, Plain and Black-headed Mountain-Finches, Dark-breasted and White-browed Rosefinches, Crimson-browed Finch, Collared and White-winged Grosbeaks.

The trail to Gosainkund Lakes is accessible via a short-cut from Syabru on the Langtang Valley Trek. From the short-cut the trail ascends through coniferous forest to **Sing Gompa** at 3255 m (10,679 ft). Species recorded along this stretch include White-bellied Redstart, Rusty-flanked Treecreeper and Collared Grosbeak, while Satyr Tragopan* occurs near Sing Gompa. Above Sing Gompa the trail climbs to the **Gosainkund Lakes**. These lakes may lie in a remote area above 4267 m (14,000 ft), but they are a very popular tourist attraction and birders who are hoping to get 'away from it all' will be disappointed to discover that there is a 'village pub' in Gosainkund. Other birders will no doubt welcome the thought of a beer after a hard day's climbing. The most important thing to know, however, is that three high-altitude specialities occur just above here: Red-fronted Rosefinch *en route* to the

4600 m (15,092 ft) **Laurebina Pass** and Wood Snipe* and Grandala on the barren, boulder-strewn slopes between the pass and **Phedi**. Below the pass on the Phedi side also look out for Snow Partridge and Himalayan Monal, while the low juniper scrub supports Smoky Warbler and White-winged Grosbeak. Beyond Phedi the trail reaches **Gapte** at 3565 m (11,696 ft), where the rhododendron's flower in May and attract the fantastic Fire-tailed Myzornis.

Instead of returning from Gapte on the same route, it is possible to join the **Helambu Circuit** and return to Kathmandu the same day by bus, or, better still, to carry on trekking, to **Thore Pati** via remnant forest patches, which support Hoary-throated Barwing and Red-tailed Minla, and from Thore Pati to the **Sheopuri Ridge Reserve** where the endemic Spiny Babbler occurs. From here the trail descends steeply to Sundarijal, where it is possible to return to Kathmandu by road.

Accommodation: lodges at Sing Gompa (e.g. 'Stuffed Yak' Lodge), Gosainkund, Phedi, Gapte and Thore Pati, camping.

The small town of **Pokhara** lies at 915 m (3002 ft) in a magnificent setting below the immense Annapurna Massif, all peaks of which exceed 6500 m (21,326 ft). Although the surrounds of Pokhara are heavily cultivated and much of the remaining forest is heavily degraded, this is still a good birding area. Species recorded in the area include Falcated Duck (Nov–Mar), Lammergeier, Pied Harrier (Nov–Mar), Brown Fish-Owl, Long-tailed Broadbill, Green Magpie, Maroon Oriole, Long-tailed Thrush, Pale Blue-Flycatcher, Black-backed Forktail, Chestnut-headed and Grey-bellied Tesias, White-crested and Rufous-chinned Laughingthrushes, White-browed Scimitar-Babbler and Red-billed Leiothrix. Pokhara is accessible by road (8 hours) and air from Kathmandu. Bird the forest at the southwest corner of Phewa Tal lake (behind Fishtail Lodge), the marshy area at the northern end (Falcated Duck, Pied Harrier) and the lake known as Begnas Tal, 15 km southeast of Pokhara (Falcated Duck).

Accommodation: Pokhara — Hotel Tragopan. Phewa Tal — Fishtail Lodge (A+), Hotel Nirvana (C) and various other, much cheaper, options.

JOMOSOM TREK

This trek has been nicknamed the 'Apple Pie Trek' because this is on the menu of virtually all the lodges *en route* and it reflects the almost ridiculous ease with which the trek can be accomplished, despite its remote location. The trail traverses the Kali Gandaki Gorge, subtropical and temperate forests as well as mountain meadows at the edge of the Tibetan Plateau. The birdlife is spectacular and includes Tibetan Partridge, Koklass and Cheer* Pheasants, Solitary Snipe, Rufous-backed, White-throated and White-winged Redstarts, White-browed Tit-Warbler, Blanford's and Red-fronted Rosefinches and Maroon-backed Accentor. It is possible to see around 200 species over a period of two to three weeks, although the trek can be completed in ten days.

JOMOSOM TREK

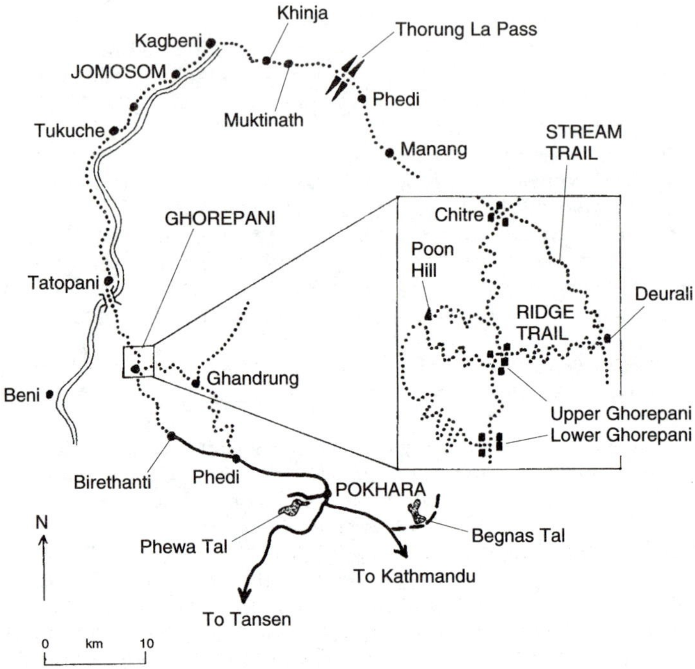

Most of the birds listed below are only present during the spring and summer, and late March is the best time to go as some winter visitors such as White-winged Redstart are still present.

Nepalese Endemics

Spiny Babbler.

Specialities

Tibetan Partridge, Satyr Tragopan*, Koklass and Cheer* Pheasants, Solitary Snipe, Yellow-rumped Honeyguide*, Grandala, Rufous-backed and White-throated Redstarts, White-browed Tit-Warbler, Spotted and Variegated Laughingthrushes, Hoary-throated Barwing, Nepal Fulvetta, Rufous-vented Yuhina, Spectacled Finch, Blanford's, Pink-browed, Spot-winged, Red-fronted and Streaked Rosefinches, Red-headed Bullfinch.

Others

Lammergeier, Himalayan Griffon, Tibetan and Himalayan Snowcocks, Chukar, Hill Partridge, Blood Pheasant, Himalayan Monal, Snow Pigeon, Speckled Wood-Pigeon, Slaty-headed Parakeet, Crested Kingfisher, Chestnut-headed Bee-eater, Speckled Piculet, Rufous-bellied, Crimson-breasted and Scaly-bellied Woodpeckers, Gold-billed and Green Magpies, Maroon Oriole, Long-tailed and Short-billed Minivets, Orange-bellied Leafbird, Grey-backed Shrike, Chestnut-bellied Rock-Thrush, Plain-backed, Long-tailed, Long-billed*, Indian Grey and

Chestnut Thrushes, Slaty-blue Flycatcher, Small Niltava, Pygmy Blue-Flycatcher, Golden, White-browed and Rufous-breasted* Bush-Robins, Blue-capped, Hodgson's and White-winged Redstarts, Little, Slaty-backed and Spotted Forktails, White-tailed Nuthatch, Wallcreeper, Bar-tailed and Rusty-flanked Treecreepers, Black-throated and Black-browed Tits, Striated Prinia, Chestnut-headed Tesia, Yellowish-bellied and Grey-sided Bush-Warblers, Tickell's Leaf-Warbler, Buff-barred, Ashy-throated and Black-faced Warblers, White-throated, White-crested, Striated, Streaked and Black-faced Laughingthrushes, White-browed Scimitar-Babbler, Red-billed Leiothrix, Green and Black-eared Shrike-Babblers, Blue-winged and Chestnut-tailed Minlas, Rufous-winged and White-browed Fulvettas, Rufous Sibia, Whiskered and Stripe-throated Yuhinas, Great, Brown and Black-throated Parrotbills, Rufous-vented, Grey-crested, Black-lored and Yellow-browed Tits, Russet Sparrow, Rosy and Upland Pipits, Himalayan, Robin, Rufous-breasted, Brown and Maroon-backed Accentors, Gould's, Green-tailed and Fire-tailed Sunbirds, Fire-fronted Serin, Yellow-breasted Greenfinch, Plain Mountain-Finch, Beautiful and White-browed Rosefinches, Crimson-browed Finch, Brown Bullfinch, Collared and White-winged Grosbeaks, Gold-naped Finch.

Other Wildlife

Bharal, common goral, yellow-throated marten.

(Other species recorded here include Demoiselle Crane, Long-billed Plover*, Tibetan Ground-Jay (around Manang on the other side of Thorung La), Dusky Thrush (Lete), Fire-capped Tit (Lete) and Great Rosefinch (north of Kalopani).)

Downhill, this trek begins at **Jomosom**, which is accessible by air from Pokhara. Jomosom lies at 2715 m (8908 ft) at the edge of the Tibetan Plateau, and the fields around here and Marpha support Rufous-backed, White-throated and White-winged Redstarts, and White-browed Tit-Warbler. Before beginning the descent, it is worth birding above Jomosom. Demoiselle Crane has been recorded in the fields around **Kagbeni** at 2805 m (9203 ft). From here the trail ascends the Jhong Khola Valley, a good stretch for White-winged Redstart and White-browed Tit-Warbler, before reaching **Muktinath** at 3800 m (12,467 ft). High-altitude specialities such as Tibetan and Himalayan Snowcocks, Solitary Snipe and Snow Pigeon occur around Muktinath, in the fields surrounding the village (Snow Pigeon), the area around the monastery (White-winged Grosbeak) and pool (Solitary Snipe) and the Thorung La Pass (snowcocks and Bharal).

From Jomosom the main trail descends to Kalopani, then through fairly good forest (Yellow-rumped Honeyguide) before reaching **Ghasa**. Many of the trek's specialities occur in the excellent forest around Ghasa, including all six Nepalese pheasants. Seeing these birds, however, involves a considerable amount of time (at least three days) and effort, as the valley sides here are very steep and dangerous (beware). To the east of Ghasa leave the main trail just east of the bridge across the Kali Gandaki River and explore the valley sides to the north for Blood Pheasant, Satyr Tragopan*, Cheer Pheasant* and Grandala. To the west of Ghasa leave the main trail just north of Mustang Lodge (north of Ghasa) and explore the valley sides to the west for Koklass and Cheer* Pheasants and Maroon-backed Accentor. Below Ghasa the trail to enters the Kali Gandaki Gorge, where the endemic Spiny Babbler occurs to the north and south of **Tatopani**. From Tatopani the trail climbs to **Ghorepani** and the Ghandrung Ridge, a particularly good stretch where Great Parrotbill occurs. It is worth spending a few days around Ghorepani where Blanford's Rosefinch occurs along the **Poon Hill Trail** from Upper Ghorepani to Lower Ghorepani, Koklass Pheasant, Black-throated Parrotbill and Spectacled Finch occur along the **Ridge Trail** which leads to Deurali, and Solitary Snipe, and Long-tailed and Long-billed* Thrushes have been recorded along the **Stream Trail** between Deurali and Chitre. From Ghorepani the trail descends through oak–rhododendron forests before reaching Birethanti at 1065 m (3494 ft). This is the end of the main trail, but don't forget to look along the river here for Crested Kingfisher, Little, Slaty-backed and Spotted Forktails and Wallcreeper, or at Phedi for Long-billed Plover*. Pokhara is accessible by road from Birethanti.

Accommodation: Muktinath — North Pole Lodge. Ghasa — Eagle's Nest Guest House. Tatopani — Namaste Lodge.

The amazing White-crested Laughingthrush is widespread throughout Nepal and southeast Asia

It is possible to cut across to the bottom of the **Annapurna Sanctuary Trek** from Ghorepani and return along there to Pokhara via Ghandrung and Landrung. This is worth birding in late winter when the resident pheasants are calling and wintering species are still present, especially the forest between Ghorepani and Tadapani via Deurali (Chestnut Thrush), the forest between Tadapani and Tolka via Ghandrung and Landrung, and the forest between Tolka and Phedi (Scarlet Finch).

Jomosom is also the starting and ending point for the **Mustang Trek**, which usually takes 16 days to complete and is at its best in August. The Mustang trail passes through a land which is geographically, culturally and ornithologically Tibetan, traversing the southern edge of the desolate but beautiful Tibetan Plateau, where the high-altitude specialities include Tibetan Partridge, Tibetan Sandgrouse, Tibetan Ground-Jay, White-browed Tit-Warbler, Hume's Lark, Mongolian Finch, Black-winged, White-rumped, Rufous-necked and Blandford's Snowfinches, and Great Rosefinch, as well as bharal, snow leopard and wolf.

The massive **Shey-Phoksundo National Park** (3555 sq km) is Nepal's largest park and the scene for much of Peter Matthiessen's excellent book, *The Snow Leopard*. It is situated in the far northwest in a rugged, remote land of forests, mountain meadows and the near-desert terrain of the Tibetan Plateau. Species recorded here include Tibetan Partridge, Wood Snipe* (at Pani Palta), Tibetan Ground-Jay, White-cheeked Nuthatch, White-throated Tit*, White-browed Tit-Warbler, Variegated Laughingthrush, Black-winged Snowfinch, Streaked Rosefinch and Red-headed Bullfinch, as well as bharal, musk deer, snow leopard and wolf. The park is only accessible via the airport at Juphaal; special permits are required and the trekking fees are high.

Surkhet, two days by road west of Kathmandu, is the starting point for the **Rara Lake Trek**. This is a rather strenuous 18-day camping trek, best tackled in March, where it is possible to see a number of west Himalayan specialities such as Kashmir and White-cheeked Nuthatches, as well as Himalayan Snowcock, Cheer Pheasant*, Rufous-backed Redstart, Black-crested Tit and Black-throated Accentor. From Surkhet the trail crosses two high ridges and the Tila Valley before reaching Sinja at 2134 m (7000 ft). From here the trail ascends to the 3962 m (13,000 ft) Chuchmara Pass before dropping to Rara Lake at 3048 m (10,000 ft). It is worth spending a few days here before returning to the trail, which then traverses two more high passes before reaching Jumla at 2347 m (7700 ft). From Jumla it is possible to return to Kathmandu by air.

The **Everest Trek**, which is best in May for birds and in autumn for mountain views, passes through farmland, meadows and rhododendron stands where Tibetan Snowcock, Blood Pheasant, Himalayan Monal, Snow Pigeon, Black-headed Mountain-Finch and Great and Red-fronted Rosefinches occur, along with musk deer and tahr. The trek begins and ends at Lukla, which is accessible by air from Kathmandu. It follows the Dudh Kosi Valley to Namche Bazaar, Khumjing, Thyangboche (high-altitude specialities) and Upper Pangboche, beyond which lie high pastures and rocky river valleys surrounded by magnificent mountain scenery, including Everest, which rises to 8848 m (29,029 ft). The trail then ascends to the Gokyo Lakes at 4572 m (15,000 ft), where Red-fronted Rosefinch occurs and from where it is possible to climb Kala Pattar, which rises to 5182 m (17,000 ft).

The 18-day **Barun Valley Trek**, best in May, ascends through the subtropical, temperate and subalpine zones where Satyr Tragopan*, Wood Snipe*, Spot-bellied Eagle-Owl*, Brown Wood-Owl, Dark-sided Thrush, Gould's Shortwing*, Sapphire Flycatcher, Broad-billed Warbler*, Blue-winged Laughingthrush, Slender-billed Scimitar-Babbler*, Rufous-throated* and Spotted* Wren-Babblers, Rusty-fronted Barwing, Fire-tailed Myzornis and Maroon-backed Accentor occur, along with bharal and snow leopard. This trek begins and ends at Tumlingtar, accessible by air from Kathmandu. It follows the Arun Valley northwards before ascending to the 4267 m (14,000 ft) Barun Pass, the gateway to Mount Makalu basecamp.

The long, tough 23-day **Kangchenjunga Trek**, best in May or June, in extreme northeast Nepal, approaches Mount Kangchenjunga, the world's third highest mountain at 8598 m (28,209 ft). Little is known about the birds here, but possibilities include Blue-fronted Robin*, Purple Cochoa*, Red-faced Liocichla, Long-billed* and Spotted* Wren-Babblers and Yellow-throated Fulvetta*. The trek begins north of Ilam, accessible by road from Biratnagar and Birtamod, or from Darjeeling, in India.

HANGA THAM TREK

This trek in extreme east Nepal passes through heavily cultivated, terraced hillsides, vegetated ravines and oak–rhododendron forest which support a number of east Himalayan specialities, including the rare Rufous-throated Wren-Babbler*. The best time to tackle this trek is May and it will take at least a week.

Most of the species listed below are only present in summer (May– Sep).

Specialities

Gould's Shortwing*, Rufous-throated Wren-Babbler*, Cutia, Rusty-fronted Barwing.

Others

Blue-capped Rock-Thrush, Long-tailed Thrush, Grey-winged Blackbird, Sapphire and Blue-throated Flycatchers, Chestnut-headed Tesia, Brownish-flanked Bush-Warbler, Broad-billed Warbler*, White-crested and Scaly Laughingthrushes, Slender-billed Scimitar-Babbler*, Rufous-capped Babbler, Black-headed Shrike-Babbler*, Rufous-backed Sibia, Brown Parrotbill, Upland Pipit, Maroon-backed Accentor.

From Ilam, accessible by road from Birtamod, or Darjeeling, in India, walk north and ask any passing locals to point out the route as often as possible, since the trail is not always obvious. It takes a day to get to Jamuna and 2–3 hours to reach the settlement of Hanga Tham, beyond which lies excellent mossy oak–rhododendron forest worth prolonged birding. It is possible to return to Ilam in a day.

Accommodation: Ilam — Deurali Lodge. Trek — camping, village houses.

The short **Sunischare Trek**, best covered over the period of at least three days, is good for Pin-tailed Pigeon, Crested Kingfisher, Long-tailed Broadbill, Pale-chinned Blue-Flycatcher, Black-backed Forktail and White-throated Bulbul, while Pale-headed Woodpecker has also been recorded. Walk south from Ilam, beginning on the hairpin bend just below Deurali Lodge. The best birding areas are around the Modi Khola River and the Garuwa–Sukhani stretch. It takes a day to get from Ilam to Chisapani, allowing a few hours to bird the river area thoroughly, and another day to get to Sukhani, from where it is a short distance to Sunischare which is connected by road to Birtamod.

Accommodation: Ilam — Deurali Lodge. Trek — camping, village houses.

ADDITIONAL INFORMATION

Addresses

Nepal Bird Watching Club, c/o Valley Brook Centre, Chetrapati, Kathmandu.

Books and Papers

A Pictorial Guide to the Birds of the Indian Subcontinent. Ali S *et al.*, 1983. Bombay Natural History Society/Oxford University Press.
A Birdwatcher's Guide to Nepal. Inskipp C, 1988. Prion.
A Guide to the Birds of Nepal, 2nd Edition. Inskipp C and T, 1991. Helm.

ENDEMICS (2)

Immaculate Wren-Babbler*	Central: Langtang Valley Trek
Spiny Babbler	West and Central: Sheopuri Ridge Reserve, Gosainkund Trek and Jomosom Trek

Near-endemics

Swamp Francolin*, Tibetan Partridge, Satyr Tragopan*, Cheer Pheasant*, Bengal* and Lesser* Floricans, Indian Courser, Brown-fronted, Himalayan and White-naped Woodpeckers, White-bellied Drongo, Black-headed Jay, Tibetan Ground-Jay, Pied* and Indian Grey Thrushes, Rusty-tailed Flycatcher, Pale-chinned Blue-Flycatcher, Rufous-breasted Bush-Robin*, Kashmir and White-cheeked Nuthatches, White-throated Tit*, Grey-crowned* and Jungle Prinias, Smoky Warbler, Tytler's Leaf-Warbler*, Western Crowned-Warbler, Bristled Grassbird*, Striated, Rufous-necked, Grey-sided and Variegated Laughingthrushes, Rufous-throated Wren-Babbler*, Black-chinned, Tawny-bellied, Jerdon's*, Slender-billed* and Large Grey Babblers, Rusty-fronted and Hoary-throated Barwings, Nepal Fulvetta, White-naped and Rufous-vented Yuhinas, Fire-tailed Myzornis, Great, Brown, Black-breasted* and Fulvous Parrotbills, Black-crested and Black-lored Tits, Tibetan Lark, Black-winged, Rufous-necked and Blanford's Snowfinches, Robin, Rufous-breasted and Maroon-backed Accentors, Fire-tailed Sunbird, Tibetan Serin, Spectacled Finch, Blanford's, Beautiful, Pink-browed, Vinaceous, Dark-rumped and Streaked Rosefinches, Crimson-browed and Scarlet Finches, Red-headed Bullfinch, Gold-naped Finch.

NORTH KOREA

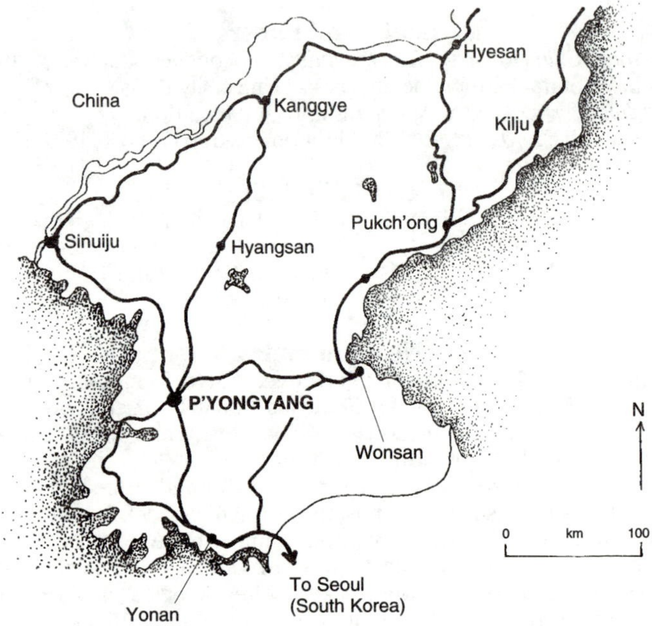

North Korea is one of the world's most secretive countries and certainly one of the hardest to get into. Only 40 tourists were rumoured to have made it in 1994 and most of those were on tours organised in Beijing. Official guides and designated expensive hotels are compulsory. All of which is disappointing, because the country's birds include such spectacular species as White-naped Crane*.

At 120,538 sq km, North Korea is a little smaller than England and nearly six times smaller than Texas. There are no regular domestic flights, few public buses and a small rail network. In 1995 there were serious food shortages due to crop failures compounded by floods. Immunisation against hepatitis, polio and typhoid is recommended. Winters are dry and cold, summers warm and wet. Very little is known about the birds of North Korea or their status and one can only hope that the 26 threatened and near-threatened species which occur in this country are afforded some form of protection. Non-endemic specialities and spectacular species include Mandarin Duck*, Baikal Teal* (winter visitor), Baer's Pochard* (winter visitor), Scaly-sided Merganser* (breeding summer visitor), Chinese Egret* (breeding summer visitor), Black-faced Spoonbill* (breeding summer visitor), Oriental Stork*, Steller's Sea-Eagle* (winter visitor), Swinhoe's Rail*, Hooded*, Red-crowned* and White-naped* Cranes, Nordmann's Greenshank*, Spoonbill Sandpiper*, Long-billed Plover*, Japanese Paradise-Flycatcher* (breeding summer visitor), Japanese Waxwing* (winter visitor), Varied Tit, Yellow-billed and Japanese Grosbeaks and Rufous-backed* (breeding), Ochre-rumped* and Yellow* Buntings. There is no endemic species.

The area around **Kumya** on the east coast and the **Tumen River Valley** along the northeast border are important refuelling stops for White-naped Cranes* on their flight from their wintering quarters at Arasaki in Japan to their breeding grounds further north. Rocky islets such as **Tegam**, **Sogam** and **Sorap** off the west coast support breeding Chinese Egret* (probably the bulk of the world population) and Black-faced Spoonbill*. One of the last sightings of Crested Shelduck*, now thought to be extinct, involved a flock of six birds in the northeast in 1971.

ADDITIONAL INFORMATION

Books and Papers

Report on the Hungarian Scientific Expedition in North Korea. Waliczky Z and Baldi A, 1991. Hungarian Ornithological Society.

Near-endemics

Japanese Cormorant, Scaly-sided Merganser*, Steller's Sea-Eagle*, Swinhoe's Rail*, Hooded*, Red-crowned* and White-naped* Cranes, Black-tailed Gull, Spectacled Guillemot, Bull-headed and Chinese Grey Shrikes, Japanese Waxwing*, Snowy-browed Nuthatch*, Varied Tit, Chinese Penduline-Tit, Black-backed and Japanese Wagtails, Grey-capped Greenfinch, Japanese Grosbeak, Rufous-backed*, Ochre-rumped*, Tristram's, Yellow-throated and Yellow* Buntings.

PAKISTAN

INTRODUCTION

Summary

Pakistan deserves to be a popular birding destination because the wondrous mountains of the Karakoram Range in the north support many west Himalayan specialities such as Western Tragopan*. However, few birders have been here and many are probably put off by the fact that seeing such birds involves a mini-expedition, for while getting around these mountains is not too difficult, there are few places to stay. However, it is possible that the tourist infrastructure may be improved in the future, paving the way for birders to see some rare and beautiful birds in one of world's most dramatic landscapes.

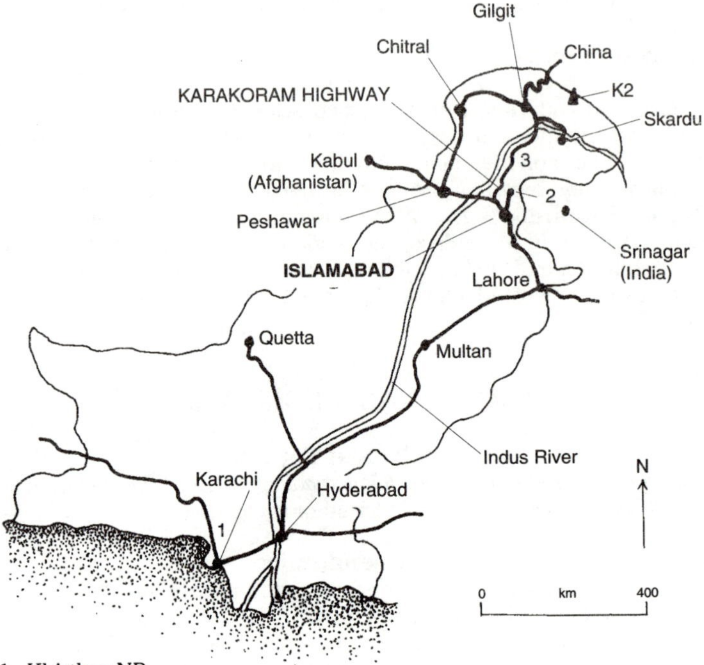

1 Khirthar NP
2 Murree
3 Palas Valley

Size

At 746,045 sq km, Pakistan is nearly six times the size of England and a little larger than Texas.

Getting Around

There is an excellent, cheap bus network, but travelling around on public transport, especially in the north, can be very time consuming. There are some 'flying coaches' which, along with the other vehicles on the often rough roads, do try to 'fly'. However, the amazing amount of traffic on major roads means that the locals cannot drive fast — just dangerously. There is also a good air network, although this is subject to the weather in the north, where flying to Skardu from Islamabad, for example, could take numerous attempts. This is reputed to be the most dangerous flight in the world and it is well worth waiting for if you want to see the endless snow-capped peaks of the Karakoram at close range. Major towns and cities between Karachi in the south and Islamabad in the north are connected by the slow rail network. Check with the most convenient tourist office before embarking on a major trek in the north to see what conditions need to be met.

Accommodation and Food

Accommodation is thin on the ground in the remoter regions of the north, hence it is not possible to take on long treks in Pakistan without camping equipment. Birders who like curries will enjoy the wonderful selection of such dishes in the towns, but prepare to survive on dal (lentils) with chapati in most places, washed down with copious amounts of green tea.

Health and Safety

Immunisation against hepatitis, meningitis, polio, typhoid and yellow fever is recommended, as are precautions against malaria and, in the north, altitude sickness.

Climate and Timing

The best time to visit north Pakistan is between May and September. It is hot all year round in central and south Pakistan, especially in June and July.

Habitats

Four mountain ranges (the Karakoram, Pamirs, Hindu Kush and Himalayas) meet in north Pakistan to form a magnificent part of the world. The numerous spectacular mountains rise to 8611 m (28,251 ft) at K2, which is just 237 m (778 ft) shorter than Mount Everest. They support barren scree slopes, mountain meadows and remnant coniferous and mixed forests, while the valleys in the foothills are filled with orchards. The Indus River flows south from here to the coast near Karachi, providing the Punjab's agricultural plains with water. Beyond these plains lies semi-desert and desert.

Conservation

Only a fraction (4%) of Pakistan's original forest cover remains and if any more is lost many of the country's birds, especially the 39 threatened and near-threatened species, will be in severe danger of extinction.

Bird Species

Over 660 species have been recorded in Pakistan. Non-endemic specialities and spectacular species include Himalayan Snowcock, Western Tragopan*, Koklass Pheasant, Demoiselle Crane, Sind Woodpecker, Black-headed Jay, White-winged Redstart, Hume's Wheatear, Kashmir and White-cheeked Nuthatches, White-cheeked and White-throated* Tits, Hypocolius, Long-billed Bush-Warbler*, White-browed Tit-Warbler, Plain and Tytler's* Leaf-Warblers, Spectacled Finch, Red-fronted Rosefinch, Orange Bullfinch* and Black-and-yellow Grosbeak.

Endemics

There is no endemic species, but around 20 west Himalayan specialities occur in the north.

KHIRTHAR NATIONAL PARK

A number of localised species, including Sind Woodpecker, Hypocolius and Plain Leaf-Warbler, have been recorded in this desert oasis, 80 km northwest of Karachi.

Specialities

Demoiselle Crane (late Sep–early Oct), Sociable Lapwing* (Nov–Mar),

Sykes' Nightjar, Sind Woodpecker, Hume's Wheatear, Hypocolius (Nov–Mar), Rufous-fronted Prinia, Plain Leaf-Warbler (Nov–Mar).

Others

Red-necked*, Laggar (Nov–Mar) and Barbary (Nov–Mar) Falcons, See-see Partridge, Grey Francolin, Greater Painted-Snipe, Cream-coloured Courser, Yellow-wattled Lapwing, Chestnut-bellied and Lichtenstein's Sandgrouse, Spotted Owlet, Indian Nightjar, Green and Blue-cheeked (Apr–Sep) Bee-eaters, Indian Roller, Small Minivet, Bay-backed Shrike, Common Woodshrike, Variable and Red-tailed Wheatears, Streaked Scrub-Warbler, Blyth's Reed-Warbler (Sep–Oct), Singing Bushlark, Black-crowned and Ashy-crowned Sparrow-Larks, Greater Hoopoe-Lark, Chestnut-shouldered Petronia (Apr–Sep), White-throated Munia, Trumpeter Finch, Grey-hooded (Sep–Oct) and House Buntings.

The Sind Wildlife Department may provide transport and a guide to the visitor centre at Khar, where there are desert plains, hills, a farm and a reservoir (Hab Dam), all of which are worth exploring. Sykes' and Indian Nightjars feed on the insects attracted to the lights across the top of Hab Dam.

Accommodation: resthouse.

Previous good birding sites near **Karachi** include Cape Monze (White-tailed Lapwing, Sooty Gull, Variable Wheatear), Korangi Creek (shorebirds including Great Knot), Hub river mouth (terns and desert species), Haleji Lake near Gujo, which is 87 km east of Karachi, and Keenjhar Lake (Pallas' Fish-Eagle*), 125 km east of Karachi and 83 km south of Hyderabad.

Good birding sites near **Islamabad** in north Pakistan include Rawal Lake to the southeast of the city (Cinnamon Bittern (Apr–Sep) on north side, Great Thick-knee and Small Pratincole at the eastern end) and the Margalla Hills NP on the northern edge of the city. The vegetated ravines and remnant pine forest here support Kalij Pheasant, Blue-throated Barbet, Indian Pitta (May–Sep), Chestnut Thrush (Nov–Mar), Golden Bush-Robin, Variegated Laughingthrush, Black-chinned Babbler, Rufous-breasted (Nov–Mar) and Black-throated (Nov–Mar) Accentors and Chestnut-breasted Bunting.

MURREE

The forested hills near Murree, an old hill station situated at 2291 m (7515 ft) 60 km northeast of Islamabad, support a few west Himalayan specialities including Black-headed Jay and Black-and-yellow Grosbeak.

Specialities

Koklass Pheasant, Black-headed Jay, White-cheeked Nuthatch, Variegated Laughingthrush, White-cheeked Tit, Black-and-yellow Grosbeak.

Others

Slaty-headed Parakeet, White-throated Needletail, Great Barbet, Yellow-crowned, Himalayan, Rufous and Scaly-bellied Woodpeckers, Gold-billed Magpie, Long-tailed Minivet, Blue-capped (May–Sep) and Chestnut-bellied (May–Sep) Rock-Thrushes, Chestnut Thrush (Nov–Mar), Ultramarine Flycatcher, Rufous-bellied Niltava, Black-throated Tit, Western Crowned-Warbler (May–Sep), Streaked Laughingthrush, Black-crested and Green-backed Tits, Russet Sparrow, Yellow-breasted Greenfinch.

Murree is accessible by road from Islamabad. Although any of the forested slopes around here are worth birding, Ayubia NP, 26 km north of Murree (40 km south of Abbottabad) is a particularly good area. It is accessible from Dungagarli, a village at the western end, from where there is a 10 km trail east to Ayubia through the forest.

In the **Northwest Frontier Province**, Black-throated Accentor has been recorded in winter at the 2700 m (8858 ft) Lowarai Pass, which is situated between Dir and Drosh, south of Chitral, and Crimson-winged Finch occurs at Germ Kesma (Garm Chasma), northwest of Chitral. A permit, obtainable in Chitral, is required to visit the 322 km long Chitral Valley, which would probably reward investigation.

The 805 km long **Karakoram Highway**, which starts at Havelian, 100 km northwest of Islamabad and ends, after crossing the Khunjerab Pass at a mighty 5575 m (18,290 ft), in Sinkiang province, China, runs through some of the most awesome scenery on earth and enables access to some superb birding sites. Western Tragopan* has been recorded in the 100 km long **Neelum Valley**, north of Muzaffarabad. Western Tragopan*, Kashmir Flycatcher* (May–Sep), Kashmir and White-cheeked Nuthatches, Grey-sided Bush-Warbler, Orange Bullfinch* and Black-and-yellow Grosbeak have been recorded in the 160 km long **Kaghan Valley**, accessible from Mansehra at the south end, and the 4146 m (13,602 ft) Babusar Pass, 593 km from Rawalpindi, at the north end. For permission to visit these valleys, write well in advance to the NCCW.

PALAS VALLEY

The temperate forest in this high valley supports around 325 pairs of the very rare and beautiful Western Tragopan*, along with a number of other west Himalayan specialities such as Black-headed Jay, Tytler's Leaf-Warbler*, Orange Bullfinch* and Black-and-yellow Grosbeak. Seeing these birds and the many others which occur here will involve obtaining a permit in advance from the NCCW and organising a camping trek which lasts at least ten days during May, when the cat-like call of the tragopan can be heard at dawn.

Many of the birds listed below are only present during the summer (May–Sep).

Specialities

Western Tragopan*, Koklass Pheasant, Black-headed Jay, Rusty-tailed Flycatcher, Kashmir Nuthatch, White-cheeked and White-throated* Tits, Brooks' and Tytler's* Leaf-Warblers, Variegated Laughingthrush, Spectacled Finch, Orange Bullfinch*, Black-and-yellow Grosbeak.

Others

Lammergeier, Himalayan Griffon, Himalayan Monal, Himalayan and Scaly-bellied Woodpeckers, Blue-capped Rock-Thrush, Scaly and Chestnut Thrushes, Indian Blue Robin, Little Forktail, Western Crowned-Warbler, Streaked Laughingthrush, Black-crested Tit, Russet Sparrow, White-browed Rosefinch, Chestnut-breasted Bunting.

Other Wildlife

Black bear, common goral, musk deer, wolf, yellow-throated marten.

This valley is accessible from the village of Pattan, north of Abbottabad on the Karakorum Highway. After crossing the Indus River the trail through the valley follows the Palas River and ascends through scrub to the coniferous forests where Western Tragopan* occurs.

*The Palas Valley supports the beautiful black and red Western Tragopan**

Western Tragopan* also occurs in the **Pattan Valley**, opposite the Palas Valley, along with White-bellied Redstart. From Pattan it is a two-day walk to Dukal, where the steep slopes still support some forest. The rarely reported Long-billed Bush-Warbler* has been recorded in the **Naltar Valley**, north of Gilgit, as well as Himalayan Snowcock, Snow Pigeon and White-browed Tit-Warbler. This valley is accessible from the village of Nomal or via the suspension bridge over the River Hunza from Rahimabad on the Karakoram Highway. From Nomal it is a 16 km walk to the settlement of Naltar where the bush-warbler occurs, and it is possible to stay in a basic guesthouse. White-browed Tit-Warbler and White-winged Grosbeak have been recorded in the **Minapin Valley**, which is accessible from Minapin Village between Gilgit and Karimabad (Hunza). From the village it is possible to walk to the Minapin Glacier and Rakaposi Base Camp at 3700 m (12,139 ft). The towering 7800 m (25,591 ft) peak of Rakaposi is visible from here. The intricately irrigated small fields and orchards of the **Hunza Valley** near Karimabad (Hunza) support birds such as Indian Grey Thrush, Mongolian Finch and Chestnut-breasted Bunting. From the small village of **Passu**, 35 km north of Karimabad (Hunza) on the Karakoram Highway, it is possible to visit the Passu and Batura Glaciers, via a trail which begins near the Shispar Hotel. Birds recorded along this trail include Plain Mountain-Finch, Mongolian Finch and Great Rosefinch. Eventually, at Dhee Sar in extreme north Pakistan next to the Chinese border, the Karakoram Highway enters **Khunjerab NP**, where the avifauna includes Himalayan Snowcock, Snow Pigeon, White-winged

Redstart, Black-headed Mountain-Finch and Red-fronted Rosefinch. However, the park is more famous for the rare Marco Polo sheep, which are occasionally seen at the Khunjerab Pass on the Chinese border. To bird away from the road it is necessary to obtain permission from the Director of the park and the District Chief of Police, both of which are based in Gilgit.

Species recorded in and around **Skardu**, which is situated at 2438 m (7500 ft) and is the starting point for mountaineering expeditions to K2, include Wood Snipe*, as well as Great Black-headed Gull, White-winged Redstart, Wallcreeper, White-browed Tit-Warbler, Streaked Laughingthrush and Brown Accentor. Skardu is a remote town accessible via what is reputed to be the most dangerous, but wonderful, flight in the world (past Nanga Parbat, the world's fourth highest peak, which rises far above endless other snow-capped peaks to 8126 m (26,660 ft)), or by what is arguably an even more dangerous 241 km track from Gilgit. Bird the orchards and fields surrounding the town, the wood below the K2 Motel (White-browed Tit-Warbler) and the stream on the far side of Kharpocho (the mountain next to town) where Wood Snipe* has been recorded in January. Mountaineers head for K2 base camp along the **Shigar Valley**, 32 km from Skardu. Birders have seen White-winged Redstart and White-browed Tit-Warbler in this valley, and Ibisbill at the Chu Tran hot springs, in the side valley near the head of the Shigar Valley. Other species seen around Chu Tran include Himalayan Snowcock, Wallcreeper and Rufous-vented Tit.

ADDITIONAL INFORMATION

Addresses

National Council for Conservation of Wildlife (NCCW), House No. 485, Street 84, Sector G-6/4, Islamabad.

Books and Papers

A Pictorial Guide to the Birds of the Indian Subcontinent. Ali S, 1983. Bombay Natural History Society/Oxford University Press.
The Birds of Pakistan, volumes 1 and 2. Roberts T, 1991–92. Oxford University Press.

Near-endemics

Western Tragopan*, Cheer Pheasant*, Indian Courser, Tibetan and Painted Sandgrouse, Pale-backed Pigeon*, Sykes' Nightjar, Brown-fronted, Sind and Himalayan Woodpeckers, Black-headed Jay, White-tailed Iora, Indian Grey Thrush, Rusty-tailed and Kashmir* Flycatchers, White-browed Bushchat*, Indian Chat, Kashmir and White-cheeked Nuthatches, White-cheeked and White-throated* Tits, Streak-throated Swallow, Rufous-vented*, Rufous-fronted and Jungle Prinias, Long-billed Bush-Warbler*, Tytler's Leaf-Warbler*, Western Crowned-Warbler, Bristled Grassbird*, Variegated Laughingthrush, Black-chinned and Jerdon's* Babblers, Black-crested and Yellow-breasted Tits, Rufous-tailed Lark, Sind Sparrow, Blanford's Snowfinch, Robin and Rufous-breasted Accentors, Spectacled Finch, Orange Bullfinch*, Black-and-yellow Grosbeak.

THE PHILIPPINES

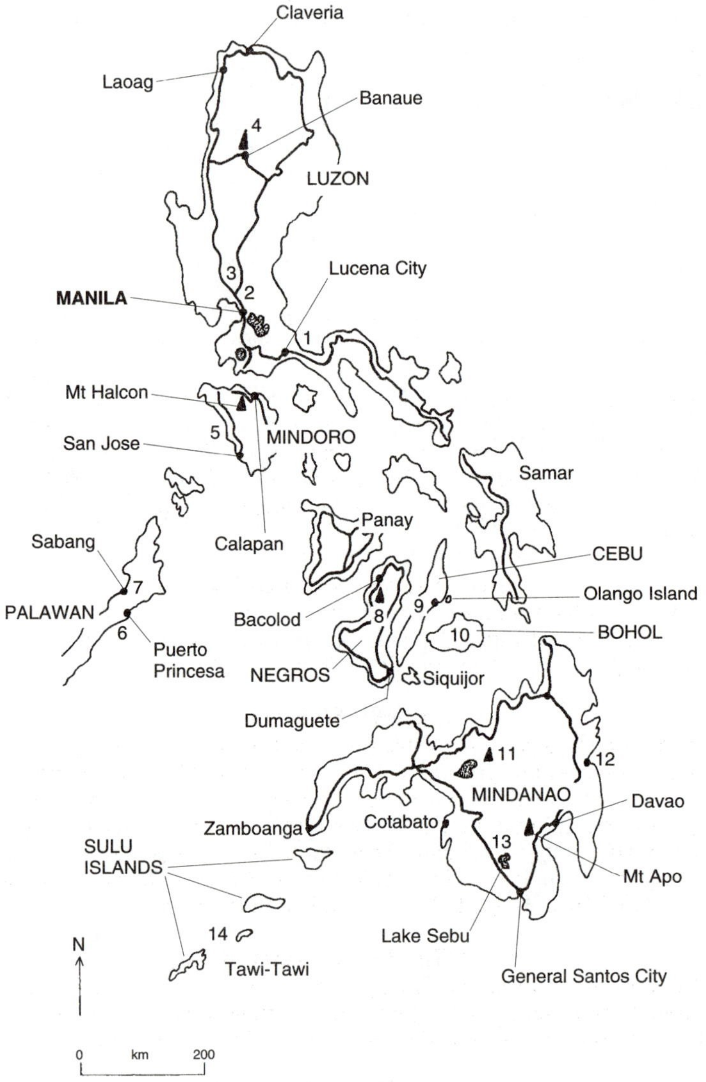

1 Quezon NP (Luzon)
2 Angat (Luzon)
3 Candaba Swamp (Luzon)
4 Mount Polis (Luzon)
5 Siburan (Mindoro)
6 Balsahan Trail (Palawan)
7 St Paul's NP (Palawan)
8 Mount Canlaon NP (Negros)
9 Cebu
10 Rajah Sikatuna NP (Bohol)
11 Mount Katanglad NP (Mindanao)
12 Mangagoy (Mindanao)
13 Sitio Siete (Mindanao)
14 Sulu Islands

INTRODUCTION

Summary

Nearly half of the resident Philippine avifauna is endemic, but many of the 185 birds which are unique to these islands are rare because only a fraction of the original forest cover remains. Although the country's infrastructure makes getting around fairly easy, those birders wishing to see over 100 endemics should allow at least three weeks for a trip which will need to cover the whole archipelago.

Size

At 300,000 sq km, the Philippine archipelago is over twice the size of England, and a little under half the size of Texas. It extends nearly 2000 km from north to south across the western Pacific.

Getting Around

Before venturing to the Philippines it is wise to decide which sites to visit before scrutinising the timetables of the efficient internal air network, drawing up an itinerary, then purchasing the cheap airpass and booking all flights well in advance. Once there it is possible to reach virtually every site by bus and taxi. Negotiate taxi fares before setting off and aim to haggle down to a third of what the driver demands. Ferries run daily between most islands, but they are not the safest form of transport.

Accommodation and Food

Most towns have a range of accommodation and there are resthouses in some National Parks. The wide variety of food is cheap and the local 'San Mig' may be the cheapest beer in the world.

Health and Safety

Immunisation against hepatitis, polio, typhoid and yellow fever is recommended, as are precautions against malaria. Most Philippinos are exceptionally friendly, but there are a number of fanatical religious groups and up until the early 1990s it was still dangerous to travel in some parts of the archipelago (e.g. north Luzon and south Mindanao) where the communist New People's Army (NPA) were active. Reports in the mid 1990s suggested this group had disbanded.

Climate and Timing

The best time to visit the Philippines is between January and March. From April onwards the temperature rises rapidly with the approach of the rainy season, which usually lasts from July to December.

Habitats

The mountainous Philippine archipelago was once heavily forested, but very little lowland or montane forest remains today in this densely populated country, where much of the lowlands has been turned over to paddies and fishponds, and most montane forests have been logged.

Conservation

Conservation is not a word one associates with the Philippines. Only 2% of the original forest cover remains and if the present rate of degradation and destruction continues there will be little point in looking for birds here after the end of this century. That joke about birders in the Philippines scouring desolate islands, hoping to find some trees where there might be some birds, isn't funny anymore. The avifauna is already one of the most endangered on earth and it includes 135 threatened and near-threatened species. Eighty-six of these extremely rare birds are threatened with extinction, the third highest total, with China, for any country in the world.

Bird Families

The Philippine islands are unique in Asia in supporting an endemic family: three species of rhabdornises.

Bird Species

Over 565 species have been recorded in the Philippines, of which around 400 are resident. Non-endemic specialities and spectacular species include Chinese Egret*, Great-billed Heron*, Tabon Scrubfowl*, Barred and Buff-banded Rails, Swinhoe's Snipe, Malaysian Plover*, Australasian Grass-Owl, Blyth's Frogmouth, Whiskered Treeswift, Purple Needletail, Ruddy Kingfisher, Hooded and Red-bellied Pittas, Rufous Paradise-Flycatcher*, Island and Brown-headed Thrushes, Chestnut-cheeked Starling*, Siberian Rubythroat, Middendorff's and Sakhalin Warblers, Streaked Reed-Warbler* and Ijima's Leaf-Warbler*.

Endemics

The 185 endemics include Great Philippine Eagle*, a peacock-pheasant, five fruit-doves, a trogon, six cracking kingfishers, ten hornbills, two pittas, a strange broadbill, a nuthatch, 18 babblers, 12 flowerpeckers and five sunbirds. Fifty-eight species are single-island endemics: Luzon (18), Mindanao (18), Mindoro (6), Palawan (6), Negros (3), Sulu Archipelago (3), Cebu (2) and Panay (1).

Expectations

It is possible to see over 300 species in a month, including 120–130 endemics, so long as at least five islands (Luzon, Mindoro, Negros, Palawan and Mindanao) are visited, while a more extensive trip that takes in seven islands may yield 350 species, including over 130 endemics.

LUZON

The specialities of this, the largest and most northerly island in the Philippine archipelago, are Cream-breasted Fruit-Dove*, Luzon Bleeding-heart*, Luzon* and Green* Racquet-tails, Red-crested and Scale-feathered Malkohas, Rufous Coucal*, Luzon Scops-Owl*, River* and Philippine* Kingfishers, Luzon Hornbill*, Sooty Woodpecker, Green-backed Whistler, Celestial Monarch*, Rufous Paradise-Flycatcher*, White-lored Oriole, Blackish Cuckoo-Shrike*, Black-and-white Triller, Ashy Thrush*, Blue-breasted Flycatcher*, White-browed Shama, Luzon Redstart*, Lowland White-eye, Philippine Bush-Warbler, Grey-backed Tailorbird, Luzon Wren-Babbler*, Chestnut-faced Babbler*, Long-billed Rhabdornis*, White-fronted Tit*, and Olive-backed and Pygmy Flowerpeckers. Other species most likely to be found on Luzon include Spotted* and Luzon* Buttonquails, Luzon Rail*, Flame-breasted Fruit-Dove*, Whiskered Pitta*, Isabela Oriole*, Rusty-flanked Jungle-Flycatcher*, Ash-breasted Flycatcher*, Golden-crowned Babbler*, Luzon Striped-Babbler* and Green-faced Parrotfinch*.

In **Manila**, sites worth visiting include the leafy **American Cemetery** (open 0700 to 1700), which is at Fort Bonifacio and supports Barred Rail, Chestnut-cheeked Starling* (Nov–Mar) and Lowland White-eye, and the **Philippine Cemetery**, a mile or so further on, where possibilities in the grassland and scrub include Spotted Buttonquail*, as well as Blue-breasted Quail and Australasian Grass-Owl. Species present in both include Grey-faced Buzzard (Nov–Mar), Golden-bellied Gerygone, Pied Triller and Striated Grassbird.

Accommodation: Manila — Malate Pensionne.

The fishponds and paddies just south of **Pagbilao**, halfway between Lucena City and Malicboy, support Yellow and Cinnamon Bitterns, Barred, Buff-banded and Slaty-breasted Rails, White-browed Crake, Watercock, Australasian Grass-Owl, Great Eared-Nightjar, Siberian Rubythroat (Nov–Mar) and Striated Grassbird, while Philippine Duck* and Lowland White-eye have also been recorded.

QUEZON NATIONAL PARK

The degraded forest in this tiny park (10 sq km) is the best on the island for Cream-breasted Fruit-Dove*, Philippine Eagle-Owl*, River* and Spotted* Kingfishers, Sooty Woodpecker, Ashy Thrush* and Blue-breasted Flycatcher*. Otherwise the species present are similar to those at Angat (p. 256).

Philippine Endemics

Philippine Serpent-Eagle, Philippine Hawk-Eagle*, Philippine Falconet, Luzon Bleeding-heart*, Cream-breasted Fruit-Dove*, Guaiabero, Green Raquet-tail*, Red-crested and Scale-feathered Malkohas, Rufous Coucal*, Luzon* and Philippine Scops-Owls, Philippine Eagle-Owl*, Philippine Hawk-Owl, Philippine Trogon, River*, Philippine* and Spotted* Kingfishers, Rufous* and Luzon* Hornbills, Sooty Woodpecker, Yellow-bellied Whistler, Blue-headed Fantail, Balicassiao, Blackish Cuckoo-Shrike*, Black-and-white Triller, Philippine Fairy-bluebird, Ashy Thrush*, Coleto, Blue-breasted Flycatcher*, White-browed Shama, Yellow-wattled Bulbul, Yellowish White-eye, Grey-backed Tailorbird, Lemon-throated Warbler, Luzon Wren-Babbler*, Black-crowned Babbler, Stripe-sided Rhabdornis, Elegant Tit, Olive-backed, Striped, Red-striped, White-bellied and Pygmy Flowerpeckers, Flaming Sunbird.

Specialities

Rufous Paradise-Flycatcher*.

Others

Rufous-bellied Eagle, Greater Flameback, Narcissus Flycatcher Nov–Mar).

QUEZON NP

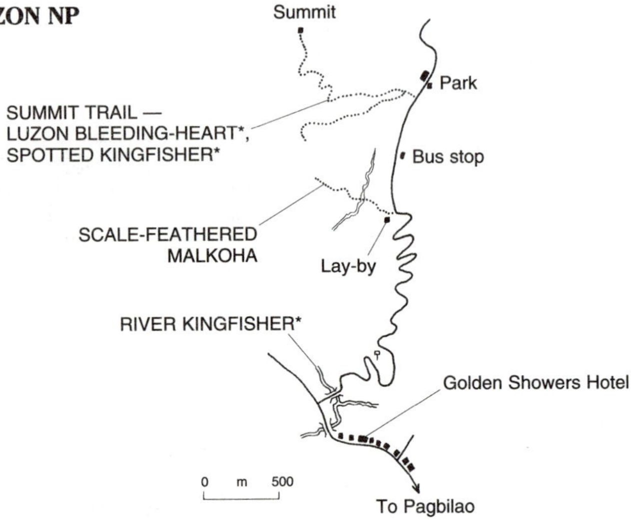

To reach this park, head south from Manila to Malicboy or Pagbilao (where the accommodation is better) via Lucena City, a journey of 3–4 hours by bus. About 400 m beyond the Golden Showers Hotel in Malicboy, turn right on to the road up to the park. River Kingfisher* occurs on the small river to the left here. Most of the endemics occur along the **Summit Trail**, which is on the left just over the brow of a hill about 3 km up from the river. Also bird along the road, especially the 200 m stretch above the Summit Trail to the park, and the trail to the left by a lay-by lower down the mountain (Scale-feathered Malkoha).

Stripe-sided Rhabdornis is one of three members of the Rhabdornis family which is endemic to the Philippines

ANGAT

The Sierra Madre Mountains extend for 500 km parallel to the east coast of Luzon and are most accessible near Angat, northeast of Manila. This is the best site for Luzon Bleeding-heart*, Philippine Kingfisher*, Celestial Monarch*, White-lored Oriole, Long-billed Rhabdornis* and White-fronted Tit*. Otherwise the species are similar to those at Quezon NP (p. 255).

ANGAT

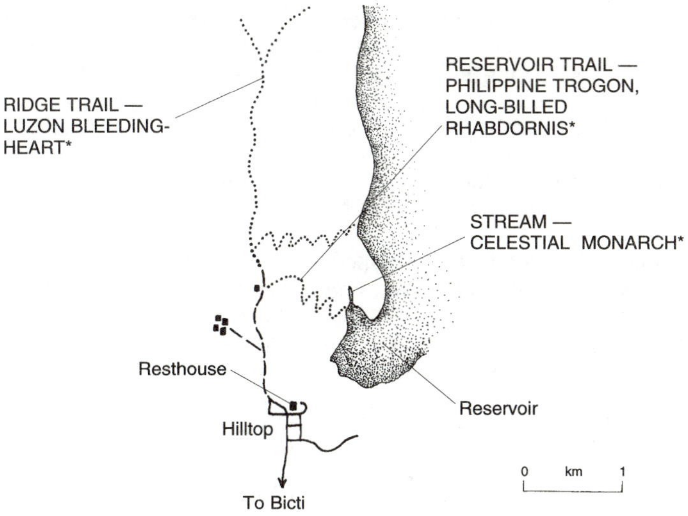

Philippine Endemics

Philippine Serpent-Eagle, Philippine Hawk-Eagle*, Philippine Falconet, Luzon Bleeding-heart*, White-eared and Amethyst Doves, Yellow-breasted Fruit-Dove, Spotted Imperial-Pigeon*, Guaiabero, Green Raquet-tail*, Philippine Hanging-Parrot, Red-crested and Scale-feathered Malkohas, Philippine and Rufous* Coucals, Philippine Scops-Owl, Philippine Eagle-Owl*, Pygmy Swiftlet, Philippine Trogon, River*, Philippine* and Spotted* Kingfishers, Rufous* and Luzon* Hornbills, Philippine and Sooty Woodpeckers, Yellow-bellied Whistler, Blue-headed Fantail, Celestial Monarch*, Balicassiao, White-lored Oriole, Blackish Cuckoo-Shrike*, Black-and-white Triller, Philippine Fairy-bluebird, Ashy Thrush*, Coleto, White-browed Shama, Yellow-wattled and Philippine Bulbuls, Philippine and Grey-backed Tailorbirds, Lemon-throated Warbler, Luzon Wren-Babbler*, Stripe-sided and Long-billed* Rhabdornises, Elegant and White-fronted* Tits, Striped, White-bellied and Pygmy Flowerpeckers, Lovely Sunbird, Naked-faced Spiderhunter*.

Specialities

Philippine Cuckoo-Dove, Purple Needletail, Rufous Paradise-Flycatcher*.

Others

Rufous-bellied Eagle, Red Junglefowl, Pompadour Green-Pigeon, Drongo Cuckoo, Great Eared-Nightjar, Whiskered Treeswift, White-bellied Woodpecker, Greater Flameback, White-breasted Woodswallow, Bar-bellied Cuckoo-Shrike, Purple-throated Sunbird.

(Other species recorded here include Ash-breasted* (once) and Russet-tailed* (Furtive) Flycatchers and Luzon Redstart*.)

Angat is 60–70 km by road from Manila. Head for Sapang Palay, Bicti and

Hilltop (making sure taxis don't go to Angat Dam). Most birds occur along the **Ridge Trail**, which starts beyond the army post above the village, and on the **Reservoir Trail**, which leads off to the right from the Ridge Trail, 1 km above the army post. It is necessary to walk several kilometres along the Ridge Trail before reaching good habitat (take right fork). Celestial Monarch* has been recorded along the usually dry stream at the bottom of the Reservoir Trail, along with River Kingfisher*.

Accommodation: resthouse (basic), best booked in advance by phoning 9213 541/458.

Middendorff's Warbler and Streaked Reed-Warbler* winter at **Candaba Swamp**, 56 km north of Manila Airport. This extensive area of paddies, fishponds and marshes also supports Yellow and Cinnamon Bitterns, Pied Harrier (Nov–Mar), Barred and Buff-banded Rails, White-browed Crake, Pheasant-tailed Jacana, Greater Painted-Snipe, Swinhoe's Snipe (Nov–Mar), Oriental Pratincole, Australasian Grass-Owl, Blue-tailed Bee-eater, Lanceolated Warbler (Nov–Mar) and Striated Grassbird. Head up the northern highway to the Santa Rita turn, through Ploridel, and after a further 10 km or so turn left. After 5–6 km there are two bridges. Turn right after the second (before Candaba town) and head for Bahay Pare village, a kilometre or so further on. Turn left here on to a track for 3 km to a T-junction, from where it is possible to explore on foot.

Similar species to those found at Angat and Quezon NP, including Luzon Bleeding-heart*, Ashy Thrush* and Blue-breasted Flycatcher*, can be found at **Makiling NP**, a mountain to the south of Manila near Los Banos. However, it is necessary to cover more ground on foot here.

The Manila–Banaue road passes through open country and **Lagawe Gorge**, where River Kingfisher* (on boulders in the river) and Luzon Redstart* occur.

MOUNT POLIS

The remnant oak and pine forests in north Luzon support some montane and north Luzon specialities, hence this is the best site for Flame-breasted Fruit-Dove*, Luzon Racquet-tail*, Luzon Scops-Owl*, Green-backed Whistler, Grey-capped Shrike*, Luzon Redstart*, Philippine Bush-Warbler and Chestnut-faced Babbler*.

Philippine Endemics

Flame-breasted Fruit-Dove*, Spotted Imperial-Pigeon*, Luzon Racquet-tail*, Luzon Scops-Owl*, Philippine Swiftlet, Green-backed Whistler, Blue-headed Fantail, Grey-capped Shrike*, Luzon Redstart*, Sulphur-billed Nuthatch, Philippine and Long-tailed* Bush-Warblers, Chestnut-faced Babbler*, Elegant Tit, Flame-crowned Flowerpecker*, Metallic-winged Sunbird, White-cheeked Bullfinch*.

Specialities

Island and Brown-headed Thrushes.

Others

Island Flycatcher, Citrine Canary-Flycatcher, Mountain White-eye, Mountain Leaf-Warbler.

(Other species recorded here include River Kingfisher*, Whiskered Pitta*, Rusty-flanked Jungle-Flycatcher* and Long-billed Rhabdornis*.)

Mount Polis is accessible from Banaue, famous for its 2,000 year old paddies and popular with tourists, which is 10 hours by bus north of Manila. From Banaue head up towards Bontoc for 1 hour to the 2300 m (7546 ft) pass on Mount Polis and bird alongside the road either side of the pass. Otherwise, Luzon Redstart occurs on the river below Bay-Yo village, the first village some 6 km beyond the army post (KM 362) at the pass. There is little public transport up to the pass, but motor-trikes can be hired in Banaue.

Accommodation: Banaue — Banaue Hotel (A+), Greenview Hotel (C).

The **Dalton Pass** is an important flyway for migrants, a fact long appreciated by the local people who trap the birds for food. The birdcatchers have reported trapping (mainly at night between August and January) such rarities as Luzon Buttonquail*, Luzon Rail* and Green-faced Parrotfinch*, as well as Rusty-breasted Cuckoo and Ruddy Kingfisher. The pass is accessible by road north from Manila. Spotted* and Luzon* Buttonquails, Whiskered Pitta*, Isabela Oriole*, Rusty-flanked Jungle-Flycatcher*, Golden-crowned Babbler*, Luzon Striped-Babbler* and Green-faced Parrotfinch* are only likely to be encountered in north Luzon, where they inhabit the relatively remote parts of the Philippines, well away from the beaten birding track and in some cases, within the former strongholds of the NPA where birders have been kidnapped in the past. Whiskered Pitta* occurs in the montane forests of the **Sierra Madre Mountains**, which rise to 1800 m (5,906 ft) and extend 500 km along the east coast of Luzon, and the 300 km long **Cordillera Central** which rises to 2930 m (9,613 ft) at Mount Pulog, the highest peak on Luzon. Sites in the Sierra Madre where it has been recorded recently include Mount Cagua (Cagayan Province), Mount Halmut (Isabela Province), Minuma Creek (along with Celestial Monarch*, Isabela Province) and Mount Isarog (Camarines Sur Province). In the Cordillera Central it is has been recorded recently in Mount Pulog National Park. The best time to track down this rare pitta is in late April and early May when they are at their most vocal. The very rare Isabela Oriole* was recorded halfway between Baguio and Don Mariano Perez, about 15 km south of Diffun (Quivino Province) in 1993, and at Mansarong near Baggao (Cagayan Province) in 1994, the first records since 1961. Green-faced Parrotfinch* has been recorded at Dumalneg, accessible by road from Laoag, and Whiskered Pitta* at Adams, 20 km to the south.

MINDORO

It is possible to see the six single-island endemics unique to this island (Mindoro Bleeding-heart*, Mindoro Imperial-Pigeon*, Black-hooded Coucal*, Mindoro Scops-Owl*, Mindoro Hornbill* and Scarlet-collared Flowerpecker*) by visiting two sites.

SIBURAN

The largest remnant of lowland forest on Mindoro (50 sq km) lies next to Siburan sub-prison in the Sablayan Prison and Penal Farm. It may be an unlikely birding spot, but this is the only known site for Mindoro Bleeding-heart* and all of the other lowland Mindoro endemics also occur here.

It is crucial to obtain permission to visit this site in advance by writing to Leonardo Gabutero, Kalikasan Mindoro Foundation Incorporated (KMFI), 2266 Mabini Street, San Jose, Occidental Mindoro 5100, who will write the necessary letter of introduction to the penal farm.

Philippine Endemics

Philippine Duck*, Mindoro Bleeding-heart*, Blue-crowned Racquet-tail*, Black-hooded* and Philippine Coucals, Philippine Hawk-Owl, Grey-rumped Swiftlet, Mindoro Hornbill*, Balicassiao, Black-bibbed Cuckoo-Shrike*, Black-and-white Triller, Coleto, Elegant Tit, Bicoloured and Scarlet-collared* Flowerpeckers.

Specialities

Malayan Night-Heron, Blue-naped Parrot*, Swinhoe's Snipe (Nov–Mar).

Others

Yellow and Cinnamon Bitterns, Wandering Whistling-Duck, Rufous-bellied Eagle, Red Junglefowl, Buff-banded Rail, Pheasant-tailed Jacana, Great Eared-Nightjar, Savanna Nightjar, Whiskered Treeswift, Blue-throated Bee-eater, Red-bellied Pitta.

(There is a potential new species of scops-owl here and the hawk-owl, which has a different call from the birds on other islands, is also a potential island endemic.)

Siburan is about 65 km north of San Jose, roughly halfway along Mindoro's west coast. The penal farm HQ is 5.5 km from the main road and the forest 2.5 km further on, across a river which is not always dry. Philippine Duck*, Blue-crowned Racquet-tail*, Blue-naped Parrot*, the potential new species of scops-owl and Black-bibbed Cuckoo-Shrike* occur on and around nearby Lake Lubao.

Accommodation: Sablayan — hut (basic/take food). San Jose — Sea View Hotel.

The two remaining Mindoro endemics, Mindoro Imperial-Pigeon* and Mindoro Scops-Owl*, are montane species and occur on **Mount Halcon**, which is accessible by road from Calapan in northeast Mindoro. Head southwest to Magtibay where it is possible to stay with the village priest. It is a 5 hour walk from here to the forest and two more hours to scops-owl territory. Other species recorded here include Green-backed Whistler and Scarlet-collared Flowerpecker*. The pigeon and owl have also been recorded at Mount Hinundunang near Roxas.

PALAWAN

The specialities of this 400 km long island near Borneo are Palawan Peacock-Pheasant*, Blue-headed Racquet-tail, Palawan Scops-Owl*, Palawan Swiftlet, Palawan Hornbill, Blue Paradise-Flycatcher*, Yellow-throated Leafbird, Palawan Flycatcher*, Palawan Blue-Flycatcher, White-vented Shama, Sulphur-bellied Bulbul, Ashy-headed and Palawan* Babblers, Falcated Wren-Babbler*, Palawan Striped-Babbler*, Palawan Tit and Palawan Flowerpecker.

Chinese Egret* winters on the mud flats beyond Garceliano Beach, at the eastern end of the runway at the island's entry point, **Puerto Princesa**.

BALSAHAN TRAIL

This trail runs through a small patch of forest which is the best site for Palawan Scops-Owl*, Palawan Flycatcher*, Palawan Babbler* and Palawan Tit. The forest also supports plenty of other birds, an unusual phenomenon in the Philippines.

Philippine Endemics

Black-chinned Fruit-Dove, Blue-headed Racquet-tail, Palawan Scops-Owl*, Palawan Swiftlet, Palawan Hornbill, Blue Paradise-Flycatcher*, Yellow-throated Leafbird, Palawan Flycatcher*, Palawan Blue-Flycatcher, White-vented Shama, Sulphur-bellied Bulbul, Ashy-headed and Palawan Babblers, Falcated Wren-Babbler*, Palawan Tit, Palawan Flowerpecker, Lovely Sunbird.

Specialities

Blyth's Frogmouth, Mangrove Blue-Flycatcher.

Others

Jerdon's Baza*, Grey-faced Buzzard, Chestnut-winged Cuckoo, Chestnut-breasted Malkoha, Spotted Wood-Owl, Brown-backed Needletail, Rufous-backed Kingfisher, Hooded and Red-bellied Pittas, Dark-throated Oriole, Asian Fairy-bluebird, Olive-winged and Grey-cheeked Bulbuls, Rufous-tailed Tailorbird, Pechora Pipit (Nov–Mar), Plain-throated Sunbird.

It may be best to hire a jeepney in Puerto Princesa, as few actually go to the Iwahig Penal Farm. About 17 km from Puerto Princesa check in at the checkpoint, then head to the picnic area, from where the trail, which begins as a track, crosses a river and enters a small ravine.

Accommodation: Puerto Princesa — Casa Linda (A), Yayene Pensionne (C), Pink Silk Guesthouse (C).

ST PAUL SUBTERRANEAN NATIONAL PARK

The forest within this coastal park supports all but one (Palawan Striped-Babbler*) of the Palawan endemics and is the best site for

Palawan Peacock-Pheasant*, Philippine Cockatoo*, Palawan Hornbill and White-vented Shama.

Philippine Endemics

Palawan Peacock-Pheasant*, Blue-headed Raquet-tail, Philippine Cockatoo*, Palawan Scops-Owl*, Palawan Swiftlet, Palawan Hornbill, Blue Paradise-Flycatcher*, Yellow-throated Leafbird, Palawan Flycatcher*, Palawan Blue-Flycatcher, White-vented Shama, Sulphur-bellied Bulbul, Ashy-headed Babbler, Falcated Wren-Babbler*, Palawan Tit, Palawan Flowerpecker, Lovely Sunbird.

Specialities

Great-billed Heron*, Tabon Scrubfowl*, Malaysian Plover*, Blue-naped Parrot*, Blyth's Frogmouth, Germain's Swiftlet, Ruddy Kingfisher.

Others

Lesser Frigatebird, Pacific Reef-Egret, Pintail Snipe (Nov–Mar), Grey-tailed Tattler (Nov–Mar), Long-toed Stint (Nov–Mar), Thick-billed Pigeon, Chestnut-breasted Malkoha, Collared Scops-Owl, Brown-backed Needletail, Blue-eared, Rufous-backed and Stork-billed Kingfishers, Common Flameback, Great Slaty Woodpecker, Hooded Pitta, Mangrove Whistler, Dark-throated Oriole, Fiery Minivet, Asian Fairy-bluebird, Citrine Canary-Flycatcher, Olive-winged and Grey-cheeked Bulbuls, Rufous-tailed Tailorbird, White-bellied Munia, Plain-throated, Copper-throated and Purple-throated Sunbirds, Little Spiderhunter.

From Puerto Princesa head northwest to Sabang (5 hours by jeepney) from where it is a 30 minute walk along the beach to the park HQ. The area around the HQ is good for Philippine Cockatoo*, as well as kingfishers, Blyth's Frogmouth and babblers along the small stream at the southern edge of the HQ grounds. Otherwise bird the Ridge Trail, Mangrove Trail and the Orange Trail, which is between the Ridge Trail and the Ladder Trail (Monkey Catwalk). Palawan Peacock-Pheasant* occurs at the base of the limestone crags and Tabon Scrubfowl near the subterranean river, 3.5 km along the Orange Trail.

Accommodation: Sabang — chalets (C/basic).

Ursula Island, off southeast Palawan, supports Tabon Scrubfowl*, Nicobar Pigeon*, Malaysian Plover*, Grey* and Pied Imperial-Pigeons and Mantanani Scops-Owl. From Brooke's Point head for Rio Tuba, where boats can be hired for the one hour crossing. Palawan Striped-Babbler* has only been recorded on **Mounts Mantalingajan** and **Borangbato** in south Palawan.

PANAY

The island endemic, Panay Striped-Babbler*, has been recorded in the upper catchment of the Aklan River and Writhe-billed* and Tarictic* Hornbills, as well as Negros Jungle-Flycatcher*, occur in Hamtang Forest accessible from Iloilo via Bugasong and Nawili (where guides can be hired).

NEGROS

The nine specialities of this island are Negros Bleeding-heart*, Negros Fruit-Dove* (which has never been seen in the field), Tarictic* and Writhed-billed* Hornbills, White-vented Whistler, White-winged Cuckoo-Shrike*, Negros Jungle-Flycatcher*, Flame-templed Babbler* and Negros Striped-Babbler*.

MOUNT CANLAON NATIONAL PARK

The remnant forest in this mountain park is the best for Negros Bleeding-heart*, Tarictic Hornbill*, White-vented Whistler, White-winged Cuckoo-Shrike* and Flame-templed Babbler*.

Philippine Endemics

Negros Bleeding-heart*, Yellow-breasted Fruit-Dove, Pink-bellied Imperial-Pigeon, Blue-crowned Racquet-tail*, Philippine Hawk-Owl, Philippine Swiftlet, Philippine Needletail, Spotted Kingfisher*, Tarictic Hornbill*, White-vented Whistler, Blue-headed Fantail, White-winged Cuckoo-Shrike*, Sulphur-billed Nuthatch, Yellowish White-eye, Philippine Tailorbird, Lemon-throated Warbler, Flame-templed Babbler*, Stripe-sided Rhabdornis, Bicoloured and Red-striped Flowerpeckers, Flaming Sunbird.

Specialities

Purple Needletail, Tawny Grassbird.

Others

Red Junglefowl, Whiskered Treeswift, Bar-bellied Cuckoo-Shrike, Citrine Canary-Flycatcher, Mountain White-eye, Mountain Leaf-Warbler, Pechora Pipit (Nov–Mar), Crimson Sunbird.

(Other species recorded here include Negros Jungle-Flycatcher*, Stripe-breasted Rhabdornis and Lovely Sunbird.)

The quiet, run-down resort of Mambucal is 1 hour by road from Bacolod, the island's northern entry/exit point. Check the trees and bushes here for Spotted Kingfisher* and Red-striped Flowerpecker. The forest is an hour's walk uphill and, although degraded, the lower reaches support most of the specialities. Negros Bleeding-heart* occurs higher up and at in the Guintubdan area southwest of the NP.

Accommodation: Mambucal — Pagoda Inn, tourist lodge.

Tarictic Hornbill* and Flame-templed Babbler* have been recorded in the forested valley, known as **Casa Roro**, at the base of Mount Talinis near Dumaguete, the island's southern entry/exit point, which is 7–8 hours by bus south of Bacolod. From Dumaguete head inland a few kilometres to Valencia and Terejos (where the trees around the swimming pools attract flowerpeckers and sunbirds), then continue on a track through a residential area for 4 km until reaching a trail, signposted 'Casa Roro', which leads to a waterfall. The only known site for

Negros Striped-Babbler* is **Mount Talinis**, which can only be visited with permission from the Philippine National Oil Corporation (PNOC), and such permission must be sought on your behalf by DENR. Their offices are in Dumaguete. Take a typed letter (asking for permission), signed by senior DENR officers, to the main PNOC security office, where permission to continue to the start of the mountain trail is usually granted without a problem. Pink-bellied Imperial-Pigeon, Philippine Needletail and White-winged Cuckoo-Shrike* also occur here. The only site, albeit unreliable, where Writhed-billed Hornbill* may be seen is **Lake Balinsasayao**, some 25 km west of Dumaguete. Other species recorded here include Spotted Kingfisher*, Red-bellied Pitta, White-vented Whistler and White-winged Cuckoo-Shrike*.

Accommodation: bunkhouse (basic/take food).

Negros Jungle-Flycatcher* has been recorded at **Ban-Ban**, a small village inland of Ayungon, which is 2 hours by bus north of Dumaguete. Bird alongside the main road above the village where other species recorded include Philippine Falconet, Blue-crowned Racquet-tail*, Rufous Paradise-Flycatcher*, Philippine Oriole, White-winged Cuckoo-Shrike*, Flame-templed Babbler*, Stripe-sided and Stripe-breasted Rhabdornises and Pygmy Flowerpecker.

CEBU

The small island of Cebu, where just 0.3% (a few trees) of the original forest cover remains, may be a taste of what the Philippines as a whole will look like after the end of this century. Birders will have to read a 'Where to Find Trees in the Philippines' book before they even think about looking for any birds. The island's two endemics, Black Shama* and Cebu Flowerpecker*, somehow survive in **Talsarian Forest** near Tabunan, along with Philippine Hanging-Parrot, Philippine and Purple Needletails, Rufous-lored Kingfisher*, White-vented Whistler, Everett's White-eye and Elegant Tit. The shama also occurs at **Casili Consolacion**, near the airport. Birders should support the efforts of the Philippine Wetland and Wildlife Conservation Foundation (PWCF) to conserve Cebu's birds by arranging their visits in advance through Perla Magsalay, PWCF, c/o Cebu Zoo, Capitol Hills, Cebu City 6000 (tel: 210604). She will help to locate the birds and appreciate an appropriate donation.

Olango Island, off Cebu, is the best site for wintering shorebirds in the Philippines and species present include Far Eastern Curlew*, Grey-tailed Tattler, Asian Dowitcher* and Great Knot. The island can be reached on regular ferries which depart a few kilometres north of the airport and take 20 minutes. The birds spread out over a large area at low tide, but at high tide they usually roost near Coconut Island on the southeast coast. Chinese Egret* is also present, usually around the south coast.

BOHOL

This island has no endemic species but it hosts the best site for Samar Hornbill* and Yellow-breasted Tailorbird*.

RAJAH SIKATUNA NATIONAL PARK

Most of the remaining natural dipterocarp forest on Bohol lies within this park (90 sq km). It is the best site for Samar Hornbill* and Yellow-breasted Tailorbird*, and it also supports a fine selection of other endemics, including Black-faced Coucal, Philippine Frogmouth, Azure-breasted Pitta*, Wattled Broadbill* and Striated Wren-Babbler*.

RAJAH SIKATUNA NP

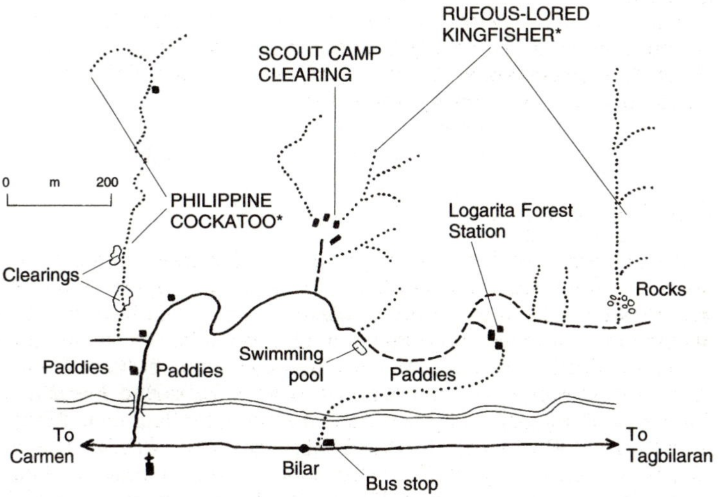

Philippine Endemics

Philippine Serpent-Eagle, Mindanao Bleeding-heart*, Amethyst Dove, Yellow-breasted and Black-chinned Fruit-Doves, Philippine Cockatoo*, Black-faced Coucal, Philippine Scops-Owl, Philippine Eagle-Owl*, Philippine Hawk-Owl, Philippine Frogmouth, Philippine Trogon, Rufous-lored Kingfisher*, Samar Hornbill*, Azure-breasted Pitta*, Wattled Broadbill*, Yellow-bellied Whistler, Blue Fantail, Philippine Oriole, Black-bibbed Cuckoo-Shrike*, Philippine Fairy-bluebird, Yellow-wattled Bulbul, Rufous-fronted and Yellow-breasted* Tailorbirds, Philippine Leaf-Warbler, Striated Wren-Babbler*, Black-crowned Babbler, Brown Tit-Babbler, Bicoloured Flowerpecker, Metallic-winged Sunbird.

Specialities

Philippine Nightjar, Grey Swiftlet, Ruddy Kingfisher, Everett's White-eye.

Others

Besra, Pompadour Green-Pigeon, Whiskered Treeswift, Greater Flameback, Red-bellied Pitta, Purple-throated Sunbird.

(Other species recorded here include Slaty-legged Crake.)

Other Wildlife

Philippine flying lemur, Philippine tarsier.

Head for the Logarita Forest Station near Bilar, a town on the Carmen–Tagbilaran road, 1 hour by bus east of Tagbilaran. Bird the several trails and the Scout Camp clearing (nightbirds).

Accommodation: resthouse (very basic).

SIQUIJOR

Streak-breasted Bulbul*, a common and widespread species, is unique to this island. Lilo-an is one good site for the bulbul, as well as Philippine Cockatoo* and Rufous-lored Kingfisher*, but the best forest is at Bandila-an and other species recorded on the island include Hooded Pitta, Yellow-bellied Whistler, Coleto and Everett's White-eye.

MINDANAO

The specialities of this, the second largest and most southerly island in the Philippine archipelago, are Great Philippine Eagle*, 'Philippine Woodcock*', Mindanao Racquet-tail*, Mindanao Lorikeet*, Mindanao Scops-Owl*, Mindanao Eagle-Owl*, Whitehead's Swiftlet*, Silvery* and Blue-capped* Kingfishers, Mindanao* and Writhed* Hornbills, Black-and-cinnamon Fantail, Short-crested Monarch*, McGregor's Cuckoo-Shrike*, Philippine Leafbird*, Apo Myna*, Mindanao Jungle-Flycatcher*, Little Slaty Flycatcher*, Zamboanga and Yellowish* Bulbuls, Mindanao and Cinnamon White-eyes, Rufous-headed, White-browed* and White-eared Tailorbirds, Bagobo*, Pygmy* and Rusty-crowned* Babblers, Miniature Tit-Babbler*, Red-eared Parrotfinch*, Whiskered* and Olive-capped Flowerpeckers and Grey-hooded and Mount Apo* Sunbirds.

MOUNT KATANGLAD NATIONAL PARK

The mountains in north Mindanao rise to nearly 3000 m (9843 ft) and they support remnant montane forests where a number of extremely rare birds occur. Most of the Mindanao montane specialities are present on Mount Katanglad and this is the best place to see Great Philippine Eagle*, as well as a probable new species of woodcock which was discovered here in February 1993. Other birds best looked for here are Black-and-cinnamon Fantail, Mindanao White-eye and Red-eared Parrotfinch*.

MOUNT KATANGLAD NP

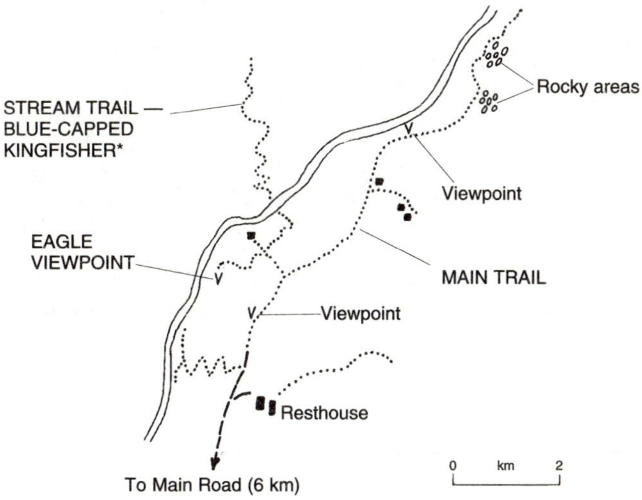

Philippine Endemics

Great Philippine Eagle*, Philippine Hawk-Eagle*, Plain Bush-hen, 'Philippine Woodcock*', Mindanao Raquet-tail*, Philippine Hanging-Parrot, Mindanao Lorikeet*, Mindanao Scops-Owl*, Mindanao Eagle-Owl*, Philippine Hawk-Owl, Philippine Swiftlet, Blue-capped Kingfisher*, Yellow-bellied Whistler, Black-and-cinnamon Fantail, McGregor's Cuckoo-Shrike*, Apo Myna*, Sulphur-billed Nuthatch, Mindanao and Cinnamon White-eyes, Long-tailed Bush-Warbler*, Rufous-headed Tailorbird, Brown Tit-Babbler, Stripe-breasted Rhabdornis, Elegant Tit, Red-eared Parrotfinch*, Striped, Olive-capped, Flame-crowned* and White-bellied Flowerpeckers, Grey-hooded Sunbird, White-cheeked Bullfinch*.

Specialities

Barred Honey-buzzard, Philippine Cuckoo-Dove, Australasian Grass-Owl, Philippine Nightjar, Tawny Grassbird.

Others

Grey-faced Buzzard, Metallic Pigeon, Whiskered Treeswift, Greater Flameback, Short-tailed Starling, Island Flycatcher, Mountain White-eye, Mountain Leaf-Warbler.

(Other species recorded here include Swinhoe's Snipe (Nov–Mar), Mindanao Jungle-Flycatcher*, Little Slaty Flycatcher* and Bagobo Babbler*.)

To reach the park head for Dalwangan from Cagayan de Oro. Constancio Maghanoy lives in the house to the left just before the huge 'Save the Eagle' sign. He will arrange guides to escort birders 6 km to the resthouse where the woodcock occurs, and onward to the best sites to look for Great Philippine Eagle*. In 1993 there were only 22 Great Philippine Eagles* left in the wild (with a further 13 in captivity) and this park is one of the last places in which this magnificent bird is seen with any regularity. Their nests are watched carefully and if there is a young bird in a nest (there was a three month old chick in a nest in April 1996) the parent birds, which prey on flying lemurs and young monkeys, usually visit it a couple of times a day. Adult birds are rarely seen away from the nest as they usually stay below the canopy. To see the other birds in this park, bird the forest patch opposite the resthouse, the scrub (Long-tailed Bush-Warbler*), farmland (Tawny Grassbird) and coffee plantations around the campsite (nightbirds), the Main Trail and the short Stream Trail.

Accommodation: resthouse (basic), bookable through Constancio Maghanoy and Carlito Gayramara, Dalwangan, Malaybalay, Bukidnon Province, Mindanao 8700.

MANGAGOY

The logged forest patches from sea level to 1200 m (3937 ft) in east Mindanao support a number of localised endemics and this is the most reliable site for Philippine Duck*, Philippine Falconet, Silvery Kingfisher*, Mindanao Hornbill*, Short-crested Monarch*, Yellowish Bulbul*, White-browed Tailorbird* and Naked-faced Spiderhunter*.

MANGAGOY

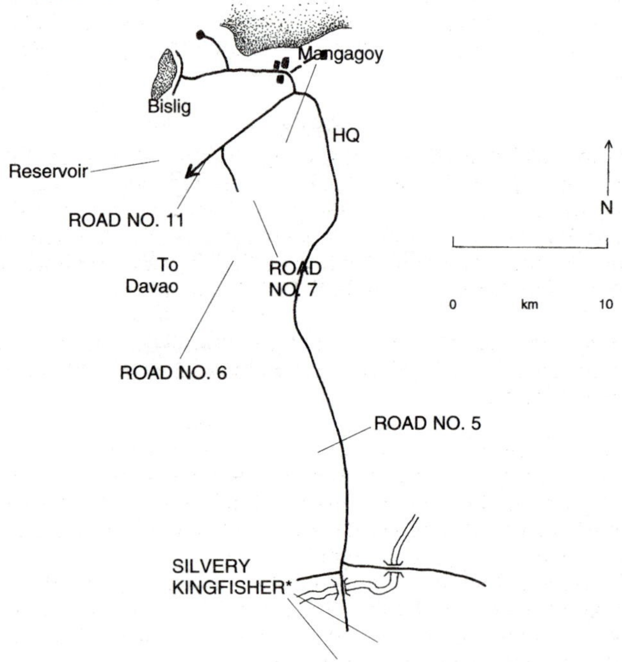

The forest here is owned by the Paper Industry Corporation of the Philippines (PICOP) and permission to visit the site may be obtained in advance by writing to them at the PICOP, Paper Country Inn, Tabon, Bislig, Surigao del Sur, Mindanao (tel/fax: 633 5949). It is also possible to obtain a permit and arrange transport at the Paper Country Inn on arrival, although this may be difficult at weekends.

Philippine Endemics

Philippine Duck*, Philippine Serpent-Eagle, Philippine Hawk-Eagle*, Philippine Falconet, Plain Bush-Hen, Mindanao Bleeding-heart*, Amethyst Dove, Yellow-breasted and Black-chinned Fruit-Doves, Pink-bellied and Spotted* Imperial-Pigeons, Guaiabero, Blue-crowned Raquet-tail*, Black-faced Coucal, Philippine Needletail, Philippine Trogon, Silvery* and Rufous-lored* Kingfishers, Rufous*, Mindanao* and Writhed* Hornbills, Philippine Woodpecker, Azure-breasted Pitta*, Wattled Broadbill*, Yellow-bellied Whistler, Blue Fantail, Short-crested* and Celestial* Monarchs, Philippine Oriole, Black-bibbed Cuckoo-Shrike*, Philippine Fairy-bluebird, Philippine Leafbird*, Coleto, Yellow-wattled and Yellowish* Bulbuls, Rufous-fronted and White-browed* Tailorbirds, Striated Wren-Babbler*, Pygmy* and Rusty-crowned* Babblers, Brown Tit-Babbler, Stripe-sided and Stripe-breasted Rhabdornises, Olive-backed, Bicoloured, White-bellied and Pygmy Flowerpeckers, Metallic-winged and Lovely Sunbirds, Naked-faced Spiderhunter*.

Specialities

Barred Honey-buzzard, Swinhoe's Snipe (Nov–Mar), Philippine Cuckoo-Dove, Azure-rumped Parrot, Australasian Grass-Owl, Philippine Nightjar, Purple Needletail, Rufous Paradise-Flycatcher*, Everett's White-eye.

Others

Wandering Whistling-Duck, Rufous Night-Heron, Cinnamon Bittern, Jerdon's Baza*, Grey-headed Fish-Eagle*, Rufous-bellied Eagle, Red Junglefowl, Pintail Snipe (Nov–Mar), Violet Cuckoo, Whiskered Treeswift, White-bellied Woodpecker, Greater Flameback, Asian Glossy Starling, Striated Grassbird, White-bellied Munia, Pechora Pipit (Nov–Mar), Purple-throated Sunbird, Little Spiderhunter.

(Other species recorded here include Schrenck's Bittern*, Great Philippine Eagle*, Little Slaty* and Russet-tailed* Flycatchers and Philippine Leaf-Warbler.)

Mangagoy, a few kilometres from Bislig, is accessible by road from Davao (5 hours by bus). The best birding is along the roads, especially Road No. 5, around KM 26 (Rufous-lored Kingfisher*), KM 28 (Celestial Monarch*, Rufous Paradise-Flycatcher*), KM 38 (Silvery Kingfisher*) to KM 40, and KM 56 (Great Philippine Eagle*, rarely). Also bird Road No. 7 (Wattled Broadbill*, Short-crested Monarch*), Road No. 11 (Philippine Duck*, Australasian Grass-Owl, White-browed Tailorbird* — in scrub by the limestone crags) and Bay View Hills, where there is a short trail, small lake and a few pools (Silvery Kingfisher*, Stripe-breasted Rhabdornis, Pechora Pipit).

Accommodation: Bislig Inn (basic), KM 38 PICOP Army Base (take some rum for the friendly soldiers, and some food).

Silvery Kingfisher is one of six brilliant kingfishers which occur only in the Philippines*

SITIO SIETE

The mossy forest near Lake Sebu in the far south of Mindanao is the best site for Amethyst and Dark-eared* Doves, Blue-capped Kingfisher*, White-eared Tailorbird* and Bagobo Babbler*. Otherwise the species are similar to those at Mangagoy (p. 268).

Philippine Endemics

Amethyst and Dark-eared* Doves, Pink-bellied and Spotted* Imperial-Pigeons, Mindanao Racquet-tail*, Black-faced Coucal, Mindanao Scops-Owl*, Philippine Frogmouth, Philippine Needletail, Blue-capped Kingfisher*, Rufous* and Writhed* Hornbills, Yellow-bellied Whistler, Blue Fantail, Philippine Oriole, McGregor's Cuckoo-Shrike*, Philippine Leafbird*, Russet-tailed Flycatcher*, Cinnamon White-eye, Rufous-headed and White-eared Tailorbirds, Philippine Leaf-Warbler, Bagobo*, Pygmy* and Rusty-crowned* Babblers, Brown Tit-Babbler, Stripe-breasted Rhabdornis, White-fronted Tit*, Olive-backed, Striped, Whiskered*, Olive-capped, Bicoloured and White-bellied Flowerpeckers, Grey-hooded and Mount Apo* Sunbirds, Naked-faced Spiderhunter*.

Specialities

Japanese Night-Heron*, Rufous Paradise-Flycatcher*.

(Other species recorded here include Mindanao Jungle-Flycatcher*, Little Slaty Flycatcher*, a potential new species of shortwing and a potential new species of *Stachyris* babbler.)

Sitio Siete is accessible from General Santos City. From there head to Lake Sebu via Koronadel and Surallah, then walk or take a motorbike 15 km to the village of Sitio Siete, from where there are trails into the forest above.

Accommodation: village houses, camping.

SITIO SIETE

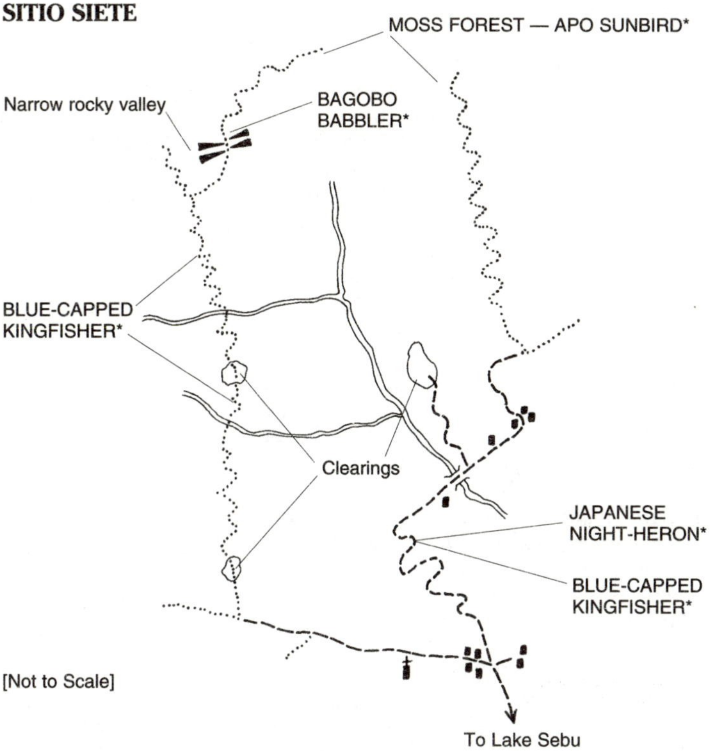

The rare Whitehead's Swiftlet* has been recorded at Lake Vernado on **Mount Apo**, accessible by road from Davao via Kidapawan, Digos and Ilomavis to Lake Agco, from where it is a 3 hour hike uphill to the Marbel River Campsite, and a further 5 hours to the lake, which is situated at 2210 m (7251 ft). It is necessary to obtain a permit in advance from the CEMRO office, and the latest information on NPA activities, at the tourist office in Kidapawan, *en route*. Guides are available (and recommended) at Lake Agco. Other species recorded on Mount Apo include Great Philippine Eagle*, Amethyst Dove, Mindanao Racquet-tail*, Mindanao Lorikeet*, Mindanao Scops-Owl*, Mindanao Eagle-Owl*, Black-and-cinnamon Fantail, Grey-capped Shrike*, Apo Myna*, Mindanao Jungle-Flycatcher*, Little Slaty* and Russet-tailed* Flycatchers, Mindanao and Cinnamon White-eyes, Long-tailed Bush-Warbler*, Rufous-headed Tailorbird, Bagobo Babbler*, Stripe-breasted Rhabdornis, Red-eared Parrotfinch*, Whiskered* and Olive-capped Flowerpeckers, Grey-hooded and Mount Apo* Sunbirds and White-cheeked Bullfinch*, all of which have been recorded at Baracatan village, an old eagle project site, accessible from Davao via Toril.

Zamboanga Bulbul occurs near Zamboanga at the southwestern tip of Mindanao. To look for this bird visit the regional forestry office and ask for directions to the 'Watershed Reforestation Project'. Once there walk on, past two villages, for a few kilometres, until reaching some huts around which the bulbul has been seen.

SULU ISLANDS

These islands, at the southwest corner of the Philippine archipelago, support three endemics: Sulu Bleeding-heart*, Blue-winged Racquet-tail* and Sulu Hornbill*. The entry point is Bongao from where boats can be taken to **Balimbing** on Tawi-Tawi, the main island. The three endemics plus Rufous-lored Kingfisher* occur at Balimbing, while Grey-rumped Swiftlet and Celestial Monarch* have been recorded at Barangay Buan, Tabon Scrubfowl* and Gray's Warbler (Nov–Mar) on Bongao Peak and Dark-eared Dove*, Rufous-lored Kingfisher* and Sulu Hornbill* in Balobok Forest near Lakit-Lakit.

ADDITIONAL INFORMATION

Books and Papers

Birds of the Philippines. du Pont J, 1971. Delaware Museum of Natural History.
The Birds of the Philippines. Dickinson E *et al.*, 1991. BOU.
Report of the Cambridge Philippines Rainforest Project 1991. Evans T *et al.*, 1993. BirdLife International.
Birdwatching in the Philippines. Hornbuckle J, 1994. Available from the author at 30 Hartington Road, Sheffield S7 2LF, UK.

PHILIPPINE ENDEMICS (185)

Philippine Duck*	Pagbilao (Luzon), Siburan (Mindoro) and Mangagoy (Mindanao)
Philippine Serpent-Eagle	Widespread (not Palawan)
Great Philippine Eagle*	Mt Katanglad NP (Mindanao) (also known from Luzon, Mangagoy and Mt Apo, Mindanao, and Leyte and Samar Islands)
Philippine Hawk-Eagle*	Forested sites on Luzon and Mindanao
Philippine Falconet	Quezon NP and Angat (Luzon), Ban-Ban (Negros) and Mangagoy (Mindanao)
Palawan Peacock-Pheasant*	St Paul's NP (Palawan)
Spotted Buttonquail*	Rare, Manila cemeteries (Luzon) and recorded in far north Luzon, 1994
Luzon Buttonquail*	Luzon: only known from several specimens, but reported by bird catchers at Dalton Pass
Luzon Rail*	Luzon: reported by birdcatchers at Dalton Pass up to 1970 and no records anywhere since 1979
Plain Bush-Hen	Widespread (not Palawan)
Luzon Bleeding-heart*	Quezon NP, Angat and Makiling NP (Luzon) (also known from Polillo and Catanduanes Islands)
Mindoro Bleeding-heart*	Siburan (Mindoro)
Negros Bleeding-heart*	Rare, Mt Canlaon NP (Negros)

Mindanao Bleeding-heart*	Rajah Sikatuna NP (Bohol) and Mangagoy (Mindanao) (also known from Samar, Leyte and Basilan Islands)
Sulu Bleeding-heart*	Rare, Balimbing (Tawi-Tawi Island, Sulu Archipelago)
White-eared Dove	Widespread (not Palawan)
Amethyst Dove	Angat (Luzon), Rajah Sikatuna NP (Bohol) and Mangagoy, Sitio Siete and Mt Apo (Mindanao)
Dark-eared Dove*	Rare at Sitio Siete (Mindanao) (also known from Basilan and Tawi-Tawi Islands)
Flame-breasted Fruit-Dove*	Mt Polis (Luzon) (also known from northeast Luzon and Polillo Island)
Cream-breasted Fruit-Dove*	Quezon NP (Luzon) (also known from Polillo Island)
Yellow-breasted Fruit-Dove	Widespread (not Palawan)
Black-chinned Fruit-Dove	Balsahan Trail (Palawan), Rajah Sikatuna NP (Bohol) and Mangagoy (Mindanao)
Negros Fruit-Dove*	Known only from a single specimen taken in Mt Canlaon NP (Negros) in 1953, and possibly a runt specimen of Yellow-breasted)
Pink-bellied Imperial-Pigeon	Mt Canlaon NP and Mt Talinis (Negros) and Mangagoy and Sitio Siete (Mindanao)
Mindoro Imperial-Pigeon*	Mt Halcon (Mindoro)
Spotted Imperial-Pigeon*	Angat and Mt Polis (Luzon), and Mangagoy and Sitio Siete (Mindanao)
Guaiabero	Widespread
Luzon Racquet-tail*	Mt Polis (Luzon)
Mindanao Racquet-tail*	Mt Katanglad NP, Sitio Siete and Mt Apo (Mindanao)
Blue-headed Racquet-tail	Balsahan Trail and St Pauls NP (Palawan) (also known from Balabac and Calamian Islands)
Green Racquet-tail*	Rare, Quezon NP and Angat (Luzon) (also known from Subic Bay Naval Forest Reserve, Luzon and Marinduque Island)
Blue-crowned Racquet-tail*	Siburan (Mindoro), Negros and Mangagoy (Mindanao)
Blue-winged Racquet-tail*	Balimbing, Tawi-Tawi Island (Sulu Islands)
Philippine Hanging-Parrot	Widespread
Philippine Cockatoo*	St Paul's NP (Palawan), Rajah Sikatuna NP (Bohol) and Siquijor
Mindanao Lorikeet*	Mt Katanglad NP and Mt Apo (Mindanao)
Red-crested Malkoha	Quezon NP and Angat (Luzon)
Scale-feathered Malkoha	Quezon NP and Angat (Luzon) (also known from Marinduque

	Island
Black-hooded Coucal*	Siburan (Mindoro)
Philippine Coucal	Widespread
Black-faced Coucal	Rajah Sikatuna NP (Bohol) and Mangagoy and Sitio Siete (Mindanao)
Rufous Coucal*	Quezon NP and Angat (Luzon) (also known from Polillo and Catanduanes Islands
Mindanao Scops-Owl*	Mt Katanglad NP, Sitio Siete and Mt Apo (Mindanao)
Luzon Scops-Owl*	Quezon NP and Mt Polis (Luzon)
Mindoro Scops-Owl*	Mt Halcon (Mindoro)
Philippine Scops-Owl	Quezon NP and Angat (Luzon) and Rajah Sikatuna NP (Bohol)
Palawan Scops-Owl*	Balsahan Trail and St Paul's NP (Palawan)
Mindanao Eagle-Owl*	Mt Katanglad NP and Mt Apo (Mindanao) (also known from Marinduque Island)
Philippine Eagle-Owl*	Quezon NP and Angat (Luzon) and Rajah Sikatuna NP (Bohol)
Philippine Hawk-Owl	Widespread
Philippine Frogmouth	Rajah Sikatuna NP (Bohol) and Sitio Siete (Mindanao)
Grey-rumped Swiftlet	Widespread
Pygmy Swiftlet	Widespread
Whitehead's Swiftlet*	Rare, Mt Apo (Mindanao) (also known from Mt Data, Luzon)
Palawan Swiftlet	Balsahan Trail and St Paul's NP (Palawan)
Philippine Swiftlet	Widespread at high altitude
Philippine Needletail	Mt Canlaon NP and Mt Talinis (Negros) and Mangagoy and Sitio Siete (Mindanao) (also known from Cebu and Leyte Islands)
Philippine Trogon	Quezon NP and Angat (Luzon), Rajah Sikatuna NP (Bohol) and Mangagoy (Mindanao)
River Kingfisher*	Quezon NP, Angat and Mt Polis (Luzon)
Silvery Kingfisher*	Mangagoy (Mindanao)
Philippine Kingfisher*	Quezon NP and Angat (Luzon)
Rufous-lored Kingfisher*	Rajah Sikatuna NP (Bohol), Siquijor, Mangagoy (Mindanao) and Balimbing, Tawi-Tawi Island (Sulu Islands) (also known from Cebu)
Spotted Kingfisher*	Quezon NP and Angat (Luzon) and Negros (also known from Marinduque Island)
Blue-capped Kingfisher*	Mt Katanglad NP and Sitio Siete (Mindanao)
Palawan Hornbill	Balsahan Trail and St Paul's NP

	(Palawan) (also known from Balabac and Calamian Islands)
Sulu Hornbill*	Balimbing, Tawi-Tawi Island (Sulu Islands)
Rufous Hornbill*	Quezon NP and Angat (Luzon) and Mangagoy and Sitio Siete (Mindanao)
Luzon Hornbill*	Quezon NP and Angat (Luzon)
Mindoro Hornbill*	Siburan (Mindoro)
Tarictic Hornbill*	Mt Canlaon NP and Casa Roro (Negros) and Hamtang Forest (Panay)
Samar Hornbill*	Rajah Sikatuna NP (Bohol) (also known from Samar and Leyte Islands)
Mindanao Hornbill*	Mangagoy (Mindanao)
Writhe-billed Hornbill*	Rare, Lake Balinsasayao (Negros) and Hamtang Forest (Panay)
Writhed Hornbill*	Mangagoy and Sitio Siete (Mindanao) (also known from Camiguin Island)
Philippine Woodpecker	Widespread
Sooty Woodpecker	Quezon NP and Angat (Luzon)
Azure-breasted Pitta*	Rajah Sikatuna NP (Bohol) and Mangagoy (Mindanao) (also known from Samar and Leyte Islands)
Whiskered Pitta*	Sierra Madre Mountains and Cordillera Central (Luzon)
Wattled Broadbill*	Rajah Sikatuna NP (Bohol) and Mangagoy (Mindanao)
Green-backed Whistler	Mt Polis (Luzon) and Mt Halcon (Mindoro)
White-vented Whistler	Mt Canlaon NP and Lake Balinsasayao (Negros) (also known from Cebu and Tawi-Tawi Island, Sulu Islands)
Yellow-bellied Whistler	Widespread on Luzon, Bohol, Siquijor and Mindanao
Blue Fantail	Rajah Sikatuna NP (Bohol) and Mangagoy and Sitio Siete (Mindanao) (also known from Samar, Leyte and Basilan Islands)
Blue-headed Fantail	Widespread on Luzon and Negros
Black-and-cinnamon Fantail	Mt Katanglad NP and Mt Apo (Mindanao)
Short-crested Monarch*	Rare, Mangagoy (Mindanao) (also known from Dinagat Island off north Mindanao)
Celestial Monarch*	Rare, Angat (Luzon), Mangagoy (Mindanao) and Tawi-Tawi Island (Sulu Islands)
Blue Paradise-Flycatcher*	Balsahan Trail and St Paul's NP (Palawan) (also known from Calamian Island)

Balicassiao	Widespread
White-lored Oriole	Angat (Luzon)
Philippine Oriole	Negros, Rajah Sikatuna NP (Bohol) and Mangagoy and Sitio Siete (Mindanao)
Isabela Oriole*	Rare, Quivino and Cagayan Provinces (North Luzon)
Blackish Cuckoo-Shrike*	Quezon NP and Angat (Luzon)
Black-bibbed Cuckoo-Shrike*	Siburan (Mindoro), Rajah Sikatuna NP (Bohol) and Mangagoy (Mindanao) (also known from Basilan Island)
McGregor's Cuckoo-Shrike*	Mt Katanglad NP and Sitio Siete (Mindanao)
White-winged Cuckoo-Shrike*	Widespread on Negros (also known from Guimaras and Panay Islands)
Black-and-white Triller	Quezon NP and Angat (Luzon) and Siburan (Mindoro)
Philippine Fairy-bluebird	Quezon NP and Angat (Luzon), Rajah Sikatuna NP (Bohol) and Mangagoy (Mindanao)
Philippine Leafbird*	Mangagoy and Sitio Siete (Mindanao) (also known from Cebu and Leyte Islands)
Yellow-throated Leafbird	Balsahan Trail and St Paul's NP (Palawan) (also known from Calamian and Balabac Islands)
Grey-capped Shrike*	Mt Polis (Luzon) and Mt Apo (Mindanao) (also known from Mindoro Island)
Ashy Thrush*	Quezon NP, Angat and Makiling NP (Luzon)
Apo Myna*	Mt Katanglad NP and Mt Apo (Mindanao)
Coleto	Widespread
Rusty-flanked Jungle-Flycatcher*	Rare, Mt Polis (Luzon) and extreme north Luzon
Negros Jungle-Flycatcher*	Rare, Mt Canlaon NP and Ban Ban (Negros) and Hamtang Forest (Panay)
Mindanao Jungle-Flycatcher*	Rare, Mt Katanglad NP, Sitio Siete and Mt Apo (Mindanao)
Ash-breasted Flycatcher*	Rare, Angat (Luzon) (also known from northeast Luzon)
Little Slaty Flycatcher*	Rare, at most sites on Mindanao (also known from Samar, Leyte and Basilan Islands)
Palawan Flycatcher*	Balsahan Trail and St Paul's NP (Palawan)
Russet-tailed Flycatcher*	Rare, Angat (Luzon) and Mangagoy, Sitio Siete and Mt Apo (Mindanao)
Blue-breasted Flycatcher*	Rare, Quezon NP and Makiling NP (Luzon) (also known from north-

	east Luzon and Catanduanes Island)
Palawan Blue-Flycatcher	Balsahan Trail and St Paul's NP (Palawan) (also known from Calamian and Balabac Islands)
White-browed Shama	Quezon NP and Angat (Luzon)
White-vented Shama	Balsahan Trail and St Paul's NP (Palawan) (also known from Calamian and Balabac Islands)
Black Shama*	Casili Consolacion and Talsarian Forest (Cebu)
Luzon Redstart*	Angat, Lagawe Gorge, Mt Polis and Mt Pulog (Luzon)
Sulphur-billed Nuthatch	Widespread (not Palawan)
Yellow-wattled Bulbul	Quezon NP and Angat (Luzon), Rajah Sikatuna NP (Bohol) and Mangagoy (Mindanao)
Sulphur-bellied Bulbul	Balsahan Trail and St Paul's NP (Palawan)
Philippine Bulbul	Widespread
Zamboanga Bulbul	Zamboanga (Mindanao) (also known from Basilan Island)
Streak-breasted Bulbul*	Siquijor (also known from Romblon and Tablas Islands)
Yellowish Bulbul*	Mangagoy (Mindanao)
Lowland White-eye	American Cemetery, Manila and Pagbilao (Luzon)
Yellowish White-eye	Quezon NP (Luzon) and widespread on Negros
Mindanao White-eye	Mt Katanglad NP and Mt Apo (Mindanao)
Cinnamon White-eye	Mt Katanglad NP, Sitio Siete and Mt Apo (Mindanao)
Philippine Bush-Warbler	Mt Polis (Luzon)
Long-tailed Bush-Warbler*	Mt Polis (Luzon) and Mt Katanglad NP and Mt Apo (Mindanao)
Rufous-headed Tailorbird	Mt Katanglad, Sitio Siete and Mt Apo (Mindanao)
Philippine Tailorbird	Angat (Luzon) and widespread on Negros
Rufous-fronted Tailorbird	Rajah Sikatuna NP (Bohol) and Mangagoy (Mindanao)
Grey-backed Tailorbird	Quezon NP and Angat (Luzon) (also known from Palawan and Catanduanes Islands)
Yellow-breasted Tailorbird*	Rajah Sikatuna NP (Bohol) (also known from Samar and Leyte Islands)
White-browed Tailorbird*	Mangagoy (Mindanao)
White-eared Tailorbird	Sitio Siete (Mindanao) (also known from Basilan Island)
Philippine Leaf-Warbler	Rajah Sikatuna NP (Bohol) and Mangagoy and Sitio Siete (Mindanao)

Lemon-throated Warbler	Quezon NP and Angat (Luzon) and Negros (also known from Cebu)
Bagobo Babbler*	Mt Katanglad NP, Sitio Siete and Mt Apo (Mindanao)
Ashy-headed Babbler	Balsahan Trail and St Paul's NP (Palawan) (also known from Balabac Island)
Palawan Babbler*	Balsahan Trail and St Paul's NP (Palawan) (also known from Balabac Island)
Striated Wren-Babbler*	Rajah Sikatuna NP (Bohol) and Mangagoy (Mindanao)
Falcated Wren-Babbler*	Balsahan Trail and St Paul's NP (Palawan) (also known from Balabac Island)
Luzon Wren-Babbler*	Quezon NP and Angat (Luzon)
Pygmy Babbler*	Mangagoy and Sitio Siete (Mindanao) (also known from Samar and Leyte Islands)
Golden-crowned Babbler*	Foothills of north Luzon
Black-crowned Babbler	Quezon NP (Luzon) and Rajah Sikatuna NP (Bohol) (also known from Samar and Leyte Islands)
Rusty-crowned Babbler*	Mangagoy and Sitio Siete (Mindanao)
Flame-templed Babbler*	Widespread Negros (also known from Panay)
Chestnut-faced Babbler*	Mt Polis (Luzon)
Luzon Striped-Babbler*	Northeast Luzon
Panay Striped-Babbler*	Mt Baloy (Panay)
Negros Striped-Babbler*	Mt Talinis (Negros)
Palawan Striped-Babbler*	Mt Mantalingajan and Mt Borangbato (Palawan)
Brown Tit-Babbler	Rajah Sikatuna NP (Bohol) and widespread on Mindanao
Miniature Tit-Babbler*	Rare, Mt Lobi and Mt Matutum (Mindanao) (also known from Samar and Leyte Islands)
Stripe-sided Rhabdornis	Quezon NP and Angat (Luzon), Negros and Mangagoy (Mindanao)
Long-billed Rhabdornis*	Angat and Mt Polis (Luzon) (also known from northeast Luzon)
Stripe-breasted Rhabdornis	Widespread on Negros and Mindanao
Elegant Tit	Widespread
Palawan Tit	Balsahan Trail and St Paul's NP (Palawan) (also known from Balabac Island)
White-fronted Tit*	Angat (Luzon) and Sitio Siete (Mindanao) (also known from northeast Luzon)
Green-faced Parrotfinch*	Extreme north Luzon (also reported by birdcatchers at Dalton Pass, Luzon and on NW Panay)

Red-eared Parrotfinch*	Mt Katanglad NP and Mt Apo (Mindanao)
Olive-backed Flowerpecker	Quezon NP (Luzon) and Mangagoy and Sitio Siete (Mindanao)
Palawan Flowerpecker	Balsahan Trail and St Paul's NP (Palawan) (also known from Balabac and Culion Islands)
Striped Flowerpecker	Quezon NP and Angat (Luzon) and Mt Katanglad NP and Sitio Siete (Mindanao)
Whiskered Flowerpecker*	Sitio Siete and Mt Apo (Mindanao)
Olive-capped Flowerpecker	Mt Katanglad NP, Sitio Siete and Mt Apo (Mindanao)
Flame-crowned Flowerpecker*	Mt Polis (Luzon) and Mt Katanglad NP (Mindanao)
Bicoloured Flowerpecker	Widespread on Mindoro, Negros, Bohol and Mindanao
Cebu Flowerpecker*	Rare, Talsarian Forest (Cebu)
Red-striped Flowerpecker	Widespread (not Mindoro)
Scarlet-collared Flowerpecker*	Siburan and Mt Halcon (Mindoro)
White-bellied Flowerpecker	Quezon NP and Angat (Luzon) and widespread on Mindanao
Pygmy Flowerpecker	Quezon NP and Angat (Luzon), Ban-Ban (Negros) and Mangagoy (Mindanao)
Grey-hooded Sunbird	Mt Katanglad NP, Sitio Siete and Mt Apo (Mindanao)
Mount Apo Sunbird*	Sitio Siete and Mt Apo (Mindanao)
Flaming Sunbird	Quezon NP and Makiling NP (Luzon) and widespread on Negros
Metallic-winged Sunbird	Mt Polis (Luzon), Rajah Sikatuna NP (Bohol) and Mangagoy (Mindanao)
Lovely Sunbird	Widespread
Naked-faced Spiderhunter*	Angat (Luzon) and Mangagoy and Sitio Siete (Mindanao) (also known from Samar and Leyte Islands)
White-cheeked Bullfinch*	Mt Polis (Luzon) and Mt Katanglad NP and Mt Apo (Mindanao)
Philippine Woodcock*	Mt Katanglad NP (Mindanao) (may also be present on Mt Cetaceo, north Luzon)

Near-endemics

Barred Honey-buzzard, Tabon Scrubfowl*, Philippine Cuckoo-Dove, Whistling Green-Pigeon*, Grey Imperial-Pigeon*, Blue-naped* and Azure-rumped Parrots, Mantanani Scops-Owl, Sunda Frogmouth, Philippine Nightjar, Germain's and Grey Swiftlets, Purple Needletail, Rufous Paradise-Flycatcher*, Sunda Thrush, Short-tailed Starling, Chestnut-tailed Jungle-Flycatcher, Island Flycatcher, Citrine Canary-Flycatcher, Sakhalin Warbler, Streaked Reed-Warbler*, Ijima's Leaf-Warbler*, Dusky Munia, Mountain Serin, Yellow Bunting*.

SINGAPORE

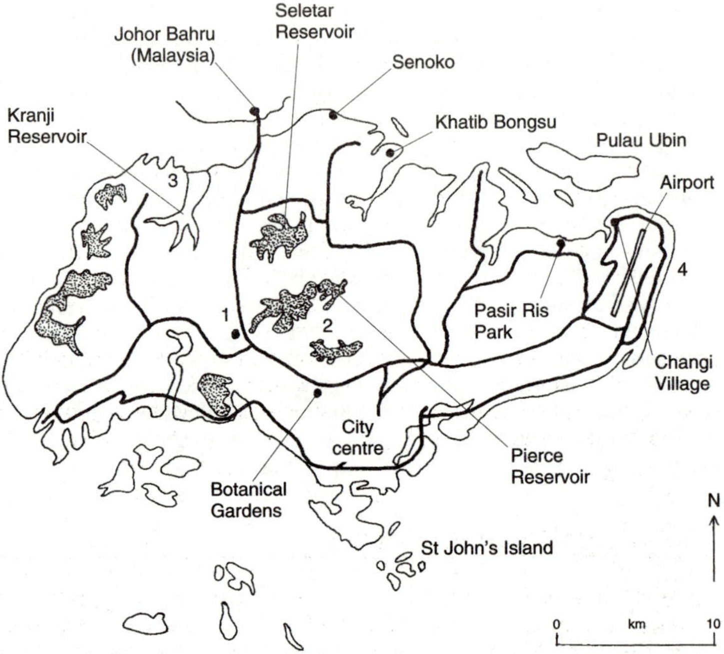

1 Bukit Timah NR
2 Sime Road Forest
3 Sungei Buloh Nature Park
4 Changi Beach

INTRODUCTION

Nearly three million people live on this tiny island (640 sq km), hence very little natural habitat is left. However, remnant forest patches still support a good selection of southeast Asian birds, including some species which are tricky to see elsewhere in Malaysia, and mangrove-lined bays and beaches support shorebirds such as Malaysian Plover*. Hence, while a full scale trip would be unnecessary, a short stopover in Singapore of two or three days could prove to be very worthwhile.

The public transport system is superb and includes taxis, buses and trains (MRT), hence hiring a vehicle would be an unnecessary expense. A wide range of accommodation is available, with the cheap but clean budget hotels concentrated on Bencoleen Street and the Katong and Geylang areas. The food is varied and cheap. Immunisation against hepatitis, polio, typhoid and yellow fever is recommended. The best time to visit is probably during the migration periods which fall between March and April, and October and November. It is humid throughout the year, with the driest time falling between May and July, and the wettest between November and March. Singapore has rapidly become one of the most densely populated countries in the world and over 80% of the land is now urbanised. Hence it is not too surprising to learn that 74 species have been lost since 1819, with an average of three species disappearing from the island every four years since 1940. This is what happens when the human population is too high. Some of the remaining forested areas and wetlands are protected in reserves totalling 5% of the land area, but other areas are being destroyed. For example, more birds have been recorded at Senoko than any other site in Singapore, but this area of forest, mangrove, mud flat and ponds is being replaced by a new town. Twenty threatened and near-threatened species occur in Singapore, out of a grand total of 335 species. Of these about 140 are resident. Non-endemic specialities and spectacular species include Chinese Egret*, Great-billed Heron*, Nordmann's Greenshank*, Asian Dowitcher*, Malaysian Plover*, Jambu Fruit-Dove, Long-tailed Parakeet, Red-crowned Barbet, Sunda Woodpecker, Hooded, Blue-winged and Mangrove* Pittas, Japanese Paradise-Flycatcher*, Daurian Starling and Brown-chested Jungle-Flycatcher*. There is no endemic species. During the peak passage month of October it is possible to see over 100 species in a few days and up to 200 in a couple of weeks.

BUKIT TIMAH NATURE RESERVE

This small reserve (81 ha) in the centre of the main island protects the only area of primary lowland forest left in Singapore. A good selection of birds, some of which are hard to see elsewhere in Asia, occur here, including Brown-chested Jungle-Flycatcher*.

Specialities

Jambu Fruit-Dove, Red-crowned Barbet*, Brown-chested Jungle-Flycatcher* (Nov).

Others

Black Baza (Oct–Apr), Blue-rumped Parrot*, Chestnut-winged (Nov–Mar) and Rusty-breasted Cuckoos, Chestnut-bellied Malkoha, Silver-backed (Nov–Mar) and Brown-backed (Nov–Mar) Needletails, Black-backed Kingfisher (Nov), Hooded (Nov–Dec) and Blue-winged (Sep–Nov) Pittas, Lesser Cuckoo-Shrike, Scarlet Minivet, Asian Fairy-bluebird, Greater Green and Lesser Green Leafbirds, White-throated Rock-Thrush (Nov–Mar), Orange-headed (Nov–Mar) and Siberian (Oct–Dec) Thrushes, Ferruginous Flycatcher (Oct–Apr), Siberian Blue-Robin (Sep–Apr), Buff-vented Bulbul, Short-tailed Babbler, Thick-billed and Yellow-vented Flowerpeckers, Crimson Sunbird, Little Spiderhunter.

To reach the reserve, head up towards Upper Bukit Timah Road from the city centre and turn right into Hindhede Drive. The reserve is at the end of here. Bird from the road leading to the summit and along the well marked trails.

SIME ROAD FOREST

Although most of the forest here is open secondary growth, resident birdwatchers believe it is the best site for forest birds on the island, especially between October and March.

Specialities

Jambu Fruit-Dove, Long-tailed Parakeet, Red-crowned Barbet*, Sunda Woodpecker.

Others

Grey-headed Fish-Eagle*, Black-thighed Falconet, Pink-necked Pigeon, Blue-rumped Parrot*, Blue-crowned Hanging-Parrot, Banded Bay and Rusty-breasted Cuckoos, Chestnut-bellied Malkoha, Spotted Wood-Owl, Malaysian and Jungle (Nov–Feb) Nightjars, Blue-eared, Black-backed (Nov) and Stork-billed Kingfishers, Rufous, White-bellied and Banded Woodpeckers, Common Flameback, Blue-winged Pitta, Asian Fairy-bluebird, Daurian Starling (Sep–Apr), Dark-sided (Oct–Mar), Ferruginous (Nov–Mar), Yellow-rumped (Nov–Mar), Narcissus (Nov–Mar) and Mugimaki (Nov–Mar) Flycatchers, Cream-vented and Red-eyed Bulbuls, White-chested*, Short-tailed and Chestnut-winged Babblers, Crimson Sunbird, Little Spiderhunter.

Bird the concrete walkway which begins at the Bukit Kalang Service Reservoir, which is accessible via Island Club Road (drive through the Singapore Island Country Club car park) or Sime Road (via a track leading east).

SUNGEI BULOH NATURE PARK

Singapore's only wetland reserve (75 ha), at the north end of the island, consists of mud flats, mangroves, ponds and scrub which attract migrant and wintering shorebirds such as Asian Dowitcher* and Great Knot, as well as Chinese Egret*.

Specialities

Chinese Egret* (Oct–Apr), Long-tailed Parakeet, Sunda and Laced Woodpeckers.

Others

Pacific Reef-Egret, Chinese Pond-Heron (Oct–Apr), Black Bittern (Nov–Apr), Watercock (Oct–May), Pintail Snipe (Oct–Mar), Asian Dowitcher* (Sep–Apr), Great Knot (Oct–Nov), Rufous-necked and Long-toed Stints, Common Flameback, White-chested Babbler*, Copper-throated Sunbird.

The park entrance is at the end of Neo Tiew Crescent, which begins just before Kranji Dam.

Similar species to those listed for Sungei Buloh occur at **Khatib Bongsu**, another area of mud flats, mangroves and ponds at the north end of the main island. This site is also particularly good for

Nordmann's Greenshank* (Mar), Grey-tailed Tattler (Oct–Mar) and Mangrove Whistler. To reach the area head for Yishun Avenue 11 and turn on to the disused road, heading up hill near the junction with Yishun Avenue 6, then follow the signs to the 'Buddha Temple'.

Species recorded in the large **Pasir Ris Park**, on the northeast coast, include Schrenck's Bittern* (Oct–Mar), Blue-breasted Quail, Ruddy-breasted Crake, Black-capped Kingfisher, Yellow-rumped Flycatcher (Oct–Dec), Forest Wagtail (Oct–Dec) and resident Copper-throated Sunbird, which occurs in the mangroves accessible via a boardwalk.

CHANGI BEACH

The beach, scrub and casuarinas on Singapore's east coast support breeding Malaysian Plover*, wintering Nordmann's Greenshank* and migrants such as Brown-chested Jungle-Flycatcher*.

Specialities

Nordmann's Greenshank* (Nov–Mar), Malaysian Plover*, Sunda Woodpecker, Brown-chested Jungle-Flycatcher* (Oct–Nov).

Others

Lesser (Feb) and Christmas Island* (Jun–Aug) Frigatebirds, Pintail Snipe (Oct–Mar), Asian Dowitcher* (Nov–Jan), Great Knot (Nov), Black-naped Tern, Horsfield's Bronze-Cuckoo (Jun–Aug), Grey-rumped Treeswift, Blue-throated Bee-eater, Pied Triller, White-throated Rock-Thrush (Nov), Daurian Starling (Sep–Mar), Forest Wagtail (Aug–Apr).

(Other species recorded here include Oriental Plover (Feb).)

Head for the Changi Coast Road, 20 km east of the city centre, and bird the area behind the Singapore Airlines hangar, 5 minutes by road from Changi Village.

Great-billed Heron* occurs on **Pulau Ubin**, a small islet 15 minutes by ferry from Changi Point, as well as Christmas Island Frigatebird* (Jul–Aug), Chinese Egret* (Sep–Apr), Red Junglefowl, Cinnamon-headed Pigeon*, Buffy Fish-Owl, Mangrove Pitta*, Mangrove Whistler and Straw-headed Bulbul*.

Migrants such as Malayan Night-Heron and other species such as Great-billed Heron* (often near the ferry terminal) occur on **St John's Island**, accessible by ferry from the World Trade Centre. Other migrants recorded here in October and November include Hooded and Blue-winged Pittas and Yellow-rumped and Narcissus Flycatchers, while Swinhoe's Storm-Petrel* is possible from the ferry at this time and Pied Imperial-Pigeon is an island resident.

While in Singapore it may be worth considering a visit to **Panti FR** in Malaysia (p. 203). This site is closer to Singapore (60 km from Johor Bahru at the north end of the island) than Kuala Lumpur and easily accessible as there are no problems crossing the border. The best way to reach this reserve from the main city if time is short is to take a taxi to Johor Bahru, just across the border, and a long-distance taxi from there. Taking a hired car into Malaysia would be more expensive.

ADDITIONAL INFORMATION

Addresses

The Nature Society (Singapore), c/o Botany Department, National University of Singapore, Lower Kent Ridge Road, Singapore 0511 (tel/fax: 65 741 2036), publishes an annnual journal, called *Iora*.
Birders who wish to be guided to the best sites and birds are recommended to contact Lim Kim Seng, Block 644 Yishun Street 61, #12-300, Singapore 760644 (tel/fax: 65 759 0873).

Books and Papers

The Birds of Singapore. Briffet C and Supari S, 1994. Oxford University Press.
Pocket Checklist of the Birds of Singapore. Lim K S, 1991. Nature Society.
Vanishing Birds of Singapore. Lim K S, 1992. Nature Society.

SOUTH KOREA

INTRODUCTION

This small, friendly country with a modern infrastructure supports many eastern Palearctic specialities, not least breeding Fairy Pitta*, and wintering Baikal Teal*, Scaly-sided Merganser* and Relict Gull*.

At 98,484 sq km, South Korea is slightly smaller than England and seven times smaller than Texas. The air, bus and rail networks are all excellent and there are even long-distance taxis, known as 'bullet taxis' for obvious reasons. Hire-cars are very expensive. There is a wide range of accommodation available, including Western and Korean (yogwans and yoinsuks) hotels. The food is also varied with hot, spicy noodles, rice, soup and vegetables being the most popular, and Posin T'ang Jip (dog-meat soup) the delicacy. Herbal teas and various vodka-like firewaters are the favourite drinks. Immunisation against hepatitis, polio and typhoid is recommended. The best times to visit South Korea are May and June, the driest months of the year, and during the very cold winters. July and August are usually hot and wet. This is a mountainous

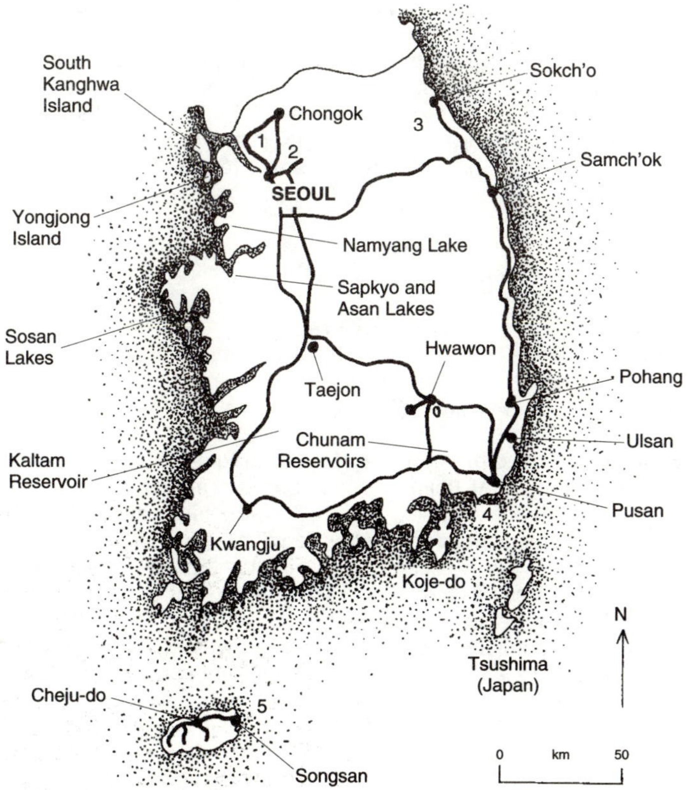

1 Han River Estuary
2 Kwangnung Forest
3 Sorak-San NP
4 Nakdong Estuary
5 Cheju-do

country with a long, indented coastline with many estuaries and offshore islands. Most low-lying areas have been turned over to agriculture and there are many paddies, but there is still plenty of forest, mainly in upland areas. Thirty-three threatened and near-threatened species out of a total of nearly 400 species have been recorded in South Korea. Non-endemic specialities and spectacular species include Swan Goose*, Mandarin Duck*, Baikal Teal*, Harlequin Duck, Scaly-sided Merganser*, Chinese Egret*, Black-faced Spoonbill*, Hazel Grouse, Hooded*, Red-crowned* and White-naped* Cranes, Spoonbill Sandpiper*, Long-billed Plover*, Black-tailed, Slaty-backed, Saunders'* and Relict* Gulls, Ruddy Kingfisher, Pygmy Woodpecker, Fairy Pitta*, Bull-headed Shrike, Vinous-throated Parrotbill, Varied Tit, Black-backed and Japanese Wagtails, Siberian Accentor, Japanese Grosbeak and Ochre-rumped* and Pallas' Buntings. There is no endemic species.

HAN RIVER ESTUARY

The Han River converges with the Imjin River to form an important estuary 25 km northwest of Seoul, where the mud flats, salt-marsh and paddies support more wintering birds (over 90,000) than any other site in South Korea, including Scaly-sided Merganser* and White-naped Crane*.

Most of the species listed below are only present during the winter (Nov–Mar).

Specialities

Swan Goose*, Scaly-sided Merganser*, White-naped Crane*.

Others

Bean Goose, White-tailed Eagle*, Bull-headed Shrike, Dusky Thrush, Daurian Redstart, Siberian Accentor, Long-tailed Rosefinch, Pine, Meadow and Yellow-throated Buntings.

The estuary is accessible from the Han–Imjin River Highway between Seoul and Imjingak. At Imjingak view the surrounding area from the roof of the restaurant complex. Birding from the highway is best heading south from Imjingak back towards Seoul, but this is a sensitive military area and it is wise to scan from inside a vehicle at various points along the road. Even this birding method is likely to attract the attention of soldiers, but they are usually friendly. Scaly-sided Merganser* has been recorded along the upper Imjin River just west of Chongok, accessible from Highway 37, and near Cholwon (Chorwon), northeast of Chongok.

KWANGNUNG FOREST

This mixed forest 70 km northeast of Seoul supports a fine selection of forest birds, including Ruddy Kingfisher and Varied Tit.

Specialities

Ruddy Kingfisher (Apr–Sep), Pygmy Woodpecker, Varied Tit.

Others

Mandarin Duck* (Sep–Apr), White-backed and Black Woodpeckers, Dusky Thrush (Oct–Apr), Daurian Redstart, Brown-eared Bulbul, Vinous-throated Parrotbill, Forest Wagtail (Apr–Sep), Yellow-throated Bunting.

(Other species recorded here include Solitary Snipe (Nov–Mar).)

Turn off Route 47 several kilometres north of Chinjop on to Route 314 to reach the forest and concentrate on the arboretum, by the second car park, where the stream has attracted Mandarin Duck* and Solitary Snipe.

Ten to 20 pairs of Black-faced Spoonbill* (Apr–Sep) breed in an egretry in the outer Han River estuary in the demilitarised zone between South and North Korea, and post-breeding flocks usually gather on the south coast of **South Kanghwa Island**, 50 km west of Seoul, between August and October. Other species recorded here include Chinese Egret*

(May–Jun), Schrenck's Bittern* (May–Sep), Red-crowned Crane* (Nov–Mar), Far Eastern Curlew* (spring), Nordmann's Greenshank* (spring), Siberian Accentor (Nov–Mar) and Pallas' Bunting (Nov–Mar). The southeast corner of this island is the best area and can be reached by turning left in Chondungsa village, then following the road to and beyond the temple to a large restaurant on the south side of the road. After passing the restaurant hang left to reach the coast (Chinese Egret* and Black-faced Spoonbill*), or right to reach wooded hillsides (Siberian Accentor). The paddies in this area support Schrenck's Bittern* in summer and Pallas' Bunting in winter.

SORAK-SAN NATIONAL PARK

This mountainous National Park in northeast Korea is one of the most scenic areas of the country and hence very popular with the South Koreans. The forests, meadows and rivers support a good range of birds, including Pale Thrush, Japanese Wagtail and Gray's Warbler.

Many of the species listed below are only present during the summer months (Apr–Sep).

Specialities

Pygmy Woodpecker, Pale Thrush, Varied Tit, Japanese Wagtail.

Others

Japanese Cormorant, Mandarin* and Spot-billed Ducks, Common Pheasant, Pintail Snipe, Grey-tailed Tattler, Black-tailed Gull, Jungle Nightjar, Black-capped Kingfisher, White-backed Woodpecker, Bull-headed Shrike, Dusky Thrush, White-cheeked Starling, Yellow-rumped Flycatcher, Siberian Blue-Robin, Daurian Redstart, Gray's Warbler, Eastern Crowned-Warbler, Grey-capped Greenfinch.

The main entrance to the park is on the east side of Sorak-dong, west of the main Naksan-Sokch'o road. Bird throughout the park, including the areas around T'owansong Falls and Sinhung-sa Temple. There is a cable-car to Kwan-gumsong Sanjang and the path down from there is usually the quietest in the park.

Accommodation: Yang-yang — hotels, hostels (minbaks), Youth Hostel and campsite. Sorak-dong — hotels.

Over 40,000 Baikal Teal* have been recorded in winter on **Namyang Lake** at the southeast edge of Namyang Bay, 45 km southwest of Seoul. The bay is a major shorebird stopover in spring when Spoonbill Sandpiper*, as well as Nordmann's Greenshank* and 3,500 Great Knot have been recorded. The teal appear to be highly mobile and have also been recorded in large numbers on **Sapkyo** and **Asan Lakes**, further south, the **Sosan Lakes** to the west, where Oriental Stork* has also been recorded in winter, and on the **Kum River Estuary**, much further south, where Saunders' Gull* also winters.

Azure-winged Magpie is a localised species in South Korea, but the surrounds of **Kaltam Reservoir** south of Chonju, is one of the best sites.

The major wintering site for Hooded Crane* (125 in 1994–95) is **Hwawon**, where they feed on the Nakdong River plain, visible from the observation tower in Hwawon Park, southwest of Taegu. The birds appear to prefer the fields west of the industrial estate to the north, but these fields seem destined to disappear under yet more concrete in the near future.

Long-billed Plover*, Japanese Wagtail, Buff-bellied Pipit and Pallas' Bunting have been recorded along the river at **Kyongju**, 21 km southwest of Pohang near the southeast coast and Siberian Accentor occurs in the village garden at nearby Yangdong. The coast from **Pohang** south to **Ulsan**, accessible via Route 31, is worth checking in winter for Pelagic Cormorant, Harlequin Duck, Black-tailed, Glaucous-winged and Slaty-backed Gulls, Marbled and Ancient Murrelets, Pacific Loon, Russet Sparrow and Siberian Accentor. The Kuryongpo Peninsula, accessible via Route 912, near Pohang is one of the best areas.

NAKDONG ESTUARY

This estuary on the western edge of Pusan in extreme southeast South Korea attracts some very rare birds throughout the year, with Black-faced Spoonbill* in summer, Relict Gull* in winter and passage shorebirds which have included Spoonbill Sandpiper*.

Specialities

Black-faced Spoonbill* (Apr–Sep), Spoonbill Sandpiper* (Apr–May/Sep–Oct), Saunders'* (Nov–Mar) and Relict* (Nov–Mar) Gulls, Chinese Penduline-Tit, Black-backed Wagtail.

Others

Bean Goose, Yellow Bittern (Apr–Sep), White-tailed Eagle*, Far Eastern Curlew* (Apr–May/Sep–Oct), Great Knot (Apr–May/Sep–Oct), Rufous-necked Stint (Apr–May/Sep–Oct), Sharp-tailed Sandpiper (Apr–May/Sep–Oct), Black-tailed Gull, Bull-headed Shrike, Siberian Accentor (Nov–Mar), Pallas' Bunting (Nov–Mar).

Pusan is 432 km southeast of Seoul (and is accessible by ferry from Japan). The estuary can be viewed from Ulsukto Island, where there is a rudimentary bird sanctuary and an observation tower (in the southwest corner) but the best viewpoint for gulls in on the southern tip of the mainland west of the island.

Baikal Teal*, White-naped Crane*, Japanese Quail and Ochre-rumped Bunting* winter on and around the **Chunam** and **Tongpan Reservoirs**, which can be reached by turning north at the Chinyong interchange, 35 km west of Pusan. Once off the expressway, follow signs to Changwon, then take the turning north towards Miryang. About 3.5 km from this turning, turn east. One kilometre along this road, turn right, cross the bridge, and turn left, to reach Chunam Reservoir. Baikal Teal* (5,000 in 1994–95) appear to prefer Tongpan Reservoir, which is to the right and is best viewed by continuing east to a village from where it is possible to walk out to the embankment around the reservoir.

Fairy Pitta* is a summer visitor to the island of **Koje-do**, which lies off the southeast coast and is accessible by road from Pusan. This rare pitta has been recorded just north of Hakdong, around the temple just to the north of the town and for a few kilometres further north. Winter visitors to Koje-do include Harlequin Duck (in Hakdong Bay on the southern coast) and Long-billed Plover* (near Koje).

CHEJU-DO

This large, mountainous island, 85 km south of the mainland, is very popular with South Koreans because of its balmy summers. The main avian attraction is the rare Fairy Pitta*, which breeds in the island's forests.

Specialities

Fairy Pitta* (Apr–Sep), Varied Tit.

Others

Mandarin Duck*, Slaty-backed Gull, White-backed Woodpecker, Bull-headed Shrike, Pale and Dusky Thrushes, Brown-eared Bulbul, Grey-capped Greenfinch, Yellow-throated Bunting.

This island is accessible by air from Seoul and by ferry from Pusan. Fairy Pitta* breeds on the southern slopes of the Hallasan volcano, where there are plenty of trails to try. The area around Mosulpo in the south-west is good for spring migrants in late April and early May.

Japanese Wood-Pigeon* is a widespread resident on **Ullung-do**, a steep, rocky island situated roughly halfway between South Korea and Japan, and accessible by ferry from Pohang. Summer visitors to this island include Lesser Cuckoo and Pleske's Warbler, while Streaked Shearwater (Apr–Sep) has been recorded from the ferry.

ADDITIONAL INFORMATION

Books and Papers

Birding South Korea in Winter. Diskin D, 1995. Privately published.
Wild Birds of Korea in Colour. Yoon Moo-Boo, 1993. Kyohak.
A Field Guide to the Birds of Korea. Won Pyong-Oh, 1993. Kyohak.
Coloured Wild Birds of Korea. Yoon Moo-Boo, 1989. Academy.
A Field Guide to the Birds of Japan. Sonobe *et al.*, 1982. Wild Bird Society of Japan.

Near-endemics

Japanese Cormorant, Scaly-sided Merganser*, Steller's Sea-Eagle*, Swinhoe's Rail*, Hooded*, Red-crowned* and White-naped* Cranes, Black-tailed, Saunders* and Relict* Gulls, Spectacled Guillemot, Japanese Murrelet*, Japanese Wood-Pigeon*, Bull-headed and Chinese Grey Shrikes, Japanese Waxwing*, Varied Tit, Chinese Penduline-Tit, Black-backed and Japanese Wagtails, Grey-capped Greenfinch, Japanese Grosbeak, Ochre-rumped*, Tristram's, Yellow-throated and Yellow* Buntings.

SRI LANKA

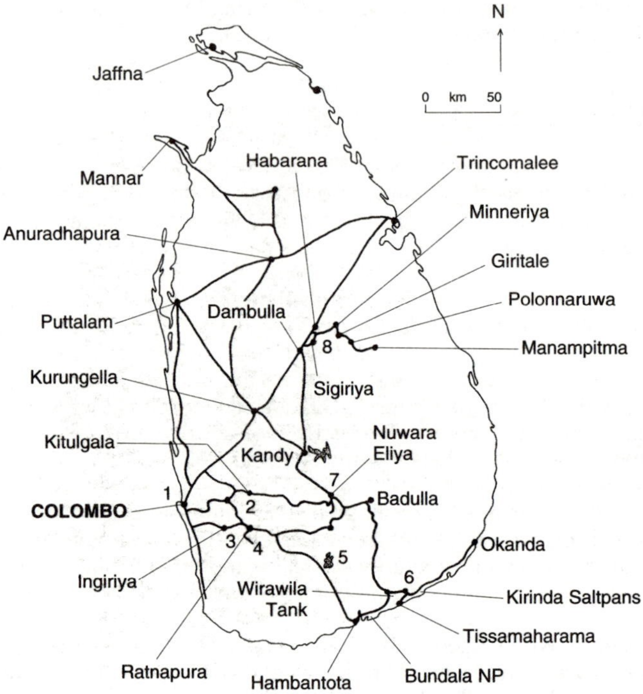

1 Bellanwila-Attidiya Sanctuary
2 Kelani River FR
3 Ingiriya FR
4 Sinharaja FR
5 Uda Walawe NP
6 Yala NP
7 Nuwara Eliya
8 Dambulla

INTRODUCTION

Summary

The island of Sri Lanka, off the south coast of India, supports 23 endemics and a further 17 species which are only shared with India. Virtually all of these birds are relatively easy to find on a short trip, especially with a hire-car and driver, and if the trip is made in winter the bonuses include Indian Pitta and the cracking Pied Thrush*.

Size

At 65,610 sq km, Sri Lanka is about half the size of England and ten times smaller than Texas.

Getting Around

The best way to get around Sri Lanka on a tight schedule is to hire a car complete with driver, alias guide and interpreter. Fortunately, this is a cheaper alternative to no driver because of the insurance costs associated with personal use of a vehicle. Hire-cars are best booked in advance and one good company is A. Baur and Co. (Travel), Baur's Building, 5 Upper Chatham Street, Colombo 1 (fax: 94 1 548493). The public transport system is less extensive and more expensive than in India, but there is a fairly good rail network.

Accommodation and Food

Most of the rather limited accommodation is much more expensive than India. Curries dominate the menus and they can be washed down with the local brew, Lion's beer.

Health and Safety

Immunisation against hepatitis, polio, typhoid and yellow fever is recommended, as are precautions against malaria.

Government troops conquered the Tamil separatists' stronghold in the extreme north of the island in late 1995, and there were no immediate reprisals. However, the Tamil Tigers are a particularly fanatical group and trouble may lie ahead, so it is best to check the latest situation with the relevant Foreign Office before venturing to Sri Lanka. Fortunately, all of the best birds occur in the south of the island, well away from the Tamils' previous strongholds, and even if they re-emerge it may still be possible to go birding in Sri Lanka.

Climate and Timing

The best time to visit Sri Lanka is in January and February when northern migrants such as Indian Pitta, Pied Thrush* and Kashmir Flycatcher* are wintering, but it can be wet at this time of year, especially in the southwest, where Ratnapura receives as much as 5 m of rain every year.

Habitats

The diverse range of habitats includes remnant and degraded lowland and foothill forests, dry deciduous forests, montane forests and grasslands and coastal lagoons. Two of the most prominent features of the Sri Lankan landscape are paddies and small reservoirs, known as 'tanks', which often support a fine variety of waterbirds.

Conservation

Although 10% of the land lies within national parks, forest reserves and various other sanctuaries, many of the important habitats are little more than degraded remnants. If what is left becomes even more degraded, or is destroyed, many birds, especially the 29 threatened and near-threatened species which occur in the country, are unlikely to survive.

Bird Species

Over 400 species have been recorded in Sri Lanka. Non-endemic specialities and spectacular species include Great Thick-knee, Small Pratincole, White-naped Woodpecker, Indian Pitta, Pied Thrush* and Kashmir Flycatcher*.

Endemics

The 23 species which are endemic to Sri Lanka include a junglefowl, a malkoha, a coucal, an owlet, a hornbill, a magpie and a thrush. The 17 species shared with southern India include Blue-faced Malkoha, Ceylon Frogmouth*, Malabar Trogon and Malabar Pied-Hornbill*.

Expectations

It is possible to see 220–250 species on a two-week trip, including all of the endemics.

BELLANWILA-ATTIDIYA SANCTUARY

The marshes in this small sanctuary near Colombo, the Sri Lankan capital, support a fine selection of marshbirds, including three species of bittern.

Sri Lankan Endemics

Yellow-fronted Barbet.

Specialities

Spot-billed Pelican*, Black Bittern, Brown-headed Barbet, White-browed Bulbul, Long-billed Sunbird.

Others

Little and Indian Cormorants, Cotton Pygmy-Goose, Indian Pond-Heron, Yellow and Cinnamon Bitterns, Painted Stork*, Asian Openbill*, Brahminy Kite, Ruddy-breasted Crake, Watercock, Pheasant-tailed Jacana, Greater Painted-Snipe, Pintail Snipe (Nov–Mar), Pied Cuckoo, Stork-billed Kingfisher, Green, Blue-tailed and Chestnut-headed Bee-eaters, Indian Roller, Black-rumped Flameback, Ashy Woodswallow, Plain Prinia, Pallas' Warbler (Nov–Mar), Blyth's Reed-Warbler (Nov– Mar), Yellow-billed Babbler, Pale-billed Flowerpecker, Black-headed Munia.

This sanctuary is just south of Colombo, near the Bellanwila Temple. Walk along the raised bund which crosses the reserve. Spot-billed Pelican*, a widespread species in Sri Lanka, also occurs on Lake Beira in Colombo.

Accommodation: Colombo.

KELANI RIVER FOREST RESERVE

The remnant lowland forest in this reserve near Kitulgala supports many of the lowland endemics, including Spot-winged Thrush*, Ashy-headed Laughingthrush* and Orange-billed Babbler.

Sri Lankan Endemics

Ceylon Spurfowl, Ceylon Junglefowl, Ceylon Hanging-Parrot, Layard's Parakeet, Chestnut-backed Owlet*, Ceylon Grey Hornbill, Yellow-fronted Barbet, Ceylon Magpie*, Spot-winged Thrush*, Ceylon Myna, Ashy-headed Laughingthrush*, Brown-capped and Orange-billed Babblers, White-throated Flowerpecker*.

Specialities

Ceylon Frogmouth*, Malabar Trogon, Indian Blue-Robin (Nov–Mar), White-browed and Yellow-browed Bulbuls, Indian Scimitar-Babbler, Dark-fronted Babbler, Black-throated Munia, Long-billed Sunbird.

Others

Rufous-bellied Eagle, Pompadour Green-Pigeon, Chestnut-winged Cuckoo, Brown Hawk-Owl, Brown-capped Woodpecker, Lesser Yellownape, Blue-winged and Golden-fronted Leafbirds, Brown-breasted Flycatcher* (Nov–Mar), Tickell's Blue-Flycatcher, White-rumped Munia, Purple-rumped Sunbird.

(Other species recorded here include Red-faced Malkoha* and Green-billed Coucal*.)

Bird the resthouse grounds and the forest on the opposite bank of the Kelani River, above the village reached by dugout canoe.

Accommodation: Kitulgala — resthouse.

INGIRIYA FOREST RESERVE

This small, degraded lowland forest is the best in Sri Lanka for the endemic Green-billed Coucal*, and a good site for the near-endemic Ceylon Frogmouth*.

Sri Lankan Endemics

Ceylon Spurfowl, Ceylon Hanging-Parrot, Green-billed Coucal*, Chestnut-backed Owlet*, Ceylon Grey Hornbill, Yellow-fronted Barbet, Brown-capped Babbler, White-throated Flowerpecker*.

Specialities

Ceylon Frogmouth*, Indian Swiftlet, Malabar Trogon, Yellow-browed Bulbul, Dark-fronted Babbler.

Others

Pompadour Green-Pigeon, Crested Treeswift, Chestnut-headed Bee-eater, Lesser Yellownape, Greater Flameback, Black-headed Cuckoo-Shrike, Small Minivet, Brown-breasted Flycatcher* (Nov–Mar), Tickell's Blue-Flycatcher, Black-crested Bulbul, Large-billed Leaf-Warbler (Nov–Mar).

Bird the track leading to the Buddhist hermitage near Bodhinagala, 5 km from Ingiriya, paying special attention to the bamboo and rattan thickets, the preferred habitat of Green-billed Coucal*.

Accommodation: Ingiriya.

SINHARAJA FOREST RESERVE

This logged, mainly secondary lowland forest is the best site for virtually all of the island's lowland endemics, especially Red-faced Malkoha* and White-faced Starling*.

Sri Lankan Endemics

Ceylon Spurfowl, Ceylon Junglefowl, Ceylon Hanging-Parrot, Layard's Parakeet, Red-faced Malkoha*, Chestnut-backed Owlet*, Ceylon Grey Hornbill, Yellow-fronted Barbet, Ceylon Magpie*, Spot-winged Thrush*, White-faced Starling*, Ceylon Myna, Ashy-headed Laughingthrush*, Orange-billed Babbler, White-throated Flowerpecker*.

Specialities

Ceylon Frogmouth*, Malabar Trogon, Crimson-fronted Barbet, Indian Pitta (Nov–Mar), Yellow-browed Bulbul, Indian Scimitar-Babbler, Dark-fronted Babbler, Long-billed Sunbird.

Others

Brown-backed Needletail, Blue-tailed and Chestnut-headed Bee-eaters, Lesser Yellownape, Greater Flameback, White-browed Fantail, Small Minivet, Blue-winged and Golden-fronted Leafbirds, Brown-breasted Flycatcher* (Nov–Mar), Velvet-fronted Nuthatch, Black-crested Bulbul, Jungle Prinia, Large-billed Leaf-Warbler (Nov–Mar), Tawny-bellied Babbler, Forest Wagtail (Nov–Mar), Pale-billed Flowerpecker.

Other Wildlife

Giant wood spider, grizzled giant squirrel, purple-faced leaf-monkey, toque macaque and butterflies such as common birdwing.

(Other species recorded here include Green-billed Coucal*.)

Sinharaja is 3 hours by rough road south of Ratnapura via Kalawana and Weddagala, where the track through the forest starts. It is best to

Red-faced Malkoha is one of Sri Lanka's most spectacular endemics*

arrive here at dawn and bird along the track up from Kudawa Base Camp to Martin's Hostel and beyond for several kilometres, looking and listening in particular for feeding flocks, as these contain most of Sri Lanka's lowland endemics. Beware of leeches.

Accommodation: Martin's Hostel (take food). Ratnapura — Ratnaloka Inn (Indian Pitta and Ceylon Magpie* in garden).

UDA WALAWE NATIONAL PARK

The extensive grasslands which surround a reservoir in this park support a good selection of arid-country specialists, including Blue-faced Malkoha and Malabar Pied-Hornbill*.

Specialities

Grey-bellied Cuckoo (Nov–Mar), Blue-faced and Sirkeer Malkohas, Jerdon's Nightjar, Malabar Pied-Hornbill*, Crimson-fronted Barbet, Indian Pitta (Nov–Mar).

Others

Oriental Darter*, Lesser Adjutant*, Grey-headed Fish-Eagle*, Pallid Harrier* (Nov–Mar), Yellow-wattled Lapwing, Plum-headed Parakeet, Brown Fish-Owl, Indian Nightjar, Blue-eared, Stork-billed and Black-capped Kingfishers, Green Bee-eater, Indian Roller, Yellow-crowned Woodpecker, Common Woodshrike, Indian Robin, Jungle and Ashy Prinias, Tawny-bellied and Yellow-eyed Babblers, White-throated Munia.

Other Wildlife

Asian elephant, barking deer, leopard, sambar.

The park is near Embilipitiya, which is 2 hours by road from Ratnapura.

Accommodation: Embilipitiya — Centuria Inn.

YALA NATIONAL PARK

The wetlands and scrub in and near this park on Sri Lanka's southeast coast support an excellent mixture of marshbirds and arid-country specialists, including Great Thick-knee, Small Pratincole, Malabar Pied-Hornbill* and White-naped Woodpecker.

Sri Lankan Endemics

Ceylon Junglefowl.

Specialities

Spot-billed Pelican*, Black Bittern, Great Thick-knee, Blue-faced and Sirkeer Malkohas, Jerdon's Nightjar, Malabar Pied-Hornbill*, White-naped Woodpecker, Indian Pitta (Nov–Mar), White-browed Bulbul, Yellow-billed Babbler, Long-billed Sunbird.

Others

Little and Indian Cormorants, Oriental Darter*, Greater Flamingo, Yellow Bittern, Painted Stork*, Asian Openbill*, Black-necked Stork, Lesser Adjutant*, Black-headed Ibis*, Indian Peafowl, Pheasant-tailed Jacana, Pintail Snipe (Nov–Mar), Long-toed Stint (Nov–Mar), Oriental (Nov–Mar) and Small Pratincoles, Yellow-wattled Lapwing, Great and Lesser Crested-Terns, Saunders' Tern, Orange-breasted Pigeon, Pompadour Green-Pigeon, Pied Cuckoo, Indian Nightjar, Crested Treeswift, Green, Blue-tailed and Chestnut-headed Bee-eaters, Indian Roller, Yellow-crowned Woodpecker, White-browed Fantail, Ashy Woodswallow, Black-headed Cuckoo-Shrike, Small Minivet, Common Woodshrike, Brahminy Starling, Indian Robin, Tawny-bellied and Yellow-eyed Babblers, Rufous-winged Bushlark, Ashy-crowned Sparrow-Lark, Forest Wagtail (Nov–Mar), White-throated Munia, Streaked and Baya Weavers, Pale-billed Flowerpecker.

Other Wildlife

Asian elephant, leopard, sambar, sloth bear, swamp crocodile, water buffalo.

Yala is only accessible via expensive jeep rides, but its speciality, Malabar Pied-Hornbill*, occurs along the Kataragama–Buttala Road on the western edge. Other sites worth birding in the Tissamaharama–Hambantota area to the west include the Bundala Sanctuary, which is accessible from Weligata between Tissamaharama and Hambantota (Black-necked Stork, Great Thick-knee, Blue-faced Malkoha), the Wirawila Tank (Black Bittern, Streaked Weaver) and the Hambantota Saltpans (Small Pratincole), which are situated a few kilometres towards Tissamaharama.

Accommodation: Lake Tissawewa (near Tissamaharama) — Tissa Resthouse (A).

NUWARA ELIYA

The old hill resort of Nuwara Eliya is situated at 1889 m (6198 ft) in the cool highlands of central Sri Lanka. All of the montane endemics can be seen in the remnant montane forests in and near this town, as well as Pied Thrush* and Indian Pittas, which have been seen feeding on open lawns in the town park.

Sri Lankan Endemics

Ceylon Wood-Pigeon*, Ceylon Magpie*, Ceylon Whistling-Thrush*, Dull-blue Flycatcher*, Yellow-eared Bulbul*, Ceylon White-eye, Ceylon Bush-Warbler*.

Specialities

Brown Wood-Owl, Indian Swiftlet, Crimson-fronted Barbet, Indian Pitta (Nov–Mar), Pied Thrush* (Nov–Mar), Kashmir Flycatcher* (Nov–Mar), Indian Blue-Robin (Nov–Mar), Indian Scimitar-Babbler, Yellow-billed Babbler, Long-billed Sunbird.

Others

Jerdon's Baza, Indian Robin, Blyth's Reed-Warbler (Nov–Mar), Purple-rumped Sunbird.

Other Wildlife

Purple-faced leaf-monkey (bear monkey).

Victoria Park, in the centre of Nuwara Eliya, is a terrific place to start birding in the highlands of Sri Lanka. Here it is possible to see Indian Pittas feeding on open lawns and Pied Thrushes* can be found around the compost heap or along the stream. The **Hakgala Botanical Gardens**, 10 km southeast of the town, is the best site for for Ceylon Bush-Warbler*. The remnant forest within the **Surrey Tea Estate**, the best site for the scarce Ceylon Wood-Pigeon*, is 6 km further southeast from here. Follow the sign for 'Paboda Guest House', which is on the south side of the road between KMS 97 and 98, just east of Welimada, and once at the guest house ask politely for permission to enter the forest, where Ceylon Wood-Pigeon* occurs, and enquire whether Brown Wood-Owl is roosting in the grounds. The shy and crepuscular Ceylon Whistling-Thrush is the hardest endemic to see. The river up and down stream from the **Hakgala Waterfall** used to be the best site, but in recent years birds have been seen more regularly at **KM 83**. Walk down the steep trail which starts at the fifth telegraph pole (No. 92) back from KM 83 towards Nuwara Eliya, cross the irrigation channel to reach the river, and check the trees on the opposite side of the river. **Horton Plains NP**, accessible via a rough track through Pattipola south of Nuwara Eliya, is another good birding area where Ceylon Wood-Pigeon*, Ceylon Magpie*, Ceylon Whistling-Thrush* and Ceylon Bush-Warbler* (on the way up from Nuwara Eliya) have been recorded. The mossy forest just before 'World's End', a spectacular 1000 m (3281 ft) inland cliff, is particularly good.

Accommodation: Nuwara Eliya — Grand Hotel (A).

Ceylon Myna, Forest Wagtail (Nov–Mar) and Long-billed Sunbird, along with Flying Foxes, occur in the Peradeniya Botanical Gardens (60 ha), southwest of **Kandy** on the Colombo Road, while Ceylon Hanging-Parrot, Chestnut-headed Bee-eater, Yellow-fronted Barbet, Indian Pitta (Nov–Mar), Indian Blue-Robin (Nov–Mar), Brown-capped Babbler and Indian Scimitar-Babbler occur in the excellent forest at the Udawattakelle Sanctuary, behind the Temple of the Tooth, a few kilometres northeast of town.

DAMBULLA

This town in central Sri Lanka lies near one of the country's main tourist areas and, while admiring the ancient buildings and impressive scenery, it is possible to see some excellent birds.

Sri Lankan Endemics

Ceylon Junglefowl, Ceylon Grey Hornbill, Brown-capped Babbler.

Specialities

Spot-billed Pelican*, Blue-faced Malkoha, Malabar Pied-Hornbill*, Crimson-fronted Barbet, Indian Pitta (Nov–Mar), White-browed Bulbul, Yellow-billed Babbler, Long-billed Sunbird.

Others

Little and Indian Cormorants, Oriental Darter*, Cotton Pygmy-Goose, Painted Stork*, Black-headed Ibis*, Grey-headed Fish-Eagle*, Pheasant-tailed Jacana, Greater Painted-Snipe, Pintail Snipe (Nov–Mar), Pied, Banded Bay and Drongo Cuckoos, Black-rumped Flameback, Large and Black-headed Cuckoo-Shrikes, Black-crested Bulbul, Tawny-bellied Babbler, Purple-rumped Sunbird.

Birding and 'culturing' can be combined very well in this area, especially at Sigiriya and Polonnaruwa. To the northeast of Dambulla Indian Pitta occurs in the old gardens around the base of the impressive 180 m (590 ft) Lion's Rock fortress at **Sigiriya**, and this lovely bird has even been recorded in the grounds of Sigiriya Village Hotel. Blue-faced Malkoha, Malabar Pied-Hornbill*, Indian Pitta and Black-headed Cuckoo-Shrike have been recorded around the ruins at **Polonnaruwa**, the ancient capital of Sri Lanka, which is 10 km southeast of Giritale.

Accommodation: Sigiriya Village Hotel, Royal Lotus Hotel.

The ruins in and around the ancient city of **Anuradhapura** in north-central Sri Lanka, as well as nearby tanks (e.g. Kanadarawa), support Spot-billed Pelican*, Blue-faced Malkoha, Brown Fish-Owl, Indian Pitta (Nov–Mar) and Long-billed Sunbird (at Mihintale).

ADDITIONAL INFORMATION

Books and Papers

A Field Guide to the Birds of Sri Lanka. Kotagama S and Prithiviraj F, 1995. WHTSL, Sri Lanka.
A Pictorial Guide to the Birds of the Indian Subcontinent. Ali S *et al.*, 1983. Bombay Natural History Society/Oxford University Press.
South India, Sri Lanka and the Andaman Islands (Trip Report). Gee B, 1995. Privately published (available via OBC).

SRI LANKAN ENDEMICS (23)

Ceylon Spurfowl	Widespread
Ceylon Junglefowl	Widespread
Ceylon Wood-Pigeon*	Nuwara Eliya
Ceylon Hanging-Parrot	Widespread
Layard's Parakeet	Widespread
Red-faced Malkoha*	Sinharaja FR (there are unconfirmed records of this species from south India)
Green-billed Coucal*	Ingiriya FR, Kelani River FR and Sinharaja FR
Chestnut-backed Owlet*	Ingiriya FR, Kelani River FR and

	Sinharaja FR
Ceylon Grey Hornbill	Widespread
Yellow-fronted Barbet	Widespread
Ceylon Magpie*	Widespread
Ceylon Whistling-Thrush*	Nuwara Eliya
Spot-winged Thrush*	Kelani River FR and Sinharaja FR
White-faced Starling*	Sinharaja FR
Ceylon Myna	Widespread
Dull-blue Flycatcher*	Nuwara Eliya
Yellow-eared Bulbul*	Nuwara Eliya
Ceylon White-eye	Nuwara Eliya
Ceylon Bush-Warbler*	Nuwara Eliya
Ashy-headed Laughingthrush*	Kelani River FR and Sinharaja FR
Brown-capped Babbler	Widespread in the lowlands
Orange-billed Babbler	Kelani River FR and Sinharaja FR
White-throated Flowerpecker*	Ingiriya FR, Kelani River FR and Sinharaja FR

Near-endemics

Species Shared with India (17)
Painted Francolin, Jungle Bush-Quail, Blue-faced Malkoha, Ceylon Frogmouth*, Jerdon's Nightjar, Indian Swiftlet, Malabar Trogon, Malabar Pied-Hornbill*, Crimson-fronted Barbet, Hill Swallow, White-browed and Yellow-browed Bulbuls, Indian Scimitar-Babbler, Dark-fronted and Yellow-billed Babblers, Black-throated Munia, Long-billed Sunbird.

Others
Indian Courser, White-naped Woodpecker, White-bellied Drongo, Pied Thrush*, Kashmir Flycatcher*, Jungle Prinia, Purple-rumped Sunbird.

TAIWAN

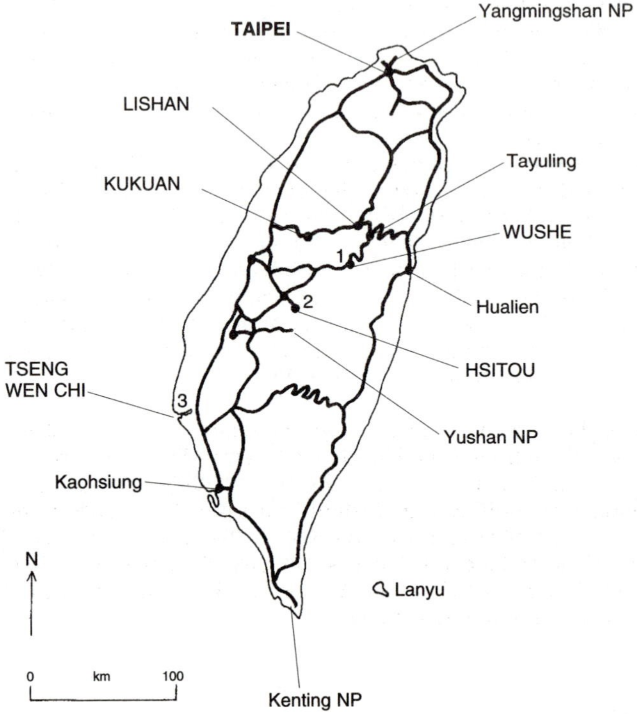

1 Wushe
2 Hsitou
3 Tseng Wen Chi

INTRODUCTION

This small, mountainous island which lies 160 km off the east coast of China, supports 14 endemics, most of which can be seen with some ease thanks to the modern infrastructure.

At 35,742 sq km, Taiwan is a quarter the size of England, and nearly 20 times smaller than Texas. It is approximately 400 km from north to south and 150 km from west to east. The island has an excellent road system and bus network. Hire-car drivers should remember that Taiwan drivers may be the worst in the world. Accommodation ranges from campsites through Youth Hostels to expensive hotels and the food, tea and beer are fine, but beware of the spirit called kaoliang which is reputed to be 65% alcohol. Immunisation against hepatitis, polio, typhoid and yellow fever is recommended. The best time to look for the endemics is late April–early May, but birds such as Black-faced

Spoonbill* are only present during the winter. Summers are hot and humid in the mainly dry lowlands. In the mountains it can rain at any time of year and in winter there is some snow on the higher forested peaks which rise to 3952 m (12,966 ft) at Mount Yushan. These mountains, which form the backbone of the island, drop steeply to the sea on the eastern side of the island, but on the western side there is a heavily cultivated narrow coastal plain. There are over 40 protected areas, including five national parks and 20 nature reserves, all of which help to conserve the island's birds, which include 32 threatened and near-threatened species.

Over 450 species have been recorded on Taiwan. Non-endemic specialities and spectacular species include Mandarin Duck*, Black-faced Spoonbill*, Chinese Bamboo-Partridge, White-bellied Pigeon*, Island Thrush, Collared Finchbill, Rusty Laughingthrush, Golden Parrotbill, Varied Tit, Vinaceous Rosefinch and Grey-headed Bullfinch. The island boasts 14 endemic species, which include two pheasants, a magpie, a bush-robin, Flamecrest, five babblers and a tit. It is possible to see around 80 species during a week and up to 150 in two or three, including 13 of the 14 endemics.

Most of the endemics occur in the mountains and the best way to approach them from **Taipei**, the capital (where Taiwan Magpie occurs in Yangming Park, adjacent to Yangmingshan NP), is to head south to **Kukuan**, then northeast to **Lishan** and south to Wushe. Mandarin Duck* (on the river and reservoir east of Kukuan), Taiwan Whistling-Thrush, Collared Finchbill, Steere's Liocichla, Streak-breasted Scimitar-Babbler, Grey-cheeked Fulvetta, White-eared Sibia and Varied Tit are all possible between Kukuan and Lishan.

WUSHE

The town of Wushe is situated in the mountains of north-central Taiwan where most of the island's endemics, as well as Island Thrush, White-browed Bush-Robin and Grey-headed Bullfinch occur.

Taiwan Endemics

Taiwan Partridge*, Swinhoe's Pheasant*, Collared Bush-Robin, Flamecrest, White-whiskered Laughingthrush, Steere's Liocichla, Taiwan Barwing, White-eared Sibia, Taiwan Yuhina, Yellow Tit*.

Specialities

Chinese Bamboo-Partridge, Island Thrush, Rusty Laughingthrush, Golden Parrotbill.

Others

Ashy Wood-Pigeon, Collared Owlet, White-throated Needletail (May–Sep), Black-browed Barbet, White-backed Woodpecker, Ferruginous Flycatcher, Vivid Niltava, White-browed Bush-Robin, Black-throated Tit, Brownish-flanked and Yellowish-bellied Bush-Warblers, Rufous-faced Warbler, Pygmy Wren-Babbler, Rufous-capped Babbler, Green-backed Tit, Vinaceous Rosefinch, Brown and Grey-headed Bullfinches.

North of Wushe, bird the roadside, the track to the left just after Mei Feng which is at the KM 15 post (Swinhoe's Pheasant*, Island Thrush), the Yuanfeng area at the KM 25 post (Flamecrest, White-whiskered Laughingthrush) and above and below the 3275 m (10,745 ft) Hohuan Shan Pass at the KM 33 post (Flamecrest, Golden Parrotbill, Vinaceous Rosefinch).

Accommodation: Wushe, Tsuifeng, Tayuling.

East of the Hohuan Shan Pass the Central Cross-Island Highway descends to the east coast via the stunning **Taroko Gorge**, where Eurasian Nutcracker, Taiwan Whistling-Thrush, Little Forktail and Collared Finchbill occur. The localised endemic, Styan's Bulbul*, occurs around the coastal town of **Hualien**, along with White-bellied Pigeon* and shorebirds such as Grey-tailed Tattler.

Flamecrest is one of Taiwan's 14 endemics

HSITOU (CHITOU)

The Hsitou Forest Recreation Area, which includes Phoenix Mountain, lies at 1100 m (3609 ft) in the mountains of central Taiwan where the avifauna is almost identical to that around Wushe to the north.

Taiwan Endemics

Taiwan Partridge*, Taiwan Whistling-Thrush, Steere's Liocichla, Taiwan Barwing, White-eared Sibia, Taiwan Yuhina, Yellow Tit*.

Specialities

Chinese Bamboo-Partridge, White-bellied Pigeon*, Island Thrush, Rusty Laughingthrush.

Others

Ashy Wood-Pigeon, Mountain Scops-Owl, Collared Owlet, Black-browed Barbet, White-backed Woodpecker, Ferruginous Flycatcher, Vivid Niltava, Black-throated Tit, Brownish-flanked Bush-Warbler, Rufous-faced Warbler, Rufous-capped Babbler, Spot-breasted and Streak-breasted Scimitar-Babblers, Pygmy Wren-Babbler, Grey-cheeked Fulvetta.

Bird the Mountain and Arboretum Trails at this popular tourist site.

Accommodation: Hsitou — lodges within the Recreation Area.

The rarest endemic, Mikado Pheasant*, as well as Swinhoe's Pheasant*, occur in the remote mountain areas of **Yushan NP** (1055 sq km). Permits are required to visit the restricted areas within this park and they may be obtained via mountaineering organisations such as the ROC Alpine Association, 10th Floor, 185 Chungshan N Road, Section 2, Taipei.

Tseng Wen Chi, an estuary in Tainan county, southwest Taiwan, supports the world's largest wintering flock of Black-faced Spoonbills* (206 in winter 1993–94). The birds can usually be found on the north and south sides of the river, west of Highway 17, although this site remains under threat from a proposed industrial park. Black-faced Spoonbill* has also been recorded at the Tatu estuary in west Taiwan and the Lanyang estuary in the northeast. Over 200 species have been recorded in **Kenting NP** (326 sq km) at the southern end of the island, including many waterbirds, most of which winter on Lungluan Lake.

ADDITIONAL INFORMATION

Addresses

The Wild Bird Society of Taiwan, No. 6, Alley 13, Lane 295, Fu-Shin (Chungshan) South Road, Section 1, Taipei, Taiwan ROC (tel: 325 9190, fax: 755 4209), is usually very helpful to visiting birders.

Books and Papers

Finding birds in Taiwan. Brazil M, 1992. *OBC Bulletin* 16: 40–44.
A Field Guide to the Birds of Taiwan (Chinese). Wild Bird Society of Taiwan. 1992. C of P: Taiwan.
A Pictorial Guide to the Birds of Taiwan. Wang J *et al.*, 1991.

ENDEMICS (14)

Taiwan Partridge*	Wushe and Hsitou
Swinhoe's Pheasant*	Wushe
Mikado Pheasant*	Yushan NP
Taiwan Magpie	Yangming Park, near Taipei
Taiwan Whistling-Thrush	Kukuan, Toroko Gorge and Hsitou
Collared Bush-Robin	Wushe
Flamecrest	Wushe
Styan's Bulbul*	Hualien
White-whiskered Laughingthrush	Wushe
Steere's Liocichla	Kukuan, Wushe and Hsitou
Taiwan Barwing	Wushe
White-eared Sibia	Kukuan, Wushe and Hsitou
Taiwan Yuhina	Wushe and Hsitou
Yellow Tit*	Wushe and Hsitou

(The Taiwan races of Island Thrush, White-browed Shortwing, White-browed Bush-Robin and Pygmy Wren-Babbler are all potentially separate species.)

Near-endemics
Chinese Bamboo-Partridge, Saunders' Gull*, Japanese Wood-Pigeon*, Philippine Cuckoo-Dove, Whistling Green-Pigeon*, Ryukyu Scops-Owl (Lanyu Island, off the southeast coast), Japanese Waxwing*, Collared Finchbill, Light-vented Bulbul, Rusty Laughingthrush, Hwamei, Golden Parrotbill, Varied Tit, Japanese Wagtail, Vinaceous Rosefinch, Grey-headed Bullfinch, Yellow Bunting*.

THAILAND

INTRODUCTION

Summary
Many of the first birders to visit Thailand went in search of wintering Siberian species which were rarities in Europe, but most of those who returned from those early sorties ended up telling tales of pittas and broadbills, rather than warblers and buntings. All types of birders, from those who are fascinated by 'little brown jobs' like Lanceolated Warbler to those who live for little more than the sight of a brightly coloured pitta bounding across a gloomy forest floor, enjoy birding in this friendly country, where the tourist infrastructure is second to none.

Size
At 514,000 sq km, Thailand is four times the size of England and a little smaller than Texas.

Getting Around
There is an extensive, fast (some say too fast), frequent and cheap bus network, and, for long distances, a reasonably priced, reliable and comfortable train service, as well as a good domestic air network. However, birders on a tight schedule will spend more time birding if they hire a vehicle. All sites except Doi Chiang Dao where Giant Nuthatch* occurs are accessible in a 2WD.

Accommodation and Food
A wide range of accommodation is available at or near most of the major birding sites and camping is possible in most national parks. Most menus are dominated by fried rice with vegetables, chicken, beef or shrimps, and Singha beer is available everywhere.

Health and Safety
Immunisation against hepatitis, polio, typhoid and yellow fever is recommended, as are precautions against malaria, which is particularly prevalent in the south.

Thailand

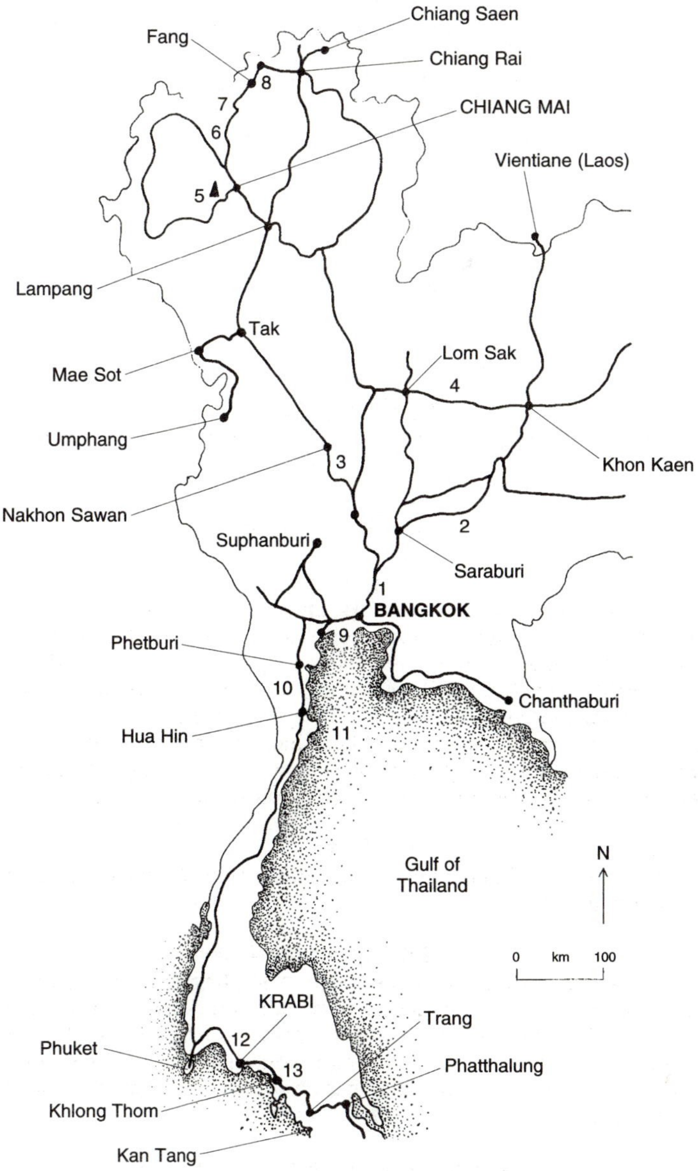

1 Rangsit
2 Khao Yai NP
3 Bung Boraphet
4 Nam Nao NP
5 Doi Inthanon NP
6 Doi Chiang Dao
7 Doi Ang Khang
8 Thaton
9 Samut Sakhon
10 Kaeng Krachan NP
11 Khao Sam Roi Yot NP
12 Krabi
13 Khao Nor Chuchi (Khao Pra Bang Khram Non-hunting Area)

Climate and Timing

The best time to visit central and north Thailand is between November and February, when northern migrants are present and it is not too hot. The best time to visit south Thailand is from April onwards, when Gurney's Pitta is easier to see. In general, the wettest period is usually June to October.

Habitats

The flat and fertile central plains where there are many paddies are surrounded by the Khorat Plateau to the northeast, mountains with remnant montane forests to the north, which rise to 2596 m (8517 ft) at Doi Inthanon, and a multitude of rubber and palm plantations to the south, relieved here and there by remnant lowland forests. There are also extensive areas of mangrove-lined mudflats and a liberal sprinkling of beautiful offshore islands along Thailand's lengthy coastline.

Conservation

Although Thailand has many National Parks and reserves, most still suffer from illegal logging, hunting and agricultural encroachment, so an awful lot more could be done to protect the country's amazing avifauna, which includes a high total of 102 threatened and near-threatened species.

Bird Species

Over 920 species have been recorded in Thailand. Non-endemic specialities and spectacular species include Bar-backed, Chestnut-headed* and Scaly-breasted Partridges, Silver Pheasant, Siamese Fireback*, Hume's Pheasant*, Masked Finfoot*, Nordmann's Greenshank*, Crab and Malaysian* Plovers, Nicobar Pigeon*, Coral-billed Ground-Cuckoo*, four trogons, Brown-winged*, Ruddy and Rufous-collared Kingfishers, Rufous-necked* and Plain-pouched* Hornbills, Black-headed, Bamboo and Heart-spotted Woodpeckers, Eared, Rusty-naped, Blue, Gurney's*, Hooded, Blue-winged and Mangrove* Pittas, six broadbills, Dark-sided and Grey-sided* Thrushes, Vinous-breasted Starling, Siberian Rubythroat, four forktails, Purple* and Green* Cochoas, Giant Nuthatch*, Red-faced Liocichla, Silver-eared Mesia, Chestnut-fronted Shrike-Babbler, Burmese Yuhina*, Black-browed Parrotbill*, Sultan Tit, Pin-tailed Parrotfinch, Gould's Sunbird and Scarlet Finch.

Endemics

Just two species are endemic to Thailand: White-eyed River-Martin*, which, sadly, has not been seen since 1980, and Deignan's Babbler*, which has not been seen for some years and may only be a form of Rufous-fronted Babbler.

Expectations

It is possible to see over 420 species on a month's trip which covers both the north and south, and around 250 species during a shorter trip to the far north.

The best birding site in **Bangkok**, the capital, is Lumpini Park, where Vinous-breasted Starling as well as Indian Roller and Streak-eared Bulbul occur, but beware of birds which have been released by the Thais, who believe setting a cage bird free will please Buddha.

RANGSIT

The marshes and paddies near Rangsit, just north of Bangkok, may not be the most picturesque birding site in Thailand, but they support a good selection of waterbirds and a few wintering passerines from Siberia.

Many of the birds listed below are only present from November to early April.

Others

Little Cormorant, Chinese and Javan Pond-Herons, Yellow and Cinnamon Bitterns, Pied Harrier, Slaty-breasted Rail, Baillon's and Ruddy-breasted Crakes, Watercock, Bronze-winged Jacana, Pintail Snipe, Long-toed Stint, Oriental Pratincole, Black-capped Kingfisher, Green and Blue-tailed Bee-eaters, Indian Roller, Siberian Rubythroat, Chestnut-tailed, White-shouldered, Asian Pied, Black-collared and Vinous-breasted Starlings, Streak-eared Bulbul, Lanceolated and Pallas' Warblers, Black-browed Reed-Warbler, Thick-billed Warbler.

(Other species recorded here include Cotton Pygmy-Goose, Black Bittern, Pheasant-tailed Jacana, Greater Painted-Snipe and Plain-backed Sparrow.)

Turn east off Highway 1, 9 km north of the Don Muang Airport, after crossing a canal, then after 1.5 km turn north in response to the 'SSTI (Siam Synthetic Textile Industries)' sign. At the end of this 1 km track explore the maze of pools and ponds.

Pied Harrier is a winter visitor to the marshes and paddies at Rangsit, near Bangkok

There is a huge heronry at **Ban Lung Chom**, near Suphanburi, about 120 km northwest of Bangkok, where the breeding birds include thousands of Asian Openbills*, and roosting rarities have included Spot-billed Pelican* and Painted Stork*. From Suphanburi head for Ban Thasadet, then Ban Lung Chom, where there is an observation tower.

En route from Bangkok to Khao Yai NP it is possible to see Limestone Wren-Babbler around the monastery at **Wat Tampraprotisat**, which is about 12 km from KM 128 on Highway 2. Try the normally dry river bed below the monastery. Other species recorded here include Green-eared Barbet, Eared and Blue-winged (Apr–Sep) Pittas and Burmese Shrike.

KHAO YAI NATIONAL PARK

The evergreen dipterocarp forest within this park supports an excellent selection of southeast Asian birds, but most of the site's specialities, including Coral-billed Ground-Cuckoo* and Eared and Blue Pittas are shy and elusive birds which take some finding.

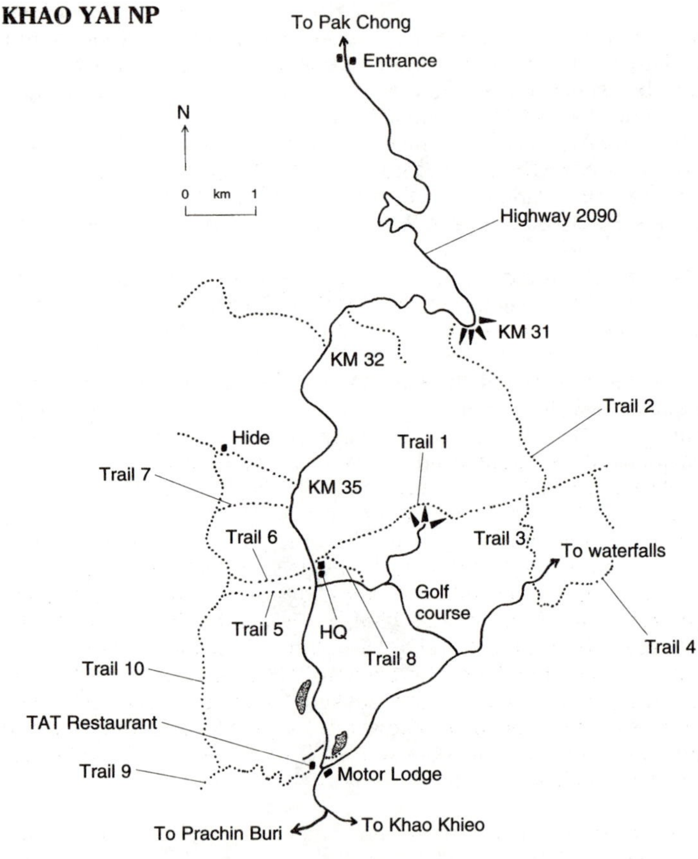

Specialities

Scaly-breasted Partridge, Siamese Fireback*, Coral-billed Ground-Cuckoo*, Green-eared and Moustached Barbets, Eared and Blue Pittas, Silver-breasted Broadbill, Indochinese Cuckoo-Shrike.

Others

Red Junglefowl, Silver Pheasant, Thick-billed Pigeon, Vernal Hanging-Parrot, Red-breasted Parakeet, Green-billed Malkoha, Collared Scops-Owl, Collared, Asian Barred and Spotted Owlets, Brown Hawk-Owl, Great Eared-Nightjar, Jungle Nightjar, Silver-backed and Brown-backed Needletails, Orange-breasted and Red-headed Trogons, Blue-eared and Banded Kingfishers, Blue-bearded and Chestnut-headed Bee-eaters,

Indian Roller, Great, Brown* and Wreathed Hornbills, Blue-eared Barbet, Greater Yellownape, Common and Greater Flamebacks, Black-and-buff, Heart-spotted and Great Slaty Woodpeckers, Blue-winged Pitta (May–Oct), Banded and Long-tailed Broadbills, Green Magpie, Ashy Woodswallow, Great Iora, Rosy Minivet (Nov–Mar), Asian Fairy-bluebird, Blue-winged Leafbird, Large Woodshrike, White-throated Rock-Thrush (Nov–Mar), Chestnut-tailed Starling, Golden-crested Myna, Yellow-rumped Flycatcher (Nov–Mar), Hainan and Hill Blue-Flycatchers, Siberian Blue-Robin (Nov–Mar), White-rumped Shama, Slaty-backed and White-crowned Forktails, Black-crested, Stripe-throated, Puff-throated and Grey-eyed Bulbuls, Rufescent Prinia, Asian Stubtail (Nov–Mar), Thick-billed Warbler (Nov–Mar), Dark-necked Tailorbird, Pale-legged (Nov–Mar) and Blyth's (Nov–Mar) Leaf-Warblers, Sulphur-breasted Warbler (Nov–Mar), White-crested and Black-throated Laughingthrushes, Abbott's and Chestnut-capped Babblers, Large and White-browed Scimitar-Babblers, Sultan Tit, Plain-backed Sparrow, Forest Wagtail (Nov–Mar), Yellow-vented Flowerpecker, Ruby-cheeked and Crimson Sunbirds, Little Spiderhunter.

Other Wildlife

Black giant squirrel, pig-tailed macaque, white-handed gibbon.

(Other species recorded here include Spot-bellied Eagle-Owl* and Pin-tailed Parrotfinch.)

Khao Yai NP is about 200 km northeast of Bangkok (buses from Bangkok serve the HQ). From Bangkok take Highway 1, then turn on to Highway 2 (1 km before Saraburi). At KM 165.5, 5 km before Pak Chong, turn right on to Highway 2090. The park entrance is at KM 23 along this road. Bird between there and the HQ at KM 37, alongside the road between the HQ and the Motor Lodge area at KM 40, and on the trails, especially Trail 1 (Eared Pitta, Silver-breasted Broadbill), Trail 6 (Siamese Fireback*, Coral-billed Ground-Cuckoo*, Red-headed Trogon, Eared and Blue (by stream) Pittas) and Trail 7 (Banded Kingfisher). Coral-billed Ground-Cuckoos* have been seen following wild pigs around. The Motor Lodge area is good for nightbirds and the lake there attracts Silver-backed and Brown-backed Needletails. Beware of leeches.

Accommodation: all accommodation within the park was closed in the early 1990s (but may be re-opened if the outcry from outraged birders has any effect). Pak Chong — Hotel Phuphaya.

The unique White-eyed River-Martin* used to be a winter visitor which associated with roosting Barn Swallows at **Bung Boraphet**, a shallow, freshwater lake which lies a few kilometres southeast of Nakhon Sawan, north of Bangkok. It has not been reliably reported since 1980 and, even though the location of its breeding grounds remains a mystery, this beautiful bird may now be extinct. However, birders who make the pilgrimage to Bung Boraphet should find plenty of waterbirds to enjoy while day-dreaming of the martin sweeping by, including Cotton Pygmy-Goose, Baer's Pochard* (Dec–Mar), Cinnamon Bittern, Pied Harrier (Nov–Mar), Ruddy-breasted and White-browed Crakes, Watercock, Pheasant-tailed and Bronze-winged Jacanas, Pintail Snipe

The elusive Coral-billed Ground-Cuckoo could be the highlight of a trip to Khao Yai*

(Nov–Mar), Oriental Pratincole, Ashy Woodswallow and Striated Grassbird. Birding is best by boat here and these can be hired at the northern and southern shores.

Accommodation: Nakhon Sawan — Vitithep Hotel (B).

Grey Peacock-Pheasant, Green Peafowl* and Rufous-necked Hornbill* occur in the **Huai Kha Khaeng WS** near Bung Boraphet, but this site is difficult to get to, does not always welcome visitors and, perhaps as a result, is threatened by a proposed dam. The research station at Khao Nang Rum is 50 km from Lam Sak (4WD recommended), accessible by road from Uthai Thani. Bird the dry forest around Khao Nang Rum (Blue-bearded Bee-eater, Black-headed Woodpecker, Dusky Broadbill), the nearby Khao Kheo Ridge (Bar-backed and Scaly-breasted Partridges, Grey Peacock-Pheasant, Rufous-necked Hornbill* and Blue Pitta) and the area around the HQ, 16 km back towards Lam Sak. Looking for Green Peafowl* involves a two-day hike. Other species recorded here include Eared and Rusty-naped Pittas, Rosy Minivet, Pygmy Blue-Flycatcher, White-throated Bulbul, Coral-billed Scimitar-Babbler and Rufous-fronted, Spot-necked and White-hooded Babblers, while mammals include dusky leaf-monkey and white-handed gibbon.

NAM NAO NATIONAL PARK

The forest within this park in north-central Thailand supports a similar avifauna to Khao Yai (p. 308), although the exceptions include Bamboo Woodpecker and Pin-tailed Parrotfinch, two species which are associated with extensive areas of bamboo.

Specialities

Bar-backed Partridge, Silver Pheasant, Moustached Barbet, Bamboo Woodpecker, Blue Pitta, Silver-breasted Broadbill, Chestnut-fronted Shrike-Babbler, Pin-tailed Parrotfinch.

Others

Chinese Francolin, Vernal Hanging-Parrot, Grey-headed Parakeet, Green-billed Malkoha, Brown Fish-Owl, Brown Wood-Owl, Orange-

NAM NAO NP

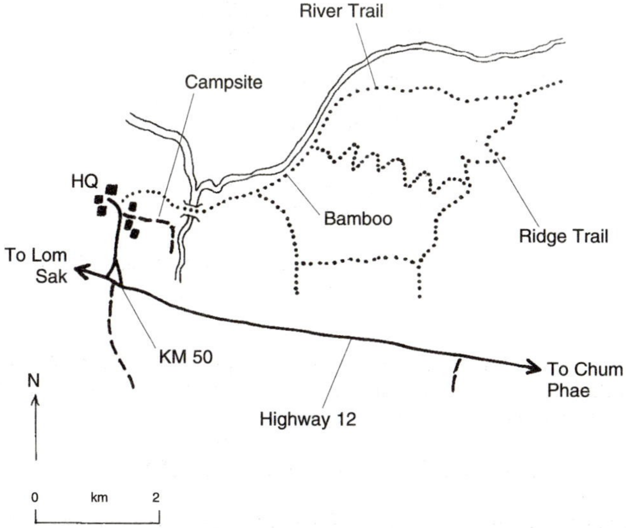

breasted and Red-headed Trogons, Blue-bearded Bee-eater, Great and Blue-throated Barbets, Speckled and White-browed Piculets, Heart-spotted and Great Slaty Woodpeckers, Long-tailed Broadbill, Blue and Green Magpies, Grey Treepie, Great Iora, Slender-billed Oriole, Small Minivet, Asian Fairy-bluebird, Golden-fronted Leafbird, Orange-headed and Scaly Thrushes, Chestnut-tailed Starling, Golden-crested Myna, Yellow-rumped (Nov–Mar) Flycatcher, Hainan and Hill Blue-Flycatchers, Slaty-backed and White-crowned Forktails, Siberian Blue-Robin (Nov–Mar), Chestnut-bellied and Velvet-fronted Nuthatches, Stripe-throated Bulbul, Brown Prinia, Pale-legged Leaf-Warbler (Nov–Mar), Eastern Crowned-Warbler (Nov–Mar), White-crested Laughing-thrush, Red-billed Scimitar-Babbler, Eyebrowed Wren-Babbler, White-hooded Babbler, Brown-cheeked Fulvetta, Sultan Tit.

Other Wildlife

Yellow-throated Marten.

(Other species recorded here include Siamese Fireback*, Coral-billed Ground-Cuckoo*, Rusty-naped Pitta and Indochinese Cuckoo-Shrike.)

The park entrance is 50 km east of Lom Sak on Highway 12. Bird the 2 km road to the HQ, the River Trail (Silver Pheasant, Bamboo Woodpecker), which starts from the picnic ground across the river from the campsite, and the Ridge Trail. It is best to avoid the campsite here, especially at weekends, because many visitors seem to enjoy staying up all night.

Accommodation: chalets (B), which must be booked in advance via the National Parks Division of the Forestry Department, Phanon Yothin Road, Bang Khen, Bangkok 10900, and campsite (C/tents for hire).

The small town of **Umphang**, 163 km south of Mae Sot near the Burmese border, lies close to extensive evergreen and dry dipterocarp forests which support a number of localised species including Olive Bulbul and Burmese Yuhina*, as well as Rufous-throated Partridge, Pin-tailed Pigeon, Brown Hornbill*, Stripe-breasted Woodpecker, White-necked Laughingthrush, Limestone Wren-Babbler and Chestnut-fronted Shrike-Babbler. Bird alongside the 50 km road south out of Umphang and any side tracks and trails.

Accommodation: Guesthouse.

DOI INTHANON NATIONAL PARK

Thailand's highest mountain is one of the best birding sites in the country. Over 380 species have been recorded in the foothill dry deciduous woodland and montane forest, including Black-headed Woodpecker, Rusty-naped Pitta, Dark-sided and Grey-sided* Thrushes and Purple* and Green* Cochoas.

DOI INTHANON NP

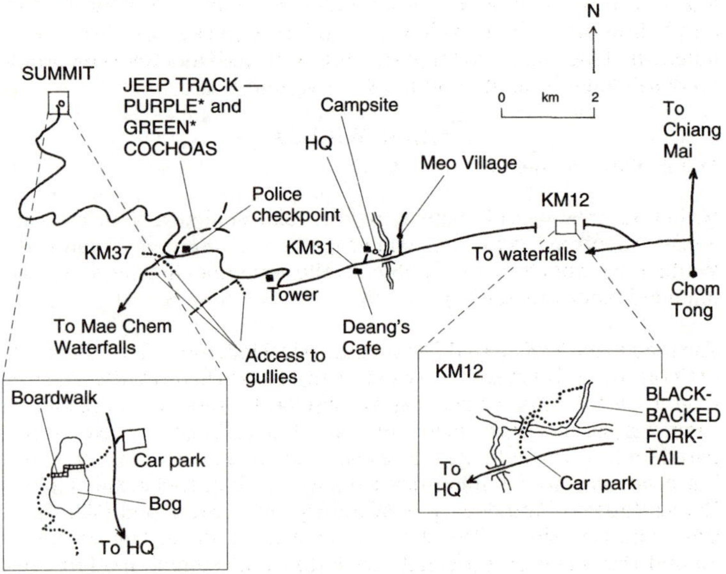

Specialities

Rufous-winged Buzzard*, White-rumped Falcon*, Rufous-throated Partridge, Stripe-breasted and Black-headed Woodpeckers, Rusty-naped Pitta, Indochinese Cuckoo-Shrike, Dark-sided and Grey-sided* (Nov–Mar) Thrushes, Purple* and Green* Cochoas, White-headed Bulbul, White-necked Laughingthrush, Rusty-cheeked Scimitar-Babbler, Chestnut-fronted Shrike-Babbler.

Others

Collared Falconet, Chinese Francolin, Mountain Bamboo-Partridge, Silver Pheasant, Ashy Wood-Pigeon, Pin-tailed Pigeon, Blossom-headed Parakeet, Asian Emerald Cuckoo, Jungle Nightjar, Red-headed Trogon, Blue-bearded Bee-eater, Lineated and Golden-throated Barbets, Speckled and White-browed Piculets, Fulvous-breasted and Bay Woodpeckers, Long-tailed Broadbill, Yellow-bellied Fantail, Blue Magpie, Ashy Woodswallow, Maroon Oriole, Rosy (Nov–Mar), Long-tailed and Short-billed Minivets, Golden-fronted Leafbird, Chestnut-bellied Rock-Thrush, Siberian (Nov–Mar), Scaly and Chestnut (Nov–Mar) Thrushes, Lesser Shortwing, Brown-breasted*, Ferruginous and Slaty-backed Flycatchers, Large, Small, Rufous-bellied and Vivid Niltavas, Daurian (Nov–Mar) and Plumbeous Redstarts, Black-backed, Slaty-backed and White-crowned Forktails, Chestnut-vented and Chestnut-bellied Nuthatches, Brown-throated Treecreeper, Asian Martin, Brown-breasted and Flavescent Bulbuls, Chestnut-flanked White-eye (Nov–Mar), Slaty-bellied Tesia, Yellow-streaked (Nov–Mar), Buff-barred (Nov–Mar) and Ashy-throated Warblers, Blyth's (Nov–Mar) and White-tailed Leaf-Warblers, Grey-cheeked Warbler, White-crested Laughingthrush, Red-billed Scimitar-Babbler, Chestnut-capped Babbler, Silver-eared Mesia, White-browed and Black-eared Shrike-Babblers, Spectacled Barwing, Blue-winged and Chestnut-tailed Minlas, Rufous-winged and Grey-cheeked Fulvettas, Rufous-backed and Black-headed Sibias, Grey-headed and Black-throated Parrotbills, Yellow-cheeked and Yellow-browed Tits, Yellow-bellied Flowerpecker, Gould's, Green-tailed and Black-throated Sunbirds, Streaked Spiderhunter, Dark-breasted Rosefinch, Chestnut Bunting (Nov–Mar).

Other Wildlife

Yellow-throated Marten.

(Other species recorded here include Black-tailed Crake, Burmese Shrike, Sapphire Flycatcher, White-capped Redstart, Pale-footed Bush-Warbler and Spot-throated Babbler, while wintering thrushes have also included Black-breasted*.)

The road to the 2596 m (8517 ft) summit of Doi Inthanon starts 1 km north of Chom Tong, 57 km southwest of Chiang Mai off Highway 108. The best time to visit the *Sphagnum* bog surrounded by rhododendrons at the summit is just after dawn, before the many tourists begin to arrive. Be prepared for a cool start to the day, as far as the temperature is concerned, but a hot start to a birding day because the bog specialities include Rufous-throated Partridge, Ashy Wood-Pigeon, Rusty-naped Pitta, Dark-sided and Grey-sided* Thrushes, Chestnut-tailed Minla, Yellow-browed Tit and Dark-breasted Rosefinch. Back down the summit road the best birding spot is the Jeep Track at KM 37.5, where Purple* and Green* Cochoas occur, along with Grey-sided Thrush*, Slaty-bellied Tesia, Grey-cheeked Warbler and Spectacled Barwing. The gullies to the right of the summit road at KM 37 are more difficult to bird, but they are good for Rusty-naped Pitta and White-necked Laughingthrush. From the road to Mae Chem Waterfalls enter the forest at the first lay-by or Pole No. 4, then scramble down to the streams and use them as trails. Good birding areas lower down include KM 34 (Jungle Nightjar, Black-throated Parrotbill), the HQ area at KM 31, Vachurathon Waterfalls at KM 20.7 (Slaty-backed

Forktail, Plumbeous Redstart) and the stream at KM 12 (Black-backed Forktail — cross the river and walk right). The dry deciduous woodland belt, which is present below KM 28, supports a different avifauna which includes Collared Falconet, White-rumped Falcon* and the lovely Black-headed Woodpecker, all of which have been seen in the KM 10 area. Most birders eat at Mr Deang's Cafe near the HQ, where they discuss tactics after reading the cafe's birding logbook.

Accommodation: HQ — chalets (B), campsite (C/tents for hire). Chiang Mai — Inthanon Highland Resort, Empress Hotel.

The partly forested mountains of **Doi Suthep** and **Doi Pui**, 16–21 km from Chiang Mai on Highway 1004, support similar birds to Doi Inthanon NP, including Rufous-winged Buzzard* and Collared Falconet, as well as Slender-billed Oriole, White-bellied Redstart, Fire-capped Tit and Spot-winged Grosbeak. Bird the track at KM 16, around the temple at Doi Suthep and the trail to Doi Pui summit from the checkpoint at the end of the road.

DOI CHIANG DAO

The remnant pine forests on Doi Chiang Dao, near the Burmese border in north Thailand, are only accessible with a 4WD, but they support two great rarities: Hume's Pheasant* and Giant Nuthatch*. This is also the only known site for the endemic Deignan's Babbler*, but this species, which may be conspecific with Rufous-fronted Babbler, has not been definitely recorded for a number of years.

Specialities

Hume's Pheasant*, Giant Nuthatch*, White-headed Bulbul, Rusty-cheeked Scimitar-Babbler, Scarlet Finch.

Others

Mountain Bamboo-Partridge, Mountain Scops-Owl, Blue-throated Barbet, Bay Woodpecker, Long-tailed Broadbill, Slender-billed Oriole, Long-tailed Minivet, Burmese Shrike, Chestnut-bellied Rock-Thrush, Sapphire Flycatcher, Daurian Redstart (Nov–Mar), Flavescent Bulbul, Chestnut-flanked White-eye (Nov–Mar), Aberrant and Russet Bush-

The world's largest nuthatch occurs at Doi Chiang Dao and Doi Ang Khang in north Thailand

Warblers, White-browed Laughingthrush, Rufous-fronted Babbler, Black-eared and Chestnut-fronted Shrike-Babblers, Grey-headed Parrotbill, Gould's Sunbird, Crested and Chestnut (Nov–Mar) Buntings.

(Other species recorded here include Hodgson's Frogmouth, White-bellied Redstart and Deignan's Babbler*.)

4WDs can be hired in Chiang Mai. Turn off Highway 107 in response to the 'Highland Forestry Development Project' sign 67.5 km north of Chiang Mai, then take the track which doubles back on the right at the KM 20 checkpoint and leads to a substation after 5 km. Park here and bird alongside the track beyond, where Giant Nuthatch* occurs in the stands of pine, usually within the first kilometre.

Accommodation: substation (basic/take food and a tip such as a bottle of whisky). Chiang Dao Resort.

DOI ANG KHANG

The rugged, largely deforested hills of the Doi Ang Khang range near the Burmese border in north Thailand support some localised rarities, including Giant Nuthatch*, Spot-breasted Laughingthrush*, Red-faced Liocichla and Spot-breasted and Black-browed* Parrotbills.

Specialities

Stripe-breasted Woodpecker, Giant Nuthatch*, Crested Finchbill, Buff-throated Warbler (Nov–Mar), Spot-breasted Laughingthrush*, Red-faced Liocichla, Rusty-cheeked Scimitar-Babbler, Spot-breasted and Black-browed* Parrotbills, Scarlet Finch.

Others

Mountain Bamboo-Partridge, Himalayan Swiftlet, Slender-billed Oriole, Burmese Shrike, Siberian Thrush (Nov–Mar), Slaty-backed Flycatcher, Vivid Niltava, Daurian Redstart (Nov–Mar), Brown-breasted and Flavescent Bulbuls, Chestnut-flanked White-eye (Nov–Mar), Hill Prinia, Slaty-bellied Tesia, Yellow-streaked Warbler (Nov–Mar), White-browed Laughingthrush, White-browed Scimitar-Babbler, Rufous-fronted Babbler, Silver-eared Mesia, Spectacled Barwing, Striated Yuhina, Grey-headed Parrotbill, Gould's Sunbird, Crested and Chestnut (Nov–Mar) Buntings.

(Other species recorded here include Hume's Pheasant*, Rusty-naped Pitta, Indochinese Cuckoo-Shrike, White-bellied Redstart, Cutia and Black-headed Greenfinch.)

About 15 km southwest of Fang, on the Chiang Mai–Thaton road (Route 107), turn west at KM 137 on to a very steep road. After about 19 km, before the checkpoint, turn south on to the road which leads to a forested ridge on the left-hand side where Giant Nuthatch* occurs. This splendid bird also occurs on the forested ridges to the south, accessible via a track. Continue along this road, or the one through the checkpoint, to reach the village of Ban Khoom, 6 km above the checkpoint.

DOI ANG KHANG

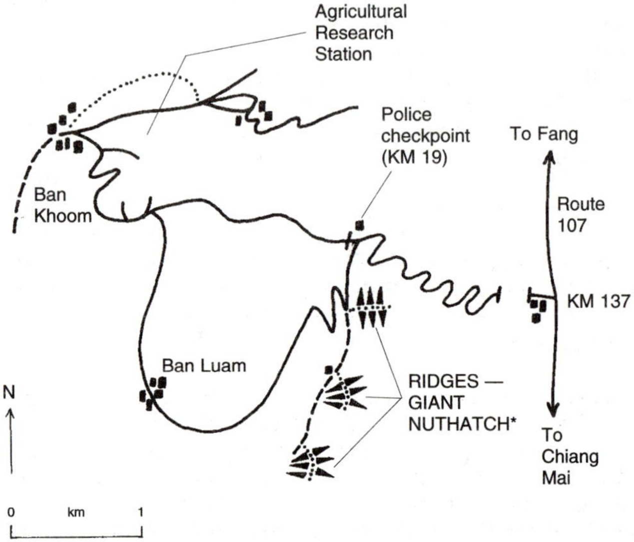

Most of the other species listed above occur around Ban Khoom, especially around the Agricultural Research Station and alongside the road just below the village.

Accommodation: Ban Khoom — huts (C/very basic). Fang — Choki Thani Hotel (B). Chiang Dao Resort.

Jerdon's Bushchat* is a winter visitor in small numbers to the grasslands alongside the Mae Kok River at **Thaton**, 170 km north of Chiang Mai. This rare chat has been seen in recent years along the north side of the river to the east of Thaton. Other wintering species recorded here, in the paddies to the southeast of Thaton, include Pied Harrier, Blue-breasted Quail, Yellow-legged Buttonquail, Greater Painted-Snipe, Pintail Snipe, Oriental Pratincole, Grey-headed Lapwing*, Siberian Rubythroat, Spotted Bush-Warbler, Lanceolated, Pallas' and Blunt-winged Warblers and Chestnut-eared Bunting.

Accommodation: Mae Kok River Lodge, Thaton House Hotel, Thip's Travellers Lodge (C).

Long-billed Plover* and Jerdon's Bushchat* winter along the Mekong River at **Chiang Saen** on the Laos border, and Baer's Pochard* occurs on the lake 7 km south of the town.

Accommodation: Chaing Saen Guesthouse (C).

In southeast Thailand, Malayan Night-Heron, Coral-billed Ground-Cuckoo*, Eared, Blue and Blue-winged (Apr–Sep) Pittas, and Short-tailed Magpie* occur in the dense secondary forest at **Khao Ang Ru**

Nai. This wildlife sanctuary, which is not officially open to the public, is about 14 km south of Bang Nong Khok, accessible from Bangkok via Chachengsao, Phanom Sarakham and Sanam Chai Khat. There is no trail, only a 12 km track to a waterfall, but this is excellent for birding and other species recorded here include Siamese Fireback*, Violet Cuckoo, Banded Kingfisher, Heart-spotted Woodpecker, Great Iora, Vinous-breasted Starling and Golden-crested Myna, plus the localised pileated gibbon.

Accommodation: chalet (basic/take food).

Also in southeast Thailand, Chestnut-headed Partridge* occurs around Khao Sabap in **Namtok Phliu NP**, and, along with Eared Pitta and Silver Oriole* (Nov–Mar), in **Khao Soi Dao WS**, which is 62.5 km north of Chanthaburi.

The marshes, mangroves, mud flats, shrimp ponds and salt-pans on the edge of the Gulf of Thailand at **Samut Sakhon**, 50 km south of Bangkok, support masses of wintering and passage shorebirds, including Grey-tailed Tattler (Apr–May), Asian Dowitcher* (Apr–May), Great Knot (Apr–May), Rufous-necked and Long-toed Stints, as well as Pink-necked Pigeon, Golden-bellied Gerygone and Plain-throated Sunbird. To reach here head southwest out of Bangkok on Route 35, then turn east at the KM 50 stone to Langan village, 2 km away, on the shore. Scan the mud flats from the pier here, or walk north and explore.

KAENG KRACHAN NATIONAL PARK

This park near the Burmese border, southwest of Bangkok, is the biggest in Thailand (3083 sq km). The main habitat is evergreen forest and this supports a mixture of birds at the southern end of their Burmese and northern Thailand ranges, and birds at the northern end of their peninsular Thailand and Malayan ranges. Over 310 species have been recorded and over 200 species are possible in five days, including Yellow-vented Pigeon*, the rarely reported Plain-pouched Hornbill*, five species of broadbill, an isolated population of Ratchet-tailed Treepie and Olive Bulbul.

Specialities

Bar-backed and Scaly-breasted Partridges, Yellow-vented Pigeon*, Plain-pouched Hornbill*, Moustached Barbet, Streak-breasted, Laced and Bamboo Woodpeckers, Dusky and Silver-breasted Broadbills, Ratchet-tailed Treepie, Chestnut-naped Forktail, Olive Bulbul.

Others

Cotton Pygmy-Goose, Black Baza, Collared and Black-thighed Falconets, Oriental Hobby, Red Junglefowl, Grey Peacock-Pheasant, Thick-billed and Pin-tailed Pigeons, Vernal Hanging-Parrot, Chestnut-winged Cuckoo, Green-billed and Chestnut-breasted Malkohas, Brown Fish-Owl, Collared Owlet, Great Eared-Nightjar, Orange-breasted and Red-headed Trogons, Red-bearded, Blue-bearded and Chestnut-headed Bee-eaters, Great, Brown* and Wreathed Hornbills, Blue-throated

Barbet, Olive-backed, Bay, Black-and-buff and Heart-spotted Woodpeckers, Blue-winged Pitta (May–Oct), Banded, Black-and-yellow and Long-tailed Broadbills, Crested Jay, Green Magpie, Great Iora, Greater Green Leafbird, Maroon-breasted Philentoma, Golden-crested Myna, Rufous-browed and White-tailed Flycatchers, Stripe-throated, Flavescent, Puff-throated, Ochraceous and Buff-vented Bulbuls, Rufescent Prinia, Sulphur-breasted Warbler (Nov–Mar), White-crested Laughingthrush, Buff-breasted and Puff-throated Babblers, White-browed and Coral-billed Scimitar-Babblers, Black-eared Shrike-Babbler, White-hooded Babbler, Sultan Tit.

Other Wildlife

Asian elephant, black giant squirrel, dusky leaf-monkey, leopard, tiger, white-handed gibbon, yellow-throated marten.

(Other species recorded here include Ferruginous Partridge, White-bellied Pigeon*, Eared, Rusty-naped and Blue Pittas, Silver Oriole* and Green Cochoa*.)

At Tha Yung, 20 km south of Phetburi (Phetchaburi), a town 160 km southwest of Bangkok, turn off Highway 4 on to the 30 km road to the HQ at Khao Phanoen Tung (turn left just before Kaeng Krachan village, below the dam). It is best to arrive at the HQ between 0900 and 1600 to find the park staff who will arrange accommodation and permits. From the HQ bird the 36 km track into the hills (park vehicles are available for hire), especially KMS 15–18 (Scaly-breasted Partridge, Blue Pitta, Silver Oriole*), KMS 24–25 (ground-dwelling species along the trails), KMS 27–28 (Bar-backed Partridge, Yellow-vented Pigeon*, Plain-pouched Hornbill*, Olive-backed Woodpecker, Ratchet-tailed Treepie), KM 32 (Ratchet-tailed Treepie, Silver Oriole*, White-hooded Babbler) and KM 36 (hornbills). Ferruginous Partridge has been recorded along the steep trail to Tho Thip Waterfall (2.5 hours away), which leads down from the end of the road. Beware of tigers.

Accommodation: chalets (B, basic), campsite (tents for hire).

The blue-billed, pink-breasted Black-and-yellow Broadbill is one of Asia's most amazing avian attractions

KHAO SAM ROI YOT NATIONAL PARK

In this park, forested limestone crags rise from the coastal mangroves and mud flats, which support a fine selection of shorebirds including Nordmann's Greenshank* and Malaysian Plover*, and tower above a maze of marshes, pools and paddies where a fine selection of marshbirds can be found.

KHAO SAM ROI YOT NP

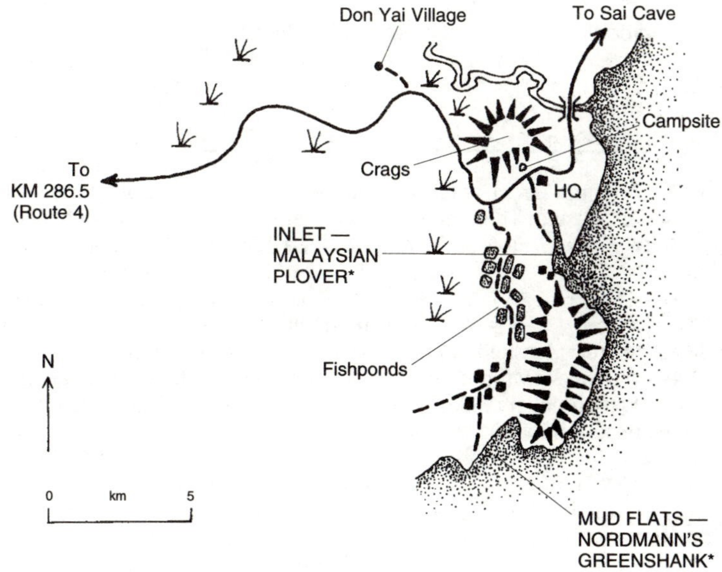

Specialities

Nordmann's Greenshank* (Oct–Apr), Malaysian Plover*, Vinous-breasted Starling.

Others

Pacific Reef-Egret, Yellow and Cinnamon Bitterns, Pied Harrier (Nov–Mar), Blue-breasted Quail, Red Junglefowl, Slaty-breasted Rail, Baillon's, Ruddy-breasted and White-browed Crakes, Pheasant-tailed and Bronze-winged Jacanas, Greater Painted-Snipe, Great Knot (Oct–Apr), Rufous-necked (Oct–Apr) and Long-toed (Oct–Apr) Stints, Oriental Pratincole (Oct–Apr), Great Crested-Tern, Indian Nightjar, Green and Blue-tailed Bee-eaters, Golden-bellied Gerygone, Racket-tailed Treepie, Golden-crested Myna, Tickell's Blue-Flycatcher, Red-eyed Bulbul, Lanceolated (Nov–Mar) and Pallas' (Nov–Mar) Warblers, Black-browed Reed-Warbler (Nov–Mar), White-crested Laughingthrush, Rufous-winged Bushlark, Plain-backed Sparrow, Forest Wagtail (Nov–Mar), Streaked and Baya Weavers, Yellow-breasted Bunting (Nov–Mar).

Other Wildlife

Crab-eating macaque, slow loris.

(Other species recorded here include Far Eastern Curlew* (Oct–Apr), Spoonbill Sandpiper* (Oct–Apr) and Black-naped Tern.)

To reach this park from Bangkok by road head south on Highway 4, through Hua Hin, to KM 286.5, 6.5 km north of Kui Buri, and turn east to the HQ, 15 km away. Malaysian Plover* occurs at the inlet southeast of the HQ and on the mud flats and beach some 10 km south of the HQ. Golden-crested Myna, Tickell's Blue-Flycatcher and White-crested Laughingthrush occur on the hills just north of the HQ. Beware of the heat.

Accommodation: chalets (C), campsite (C/tents for hire).

KRABI

The maze of mangroves below the limestone crags at Krabi on the west coast of peninsular Thailand support a number of mangrove specialists, not least Masked Finfoot*, Brown-winged Kingfisher* and Mangrove Pitta*.

Specialities

Chinese Egret*, Masked Finfoot* (Jan–Sep), Nordmann's Greenshank* (Oct–Apr), Brown-winged* and Ruddy Kingfishers, Streak-breasted and Laced Woodpeckers, Mangrove Pitta*, Mangrove Blue-Flycatcher, White-chested Babbler*.

KRABI

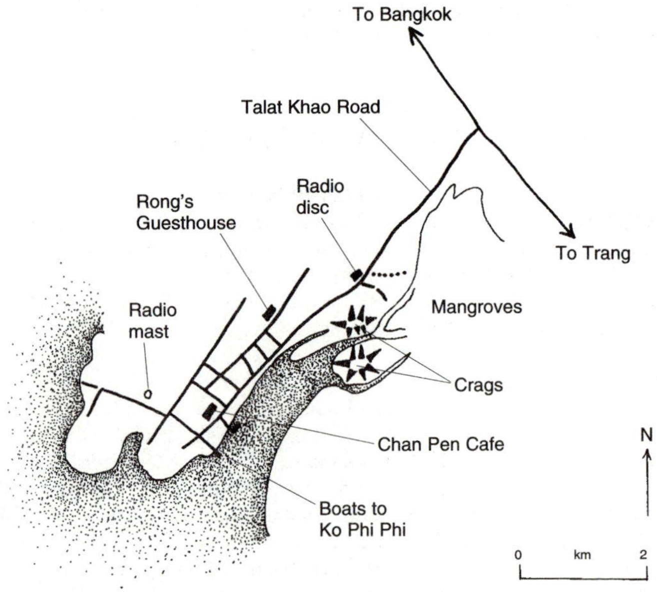

Others

Little Cormorant, Pacific Reef-Egret, Javan Pond-Heron, Brahminy Kite, Oriental Hobby, Slaty-breasted Rail, Great Knot (Oct–Apr), Great Crested-Tern, Pink-necked Pigeon, Banded Bay Cuckoo, Chestnut-bellied Malkoha, Spotted Wood-Owl, Great Eared-Nightjar, Grey-rumped Treeswift, Black-capped and Collared Kingfishers, Blue-throated Bee-eater, White-bellied, Maroon and Great Slaty Woodpeckers, Golden-bellied Gerygone, Mangrove Whistler, Asian Glossy Starling, Pacific Swallow, Olive-winged Bulbul, Ashy Tailorbird, Plain-backed Sparrow, Scarlet-backed Flowerpecker, Plain and Copper-throated Sunbirds.

Other Wildlife

Crab-eating macaque, dusky langur, small-clawed and smooth otters.

(Other species recorded here include Cinnamon and Black Bitterns, Asian Dowitcher* (Oct–Apr), Malaysian Plover*, Brown Fish-Owl, Black-and-red Broadbill and Forest Wagtail (Nov–Mar).)

Krabi, in south Thailand, is accessible by road from Bangkok (12 hours) or Phuket, which is connected to Bangkok by air. The best way to see mangrove specialities (Masked Finfoot* became very elusive in the mid-1990s) and shorebirds is to take a boat trip into the mangroves and out to mud flats and sand bars with Mr Dai, and these can be arranged at Mrs Lee's Chan Pen Cafe on the riverfront where most birders eat breakfast. Boats trips to the Ko Phi Phi Islands can also be arranged here. Without a boat it is possible to bird the mangrove edge around the town via the track east 2 km north of town, the trail opposite the radio-disc, just to the north of there, and via the track west of the radio mast, south-west of town. Malaysian Plover* has been recorded on Ao Nang Beach, in the early morning before the many sunseekers arrive.

Accommodation: River Site Hotel, just outside town, where it is much quieter at night.

At Mrs Lee's Chan Pen Cafe in Krabi it is possible to arrange boat trips (2 hours) to the **Ko Phi Phi Islands**, where Lesser and Christmas Island* Frigatebirds, Black-naped Tern, Nicobar Pigeon* and Plain-throated Sunbird occur, and the snorkelling and scuba-diving is spectacular. The pigeons occur underneath the fruit bat colony on the steep slope at the northern end of Ko Ma Island, accessible via an expensive

*Krabi is one of the most accessible sites in Asia for Masked Finfoot**

boat trip from the main island, Phi Phi Don, but these bizarre birds are much easier to see in Mu Ko Similan National Park, discussed below. The frigatebirds can be tricky, but they gather in the channel between Phi Phi Ley and Ko Bida Noy in the late afternoon, before roosting on Ko Bida Noy. Spring migrants (late March) on the Ko Phi Phi Islands have included Malayan Night-Heron, Red-legged Crake, Hooded and Blue-winged Pittas, Crow-billed Drongo, Orange-headed Thrush and Daurian Starling. There is plenty of accommodation on Phi Phi Don. Another island accessible by boat from Krabi is **Sa Pra Nang**, where Buffy Fish-Owls roost on the cliffs surrounding the tidal lagoon, visible after a short, steep, uphill walk from the resort area.

Although nowhere near as good as it used to be, the small strip of lowland forest known as **Ban Bai Chong**, alongside the road to Ao Luk, 15 km from Krabi, still supports some essentially Malayan species such as Moustached Hawk-Cuckoo, Black-bellied and Chestnut-breasted Malkohas, Whiskered Treeswift, Black-and-yellow Broadbill, Dark-throated Oriole, Fiery Minivet, Olive-winged Bulbul and Thick-billed and Spectacled Spiderhunters, while scarcer species include Banded and Hooded (Mar–May) Pittas.

One of the best sites in Asia for Nicobar Pigeon* is Island Number 4, a popular snorkelling and scuba-diving site in **Mu Ko Similan National Park**, 2.5 hours by fast boat west of Phuket, and also accessible from Thap Lamu, closer to Krabi. The pigeons can be seen foraging for scraps at the open restaurant or around the campsite, and other species which occur here include White-bellied Sea-Eagle, Pied Imperial-Pigeon and Bridled Tern.

KHAO NOR CHUCHI (KHAO PRA BANG KHRAM NON-HUNTING AREA)

The lowland forest in this immensely important reserve supports the only known viable population of Gurney's Pittas* (24–34 pairs), an extremely rare bird which is close to extinction because of the almost total obliteration of peninsular Thailand's lowland forests. Most birds are very thin on the ground here, and only a handful of species are likely to be seen during a few hours, but during a prolonged stay it is possible to see more than one species of beautiful pitta and a fine selection of mainly Malayan species, including Rufous-collared Kingfisher and Malaysian Honeyguide*.

Specialities

Rufous-collared Kingfisher, Red-crowned Barbet*, Malaysian Honeyguide*, Streak-breasted and Bamboo Woodpeckers, Gurney's Pitta*, Dusky Broadbill, Striped and Large* Wren-Babblers.

Others

Wallace's Hawk-Eagle*, Black-thighed Falconet, Violet and Drongo Cuckoos, Black-bellied, Raffles', Red-billed and Chestnut-breasted Malkohas, Spotted Wood-Owl, Great Eared-Nightjar, Whiskered

Treeswift, Silver-rumped Needletail, Diard's, Scarlet-rumped and Orange-breasted Trogons, Banded Kingfisher, Red-bearded and Blue-throated Bee-eaters, Black* and Bushy-crested Hornbills, Gold-whiskered, Red-throated, Yellow-crowned and Brown Barbets, Rufous Piculet, Checker-throated, Maroon, Orange-backed, Buff-rumped, Black-and-buff and Grey-and-buff Woodpeckers, Banded, Hooded (May–Oct) and Blue-winged (May–Oct) Pittas, Banded, Black-and-yellow and Green Broadbills, Crow-billed Drongo, Crested Jay, Black Magpie*, Green and Great Ioras, Dark-throated Oriole, Greater Green and Lesser Green Leafbirds, Tiger Shrike (Nov–Mar), Rufous-winged and Maroon-breasted Philentomas, Orange-headed Thrush, Fulvous-chested Jungle-Flycatcher, Yellow-rumped Flycatcher (Nov–Mar), Scaly-breasted, Grey-bellied, Puff-backed, Olive-winged, Cream-vented, Red-eyed, Spectacled, Grey-cheeked, Yellow-bellied, Hairy-backed and Buff-vented Bulbuls, Rufous-tailed Tailorbird, Ferruginous*, Short-tailed, Black-capped, Moustached, Scaly-crowned and Rufous-crowned Babblers, White-browed Scimitar-Babbler, Chestnut-rumped and Chestnut-winged Babblers, Sultan Tit, White-bellied and White-headed Munias, Yellow-breasted and Crimson-breasted Flowerpeckers, Plain, Red-throated, Ruby-cheeked and Purple-throated Sunbirds, Thick-billed, Spectacled, Yellow-eared and Grey-breasted Spiderhunters.

(Other species recorded here include Crested Partridge, Crested Fireback*, Red-legged Crake, Jambu Fruit-Dove, Brown Wood-Owl, Gould's Frogmouth, White-crowned Hornbill, Giant Pitta*, Malaysian Rail-babbler, Chestnut-capped Thrush, Chestnut-naped Forktail, Black-and-white Bulbul, Spot-necked Babbler, Pin-tailed Parrotfinch and Scarlet-breasted Flower-pecker.)

Turn left off Highway 4 at the Esso garage just before Khlong Thom (Chlong Thong), 40 km south of Krabi. From here it is 18 km to Ban Bang Tieo and a further 2 km to the HQ. Previously productive spots for Gurney's Pitta* include the Pole Bridge area (trails B and C) and the more open tracks along the forest edge. This species is most active and vocal in April and May. There is a beautiful natural pool near the HQ where it is possible to cool off in between bouts of birding.

Accommodation: Ban Bang Tieo — bamboo huts (C/basic/including food).

The rare and beautiful Gurney's Pitta is one of Thailand's star birds*

Nordmann's Greenshank* (Oct–Apr) and Crab Plover roost on Hat Tub, an islet off **Ko Libong Island**, which is accessible by boat (90 minutes) from Kan Tang, near Trang. Other species recorded here include Chinese Egret* (Oct–Apr), Far Eastern Curlew* (Oct–Apr), Great Knot (Oct–Apr), Great Thick-knee, Malaysian Plover*, Buffy Fish-Owl and Mangrove Pitta*.

ADDITIONAL INFORMATION

Books and Papers

A Guide to the Birds of Thailand. Lekagul B and Round P, 1991. C of P: Thailand.

ENDEMICS (2)

White-eyed River-Martin*	Central: Bung Boraphet — there has been no record since 1980 of this former winter visitor (Nov–Feb) and this species may now be extinct
Deignan's Babbler*	North: Doi Chiang Dao — there has been no record for some years of this species, which may be conspecific with Rufous-fronted Babbler

Near-endemics

Storm's Stork*, Chestnut-headed Partridge*, Siamese Fireback*, Hume's Pheasant*, Malayan Peacock-Pheasant*, Yellow-vented Pigeon*, Coral-billed Ground-Cuckoo, White-fronted Scops-Owl*, Indochinese and Germain's Swiftlets, Plain-pouched Hornbill*, Streak-breasted and Bamboo Woodpeckers, Blue-rumped* and Gurney's* Pittas, Ratchet-tailed Treepie, Silver Oriole*, Fujian Niltava*, Chestnut-vented and Giant* Nuthatches, Olive and White-headed Bulbuls, Large Wren-Babbler*, Mountain Fulvetta, Burmese Yuhina*, Short-tailed Parrotbill*.

TURKESTAN

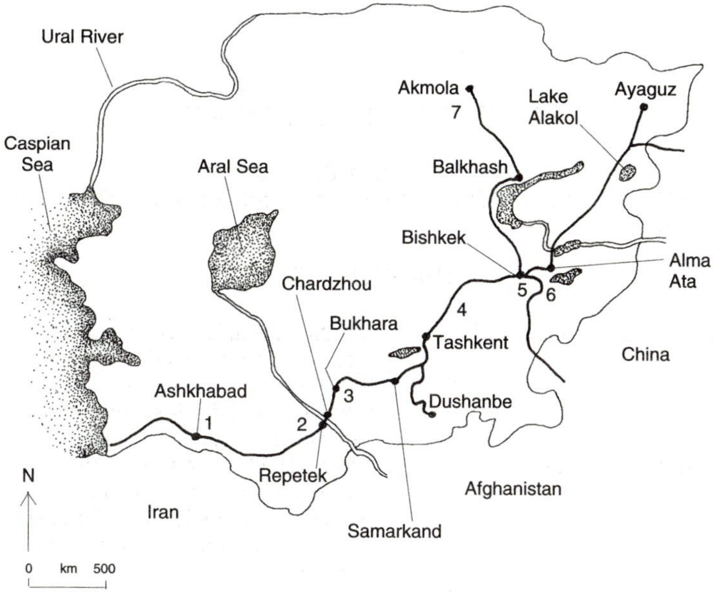

1 Ashkhabad
2 Chardzhou
3 Bukhara
4 Aksu Dzahbagly NR
5 Ala Archa Gorge
6 Alma Ata
7 Akmola

INTRODUCTION

Turkestan is the name used to cover the more or less independent states of Kazakhstan, Turkmenistan, Uzbekistan, Kirghizia and Tajikistan, which lie in central Asia, between the Caspian Sea and China. This huge area of desert, steppe, lakes and mountains supports a superb mixture of central Asian endemics, eastern Mediterranean species and Himalayan specialities at the western edge of their range, as well as an endemic ground-jay.

To get the best out of a trip to Turkestan a vehicle, preferably 4WD, is more or less essential. It is obligatory to stay in the basic tourist hotels in the towns and cities, most of which are on the flight network. The local cuisine is lightly spiced and can be washed down with local wine and vodka. Immunisation against hepatitis, polio and typhoid is recommended. The best time to visit Turkestan, which basically has hot summers and cold winters, is between May and September. Habitats range from desert and steppe through riverine woodlands and wetlands to lakes and mountains complete with spruce forests, juniper stands and alpine meadows. Twenty-three threatened and near-threatened species occur in Turkestan and around 500 species have been recorded in total. Non-endemic specialities and spectacular species include Himalayan Snowcock, Demoiselle Crane, Ibisbill, Sociable Lapwing*, Great Black-headed and Relict* Gulls, Pallas' Sandgrouse, Pale-backed Pigeon*, White-winged Woodpecker*, White-tailed Rubythroat, White-throated Robin, Rufous-backed and White-winged Redstarts, Sykes' and Upcher's Warblers, White-browed Tit-Warbler, Menetries' Warbler, Persian Nuthatch, Black-breasted, Turkestan, Azure and Yellow-breasted Tits, White-crowned Penduline-Tit, White-winged and Black Larks, Saxaul and Desert Sparrows, Black-throated Accentor, Crimson-winged and Desert Finches, and Red-mantled and Red-fronted Rosefinches. One species is endemic: Turkestan Ground-Jay. It is possible to see over 300 species, including most of those listed above, on an extensive three-week trip.

ASHKHABAD

The capital of Turkmenistan is situated at the southern edge of the Karakum Desert near the foothills of the rugged Kopet Dag mountain range. Beyond the irrigated farmland around the city lies arid, open desert, rocky gorges and wooded wadis, where the specialities include Turkestan Tit.

Many of the species listed below are only present during the summer (May–Sep).

Specialities

White-winged Woodpecker*, Persian Nuthatch, Sykes' Warbler, Turkestan Tit.

Others

Eurasian Griffon, Cinereous Vulture*, Long-legged Buzzard, See-see Partridge, Chukar, European Bee-eater, Rosy Starling, Finsch's, Variable and Isabelline Wheatears, Moustached and Paddyfield Warblers, Blyth's and Clamorous Reed-Warblers, Upcher's Warbler, Small Whitethroat, Desert and Menetries' Warblers, Desert and Bimaculated Larks, Rock Petronia, Pale Rockfinch, Trumpeter and Desert Finches, Grey-hooded and Red-headed Buntings.

Bird the riverine woodlands (White-winged Woodpecker*, Turkestan Tit), farmland and scrub around the city, and the Kopet Dag foothills, one hour away by road.

CHARDZHOU

This city in east Turkmenistan is situated on the banks of the Amu Darya (Oxus) River, which provides water for an irrigated strip of land which extends far into the surrounding desert. The *Saxaul* scrub and sand dunes in the Karakum Desert, to the south, support the endemic Turkestan Ground-Jay, as well as White-crowned Penduline-Tit and Saxaul and Desert Sparrows.

Turkestan Endemics

Turkestan Ground-Jay.

Specialities

White-winged Woodpecker*, White-crowned Penduline-Tit, Saxaul and Desert Sparrows.

Others

White-tailed Lapwing, Blue-cheeked Bee-eater (May–Sep), Brown-necked Raven, Long-tailed Shrike, Rufous-tailed Scrub-Robin (May–Sep), Streaked Scrub-Warbler, Upcher's (May–Sep) and Desert (May–Sep) Warblers, Spanish Sparrow, Desert Finch.

(Other species recorded here include Hypocolius.)

Most of the goodies occur in the **Repetek Reserve**, one hour by road to the south of Chardzhou.

See-see Partridge, Streaked Laughingthrush, Yellow-breasted Tit, White-winged Grosbeak and Chestnut-breasted Bunting occur in the **Kugitang NR**, which is situated in the mountains along the southern borders of Turkmenistan and Uzbekistan and is renowned for its flora.

Turkestan Ground-Jay is one of five species of ground-jay which are unique to Asia

BUKHARA

This town in Uzbekistan is situated in a large oasis in the Kyzylkum Desert and during spring even the gardens of the town attract migrants. However, the best birding areas are at the edge of the irrigated farmland, where there are ponds and reedbeds which support a good selection of waterbirds, including White-tailed Lapwing.

Many of the species listed below are only present in spring and summer (May–Sep).

Others

Pygmy Cormorant*, Ruddy Shelduck, Marbled Teal*, Greater Flamingo, White-tailed Lapwing, Slender-billed Gull, Long-tailed Shrike, Clamorous Reed-Warbler, Savi's and Paddyfield Warblers.

Bukhara is 2 hours by road north of Chardzhou. The best wetlands, which include fishponds, lie to the south and east of the town.

Beyond the cotton fields and orchards which surround **Samarkand**, an ancient 'Silk Road' city in Uzbekistan, east of Bukhara, the wooded valleys at the base of the Tien Shan mountain range, one hour by road south of the city, support Yellow-breasted Tit, as well as summer visitors such as Lesser Kestrel*, Asian Paradise-Flycatcher, White-throated Robin, Orphean Warbler and Chestnut-breasted Bunting. Similar species may be found around Chimgan ski resort near **Tashkent** to the northeast. To the southeast, White-capped Redstart, Little Forktail, Western Crowned-Warbler and Streaked Laughingthrush, four basically Himalayan species, occur around **Dushanbe**, the capital of Tajikistan, which is situated on the banks of the Varzob River.

AKSU DZHABAGLY NATURE RESERVE

This reserve (744 sq km) in the western Tien Shan mountain range is at its best during the summer, but the nearby Chokpak Pass, a major migrant flyway, is most exciting during late August–early September. Nearly 240 species have been recorded here, including Himalayan Snowcock and Crimson-winged Finch.

Many of the birds listed below are only present during the summer and early autumn (May–Sep).

Specialities

Himalayan Snowcock, Persian Nuthatch, Black-breasted and Yellow-breasted Tits, Crimson-winged Finch, Red-mantled Rosefinch.

Others

Great White and Dalmatian* Pelicans, Lammergeier, Cinereous Vulture*, Pallid Harrier*, Chukar, White-tailed Lapwing, Yellow-legged and Slender-billed Gulls, Oriental Turtle-Dove, Blue-cheeked Bee-eater, Asian Paradise-Flycatcher, Long-tailed Shrike, Brown Dipper, Blue Whistling-Thrush, Rosy Starling, White-throated Robin, Pied, Desert and Isabelline Wheatears, Wallcreeper, Paddyfield Warbler, Blyth's and Clamorous Reed-Warblers, Upcher's Warbler, Hume's Whitethroat, Bimaculated and Lesser Short-toed Larks, Oriental Skylark, Himalayan and Brown Accentors, Fire-fronted Serin, White-winged Grosbeak, Grey-hooded, Chestnut-breasted and Red-headed Buntings.

Other Wildlife

Arhkar (Marco Polo sheep), brown bear, ibex, red marmot.

(Other species recorded here include Demoiselle Crane, Asian Dowitcher*, Black-winged Pratincole*, Sociable Lapwing*, Pale-backed Pigeon*, White-winged Woodpecker*, Turkestan Tit and Hume's Lark.)

Dzhabagly village, the access point for the reserve, is situated in the Tien Shan foothills at 2200 m (7218 ft), 3–4 hours by road from Tashkent and about 80 km east of Chimkent. In the reserve, bird Mount

Kaskabulak, the Kshi Kaindy cascades, the Kshi Kaindy Pass, the dramatic Aksu Canyon, the juniper stands at Chuuldak and the Darbaza Gates on the Baldabrek River. Reserve vehicles are available for hire to explore these areas fully. Species seemingly confined to the Karatau Mountain slopes to the east of the reserve are Asian Paradise-Flycatcher, White-throated Robin and Upcher's Warbler. To the east of the Karatau Mountains there are many lakes among the steppe where Asian Dowitcher* has been recorded, while White-tailed Lapwing occurs at Lake Chuskakol in the steppe to the west. Autumn migrants at the nearby **Chokpak Pass**, where there is an ringing station in the autumn, include large numbers of Pallid Harrier*, Lesser Kestrel*, European Bee-eater and Grey-hooded and Red-headed Buntings, while Pale-backed Pigeon* occasionally appears.

Accommodation: Dzhabagly — hotel. It may also be possible to stay in the research houses and tents at 1981 m (6500 ft) where Red-mantled Rosefinches and White-winged Grosbeaks are 'garden birds'.

ALA ARCHA GORGE

The lowland broadleaf forests, high coniferous forests, juniper stands and alpine meadows in and around this magnificent gorge near Bishkek in the snow-capped Tien Shan support a superb range of birds, including Rufous-backed and White-winged Redstarts, White-browed Tit-Warbler and White-winged Grosbeak.

Most of the birds listed below are only present during the summer months (May–Sep).

Specialities

Himalayan Snowcock, Boreal Owl, Rufous-backed and White-winged Redstarts, White-browed Tit-Warbler, Sulphur-bellied Warbler, Black-breasted, Turkestan and Yellow-breasted Tits, Black-throated Accentor, Red-mantled Rosefinch.

Others

Lammergeier, Himalayan Griffon, Cinereous Vulture*, Lesser Kestrel*, Common Pheasant, Oriental Turtle-Dove, Long-tailed Shrike, Brown Dipper, Blue Whistling-Thrush, Rosy Starling, White-tailed Rubythroat, Blue-capped Redstart, Wallcreeper, Blyth's Reed-Warbler, Himalayan and Brown Accentors, Fire-fronted Serin, Plain Mountain-Finch, Desert Finch, White-winged Grosbeak.

Other Wildlife

Ibex.

Ala Archa Gorge is 40 km from Bishkek. There are some excellent trails here which pass through the full range of habitats up to 3000 m (9843 ft). Boreal Owl breeds in nest boxes at the valley bottom, but most of the other special birds here, including White-browed Tit-Warbler, are only found at higher altitudes, especially in the juniper stands.

Accommodation: Bishkek — Intourist Hotel.

ALMA ATA

The capital of Kazakhstan is situated in the northern Tien Shan where the mountains rise to 4951 m (16,243 ft) at Mount Talgar. The spruce forests and juniper stands on the slopes of these mountains support a similar avifauna to the Ala Archa Gorge, but the exceptions are exceptional. They include Ibisbill, Pale-backed Pigeon*, Azure Tit and Red-fronted Rosefinch.

Most of the species listed below are only present during the summer months (May–Sep).

Specialities

Himalayan Snowcock, Demoiselle Crane (May), Ibisbill, Pale-backed Pigeon*, White-winged Woodpecker*, Rufous-backed and White-winged Redstarts, Sykes' and Sulphur-bellied Warblers, White-browed Tit-Warbler, Black-breasted, Turkestan and Azure Tits, White-crowned Penduline-Tit, Saxaul Sparrow, Black-throated Accentor, Red-mantled and Red-fronted Rosefinches.

Others

Dalmatian Pelican*, Black Stork, White-tailed Eagle*, Lammergeier, Himalayan Griffon, Cinereous Vulture*, Common Pheasant, Black-bellied Sandgrouse, Oriental Turtle-Dove, Blue-cheeked Bee-eater, Three-toed Woodpecker, Eurasian Nutcracker, Brown Dipper, Blue Whistling-Thrush, White-tailed Rubythroat, Blue-capped Redstart, Wallcreeper, Paddyfield Warbler, Clamorous Reed-Warbler, Small Whitethroat, Himalayan and Brown Accentors, Fire-fronted Serin, Plain and Black-headed Mountain-Finches, White-winged Grosbeak.

Other Wildlife

Grey marmot, red pika.

(Other species recorded here include Daurian Partridge (Nov–Mar) and Pallas' Sandgrouse.)

The semi-desert, wetlands and stands of *Turanga* poplars alongside the **Ili River** near Alma Ata support Pale-backed Pigeon*, White-winged Woodpecker*, Sykes' Warbler, Small Whitethroat, White-crowned Penduline-Tit and Saxaul Sparrow. The narrow winding track from Alma Ata to the **Alma Ata Gorge** passes through spruce forest (Black-throated Accentor) before reaching the Oziorny Pass at 3507 m (11,506 ft), where Black-headed Mountain-Finch and Red-fronted Rosefinch occur. The traditional site for Ibisbill in the gorge is the Medeo Valley, but seeing this brilliant bird here involves walking 834 steps up the face of a dam. In recent years Ibisbill has also been recorded in the valley west of the Medeo Valley, along with White-winged Redstart and Plain Mountain-Finch.

Altai Falcon occurs in the **Charyn Canyons** area, southeast of Alma Ata, as well as Persian Nuthatch, Mongolian Finch, and Pine and Grey-hooded Buntings.

Accommodation: Charyn River Lodge (basic).

The **Sary Ishikotrau Desert**, just south of Lake Balkhash, supports a small isolated population of Turkestan Ground-Jay, as well as Pallas' Sandgrouse, White-winged Woodpecker*, Sykes' Warbler, White-crowned Penduline-Tit and Saxaul Sparrow.

Lake Alakol, in extreme east Kazakhstan, near the Dzungharian Gate, a natural passageway between Turkestan and China, is one of the few known breeding sites of Relict Gull*. Other species recorded here include Demoiselle Crane, Great Black-headed Gull, Paddyfield Warbler and Asian Short-toed Lark.

Accommodation: Uch Aral.

The delightful Azure Tit occurs at Alma Ata

AKMOLA

Although much of the natural steppe near this city in north-central Kazakhstan has been turned over to farmland, huge areas of untouched feather-grass plains are still within reach of the city. These grasslands support White-winged and Black Larks and, in spring, the many lakes have attracted as many as 20,000 Red-necked Phalaropes.

Most of the species listed below are only present during the summer months (May–Sep).

Specialities

Demoiselle Crane, Sociable Lapwing*, Azure Tit, White-winged and Black Larks.

Others

Dalmatian Pelican*, White-headed Duck*, Greater Flamingo, Pallid Harrier*, Red-necked Phalarope (May), Black-winged Pratincole*, Yellow-legged, Great Black-headed and Slender-billed Gulls, Blyth's Reed-Warbler.

Other Wildlife

Saiga.

(Other species recorded here include Little Crake, Asian Dowitcher* and Caspian Plover.)

The best birding areas are the **Kurgaldzhinju Reserve**, about 150 km southwest of Akmola, and the Lake Bashun area.

ENDEMICS (1)

Turkestan Ground-Jay	Chardzhou (Repetek Reserve) and Sary Ishikotrau Desert

Near-endemics

Relict Gull*, Pallas' Sandgrouse, Pale-backed Pigeon*, White-winged Woodpecker*, Mongolian Ground-Jay, Turkestan and Yellow-breasted Tits, Saxaul Sparrow.

VIETNAM

INTRODUCTION

Summary

Although the Vietnam War ended in 1975, this country only opened its doors to foreigners in the early 1990s. However, it is now possible to travel freely almost everywhere within Vietnam and to see many of its very special birds which include a superb range of pheasants and pittas, many Indochinese specialities and ten endemics.

Size

At 329,556 sq km and stretching 1600 km from north to south, Vietnam is over twice the size of England and half the size of Texas.

Getting Around

Most hire-cars are expensive and only available with drivers, but the cheap and efficient rail and bus networks enable easy access to most important sites. There are some internal flights, but it is wise to book these well in advance.

Accommodation and Food

In the major cities and towns accommodation is expensive, especially in the north, mainly because foreigners are normally shown to the best hotel available, but accommodation in the National Parks is cheap and basic. Most menus are dominated by noodle soup variations, but there is also French bread and beer, in the form of 'San Mig', and this is widely available.

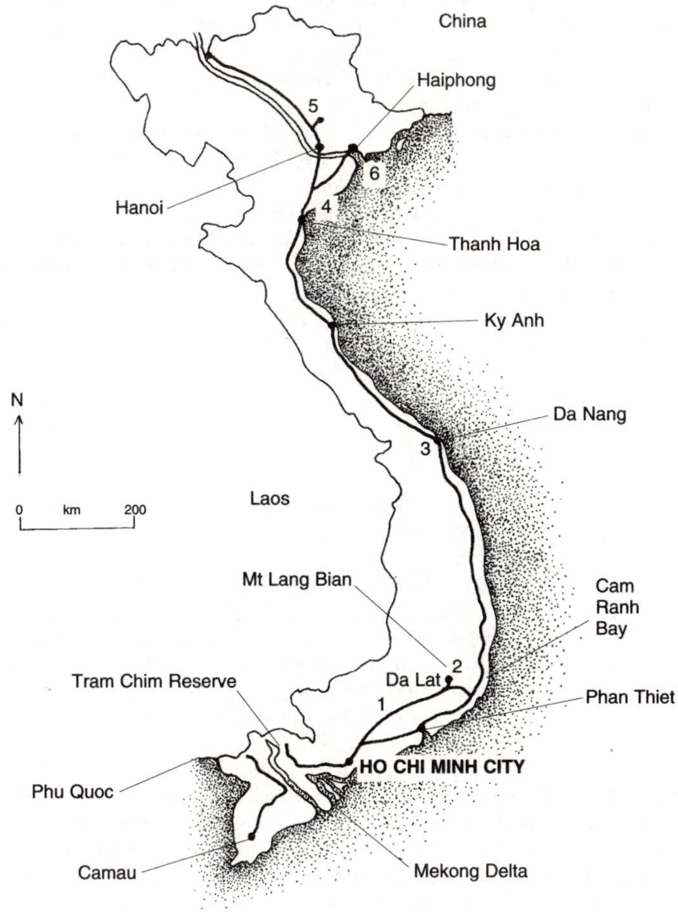

1 Nam Bai Cat Tien NP
2 Da Lat Plateau
3 Bach Ma NP
4 Cuc Phuong NP
5 Tam Dao
6 Red River Delta

Health and Safety

Immunisation against hepatitis, polio, typhoid and yellow fever is recommended, as are precautions against malaria, which is particularly prevalent in this country. Take great care when birding off the beaten track because there are still numerous unexploded land mines and other military weapons littering the land.

Climate and Timing

It can rain in the highlands at any time of the year, but the main rainy season usually lasts from May to October, hence the best time to visit is between November and April, especially towards the end of this period.

Habitats

In the 1600 km between the huge deltas of the Red River in the north and the Mekong River in the south there are a fertile coastal plain, remnant lowland forests and high plateaus rising to 3000 m (9843 ft) with montane broadleaf and pine forests.

Conservation

Forest cover in Vietnam has declined by 30% since 1945 because of the rapid rise in the human population (from 20 million in 1945 to 65 million in 1989) and the mass habitat destruction which took place during the Vietnam War. The government deserves credit for establishing several reserves and national parks to help protect some of the remaining habitat, but they need to do much more to protect the birds of Vietnam, which include a high total of 103 threatened and near-threatened species, because even so-called protected areas suffer from agricultural encroachment, the rising demand for firewood and logging. Meanwhile, coastal mangroves, especially in the Mekong Delta, are being cleared to make way for shrimp-ponds.

Bird Species

Nearly 850 species have been recorded in Vietnam. Non-endemic specialities and spectacular species include White-winged Duck*, White-shouldered Ibis*, Black-faced Spoonbill*, Bar-backed and Scaly-breasted Partridges, Silver Pheasant, Siamese Fireback*, Crested Argus*, Green Peafowl*, Red-legged Crake, Pale-capped*, Yellow-vented* and White-bellied* Pigeons, Coral-billed Ground-Cuckoo*, Blyth's* and Ruddy Kingfishers, Red-vented Barbet, Red-collared* and Heart-spotted Woodpeckers, Eared, Blue-rumped*, Rusty-naped, Blue, Bar-bellied* and Blue-winged Pittas, four broadbills, White-winged* and Short-tailed* Magpies, Collared and Ratchet-tailed Treepies, Dark-sided Thrush, Siberian Rubythroat, three forktails, Purple* and Green* Cochoas, Yellow-billed Nuthatch*, Short-tailed Scimitar-Babbler*, Sooty Babbler*, Grey-faced Tit-Babbler*, Silver-eared Mesia, Cutia, Chestnut-fronted Shrike-Babbler, Short-tailed* and Rufous-headed* Parrotbills, Sultan Tit, Gould's and Fork-tailed Sunbirds and Scarlet Finch.

Endemics

The six 'pheasants', two laughingthrushes, crocias and greenfinch which are unique to Vietnam represent the highest number of endemics for any country in southeast Asia.

Expectations

It is possible to see around 350 species on a thorough month-long trip.

The mature native trees which line the streets and fill the parks of the capital, **Ho Chi Minh City** (Saigon), in southeast Vietnam, support species such as Thick-billed Pigeon, Streak-eared Bulbul and Forest Wagtail (Nov–Mar). One particularly good site in the city worth birding if time is available is the zoo.

Small numbers of Sarus Crane* and Bengal Florican* occur in and around the **Tram Chim NR**, which is situated in the Mekong Delta, south Vietnam, but the marshes and grasslands here are a long way off the main birding circuit.

NAM BAI CAT TIEN NATIONAL PARK

Over 250 species have been recorded in the extensive lowland forest and wetlands of this large park (365 sq km) in south-central Vietnam, including two rare endemics and a big bag of goodies which are hard to see elsewhere in Asia, not least White-shouldered Ibis* and Pale-headed Woodpecker.

Vietnamese Endemics

Orange-necked Partridge*, Germain's Peacock-Pheasant*.

Specialities

White-winged Duck*, Malayan Night-Heron, White-shouldered Ibis*, Bar-backed and Scaly-breasted Partridges, Siamese Fireback*, Green Peafowl*, Red-legged Crake, Spot-bellied Eagle-Owl*, Tawny Fish-Owl*, Red-vented and Green-eared Barbets, Laced and Pale-headed Woodpeckers, Blue-rumped* and Bar-bellied* Pittas, Dusky Broadbill, Short-tailed Magpie*, Indochinese Cuckoo-Shrike, Vinous-breasted Starling, Grey-faced Tit-Babbler*.

Others

Chinese Pond-Heron, Yellow and Cinnamon Bitterns, Painted Stork*, Lesser Adjutant*, Black Baza, Grey-headed Fish-Eagle*, Grey-faced Buzzard (Nov–Mar), Rufous-bellied Eagle, Collared Falconet, Red Junglefowl, Yellow-legged Buttonquail, Watercock, Bronze-winged Jacana, Pintail Snipe (Nov–Mar), Pompadour Green-Pigeon, Vernal Hanging-Parrot, Red-breasted Parakeet, Chestnut-winged, Banded Bay, Asian Emerald and Drongo Cuckoos, Green-billed Malkoha, Great Eared-Nightjar, Silver-backed Needletail, Orange-breasted Trogon, Black-backed, Banded and Stork-billed Kingfishers, Blue-bearded and Chestnut-headed Bee-eaters, Indian Roller, Great and Wreathed Hornbills, Lineated Barbet, White-browed Piculet, White-bellied, Black-and-buff, Heart-spotted and Great Slaty Woodpeckers, Blue-winged Pitta, Black-and-red and Banded Broadbills, Racket-tailed Treepie, Ashy Woodswallow, Great Iora, Asian Fairy-bluebird, Blue-winged and Golden-fronted Leafbirds, Large Woodshrike, Chestnut-tailed Starling, Golden-crested Myna, Hainan and Tickell's Blue-Flycatchers, Rufous-tailed Robin (Nov–Mar), Siberian Rubythroat (Nov–Mar), Siberian Blue-

Heart-spotted Woodpecker is one of many widespread, but superb, Asian species which occur in Vietnam

Robin (Nov–Mar), White-rumped Shama, Slaty-backed Forktail, Velvet-fronted Nuthatch, Stripe-throated, Streak-eared and Ochraceous Bulbuls, Rufescent, Yellow-bellied and Plain Prinias, Lanceolated (Nov–Mar) and Pallas' (Nov–Mar) Warblers, Black-browed Reed-Warbler (Nov–Mar), Thick-billed Warbler (Nov–Mar), Pale-legged Leaf-Warbler (Nov–Mar), White-crested Laughingthrush, Scaly-crowned Babbler, Large Scimitar-Babbler, Chestnut-capped and White-hooded Babblers, Black-headed Munia, Streaked, Baya and Asian Golden* Weavers, Scarlet-backed Flowerpecker, Ruby-cheeked and Purple-throated Sunbirds, Little Spiderhunter, Yellow-breasted Bunting (Nov–Mar).

Other Wildlife

Crab-eating macaque, crested gibbon, douc langur.

(Other species recorded here include Pin-tailed Parrotfinch.)

This park is 170 km northeast of Ho Chi Minh City. From the capital head towards Da Lat via Bien Hoa and at KM Stone 147, in the vicinity of Phuong Lam, turn northwest. After 20 km this road reaches the Dong Nai River, where it is possible to cross to the west bank where the park HQ is situated. From the HQ, which lies at the southern end of the park, bird the track near the river, the trail to Thac Troi Waterfall and, especially, the 15 km track to the Dac Lua substation at the northern end of the park. White-shouldered Ibis* and Orange-necked Partridge* (in bamboo to the south) occur near here.

Accommodation: HQ and Dac Lua substation (basic).

DA LAT PLATEAU

The montane forests of the 2200 m (7218 ft) Da Lat Plateau, 300 km northeast of Ho Chi Minh City, support four endemics and a number of localised species such as Blue Pitta and Yellow-billed Nuthatch*.

Vietnamese Endemics

Black-hooded* and Collared* Laughingthrushes, Grey-crowned Crocias*, Vietnamese Greenfinch*.

Specialities

Rufous-throated Partridge, Pale-capped Pigeon*, Red-vented and Moustached Barbets, Rusty-naped and Blue Pittas, Indochinese Cuckoo-Shrike, Green Cochoa*, Yellow-billed Nuthatch*, White-cheeked and Spot-breasted* Laughingthrushes, Short-tailed Scimitar-Babbler*, Cutia, Chestnut-fronted Shrike-Babbler, Mountain Fulvetta.

Others

Jerdon's Baza, Grey-faced Buzzard (Nov–Mar), Chinese Francolin, Silver Pheasant, Wedge-tailed Pigeon, Golden-throated and Black-browed Barbets, Lesser and Greater Yellownapes, Greater Flameback, Bay Woodpecker, Slender-billed and Maroon Orioles, Large Cuckoo-Shrike, Long-tailed Minivet, Orange-bellied Leafbird, Burmese Shrike, Rufous-browed Flycatcher, Large Niltava, Slaty-backed and Spotted Forktails,

Chestnut-vented Nuthatch, Brown-throated Treecreeper, Black-throated Tit, Flavescent Bulbul, Hill Prinia, Grey-bellied Tesia, Dark-necked Tailorbird, Ashy-throated Warbler, Blyth's (Nov–Mar) and White-tailed Leaf-Warblers, White-spectacled Warbler, White-browed Scimitar-Babbler, Pygmy Wren-Babbler, Rufous-capped Babbler, Silver-eared Mesia, White-browed Shrike-Babbler, Blue-winged Minla, Rufous-winged Fulvetta, Rufous-backed and Black-headed Sibias, Yellow-cheeked and Yellow-browed Tits, Gould's Sunbird, Chestnut Bunting (Nov–Mar).

The popular hill resort of Da Lat is accessible by air and road from Ho Chi Minh City. Bird the 5 km road which ascends the western flank of **Mount Lang Bian**, accessible via Lac village, 10 km northeast of Da Lat, especially the forest near the peak (Short-tailed Scimitar-Babbler*), and the montane forest at the southern end of **Ho Tuyen Lam**, a large reservoir 5 km southwest of Da Lat. Boats can be hired to reach the forest, which supports Blue Pitta, Black-hooded Laughingthrush* and the very rare Grey-crowned Crocias*.

Accommodation: Da Lat — Mimosa Hotel, Cam Do Hotel.

A potential new species of fulvetta, allied to Spectacled*, was recorded in 1991 in upper montane forest on **Nui Bi Doup** near Da Lat. Black-hooded* and White-cheeked Laughingthrushes, as well as Yellow-vented Pigeon*, Blue Pitta, Dark-sided Thrush, Grey-eyed Bulbul, Spot-breasted Laughingthrush*, Buff-breasted Babbler, Grey-headed Parrotbill and Streaked Spiderhunter occur at the **Deo Nui San** pass, near Di Linh.

Black-hooded Laughingthrush is one of two laughingthrushes endemic to Vietnam which occur on the Da Lat Plateau*

BACH MA NATIONAL PARK

The selectively logged forest in this rugged park (189 sq km) near the coast in central Vietnam supports the endemic Annam Partridge* and many other rare and beautiful birds including Crested Argus*, Coral-billed Ground-Cuckoo* and Blyth's Kingfisher*.

Vietnamese Endemics

Annam Partridge*.

Specialities

Crested Argus*, Coral-billed Ground-Cuckoo*, Blyth's Kingfisher*, Red-vented Barbet, Red-collared Woodpecker*, White-winged Magpie*, Ratchet-tailed Treepie, Blue-rumped* and Bar-bellied* Pittas, Black-throated Laughingthrush, Short-tailed Scimitar-Babbler*, Grey-faced Tit-Babbler*, Rufous-throated Fulvetta*, Fork-tailed Sunbird.

Others

Silver Pheasant, Orange-breasted Pigeon, Red-headed Trogon, Banded Kingfisher, Blue-throated and Chestnut-headed Bee-eaters, Black-browed Barbet, Long-tailed Broadbill, Racket-tailed Treepie, Siberian Thrush (Nov–Mar), Pale-legged (Nov–Mar) and White-tailed Leaf-Warblers, White-crested and Lesser Necklaced Laughingthrushes, Scaly-crowned, Grey-throated and Spot-necked Babblers, Brown-cheeked Fulvetta, Sultan Tit.

The park is north of Da Nang and the forest is accessible via an old road. Blyth's Kingfisher* has been recorded in the Khe Thuong Valley, in the proposed southern extension to the NP.

Accommodation: guesthouse (basic).

Sooty Babbler*, as well as Blue-rumped* and Bar-bellied* Pittas, has been recorded at **Phong Nha**, a cultural and historical site in Quang Binh province, central Annam. Imperial Pheasant* (one bird trapped in 1990) and Vietnamese Fireback* (a few recent sightings) have been recorded in the logged hill forests up to 12 km west of the settlement of Cat Bin in north Annam. Other species recorded here and in the proposed **Ke Go NR** include Grey Peacock-Pheasant, Crested Argus*, Coral-billed Ground-Cuckoo*, Blyth's Kingfisher*, Red-vented Barbet, Red-collared Woodpecker*, Blue-rumped* and Bar-bellied* Pittas, White-winged Magpie*, Ratchet-tailed Treepie, Short-tailed Scimitar-Babbler* and Grey-faced Tit-Babbler*as well as giant muntjac. Also in north Annam, near the Laos border southwest of Ha Tinh, Blue-rumped Pitta*, White-cheeked, Rufous-vented and Red-tailed* Laughingthrushes, and Saola have been recorded in the **Vu Quang NR**.

CUC PHUONG NATIONAL PARK

The excellent lowland forest which lies below the limestone crags within this park (250 sq km) in north Vietnam supports a fine selection of localised birds, including White-bellied Pigeon*, Ruddy Kingfisher and Limestone Wren-Babbler.

Specialities

Malayan Night-Heron, White-bellied Pigeon*, Spot-bellied Eagle-Owl*, Ruddy Kingfisher, Red-vented Barbet, Red-collared Woodpecker*, Eared, Blue-rumped* and Bar-bellied* Pittas, Silver-breasted Broadbill, White-winged* and Short-tailed* Magpies, Ratchet-tailed Treepie, Fujian Niltava*, Puff-throated Bulbul, Limestone Wren-Babbler, Rufous-throated Fulvetta*, Fork-tailed Sunbird.

Others

Black Baza, Pied Falconet*, Silver Pheasant, Grey Peacock-Pheasant, Pin-tailed Pigeon, Brown-backed Needletail, Brown Hornbill*, Rufous Woodpecker, Crow-billed Drongo, Green Magpie, Long-tailed Minivet, White-tailed Flycatcher, White-crowned Forktail, Light-vented Bulbul (Nov–Mar), Russet Bush-Warbler, Sultan Tit, Forest Wagtail (Nov–Mar).

Other Wildlife

Marbled cat, red-bellied squirrel, Tonkin leaf-monkey.

This park is accessible by road 120 km south of Hanoi, the largest city in north Vietnam, which is connected by road, rail and air to Ho Chi Minh City. Turn west off Highway 1 in Ha Nam, near Ninh Binh, 80 km south of Hanoi, to the HQ. The best trails are at Bong substation, 20 km beyond the HQ.

Accommodation: HQ and Bong substation (basic).

TAM DAO

The montane forest above this hill resort, which is situated at 930 m (3051 ft) in the hills of Tonkin near Hanoi, supports Grey Laughingthrush* and Short-tailed Parrotbill*, two species which are restricted in range to south China, Laos and north Vietnam, as well as more widespread, but wonderful, birds such as Purple* and Green* Cochoas.

Specialities

Ruddy Kingfisher, Collared Treepie, Fujian Niltava*, Purple* and Green* Cochoas, Chestnut Bulbul, Grey* and Black-throated Laughingthrushes, Short-tailed* and Rufous-headed* Parrotbills, Fork-tailed Sunbird.

Others

Collared Falconet, Grey Peacock-Pheasant, Pin-tailed Pigeon, Hodgson's Hawk-Cuckoo, Mountain Scops-Owl, Red-headed Trogon, Long-tailed Broadbill, Black-winged Cuckoo-Shrike, Tiger (Mar–Apr) and Grey-backed Shrikes, White-tailed Flycatcher, Hill Blue-Flycatcher, Rufous-tailed Robin (Nov–Mar)Slaty-bellied Tesia, Greater Necklaced Laughingthrush, Streak-breasted, Red-billed and Coral-billed Scimitar-Babblers, Streaked and Eyebrowed Wren-Babblers, Spot-necked and White-hooded Babblers, Grey-cheeked Fulvetta, Striated and Black-chinned Yuhinas, Crimson Sunbird.

Tam Dao is 85 km northwest of Hanoi. Bird the track and trails above the resort.

Accommodation: chalets, hotel.

The **Red River Delta** in north Vietnam is an important wintering ground for Black-faced Spoonbill* (71 in January 1996), Nordmann's Greenshank* (14 in January 1996) and Spoonbill Sandpiper* (at least 15 in January 1996) and an equally crucial refuelling stop for migrant shorebirds including Asian Dowitcher*, Great Knot and Rufous-necked and Long-toed Stints. Black-faced Spoonbill* occurs on both the Red River and Day River estuaries, particularly at the Xuan Thuy Reserve, where up to 71 birds have been present in recent winters. It is possible to stay in the basic guesthouse here.

ADDITIONAL INFORMATION

Books and Papers

Birds of South Vietnam. Wildash P, 1968. Tuttle.
Forest Bird Surveys in Vietnam 1991. Eames J *et al.*, 1992. BirdLife International Study Report No. 51.

ENDEMICS (10)

Orange-necked Partridge*	South: Nam Bai Cat Tien NP
Annam Partridge*	Central: Bach Ma NP
Imperial Pheasant*	North: one bird trapped at Ke Go in 1990 and a pair trapped elsewhere in 1923
Edward's Pheasant*	Central: formerly recorded in the area now encompassed by Bach Ma NP, but possibly extinct and conspecific with Vietnamese Fireback*
Vietnamese Fireback*	North: Ke Go and in the Net River watershed (north Quang Binh province)
Germain's Peacock-Pheasant*	South: Nam Bai Cat Tien NP, Cat Loc NR and the lower slopes of the Da Lat and Di Linh plateaus
Black-hooded Laughingthrush*	South: Da Lat Plateau and Di Linh
Collared Laughingthrush*	South: Da Lat Plateau
Grey-crowned Crocias*	South: Da Lat Plateau
Vietnamese Greenfinch*	South: Da Lat Plateau

Near-endemics

White-shouldered Ibis*, Temminck's Tragopan*, Siamese Fireback*, Crested Argus*, Bengal Florican*, Saunders'* and Relict* Gulls, Yellow-vented Pigeon*, Coral-billed Ground-Cuckoo*, Indochinese Swiftlet, Red-vented Barbet, Red-collared Woodpecker*, Blue-rumped* and Bar-bellied* Pittas, White-winged Magpie*, Ratchet-tailed Treepie, Collared Crow, Red-billed Starling*, Crested Myna, Fujian Niltava*, Chestnut-vented and Yellow-billed* Nuthatches, Collared Finchbill, Light-vented and Chestnut Bulbuls, Masked, Grey* and White-cheeked Laughing-thrushes, Hwamei, Red-winged Laughingthrush*, Short-tailed Scimitar-Babbler*, Sooty Babbler*, Grey-faced Tit-Babbler*, Streaked Barwing*, Spectacled* and Mountain Fulvettas, White-collared Yuhina, Ashy-throated, Golden and Short-tailed* Parrotbills, Fork-tailed Sunbird, Black-headed Greenfinch.

THE MIDDLE EAST

AFGHANISTAN

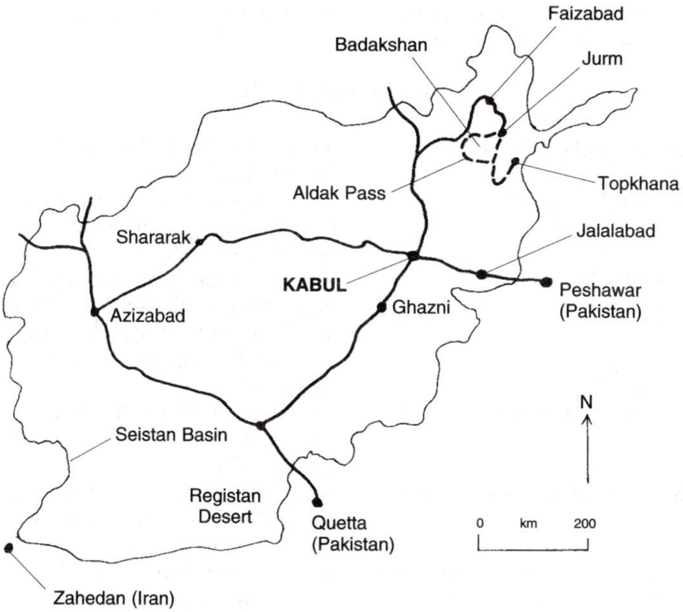

Hardly anyone has been travelling, let alone birding, in war-torn Afghanistan for 20 years, and tourist visas were still not being issued in 1996. This is bad news for birders because, apart from a number of Central Asian and west Himalayan specialities, Afghanistan also boasts an endemic snowfinch.

At 647,497 sq km, Afghanistan is five times the size of England and nearly as big as Texas. There are few roads and little traffic, although buses used to connect the major towns. It used to be possible to hire porters to explore the best areas, where stone huts were the only accommodation available. Most food consists of kebabs, omelettes and nan bread, washed down with copious amounts of tea. Immunisation against hepatitis, polio, typhoid and yellow fever is recommended, as are precautions against malaria. If anyone does manage to go birding in Afghanistan they should be aware of the millions of unexploded land mines which litter the countryside. The harsh climate ranges from sweltering summers to very cold winters. Rainfall is low except in the mountains and the almost subtropical extreme east. The best times to visit would be summer for the mountains and winter for the lowlands. This is a rugged country, with the Pamirs and Hindu Kush mountain ranges in the centre and east of the country, which rise to 7484 m (24,554 ft) at Mount Zebak in the Pamirs. Habitats range from the desert of the Seistan Basin in the southwest, through steppe and remnant forests to juniper scrub and high-altitude meadows. Many areas are heavily degraded thanks to overgrazing, wood-cutting and logging, and there are no protected areas to help conserve Afghanistan's avifauna, including the 18 threatened and near-threatened species which occur in the country.

Around 460 species have been recorded in Afghanistan, a good total for a land-locked and largely arid country. Non-endemic specialities and spectacular species include Siberian Crane*, White-winged Woodpecker*, Rufous-backed Redstart, White-browed Bushchat*, White-cheeked Tit, Tytler's Leaf-Warbler and Black-and-yellow Grosbeak. There is one endemic: Afghan Snowfinch.

Sites near the capital, **Kabul**, in the east, include the **Safed Koh** mountain range to the southeast, where species recorded include Himalayan Monal, Black-headed Jay, Kashmir and White-cheeked Nuthatches, White-cheeked Tit, Brooks' Leaf-Warbler, Black-breasted and Black-crested Tits and Black-and-yellow Grosbeak. Species recorded in the almost subtropical **Jalalabad Valley**, with its farmland and many orchards, east of Kabul, include wintering Black-headed Jay, Rufous-backed Redstart and Black-throated Accentor. The higher **Pech and Waygal Valleys**, north of Jalalabad, used to be important stopovers for migrant Siberian Cranes*. Species recorded between **Salang Kotal** and **Khinjan** at the 3658 m (12,001 ft) pass between Kabul and the north include White-winged Woodpecker*, Plain Leaf-Warbler, Sulphur-bellied Warbler, Turkestan and Yellow-breasted Tits and Red-mantled Rosefinch. The former tourist hot spot of **Bande Amir** (Band-i-Amir), an impressive valley in the Hindu Kush west of Kabul, may still support the endemic Afghan Snowfinch, as well as Himalayan Snowcock. Afghan Snowfinch has also been recorded around **Ab-i-Nawar**, a large saline lake on the Dashte Nawar plateau 55 km northwest of Ghazni, which is 150 km southwest of Kabul. A Greater Flamingo breeding colony was thought to move between this lake and **Ab-i-Istada**, 130 km south of Ghazni, which also used to be an important refuelling stop for Siberian Cranes*.

Afghan Snowfinch was recorded in 1991 between Topkhana and Magnawol, and at the Aldak Pass, in the remote province of **Badakshan**, northeast Afghanistan. Other species recorded in Badakshan at that time included Himalayan Snowcock, Snow Pigeon, Indian Scops-Owl (in Fermaquli village, Keshim Valley), White-winged Redstart (Topkhana), Little Forktail and Sulphur-bellied Warbler. It used to be possible to hire porters for the 350 km trek from Topkhana to Fermaquli via Jurm, and back to Topkhana via the Aldak Pass.

The country's most important wetland, **Hamun-i-Puzak**, which lies in the Seistan Basin in southwest Afghanistan, may still support up to a million waterfowl during the winter. Resident species used to include White-headed Duck* and Marbled Teal*, and Dalmatian Pelican* and

Great Black-headed Gull have also been recorded. Houbara Bustard used to occur in the lake's vicinity and in the **Registan Desert** to the southeast, along with White-browed Bushchat* and Hypocolius.

ENDEMICS (1)

Afghan Snowfinch	East: Bande Amir, Ab-i-Nawar and Badakshan (occasionally recorded in southeast Turkmenistan, Turkestan)

Near-endemics

Tibetan Sandgrouse, Pale-backed Pigeon*, Sykes' Nightjar, Brown-fronted, White-winged*, Sind and Himalayan Woodpeckers, Black-headed Jay, Rusty-tailed Flycatcher, White-browed Bushchat*, Kashmir and White-cheeked Nuthatches, White-cheeked Tit, Streak-throated Swallow, Tytler's Leaf-Warbler*, Western Crowned-Warbler, Black-crested, Turkestan and Yellow-breasted Tits, Dead Sea Sparrow, Rufous-breasted Accentor, Black-and-yellow Grosbeak.

BAHRAIN

INTRODUCTION

This small, low-lying, arid archipelago, which lies in the Arabian Gulf 25 km east of Saudi Arabia and 30 km west of Qatar, attracts a fine assortment of migrants and winter visitors, such as Hypocolius, as well as some Arabian Peninsula specialities including Socotra Cormorant*.

The total area covered by the islands is just over 700 sq km and the best way to get around is in a hire-car, which acts as a hide and provides air-conditioning. Most accommodation is expensive. There is a wide range of food and drink available, including beer. Health standards are high, but immunisation against hepatitis, polio, typhoid and yellow fever is recommended. The best time to see Hypocolius is during the November to February period, which also happens to be the most pleasant time of year weatherwise. April to October is very hot and humid. However, passerine migrants are most numerous in March and April, when it is still relatively cool, and shorebirds pass through in large numbers between July and October. The natural habitat of the 30 or so islands is sparsely vegetated sand and stony desert. At the northern end of the main island this has been replaced with a 3 km wide strip of cultivation, composed mainly of date palms. The coastal lowlands rise slightly to a highest point of only 134 m (440 ft) at Jabal Al Dukhan. Some areas of mud flat and mangrove, as well as reefs, surround the islands, but Bahrain's rich coastal wetlands are disappearing fast due to

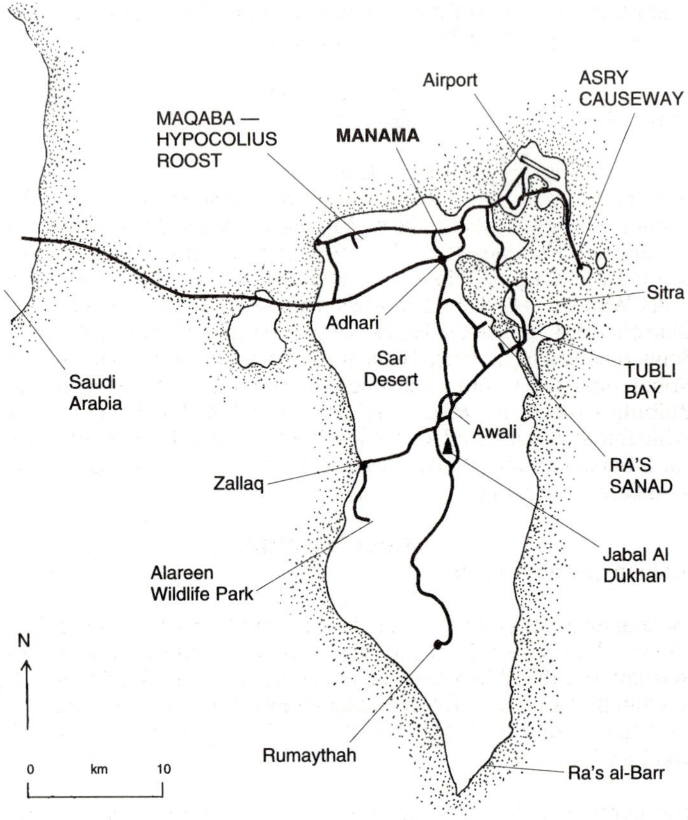

reclamation projects and increasing urbanisation. However, legislation regarding the protection of wildlife has recently been adopted and the National Committee for Wildlife Protection (NCWP) has designated a number of protected sites, such as Tubli Bay and the Hawar Islands, which will help conserve the birds of Bahrain, including the four threatened and near-threatened species which occur in the country.

Over 305 species have been recorded in Bahrain, of which only 25 or so are regular breeding species. Non-endemic specialities and spectacular species include Socotra Cormorant*, Sooty Falcon, Cream-coloured Courser, Great Black-headed Gull, White-cheeked and Saunders' Terns, Hypocolius, Upcher's and Menetries' Warblers and Cinereous Bunting*. There is no endemic species and three days is usually enough to see all of the local specialities.

BAHRAIN ISLAND

The main island (50 km by 16 km) supports a fine range of species, not least a huge wintering flock of Hypocolius, which, during the early 1990s contained over 500 birds.

Most of the species listed below are spring (Mar–Apr) and autumn (Sep–Oct) migrants and/or winter visitors.

Specialities

Hypocolius.

Others

Socotra Cormorant*, Greater Flamingo, Western Reef-Egret, Pallid Harrier*, Lesser Kestrel*, Saker Falcon, Baillon's Crake, Broad-billed Sandpiper, Cream-coloured Courser, Mongolian Plover, Greater Sandplover, Caspian Plover, Great Black-headed and Slender-billed Gulls, White-cheeked and Saunders' Terns, Namaqua Dove, Pallid Swift, Blue-cheeked Bee-eater, House Crow, Masked Shrike, Collared and Semicollared Flycatchers, White-throated Robin, Rufous-tailed Scrub-Robin (Mar–Sep), Mourning and Red-tailed Wheatears, White-eared Bulbul, Graceful Prinia, Upcher's Warbler, Small and Hume's Whitethroats, Desert and Menetries' Warblers, Black-crowned Sparrow-Lark, Bar-tailed and Desert Larks, Greater Hoopoe-Lark, Lesser Short-toed Lark.

Other Wildlife

Arabian gazelle, dugong.

(Scarce migrants and/or winter visitors include Houbara Bustard, Crab Plover, White-tailed Lapwing, Dark-throated Thrush, Rufous-backed Redstart, Hooded Wheatear, Bimaculated Lark, Dead Sea Sparrow, Pale Rockfinch, Mongolian Finch and Cinereous Bunting*, and introduced species include Grey Francolin, Alexandrine Parakeet, Common Myna and Red Avadavat.)

The northern end of this island is the best area for birds, notably the wintering flock of Hypocolius which roosts in neglected palm gardens and scrub in a small protected area at **Maqaba**, 20 minutes by road west of the capital, Manama. Peak numbers are usually recorded in December. The farmland near here, especially at **Qurayyah**, is good for migrants including Caspian Plover, and Socotra Cormorant* may be seen anywhere along the north coast. The palm plantations by the natural spring at **Adhari**, near Bahrain Fort, and alongside the **Manama–Budayyi road** are also worth checking for migrants. **Tubli Bay** (Khawr al Kabb), just south of Manama, is an excellent birding area, although infilling for development continues to encroach upon the remaining mud flat and mangrove which, especially from July to October, attract numerous shorebirds. In summer this is a good site for White-cheeked and Saunders' Terns and in winter, Great Black-headed Gull. The bay can be viewed from the Majlis al Tawon Highway south to Sitra Island and at Ra's Sanad on the southwest shoreline. To reach Ra's Sanad turn northwest off the Majlis al Tawon Highway, after crossing Sitra Island, between the villages of Al Akr and An Nuwaydirat. Waterfowl and raptors are attracted to the artificial lakes within **Alareen Wildlife Park**, some 30 km south of Manama. One of the best places for migrants is the **Sakhir Racecourse**, which is situated just off the road to Zallaq, a few kilometres west of Awali town, more or less in the centre of the island. Ask for permission to enter at the main gate. The *Prosopis* groves at the nearby **Sakhir Palace**, south of the road to

Zallag, are also attractive to spring passerine migrants including White-throated Robin and Menetries' Warbler. **Jabal Al Dukhan**, a few kilometres south of Awali on the west side of the road to Ash Shabak, supports wintering Mourning and Red-tailed Wheatears, while Hooded Wheatear is an occasional visitor, Hume's Wheatear is a rarity and Cinereous Bunting* has been recorded in the bushes at the summit during spring. Desert species are hard to find, but the **Sar Desert**, which is bisected by the Saudi Arabian Highway, is probably the best place for species such as Cream-coloured Courser and Greater Hoopoe-Lark.

The **Asry Causeway**, just south of the airport on Muharraq Island, 2 km east of Manama, is a good place to see Socotra Cormorant*, shorebirds, including occasional Crab Plovers, and terns.

The **Hawar Islands**, 18 km southeast of Bahrain Island, support the largest known breeding colony of Socotra Cormorant* (over 100,000 pairs have been present from October to February), as well as breeding Sooty Falcon (May–Nov) and the second largest population of dugong in the world. The Central Municipal Council arranges regular trips for 'tourists' to these islands.

ADDITIONAL INFORMATION

Addresses

Please send records to the Bahrain Bird Recorder, Bahrain Natural History Society, PO Box 20336, Manama, Bahrain.

Books and Papers

Birds in Bahrain: a Study of Their Migration Patterns 1990–1992. Hirschfeld E, 1995. Hobby.
The Birds of Bahrain. Nightingale T and Hill M, 1993. Immel.

IRAN

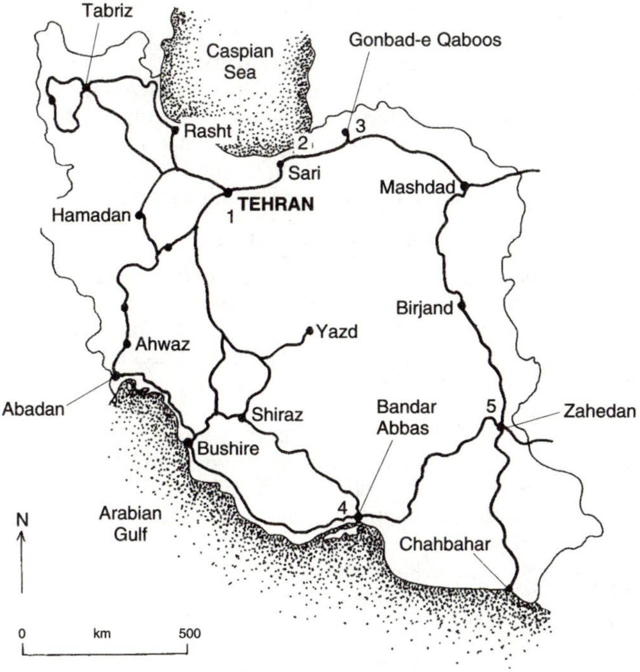

1 Kavir NP
2 Mian Kaleh Wildlife Refuge
3 Golestan NP
4 Bandar Abbas
5 Zahedan

INTRODUCTION

Summary

Few birders have been to Iran since the late 1960s and early 1970s, but with avian enticement in the form of birds such as Rufous-backed Redstart and Hypocolius, the temptation would be hard to resist if tourism was encouraged. Unfortunately, this is a difficult country to get in to and American birders, especially those with Israeli stamps in their passports, stand little chance of seeing the birds of Iran.

Size

At 1,648,184 sq km, Iran is over 12 times larger than England and 2.4 times the size of Texas.

Getting Around

The domestic air and bus networks are cheap and efficient, but flights need to be booked well in advance.

Accommodation and Food

There is a wide range of accommodation in the major cities, most of which is expensive, but it is basic at Gonbad-e Qaboos, Semnan and Kavir NP. Food and drink consists mainly of kebabs, rice, vegetables, tea and alcohol-free beer.

Health and Safety

Immunisation against hepatitis, polio, typhoid and yellow fever is recommended, as are precautions against malaria. Crime is rare and the Iranians are friendly and helpful people on the whole, but beware of the Islamic Revolutionary Guards Corps, known as the Komite, who have been known to hassle tourists, especially in the Zahedan area.

Climate and Timing

April and May, when many migrants are moving through, is the best time to visit Iran. Summers are hot and dry, winters cold and dry, except in the mountains where snow falls. It can rain at any time of the year around the Caspian Sea, but the main wet season here lasts from September to November.

Habitats

Most of Iran consists of a high plateau bordered to the north by the Elburz (Alborz) Mountains, which rise to 5500 m (18,045 ft) at Kuh-e-Damavand, and to the west by the Zagros Mountains. Much of the eastern plateau is desert and semi-desert and this covers 60% of the land surface. Otherwise, the habitats include acacia woodlands, dry deciduous and temperate forests, steppe and along the 2000 km of coastline, mud flats and mangroves.

Conservation

Up until the 1940s there were lions and tigers in Iran. They are extinct now, and as the human population has doubled since 1970, any remaining brown bears, cheetahs and leopards are likely to join them in extinction. Although overgrazing and deforestation are continuing problems, Iran has a relatively good record as far as nature conservation goes and by the end of 1991 there were 77 protected areas covering nearly 5% of the land surface. Most of these survive to this day, helping to conserve the country's birds, which include 23 threatened and near-threatened species.

Bird Species

Over 490 species have been recorded in Iran. While most of the avifauna is 'Palearctic', there are small Oriental and Afrotropical elements. Non-endemic specialities and spectacular species include Caspian Snowcock, Caucasian Grouse*, Siberian Crane*, Houbara Bustard, Crab Plover, Indian Roller, Sind Woodpecker, Rufous-backed Redstart, Hooded and Hume's Wheatears, Hypocolius, Sykes' Warbler, Plain Leaf-Warbler, Menetries' Warbler, Iraq Babbler* and Spot-throated Accentor.

Endemics

One species is endemic: Iranian Ground-Jay.

Expectations

In spring it is possible to see over 40 shorebirds and 30 warblers on a three- to four-week trip.

Caspian Snowcock and Spot-throated Accentor (May–Sep) occur in the Upper Lar Valley, 40 km to the northeast of Iran's modern capital, **Tehran**, which lies at the base of the Elburz Mountains on the edge of the desert at 1600 m (5249 ft).

KAVIR NATIONAL PARK

This large national park (4000 sq km) is situated to the southeast of Tehran in the Dasht-e Kavir (Salt Desert) and supports such desert birds as Houbara Bustard and Hume's Wheatear.

Specialities

Houbara Bustard, Hooded and Hume's Wheatears, Spot-throated Accentor (Nov–Mar).

Others

See-see Partridge, Cream-coloured Courser, Crowned Sandgrouse, Finsch's (Nov–Mar) and Red-tailed (Nov–Mar) Wheatears, Streaked Scrub-Warbler, Bar-tailed and Desert Larks, Greater Hoopoe-Lark, Mongolian Finch (Nov–Mar).

Other Wildlife

Dorcas gazelle, ibex, mouflon, wolf.

The park is 110 km southeast of Tehran. Bird throughout, especially around the vegetated springs which attract migrants in the spring.

Accommodation: Caravanserai (basic).

A few Siberian Cranes* winter at **Fereidoonkenar Marshes**, a protected area near the Caspian Sea northeast of Tehran (13 km southwest of Babolsar), along with Lesser White-fronted Goose* and Imperial Eagle*.

MIAN KALEH WILDLIFE REFUGE

This superb wetland (688 sq km) on the southeast shore of the Caspian Sea includes part of the shallow, brackish Gorgan Bay and the 60 km long sandy peninsula which almost completely separates the bay from the sea. Nearly 300 species have been recorded here and in some winters up to 100 White-tailed Eagles* have been present.

Others

Dalmatian Pelican* (Nov–Mar), White-tailed Eagle* (Nov–Mar), Pallid Harrier* (Nov–Mar), Imperial Eagle* (Nov–Mar), Saker Falcon (Nov–Mar), Black Francolin, Caspian Plover (May–Sep), White-tailed Lapwing, Great Black-headed (Nov–Mar) and Slender-billed Gulls,

Blue-cheeked (May–Sep) and European (May–Sep) Bee-eaters, Rosy Starling, Menetries' Warbler (May–Sep), Spanish Sparrow.

The refuge is near Sari, 267 km northeast of Tehran.

Accommodation: Sari.

GOLESTAN NATIONAL PARK

The deciduous forests, semi-arid steppe and juniper stands in this National Park, at the eastern end of the Elburz Mountains, support breeding Rufous-backed Redstart and Plain Leaf-Warbler, as well as a fine variety of large mammals, including brown bear.

Most of the species listed below are only present during the summer (May–Sep).

Specialities

Caspian Snowcock, Rufous-backed Redstart, Plain Leaf-Warbler, Crimson-winged Finch.

Others

Lammergeier, Cinereous Vulture*, Lesser Spotted and Imperial* Eagles, See-see Partridge, Chukar, Little Bustard, Black Woodpecker, Semicollared Flycatcher, White-throated Robin, Finsch's and Variable Wheatears, Persian Nuthatch, Hume's Whitethroat, Menetries' Warbler, Bimaculated Lark, Pale Rockfinch, Fire-fronted Serin, Grey-hooded and Red-headed Buntings.

Other Wildlife

Brown bear, goitred gazelle, ibex, leopard, lynx, Persian wild goat, wild sheep, wolf.

The park is situated between Gonbad-e Qaboos and Bojnurd.

Accommodation: Gonbad-e Qaboos (basic).

Most of the species listed under Golestan NP, as well as Red-tailed Wheatear, Spot-throated Accentor and White-winged Grosbeak, occur in **Pavar**, a protected area in the Elburz Mountains east of Tehran and 35 km north of Semnan, where it is possible to stay in basic accommodation.

There are some good birding areas in northwest Iran. The marshes alongside the Caspian Sea near the city of **Rasht**, 324 km northwest of Tehran, support over 500 Pygmy Cormorants* in winter, as well as small numbers of Dalmatian Pelican*, Lesser White-fronted Goose*, and White-tailed* and Imperial* Eagles. **Gori Gol**, a lake which lies on the north side of the Tehran–Tabriz road, 40 km southeast of Tabriz, supports breeding White-headed Duck*; the **Arasbaran** protected area, 90 km northeast of Tabriz, supports Caucasian Grouse*; and Great Bustard* occurs on the plains between the villages of Nowruzlu and Ghazanlu, 45 km northeast of **Mahabad**.

In southwest Iran Hypocolius breeds in the **Ahwaz** region, in the scrub surrounding the reedy lake (where Iraq Babbler* is resident) on the Hamidieh Plains 30 km northwest of Ahwaz, along the Karkheh River Valley 35–90 km northwest of Ahwaz and in the Dez River Valley, 35–90 km north of Ahwaz. The **Shadegan Marshes**, to the south of Ahwaz near Abadan, are thought to be the most important site in the world for Marbled Teal* (up to 20,000 have been recorded here in winter).

The lakes, acacia woodland and open oak forests within the protected area known as **Arjan**, located in the Zagros Mountains between Shiraz and Bushire in south-central Iran, support Great White and Dalmatian* Pelicans, White-headed Duck*, Marbled Teal*, Greater Flamingo, Indian Roller, Syrian Woodpecker and Upcher's Warbler. Bird Dasht-e Arjan lake, the open oak forests in Dasht-e Barm, a long narrow valley, and the brackish Parishan Lake and its surrounds.

Accommodation: Shiraz and Bushire.

Hypocolius breeds in the coastal hills near **Bushire**, a large port on the Arabian Gulf coast in south Iran, while the bay to the south of the town supports breeding Saunders' Tern and wintering Crab Plover and Great Black-headed Gull.

BANDAR ABBAS

Iran's busiest port is a good base from which to explore nearby woodlands where Sind Woodpecker occurs, and Kuh-e Geno, an isolated mountain which attracts an excellent variety of wintering Central Asian specialities such as Rufous-backed Redstart.

Specialities

Persian Shearwater, Socotra Cormorant*, Crab Plover, Great Thick-knee, Sind Woodpecker, Rufous-backed Redstart (Nov–Mar), Plain Leaf-Warbler (Nov–Mar), Spot-throated Accentor (Nov–Mar).

Others

Goliath Heron, Indian Pond-Heron, White-eyed Buzzard, See-see Partridge, Grey Francolin, Sooty Gull, White-cheeked, Bridled and Saunders' Terns, Chestnut-bellied and Lichtenstein's Sandgrouse, Spotted Owlet, Bay-backed Shrike, Variable (Nov–Mar) and Red-tailed (Nov–Mar) Wheatears, Paddyfield Warbler (Apr–May), Blyth's Reed-Warbler (Apr–May), Small (Nov–Mar) and Hume's (Nov–Mar) Whitethroats, Sand Lark, Purple Sunbird, House Bunting.

Bandar Abbas is accessible by air. Bird the three river deltas and their surrounding woodlands which lie between 10 and 70 km east of Bandar Abbas (Sind Woodpecker, Plain Leaf-Warbler) and the road which ascends the south side of Kuh-e Geno to the summit at 2370 m (7776 ft), 25 km northwest of Bandar Abbas. It is also possible to hire a dhow to visit the island of Hormoz (Great Thick-knee) and to look for seabirds, which have included Persian Shearwater as well as rarities such as Wilson's Storm-Petrel, Red-billed Tropicbird and Masked Booby.

ZAHEDAN

The barren volcanic hills, stony plains and desert scrub south of this town, which lies close to the Afghanistan and Pakistan borders in south-east Iran, support the localised endemic, Iranian Ground-Jay, as well as Houbara Bustard and Sykes' Warbler.

Iranian Endemics

Iranian Ground-Jay.

Specialities

Houbara Bustard, Sykes' Warbler, Plain Leaf-Warbler, Spot-throated Accentor.

Others

Spotted Sandgrouse, Bay-backed Shrike, Variable Wheatear, Small and Hume's Whitethroats, Desert Warbler, Pale Rockfinch, Grey-hooded Bunting.

Zahedan is accessible by air. The road south to Chahbahar passes the eastern edge of Hamoun-i Gabi, 30 km southeast of Khash, a large salt flat where the *Zygophyllum*-dominated desert scrub supports Iranian Ground-Jay. The Chahbahar road also passes over the western flank of the isolated dormant volcano, Kuh-i Taftan which rises to 4042 m (13,261 ft) 100 km southeast of Zahedan. The farmland, pistachio and almond scrub and boulder fields on its slopes support Sykes' Warbler. To the north of Zahedan, Hormak oasis, a few kilometres from the Afghanistan border, is an excellent place for migrants in spring (Apr–May).

ADDITIONAL INFORMATION

Books and Papers

The Birds of Iran. Scott D *et al.*, 1975. Department of Environment, Tehran.

ENDEMICS (1)

Iranian Ground-Jay	Zahedan

Near-endemics

Caspian Snowcock, Caucasian Grouse*, Siberian Crane*, Sykes' Nightjar, Sind Woodpecker, Iraq Babbler*, Turkestan Tit, Sind and Dead Sea Sparrows, Spot-throated Accentor, Cinereous Bunting* (breeding).

IRAQ

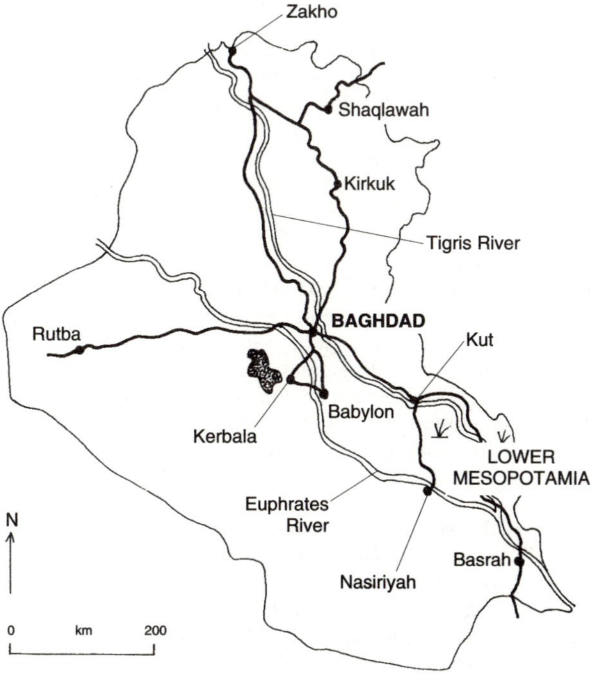

If Iraq was open to travellers it would probably be popular with birders, especially the marshes of Lower Mesopotamia where one of the world's most spectacular concentrations of waterbirds may still exist. However, the chances of birding in Iraq, even in the distant future, seem slim to say the least, especially in a country where at present it is possible to be arrested for looking at birds *without* binoculars.

At 434,924 sq km, Iraq is three times the size of England and 1.6 times smaller than Texas. Before the Gulf War there was a good bus system and shared taxi network, while regular air and rail services used to connect Baghdad with Basrah in the south. There were few budget hotels willing to accept foreigners even before the war. Immunisation against hepatitis, polio, typhoid and yellow fever is recommended, as are precautions against malaria. The summers are hot and the best time to visit would be during the cooler winter months when the marshes of Lower Mesopotamia in the south may still attract masses of waterbirds. This is the main wet season, but most of the rain falls in the north and north-east where the mountains rise to over 3500 m (11,483 ft). The slopes of these mountains support steppe and farmland, but most of the country consists of desert, except for the marshes of the south which lie on the floodplains of the Tigris and Euphrates rivers. This huge area of massive shallow lakes (haurs), reedbeds and marshes is still considered to be an immensely important wintering ground for Palearctic waterfowl, but by all accounts these wetlands are disappearing fast due to oil exploration, massive flood-control projects and irrigation schemes. Iraq has no protected areas despite its importance to many birds, which include 16 threatened and near-threatened species.

Non-endemic specialities and spectacular species include Slender-billed Curlew*, Pallid Scops-Owl, Hypocolius, Basra Reed-Warbler* and Dead Sea Sparrow. There is no endemic species, but Iraq Babbler* is virtually confined to the marshes of Lower Mesopotamia.

Persian Nuthatch has been recorded around **Shaqlawah**, a mountain village 134 km east of Mosul in northeast Iraq. Good sites around **Baghdad** may still include the farmland alongside the Tigris River and on the island of Umm Al Khanazeer near Al Jadriyah on the southwest outskirts of the city. Species recorded here include Marbled Teal*, Black Francolin, Red-wattled and White-tailed Lapwings, Blue-cheeked Bee-eater (May–Sep), Indian Roller, Hypocolius, Basra Reed-Warbler* (May–Sep), Iraq Babbler* and Dead Sea Sparrow. Similar species, as well as Pallid Scops-Owl and Egyptian Nightjar, have been recorded in the farmland and palm groves 12 km west of **Mahmudiya** and at **Salman Pak** (Ctesiphon), southeast of Baghdad. Spur-winged Plover and Pied Kingfisher have been recorded at **Babylon**, 90 km south of Baghdad.

The marshes of **Lower Mesopotamia** lie between Amara, Nasiriyah and Basrah in south Iraq. They have been inhabited by the Ma'dan (Marsh Arabs) for at least 5000 years and are probably still the most important breeding area in the world for Marbled Teal*, possibly an important wintering ground for Slender-billed Curlew* (six were seen during the last survey in 1979 at Haur Al Hammar) and an important site for Great White and Dalmatian* Pelicans. The region, which used to cover 10,000 sq km, also probably still supports Pygmy Cormorant*, African Darter, White-tailed* and Imperial* Eagles, Red-wattled, Sociable* and White-tailed Lapwings, Pied Kingfisher, Indian Roller, Basra Reed-Warbler* and Iraq Babbler*.

ADDITIONAL INFORMATION

Books and Papers

The Bird Fauna of Semi-desert Areas of Central Iraq. Al-Dabbagh K, in prep. Sandgrouse.
Migration in Iraq. Marchant S, 1963. *Ibis* 105: 369–398.
The Avifauna of Iraq. Allouse B, 1953. Iraq Natural History Museum Publication No. 3.

Near-endemics

Caspian Snowcock, Iraq Babbler*, Dead Sea Sparrow.

ISRAEL

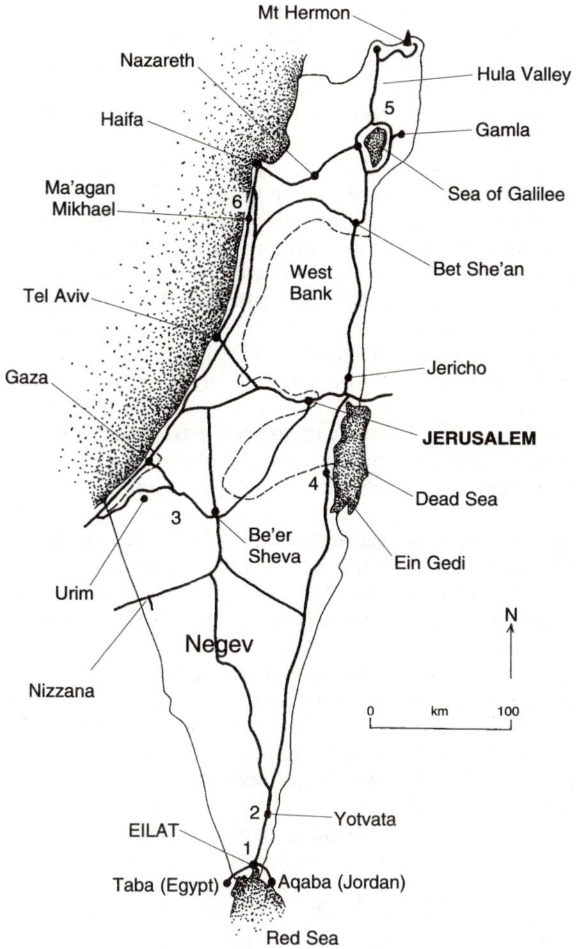

1 Eilat
2 Arava Valley
3 Negev Desert
4 Ein Gedi
5 Galilee, Golan Heights and Mount Hermon
6 Ma'agan Mikhael

INTRODUCTION

Summary

Israel is a modern country situated on a major migration route and, especially in spring, attracts numerous birders in search of numerous birds, which, as well as migrants, include many desert specialities.

Size

At 20,770 sq km (including the occupied territories of the Golan Heights, West Bank and Gaza Strip), Israel is just one-sixth the size of England and 33 times smaller than Texas.

Getting Around

On entering Israel the authorities will stamp a separate piece of paper instead of your passport if you ask politely. This is a good idea as an Israeli stamp in your passport may make it difficult, if not impossible, to enter some Middle Eastern Arab states.

Distances are mercifully small in Israel so the domestic flight network will be of little use. A hire-car is the best way to get around as buses and shared taxis (sheruts) don't reach all of the best birding sites, especially in the desert, and the road network is excellent. However, driving has its hazards. Before the peace process began to liberate the occupied territories in autumn 1995, Israeli cars were the target of people armed with stones when they passed through the West Bank. Such 'stonings' may have ceased, but it pays to be aware of such a possibility in the future, and of the notoriously carefree Israeli drivers.

Accommodation and Food

Hostels and well-equipped campsites are available for budget birders, but it may be just as cheap to take a package hoilday to Eilat and use what would otherwise be a very expensive hotel as a convenient base. Hotels and kibbutz guesthouses are expensive throughout the country. On the food front, you name it you can get it, in most places, but it may be expensive if it is not along the lines of felafel (chick pea and salad sandwiches), hummus and kebabs. Goldstar beer is the most popular.

Health and Safety

Immunisation against hepatitis, polio and typhoid is recommended. In early 1996 the Hizbullah militia, based in southern Lebanon, fired Katyusha missiles into north Israel. A ceasefire was negotiated in April 1996 but how long this will last is anybody's guess.

Climate and Timing

Mid-March to early April, the early spring, is the peak time to visit Israel. At this time, lingering winter specialities mix with summer visitors and many migrants. Autumn is also a good time, with the best period for migrants being September to mid-November, and in winter the north sees the arrival of many winter visitors such as waterbirds and raptors, although it is usually cool and wet here at this time of year.

Habitats

Although the majority of the land surface is desert (50%) and farmland (28%), there are also wetlands, woodlands, wooded wadis and mountain meadows packed into this tiny country. The north is typically Mediterranean with wooded mountain slopes, scrubby valleys and wetlands, but the south, in stark contrast, is mainly an arid land of barren rocky outcrops and desert dotted with irrigated kibbutz fields and orchards.

Conservation

Israel's network of reserves and hunting restrictions help to conserve the varied avifauna, which includes 15 threatened and near-threatened species.

Bird Species

Over 500 species have been recorded in Israel, although over 100 of these are scarce visitors and vagrants. Non-endemic specialities and spectacular species include Pygmy Cormorant*, Sooty Falcon, Sand Partridge, Houbara Bustard, Cream-coloured Courser, White-eyed* and Great Black-headed Gulls, five species of sandgrouse, Green Bee-eater, Masked Shrike, Tristram's Starling, White-throated Robin, Hooded Wheatear, Blackstart, Red Sea and Cyprus Warblers, a fine selection of larks, Dead Sea Sparrow, Palestine Sunbird, Syrian Serin, Crimson-winged Finch, Trumpeter and Desert Finches, and Pale Rosefinch.

Endemics

There is no endemic species.

Expectations

It is possible to see between 160 and 175 species on a spring trip of one or two weeks to Eilat and its environs in the south, including five species of sandgrouse, seven wheatears, over 20 warblers and ten larks. A similar total is possible in autumn but there are smaller numbers of most species. Over 200 species are possible on a two-week spring or winter trip to both the north and south.

EILAT

This popular tourist resort in south Israel is situated at the northernmost point of the Red Sea on one of the world's major migration routes, and is one of the most exciting birding sites in the Palearctic. Apart from desert specialities, which include Hooded Wheatear and wintering rarities such as Cyprus Warbler, the major attraction is the spring migrants, which include numerous shorebirds, terns (50,000 White-winged Terns have been recorded in one spring) and passerines, which are attracted to the wide variety of habitats forming a desert oasis. These habitats include salt-pans, fields, palm plantations and sparsely vegetated wadis. Over 420 species have been recorded in the Eilat area, but the vast majority are migrants so there are quiet days and only the most fanatical birders will be able resist snorkelling or scuba-diving on the fantastic coral reefs which are just offshore.

Eilat is a wonderful place for raptors and each spring more birds pass over here than any other site on earth. In the 1980s spring raptor totals ranged from nearly 500,000 to 1.2 million in autumn the peak count is 26,000. The majority of birds in spring are European Honey-buzzards and 'Steppe' Buzzards, but they have included over 50,000 Levant Sparrowhawks and Steppe Eagles. Over 25,000 Levant Sparrowhawks have been counted in a single day in late April.

Many of the species listed below are spring and/or autumn migrants, or winter visitors which linger into early spring.

Specialities

White-eyed Gull*, Namaqua Dove, Tristram's Starling, Hooded Wheatear, Cyprus Warbler, Palestine Sunbird, Pale Rosefinch, Cinereous Bunting*.

EILAT

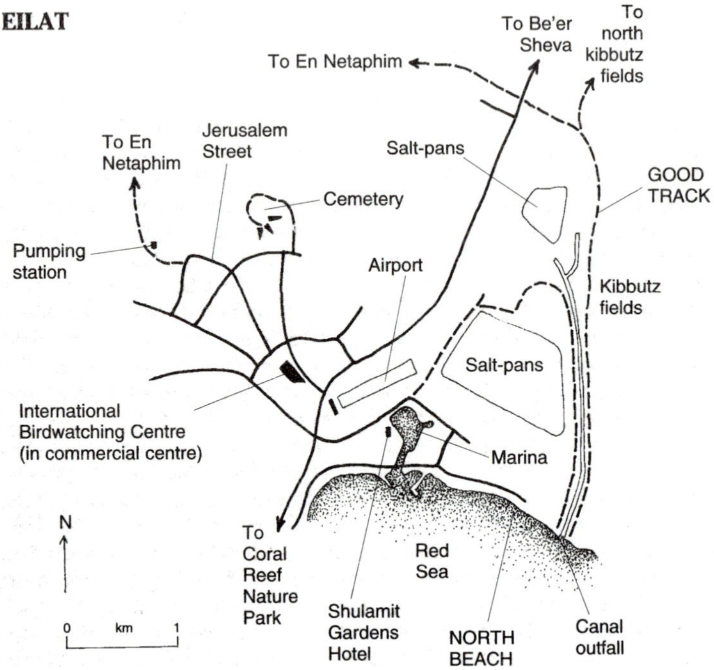

Others

Brown Booby, Great White Pelican, Greater Flamingo, Western Reef-Egret, White Stork, Egyptian Vulture, Eurasian Griffon, Long-legged Buzzard, Lesser Spotted, Steppe and Imperial* Eagles, Lesser Kestrel*, Lanner and Barbary Falcons, Sand Partridge, Little Crake, Greater Sandplover, Great Black-headed and Slender-billed Gulls, Lichtenstein's Sandgrouse, Laughing Dove, White-throated Kingfisher, Green and European Bee-eaters, House Crow, Masked Shrike, Collared and Semicollared Flycatchers, Rufous-tailed Scrub-Robin, White-tailed, Mourning and Isabelline Wheatears, Blackstart, Pale Crag-Martin, White-spectacled Bulbul, Streaked Scrub-Warbler, Graceful Prinia, Savi's, Moustached, Desert, Orphean and Rueppell's Warblers, Arabian Babbler, Desert and Bimaculated Larks, Oriental Skylark, Spanish Sparrow, Yellow Wagtail (including the black-headed *feldegg* race), Red-throated Pipit, Trumpeter and Desert Finches, Cretzschmar's and House Buntings.

Other Wildlife

Dorcas gazelle, nubian ibex, rock hyrax.

(Many other species are possible, especially in spring, and these include Streaked Shearwater, Red-billed Tropicbird, Striated Heron, Verreaux's Eagle, Sooty Falcon, Baillon's Crake, Caspian and Spur-winged Plovers, White-tailed Lapwing, Sooty Gull, White-cheeked Tern, Dideric Cuckoo, Pallid Scops-Owl (winters 1993–94 and 1994–95), Hume's Owl, Egyptian and Nubian Nightjars, Black Scrub-Robin, Cyprus Wheatear, Upcher's and Olive-tree Warblers, Dunn's Lark and Buff-bellied Pipit, as well as 'Mascarene Shearwater', a probable new species which was recorded in June 1992.)

Eilat is accessible by air and around 350 km south of Tel Aviv. Before dashing out into the field it may be best to visit the International Birdwatching Centre on Hatmarin Boulevard in the town centre. This is open from 1700 to 1900 daily and has details on all the latest sightings in Eilat and elsewhere. The centre also organises trips to local rarities such as Hume's Owl. Most of the hotels are situated around the marina at the western end of **North Beach**. The area east of Sun Bay campsite at the eastern end of this beach is the best site for Western Reef-Egret and White-eyed Gull*, while seawatching from here in strong southerlies may produce rarities such as Red-billed Tropicbird. Many birders gather at the mouth of the canal here in the late afternoon to seawatch and socialise. Some of the best habitats for migrants are within walking distance of the hotel complex at North Beach. Passerine migrants are even attracted to the gardens and parks in town (e.g. opposite the Shulamit Gardens Hotel), but the **south fields** to the north of the hotel complex, between the main road north and the Jordanian border to the east, are the best place for migrants. These fields are accessible via the tracks which run alongside the canal, as are the salt-pans where shorebirds and gulls tend to congregate in spring and where Sooty and Barbary Falcons have been recorded in autumn. The canal itself is good for migrant crakes. The track on the east side of the canal passes a palm plantation (White-throated Kingfisher, Green Bee-eater) before reaching the kibbutz fields (Namaqua Dove, Desert Finch). Further north the track reaches the **north fields**, where Oriental Skylarks occur in most winters, and Caspian Plover is possible in spring.

To the west of the town there is a **pumping station** with a small pool which attracts desert species such as Lichtenstein's Sandgrouse, Trumpeter Finch and House Bunting. The sandgrouse usually come to drink at dusk, but access may be restricted (check latest details at the International Birdwatching Centre). To reach the station take the track to the right at the top of Jerusalem Street, just round the bend beyond the Edomit Palace Hotel. The station is 500 m or so along here on the right. Keep right at all major junctions beyond the pumping station to reach an area of wadis where Sand Partridge, Tristram's Starling, Hooded Wheatear and Cyprus Warbler occur. The cemetery, reached by turning right at the top of Hatmarin Boulevard and following the road around to the left, is an excellent raptor viewpoint (especially the hill to the south, where birds may pass at eye level) and a good shady site for Sand Partridge and House Bunting.

The **Moon Valley Mountains**, to the west of Eilat, can be reached by taking the road to Ovda. Many raptors pass over these mountains and the best viewpoints are usually the hill behind the oil storage tanks to the south of the road 2 km west of Eilat, the hill to the east of the highest point of the road (accessible via a track) and the roadside 1 km beyond the En Netaphim turn-off. These mountains also support Hume's Owl (rare). The spring and 30 m waterfall at **En Netaphim**, which is accessible via a path from the car park, is a good site for Pale Rosefinch in winter, and other species in this area include Sand Partridge, Tristram's Starling, Hooded Wheatear, Streaked Scrub-warbler and Trumpeter Finch.

South of town turn west in response to the 'Texas Ranch' sign to enter **Wadi Shlomo**, where Hooded Wheatear occurs on the cliffs after 2–3 km.

Birding at Eilat can be spectacular, but some of those birders who have ventured on to the reefs have ended up admitting that the unbelievable variety of underwater life is even better. The best reef is at **Coral Reef Nature Park**, just south of town. There is an underwater observatory here and glass-bottomed boat trips for those who have problems snorkelling or scuba-diving.

Accommodation: Sun Bay campsite (C) and bungalows (A), Max and Merran's hostel (C), Youth Hostel (B), hotels (A+).

Hooded Wheatear is one of Eilat's star birds

ARAVA VALLEY

The desert and its acacia oases in the Arava Valley north of Eilat support a fine selection of desert specialities, including resident Red Sea Warbler, and attract some localised winter visitors such as Cyprus Warbler and Pale Rosefinch. In some springs the desert is alive with larks, including Thick-billed, Dunn's and Temminck's Larks.

Specialities

Tristram's Starling, Red Sea and Cyprus (Nov–Mar) Warblers, Dead Sea Sparrow (Oct–Apr), Pale Rosefinch (Nov–Mar).

Others

Lesser Kestrel*, Sand Partridge, Cream-coloured Courser, Green Bee-eater, Brown-necked Raven, White-tailed, Desert and Isabelline Wheatears, Blackstart, Streaked Scrub-Warbler, Desert (Nov–Mar) and Orphean Warblers, Arabian Babbler, Bar-tailed and Desert Larks, Greater Hoopoe-Lark, Bimaculated and Lesser Short-toed Larks, Trumpeter and Desert Finches.

(Other species recorded here include Lappet-faced Vulture, Sooty Falcon, Houbara Bustard, Caspian Plover, Sociable Lapwing*, Crowned Sandgrouse, Thick-billed, Dunn's and Temminck's Larks and Pale Rockfinch, as well as wolf.)

Pale Rosefinches usually winter around the parking area at **Amram's Pillars**, 25 km north of Eilat. To reach here take the track west at the KM 20 post and the right fork after 5 km. Other species which occur here include Sand Partridge and Blackstart. Opposite the turning to Amram's Pillars there is a 400 m track to some salt-pans. Dead Sea Sparrow occurs in the Acacias at the end of this track. The area around the **KM 33** post is the best site for desert specialities near Eilat, even though part of this site was ploughed up in 1994 and more desert is likely to be lost to agricultural encroachment in the future. The east side of the road is the best for desert species and is accessible via track and trail. To bird this area turn east and park at the T-junction pumping station, then walk along the tracks to the north and south. There are usually plenty of larks here and wintering Desert Warbler. In summer Sooty Falcon has been recorded in the **Timna Valley**, which lies to the west of the road a few kilometres south of the KM 40 post. **KM 40** is another good area for desert species and Houbara Bustard has been recorded here. Take the track east and bird beyond the palm plantations. Further north, between KM posts 50 and 53, in the area known as **Yotvata**, Red Sea Warbler occurs in the acacias to the west of the road at the KM 50 post (along with Cyprus Warbler in winter) and in the bushy scrub (especially around the rubbish dump) just southeast of the cafe on the east side of the road to the north of the KM 50 post. Houbara Bustard has been recorded in the fields to the east of the road at the KM 53 post and the elusive Crowned Sandgrouse occurs at the sewage works at **Shizzafon**. To reach here turn west 10 km north of Yotvata (towards Be'er Sheva) and look for the pools on the north side of the road after about 5 km.

NEGEV DESERT

There are numerous military camps in the Negev Desert, northwest of Eilat, but most areas beyond these camps are accessible and this is one of the most reliable sites in the world for Houbara Bustard. Irrigation has enabled much of the western Negev to be cultivated, but the fields attract an impressive variety of wintering raptors as well as four species of sandgrouse.

Specialities

Sooty Falcon (Sep–Oct), Sand Partridge, Houbara Bustard, Sociable Lapwing* (Nov–Mar), Tristram's Starling, Pale Rosefinch (Oct–Apr).

Others

Pallid Harrier* (Sep–Apr), Lesser Spotted (Sep–Oct/Mar–Apr), Steppe (Oct–Apr) and Imperial* (Nov–Mar) Eagles, Lesser Kestrel* (Sep–Oct/Mar), Lanner, Saker (Nov–Mar) and Barbary Falcons, Chukar, Common Crane (Oct–Apr), Eurasian Thick-knee, Cream-coloured Courser, Eurasian Dotterel (Nov–Mar), Spur-winged Plover, Pin-tailed, Spotted, Black-bellied and Crowned Sandgrouse, Brown-necked Raven, White-tailed, Mourning, Finsch's (Nov–Mar), Desert and Isabelline Wheatears, Streaked Scrub-Warbler, Bar-tailed and Desert Larks, Greater Hoopoe-Lark, Calandra and Lesser Short-toed Larks, Trumpeter and Desert Finches.

Other Wildlife

Dorcas gazelle, wolf.

(Other species recorded here include Lappet-faced Vulture, Pharaoh Eagle-Owl and Hume's Owl.)

The line of pylons which crosses Route 234 to Ze'elim, 4 km south of **Urim**, is the best place to look for wintering raptors, and Sociable Lapwing* has been recorded in this area. The best area for Houbara Bustard is around **Nizzana**, near the Egyptian border, in the south Negev. This is a sensitive part of Israel with a heavy military presence and access may be difficult at times (check at International Birdwatching Centre in Eilat). *En route* to Nizzana from Be'er Sheva it is worth stopping at Ashalim, where the pools attract sandgrouse at dawn, and a walk along the nearby wadi may produce Houbara Bustard and Cream-coloured Courser. Sewage pools at Nizzana also attract sandgrouse, but their location varies from year to year. The road south to Azzuz from Nizzana Castle runs through excellent desert country which is worth a prolonged look. Lappet-faced Vulture is a rare bird in Israel, but one site where this species may still occur is at the feeding station and roost site for vultures, in Nahalzin Gorge just south of Sdeh Boker, 50 km south of Be'er Sheva. To reach the feeding station turn east before reaching Metzad Ma'agura. Sooty Falcon, Pharaoh Eagle-Owl and Hume's Owl have been recorded in **Wadi Zin** to the south of the gorge.

Accommodation: Be'er Sheva — Desert Inn. Nizzana — educational settlement. Izuz — campsite. Sdeh Boker — Desert Inn.

EIN GEDI

The vegetated wadis at Ein Gedi on the west shore of the Dead Sea may still support the rare Hume's Owl and usually attract migrants and winter visitors which include Wallcreeper, Cyprus Warbler and Syrian Serin.

Specialities

Fan-tailed Raven, Tristram's Starling, Cyprus Warbler (Oct–Apr), Palestine Sunbird, Syrian Serin (Nov–Mar).

Others

Egyptian Vulture, Eurasian Griffon, Barbary Falcon, Sand Partridge, Pallid and Little Swifts, Green Bee-eater, Brown-necked Raven, Blackstart, Wallcreeper (Nov–Mar), Pale Crag-Martin, Arabian Babbler, House Bunting.

(Other species recorded here include Hume's Owl.)

Ein Gedi is 3 hours by road north of Eilat (about 240 km) and one hour by road south of Jerusalem. Hume's Owl has been recorded on the floodlit fences north of the entrance to the main wadi (Nahal David NR) and around the nearby amphitheatre, hunting moths attracted to the lights. Wintering Wallcreeper and Cyprus Warbler occur in the wadi (Nahal Arugot NR) south of here and the warbler also occurs in the scrub on the right-hand side of the road near the Ein Gedi Kibbutz Hotel. The ruins of the nearby hilltop fortress at Masada, accessible by cable-car, afford a splendid view of the Dead Sea and migrating raptors, and are a good site for Fan-tailed Raven.

Accommodation: field centre/Youth Hostel (C), Ein Gedi Kibbutz Hotel (A).

A large colony of Lesser Kestrels* (70–80 pairs) breeds in the old city, **Jerusalem**, and many birds appear to feed in the city parks.

GALILEE, GOLAN HEIGHTS AND MOUNT HERMON

The desert of south Israel gives way to orchards, fields, fishponds and lakes in the north. These habitats attract a fine selection of wintering waterbirds and raptors, as well as a number of birds which do not occur in the south, including Pygmy Cormorant*, while the mountains of the extreme northeast, which rise to 2814 m (9232 ft) at Mount Hermon, support the localised Syrian Serin and Crimson-winged Finch.

Specialities

Armenian Gull (Nov–Mar), Dead Sea Sparrow, Syrian Serin, Crimson-winged Finch.

Others

Pygmy Cormorant*, Great White Pelican, White-headed Duck*, Marbled Teal*, Little Bittern, Glossy Ibis, Black Stork (Sep–Apr), White-tailed Eagle* (Nov–Mar), Egyptian Vulture, Eurasian Griffon, Cinereous Vulture* (Nov–Mar), Pallid Harrier (Nov–Mar), Lesser Spotted (Sep–Oct/Mar–Apr), Greater Spotted* (Sep–Apr) and Imperial* (Oct–Apr) Eagles, Lesser Kestrel*, Black Francolin, Chukar, Little Crake (Nov–Mar), Common Crane (Nov–Mar), Little Bustard* (Nov–Mar), Great Black-headed Gull (Nov–Mar), Little Swift, White-throated and Pied Kingfishers, Blue-cheeked Bee-eater (Apr–Sep), Syrian Woodpecker, White-throated Robin (May–Sep), Finsch's Wheatear (Nov–Mar), Wallcreeper (Nov–Mar), Graceful Prinia, Moustached Warbler, Clamorous Reed-Warbler, Upcher's (May–Sep) and Orphean (May–Sep) Warblers, Sombre Tit, Eurasian Penduline-Tit (Nov–Mar), Oriental Skylark (Nov–Mar), Spanish Sparrow, Rock Petronia, Pale Rockfinch, Alpine Accentor (Nov–Mar), Long-billed Pipit, Fire-fronted Serin (Nov–Mar), Cretzschmar's Bunting (May–Sep).

(Other species recorded here in winter include Sociable Lapwing*, Buff-bellied Pipit, Spot-throated Accentor and Pine Bunting.)

To the south of the Sea of Galilee (Lake Tiberias), the fishponds at Kefar Ruppin and Tirat Zevi in the heavily cultivated Jordan Valley, southeast of **Bet She'an**, and the roadside fishponds, reservoirs and fields north-west of Bet She'an, are all worth prolonged birding. There were around 2,000 Great Black-headed Gulls in the area during December 1994.

GALILEE AREA

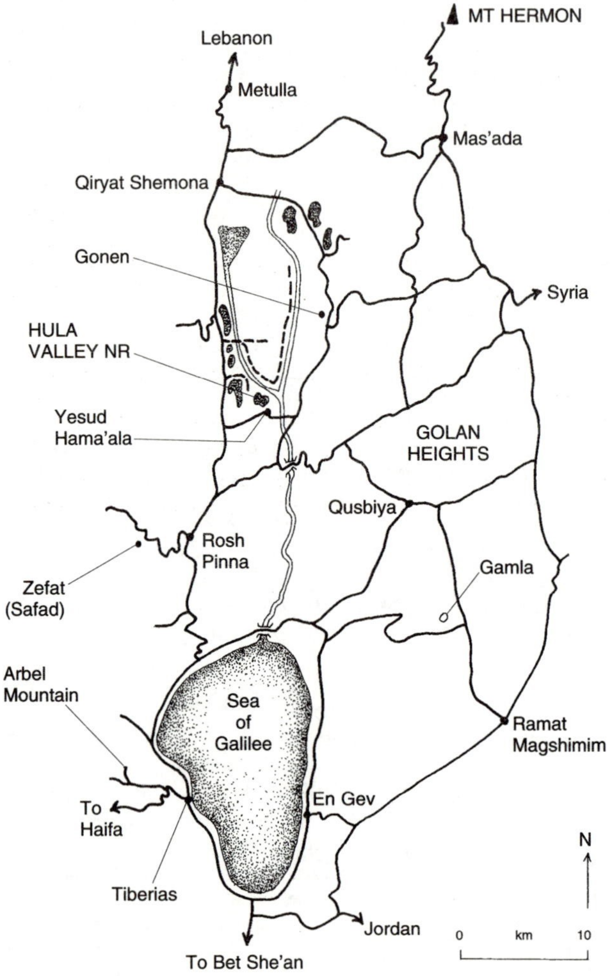

Tishlovit Reservoir, south of Afula, is a good site for White-headed Duck* (Nov–Mar) and Marbled Teal*, while the Ma'aleh Kishon Reservoirs, 7 km southwest of Gvat, are also worth checking. North of Afula, west of Nazareth, many raptors on autumn migration roost in the woods north of the Kefar Hahoresh road, and the hillsides north of nearby Gevat are favoured by migrant raptors on autumn mornings. To the west of the Sea of Galilee, the gorge leading to **Arbel Mountain** supports Long-billed Pipit and occasionally attracts wintering Wallcreeper. The **Hula Valley** NR (775 ha), which lies to the north of the Sea of Galilee, supports wintering Pygmy Cormorant*, migrant Great White Pelicans (up to 70,000), resident Marbled Teal*, wintering White-tailed Eagle*, up to 5,000 wintering Common Cranes and Dead Sea Sparrow. To reach the reserve turn east off the road to Qiryat Shemona, 10 km north of Rosh Pinna (where there is a Lesser Kestrel* colony). Dead Sea Sparrow occurs alongside the entrance track. The fishponds to the east of the Qiryat Shemona road, 1 km north of the reserve turn-off, accessible via a track, are also worth checking. About 4 km north of the reserve turn-off there is another track east which leads to fields favoured by raptors and cranes. Along the road up to **Mount Hermon** White-throated Robin and Upcher's Warbler occur in the orchards just north of Mas'ada on Route 98. There are two military checkpoints on the final approach to the mountain where it may be necessary to obtain permission to continue the ascent to the ski centre, situated at 2000 m (6562 ft), and beyond. Syrian Serin may be found around the car park at the ski centre, while Crimson-winged Finch is best looked for at the summit which can be reached via the ski-lift. Species recorded on Mount Hermon in winter include Finsch's Wheatear, Wallcreeper, Spot-throated Accentor and Fire-fronted Serin. To the east of the Sea of Galilee, Finsch's Wheatear, Spot-throated Accentor and Fire-fronted Serin are winter visitors to the rocky hills of the **Golan Heights**, which rise to 1500 m (4921 ft). Cinereous Vulture* occurs at the historical site of Gamla, and at Wadi Meizar to the south, which overlooks the spectacular Wadi Yehudiyya. The best time to look for this rarity is during the early morning when roosting birds leave their roosting cliffs to join the first thermals of the day.

Accommodation: Bet She'an — Newe Etan Kibbutz Guesthouse (A+). Kefar Blum Kibbutz Guesthouse (A+) (tel: 943666).

Great Black-headed Gull winters in the Bet She'an area

MA'AGAN MIKHAEL

The sandy beaches and fishponds near Ma'agan Mikhael, 50 km north of Tel Aviv, on Israel's northern Mediterranean coast, support wintering Great Black-headed and Armenian Gulls.

Specialities

Armenian Gull (Oct–Apr).

Others

Yelkouan Shearwater, Great White Pelican, Glossy Ibis, Black Stork (Nov–Mar), Little Crake (Nov–Mar), Greater Sandplover, Spur-winged Plover, Yellow-legged (Oct–Apr), Great Black-headed (Nov–Apr) and Slender-billed Gulls, White-throated and Pied Kingfishers, Graceful

Prinia, Clamorous Reed-Warbler, Rueppell's Warbler (May–Sep).

(Other species recorded here include Kittlitz's Plover, up to three of which were recorded in winter from 1989 to 1994.)

The fishponds, just north of Nasholim, are most easily reached via the old Tel Aviv–Haifa road. From this road turn west in response to the Ma'agan Mikhael signpost, then north at the football pitch. After 200 m turn east to the cemetery where a rocky area to the north supports Rueppell's Warbler, or continue on the main track to the 'No Entry' sign. Proceed on foot from here to the beach and walk north to look for Great Black-headed Gull and Yelkouan Shearwater offshore.

Accommodation: Ma'agan Field Centre.

ADDITIONAL INFORMATION

Addresses

Israel Rare Birds Committee, PO Box 4168, Eilat 88102, Israel. (Fax: 972 7 379326.)
International Birdwatching Centre, PO Box 774, City Centre, Eilat. (Tel: 74276.)

Hadoram Shirihai, one of Israel's most experienced birders, offers a number of guided tours in search of the country's best birds. While he is happy to arrange individual itineraries, some examples of the more regular trips include the following (prices are based on at least three participants using their own vehicles and paying for petrol and food, but include accommodation in kibbutz guesthouses: an evening excursion from Eilat in search of owls and/or nightjars (£15); a day in the Negev in search of Houbara Bustard, Cream-coloured Courser, five species of sandgrouse and many larks and wheatears (£30); a two-day trip to the Negev searching for those species above as well as other species such as Lappet-faced Vulture (£55); a three-day trip to the Arava Valley, Dead Sea, Bet She'an and Ma'agan Mikhael (£85); and a five-day trip to north Israel (£140). It is best to book well in advance and Hadoram can be reached at PO Box 4168, Eilat 88102. (Tel/fax: 972 7 379326; mobile phone: 052 624063.)

Books and Papers

The Birds of Israel. Edited by Shirihai H, 1996. Academic Press.
Birdwatching in the Deserts of Israel. Shirihai H, 1993. IOC/IRIC/IBCE.
Birdwatching in Eilat (2nd edition). Yosef R, 1995. Privately published.

Near-endemics

Armenian Gull, Cyprus Warbler, Dead Sea Sparrow, Spot-throated Accentor, Syrian Serin, Cretzschmar's Bunting (breeding).

JORDAN

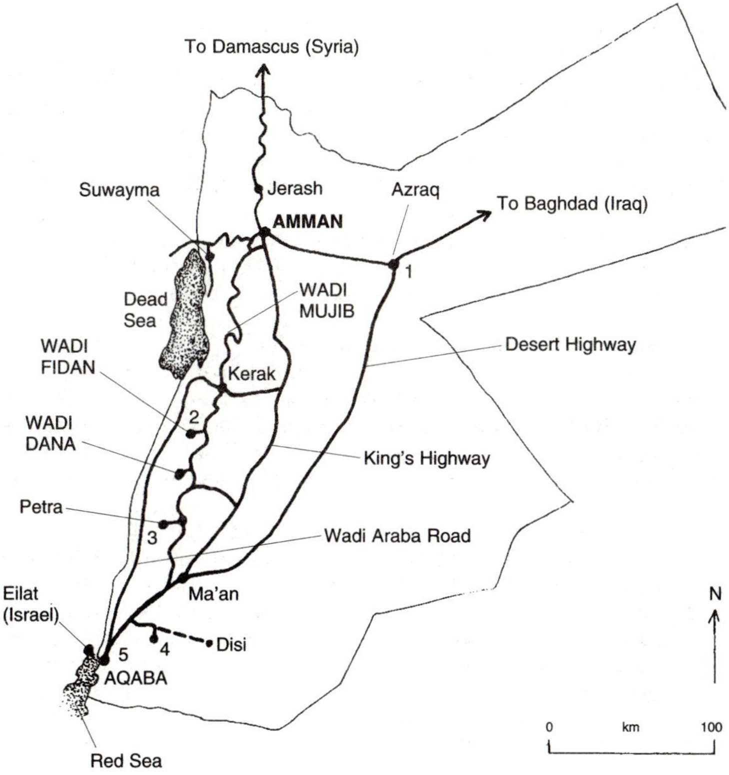

1 Azraq Oasis
2 Wadis Mujib, Fidan and Dana
3 Petra
4 Wadi Rum
5 Aqaba

INTRODUCTION

Summary

Jordan supports a similar avifauna to Israel, although birds such as Verreaux's Eagle, Sooty Falcon and the scarcer larks are more likely to be seen in this country than in its smaller, more modern neighbour. Now the border between the two countries is open it may be worth considering a trip to both.

Size

At 89,210 sq km, Jordan is a little smaller than England and a seventh the size of Texas.

Getting Around

It is possible to hire vehicles in Amman and Aqaba and using personal transport would be the best way to go birding in Jordan. A good map is essential as many roadsigns are only in Arabic. Otherwise there is an adequate bus and shared taxi network, but long-distance buses are often full and need to be booked in advance.

Accommodation and Food

A wide range of accommodation is available in Amman, Azraq, Petra and Aqaba, whereas there are only campsites (where tents can be hired) at Wadi Rum and Wadi Dana. It is also possible to camp away from towns so long as it is not in a military area. Local food such as felafel (chick pea and salad sandwiches), hummus and shawarma (spiced lamb) is cheap, but beer is relatively expensive.

Health and Safety

Immunisation against hepatitis, polio, typhoid and yellow fever is recommended.

Climate and Timing

The climate is harsh, with very hot summers and cold winters, and the best time to visit is the spring, between late March and early May, especially the last two weeks of April.

Habitats

Jordan is landlocked apart from a 27 km stretch of coastline in the south and almost entirely composed of desert (Badia), which lies on a gently undulating plateau and is composed of gravel plains (hammada), black boulder fields (harrat) and sand dunes. The Rift Valley scarp, which rises to 1736 m (5696 ft) is relatively well vegetated and there are also a few oases and some cultivation, which is mainly confined to the Jordan Valley, north of the Dead Sea.

Conservation

There are three national parks, six wildlife reserves and 18 grazing reserves, but more are needed to conserve the birds of Jordan, which include six threatened and near-threatened species.

Bird Species

Over 370 species have been recorded in Jordan. Non-endemic specialities and spectacular species include Verreaux's Eagle, Sooty Falcon, Sand Partridge, Cream-coloured Courser, White-eyed* and Great Black-headed Gulls, Hume's Owl, Masked Shrike, Tristram's Starling, White-throated Robin, Hooded and Red-rumped Wheatears, Upcher's, Red Sea and Menetries' Warblers, Blackstart, Greater Hoopoe-Lark, Thick-billed, Dunn's and Temminck's Larks, Dead Sea Sparrow, Palestine Sunbird, Syrian Serin, Trumpeter Finch, Pale Rosefinch and Cinereous Bunting*.

Endemics

There is no endemic species.

The best birding site near **Amman**, the busy modern capital in north Jordan, is **Dibbin Forest**, the best remaining pine forest in the country. Species recorded here include Syrian Woodpecker and Sombre Tit.

Good sites for migrants include the environs of **Suwayma**, on the shores of the Dead Sea southwest of Amman, and the area around the Roman city of **Jerash**, 50 km north of Amman. Brown Fish-Owl has been recorded in the **Yarmuk Valley** along the Syrian border, north of Amman.

The 85 km **Amman–Azraq Road** passes through desert east of Amman which supports Cream-coloured Courser, Red-rumped and Isabelline Wheatears and Bar-tailed, Thick-billed, Lesser Short-toed, Dunn's and Temminck's Larks. About 40 km west of Azraq a track to the east of Qasr el-Kharaneh Castle (check grounds for migrants) leads south through a good stretch of desert where Red-rumped Wheatear (at the end of the wadi to the east, just south of the pylons) and Thick-billed, Dunn's and Temminck's Larks have been recorded. Further east towards Azraq Desert Finch occurs in the trees at the back of the hunting lodge at Qasr Amra.

AZRAQ OASIS

This sadly degraded oasis, which was once a maze of marshes among many miles of desert, supported as many as 350,000 wintering waterfowl in the 1960s. Today, hardly any wetland remains thanks to the demand for water from the nearby farmland and the cities of Amman and Irbid. However, the bushy areas still attract spring migrants and up to nine species of lark breed in the surrounding hammada desert.

Most of the species listed below are usually only present in the spring.

Specialities

Thick-billed, Dunn's and Temminck's Larks, Cinereous Bunting*.

Others

Black Stork, Pallid Harrier*, Levant Sparrowhawk, Long-legged Buzzard, Lesser Spotted, Greater Spotted*, Steppe and Imperial* (Nov–Mar) Eagles, Lesser Kestrel*, Red-footed and Barbary Falcons, Little Crake, Cream-coloured Courser, Greater Sandplover, Caspian and Spur-winged Plovers, White-tailed Lapwing, Pin-tailed and Spotted Sandgrouse, Pied Kingfisher, Masked Shrike, Collared and Semicollared Flycatchers, Thrush Nightingale, White-throated Robin, Rufous-tailed Scrub-Robin, Red-rumped, Mourning and Isabelline Wheatears, Streaked Scrub-Warbler, Savi's, Moustached, Aquatic, Booted, Upcher's, Desert, Orphean, Rueppell's and Menetries' Warblers, Bar-tailed and Desert Larks, Greater Hoopoe-Lark, Bimaculated and Lesser Short-toed Larks, Desert Finch, Cretzschmar's Bunting.

(Other species recorded here include Cyprus Wheatear (Nov–Mar).

Azraq Oasis is about 100 km east of Amman and surrounds the villages of South Azraq and North Azraq. Cinereous Bunting* has been recorded in spring in and around the Shaumari Wildlife Reserve, 10 km to the south of South Azraq (ostrich and Arabian oryx are being reintroduced here). The tiny Azraq Wetland Reserve, just east of South Azraq, is worth checking, and to the east of the reserve there is a seasonally flooded pan (known as Qa al Azraq), which in normal circumstances is wet until May and a major magnet for migrants. The area around the resthouse, a few kilometres north of North Azraq, is good for migrants, and the dark form of Desert Lark, which has evolved in line with its black basalt habitat, occurs in the desert to the north, alongside the road between As Safawi and Iraq.

Accommodation: resthouse (run by the Royal Society for Nature Conservation, PO Box 6345, Amman. tel: 811689), Al-Zoubi Hotel (C).

Lanner and Barbary Falcons, Sand Partridge, Hume's Owl, Tristram's Starling, Hooded Wheatear, Blackstart, Upcher's Warbler and Dead Sea Sparrow occur in **Wadi Mujib** near Kerak in central-west Jordan, south of Amman. This wadi is accessible from the King's Highway just north of Ariha and most birds can be found by following the river up to the waterfall.

Accommodation: Kerak — Castle Hotel (C).

In Kerak it is possible to obtain a permit (from the office next to the hospital compound) to visit **Wadi Fidan**, which is only accessible from the Wadi Araba road (which runs along the Israeli border), 50 km south of Kerak. This is an excellent site for Cream-coloured Courser, Spotted Sandgrouse, Upcher's and Red Sea Warblers and Dunn's Lark. Further south, some 60 km north of Wadi Musa (near Petra), is **Wadi Dana NR**, where Upcher's Warbler, Pale Rockfinch, Long-billed Pipit, Syrian Serin and Pale Rosefinch occur. To reach this leafy wadi follow the road west from the King's Highway to the small village of Dana and ascend the very rough track beyond.

Accommodation: campsite.

PETRA

The 2,000 year old rosy remains of the ancient city of Petra are a major tourist attraction, and not even a birding trip to Jordan would be complete without seeing it as this happens to be an excellent site for Pale Rosefinch.

Specialities

Tristram's Starling, Temminck's Lark, Palestine Sunbird, Pale Rosefinch.

Others

Barbary Falcon, Sand Partridge, Chukar, Pallid Swift, Fan-tailed Raven, White-tailed and Mourning Wheatears, Blackstart, Pale Crag-Martin, Streaked Scrub-Warbler, Arabian Babbler, Desert Lark, Rock Petronia, House Bunting.

(Other species recorded here include Sooty Falcon (Oct), Hume's Owl and Syrian Serin (Nov–Mar).)

Petra, which is best seen in the late afternoon, can only be approached on foot or horseback through the narrow Siq Gorge, a good area for Pale Rosefinch, from the village of Wadi Musa about 6 km away. The area around Wadi Musa is also worth birding. Hume's Owl has been recorded at the Corinthian Tomb, Palace Tomb, Urn Tomb, Amphitheatre and Siq, usually at dusk, but tourists are supposed to leave the ruins by nightfall.

Accommodation: Wadi Musa — Moussa Spring Hotel (C).

WADI RUM

This huge wadi in south Jordan is an impressive natural wonder and a major tourist attraction. However, it is easy to get away from the hoards here, in search of such great birds as Verreaux's Eagle, Sooty Falcon and Hooded Wheatear.

Specialities

Verreaux's Eagle, Sooty Falcon (May–Oct), Tristram's Starling, Hooded Wheatear, Palestine Sunbird, Pale Rosefinch.

Others

Long-legged Buzzard, Lesser Kestrel*, Barbary Falcon, Sand Partridge, Chukar, Brown-necked Raven, White-tailed and Mourning Wheatears, Blackstart, Pale Crag-Martin, Streaked Scrub-Warbler, Bar-tailed and Desert Larks, Greater Hoopoe-Lark, Rock Petronia, Trumpeter Finch, House Bunting.

(Other species recorded here include Lappet-faced Vulture and Lammergeier.)

The Resthouse is 28 km from the Desert Highway. Turn east at Ar Rashidiyya and take the right fork after 16 km. Bird Lawrence's Well, a spring at the base of the cliffs behind the Resthouse, Wadi Rum village (Pale Rosefinch), and the bushy desert and boulder slopes 3 km north of Wadi Rum village. 4WD vehicles with drivers can be hired in the village to explore further.

Accommodation: Government Resthouse/Campsite (C — including tents for rent).

The irrigation schemes at **Disi** and **Sahl as Suwann**, east of Bedu village in Wadi Rum, attract migrants and Dunn's Lark has been recorded at Disi.

AQABA

This port at the northern tip of the Red Sea in south Jordan lies a few kilometres to the east of Eilat, its more famous neighbour in Israel. However, although over 350 species have been recorded within a few kilometres of Aqaba and there are some palm groves and gardens fed by natural springs at the base of the mountains, there is much less suitable habitat here than in Eilat. Even the spring raptor passage which involves around 50,000 birds pales into insignificance when compared with Eilat's (p. 357).

Many of the species listed below are only present in spring and/or autumn.

Specialities

White-eyed Gull*, Tristram's Starling, Hooded Wheatear, Red Sea Warbler, Dead Sea Sparrow, Palestine Sunbird.

Others

Brown Booby, Western Reef-Egret, Barbary Falcon, Great Black-headed Gull, Green Bee-eater, Fan-tailed Raven, Masked Shrike, Rufous-tailed Scrub-Robin, White-tailed Wheatear, Blackstart, Graceful Prinia, Clamorous Reed-Warbler, Arabian Babbler, Greater Hoopoe-Lark, Trumpeter Finch, House Bunting.

(Other species recorded here include Nubian Nightjar and Cyprus Warbler.)

Aqaba is accessible by air or road (3–4 hours) from Amman. Virtually anywhere in and around the town attracts migrants, even traffic islands. Seawatching has been fruitful from the jetty at the Aquamarina Hotel, while White-eyed Gulls* have been seen in the yacht harbour and at the Royal Diving Centre, 15 km south of town. Aqaba is popular with scuba-divers as one of the best reefs in the world lies just offshore.

ADDITIONAL INFORMATION

Addresses

Royal Society for the Conservation of Nature, PO Box 6354, Amman (tel: 811689; fax: 847411).

Books and Papers

The Birds of the Hashemite Kingdom of Jordan. Andrews I, 1995. Available from I Andrews, 39 Clayknowes Drive, Musselburgh, Midlothian EH21 6UW, UK.
Portrait of a Desert. Mountfort G, 1965. Collins (out of print, but well worth tracking down and reading, if only to discover what Azraq Oasis used to be like).

Near-endemics

Dead Sea Sparrow, Syrian Serin.

KUWAIT

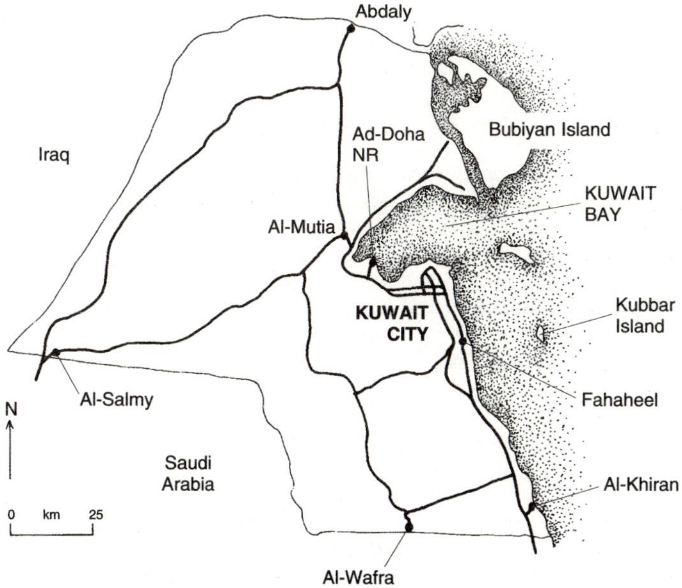

This tiny country is situated at the northeastern end of the Arabian Peninsula and supports an avifauna more or less typical of that for a small piece of land next to the Arabian Gulf: a mixture of seabirds, desert specialists and passage migrants in search of oases.

Few birders have been to Kuwait and tourism is not encouraged. However, those that do get there will find that a vehicle is more or less essential as there are few buses or taxis. When driving there are two crucial safety considerations to remember: stay on the roads and major tracks because there are still many unexploded land mines littering the desert, and do not go anywhere near the Iraq border. Accommodation is expensive in Kuwait and alcohol is banned. Immunisation against hepatitis, polio and typhoid is recommended. The summers are baking hot, but the winters are pleasant to rather cool and wet. The best time to visit is probably in the spring when lingering winter visitors mix with migrants, which may include Hypocolius. Kuwait has a long coastline which gives way to the 80 km long Jal Az-Zor escarpment, which rises to 145 m (476 ft), and a mainly flat, gravelly desert. Until the Gulf War, Kuwait's major conservation problems revolved around overgrazing, but by the end of March 1991 over 850 oil fires were burning, forming a huge black cloud up to 200 km wide and 600 km long, and in August of the same year 500 fires continued to light up the otherwise darkened sky. Lakes of oil littered the landscape, causing the death of many birds and yet, remarkably, 95% of the coastline remained free from oil after the war. Five threatened and near-threatened species occur in Kuwait.

Over 280 species have been recorded in Kuwait, but only eight species breed on a regular basis. The majority of species are migrants and/or winter visitors, and include Persian Shearwater, Socotra Cormorant*, Crab Plover, Cream-coloured Courser, Caspian Plover, White-tailed Lapwing, Great Black-headed Gull, White-cheeked (Apr–Sep) and Bridled (Apr–Sep) Terns, Blue-cheeked Bee-eater, Semicollared Flycatcher, Mourning (Sep–Apr) and Red-tailed (Sep–Apr) Wheatears, Hypocolius (on passage along the coast in spring), Basra Reed-Warbler* Apr–Sep), Upcher's and Olive-tree Warblers, Small Whitethroat and Menetries' Warbler.

Over 100 Crab Plovers have wintered in **Kuwait Bay**, where spring raptor passage has run to over 400 birds of 17 species in a single day. One of the best birding sites around this bay is Jahra Pool on the south shore. where Basra Reed-Warbler* occurs. **Kubbar Island** is a popular recreational area where White-cheeked and Bridled Terns have bred. Farmland at **Al-Abraq** and **Al-Khabari** attracts migrants, including warblers. The desert, bordered to the north by **Wadi Al-Batin**, used to support Houbara Bustard and Temminck's Lark, but it has probably still not recovered from overgrazing in the 1980s and the ravages of the Gulf War.

ADDITIONAL INFORMATION

Addresses

Kuwait Ornithological Records Committee, c/o Charles Pilcher, Faculty of Medicine, PO Box 24923, Safat, Kuwait.

LEBANON

Before Lebanon was torn apart by civil war, this small country in the east Mediterranean was one of the most popular tourist destinations in the Middle East. Now the war seems to be over it is opening up again and birders may be tempted by the presence of such birds as Syrian Serin.

Cheap buses and shared taxis reach most destinations, but birding would be better with a hire-car. Accommodation appears to be limited to expensive hotels, but the food is very varied and tasty, with such delights as kebabs and tabouleh (crushed wheat with salad and mint), which can be enjoyed with a beer or two. Immunisation against hepatitis, polio, typhoid and yellow fever is recommended. Southern Lebanon is the base for the Hizbullah militia which fired Katyusha missiles into northern Israel in early 1996, sparking retaliation by Israeli warplanes

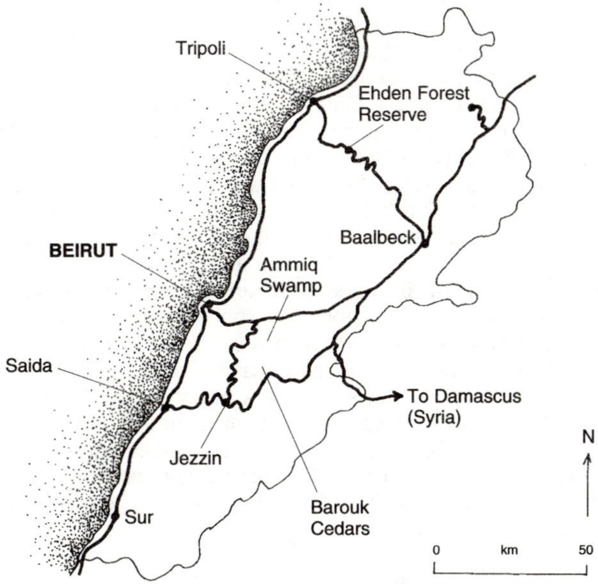

which attacked the south and the suburbs of Beirut. A ceasefire came into effect in April 1996 but it is a fragile one. Hot, dry summers give way to cool, wet winters with snow in the mountains and the migration seasons are the best times to visit. The 225 km long coastline and densely populated narrow coastal plain give way to the Lebanon Mountains, which rise to 3090 m (10,138 ft) at Qornet es-Sawda and the Cedars of Lebanon. The western slopes of these mountains support olive groves, maquis and small areas of remnant pine forest. The narrow, fertile Beka'a Valley separates these mountains from the Anti-Lebanon Mountains in the east, which rise to 2814 m (9232 ft) at Jebel ash-Sheikh (Mount Hermon) and support drier, scrubbier vegetation and remnant deciduous forests on their western slopes. Numerous birds, mainly pelicans, storks and raptors, pass through Lebanon, especially in the autumn, and millions of larks migrate through the northern Beka'a Valley, but many migrants had to dodge the many hunters until a shooting ban was introduced in early 1995. Even this ban may not last long, judging by the public outcry. Another conservation problem is overgrazing, which has led to the widespread degradation of the natural habitats and not helped the protection of Lebanon's birds, which include seven threatened and near-threatened species. Non-endemic specialities and spectacular species include Syrian Serin and Crimson-winged Finch. There is no endemic species.

Audouin's* and Yellow-legged Gulls and Lesser Crested-Tern used to breed at the **Palm Islands Marine Reserve**, northwest of Tripoli, but this is now a popular recreation area and it is doubtful if any of these birds remain. Eurasian Griffon and Chukar have been recorded in the **Ehden FR**, high in the rocky mountains southeast of Tripoli, but the habitats and birds here are under serious threat from hunting, logging and overgrazing. In south Lebanon the best cedar forest left in the country is near **Barouk** and species recorded here include Finsch's Wheatear, Orphean Warbler, Sombre Tit, Long-billed Pipit, Syrian Serin, Crimson-winged Finch and Cretzschmar's Bunting, while migrant raptors have included Eurasian Griffon, Levant Sparrowhawk, Lesser Spotted and Imperial* Eagles, Lesser Kestrel* and Saker Falcon. As with the Ehden FR this site is snow-covered in winter. The largest remaining wetland is also in the south at **Ammiq**, on the west side of the Beka'a Valley. In February and March, helped by melting snow from the mountains, this wetland has been known to flood beyond 280 ha, but by August it is usually dry. The area, which includes extensive reedbeds, is the only sizeable wetland between Israel and Turkey, and large numbers of pelicans, storks and raptors have been observed flying over. However, this used to be a very popular hunting area from autumn to spring, and the presence of so many guns probably prevented these birds from stopping off here. Nevertheless, breeding species include Little Bittern, Graceful Prinia, Savi's and Moustached Warblers and, in the surrounding area, Lesser Short-toed Lark. Spring migrants have included Great Snipe*. The nearby **Qaraoun Lake**, formed by a dam on the Litani River, is also probably worth exploring. The best base for birding the Beka'a Valley is Zahleh.

Near-endemics

Syrian Serin, Cretzschmar's Bunting (breeding).

OMAN

INTRODUCTION

Oman occupies the southeast corner of the Arabian Peninsula. Although it supports far fewer of the peninsula's endemics than neighbouring Yemen, this country is rich in seabirds and with tourism being encouraged, birders may be tempted to taste some Arabian seawatching.

There are daily flights between Muscat and Salalah, the two cities which lie at opposite ends of this small country, as well as an extensive, cheap bus network, but a vehicle, preferably 4WD, is needed to reach most of the best birding sites. Accommodation at both ends of the expenses scale is available in Muscat and Salalah, but otherwise there are few places to stay. Although there are no official campsites, it is possible to camp almost anywhere once permission to pitch has been obtained in the nearest settlement. European, Chinese, Indian and Arabic food is available in major towns, but beer is usually limited to expensive restaurants and hotels. Immunisation against hepatitis, polio,

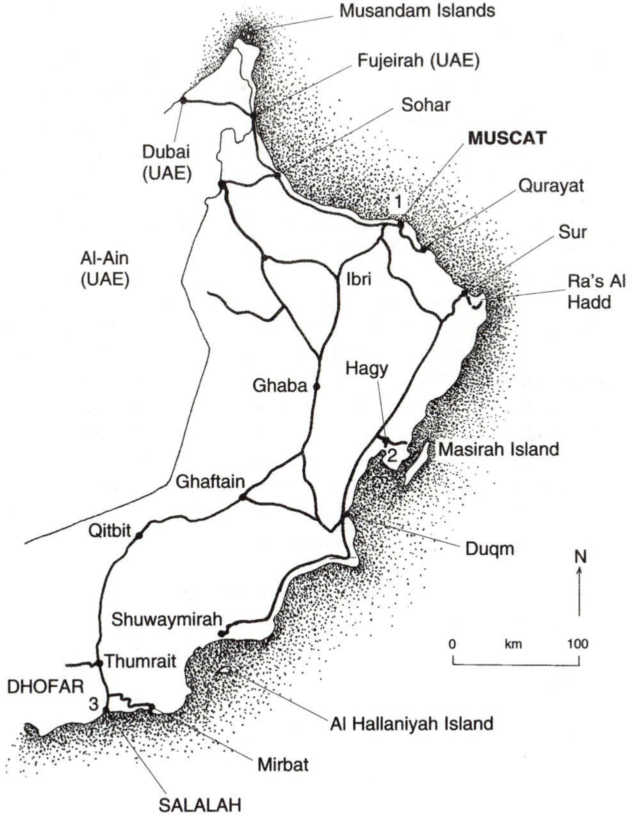

1 Muscat
2 Barr Al Hikman
3 Dhofar

typhoid and yellow fever is recommended, as are precautions against malaria. The climate is generally hot and humid during long summers and warm during short winters. The east coast is wet, windy and often foggy from June to September, but this is the best time for seabird enthusiasts as the southwest monsoon causes an upwelling of nutrients offshore, which attracts large numbers of seabirds and cetaceans. Inland from Oman's 1700 km long coastline, complete with many mangrove-lined bays, lie extensive gravel and sand deserts, and two major highlands. The Hajar Mountains in the north are sparsely vegetated and rise to 2980 m (9777 ft), but the Dhofar Highlands in the south support a narrow belt of deciduous woodland on their southern slopes and rise to 1812 m (5945 ft). There are a number of proposed nature reserves which will help to conserve the birds of Oman, which include nine threatened and near-threatened species.

Over 435 species have been recorded in Oman. Non-endemic specialities and spectacular species include Jouanin's Petrel, Persian Shearwater, Red-billed Tropicbird, Masked Booby, Socotra Cormorant*, Sooty Falcon, Houbara Bustard, Crab Plover, Sooty and Great Black-headed Gulls, Brown and Lesser Noddies, Tristram's Starling, Hume's Wheatear, Blackstart, Red Sea Warbler, Rueppell's Weaver, Palestine Sunbird and Golden-winged Grosbeak. There is no endemic species, but two of the 11 Arabian Peninsula endemics occur: Arabian Partridge and Arabian Wheatear.

The best site near **Muscat**, on the north coast, is, unfortunately, the Al Ansab Sewage Treatment Plant, where about 200 species have been recorded. At the Ghala Azaiba roundabout at the west side of the city, turn south towards the Royal Hospital then right before the next roundabout. After 2.5 km turn south again through an industrial area and continue to beyond the plant where there is a track to the right which leads to the lagoons. Inland from Muscat, Arabian Partridge, Lappet-faced Vulture (Jabal Shams), Lichtenstein's Sandgrouse, Hume's Wheatear and Long-billed Pipit occur in the mountains at **Al Jabar al Akhdar**.

AL ANSAB, MUSCAT

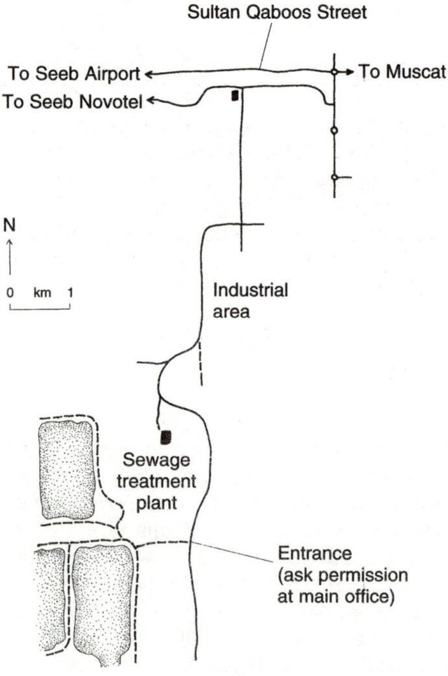

To the northwest of Muscat any tidal inlets and coastal lagoons are worth exploring along the 230 km road to Sohar. About 5 km before Sohar turn left to explore the **Sun Farms** area (ask for permission to enter at the gate), where Amur Falcon occurs on spring passage. About 70 km north of Sohar, turn right to reach **Shnass** (Shinas) from where there is a 2 km track south to a creek where the rare *kalbaensis* race of Collared Kingfisher occurs. A further 20 km or so north from the Shnass turning the road crosses a wadi where the woodland, to the west of the road, supports Variable Wheatear and Plain Leaf-Warbler in winter. North of this wadi is the border post with the UAE and **Khawr Kalba**, a site shared with the UAE, where the rare race of Collared Kingfisher also occurs (p. 413). The **Musandam Islands**, off the extreme northerly tip of Oman, support breeding Red-billed Tropicbird, Socotra Cormorant* and Sooty Falcon, but these lie in a closed military zone and are difficult to visit. **Jebel Qatar**, near the UAE border west of Sohar, supports Hume's Wheatear and wintering Plain Leaf-Warbler. For more details of this site, see p. 415.

To the southeast of Muscat Red-billed Tropicbird and Sooty Falcon occur at **Bandar Jussah** headland and island. Further southeast the rocky hills inland from the 12 km coastal stretch between Quriyat and Daghmar support Arabian Partridge and Hume's Wheatear. At the northeastern tip of Oman the lagoon at **Sur** and the **Ra's Al Hadd** headland area 30 km to the east are worth birding and birds include Red-billed Tropicbird, Crab Plover and Great Black-headed Gull (Jan–Mar), as well as migrants in September.

BARR AL HIKMAN

The extensive mud flats that surround the peninsula of Barr al Hikman and the nearby offshore island of Masirah on Oman's east coast form one of the most important sites for shorebirds, gulls and terns in west Asia. Over 220,000 birds of over 50 species have been counted during the winter, including Slender-billed Curlew*, and there are almost certainly more during migration. From April to November seabirds, including Jouanin's Petrel, occur offshore.

Specialities

Jouanin's Petrel (Apr).

Others

Flesh-footed (Jun–Aug) and Persian (May) Shearwaters, Wilson's Storm-Petrel (Nov), Socotra Cormorant*, Western Reef-Egret, Greater Flamingo, Crab Plover, Great Knot, Broad-billed Sandpiper, Mongolian Plover, Greater Sandplover, Sooty, Great Black-headed and Slender-billed Gulls, Great and Lesser Crested-Terns, Saunders' Tern, Brown (Jun–Aug) and Lesser (Jun–Aug) Noddies, Blue-cheeked Bee-eater (Apr–May), White-breasted White-eye.

(Other species recorded here include at least three Slender-billed Curlews* in January 1990.)

From Shannah, 46 km east of Hagy, head south for a few kilometres and walk out to Ma'awil Island at low tide for shorebirds, etc. There is a ferry from Shannah to Masirah Island, 20 km offshore, which is the best place to seawatch from. White-breasted White-eye occurs on Mahawt Island, off Filim, 20 km south of Hagy. 180 km south of Hagy, via the the main route south, the fish factory at Ras Duqm attracts thousands of gulls and terns, and the lagoon to the north supports Crab Plover.

Wadi Shuwaymirah on Oman's southeast coast supports Hume's Owl and Hooded Wheatear. From Shuwaymirah, 40 km south of Sheliw, take the 20 km track north then west into the wadi and explore the far end 2 km from the village for the owl and wheatear. The track which runs directly west from Shuwaymirah for 20 km allows access to cliffs where 10,000 Socotra Cormorants* roost at night and Masked Booby can be seen offshore. **Al Hallaniyah Island**, off Oman's southeast coast, is a very important breeding ground for seabirds including Persian Shearwater, Red-billed Tropicbird (300 pairs), Masked Booby (over 13,000 pairs), Socotra Cormorant* and Sooty Gull. Furthermore, Jouanin's Petrel may breed here (there is no known breeding site for this species) as up to 200 have been seen offshore in May. Other seabirds seen offshore include Flesh-footed Shearwater and Wilson's Storm-Petrel, while Arabian Wheatear is resident on the island. The island is accessible by air and it may be possible to stay in the small village near the airstrip, but expect rough weather from June to August.

The inland **Muscat–Salalah Road** passes through some good birding country. South of Ghaba the desert around **Jaaluni** (Yalooni) supports Houbara Bustard, Spotted Thick-knee, Chestnut-bellied and Crowned Sandgrouse, Black-crowned Sparrow-Lark and Greater Hoopoe-Lark. The sandgrouse come in for a dawn drink at the small pond at the Oryx Project compound. Southwest of Ghaftain there is permanent water at **Montasar**, which attracts Spotted Sandgrouse. South of Qitbit the **Dauka** area, 200 km north of Salalah, is one of Oman's best sites for spring (Apr–May) and autumn (Sep–Oct) migrants and Spotted Sandgrouse.

Accommodation: guesthouses at Ghaba, Ghaftain and Qitbit, all with gardens which attract migrants.

DHOFAR

The southwest corner of Oman is known as the Dhofar Region and it is accessible from Salalah. The fine selection of birds here includes Jouanin's Petrel, Pheasant-tailed Jacana, Rueppell's Weaver and Golden-winged Grosbeak, and it is possible to see 100 species on a good day.

Arabian Peninsula Endemics

Arabian Partridge, Arabian Wheatear.

Specialities

Jouanin's Petrel, Persian Shearwater, Tristram's Starling, Red Sea Warbler, Rueppell's Weaver, Palestine Sunbird, Golden-winged Grosbeak.

Others

Cory's, Flesh-footed and Audubon's Shearwaters, Wilson's Storm-Petrel, Red-billed Tropicbird, Masked and Brown Boobies, Socotra Cormorant*, Cotton Pygmy-Goose, Greater Flamingo, Western Reef-Egret, Greater Spotted* (Nov–Mar) and Imperial* (Nov–Mar) Eagles, Amur (Apr–May) and Barbary Falcons, Pheasant-tailed Jacana, Mongolian Plover,

Greater Sandplover, White-eyed*, Sooty and Slender-billed Gulls, Great and Lesser Crested-Terns, White-cheeked, Bridled and Saunders' Terns, Brown Noddy, Chestnut-bellied Sandgrouse, Bruce's Green-Pigeon, Dideric Cuckoo (May–Oct), Spotted Eagle-Owl, Grey-headed Kingfisher (May–Nov), Green Bee-eater, African Paradise-Flycatcher, Fan-tailed Raven, Black-crowned Tchagra, Rufous-tailed Scrub-Robin, Blackstart, White-breasted White-eye, Graceful Prinia, Singing Bushlark, Black-crowned Sparrow-Lark, Desert Lark, African Silverbill, Long-billed Pipit, Shining Sunbird, Cinnamon-breasted Bunting.

Other Wildlife

Hooded malpolon, humpback whale (Sep), sea turtle (Sep).

(Other species recorded include Greater Painted-Snipe (Khawr Sawly) and Pied Cuckoo (Ain Hamran).)

Salalah is accessible by air and road from Muscat. Around Salalah bird the Sun Farms area to the west of the Thumrait road just north of town, Ain Sahanawt, which is signposted further north (Spotted Eagle-Owl and Arabian Wheatear), the Salalah Bird Sanctuary at the western edge of town, which can be viewed from outside the fence (Cotton Pygmy-Goose) and Khawr Dahariz at the eastern edge of town. There are many excellent birding sites east of Salalah. Rueppell's Weaver occurs at **Ain Hamran**, which can be reached by turning north 13 km east of Salalah and continuing north for 7 km. Arabian Partridge and Arabian Wheatear occur in **Wadi Darbat**, which can be reached by turning north on to the Tawi Attair road, just north of Taqah. East of the Wadi Darbat turning the main road passes **Khawr Rouri**, a good site for Pheasant-tailed Jacana. About 10–15 km east of here there is a track south to some high cliffs where Red-billed Tropicbirds occur. East of this track the main road ascends a plateau where by turning on to the track north, signposted 'Tawi Attair', and turning west at the baobab trees, it is possible to reach **Wadi Hinna**, which supports Golden-winged Grosbeak. To seawatch continue east on the main road to the village of Mirbat (60 km east of Salalah), through the village and south to **Ras Mirbat**, or better still, **Ras Janjali**, 30 minutes by vehicle further east. Beware of the poisonous hooded malpolon snake on these headlands. Good sites to the west of Salalah include the two khawrs either side of the Muhit Restaurant, the rocky inlet reached by turning south on to a track 10 km west of the restaurant (White-eyed Gull*), **Khawr al Mughsayl**, 30 km west of the turning to the rocky inlet, just to the west of a housing area (Pheasant-tailed Jacana) and the blow holes reached by turning south just west of the khawr (Red-billed Tropicbird).

Accommodation: Salalah — Holiday Inn (A+), Redan Hotel (A), both of which should be booked in advance through a travel agent.

ADDITIONAL INFORMATION

Addresses

Please send all records to the Oman Bird Group, PO Box 246, Muscat 113, Sultanate of Oman, which publishes *Oman Bird News*.

Books and Papers

Important Bird Areas: the Sultanate of Oman (a birding guide). Available from Hanne and Jens Eriksen, SQU — Science, PO Box 36, Al Khod 123, Sultanate of Oman.
The Birds of Oman. Gallagher M and Woodcock M, 1980. Quartet.

Near-endemics

Jouanin's Petrel, Arabian Partridge, Arabian Wheatear, Nile Valley Sunbird, Golden-winged Grosbeak.

QATAR

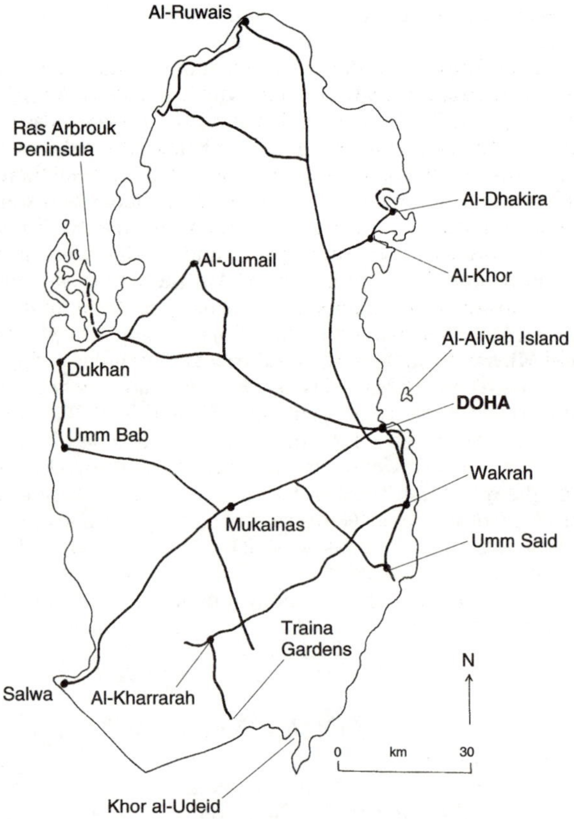

This small, low-lying country occupies a peninsular, 160 km from north to south and 90 km from west to east, midway along the west coast of the Arabian Gulf. The avifauna is more or less typical for this part of the world: a mixture of seabirds, desert specialists and migrants which, in spring, may include Hypocolius.

Qatar is an expensive country to visit because tourist visas can usually only be obtained through the most expensive hotels, where applicants are obliged to stay. Taxis are the only form of public transport. They enable access to most sites near Doha, the capital, but to explore further afield a 4WD is essential. Immunisation against hepatitis, polio, typhoid and yellow fever is recommended. The summers are hot and humid, but winter can be pleasant and there is little rain. The best time to visit is in the spring when migrants may include Hypocolius. Qatar is composed mainly of flat, stony desert, rising to a mere 40 m (131 ft). Most of the remaining natural vegetation (sparse, open desert scrub) is confined to the north, but there is little left, due mainly to overgrazing. There are no protected areas and the birds of Qatar, which include two threatened species, must survive in palm plantations, farmland, gardens, parks and, along the coast, some areas of mangrove and mud flat. Over 250 species have been recorded in Qatar, mostly migrants and winter visitors, and these include Socotra Cormorant*, Crab Plover, Great Black-headed Gull, Hypocolius and Greater Hoopoe-Lark. There is no endemic species.

The capital, **Doha**, lies on the east coast, near mangrove-lined muddy bays which support Socotra Cormorant*, Greater Flamingo, Western Reef-Egret, Crab Plover, Great Black-headed and Slender-billed Gulls, Lesser Crested-Tern and White-cheeked and Bridled Terns. Bird the shore north of the Doha Sheraton (Socotra Cormorant* breeds on Al-Aliyah Island, a few kilometres offshore from here), and south towards the Ras Abu Funtas power station. There are plenty of old and new sewage works with associated pools and reedbeds in the vicinity of Doha for diehards to delight in. The bay at **Al-Dhakira**, 50 km north of Doha, is excellent for shorebirds from August to May. Another good spot for shorebirds, including Crab Plover, is the coast southwest of **Al-Jumail** in north Qatar. Hypocolius is a fairly regular spring migrant at **Traina Gardens**, 77 km southwest of Doha. To reach Traina head southwest out of Doha on the Salwa Road. About 12 km beyond the Fort Roundabout turn left towards Umm Said, then right at the crossroads after 12 km and continue for 35 km to the track which heads left just before the village of Al Kharrarah. From here it is 17 km to Traina, where the palm grove is the best area for Hypocolius. On the west coast of the peninsula, an hour's drive from Doha, there is a good oasis for migrants at the northern end of the **Ras Abrouk Peninsula**.

ADDITIONAL INFORMATION

Books and Papers

A Birdwatcher's Guide to Qatar. Oldfield C and J, 1994. Available from the authors, 21 Learmouth Gardens, Edinburgh, UK.

SAUDI ARABIA

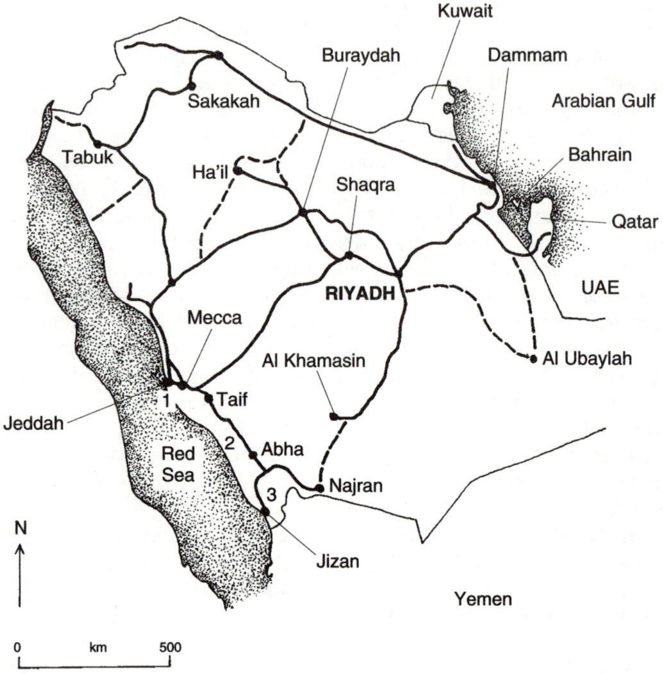

1 Jeddah
2 Wadi Turabah and Jabal Ibrahim
3 Jizan

INTRODUCTION

Saudi Arabia is a very difficult country to visit because visitors visas are normally only issued on receipt of a formal letter of invitation. Even birders on business must obtain permits to travel in many areas, but these bureaucratic barriers are worth overcoming because Saudi Arabia supports ten of the 11 Arabian Peninsula endemics, many desert specialities and a good selection of Afrotropical species.

This huge country (2,149,640 sq km), which is 16 times larger than England and three times the size of Texas, takes up 70% of the Arabian peninsula. Internal travel within Saudi Arabia is only possible if an employer's letter of introduction is presented to the authorities which issue the relevant permits, but expatriates will find cheap internal flights, a good bus system, an excellent road network and a wide range of accommodation and food. However, beer is illegal. Immunisation against hepatitis, meningitis, polio, typhoid and yellow fever is recommended, as are precautions against malaria. Beware of the occasionally over-zealous 'religious police', known as the matawwa. Anyone who scans the weather charts in the national newspapers will have come across Riyadh, the city which regularly records temperatures far in excess of all the other cities listed. Riyadh lies in the centre of this extremely hot country, which also experiences very humid summers (May–Sep) along the Red Sea coast. The winter period is more pleasant, although the Red Sea coast receives much of its rainfall at this time. The best times to visit are March–April and September–October when migrants are moving through and it is not so hot. The largest sand desert in the world, the Rub' Al-Khali (Empty Quarter), covers about 50% of the land surface of Saudi Arabia and much of the rest of the country is composed of desert. However, there are lagoons and mangrove-lined muddy bays along the long Red Sea and shorter Arabian coasts; the narrow Red Sea coastal plain, known as the Tihamah, supports remnant acacia scrub and palm thickets; there are some vegetated wadis in the western foothills of the Sarawat Mountains; and remnant juniper stands still survive in these mountains which rise to 3050 m (10,007 ft) at Jebel Souda. There are ten protected areas (a further 88 are proposed) helping to conserve the birds of Saudi Arabia, which include 19 threatened and near-threatened species.

Non-endemic specialities and spectacular species which occur in Saudi Arabia include Socotra Cormorant*, Hamerkop, Dark Chanting-Goshawk, Verreaux's Eagle, Sand Partridge, Demoiselle Crane, Houbara Bustard, Crab Plover, White-eyed Gull*, Egyptian, Nubian, Montane and Plain Nightjars, White-throated Bee-eater, Abyssinian Roller, Tristram's Starling, Black Scrub-Robin, Blackstart, Hypocolius, Upcher's Warbler, Brown Woodland-Warbler, Red Sea and Menetries' Warblers, Thick-billed, Dunn's and Temminck's Larks, Rueppell's Weaver, Arabian Golden-Sparrow, Palestine Sunbird and Golden-winged Grosbeak. There is no endemic species but ten of the 11 Arabian Peninsula endemics are present.

The best birding area near **Riyadh** in central Saudi Arabia is the **Wadi Hanifah Reserve**, 25 km to the south (Little Bittern in summer and Greater Spotted Eagle* in winter). **Hawtat Bani Tamim**, an isolated hill 200 km to the south, supports resident species such as Sand Partridge and Pharaoh Eagle-Owl, winter visitors including Menetries' Warbler and migrants which have included 200–300 Hypocolius in March (much smaller numbers in October).

There are a few good birding sites along the Arabian Gulf coast northeast of Riyadh, although a third of this coast was badly oiled during the 1991 Gulf War. The best site is probably **Tarut Bay**, which lies between Qatif and Dammam. Although the numbers of birds are maintained at an artificially high level by the input of nutrient waste, over 50,000 waterfowl have been recorded here in winter, and Great Knot occurs on passage.

Over 5,500 Demoiselle Cranes have been recorded in spring (mainly in the second half of March) at Jibal al-Tuwal and Dilan al-Jilf on the edge of the Nafud Desert west and southwest of **Ha'il**, which is 640 km northwest of Riyadh in the country's 'wheat belt'. Other species recorded here include Dunn's and Temminck's Larks and, in spring, Cinereous

Bunting*. In extreme north Saudi Arabia the **Harrat al-Harrah Reserve**, a huge area of desert 80 km northwest of Sakakah, supports the most diverse breeding assemblage of larks in the Middle East. In good years ten species are present including Thick-billed, Dunn's and Temminck's. Other species which occur here include Houbara Bustard, Cream-coloured Courser and Pharaoh Eagle-Owl, while winter visitors include Eurasian Dotterel. Ostrich was present up to 1930.

JEDDAH

The surrounds of this city on the Red Sea coast support Egyptian and Nubian Nightjars and, in spring thousands of Demoiselle Cranes have been seen passing directly over the city.

Specialities

Demoiselle Crane (Mar/Sep), Egyptian (Jan–Mar) and Nubian (Sep–Dec) Nightjars, Rueppell's Weaver.

Others

Crab, Caspian (Apr–May/Sep–Oct) and Spur-winged Plovers, White-eyed Gull* (Mar–Sep), White-cheeked Tern, Namaqua Dove, Green and Blue-cheeked (Sep–Oct) Bee-eaters, Masked Shrike (Sep), Black Scrub-Robin, White-spectacled Bulbul, Upcher's (Sep) and Menetries' (Apr–May/Sep–Oct) Warblers, African Silverbill, White-throated Munia, Nile Valley Sunbird.

Migrants occur in the gardens and parks in and around the city; Egyptian and Nubian Nightjars occur in and around the US Geological Survey compound at the eastern edge of the city; White-eyed Gull* and White-cheeked Tern can be seen from the North Corniche; and Crab Plover occurs just south of the city.

White-tailed Lapwing and Red-rumped and Red-tailed Wheatears winter in **Wadi Uranah**, 80 km southeast of Jeddah towards Taif, and migrants recorded here include Olive-tree Warbler.

Hypocolius is an irregular winter visitor to the National Wildlife Research Centre 40 km southeast of **Taif**, but one year saw the arrival of 850 birds. This centre lies on the edge of the desert and supports resident Sand Partridge, Arabian Woodpecker* and Red Sea Warbler, wintering Arabian and Red-tailed Wheatears, Small Whitethroat and Menetries' Warbler, and in spring (Mar–May) Waldrapp* has also been recorded. Hypocolius also occurs at **Mahazat as-Sayd Reserve**, 175 km northeast of Taif, along with Lappet-faced Vulture, Houbara Bustard (introduced) and Dunn's Lark.

WADI TURABAH AND JABAL IBRAHIM

Eight of the 11 Arabian Peninsula endemics occur at this site as well as a fine selection of Afrotropical species including Montane Nightjar.

Arabian Peninsula Endemics

Philby's and Arabian Partridges, Arabian Woodpecker*, Yemen Thrush*, Arabian Wheatear, Arabian Waxbill, Olive-rumped Serin, Yemen Linnet.

Specialities

Tristram's Starling, Red Sea Warbler, Palestine Sunbird.

Others

Hamerkop, Black Stork (Nov–Mar), Verreaux's Eagle, Sand Partridge, Montane Nightjar, Grey-headed Kingfisher (May–Sep), Little Rock-Thrush, White-spectacled Bulbul, Brown Woodland-Warbler, Arabian Babbler, Cinnamon-breasted Bunting.

The wadi and jabal are 150 km southeast of Taif, 80 km north of al-Baha, between the Bani Saad to al-Baha road and the Taif to al-Baha road.

Golden-winged Grosbeak, as well as Arabian Woodpecker*, Yemen Thrush*, Violet-backed Starling, Little Rock-Thrush, Olive-rumped and Yemen Serins and Yemen Linnet have been recorded near the village of **Bani Yazid**, 50 km north of al-Baha (18 km north of Mandaq), which lies on the Taif road at 2000 m (6562 ft). Bird the valley and escarpment rim either side of the road 0.5 km north of the village.

Forty pairs of Sooty Falcon breed at **Qishran Bay**, on the Red Sea coast southwest of Taif, in what is probably the densest breeding concentration of this delightful raptor in the world.

At **Dhi-Ain**, south of al-Baha, a permanent stream irrigates banana and palm plantations which support Bruce's Green-Pigeon, Grey-headed Kingfisher (May–Sep), African Grey Hornbill, Violet-backed Starling (May–Sep) and Shining Sunbird. The valley around the **Al Dahna Waterfall**, just south of Tanuma, 11 km north of Abha, supports Spotted Eagle-Owl, the *asirensis* race of Black-billed Magpie, Little Rock-Thrush, Yemen Thrush*, Violet-backed Starling and White-breasted White-eye, while Waldrapp* has also been recorded here in November. Seven Arabian Peninsula endemics including Yemen Warbler* occur at the **Raydah Escarpment Reserve**, 15 km west of Abha, as well as Gabar Goshawk, Hume's Owl and the *asirensis* race of Black-billed Magpie.

JIZAN

The coast, inland wadis and heavily terraced mountains with remnant juniper stands near Jizan in the extreme south of Saudi Arabia support one of the most diverse avifaunas in Arabia. Nearly 300 species have been recorded here, including a fine mixture of Arabian Peninsula endemics and Afrotropical species such as Botta's Wheatear and Arabian Golden-Sparrow.

Arabian Peninsula Endemics

Arabian Partridge, Arabian Woodpecker*, Arabian Wheatear, Arabian Waxbill, Olive-rumped Serin, Yemen Linnet.

MALAKI DAM and WADI JAWWAH

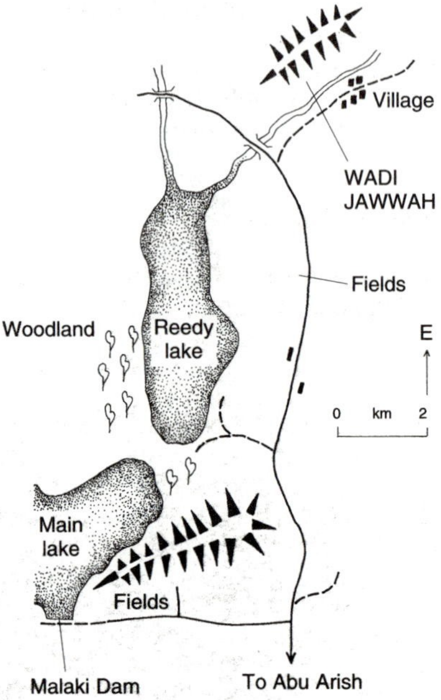

Specialities

Nubian Nightjar, Botta's Wheatear, Red Sea Warbler, Arabian Golden-Sparrow, Palestine Sunbird.

Others

Pink-backed Pelican, Western Reef-Egret, Abdim's Stork, Dark Chanting-Goshawk, Gabar Goshawk, Barbary Falcon, Helmeted Guineafowl, Harlequin Quail, Crab Plover (Nov–Mar), Spotted Thick-knee, White-eyed*, Sooty and Slender-billed Gulls, Lichtenstein's Sandgrouse, Dusky Turtle-Dove, Red-eyed Dove, African Collared-Dove, Bruce's Green-Pigeon, White-browed Coucal, Spotted Eagle-Owl, Plain Nightjar, African Palm-Swift, Grey-headed Kingfisher, White-throated and Blue-cheeked (Sep) Bee-eaters, Abyssinian Roller, African Grey Hornbill, Masked Shrike (Sep), Black-crowned Tchagra, Little Rock-Thrush, Violet-backed Starling, Gambaga Flycatcher, White-breasted White-eye, Graceful Prinia, Brown Woodland-Warbler, Arabian Babbler, Black-crowned Sparrow-Lark, Greater Hoopoe-Lark, Long-billed Pipit, Nile Valley and Shining Sunbirds, Cinnamon-breasted Bunting.

(Other species recorded here include Bateleur, Slender-billed Curlew* (one in Jizan Bay, January 1990) and Pied Cuckoo.)

White-eyed* and Sooty Gulls are attracted to the fishing boats returning to Jizan, a coastal town accessible by air from Jeddah. Crab Plover has been recorded just south of town in Jizan Bay, and 40 km further south. Spotted Thick-knee and Nubian Nightjar occur around **Malaki Dam**, about 50 km inland from Jizan, via Abu Arish. To reach here turn east 16.5 km northeast of Abu Arish. Bird the dam, the fields and woodland around the 'Reedy Lake', and **Wadi Jawwah**, further east (Plain Nightjar). Most of the Arabian Peninsula endemics as well as Botta's Wheatear occur on **Jabal Faifa**, an isolated terraced mountain to the north of this area. Dark Chanting-Goshawk and Arabian Golden-Sparrow occur in the vicinity of **Sabya**, on the Abha road, northwest of Abu Arish.

Accommodation: Jizan — Atheel Hotel.

Red-billed Tropicbird, Sooty Falcon and Brown Noddy breed on the **Farasan Islands**, 40 km offshore from Jizan.

ADDITIONAL INFORMATION

Addresses

National Wildlife Research Centre (NWRC), PO Box 1086, Taif, Saudi Arabia (tel: 02 7455 188; fax: 02 7455 176).

Books and Papers

Birds of Southern Arabia. Robinson D and Chapman A, 1993.
Birds of the Eastern Province of Saudi Arabia. Bundy G *et al.*, 1989. Witherby.
Birds of western Saudi Arabia. Lobley G, 1995. *Arabian Wildlife* 2(1): 10–12 and 2(2): 12–13.
Arabian endemics for lumpers and splitters. Jennings M, 1991. *Phoenix* 8: 10–11.

Near-endemics

Philby's and Arabian Partridges, Arabian Woodpecker*, Yemen Thrush*, Arabian Wheatear, Yemen Warbler*, Arabian Golden-Sparrow, Arabian Waxbill, Yemen Accentor*, Nile Valley Sunbird, Olive-rumped and Yemen Serins, Yemen Linnet, Golden-winged Grosbeak.

SYRIA

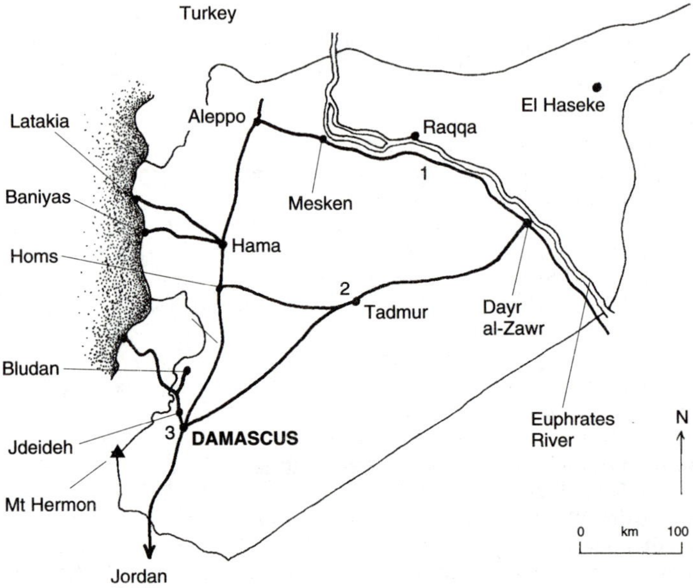

1 Aleppo to Dayr al-Zawr
2 Tadmur
3 Damascus

Syria is a popular tourist destination thanks to its excellent historical sites, but this country attracts few birders, despite the presence of a number of desert specialities and localised birds such as White-tailed Lapwing and Syrian Serin.

This small country has a good road system, a cheap bus network and taxis which can be hired for the day at reasonable cost. Cheap accommodation is available in most towns. The favourite food seems to be shawarma (spiced lamb) and felafel (chick pea and salad sandwiches). Immunisation against hepatitis, polio, typhoid and yellow fever is recommended, as are precautions against malaria. Even minor crimes such as theft are refreshingly rare in this friendly country. Summers are hot and dry, winters mild and wet, and spring is probably the best time to visit. The 40 km wide and 180 km long Mediterranean coastal plain is heavily cultivated. Inland, the Jibal al-Nusayriyan range rises to 1562 m (5125 ft) before falling away to the Al-Ghab basin, a sparsely vegetated land of steppe and stony desert with black boulder fields in the southeast. In the northeast the Euphrates River and its fertile floodplain forms a green ribbon through the barren desert. There are few reserves in Syria and raptors are heavily persecuted, hence its avifuana, which includes nine threatened and near-threatened species, could be better protected. Non-endemic specialities and spectacular species include Sand Partridge, Houbara Bustard, Cream-coloured Courser, White-tailed Lapwing, White-throated Robin, Upcher's Warbler, Temminck's Lark, Syrian Serin and Crimson-winged and Desert Finches. There is no endemic species.

From **Aleppo** (Halab) in northwest Syria, east to the Euphrates River and south along its floodplain to **Dayr al-Zawr**, there are a number of a good birding sites. The large salt-lake, Sabkhat al-Jabbul, and its steppe surrounds, just south of Jabbul village, 35 km southeast of Aleppo, support breeding Chukar, Cream-coloured Courser, Greater Sandplover and Desert Finch. Good sites along the Euphrates include: Halabiyat Zulbiyat, 40 km northwest of Dayr al-Zawr on the east bank; Shumaytiyah, an oxbow lake 20 km northwest of Dayr al-Zawr; Mayadin Pool, 2 km southeast of Mayadin; and the small marsh some 10 km south of Al-Ashara Bridge, southeast of Dayr al-Zawr, towards the Iraq border. Breeding species of the floodplain include Ruddy Shelduck, Marbled Teal*, Squacco Heron, Little Bittern, Spur-winged Plover, White-tailed Lapwing, Pied Kingfisher, Blue-cheeked Bee-eater and Graceful Prinia.

Sand Partridge and Houbara Bustard have been recorded around **Jabal al-Bishri**, an isolated mountain in semi-desert 80 km west of Dayr al-Zawr. **Tadmur** (Palmyra) in central Syria is one of the world's best historical sites. It is also a large desert oasis which is probably good for migrants. The seasonal salt-lake, Sabkhat Muh, and its steppe surrounds, to the south of Tadmur, support wintering Eurasian Dotterel and Finsch's Wheatear. Species recorded at Qasr el-Hair es-Sharqi, a ruined castle in the desert 35 km northeast of Tadmur, include Lesser Kestrel*, Cream-coloured Courser, Pin-tailed Sandgrouse and Desert and Temminck's Larks.

Accommodation: Tadmur — New Tourist Hotel (C).

Cream-coloured Courser, Pin-tailed Sandgrouse and Isabelline Wheatear have been recorded alongside the Tadmur–Damascus road.

DAMASCUS

The mountains west of Damascus in southwest Syria support a good selection of eastern Mediterranean species, including Syrian Serin and the more widespread but localised Crimson-winged Finch.

Specialities

Syrian Serin, Crimson-winged Finch.

Others

Eurasian Griffon, Long-legged Buzzard, Chukar, White-throated Robin (May–Sep), Finsch's Wheatear (May–Sep), Upcher's (May–Sep) and Orphean (May–Sep) Warblers, Sombre Tit, Bimaculated Lark, Pale Rockfinch (May–Sep), Alpine Accentor (Nov–Mar), Cretzschmar's (May–Sep) and Black-headed (May–Sep) Buntings.

Bird around the small village of Abu Zad, which lies at 1500 m (4921 ft), above the resort of Bludan, 50 km northwest of Damascus, the steep hillside at the northwest end of Wadi al-Qarn on the north side of the Damascus–Beirut road, 1–2 km southeast of Jdeideh, and around Burqush on Mount Hermon.

ADDITIONAL INFORMATION

Books and Papers

Notes on some summer birds of Syria. Baumgart W and Kasparek M, 1992. *Zoological Middle East* 6: 13–19.

Near-endemics

Syrian Serin, Cretzschmar's Bunting (breeding).

TURKEY

INTRODUCTION

Summary

Turkey supports most of the birds of the Mediterranean and much more besides. However, apart from the virtually endemic Krueper's Nuthatch, the majority of the birds which occur here but not west of the Bosphorus in Europe can only be found in the more rugged and remote eastern third of the country.

Size

At 756,953 sq km, Turkey is nearly six times the size of England and slightly larger than Texas.

Getting Around

The air and bus networks are cheap, efficient and far-reaching in the west, but a hire-car is required for serious birding in the extreme east. Beware of bad roads in the east and of crazy drivers throughout.

Accommodation and Food

There is a wide range of accommodation and food available in the west and along the south coast, but both are generally cheaper away from the main tourist resorts. In the extreme east both accommodation and food are more limited, but even the remotest towns usually have basic

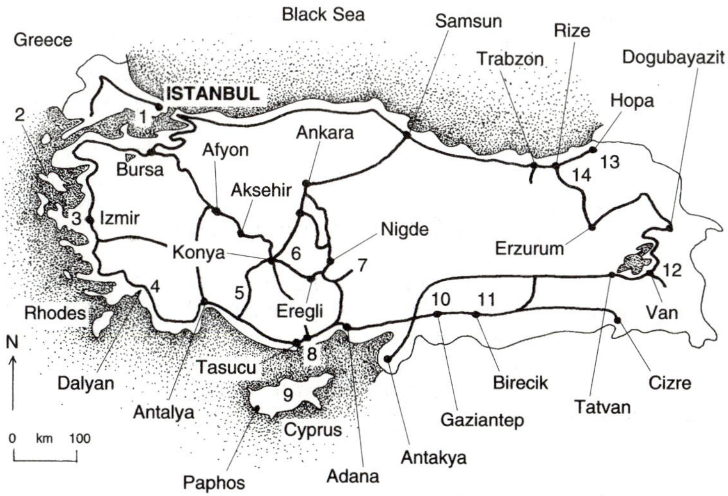

1 Istanbul
2 Lesbos
3 Izmir
4 Dalyan
5 Akseki
6 The Lakes of Central Turkey
7 Mount Demirkazik
8 Goksu Delta
9 Cyprus
10 Yesilice
11 Birecik
12 Van
13 Coruh Valley
14 Ispir and Sivrikaya

hotels and *pansiyons*. The food is excellent and includes kebabs and baklava, a very sweet 'sweet'. Beer is widely available and the legendary Turkish coffee is a particularly useful early morning boost of energy for birders starting another long day in the field.

Health and Safety

Immunisation against hepatitis, polio and typhoid is recommended, as are precautions against malaria in the far east of the country. Southeast Turkey became subject to skirmishes between Kurdish separatists and the Turkish army in the mid 1990s, making travel in this area very dangerous, so it is wise to check with the relevant Foreign Office before venturing to this region.

Climate and Timing

The best times to visit Turkey are spring (May) and autumn (late September–early October). Earlier in spring and later in autumn bad weather may make birding in the Caucasus and other mountain ranges very difficult. In winter many mountainous areas are impenetrable and even in summer the weather can be bad in such places. Lowland Turkey has very hot, dry summers and mild, wet winters.

Habitats

Turkey is primarily a high plateau bordered by mountains to the northeast, east and southeast, rising to 5165 m (16,946 ft) at Agri Dagi (Mount Ararat) near the Iranian border. There are numerous lakes (known as Golus) with highly variable water levels on this plateau, as well as steppe grasslands, forested slopes and alpine meadows on the higher peaks. The lengthy Black Sea, Aegean and Mediterranean coastlines are liberally sprinkled with beaches, cliffs, lagoons, marshes and estuaries, while inland from the Aegean and Mediterranean lie slopes of maquis and pine forests.

Conservation

Many of Turkey's lakes and wetlands need protecting to conserve the country's birds, which include 23 threatened and near-threatened species.

Bird Species

Approximately 440 species have been recorded in Turkey and at least 300 have bred. Non-endemic specialities and spectacular species include Pygmy Cormorant*, See-see Partridge, Caspian Snowcock, Caucasian Grouse*, Demoiselle Crane, Great Bustard*, Audouin's* and Armenian Gulls, Pallid Scops-Owl, Blue-cheeked Bee-eater, White-throated Robin, Red-tailed Wheatear, Persian Nuthatch, Upcher's, Olive-tree and Menetries' Warblers, Dead Sea Sparrow, Chestnut-shouldered Petronia, Spot-throated Accentor, Crimson-winged and Desert Finches and Grey-hooded and Cinereous* Buntings.

Endemics

There is no endemic species but Krueper's Nuthatch is a virtual endemic to Turkey and two species are confined to Cyprus during the breeding season: Cyprus Wheatear and Cyprus Warbler.

Expectations

It is possible to see about 250 species on an extensive two-week trip which includes the east. During spring it is possible to see up to 140 species during a two-week trip to Lesbos and over 150 during a similar period on Cyprus.

The ancient city of **Istanbul** lies in Europe *and* Asia, and thanks mainly to its splendid old buildings such as the Blue Mosque and Topkapi Palace is a major tourist destination. In ornithological circles the city is famous for being on the autumn migration route of raptors and storks. Mid-March to early April and, more especially, the second half of September, are the peak passage times, and species include Black and White Storks, Levant Sparrowhawk and Lesser Spotted Eagle. Other species which occur in the vicinity of Istanbul include Cory's and Yelkouan Shearwaters and Semicollared Flycatcher, which breeds in the Forest of Belgrade, north of the city on the European side. The best place to observe autumn migration is the viewpoint complete with cafe on **Buyuk Camlica** (pronounced Shanlisha) which rises to 282 m (925 ft) and lies on the Asian side of the Bosphorus. It is accessible via the suburb of Uskudur.

Accommodation: Asian side — Hotel Paris (adjacent to bus terminal for getting to Buyuk Camlica), Harem Hotel (A).

Further afield from Istanbul there is a small breeding colony of Dalmatian Pelicans* (around 30 pairs) at the tiny **Manyas-Kus Cenneti NP**, 15 km south of Bandirma. The park protects just 64 ha of the 16,800 ha Manyas Golu and there is a hide from which it is possible

ISTANBUL AREA

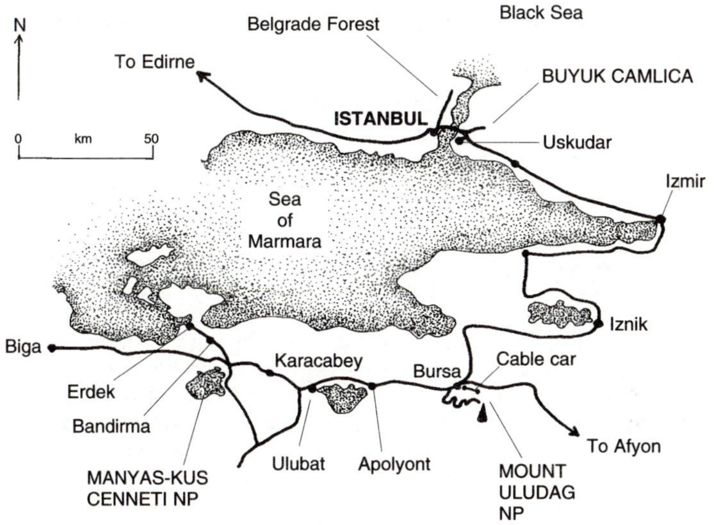

to see the colony, albeit at some distance. The area around the nearby village of **Eskisigirci** is also worth birding. To the east of Manyas Golu the large **Apolyont Golu**, 35 km west of Bursa, supports similar birds, as well as Pygmy Cormorant* and Lesser Spotted Eagle in summer, and can be viewed from near the village of Ulubat or from the Ulubat–Kumkadi track. Lammergeier, Syrian and Black Woodpeckers, Krueper's Nuthatch, Alpine Accentor and Fire-fronted Serin occur in **Mount Uludag NP**, 22 km south of Bursa. It is easy to get above the tree-line here, via a cable-car to Sanalan or via the road to the ski resort, which passes through beech and pine forests.

Although it is politically part of Greece, the island of **Lesbos** lies a few kilometres off the west coast of Turkey. This large, rugged island, 80 km across, supports resident Krueper's Nuthatch, Sombre Tit and Rock Petronia, and hosts breeding summer visitors which include Masked Shrike, Rueppell's Warbler and Cretzschmar's Bunting, but the island is perhaps better known for its spring migrants (early May is peak time), which include Red-footed Falcon and Little Crake, and its two special summer visitors: Olive-tree Warbler and Cinereous Bunting*. The best birding areas are around **Skala Kalloni**, the southern bay, where there are rivers, salt-pans and olive groves (those near the Potamia River on the northwest shore of the bay are perhaps the best for Olive-tree Warbler), the rough road between **Eressos** and **Sigri** at the west end of the island (Cinereous Bunting*, especially near Antissa) and **Plomari**, north of Agiasso, where the pine forests support Krueper's Nuthatch. Lesbos is accessible by air from most European countries and the small resort of Skala Kalloni on the south coast is a good base.

The popular tourist destination of **Izmir** in southwest Turkey lies near two lakes, an estuary and hillsides where, in summer, it is possible to see Pygmy Cormorant*, Great White and Dalmatian* Pelicans, Ruddy

Shelduck, Greater Flamingo, White-tailed Eagle*, Long-legged Buzzard, Eleonora's Falcon, Spur-winged Plover, Great Spotted Cuckoo, White-throated and Pied Kingfishers, European Bee-eater, White-throated Robin, Rufous-tailed Scrub-Robin, Eurasian Penduline-Tit and Cinereous* and Cretzschmar's Buntings. The salt-pans, lagoons and reedbeds of Camalti Tuzlasi support breeding Dalmatian Pelican*, White-throated Robin is fairly common on hillsides to the south and east of Izmir and the highly localised Cinereous Bunting* has been recorded at Emiralem and near Bafa Golu, a particularly good birding area.

The reedy delta, beaches, maquis and pine forests around the popular tourist resort of **Dalyan** in southwest Turkey support, in summer, Pygmy Cormorant*, Greater Flamingo, White-tailed Eagle* (Koycegiz Golu), Eleonora's Falcon, European Bee-eater, European Roller, Syrian Woodpecker, Masked Shrike, Rufous-tailed Scrub-Robin, Finsch's Wheatear (Kaunos ruins), Krueper's (inland, around villages of Agla and Akkopru) and Rock Nuthatches, Olive-tree and Rueppell's Warblers, Sombre Tit, Eurasian Penduline-Tit, and Cretzschmar's and Black-headed Buntings, as well as Green, Loggerhead and Nile Soft-shelled Turtles (Iztuzu Beach). The Dalyan area is particularly good in mid-May, when spring migrants such as Red-footed Falcon are moving through. Dalyan is accessible by air from most European countries.

Accommodation: Kaunos Hotel (A).

AKSEKI

This small town in the Taurus Mountains, south-central Turkey, lies just below a large area of pine forest which supports White-backed Woodpecker, a rare bird in Turkey, and the delightful Krueper's Nuthatch.

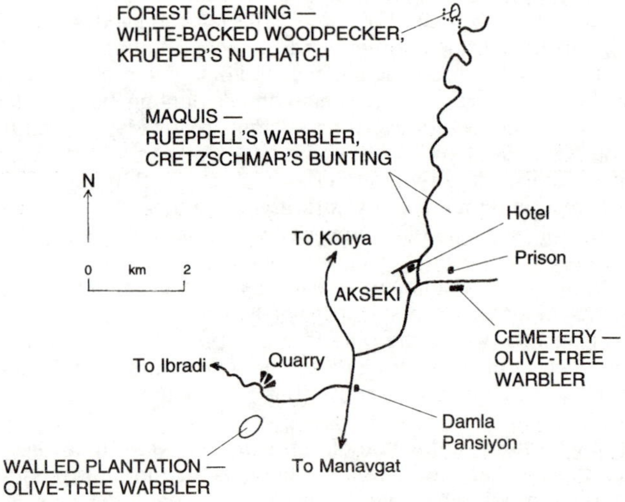

The dapper little Krueper's Nuthatch is virtually endemic to Turkey

Specialities
White-backed Woodpecker, Krueper's Nuthatch.

Others
European Roller (May–Sep), Syrian Woodpecker, Masked Shrike (May–Sep), Rock Nuthatch, Orphean (May–Sep) and Rueppell's (May–Sep) Warblers, Sombre Tit, Cretzschmar's (May–Sep) and Black-headed (May–Sep) Buntings.

(Other species recorded here include Olive-tree Warbler (May–Sep).)

Akseki is accessible from the Manavgat–Konya road. Olive-tree Warbler has been recorded around the walled plantation 1 km west of the Damla Pansiyon, 8 km south of Akseki, and in the cemetery a few hundred metres east of the town, opposite the prison. To look for White-backed Woodpecker and Krueper's Nuthatch, take the old Konya road and park 8 km north of the town on a sharp right-hand bend where there is an obvious track to the left. Take this track and bird around the first clearing, or continue on the track for 50 m to a trail on the left which leads to another clearing after 500 m. The rocky, bushy hillsides either side of the road up to this site support Rock Nuthatch, Rueppell's Warbler and Cretzschmar's Bunting.

Accommodation: Star Hotel.

THE LAKES OF CENTRAL TURKEY

Central Turkey has many ephemeral lakes, known as golus, which support a splendid range of waterbirds, including breeding Armenian Gull and Greater Sandplover.

Specialities
Armenian Gull (May–Sep).

Others
Pygmy Cormorant*, Great White and Dalmatian* Pelicans, Ruddy Shelduck, White-headed Duck*, Marbled Teal*, Greater Flamingo, Lesser Kestrel* (May–Sep), Collared Pratincole (May–Sep), Greater Sandplover (May–Sep), Spur-winged Plover, Slender-billed Gull,

Eurasian River (Apr–May), Savi's (May–Sep) and Moustached (May–Sep) Warblers, Lesser Short-toed Lark.

(Other species recorded here include Great Bustard* and Thrush Nightingale (Apr–May).)

Particularly productive lakes include **Aksehir Golu**, which is situated to the north of Aksehir, a town 93 km east of Afyon on the Afyon–Konya road. The lake is best viewed from the western shore near Ishakli, accessible from Sultandagi. Great Bustard* has been recorded in the fields near the northwest corner and Dalmatian Pelican* on the lake, while spring migrants, attracted to the extensive orchards between the Afyon–Konya road and the lake, have included Thrush Nightingale and Eurasian River Warbler. **Akgol Golu** is an internationally important wetland 20 km southwest of Eregli. When full there are many birds here, including Dalmatian Pelican*, White-headed Duck*, Marbled Teal*, Greater Sandplover and Armenian Gull. The lake can be viewed from the north side, which can be reached by heading west out of Eregli towards Hortu and turning south on to a track just before Hortu, or from the south side by heading south out of Eregli towards Karaman and turning west after 17 km (via Adabag where there is a Lesser Kestrel* colony) or 20 km (via Bogecik). Beware of soft mud. The **Hotamis Golus** have supported breeding White-headed Duck* and Marbled Teal*. To reach these lakes turn south from the Konya–Eregli road, 12 km west of Karapinar, to Hotamis 11.5 km away, then continue south (ignoring the turning east to Karaman) for 35 km before turning west to Adakale where there are marshes to the west (Marbled Teal*), or head further south to Suleimanhaci and Lake Acigol, on the east side of the road (White-headed Duck*). The small **Kulu Golu** between Ankara and Konya is also worth exploring for White-headed Duck*. To reach this golu turn east off Route 35, 108 km south of Ankara.

Accommodation: Eregli — Mac Hotel. Nigde — Hotel Evim.

The largest known wintering population of White-headed Duck has been recorded on **Burdur Golu**. Up to 11,000 birds were counted here in 1991, although numbers have fallen to as low as 3,000 since.

MOUNT DEMIRKAZIK

The Aladag Mountains rise to 3910 m (12,828 ft) at Mount Demirkazik in south-central Turkey where the high slopes support Caspian Snowcock, Spot-throated Accentor and Crimson-winged Finch. The weather here can be bad, even in the summer, and it is not always possible to get high enough to see the specialities.

Specialities

Caspian Snowcock, Spot-throated Accentor, Crimson-winged Finch.

Others

Lammergeier, Eurasian Griffon, Golden Eagle, Chukar, White-throated Robin (May–Sep), Finsch's (May–Sep) and Isabelline (May–Sep)

MOUNT DEMIRKAZIK

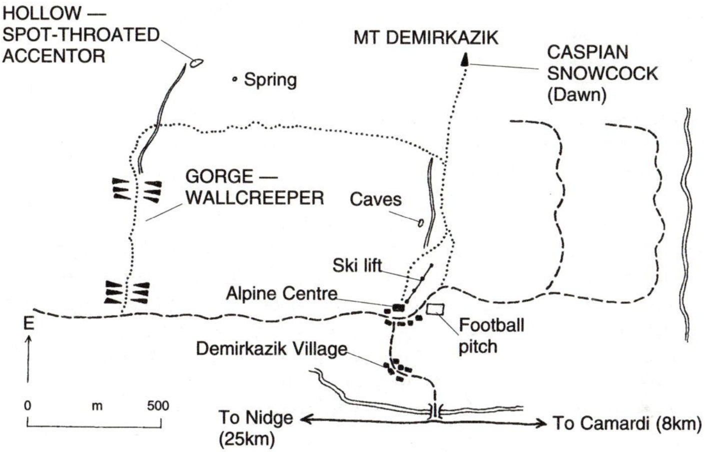

Wheatears, Rock Nuthatch, Wallcreeper, Bimaculated (May–Sep), Lesser Short-toed and Horned Larks, Rock Petronia, White-winged Snowfinch, Alpine Accentor, Fire-fronted Serin.

Other Wildlife

Ibex.

To reach Mount Demirkazik, turn right north of Nigde, just beyond Ovacik, towards Baldaras and Camardi. About 8 km before Camardi turn left on to the track to Demirkazik village and the ski centre. For the best chance of Caspian Snowcock it is necessary to be on the high scree slopes and snowfields at dawn, before the birds start climbing even higher. This means leaving the ski centre at 0300.

Accommodation: Demirkazik — ski centre. Nigde — Hotel Evim.

GOKSU DELTA

Over 310 species have been recorded in and around this important delta on the Mediterranean in southeast Turkey, including Black Francolin and Audouin's Gull*, but it is a difficult area to get around and it is best to allow plenty of time for a thorough exploration.

Specialities

Audouin's Gull*.

Others

Pygmy Cormorant*, Great White Pelican, Ruddy Shelduck, White-headed Duck*, Marbled Teal*, Lesser Kestrel* (May–Sep), Eleonora's Falcon (May–Sep), Black Francolin, Little (Apr–May) and Baillon's (Apr–May) Crakes, Purple Swamphen, Collared Pratincole (May–Sep),

Spur-winged Plover, Yellow-legged and Slender-billed Gulls, White-throated and Pied Kingfishers, Syrian Woodpecker, Rufous-tailed Scrub-Robin (May–Sep), Isabelline Wheatear (May–Sep), Graceful Prinia, Savi's (May–Sep) and Moustached Warblers, Lesser Short-toed Lark, Spanish Sparrow.

(Other species recorded here include Cyprus Wheatear (mid-April) and rarities such as Yellow-billed Stork, Slender-billed Curlew*, Crab Plover and White-tailed Lapwing.)

The towns of Tasucu and Silifke are the best bases from which to explore the delta. Audouin's Gull* occurs in Tasucu harbour, off the pier and along the beaches by the coast road to the west. The delta area is a few kilometres east of Tasucu, but a very tricky area to work and it may be wise to call in at the Information Centre in Tasucu for some help. The centre is on the ground floor of a three-storey building opposite the Tastur Hotel on the main road to Antalya (Address: DHKD, Goksu Delta Projesi, PK 38, 33900 Tasucu, Icel).

Accommodation: Silifke — Hotel Altinorfoz.

Olive-tree Warbler, as well as Masked Shrike, Krueper's Nuthatch and Rueppell's Warbler occur in summer near **Uzuncabera**. Head north from Silifke to the fork signposted 'Uzuncabera 7 km', take the left fork and stop after 1.5 km to check the open woods either side of the road for the noisy but frustratingly elusive Olive-tree Warbler.

CYPRUS

This large, rugged Mediterranean island, which rises to 1951 m (6401 ft) at Mount Olympos in the pine-clad Troodos Mountains, supports two widespread breeding endemics and is an important refuelling stop for migrants, especially in spring. From late March to mid April, the peak migration period, it is possible to see around 150 species in a week. Unfortunately many of the migrants, even the smallest passerines, are blasted out of the skies by gun-crazy locals, despite the strenuous efforts of local and international conservationists. Those with the guns argue that they are merely carrying out a long established tradition, but this is a pathetic excuse for such an archaic and barbaric slaughter.

Most of the species listed below are present from late March to mid-April.

Cyprus Breeding Endemics

Cyprus Wheatear, Cyprus Warbler.

Non-endemic Specialities

Dead Sea Sparrow.

Others

Greater Flamingo (Oct–Apr), Squacco Heron, Little Bittern, Glossy Ibis, Eurasian Griffon, Pallid Harrier*, Lesser Kestrel*, Red-footed and Eleonora's Falcons, Chukar, Black Francolin, Marsh Sandpiper, Collared

Pratincole, Spur-winged Plover, Slender-billed Gull, Great Spotted Cuckoo, European Scops-Owl, Alpine and Pallid Swifts, European Bee-eater, European Roller, Lesser Grey and Masked Shrikes, Blue Rock-Thrush, Collared and Semicollared Flycatchers, Thrush Nightingale, Finsch's (Oct–Apr), Pied and Isabelline Wheatears, Short-toed Treecreeper, Eurasian Crag Martin, Moustached, Olivaceous, Orphean, Rueppell's, Subalpine and Spectacled Warblers, Calandra and Greater Short-toed Larks, Spanish Sparrow, Tawny and Red-throated Pipits, Cretzschmar's and Black-headed Buntings.

(Other species recorded on Cyprus, mainly in spring, include Pygmy Cormorant*, Long-legged Buzzard, Imperial* and Bonelli's Eagles, Saker Falcon, Little and Baillon's Crakes, Common and Demoiselle Cranes, Great Snipe, Broad-billed Sandpiper, Cream-coloured Courser, Greater Sandplover, Caspian Plover, White-tailed Lapwing, Audouin's* and Great Black-headed Gulls, Blue-cheeked Bee-eater, Bimaculated Lark and Cinereous Bunting*.)

It is possible to take a day-trip by ferry from Tasucu on the Turkish coast to **Girne** (Kyrenia) in north Cyprus and to see the two endemic breeding species above the nearby Bellapais Monastery. Audouin's Gull* is a possibility on the ferry crossing or in Girne harbour. However, most birding visitors to Cyprus base themselves at **Paphos** in the southwest corner of the island; a resort which is accessible on direct flights from England. The endemic twosome are both widespread around Paphos and the adjacent headland, especially around the lighthouse, is a migrant hotspot. The best site for Black Francolin is alongside the Dhiarizos River downstream from Kouklia, east of Paphos. Further east the sea cliffs at **Episkopi** support Eurasian Griffon and, from mid April onwards, Eleonora's Falcon. Birders struggling with the two endemics may catch up with them at the nearby Curium ruins. One of the best birding areas on the island is the **Akrotiri Salt Lake** and nearby **Phasouri Wetland**, south of Limassol. The lake and the surrounding reedy marshes support Greater Flamingo and migrant shorebirds, as well as Moustached Warbler and Dead Sea Sparrow (in reeds at northwest corner). In early September 1995 a total of 345 Demoiselle Cranes roosted here. Take the road to the RAF base from Kolossi, west of Limassol, to reach the lake and explore the whole area. At the northwest corner of Cyprus the olive groves near the Baths of Aphrodite on the **Akamas Peninsula** attract migrants. At the east end of the island Greater Flamingo occurs on **Larnaca Salt Lake** just southwest of Larnaca airport. This is a good site for rarities and in recent years these have included Cream-coloured Courser and White-tailed Lapwing. The endemic wheatear and warbler occur on **Cape Greco** to the east and this is another good site for migrants.

Brown Fish-Owl was recorded in the **Adana** area, southeast Turkey up until 1990 and may still be present.

YESILICE

The *garrigue* hillsides near the village of Yesilice in southeast Turkey support a distinctly eastern Mediterranean avifauna, including Red-tailed Wheatear and Persian Nuthatch.

YESILICE

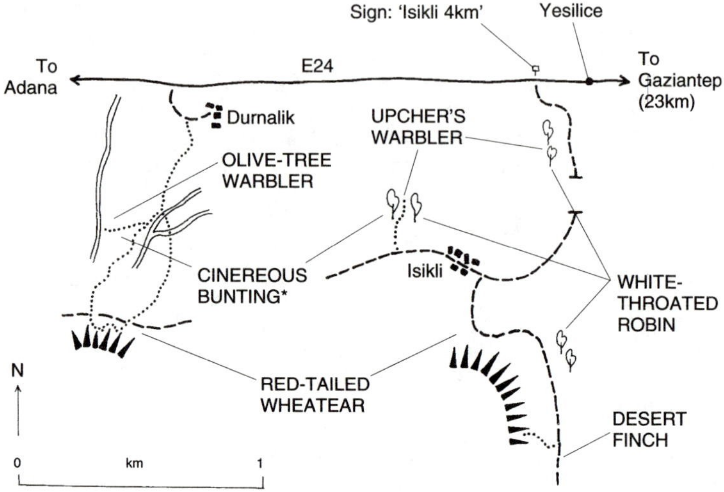

Specialities

Red-tailed Wheatear, Persian Nuthatch, Olive-tree Warbler (May–Sep), Cinereous Bunting* (May–Sep).

Others

Syrian Woodpecker, White-throated Robin, Rufous-tailed Scrub-Robin (May–Sep), Upcher's Warbler (May–Sep), Rock Nuthatch, Sombre Tit, Bimaculated Lark (May–Sep), Pale Rockfinch (May–Sep), Desert Finch, Cretzschmar's Bunting (May–Sep).

Yesilice (Buyuk Arapter) is 23 km northwest of Gaziantep and is accessible from Adana, which is connected to Istanbul by air. If approaching Yesilice from Gaziantep, try the gorge beyond the cafe 1.5 km after the Maras fork, or, after passing through Yesilice, take the track to the left after 200 m for 4 km to **Isikli** village and explore the valleys above the village, or 1.5 km beyond Yesilice take the track left to **Durnalik** village and continue on foot through the valley beyond. Upcher's Warbler and Pale Rockfinch occur in the thorn hedges lining the fields and Red-tailed Wheatear and Persian Nuthatch on the rocky slopes above the tree-line.

BIRECIK

This small town in southeast Turkey, just north of the Syrian border, is situated alongside the Euphrates River, which helps to maintain a linear oasis in an otherwise arid land of rocky, scrub-covered hills and rolling semi-desert. This is one of the best birding areas in the country, with such Turkish delights as Pallid Scops-Owl and Menetries' Warbler heading a fine supporting cast, which includes Blue-cheeked Bee-eater and Dead Sea Sparrow.

BIRECIK

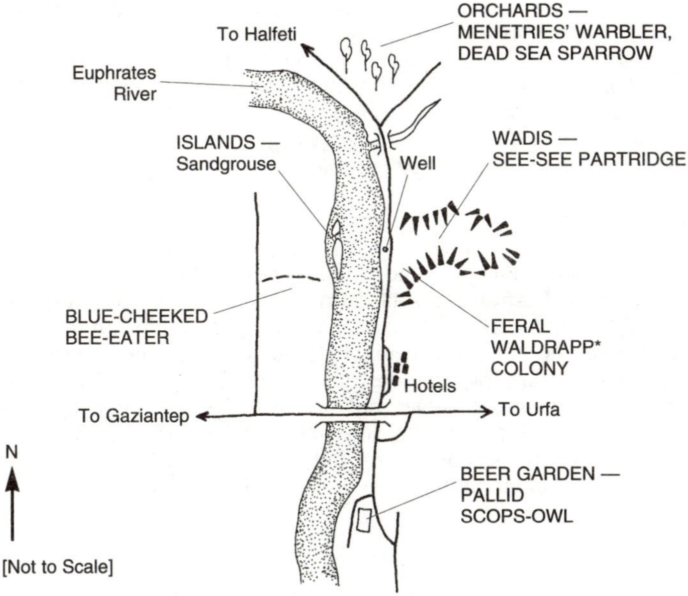

Many of the species listed below are only present during the summer (May–Sep).

Specialities

Pallid Scops-Owl, Red-tailed Wheatear, Menetries' Warbler, Persian Nuthatch, Dead Sea Sparrow, Chestnut-shouldered Petronia, Cinereous Bunting*.

Others

Lesser Kestrel*, Barbary Falcon, See-see Partridge, Chukar, Black Francolin, Spur-winged Plover, Pin-tailed and Black-bellied Sandgrouse, European Scops-Owl, Eurasian Eagle-Owl, Pied Kingfisher, Blue-cheeked and European Bee-eaters, European Roller, Syrian Woodpecker, White-throated Robin, Rufous-tailed Scrub-Robin, Graceful Prinia, Upcher's and Orphean Warblers, Rock Nuthatch, Sombre Tit, Desert, Bimaculated and Lesser Short-toed Larks, Spanish Sparrow, Rock Petronia, Pale Rockfinch, Desert Finch, Black-headed Bunting.

(Other species recorded here include Waldrapp* and Cream-coloured Courser. Birecik was once a stronghold of Waldrapp*, but sadly the only birds remaining are part of a feral colony.)

Birecik is accessible by road from Adana, which is connected to Istanbul by air. The small 'Beer Garden' just south of town is probably the most reliable site in the world for Pallid Scops-Owl (beware of European Scops-Owl which also occurs here). Ask at the cafe for the exact roosting site and repay the employees by eating and drinking there. Blue-cheeked Bee-eaters are usually more reliably seen on the west side of the Euphrates, accessible from the Gaziantep road. The feral Waldrapps* breed on the cliff just north of town, at the western end of a wadi where See-see Partridge, Eurasian Eagle-Owl and Pale Rockfinch occur. Both species of sandgrouse visit the islands in the Euphrates opposite the Waldrapp* colony to drink, usually between 0730 and 0900. North of the colony the track passes through an area of gardens and orchards where Menetries' Warbler, Dead Sea Sparrow, Chestnut-shouldered Petronia and Desert Finch occur. Cream-coloured Courser has been recorded east of Halfeti.

Accommodation: hotel (with swimming pool) at the bridge.

Little* and Great* Bustards and Cream-coloured Courser have been recorded at **Ceylanpinar**, a state farm on the Syrian border near the Birecik–Cizre road. **Cizre** is the only known site within the Western Palearctic for Red-wattled Lapwing, but seeing the few birds present is not easy because this town on the Tigris River is close to the Syrian and Iraq borders and there is a heavy military presence in the area. It is crucial to obtain permission in town to visit the bridge over the river, from where the birds can usually be seen, but even birders who have gained such permission in the past have ended up being arrested.

VAN

The water level in Van Golu, the huge lake west of Van, rose by 2.5 m between 1993 and 1995, flooding many of the surrounding marshes, but any remaining reedbeds may still support Paddyfield Warbler. To the east of Van, Grey-hooded Bunting occurs on the rocky mountain slopes.

Many of the species listed below are only present during the summer (May–Sep).

Specialities

Armenian Gull, Persian Nuthatch, Paddyfield Warbler, Chestnut-shouldered Petronia, Grey-hooded Bunting.

Others

Pygmy Cormorant*, Great White Pelican, Ruddy Shelduck, White-headed Duck*, Marbled Teal*, Lesser Kestrel*, Chukar, Black-winged Pratincole*, Eurasian Eagle-Owl, White-throated Robin, Finsch's, Pied and Isabelline Wheatears, Rock Nuthatch, Savi's and Moustached Warblers, Bimaculated Lark, Rock Petronia, Fire-fronted Serin.

(Other species recorded here include Lanner and Saker Falcons, Demoiselle Crane, Great Snipe* (May/Sep–Oct) and Crimson-winged Finch.)

White-headed Duck* and Paddyfield Warbler have been recorded west of Van town, beyond the two ruined mosques at Vankalesi. Turn south off the Ercek road, before the railway cutting by the quarry (Eurasian Eagle-Owl), about 7 km northeast of town, on to a track, to look for Grey-hooded Bunting, but beware of shepherds' dogs in this area.

Accommodation: Van — Bavram Hotel.

Spot-throated Accentor occurs in the juniper stands in the **Nemrut Dag Crater**, near Tatvan, at the western end of Van Golu. Turn west 4 km north of Tatvan on to the 25 km track down into to the crater. White-winged Scoter breeds on the larger of the two crater lakes here, and other species recorded include White-throated Robin, Finsch's Wheatear, Fire-fronted Serin, Crimson-winged Finch and Cinereous Bunting*.

Pygmy Cormorant*, White-headed Duck* and Black-winged Pratincole* have been recorded at the **Bendimahi Marshes**, 85 km north of Van at Muradiye, but this site was mostly flooded in the mid 1990s when the level of Lake Van rose dramatically. Demoiselle Crane (May–Sep) and Great Bustard* occur in the fields around the village of **Bulanik** and alongside the River Murat to the north (up to 12 birds in 1994). The river may still be accessible via a 6 km track north from the village of Balotus. Explore east and west once at the river and check the islands in the river. The most reliable site in Turkey for Mongolian Finch is 6 km east of **Dogubayazit**, around the castle of Ishak Pasa Sarayi, near the cafe at the end of the road, or along the track south from the cafe. Grey-hooded Bunting also occurs here.

Over 400,000 raptors have been seen migrating over the eastern Pontic Mountains in autumn, a total which far exceeds that for the Bosphorus. Many of these birds (30,000 on a good day and 50,000 on a rare day) pass a watchpoint in the **Coruh Valley** and they include White-tailed*, Lesser Spotted, Greater Spotted* and Imperial* Eagles and Saker Falcon. The adjacent beech forests support White-backed and Black Woodpeckers, the 'mountain' form of Chiffchaff and the 'green' form of Greenish Warbler. The watchpoint is a long uphill walk from the small town of Borcka, and best before 0800 and 1000.

Accommodation: Borcka — hotel (basic).

ISPIR AND SIVRIKAYA

These two small villages in northeast Turkey are situated in the Pontic Mountains where the high, remote scree slopes and alpine meadows support two highly localised and very elusive species: Caspian Snowcock and Caucasian Grouse*.

Specialities
Caspian Snowcock, Caucasian Grouse*, Grey-hooded Bunting.

Others
Lammergeier, Eurasian Griffon, Golden Eagle, Semicollared Flycatcher, Wallcreeper, Alpine Accentor, Fire-fronted Serin, White-winged Snowfinch.

Other Wildlife
Brown bear.

Caspian Snowcock occurs near the village of Ispir, south of Rize on Route 925. Turn north on to a track 2 km west of Ispir and look in the

SIVRIKAYA

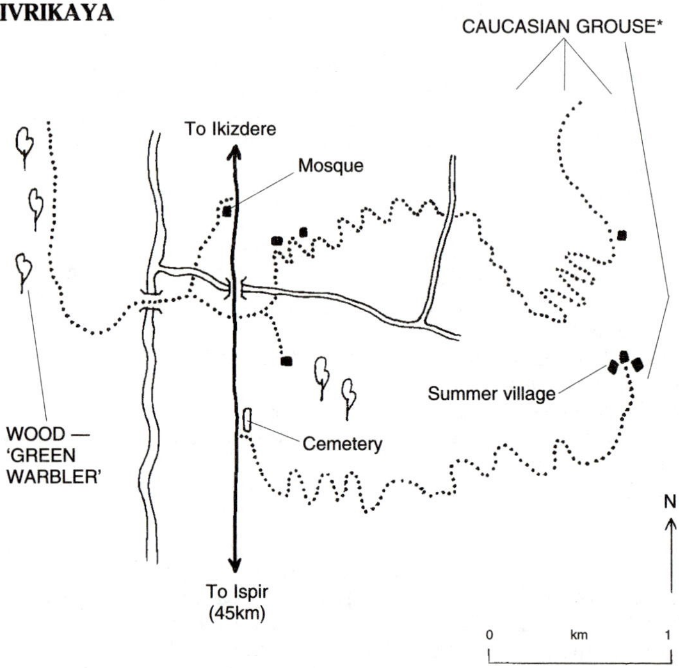

area of the pass (2600 m/8530 ft) higher up the track at dawn. Caucasian Grouse* occurs near the village of Sivrikaya, 45 km north of Ispir. This elusive rarity has been observed from the road 5 km south of the village, along with Wallcreeper, but most birders find that they have to make the long climb up the mountain slopes east of the village, via the inconspicuous path which begins 750 m south of the village bridge by the cemetery, or via the path which starts just south of the bridge, to see this bird. There are guides in the village who know the birds well and getting as high up the mountain as possible, as early as possible, with a guide, will present the best chance of success. However, this will mean starting out at 0330 in subzero temperatures. The woods west of the village support the 'green' form of Greenish Warbler and the 'mountain' form of Chiffchaff.

Accommodation: Sivrikaya — tearooms. Ikizdere. Rize.

There are a few good birding sites between the far northeast and Istanbul. The mixed forests around the **Sumela Monastery** ruins, south of Trabzon, support Boreal Owl, Black Woodpecker, Red-throated Flycatcher and the 'green' form of Greenish Warbler. Inland, the E80 passes through a valley 70 km west of Erzincan (10 km east of Refahiye) where Lesser Spotted and Imperial* Eagles, Saker Falcon and Semicollared Flycatcher (along the stream) have been recorded. The small **Todurge Golu**, on the north side of the E88, 50 km east of Sivas, supports Pygmy Cormorant* and Marbled Teal*. Further west, Black Stork, Cinereous Vulture*, and Lesser Spotted and Imperial* Eagles have been recorded between Abant and Ankara.

ADDITIONAL INFORMATION

Addresses

Please send records of Cyprus rarities to the Cyprus Ornithological Society, A E Sadler, Yiangon Souroulla 6, 6037 Larnaca (tel/fax: 4651002). Please send records of Turkish rarities to OSME, c/o The Lodge, Sandy, Beds, SG19 2DL, UK.
Cyprus Birdline: tel: 66522031.

Books and Papers

A Birdwatcher's Guide to Turkey. Green I and Moorhouse N, 1995. Prion.
A Birdwatcher's Guide to the Birds of Cyprus. Oddie B and Moore D, 1993. Suffolk WT.
Birding in Lesbos. Brooks R, 1995. Privately published.
Where to Watch Birds in Turkey, Greece and Cyprus. Welch H *et al*., 1996. Mitchell Beazley.
Songbirds of Turkey: an Atlas of Biodiversity of Turkish Passerine Birds. Roselaar, 1995. Pica Press.
The Birds of Cyprus: An Annotated Checklist. Flint P and Stewart P, 1992. BOU.

Near-endemics

Caspian Snowcock, Caucasian Grouse*, Armenian Gull, Krueper's Nuthatch, Dead Sea Sparrow, Spot-throated Accentor, Cinereous* (breeding) and Cretzschmar's (breeding) Buntings.

Cyprus

Cyprus Wheatear and Cyprus Warbler only breed on Cyprus.

UNITED ARAB EMIRATES

INTRODUCTION

Summary

The United Arab Emirates form one of the best birding areas in the Middle East and, fortunately, this is one of the easiest countries in the region for the independent birder to visit. The Emirates lie at the south-east corner of the Arabian Gulf, on a major migration route, and some birders believe this country could replace Israel as a major spring destination for birders in the future. With the possibilities ranging from Great Knot and Crab Plover to Hypocolius and Plain Leaf-Warbler, they may well be right.

Size

At 83,600 sq km, the United Arab Emirates cover an area a little smaller than England and eight times smaller than Texas.

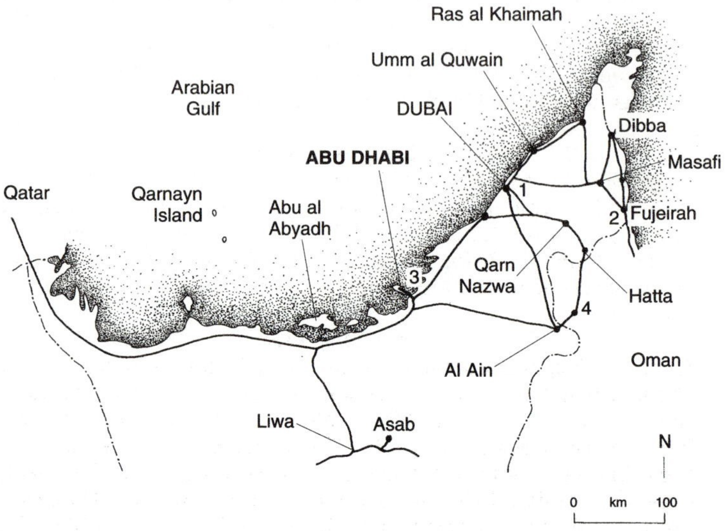

1 Dubai
2 Fujeirah
3 Abu Dhabi
4 Jebel Qatar

Getting Around

A vehicle, preferably 4WD, is more or less essential for serious birding, and hiring one is expensive. There are shared taxis, but these rarely reach the best birding sites and there is only one regular bus service, between Dubai and Abu Dhabi.

Accommodation and Food

Unfortunately, accommodation is rather limited and expensive, but there are three Youth Hostels (in Dubai, Sharjah and Fujeirah) and a few cheap hotels in Dubai. The wide range of food is good value. Beer is usually only available in expensive restaurants and hotels, and is strictly prohibited in the Emirate of Sharjah.

Health and Safety

Immunisation against hepatitis, polio and typhoid is recommended, as are precautions against malaria.

Climate and Timing

The best times to visit are in the early spring (late March to early April) and the late autumn (November), when it is hot and humid, but not excessively so, and migration is in full swing. Most shrikes, chats and warblers are much more common in the spring, while shorebirds are more numerous in the autumn.

Habitats

Many mangrove-lined muddy bays (known as khawrs) and beaches are present along the coast. Inland, the Emirates are composed mainly of sand desert, gravel plains and salt-flats with remnant patches of natural ghaf (*Prosopis*) woodland and acacia scrubland, although much of the desert near the coast and in some places inland has been turned over to gardens and parks, fodder fields, palm plantations and even forestry. In the east the Hajar Mountains rise to 1219 m (4000 ft).

Conservation

The area of built development, cultivation and afforestation continues to grow, but while new, artificial oases benefit many migrants, some desert specialists such as Houbara Bustard, which has also been heavily hunted, are not being protected. Eight threatened and near-threatened species occur in the Emirates.

Bird Species

A total of 389 species has been recorded in the Emirates, of which about 350 are migrants. Non-endemic specialities and spectacular species include Persian Shearwater, Socotra Cormorant*, Sand Partridge, Great Knot, Crab Plover, Cream-coloured Courser, Sooty and Great Black-headed Gulls, Pallid Scops-Owl, Green and Blue-cheeked Bee-eaters, Indian Roller, White-throated Robin, Hooded, Hume's and Red-tailed Wheatears, Hypocolius, Sykes' and Upcher's Warblers, Plain Leaf-Warbler, Menetries' Warbler, Greater Hoopoe-Lark and Chestnut-shouldered Petronia.

Endemics

There is no endemic species.

Expectations

It is possible to see over 190 species on an extensive two-week trip.

DUBAI

The parks, gardens and golf course in and around this modern desert city on the Arabian Gulf attract a superb selection of migrants, including Menetries' Warbler, while the tidal creek the city lies next to attracts shorebirds, notably Broad-billed Sandpiper, and terns.

Many of the species listed below are migrants and/or winter visitors.

Others

Socotra Cormorant*, Greater Flamingo, Western Reef-Egret, Greater Spotted Eagle*, Pintail Snipe, Broad-billed Sandpiper, Crab Plover, Cream-coloured Courser, Mongolian Plover, Greater Sandplover, Red-wattled and White-tailed Lapwings, Sooty, Yellow-legged, Great Black-headed and Slender-billed Gulls, White-cheeked and Saunders' Terns, Chestnut-bellied Sandgrouse, European Scops-Owl, Pallid Swift, Green Bee-eater, Indian Roller, Semicollared Flycatcher, White-throated Robin, Rufous-tailed Scrub-Robin, Pied and Isabelline Wheatears, Graceful Prinia, Orphean and Menetries' Warblers, Small and Hume's Whitethroats, Arabian Babbler, Black-crowned Sparrow-Lark, Greater Hoopoe-Lark, Chestnut-shouldered Petronia, Pale Rockfinch, Purple Sunbird.

DUBAI

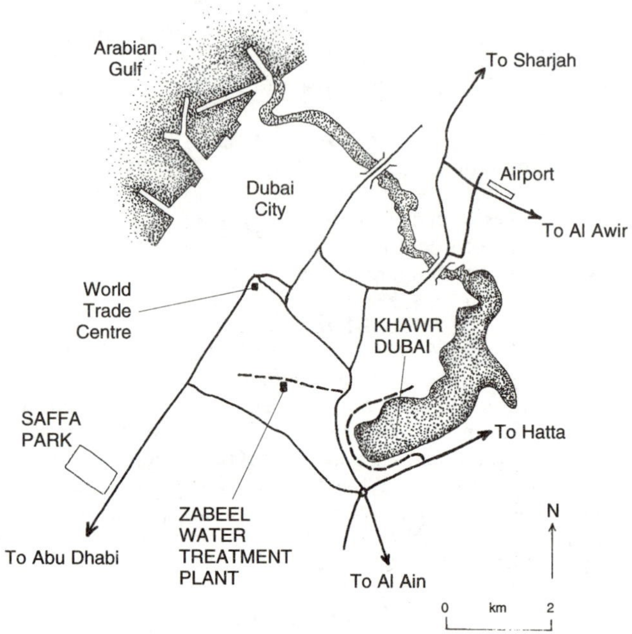

(Other species recorded here include Oriental Honey-buzzard, Lesser Spotted Eagle, Pallid Scops-Owl, Hypocolius, Blyth's Reed-Warbler and Forest Wagtail, while introduced species include Grey Francolin, Rose-ringed Parakeet, Brahminy and Asian Pied Starlings, Common Myna, Red Avadavat and, possibly, White-throated Munia.)

One of the best wetlands in the Emirates is just a few minutes drive south of the city centre. Greater Flamingo, shorebirds, Great Black-headed Gull and terns occur at **Khawr Dubai**, accessible via the track north from the Hatta road. This site is best when the sun is in the west, hence a good birding strategy in spring is to check for passerine migrants elsewhere during the morning and visit here in the afternoon (perhaps before the Pallid Swifts perform above the Dubai Museum at dusk). The Oud Metha road to Khawr Dubai passes the **Zabeel Water Treatment Plant**, which lies to the west. This is a good site for wintering Greater Spotted Eagle*, as well as other raptors and White-tailed Lapwing on passage. Over 230 species, mostly migrants, have been recorded in **Saffa Park**, on the north side of the Abu Dhabi road 5 km southwest of the city. Dubai is also close to one of the best sites for migrants in the Emirates. Over 225 species have been recorded at the 100 ha **Emirates Golf Course**, which is on the south side of the Abu Dhabi road, about 25 km southwest of Dubai. There is a driveable track around the edge of the golf course which leads to pools outside the perimeter fence where Chestnut-bellied Sandgrouse may be seen near dawn. The pools inside the fence at the south side of the complex and the nearby wood are the best sites for wintering Pintail Snipe, while the fairways are the haunt of post-breeding Cream-coloured Coursers and

EMIRATES GOLF COURSE

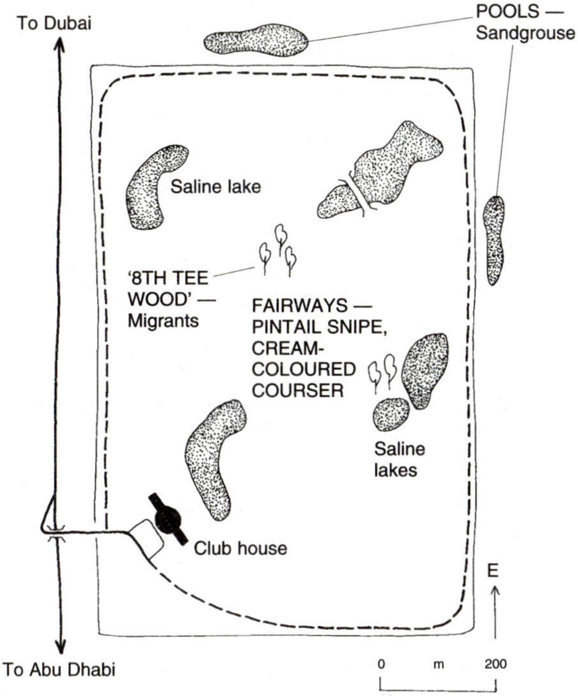

Greater Hoopoe-Lark. It is crucial to arrange permission to visit here in advance by phoning the manager on 480–222 and asking him to leave your name with the security guards at the entrance. Do not walk across the 27 fairways.

Over 120 species have been recorded in the gardens of the **Jebel Ali Hotel**, on the north side of the Abu Dhabi road, 20 km further southwest from the golf course. Ask permission to enter before wandering around the grounds in search of migrants such as Semicollared Flycatcher and White-throated Robin. The hotel lies next to the coast and from the marina it is possible to see Socotra Cormorant*, Sooty Gull and White-cheeked and Saunders' Terns. The 100 ha of natural ghaf woodland in **Mushrif NP**, a popular recreational area on the west side of the Al Awir road, 12 km southeast of Dubai airport, is also good for migrants, as well as Pallid and European Scops-Owls, wintering Small Whitethroat and Menetries' Warbler, Arabian Babbler and summering Chestnut-shouldered Petronia.

Accommodation: Ambassador Hotel, Al Falah Street, PO Box 3226, Dubai. Tel: 9714 531000.

To the north of Dubai along the coast lies the foul **Ramtha Tip**, 5 km inland from Sharjah, where the pools are a particular favourite of migrant White-tailed Lapwings. The best site for shorebirds in the Emirates is **Khawr al Beidah**, 30 km northeast of Sharjah. Great Knot

(Nov–Mar), Crab Plover (peak numbers in mid-winter) and Cream-coloured Courser (May–Sep) occur here and this is the best site in spring for Socotra Cormorant*. To reach the khawr, turn west at the roundabout 25 km northeast of Sharjah, then turn northeast on to a 2 km track to the village of Al Salamh. Continue north for 3 km from the village to reach the maze of mangrove and mud flat, then east between the dunes and the sea, checking the area around the large island off-shore 3 km along here for roosting shorebirds.

The 15 km-long bay lined with 30 m (100 ft) dunes known as **Al Jazirah Khawr**, 40 km northeast of Khawr al Beidah and 10 km south of Ras al Khaimah, also attracts numerous shorebirds, as well as passerine migrants which favour the scrub on the dunes. Turn off the Dubai–Ras al Khaimah road 3 km north of the Jazeerah al Hamra junction to reach the khawr. **Wadi Bih**, east of Ras al Khaimah, supports the highly elusive Long-billed Pipit, as well as Long-legged Buzzard, Bonelli's Eagle, Sand Partridge, Lichtenstein's Sandgrouse, Pallid Scops-Owl (rare), Hume's and Red-tailed (Oct–Mar) Wheatears, Plain Leaf-Warbler (Nov–Mar), Trumpeter Finch and House Bunting. To reach the wadi, head east opposite the main turning into Ras al Khaimah. Once on the track that leads into the wadi, proceed past the dams (Lichtenstein's Sandgrouse visit the pool here at dusk), bear left and follow the telegraph poles. Long-billed Pipit has been recorded on high ground along the right fork (east) from the Omani Police Post. Sociable Lapwing* has been recorded in winter in the extensive fields at **Hamraniyah**, south of Ras al Khaimah, as well as Pallid Harrier* (Nov–Apr), Green Bee-eater, Indian Roller and Spanish Sparrow.

On the way through the Hajar Mountains from Ras al Khaimah to Fujeirah on the east coast it is worth birding **Masafi Wadi**, which is situated in a pass at 400 m (1313 ft) and supports wintering Red-tailed Wheatear, Plain Leaf-Warbler and Small Whitethroat. Resident species include Sand Partridge, Lichtenstein's Sandgrouse, Streaked Scrub-Warbler, Desert Lark and the scarce Long-billed Pipit.

FUJEIRAH

This city on the Gulf of Oman coastline, 150 km east of Dubai, lies close to a superb mangrove-lined khawr where the rare and isolated *kalbaensis* subspecies of Collared Kingfisher occurs alongside summer visitors such as Blue-cheeked Bee-eater and Sykes' Warbler.

Specialities

Sykes' Warbler (Apr–Sep).

Others

Indian Pond-Heron (Nov–Mar), Lesser Kestrel* (Mar–Apr/Nov), Red-wattled Lapwing, Sooty (Feb–Oct), Yellow-legged (Nov–Mar) and Great Black-headed (Oct–May) Gulls, Great Crested-Tern, White-cheeked (Apr–Oct), Bridled (May–Oct) and Saunders' (Mar–Oct) Terns, Pallid Swift, Collared Kingfisher, Indian Roller, Blue-cheeked Bee-eater (Apr–Sep), Clamorous Reed-Warbler, Arabian Babbler, Black-crowned

Sparrow-Lark, Chestnut-shouldered Petronia (Apr–Sep), Pale Rockfinch (Mar–Apr).

(Other species recorded here include Persian Shearwater, Variable Wheatear (Nov–Mar), Small Whitethroat (Oct–Mar), Oriental Skylark (Nov–Mar) and Blyth's Pipit (Oct).)

The 5 km-long **Khawr Kalba**, 12 km south of Fujeirah, supports wintering Indian Pond-Heron, a tiny population of Collared Kingfisher (no more than 20 birds have ever been counted) and a few breeding pairs of Sykes' Warblers. The kingfisher is easiest to see at low tide, on the south side of the mangroves. The acacia savanna which stretches for 5 km inland from the khawr attracts spring migrants such as Pale Rockfinch, and Chestnut-shouldered Petronia in the summer. North of Fujeirah, the fodder fields just north of Khawr Fakkan, on the right-hand side of the road to Dibba, are worth a look *en route* to the fields around Fujeirah Dairy Farm, which are good for scarce species such as Oriental Skylark and Blyth's Pipit, but access to these fields is not always granted. To the north of here the road reaches **Dibba Bay**, where seawatching may produce Persian Shearwater, Sooty Gull and Bridled Tern, and a wander across the gravel plains inland may turn up Variable Wheatear and Small Whitethroat.

Accommodation: Fujeirah Beach Motel, PO Box 5445, Fujeirah. Tel: 9719 228051.

Southeast of Dubai towards Haffa, the road passes a series of rocky outcrops, of which **Qarn Nazwa** is the best for birds. This outcrop, 50 km southeast of Dubai, rises to 80 m (263 ft) and supports Pharaoh Eagle-Owl and wintering Variable and Red-tailed Wheatears. To reach it turn south off the Hatta road a few kilometres southeast of the Al Haba junction. The owl is usually seen at dusk at the southern end of the outcrop. Hume's Wheatear has been recorded in the gardens of the Hatta Fort Hotel, in **Hatta**, on the border with Oman 120 km southeast of Dubai.

ABU DHABI

This modern city lies on a coastal island and is surrounded by lagoons where shorebirds, gulls and terns occur. However, the Abu Dhabi area is more renowned for the mysterious Hypocolius, which has appeared in good numbers at the nearby camel racetrack in recent springs.

Most of the species listed below are migrants and/or winter visitors.

Specialities

Hypocolius (Feb–Mar).

Others

Western Reef-Egret, Pallid Harrier*, Lesser Kestrel*, Crab Plover, Great Knot, Great Black-headed and Slender-billed Gulls, White-cheeked and Saunders' Terns, Chestnut-bellied Sandgrouse, Masked Shrike, Semicollared Flycatcher, Rufous-tailed Scrub-Robin, Graceful Prinia, Clamorous Reed-Warbler, Upcher's Warbler, Small Whitethroat, Desert and Menetries' Warblers, Bimaculated Lark, Pale Rockfinch, Purple Sunbird.

(Other species recorded here include Caspian Plover, Blyth's Reed-Warbler, Oriental Skylark, Forest Wagtail and Blyth's Pipit.)

Abu Dhabi is about 160 km southwest of Dubai. In the city centre many good birds have turned up at Bateen Wood and the adjacent Mushref Gardens, including spring migrants such as Upcher's and Menetries' Warblers, and winter visitors including Small Whitethroat. The shallow lagoons along the southern and northern shores of the island support Crab Plover and Great Black-headed Gull, while the bushes on Khalidiyah Spit at the western tip can be good for passerine migrants. The regular September passage of Great Knot through Mirawah Island has involved over 600 birds.

Hypocolius has been recorded in recent springs at the **Al Wathba Camel Racetrack**, accessible via the Abu Dhabi–Al Ain Truck Road (not the road for passenger vehicles), about 40 km inland from Abu Dhabi. Once there, pass the Ladies Stand and explore the small plantation on the right, just before the Main Stand. This is where the largest flock (60+) of Hypocolius ever recorded in the Emirates appeared in late March 1994, followed by a similar number at the beginning of March 1995 and up to 32 in February and March 1996 (seven were also recorded in November 1995). The fodder fields enclosed by the track support Chestnut-bellied Sandgrouse and wintering Pallid Harrier*.

Accommodation: Khalidiyah Palace Hotel (A+), PO Box 4010, Abu Dhabi. Tel: 9712 662 470.

The unique Hypocolius, in a family of its own, is a spring visitor to the United Arab Emirates

Inland from Abu Dhabi, Cream-coloured Courser has been recorded around the town of **Sweihan**, in the farmland on the northern outskirts and near the National Avian Research Centre, 8 km to the south.

Hooded and Hume's Wheatears occur alongside the road to the top of the isolated **Jebel Hafit**, which rises to 1300 m (4265 ft), 30 km southeast of Al Ain, near the border with Oman. Other species recorded here include Egyptian Vulture, Long-legged Buzzard, Barbary Falcon, Brown-necked Raven and Trumpeter Finch. Other sites near Al Ain include the fodder fields enclosed by the **Al Ain Camel Racetrack**, which is sign-posted from the Abu Dhabi road south of Al Ain, where Hypocolius was recorded here in February 1996, and wintering species include Pallid Harrier* and Bimaculated Lark. The reedy pools in the **Al Ain Al Fayidah Park**, attract migrants.

JEBEL QATAR

This escarpment, northeast of Al Ain, is a good site for Hume's Wheatear and wintering Plain Leaf-Warbler.

Specialities

Hume's Wheatear, Plain Leaf-Warbler (Nov–Mar).

Others

Egyptian and Lappet-faced Vultures, Bonelli's Eagle, Barbary Falcon, Sand Partridge, Lichenstein's Sandgrouse, Pale Crag-Martin, Streaked Scrub-Warbler, Upcher's Warbler (Mar–Apr/Aug–Sep), Small Whitethroat (Oct–Mar), Menetries' Warbler (Mar–Apr/Nov), Desert Lark, Greater Hoopoe-Lark, Trumpeter Finch, House Bunting.

Jebel Qatar is actually in Oman, but this site is much more accessible from the Emirates and crossing the border is not a problem. To reach the best site, a relatively lush ravine near Mahdah known as the 'hanging gardens', head towards Mahdah from Al Ain via Buraimi, then turn right on to a track after passing the 'Welcome to Mahdah' sign. This 5 km track leads to a pool where the surrounding vegetation attracts migrants and wintering Plain Leaf-Warbler, while the adjacent escarpment supports Hume's Wheatear.

The isolated **Liwa Oases**, which lie in the southwest desert region, about 200 km southwest of Abu Dhabi via Tarif, attract migrants, while the surrounding desert may still support the odd wintering Houbara Bustard.

Red-billed Tropicbird (Oct–May) and Sooty Falcon (Apr–Oct) breed, along with many terns and gulls, on rocky islets such as Qarnayn, in the Arabian Gulf north of the Emirates.

ADDITIONAL INFORMATION

Addresses

Please send all records to the Emirates Bird Records Committee, PO Box 50394, Dubai (tel/fax: 971 4 313378), which publishes an excellent annual Bird Report in English.

Books and Papers

The Birds of the United Arab Emirates. Richardson C, 1990. Hobby.
Status and Conservation of the Breeding Birds of the United Arab Emirates. Aspinall S, 1995. Hobby.

YEMEN

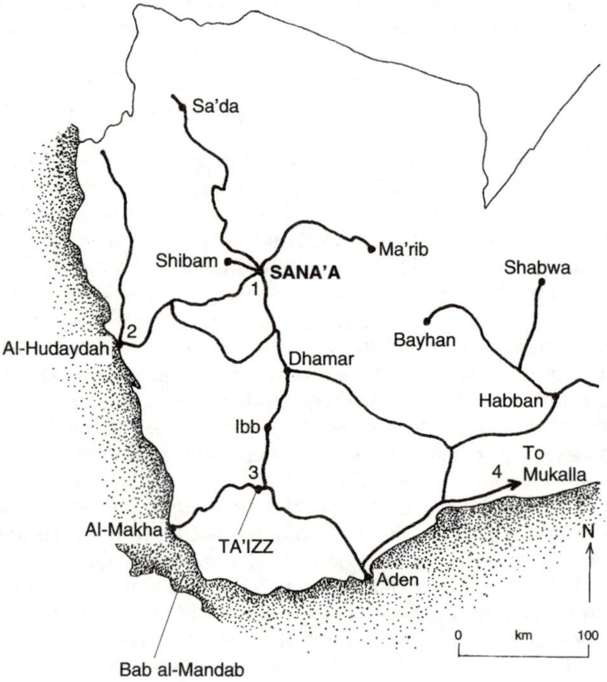

1 Sana'a
2 Al Hudaydah
3 Ta'izz
4 Mukalla

INTRODUCTION

Summary

Yemen arguably offers the best birding on the Arabian Peninsula, at least in terms of diversity. All 11 Arabian Peninsula endemics are relatively easy to see, alongside a superb selection of seabirds and some spectacular Afrotropical species. Yemen is also renowned for its cultural, archaeological and historical interest, and is very popular with tourists, but there are few facilities away from the main towns.

Size

At 527,696 sq km, Yemen is four times the size of England and a little smaller than Texas.

Getting Around

The travel situation in Yemen changes quickly. Before 1992 it was necessary for independent travellers to draw up a detailed itinerary before arriving in the country and, once there, to visit the General Tourist Company office in Sana'a to obtain the necessary travel permits. Such restrictions could easily be reinstated — check details with the nearest embassy. As most of the best known birding sites lie near the three main towns (Sana'a, Ta'izz and Al Hudaydah (Hodeidah)), the simplest way to get around is by bus and shared long-distance taxis, a much cheaper alternative than hire-vehicles which are also available.

Accommodation and Food

There is a wide range of accommodation in the main towns, where restaurants serve kebabs, spicy hot stews known as salta, bean dishes, coffee and beer.

Health and Safety

Immunisation against hepatitis, polio, typhoid and yellow fever is recommended, as are precautions against malaria. Avoid birding around ports and military bases. Birders have been arrested in such areas as recently as 1992.

Climate and Timing

The best times to visit Yemen are November or March, when migrants mix with winter and summer visitors and it is not so hot and humid on the Red Sea coastal plain as it is during the summer. March–April and August–September are the main rainy seasons, although it can rain any time of the year in the Ta'izz area.

Habitats

Yemen is a scenically spectacular country, dominated by a rugged mountain range which rises to 3666 m (12,028 ft) at Jabal al-Nabi Shu'ayb, the highest peak in Arabia. These mountains, which form the eastern rim of the Rift Valley, support remnant acacia and fig forests, and juniper stands which survive among the coffee and qat plantations. The high, fertile plateau is heavily cultivated. The coastal plain, known as the Tihamah, lies to the west of these mountains alongside the Red Sea, while to the north and east lies the world's largest sand desert, known as the Rub' Al-Khali or Empty Quarter. Most of Yemen's coastline is sandy, but there are some mud flats and mangroves. The southern coastal plain supports remnant acacia savanna and there are relatively luxuriant forests, fed by the southwest monsoon, in the mountain foothills of the south, especially in the east near the border with Oman.

Conservation

There are no protected sites, despite the fact that 19 threatened and near-threatened species occur in Yemen.

Bird Species

Over 350 species have been recorded in Yemen. Non-endemic specialities and spectacular species include Jouanin's Petrel, Red-billed Tropicbird, Masked Booby, Socotra Cormorant*, Verreaux's Eagle, Sand Partridge, Arabian Bustard, Crab Plover, Spotted Thick-knee, White-eyed* and Sooty Gulls, Nubian and Plain Nightjars, White-throated Bee-eater, Abyssinian Roller, Little Rock-Thrush, Tristram's Starling, Black Scrub-Robin, Red-tailed and Botta's Wheatears, Blackstart,

Upcher's Warbler, Brown Woodland-Warbler, Red Sea and Menetries' Warblers, Arabian Golden-Sparrow, Rueppell's Weaver, Palestine Sunbird and Golden-winged Grosbeak.

Endemics

There is no endemic species, but Yemen Accentor* is virtually so, and all of the other ten Arabian Peninsula endemics are present.

Expectations

It is possible to see over 200 species on a two-week trip, including all 11 Arabian Peninsula endemics.

SANA'A

All 11 Arabian Peninsula endemics, notably Philby's Partridge and Arabian Woodpecker*, have been recorded near Yemen's capital, which is situated at the foot of the highest mountains in Arabia at 2250 m (7382 ft).

Arabian Peninsula Endemics

Philby's and Arabian Partridges, Arabian Woodpecker*, Yemen Thrush*, Arabian Wheatear, Yemen Warbler*, Arabian Waxbill, Yemen Accentor*, Olive-rumped and Yemen Serins, Yemen Linnet.

Specialities

Tristram's Starling, Botta's Wheatear, Rueppell's Weaver, Palestine Sunbird.

Others

Hamerkop, Lammergeier, Verreaux's Eagle, Lanner and Barbary Falcons, Dusky Turtle-Dove, Red-eyed Dove, Bruce's Green-Pigeon (Apr–Oct), African Scops-Owl, Grey-headed Kingfisher (Apr–Oct), Green Bee-eater, Abyssinian Roller, African Grey Hornbill, Brown-necked and Fan-tailed Ravens, Masked Shrike (Oct–Nov), Little Rock-Thrush, Violet-backed Starling (Apr–Oct), Gambaga Flycatcher (Apr–Oct), White-throated Robin (Apr and Oct), Blackstart, Pale Crag-Martin, White-spectacled Bulbul, White-breasted White-eye, Brown Woodland-Warbler, Small Whitethroat (Oct–Mar), Arabian Babbler, Red-capped Lark, Bush Petronia, African Silverbill, Long-billed Pipit, Shining Sunbird, Cinnamon-breasted Bunting.

(Other species recorded here include Hume's Owl.)

Most of the Arabian Peninsula endemics have been recorded near the town of **Shibam**, a popular tourist site 35 km northwest of Sana'a. Bird along the path which starts behind the big mosque in Shibam and ascends the scrubby hillsides to the terraced fields around **Kawkaban**, a fortress which is perched spectacularly on the top of a 350 m (1148 ft) cliff at 2850 m (9350 ft). Philby's Partridge also occurs just to the south and east of Quratil, *en route* to Shibam, and at **Jabal al-Nabi Shu'ayb**, 35 km southwest of Sana'a off the Al Hudaydah road, just before Suq Baw'an. The best place to look for Arabian Woodpecker* is in the acacia woodlands in the roadside valley 3 km west of **Al Mahwit**, which is two hours by taxi west of Shibam. Other sites worth visiting include the wide and fertile **Wadi Dahr**, a place taxi drivers may know as 'Dar-al-Hajar' or 'Rock Palace', 15 km northwest of Sana'a (Arabian Waxbill, Olive-rumped Serin), around the village of **Haddah** in the southwest outskirts (Hamerkop and African Scops-Owl), the riverside at **Khamis bani Sa'd** (Hamerkop, Grey-headed Kingfisher, Blackstart), any vegetated wadis (Arabian Woodpecker*) and, if necessary, the rubbish tip (raptors).

Accommodation: Sana'a — Hotel Hadda, Sultan Palace Hotel (C). Shibam — Hotel Shibam (C). Al Mahwit — Hotel Nile (C).

Sand Partridge, Crowned and Lichtenstein's Sandgrouse, Red-tailed Wheatear (Nov–Mar), Small Whitethroat (Nov–Mar), Greater Hoopoe-Lark, Trumpeter Finch and House Bunting occur in the desert and the vegetated wadi around the old dam near **Ma'rib**, 160 km east of Sana'a. Hypocolius has been recorded here in April and winter visitors have included Cream-coloured Courser, Menetries' Warbler and Dunn's Lark (which also occurs alongside the road east to Sayun).

Accommodation: Brothers Hotel (C).

Waldrapp* (Nov/May) and Arabian Bustard have been recorded near **Al-Kadan**, north of Bajil. There is permanent water at Wadi al-Haud, 8 km north of Al-Kadan, and at the farmland centred on Al-Gerabi, 6 km west of Al-Kadan. The Bajil area is particularly good for raptors, including Dark Chanting-Goshawk.

AL HUDAYDAH

This port on the Red Sea coast in west Yemen lies near beaches, lagoons and mangrove-lined mudflats which support White-eyed* and Sooty Gulls, while Arabian Bustard and Arabian Golden-Sparrow occur inland in the best area of Sudanian savanna left in the country.

Arabian Peninsula Endemics

Arabian Partridge, Arabian Wheatear, Arabian Waxbill (Oct–Mar).

Specialities

Arabian Bustard, Nubian Nightjar, Tristram's Starling, Arabian Golden-Sparrow, Rueppell's Weaver.

Others

Brown Booby, Pink-backed Pelican, Greater Flamingo, Western Reef-Egret, Glossy Ibis, Abdim's Stork (Apr–Oct), Dark Chanting-Goshawk, Verreaux's Eagle, Helmeted Guineafowl, Crab Plover, Spotted Thick-knee, Spur-winged Plover, White-eyed*, Sooty and Slender-billed Gulls, White-cheeked and Saunders' Terns, Chestnut-bellied Sandgrouse, Red-eyed Dove, African Collared-Dove, Namaqua Dove, Bruce's Green-Pigeon (Apr–Oct), Pied Cuckoo (Apr–Oct), White-browed Coucal, Spotted Eagle-Owl, Plain Nightjar (Apr–Oct), Grey-headed Kingfisher

(Apr–Oct), White-throated (Apr–Oct) and Green Bee-eaters, Abyssinian Roller, Masked Shrike (Oct–Nov), Black-crowned Tchagra, Black Scrub-Robin, Upcher's Warbler (Jul–Oct), Brown Woodland-Warbler, Menetries' Warbler (Oct–Mar), Arabian Babbler, Black-crowned Sparrow-Lark, Greater Hoopoe-Lark, Bush Petronia, African Silverbill, Nile Valley Sunbird.

Other Wildlife

Hamadryas baboon.

(Other species recorded here include Lesser Flamingo*, Bateleur, Gabar Goshawk, White-tailed Lapwing.)

The People's Garden, beach, small harbour and anywhere along the coast 30 km to the north are all worth birding. Inland, Arabian Bustard, Spotted Thick-knee, White-throated Bee-eater and Black Scrub-Robin occur in the farmland east of **Al Qutay** and the acacia thickets around **Al Midman**, while **Jebel Bura**, 35 km east of Al Qutay, is also a good birding site, and the acacia savanna and gallery forest in **Wadi Rijaf**, 60 km to the east of Al-Hudaydah, support Nubian and Plain Nightjars.

Accommodation: Ambassador Hotel (A). Al Rawdah Hotel (B).

The Sana'a-Ta'izz road passes **Naqil Sumarah**, which rises to 2800 m (9186 ft), 160 km south of Sana'a (30 km north of Ibb). This mountain supports all 11 Arabian Peninsula endemics, as well as Golden-winged Grosbeak and a fine assortment of Afrotropical species. It is difficult to cover thoroughly but the Sumarah Pass is easily accessible by taxi from Ibb (to Yarim) and Philby's Partridge and Yemen Accentor* occur here.

TA'IZZ

This popular tourist town lies at an elevation of 1400 m (4593 ft) at the southern end of the Red Sea escarpment. The diversity of habitats, which include rocky outcrops, wide wadis, permanently wet marshes and juniper stands, within easy reach of the town, support most of the Arabian Peninsula endemics, as well as Red Sea Warbler and Golden-winged Grosbeak.

Arabian Peninsula Endemics

Arabian Partridge, Yemen Thrush*, Arabian Wheatear, Yemen Warbler*, Arabian Waxbill, Yemen Accentor*, Olive-rumped and Yemen Serins, Yemen Linnet.

Specialities

Tristram's Starling, Red Sea Warbler, Rueppell's Weaver, Palestine Sunbird, Golden-winged Grosbeak.

Others

Hamerkop, Glossy Ibis, Abdim's Stork (Apr–Oct), Dark Chanting-Goshawk, Greater Spotted* (Oct–Mar) and Imperial* (Oct–Mar) Eagles, Lanner and Barbary Falcons, Spotted Thick-knee, Dusky Turtle-Dove,

Bruce's Green-Pigeon (Apr–Oct), White-browed Coucal, Spotted Eagle-Owl, Plain Nightjar (Apr–Oct), Grey-headed Kingfisher (Apr–Oct), White-throated (Apr–Oct) and Green Bee-eaters, African Grey Hornbill, Black-crowned Tchagra, Little Rock-Thrush, Violet-backed Starling (Apr–Oct), Gambaga Flycatcher (Apr–Oct), Black Scrub-Robin, Blackstart, White-breasted White-eye, Graceful Prinia, Arabian Babbler, Bush Petronia, Zebra Waxbill, African Silverbill, Long-billed Pipit, Shining Sunbird, Cinnamon-breasted Bunting.

(Other species recorded here in winter include Waldrapp*: 14 in 1985, nine in 1990, three in 1992, but none in 1993.)

Ta'izz is 258 km south of Sana'a. One of the best inland wetlands in Yemen happens to be **Ta'izz Sewage Ponds**, which are about 5 km north of the market (at the end of At Tahir Street), west of the road. This is where Waldrapp* occasionally occurs and a good site for waterbirds and raptors. One of the best sites in Yemen for Golden-winged Grosbeak is on the hillsides west of the Ta'izz–Ibb road, 14 km north of Ta'izz, behind the quarry and factories. Turn west in response to the 'Arabia Felix Industries' sign. Also bird **Jabal Sabir** to the south where most of the Arabian Peninsula endemics occur. The summit of this mountain, which rises to 3006 m (9862 ft), can be reached by 4WD taxi from the Bab al Kabir (the gate of the suq). Ask to be taken to the village of Al Arus and explore the cultivated areas with remnant juniper stands below the summit.

Accommodation: Ta'izz.

The 70 km stretch of coast between **Al-Makha** and **Al-Khawkhah** in southwest Yemen supports large numbers of shorebirds, gulls and terns. Slender-billed Curlew* was recorded at both Al-Makha and Al-Khawkhah in October 1988, while seawatching from these sites has produced Persian Shearwater, Red-billed Tropicbird and Masked Booby. Al-Makha is accessible by taxi from Ta'izz. Pink-backed Pelican and White-eyed* and Sooty Gulls occur here, but at least one birder has been arrested in this sensitive port area so it may be wise to report to the police first.

The mud flats and beaches in and around the city of **Aden**, on Yemen's south coast, support shorebirds and gulls, including Crab Plover and White-eyed Gull*, while the as yet unidentified swift species seen over the city between April and July may well be Forbes-Watson's Swift. Near the port of **Mukalla** (accessible by air from Sana'a) on Yemen's south coast east of Aden it is possible to see Socotra Cormorant*, as well as Wedge-tailed, Flesh-footed and Audubon's Shearwaters, Wilson's Storm-Petrel, Red-billed Tropicbird, Masked and Brown Boobies and Bridled Tern, while scarce species include Goliath Heron and Jouanin's Petrel. It is possible to hire boats here to do some serious seawatching, although it may be more worthwhile to continue east to **Ra's Fartak**, Yemen's easternmost headland, where, during the southwest monsoon (Jun–Aug), Jouanin's Petrel is more likely, Persian Shearwater is a possibility, and rarities recorded include White-faced, Black-bellied and Swinhoe's* Storm-Petrels. Near Ra's Fartak, up to 30,000 Socotra Cormorants have been recorded off Qishn Beach to the west, Lappet-faced Vulture and Crowned Sandgrouse occur in the desert 60 km west of Al-Ghayda to the north, and Golden-winged Grosbeak occurs on the Mahra escarpment to the east, near the border with the Dhofar region of Oman (p. 380).

ADDITIONAL INFORMATION

Books and Papers

The status of birds in North Yemen, and the records of the OSME Expedition in autumn 1985, Brooks D *et al.*, 1987. *Sandgrouse* 9: 4–66.

Near-endemics

Jouanin's Petrel, Philby's and Arabian Partridges, Arabian Woodpecker*, Yemen Thrush*, Arabian Wheatear, Yemen Warbler*, Arabian Golden-Sparrow, Arabian Waxbill, Yemen Accentor*, Nile Valley Sunbird, Olive-rumped and Yemen Serins, Yemen Linnet, Golden-winged Grosbeak.

REQUEST

This book is intended to be a first edition. If you would like to contribute to the second edition, please send details of any errors or changes to the site details and species lists included in this edition, and information on any new sites you feel deserve inclusion, to:

Nigel Wheatley, c/o A & C Black (Publishers) Limited, 35 Bedford Row, London WC1R 4JH, UK.

It would be extremely helpful if information could be submitted in the following format:

1 A summary of the site's position (in relation to the nearest city, town or village), altitude, access arrangements, habitats, number of species recorded (if known), best birds, best time to visit and its richness compared with other sites.
2 A species list, preferably using the names and taxonomic order in *Clements*' Check List and supplements.
3 Details of how to get to the site and where to bird once there, with information on trails, etc.
4 A map complete with scale and compass point.
5 Any addresses to write to for permits, etc.
6 Any details of accommodation.

Any information on the following species would also be very useful:

White-eared Night-Heron*, Rock Bush-Quail, Red-legged, Slaty-legged, Black-tailed and Band-bellied* Crakes, Solitary Snipe, Indian Courser, Painted Sandgrouse, Oriental Bay-Owl, Blue-banded Kingfisher, Plain-pouched Hornbill*, Blue-naped Pitta*, Broad-tailed Grassbird*, Tawny Lark and Green Avadavat*.

I would be extremely grateful if you could also include a statement outlining your permission to use your information in the next edition and, finally, your name and address, so that you can be acknowledged appropriately.

I should like to take this opportunity to thank you in anticipation of your help. The usefulness of the next edition depends on your efforts!

CALENDAR

The following is a brief summary of the best countries and regions to visit according to the time of the year. This calendar is aimed to help those birders who have set holidays to choose the best destination. Alternatively, if there are birders out there fortunate enough to have a year to go birding in Asia, then following this schedule could produce the best birding and the most birds!

If anyone tries this, please let me know how they get on! Better still, if there is a willing sponsor out there, contact me immediately! Were such a dream to come true, the following route may prove to be the most exciting: get the year off to a flying start with three weeks in north and south India, moving on to Sri Lanka and the Andaman Islands for a couple of weeks at the end of January and beginning of February, then head north to much colder climes for a week or so on Hokkaido, Japan, before returning to the warmer Philippines for a month. In the second half of March travel to Thailand and work your way from north to south until early April, then take a trip to Taiwan and Hong Kong for a couple of weeks before birding southeast China for a few days. At the beginning of May move north to Beidaihe and, after a week or so, head inland to Sichuan and Tibet. Wind down a little in the middle of June with a relaxing trek in Nepal, then end the month in northeast India. In mid July return to Japan to look for the summer visitors and endemics, then go for a complete change of scene in Turkey and Turkestan to catch up with a few of the Central Asian species and perhaps the first six month's notes before a mammoth excursion across Indonesia in late August and September. In October, hop across to Borneo and Peninsular Malaysia before mopping up the Middle East specialities, taking in Yemen, the United Arab Emirates and Bahrain where the wintering Hypocolius should have arrived by the end of November. At the end of the year return to the forests of southeast Asia in Burma and Vietnam to round off what would surely be the experience of a birding lifetime!

JANUARY: Bhutan, Burma, India, Nepal (lowlands), Philippines, Sri Lanka, Thailand (north), Vietnam, Bahrain and Israel.
FEBRUARY: Bhutan, Burma, India, Andaman Islands, Japan (Hokkaido), Nepal (lowlands), Philippines, Sri Lanka, Thailand (north), Vietnam and Israel.
MARCH: Bhutan, India, Andaman Islands, Malaysia, Nepal (lowlands), Philippines, Vietnam, Israel (end of month), Jordan (end of month), UAE and Yemen (end of month).
APRIL: Bhutan, Cyprus, Hong Kong, India (northeast), Andaman Islands, Malaysia (including Borneo), Nepal (treks), Pakistan (north), Taiwan (end of month), Thailand (south), Vietnam, Israel (beginning of month), Jordan and UAE (beginning of month).
MAY: China (Beidaihe at beginning of month, Sichuan and Tibet at end of month), Nepal (treks), Pakistan (north), Taiwan (beginning of month), Thailand (south), Turkestan and Turkey.
JUNE: China (Sichuan and Tibet), Japan, Mongolia, Nepal (treks) and Turkey.

JULY: China (Tibet) and Oman.
AUGUST: Indonesia.
SEPTEMBER: China (Beidaihe/end of month), Indonesia and Malaysia (including Borneo).
OCTOBER: China (Beidaihe), Malaysia (including Borneo), Israel (end of month) and Yemen (end of month).
NOVEMBER: Bhutan, China (Beidaihe/beginning of month), India, Nepal (lowlands), Thailand (north), Vietnam, Israel, UAE and Yemen (beginning of month).
DECEMBER: Bhutan, Burma, India, Nepal (lowlands), Thailand (north), Vietnam, Bahrain and Israel.

USEFUL ADDRESSES

Clubs and Conservation Organisations

The Oriental Bird Club (OBC), c/o The Lodge, Sandy, Bedfordshire SG19 2DL, UK, aims to encourage an interest in the birds of the Oriental region and their conservation, and publishes an excellent biannual bulletin, as well as an annual journal called *Forktail*. **Join now**!
Web site: http//:www.gold.net/users/dj10/obchome.html

The Ornithlogical Society of the Middle East (OSME), c/o The Lodge, Sandy, Bedfordshire SG19 2DL, UK, publishes an excellent journal called *Sandgrouse*. **Join now**!

The Asian Wetland Bureau (AWB), c/o Institute of Advanced Studies, University of Malaya, 59100 Kuala Lumpur, Malaysia, has produced a number of excellent publications.

BirdLife International Wellbrook Court, Girton Road, Cambridge CB3 0NA, UK. Membership of this vitally important organisation costs from £25 per year and members receive a quarterly magazine and an annual report.

Operation Wallacea, c/o Ecosurveys Ltd, Priory Lodge, Hagnaby, Spilsby, Lincs PE23 4BP, UK (tel: 01790 763665; fax: 01790 763417), caters for volunteers who wish to help with survey work in Wallacea (volunteers must meet all their own costs).

Trip Reports

Dutch Birding Travel Report Service (DBTRS), PO Box 737, 9700 AS Groningen, The Netherlands (tel: 31 50 145 925; fax: 31 50 144 717). To obtain a copy of the catalogue, which lists an extensive selection of reports covering most Asian countries, send £3 or $5.

Foreign Birdwatching Reports and Information Service (FBRIS) (organised and owned by Steve Whitehouse), 6 Skipton Close, Worcester WR4 0LG, UK (tel: 01905 454541). To obtain a copy of the catalogue, which lists 400 reports from around the world and covers most Asian countries, send £1.

Tour Companies

Avian Adventures, 49 Sandy Road, Norton, Stourbridge DY8 3AJ, UK (tel: 01384 372013; fax: 01384 441340).
Birding, Periteau House, Winchelsea, East Sussex TN36 4EA, UK (tel: 01797 223223; fax: 0797 222911).
Birdquest, Two Jays, Kemple End, Birdy Brow, Stonyhurst, Lancashire BB6 9QY, UK (tel: 01254 826317; fax: 01254 826780; telex: 635159 BIRDQ).
Birdwatching Breaks, 26 School Lane, Herne, Herne Bay, Kent CT6 7AL, UK (tel: 01227 740799).
Branta, 7 Wingfield Street, London SE15 4LN, UK (tel: 0171 635 5812; fax: 0171 277 7720).

Budget Bird Tours, 8 Wolfreton Villas, Anlaby, Hull, East Yorkshire HU10 6QS, UK (tel: 01482 650941).
Cygnus Wildlife Holidays, 57 Fore Street, Kingsbridge, Devon TQ7 1PG, UK (tel: 01548 856178; fax: 01548 857537; telex: 45795 WSTTLX G).
Field Guides, PO Box 160723, Austin, TX 78716-0723, USA (tel: 512-327-4953; fax: 512-327-9231).
KingBird Tours Inc., PO Box 196, Planetarium Station, New York, NY 10024, USA (tel: 1 212 866 7923; fax: 1 212 866 4225).
Limosa Holidays, Suffield House, Northrepps, Norfolk NR27 0LZ, UK (tel: 01263 578143; fax: 01263 579251).
Naturetrek, Chautara, Bighton, nr. Alresford, Hampshire SO24 9RB, UK (tel: 01962 733051; fax: 01962 733368).
Ornitholidays, 1 Victoria Drive, Bognor Regis, West Sussex PO21 2PW, UK (tel: 01243 821230; fax: 01243 829574).
Pingrum Tours, Scots Meadow, Little Horwood, Milton Keynes MK17 0PD, UK (tel/fax: 01296 713355).
Regulus Travel, Lankharvsgatan 26, 424 66 Angered, Sweden.
Sunbird/Wings, PO Box 76, Sandy, Bedfordshire SG19 1DF, UK (tel: 01767 682969; fax: 01767 692481) and PO Box 31930, Tucson, AZ 85751, USA (tel: 602-749-1967; fax: 602-749-3175).
The Travelling Naturalist, 9 Little Britain, Dorchester, Dorset DT1 1NN, UK (tel/fax: 01305 267994).

Travel Agents

Wildwings, International House, Bank Road, Bristol BS15 2LX, UK (tel: 0117 984 8040; fax: 0117 967 4444). This company also organises its own tours, which in 1996 included Eilat, Hong Kong and Beidaihe (China).

USEFUL GENERAL BOOKS

Regional Field Guides

A Pictorial Guide to the Birds of the Indian Subcontinent. Ali S *et al.*, 1983. BNHS/Oxford University Press.
A Guide to the Birds of Borneo, Sumatra, Java and Bali. MacKinnon J and Phillipps K, 1993. Oxford University Press.
A Guide to the Birds of Wallacea. Bishop D, Coates B and Gardner D, in press. Dove.
An Identification Guide to the Birds of Europe and the Western Palearctic. Beaman M *et al.*, in press. Helm.
Birds of Europe with North Africa and the Middle East. Jonsson L, 1992. Helm.
Birds of the Middle East and North Africa. Hollom P, 1988. Poyser.
Collins Field Guide: Birds of South-East Asia. King B *et al.*, 1975 (1995). HarperCollins.
Collins Pocket Guide to Birds of Britain and Europe, with North Africa and the Middle East. Heinzel H, Fitter R and Parslow J, 1995. HarperCollins.
The Macmillan Birder's Guide to European and Middle Eastern Birds. Harris A, Shirihai H and Christie D, 1996. Macmillan.

Handbooks and Reference Works

Handbook of the Birds of India and Pakistan, Together With Those of Bangladesh, Nepal, Bhutan and Sri Lanka. Volumes 1 to 6 and continuing to 10. Ali S *et al.*, continuing. Oxford University Press.
Compact Handbook of the Birds of India and Pakistan, Together With Those of Bangladesh, Nepal, Bhutan and Sri Lanka. Ali S. *et al.*, 1987. Oxford University Press.
Handbook of the Birds of the World, volumes 1 to 3 and continuing. del Hoyo *et al.*, continuing. Lynx Edicions.
The Birds of the Western Palearctic (nine volumes). Cramp S (Ed.), completed in 1994.
Important Bird Areas in the Middle East. Evans M *et al.*, 1994. BirdLife International.
Birds to Watch 2: the World List of Threatened Birds. Collar N *et al.*, 1994. BirdLife International.

Bird Families

Buntings and Sparrows. Olsson U *et al.*, 1996. Pica Press.
Crows and Jays. Madge S and Burn H, 1992. Helm.
Finches and Sparrows. Clement P *et al.*, 1993. Helm.
Kingfishers, Bee-eaters and Rollers. Fry C *et al.*, 1992. Helm.
Pittas, Broadbills and Asities. Lambert F and Woodcock M, 1996. Pica Press.
Pheasants of the World. Johnsgard P, 1986. Oxford University Press.
Seabirds. Harrison P, 1985. Helm.
Shorebirds. Hayman P, Marchant J and Prater T, 1986. Helm.
The Hamlyn Photographic Guide to the Waders of the World. Rosair D and Cotteridge D, 1995. Hamlyn.
Munias and Mannikins. Restau R, due October 1996. Pica Press.
Swallows and Martins. Turner A and Rose C, 1989. Helm.

Swifts. Chantler P and Driessens G, 1995. Pica Press.
The Herons Handbook. Hancock J and Kushlan J, 1984. Helm.
The Hornbills. Kemp A, 1995. Oxford University Press.
Tits, Nuthatches and Treecreepers. Harrap S and Quinn D, 1995. Helm.
Wildfowl. Madge S and Burn H, 1988. Helm.
Woodpeckers. Winkler H *et al*., 1995. Pica Press.

Lists

An Annotated Checklist of the Birds of the Oriental Region (2,600 species). Inskipp T *et al*., in press. OBC.
Birds of the World: a Check List. Clements J, 1991. Ibis.
Birds of the World: a Check List, Supplement No. 1. Clements J, 1992. Ibis.
Birds of the World: a Check List, Supplement No. 2. Clements J, 1993. Ibis.
Palearctic Birds. Beaman, M, 1994. Harrier.

Other Wildlife

Mammals of South-East Asia, 2nd Edition. The Earl of Cranbrook, 1992. Oxford University Press.
The Book of Indian Animals, 3rd Edition. Prater, 1971 (1990). BNHS/ Oxford University Press.

Travel

Pheasant Jungles. Beebe W, 1994. WPA.
The Malay Archipelago. Wallace A R, 1986. Oxford University Press.
The Snow Leopard. Matthiessen P, 1979. Picador.

The Lonely Planet guides to many of the countries and regions within Asia are all, on the whole, excellent, although they do not usually cover the more remote birding areas.

Sounds

Learn the calls and songs before you go from recordings on sale from **WildSounds**, Dept. 8–10, Cross Street, Salthouse, Norfolk NR25 7XH, UK (tel/fax: 01263 741100).

BIRD NAMES WHICH DIFFER BETWEEN *CLEMENTS* AND VARIOUS ASIAN BIRD BOOKS

Only those name differences which are not immediately obvious are given.

Name used by *Clements*	**Name used by Asian books**	**Latin name**
Waldrapp	Bald Ibis	*Geronticus eremita*
Black Ibis	Red-naped Ibis	*Pseudibis papillosa*
Cinereous Vulture	Black Vulture	Aegypius monachus
Collared Falconet	Red-breasted Falconet	*Microhierax caerulescens*
Pied Falconet	White-legged Falconet	*Microhierax melanoleucus*
Red-necked Falcon	Red-headed Merlin	*Falco chicquera*
Amur Falcon	Eastern Red-footed Falcon	*Falco amurensis*
Szecheny's Partridge	Pheasant-Grouse	*Tetraophasis szechenyii*
Himalayan Monal	Impeyan Pheasant	*Lophophorus impejanus*
Mongolian Plover	Lesser Sandplover	*Charadrius mongolus*
Great Crested-Tern	Swift Tern	*Sterna bergii*
Pale-backed Pigeon	Eastern Stock Pigeon	*Columba eversmanni*
Oriental Turtle-Dove	Rufous Turtle-Dove	*Streptopelia orientalis*
Slaty Cuckoo-Dove	Black Cuckoo-Dove	*Turacoena modesta*
Emerald Dove	Green-winged Pigeon	*Chalcophaps indica*
Zebra Dove	Peaceful Dove	*Geopelia striata*
White-bellied Pigeon	Japanese Green-Pigeon	*Treron sieboldii*
Vernal Hanging-Parrot	Indian Lorikeet	*Loriculus vernalis*
Ceylon Hanging-Parrot	Ceylon Lorikeet	*Loriculus beryllinus*
Pygmy Hanging-Parrot	Red-billed Hanging-Parrot	*Loriculus exilis*
Grey-headed Parakeet	Eastern Slaty-headed Parakeet	*Psittacula finschii*
Plum-headed Parakeet	Blossom-headed Parakeet	*Psittacula cyanocephala*
Blossom-headed Parakeet	Eastern Blossom-headed Parakeet	*Psittacula roseata*
Malabar Parakeet	Blue-winged Parakeet	*Psittacula columboides*
Long-tailed Parakeet	Red-cheeked Parakeet	*Psittacula longicauda*
Pied Cuckoo	Jacobin Cuckoo	*Clamator jacobinus*
Chestnut-winged Cuckoo	Red-winged Crested Cuckoo	*Clamator coromandus*
Blue-faced Malkoha	Small Green-billed Malkoha	*Phaenicophaeus viridirostris*
Pallid Scops-Owl	Striated or Bruce's Scops-Owl	*Otus brucei*
Jungle Nightjar	Grey Nightjar	*Caprimulgus indicus*
Savanna Nightjar	Franklin's Nightjar	*Caprimulgus affinis*
Waterfall Swift	Giant Swiftlet	*Hydrochous gigas*
Silver-backed Needletail	White-vented Needletail	*Hirundapus cochinchinensis*
Brown-backed Needletail	Large Brown-throated Needletail	*Hirundapus giganteus*
Blyth's Kingfisher	Great Blue Kingfisher	*Alcedo hercules*
River Kingfisher	Indigo-banded Kingfisher	*Alcedo cyanopecta*
Blue-capped Kingfisher	Hombron's Kingfisher	*Actenoides hombroni*
Green-backed Kingfisher	Celebes Green Kingfisher	*Actenoides monachus*
Scaly Kingfisher	Regent Kingfisher	*Actenoides princeps*
Brown-headed Barbet	Large Green Barbet	*Megalaima zeylanica*
White-cheeked Barbet	Small Green Barbet	*Megalaima viridis*
Bornean Barbet	Black-throated Barbet	*Megalaima eximia*
Yellow-crowned Woodpecker	Yellow-fronted Pied Woodpecker	*Dendrocopos mahrattensis*
Streak-throated Woodpecker	Little Scaly-bellied Woodpecker	*Picus xanthopygaeus*
Common Flameback	Indian Goldenback	*Dinopium javanense*
Black-rumped Flameback	Lesser Goldenback	*Dinopium benghalense*
Greater Flameback	Large Goldenback	*Chrysocolaptes lucidus*
White-naped Woodpecker	Black-backed Woodpecker	*Chrysocolaptes festivus*
Azure-breasted Pitta	Steere's Pitta	*Pitta steerii*
Red-bellied Pitta	Blue-breasted Pitta	*Pitta erythrogaster*
Golden-bellied Gerygone	Flyeater	*Gerygone sulphurea*
Moluccan Flycatcher	Slaty Monarch	*Myiagra galeata*
Black-headed Jay	Black-throated or Lanceolated Jay	*Garrulus lanceolatus*

Rufous Treepie	Indian Treepie	*Dendrocitta vagabunda*
Grey Treepie	Himalayan Treepie	*Dendrocitta formosae*
Collared Treepie	Black-browed Treepie	*Dendrocitta frontalis*
Mongolian Ground-Jay	Henderson's Ground-Jay	*Podoces hendersoni*
Xinjiang Ground-Jay	Biddulph's Ground-Jay	*Podoces biddulphi*
Turkestan Ground-Jay	Pander's Ground-Jay	*Podoces panderi*
Iranian Ground-Jay	Pleske's Ground-Jay	*Podoces pleskei*
Tibetan Ground-Jay	Hume's Ground-Jay	*Podoces humilis*
White-tailed Iora	Marshall's Iora	*Aegithina nigrolutea*
Timor Oriole	Olive-brown Oriole	*Oriolus melanotis*
Halmahera Oriole	Dusky-brown Oriole	*Oriolus phaeochromus*
Brown-rumped Minivet	Swinhoe's Minivet	*Pericrocotus cantonensis*
Long-tailed Shrike	Rufous-backed Shrike	*Lanius schach*
Grey-backed Shrike	Tibetan Shrike	*Lanius tephronotus*
Rufous-winged Philentoma	Rufous-winged Flycatcher	*Philentoma pyrhopterum*
Maroon-breasted Philentoma	Maroon-breasted Flycatcher	*Philentoma velatum*
Scaly Thrush	White's Thrush	*Zoothera dauma*
Indian Grey Thrush	Tickell's Thrush	*Turdus unicolor*
Japanese Thrush	Grey Thrush	*Turdus cardis*
Island Thrush	Mountain Blackbird	*Turdus poliocephalus*
Chestnut Thrush	Grey-headed Thrush	*Turdus rubrocanus*
White-backed Thrush	Kessler's Thrush	*Turdus kessleri*
Asian Glossy Starling	Philippine Glossy Starling	*Aplonis panayensis*
Metallic Starling	Shining Starling	*Aplonis metallica*
Chestnut-tailed Starling	Grey-headed Myna	*Sturnus malabaricus*
Daurian Starling	Purple-backed Starling	*Sturnus sturninus*
White-shouldered Starling	Chinese Starling	*Sturnus sinensis*
White-cheeked Starling	Grey Starling	*Sturnus cineraceus*
Flores Jungle-Flycatcher	Russet-backed Jungle-Flycatcher	*Rhinomyias oscillans*
Grey-chested Jungle-Flycatcher	White-throated Jungle-Flycatcher	*Rhinomyias umbratilis*
Dark-sided Flycatcher	Sooty Flycatcher	*Muscicapa sibirica*
Indian Blue Robin	Blue Chat	*Luscinia brunnea*
Rufous-backed Redstart	Eversmann's Redstart	*Phoenicurus erythronota*
White-winged Redstart	Guldenstadt's Redstart	*Phoenicurus erythrogaster*
White-capped Redstart	River Chat	*Chaimarrornis leucocephalus*
White-browed Bushchat	Stoliczka's Whinchat	*Saxicola macrorhyncha*
White-throated Bushchat	Hodgson's Stonechat	*Saxicola insignis*
White-tailed Wheatear	White-crowned Black Wheatear	*Oenanthe leucopyga*
Variable Wheatear	Eastern Pied Wheatear	*Oenanthe picata*
Indian Chat	Brown Rock Chat	*Cercomela fusca*
Snowy-browed Nuthatch	Chinese Nuthatch	*Sitta villosa*
Persian Nuthatch	Eastern Rock Nuthatch	*Sitta tephronota*
Black-throated Tit	Red-headed Tit	*Aegithalos concinnus*
Streak-throated Swallow	Indian Cliff Swallow	*Hirundo fluvicola*
Black-crested Bulbul	Black-headed Yellow Bulbul	*Pycnonotus melanicterus*
Light-vented Bulbul	Chinese Bulbul	*Pycnonotus sinensis*
White-spectacled Bulbul	Yellow-vented Bulbul	*Pycnonotus xanthopygos*
Dark-crowned White-eye	Crested White-eye	*Lophozosterops dohertyi*
Flores White-eye	Thick-billed White-eye	*Heleia crassirostris*
Timor White-eye	Spot-breasted White-eye	*Heleia muelleri*
Grey-crowned Prinia	Hodgson's Prinia	*Prinia cinereocapilla*
Grey-breasted Prinia	Franklin's Prinia	*Prinia hodgsonii*
Grey-bellied Tesia	Dull Slaty-bellied Tesia	*Tesia cyaniventer*
Brownish-flanked Bush-Warbler	Strong-footed Bush-Warbler	*Cettia fortipes*
Sunda Bush-Warbler	Muller's Bush-Warbler	*Cettia vulcania*
Ceylon Bush-Warbler	Palliser's Warbler	*Bradypterus palliseri*
Pallas' Warbler	Pallas' Grasshopper Warbler	*Locustella certhiola*
Pleske's Warbler	Styan's Grasshopper Warbler	*Locustella pleskei*
White-browed Tit-Warbler	Stoliczka's or Severtzov's Tit-Warbler	*Leptopoecile sophiae*
Sulphur-bellied Warbler	Olivaceous Leaf-Warbler	*Phylloscopus griseolus*
Ashy-throated Warbler	Grey-faced Leaf-Warbler	*Phylloscopus maculipennis*
Yellow-vented Warbler	Black-browed Leaf-Warbler	*Phylloscopus cantator*
Marsh Grassbird	Japanese Marsh Warbler	*Megalurus pryeri*
Striated Grassbird	Striated Marsh Warbler	*Megalurus palustris*
Bristled Grassbird	Bristled Grass Warbler	*Chaetornis striatus*
Rufous-rumped Grassbird	Large Grass Warbler	*Chaetornis bengalensis*
Small Whitethroat	Desert Whitethroat	*Sylvia minula*
Red Sea Warbler	Arabian Warbler	*Sylvia leucomelaena*
Sunda Laughingthrush	Grey-and-brown Laughingthrush	*Garrulax palliatus*
Wynaad Laughingthrush	Yellow-breasted Laughingthrush	*Garrulax delesserti*
Rufous-breasted Laughingthrush	Nilgiri Laughingthrush	*Garrulax cachinnans*
Grey-breasted Laughingthrush	White-breasted Laughingthrush	*Garrulax jerdoni*

Indian Scimitar-Babbler	Slaty-headed Scimitar-Babbler	*Pomatorhinus horsfieldii*
Pygmy Wren-Babbler	Lesser Scaly-breasted Wren-Babbler	*Pnoepyga pusilla*
Rufous-throated Wren-Babbler	Tailed Wren-Babbler	*Spelaeornis caudatus*
Tawny-breasted Wren-Babbler	Long-tailed Wren-Babbler	*Spelaeornis longicaudatus*
Black-chinned Babbler	Red-billed Babbler	*Stachyris pyrrhops*
Crescent-chested Babbler	Pearl-cheeked Babbler	*Stachyris melanothorax*
Dark-fronted Babbler	Black-headed Babbler	*Rhopocichla atriceps*
Orange-billed Babbler	Ceylon Rufous Babbler	*Turdoides rufescens*
Yellow-billed Babbler	White-headed Babbler	*Turdoides affinis*
Red-billed Leiothrix	Pekin Robin	*Leiothrix lutea*
White-hooded Babbler	White-headed Shrike-Babbler	*Gampsorhynchus rufulus*
Rusty-fronted Barwing	Spectacled Barwing	*Actinodura egertoni*
Streak-throated Barwing	Austen's Barwing	*Actinodura waldeni*
Blue-winged Minla	Blue-winged Siva	*Minla cyanouroptera*
Chestnut-tailed Minla	Bar-throated Siva	*Minla strigula*
Yellow-throated Fulvetta	Dusky-green Tit-Babbler	*Alcippe cinerea*
Rufous-winged Fulvetta	Chestnut-headed Tit-Babbler	*Alcippe castaneceps*
Streak-throated Fulvetta	Brown-headed Tit-Babbler	*Alcippe cinereiceps*
Dusky Fulvetta	Rufous-headed Tit-Babbler	*Alcippe brunnea*
Rufous Sibia	Black-capped Sibia	*Heterophasia capistrata*
Whiskered Yuhina	Yellow-naped Yuhina	*Yuhina flavicollis*
Grey-hooded Parrotbill	Crested Parrotbill	*Paradoxornis zappeyi*
Black-throated Parrotbill	Orange or Nepal Parrotbill	*Paradoxornis nipalensis*
Black-browed Parrotbill	Lesser Red-headed Parrotbill	*Paradoxornis atrosuperciliaris*
Rufous-headed Parrotbill	Greater Red-headed Parrotbill	*Paradoxornis ruficeps*
Black-breasted Tit	Rufous-naped Tit	*Parus rufonuchalis*
Black-crested Tit	Spot-winged Black Tit	*Parus melanolophus*
White-winged Tit	White-naped Tit	*Parus nuchalis*
Tibetan Lark	Long-billed Calandra Lark	*Melanocorypha maxima*
Russet Sparrow	Cinnamon Tree Sparrow	*Passer rutilans*
Chestnut-shouldered Petronia	Yellow-throated Sparrow	*Petronia xanthocollis*
Bush Petronia	Lesser Rock Sparrow	*Petronia dentata*
Pale Rockfinch	Pale Rock Sparrow	*Carpospiza brachydactyla*
White-winged Snowfinch	(European) Snow Finch	*Montifringilla nivalis*
Black-winged Snowfinch	Tibet or Adams' Snow Finch	*Montifringilla adamsi*
White-rumped Snowfinch	Mandelli's Snow Finch	*Montifringilla taczanowskii*
White-throated Munia	Indian or Common Silverbill	*Lonchura malabarica*
Black-throated Munia	Rufous-bellied Munia	*Lonchura kelaarti*
Spot-throated Accentor	Radde's Accentor	*Prunella ocularis*
Bengal Weaver	Black-throated Weaver	*Ploceus benghalensis*
Yellow Weaver	Finn's Baya Weaver	*Ploceus megarhynchus*
Plain-throated Sunbird	Brown-throated Sunbird	*Anthreptes malacensis*
Crimson-backed Sunbird	Small Sunbird	*Nectarinia minima*
Palestine Sunbird	Orange-tufted Sunbird	*Nectarinia osea*
Long-billed Sunbird	Loten's Sunbird	*Nectarinia lotenia*
Green-tailed Sunbird	Nepal Yellow-backed Sunbird	*Aethopyga nipalensis*
White-flanked Sunbird	Kuhl's Sunbird	*Aethopyga eximia*
Olive-rumped Serin	Arabian Serin	*Serinus rothschildi*
Plain Mountain-Finch	Hodgson's Mountain-Finch	*Leucosticte nemoricola*
Black-headed Mountain-Finch	Brandt's Mountain-Finch	*Leucosticte brandti*
Spectacled Finch	Red-browed Finch	*Callacanthis burtoni*
Dark-breasted Rosefinch	Nepal or Dark Rosefinch	*Carpodacus nipalensis*
Pink-rumped Rosefinch	Stresemann's Rosefinch	*Carpodacus eos*
Pale Rosefinch	Sinai Rosefinch	*Carpodacus synoicus*
Streaked Rosefinch	Eastern Great Rosefinch	*Carpodacus rubicilloides*
Red-fronted Rosefinch	Red-breasted Rosefinch	*Carpodacus puniceus*
Crimson-browed Finch	Red-headed Rosefinch	*Pinicola subhimachalus*
Grey-headed Bullfinch	Beavan's Bullfinch	*Pyrrhula erythaca*
Yellow-billed Grosbeak	Chinese Grosbeak	*Eophona migratoria*
Rufous-backed Bunting	Jankowski's Bunting	*Emberiza jankowskii*
Grey-hooded Bunting	Grey-necked Bunting	*Emberiza buchanani*
Chestnut-breasted Bunting	White-capped Bunting	*Emberiza stewarti*
Ochre-rumped Bunting	Japanese Reed Bunting	*Emberiza yessoensis*
Chestnut-eared Bunting	Grey-headed Bunting	*Emberiza fucata*

INDEX TO SITES

INDEX TO SPECIES

Clements English index, incorporating Supplements 1–3.